Psychotherapy for Children and Adolescents

Evidence-Based Treatments and Case Examples

D1330690

Psychotherapy for Children and Adolescents

Evidence-Based Treatments and Case Examples

By

JOHN R. WEISZ

CAMBRIDGE
UNIVERSITY PRESS

PUBLISHED BY THE PRESS SYNDICATE OF THE UNIVERSITY OF CAMBRIDGE
The Pitt Building, Trumpington Street, Cambridge, United Kingdom

CAMBRIDGE UNIVERSITY PRESS
The Edinburgh Building, Cambridge CB2 2RU, UK
40 West 20th Street, New York, NY 10011-4211, USA
477 Williamstown Road, Port Melbourne, VIC 3207, Australia
Ruiz de Alarcón 13, 28014 Madrid, Spain
Dock House, The Waterfront, Cape Town 8001, South Africa

http://www.cambridge.org

First published 2004

Printed in the United States of America

Typeface Palatino 10/12 pt.   *System* LATEX 2_ε [TB]

A catalog record for this book is available from the British Library.

Library of Congress Cataloging in Publication Data

Weisz, John R.
    Psychotherapy for children and adolescents : evidence-based treatments and case
examples / John R. Weisz.
        p. cm.
    Includes bibliographical references and index.
    ISBN 0-521-57195-2 (hbk.) – ISBN 0-521-57672-5 (pbk.)
        1. Child psychotherapy–Case studies.   2. Adolescent psychotherapy–Case studies.
3. Evidence-based medicine.   I. Title.

RJ504.W355   2003
618'.92'8914–dc21

                                                                                    2003048552

ISBN 0 521 57195 2   hardback
ISBN 0 521 57672 5   paperback

For Dawn, Alli, Danny, and Tammy,
family treasures

Contents

Preface

The practice of treating children and adolescents for emotional and behavioral problems is at least a century old. In its early years, at the turn of the twentieth century, youth treatment was a rarity, but in recent decades the practice has surged in scope and cost to become a major component of care for young people. Now, early in the twenty-first century, millions of girls and boys receive psychotherapy every year in countries and cultures around the world, and significant portions of many national budgets are devoted to the mental health care these young people receive. Youth psychotherapy is remarkably diverse in its forms and methods. Hundreds of schools of therapy are brought to bear by professionals in their work with young people, and many of these professionals are highly eclectic, drawing goals and methods from a broad array of sources and using their best judgment to help the youngsters they see.

The practice of testing the effects of youth psychotherapies, using clinical trials, is naturally much younger than the treatment tradition. And at any point in time, many more professionals are providing youth psychotherapy than conducting research to test it. However, like youth treatment, youth treatment research has surged in recent decades. Well over 1,500 studies of youth psychotherapy effects have been completed to date, and hundreds of these meet standards for inclusion in scientific reviews, including quantitative syntheses called meta-analyses. Emerging from this body of treatment outcome research is a growing number of specific treatments that have significant evidence in their support, replicated across studies. These evidence-based treatments reflect the interplay of clinical care and scientific scrutiny. They are treatments that have been tested with young people who have emotional or behavioral problems or disorders, and that have been shown to work. This book is about such treatments.

In what might be seen as an ideal world, the dedicated practitioners who care for children and the dedicated researchers who test that care would be first cousins, or at least close personal friends. And the work of these two groups would be complementary, fostering crosspollination. The work of practitioners would inform research, keeping researchers alert to treatments that are widely used and in need of testing, and to the realities of youth clinical care that should be reflected in their study designs. And the work of treatment researchers would be used by practitioners in selecting the strongest interventions, those that hold up best in controlled trials.

In the real world though, things haven't worked out quite this way. Instead, as in many fields that encompass both science and practice, youth treatment research and youth clinical practice have operated in rather insular fashion, developing quite different cultures and perspectives, and even different lexicons over the years. Beyond these differences, the findings of treatment outcome research have not always been disseminated in ways that reach the practice community. And the tested treatments have not always been described in ways that convey their essence to potential users. A recurring issue is that conditions arranged for some of the research are different enough from the conditions of practice that clinicians wonder about the transportability of tested treatments to the everyday clinical care they provide. Researchers, for their part, are sometimes frustrated by the slow pace of uptake and deployment of treatments they perceive as tested and ready for use. It is this hiatus between research and practice that this book is intended to address.

In this book, I examine evidence-based treatments for children and adolescents from the two perspectives I know best: researcher and clinician. For each treatment, I describe the clinical condition it addresses, its theoretical and conceptual underpinnings, and its procedures in sufficient detail to convey the primary elements and methods used in intervening. I illustrate each treatment with a case study to elaborate how the procedures would look when actually employed with a specific youngster. I also discuss strengths and limitations of each treatment from a clinical practice perspective, noting issues likely to arise for practitioners who consider using the treatment. From a research perspective, I summarize the outcome studies, review and critique the evidence bearing on each treatment, and highlight issues and questions for further study. Overall, the goal is to describe each treatment and its applications, together with a balanced analysis of the treatment's scientific standing and its potential for everyday clinical use.

The book should be useful to several audiences and for several purposes. For practitioners, the descriptions and illustrations of treatment procedures, and the discussions of clinical practice issues and potential, can help inform decisions about whether the treatments warrant use in their own work as therapists. Those in clinical practice careers, including program directors and administrators, who want treatment choices to be informed by the scientific evidence will find the reviews of outcome studies and critiques of the evidence base of each treatment relevant to their decision making. Treatment researchers should find these features useful as well, and the analyses of strengths and gaps in the evidence and questions for future study can add to the scientific dialectic that provokes advances in research design and quality. For investigators in training or in early career, the chapters illustrate several excellent models for how clinical scientists develop treatments, select participants, train therapists, and progress from study to study to refine treatment and enrich what is known about the treatments and their effects. Training directors and teachers in such professional traditions as clinical psychology, child and adolescent psychiatry, social work, counseling, and pediatrics will find that the book conveys not only an overview of evidence-based youth practice, but also specific information needed to guide decisions about which evidence-based treatments warrant incorporation into training, practicum, supervision, and instructional programs. Finally, concerned family members can find information here on treatments relevant to special young people in their lives, youths who face difficulties and need help. Judgments about what kind of treatment to seek for a family member may be guided by a number of important considerations, but certainly the kinds of descriptions and evidence provided in this book should enter into decisions about what kind of help to seek.

A book of this type is not completed without help and support from many sources. I owe more than I can say to my wife Jenny. Her loving support means so much, and her experiences in advocating for children in court keeps me mindful of the risks that make good mental health care for youth important. Our four children, who span the range from elementary school through adolescence and into young adulthood, are sources of great joy and inspiration, not to mention fresh information about real life along the developmental trajectory.

On the professional front, I am very grateful to Julia Hough of Cambridge University Press for her interest in the project, her very thoughtful feedback on a number of chapter drafts, and her patient guidance through this lengthy process. I also extend sincere thanks to the many experts in the treatments, problems, and disorders described in the book for taking time to prepare excellent feedback, sometimes in multiple waves, on the chapters relevant to their expertise. The experts – a Who's Who of evidence-based treatment – include Russell Barkley, Paula Barrett, Caryn Carlson, Patti Chamberlain, Bruce Chorpita, Andrea Chronis, Greg Clarke, Vanessa Cobham, Phillippe Cunningham, Mark Dadds, Sheila Eyberg, Eva Feindler, Marion Forgatch, Scott Henggeler, Hyman Hops, Alan Kazdin, Philip Kendall, Pete Lewinsohn, John Lochman, Peter Loft, Bob McMahon, Tom Ollendick, Gerald Patterson, Sonja Schoenwald, Michael Southam-Gerow, Ron Rapee, Paul Rohde, Melisa Rowland, Kevin Stark, and Carolyn Webster-Stratton. In addition, Stephen Shirk provided very thoughtful comments on the book as a whole, and Bahr Weiss offered valuable insights on important issues in the field. The feedback from all these experts helped immeasurably, and the process left me touched by the generosity of these fine colleagues, so busy but so willing to share their time and ideas.

I am also pleased to acknowledge, with gratitude, support from the National Institute of Mental Health (R01 MH49522, R01 MH57347, K01 MH 01161) and the John D. and Catherine T. MacArthur Foundation. And finally, a special note of thanks to members of my UCLA research team during the years the writing took place: Tamara Altman, Vickie Chang, Brian Chu, Jennifer Connor-Smith, Trilby Cox, Samantha Fordwood, Kristin Hawley, Stan Huey, Jr., Alanna Gelbwasser, Elana Gordis, Mandy Jensen, Eunie Jung, Anna Lau, Cari McCarty, Bryce McLeod, Antonio Polo, Michael Southam-Gerow, Sylvia Valeri, and Robin Weersing. This bright, energetic group was the source of countless good ideas and lively discussions, much of the content of which has made its way into the pages of this volume. It is an honor to have worked with such a distinguished group.

J.R.W.
Los Angeles, California
August, 2002

GENERAL INTRODUCTION

1

Child and Adolescent Psychotherapies

The Lay of the Land

Sean

Nine-year-old Sean has been a worrier since early childhood. In the preschool years, he was afraid to be left alone in his room, and dropoffs at preschool were sheer trauma with Sean terrified of separation. Now a fourth grader, he is shy and withdrawn at recess, certain that he will do something "dumb" and suffer ridicule. When his teacher assigned an oral report, Sean was paralyzed by fear that he would make a fool of himself in front of the class. He trembled throughout the report, forgot his main points, and was mortified afterward. Fear robs Sean of peer connections as well. He avoids play dates, certain that other kids see him as "weird" or "a loser." He is also too afraid of separation to leave home for sleepovers. Recently, Sean has developed a fear of eating in the school cafeteria; he says his hands tremble, and other kids will see and mock him. So he looks for empty classrooms where he can eat hidden from view.

Megan

Thirteen-year-old Megan is both miserable and angry. She mopes around the house, snaps at her parents, and complains bitterly when asked to help with housework. She resents family rules and recently told her mother, "When I'm at home, I feel like a prisoner." For years, Megan has had an eye for dark clouds rather than silver linings. Her current bout with depression began when members of her clique began to exclude her. She lost confidence in herself and seemed adrift socially. Since then, her parents have heard her crying behind her locked bedroom door, and she has tearfully told her mother, "No one likes me anymore. I'm an outcast." Once a good student, Megan now lacks energy or motivation for schoolwork and her grades have dropped sharply. Her teacher and school counselor recently called her parents to express concern, and her little sister has been asking, "What's wrong with Megan?"

Kevin

Eleven-year-old Kevin zigs and zags through his house in an unpredictable course, leaving a path of destruction in his wake. Kevin is not malicious, but he is so scattered and impulsive that each day is a series of collisions, spills, scars on the wall, and broken objects. Simple daily routines such as teeth-brushing and hair care seem to elude Kevin, and he has major difficulty obeying his parents' instructions. Kevin's distractible, impulsive, disobedient style has a major impact at school. Unable to attend to his teacher or a class discussion for more than a few minutes, he fidgets at his desk and he blurts out inappropriate comments. His behavior also devastates peer relationships. Recently, when a group was discussing a favorite TV show, Kevin blurted out, "I'm getting a new bike for my birthday!" Two of the kids rolled their eyes, and the others smiled knowingly. His impulsive comments to peers (e.g., "You look like a monkey") have sparked fights. His poor concentration makes him error-prone in sports. Some of his little league teammates say Kevin is "from outer space." He is rarely invited for play dates or birthday parties, and when he wants to invite another child over, there is usually no one who wants to come.

Sal

Thirteen-year-old Sal has a reputation to protect: his own, as a bad dude. He gets in trouble at school almost every week, sometimes for disobeying a school rule, sometimes for getting into shoving matches or outright fights with other kids. He has been suspended three times, once for stealing money, once for hitting another child with a stick and drawing blood, and once for shouting profanity at a teacher who was disciplining him. Sal has a short fuse. He is quick to take offense, quick to assume that others mean him harm, and quick to strike out in fury. Understandably, most of Sal's peers at school actively avoid him, and his only friends are other youngsters with serious conduct problems; two of these youths have already been arrested and both are suspected of being gang members. At home, Sal is also disobedient, disruptive, and full of attitude. He insults and mocks his mother, refuses to lift a finger with household chores, and stays out as late as he wants. He and his uninvolved father maintain a sort of mutual ignoring relationship. In this climate, Sal is out of control and exploring ever-riskier behavior with his delinquent peers. The neighbors watch nervously, expecting to see Sal on the evening news, and not for anything good.

Young people like Sean, Megan, Kevin, and Sal can be found in homes and schools all around the world. For most such troubled children there are concerned parents and other caregivers, some at wit's end, knowing their children need help, but not sure where to turn. Eventually, many parents and youngsters make their way to mental health professionals who provide help in a variety of forms collectively labeled psychotherapy. Given the many forms that psychotherapy can take, how is one to decide which approach will really help? It is that question to which this book is addressed.

Nature, Philosophical Roots, and Evolution of Child and Adolescent Psychotherapy

This book focuses on *psychotherapy*, an array of nonmedical interventions designed to relieve psychological distress, reduce maladaptive behavior, or enhance adaptive functioning through counseling, structured or unstructured interactions, training programs, or specific environmental changes. We will concentrate specifically on children and adolescents, sometimes referred to collectively as *children* or *youth*.

Tracking psychotherapy back to its origins is not easy. The tradition of helping by listening and discussing is certainly older than recorded history. When the process began to be a profession is debatable, but a case could be made for the era of the classical Greek philosophers, who used discourse to probe the life of the mind. Socrates (469–399 BCE) developed both a method and a thesis that are arguably precursors to some modern forms of psychotherapy (see Plato's *Apology*). His philosophical dialectic, later called the Socratic method, involved questioning others in ways designed to prompt examination of their beliefs and bring them closer to truth. His "midwife thesis," the notion that the philosopher's role was to deliver the truth that is already within others, much like the midwife delivers the baby that is within a mother, is not far from the view many modern therapists have of their role. By asking others to tell him what they thought rather than telling them what to think, Socrates sought to reach the rational soul or *psyche* of those he talked with. The term *psyche* denoted the mind, inner nature, and capacity for feeling, desire, and reasoning, and was a precursor to the word *psychology*. Finally, Socrates maintained that thought and outward behavior are closely connected (see Brettschneider, 2001), presaging a tenet of many modern therapies.

The ideas of other early Greeks and many who came after the Greek era have contributed to the evolution of psychotherapy. For example, Aristotle (384–322 BCE) emphasized the role of catharsis in tragic drama, comedy, and other arts in arousing and alleviating emotional states (*Poetics*, 350 BCE; *Politics* VIII, 350 BCE; see discussion in Kazdin & Weisz, 2003). Centuries of subsequent work in philosophy, religion, medicine, and other contemplative and healing traditions have opened up a panoply of practices encompassing meditation, expert directives, subtle suggestion, hypnosis, expectancy manipulation, and persuasion, all intended to alleviate distress or dysfunction in various forms or change unwanted behavior (Shapiro & Shapiro, 1998).

Formal designation of psychotherapy as a type of professional intervention and an area of study can be traced back about 100 years (Freedheim,

1992). Arguably, contemporary psychotherapy grows out of the work of Sigmund Freud (1856–1939) and his intellectual heirs. Early markers in the application to children were Freud's treatment of a boy known as Little Hans who was afraid of horses (and much more) by consulting with the boy's father, and Freud's psychoanalysis of his own daughter, Anna (1895–1982), who became a prominent child analyst in her own right beginning in the 1920s. Anna Freud and others such as Berta Bornstein continued to apply psychoanalytic precepts and methods to children and adolescents well into the latter half of the century. The acceleration of child psychotherapy through the century was propelled by other models and methods as well, including a radically different behavioral approach. Emblematic of this new approach, Mary Cover Jones (1924a,b) used modeling and *direct conditioning* to help two-year-old Peter overcome his fear of a white rabbit. The decades beyond saw a remarkable burgeoning of behavioral psychotherapies for children and adolescents, complementing the psychoanalytic and other treatments that took shape in other quarters. By the late twentieth century, child and adolescent psychotherapy had expanded remarkably in the variety of its forms and the extent of its reach.

Evolution of Research on Psychotherapy with Young People

With the growth of psychotherapy came a growing curiosity about its potential benefits. Although research on psychotherapy developed later and more slowly than the practice itself, studies began to accumulate. Eysenck (1952) reviewed studies of adult psychotherapy and concluded that the evidence did not show it to be effective. Complementing Eysenck's work, Levitt (1957, 1963) reviewed studies that included children or adolescents and concluded that the rate of improvement among children (67–73%) was about the same with or without treatment. This conclusion was reinforced by Eysenck (1960, 1966) in later reviews encompassing studies of therapy for children and adolescents as well as adults; Eysenck's interpretation of the findings was that they provided no firm evidence that treatment led to greater improvements than the mere passage of time (i.e., no treatment).

These early reviews were highly influential, but many of the studies they relied on were methodologically weak. Subsequent research has grown stronger, and much more plentiful. Indeed, by the year 2000, about 1500 treatment outcome studies of child and adolescent psychotherapy had been completed (Durlak et al., 1995; Kazdin, 2000a). The studies have grown increasingly sophisticated over the years, more and more meeting the standards of randomized clinical trials, what has been called the "methodological Esperanto" of all disciplines that test the effects of interventions (Kazdin & Weisz, 2003, p. 4).

Another important development is that research has shifted more and more from tests of unspecified "treatment" or generic "psychotherapy" to tests of well-delineated therapies with specific treatment procedures described in detailed outlines or manuals. Of course, tests of therapy that are *not* manualized but rather done as a part of usual clinical care with therapists free to choose the methods they prefer, are potentially very useful in helping us understand whether usual care is beneficial (see Weisz et al., 1992; Weisz, Donenberg et al., 1995; and see later discussion under "Clinically Derived Treatment in Usual Clinical Care"). However, the now much more numerous studies in which treatment procedures are specified in advance and therapists follow those procedures make it possible to know, when results are published, *which specific intervention methods* worked and which did not. This, of course, is a major strength, bolstering prospects for both understanding and disseminating what works. In summary, as a consequence of several important trends over time, we are now in a position at the turn of the new century to pool and evaluate rapidly accumulating evidence on youth psychotherapies and their effects.

Forms, Scope, and Cost of Youth Psychotherapy

Just how many specific psychotherapies are practiced with children and adolescents? One recent count found 551 named therapies used with this age group (Kazdin, 2000b). The list includes familiar approaches such as play therapy and behavior modification, as well as less familiar treatments, some with intriguing names, such as "Alf group," "Barb technique," "blindfold treatment," "Let's pretend hospital," "pal program," "paraverbal therapy," "release therapy," and "Zaraleya psychoenergetic technique." Even the number 551 greatly understates the array of approaches used with young people, because few therapists limit themselves to one specific treatment approach. Instead, most therapists use eclectic mixtures of treatment methods, fashioned from their own previous clinical work, clinical supervision, and other learning experiences, and the mixtures differ from case to case. The resulting combination of adherence to specific treatments and clinically guided eclecticism means that a virtually countless array of specific psychotherapies is practiced. Moreover, any two therapists chosen at random may well have markedly different views as to what treatment is needed for any specific child, such as the four introduced at the beginning of this chapter.

Like most labor-intensive activities, psychotherapy for young people costs money. In the United States alone, the most recent figures available indicate that about 6% of youth under age 18 receive mental health care each year, at an annual cost of $11.75 billion (Sturm et al., 2000). About 10% of this cost is explicitly for medication, but most is for psychotherapy. Outpatient care accounts for about twice as much of the cost as inpatient (67% vs. 33%). And costs increase sharply with age, from 7% of the total at ages 1–5, to 34% at ages 6–11, to 59% for adolescents ages 12–17.

Problems Addressed in Psychotherapy with Children and Adolescents

Psychotherapy is used to address diverse problems and disorders that cause emotional distress, interfere with daily living, undermine development of adaptive skills, or threaten the well-being of others. Many of the problems addressed with children and adolescents fit within two broad groupings, or *syndromes*: *internalizing* (e.g., sadness, fears, shyness) and *externalizing* (e.g., temper tantrums, disobedience, fighting, stealing; Achenbach, 1991). Problems within both syndromes are frequent reasons for referral to clinics. North American youngsters are more likely to be referred for externalizing rather than internalizing problems, but not all cultures show such a strong tilt toward externalizing (see Weisz, Suwanlert et al., 1987; Weisz & Weiss, 1991). Problems that undermine school performance also generate many treatment referrals (see   Burns et al., 1995; Bussing et al., 1998; Leaf et al., 1996; Weisz, McCarty et al., 1997). These include internalizing problems such as fears that prevent school attendance, externalizing problems such as disrupting class or disobeying teachers, and other problems that do not fall neatly into either category, such as serious difficulty paying attention in class.

Another way to describe the targets of treatment is to focus on categorical diagnoses within the formal Diagnostic and Statistical Manual of Mental Disorders tradition (American Psychiatric Association, 1987, 1994, 2000). Recent evidence (e.g., Jensen & Weisz, 2002) suggests that four clusters of disorders account for a very high percentage of youth referrals:

- **Anxiety Disorders** (Social Phobia, Separation Anxiety Disorder, Generalized Anxiety Disorder, and others)
- **Depressive Disorders** (i.e., Dysthymic Disorder, Major Depressive Disorder)
- **Attention Deficit/Hyperactivity Disorder** (ADHD)
- **Conduct-related Disorders** (i.e., Oppositional Defiant Disorder, Conduct Disorder)

In this book, we will concentrate on treatments for disorders and related referral problems associated with these four clusters.

Youth versus Adult Psychotherapy: Social, Developmental, and Cultural Factors

Although psychotherapy with children and adolescents bears obvious similarities to work with adults, some important differences warrant emphasis. First, because children rarely perceive themselves as disturbed or as candidates for therapy, most referrals for treatment up until late adolescence tend to be made by parents, teachers, or other adults. These adults may thus be construed as clients in the sense that they commission the therapy, pay for it, and identify some or all of the goals. The child may or may not participate in identifying target problems or setting treatment goals, and even when he or she does participate, adult input may be weighted more heavily (Hawley & Weisz, 2002). With therapy commissioned by adults and goals shaped mostly by adults, it makes sense that children often enter the process with little motivation for treatment or personal change, or with objectives that differ from those of the adults involved.

Given marked developmental differences in the self-awareness, psychological mindedness, and expressive ability of their clientele, child therapists must often rely on adults for information about the youngsters they treat, and this can present problems of several types. First, parents' and teachers' reports may be inaccurate, based on distorted samples of child behavior, influenced by their own adult agendas, calculated to conceal their own failings as parents (including neglect or abuse), or even influenced by their own pathologies (see e.g., Goodman et al., 1994); and levels of agreement among different adults reporting on the same child tend to be low (Achenbach et al., 1989; Yeh & Weisz, 2001). In addition, adults' reports of child behavior, identification of referral concerns, and views on the acceptable process and outcome of therapy are all apt to reflect beliefs, values, practices, and social ideals of the adults' cultural reference group (see Weisz, McCarty et al., 1997).

Finally, children tend to be captives of their externally engineered environments to a much greater extent than are adults. One consequence may be that the pathology the child therapist treats may reside as much in a chaotic or disturbed environment from which the child cannot escape as in the child himself or herself. This may limit the impact of interventions involving the child as solo or primary participant. It may also argue for involvement of parents, teachers, or others from the child's social context, but such significant others are not always willing or cooperative. So, in a number of ways, the youth therapist faces challenges that are rather different from those the adult therapist confronts.

Outcomes of Youth Psychotherapy: Who Cares?

Many individuals and interest groups have a stake in the outcome of youth psychotherapy. As the focus of the intervention, the treated youth is a major stakeholder. In addition, parents and other family members who seek treatment for the youngster, and frequently for the family, are also invested in psychotherapy. Teachers' interests as well may include both concern for the treated youth and for the classroom of which that youth is a part. Those who finance the treatment – including family members, government agencies, insurance carriers, and others – have a clear stake. Finally, the therapists, clinical staff, administrators, and others in the provider community have a clear interest in the outcomes of the care in which they invest their careers. All these parties to the process of treatment have a clear stake in the question, "How effective is youth psychotherapy?"

How Are the Effects of Child and Adolescent Psychotherapy Assessed?

Questions about effects of youth psychotherapy are answered using several different methods. The most widely accepted approach involves *group comparison* designs: outcomes for a group who received a target treatment are compared with outcomes for others who received either an alternative treatment or some kind of inert control condition (e.g., placement on a waiting list). A particularly strong form of the group comparison study is the *randomized clinical trial*; here, the participants' group membership (e.g., treatment vs. control group) is determined randomly, say, by a coin toss. Such trials constitute most of the evidence discussed in this chapter. We will also review some evidence from *within-group* or *within-subject* designs, in which all study participants receive treatment. In most of these designs (reviewed in Kazdin, 1998; Kratochwill & Levin, 1992), treatments are alternately applied and withdrawn, or switched (i.e., from one treatment to another), and treatment effects are inferred from differences in behavior across the various conditions. Such approaches might be used, for example, when an entire classroom is the target of an intervention (e.g., Wurtele & Drabman, 1984), or when treated conditions are so rare that only one or two children will be treated (e.g., McGrath et al., 1988; Tarnowski et al., 1987).

Specific findings from within-group and within-subject studies will be described in later chapters of this book when relevant to particular treatment programs. However, for our overview of treatment outcome evidence, we will focus on group comparison studies, which have been reviewed much more thoroughly, and which arguably yield the strongest inferences about treatment impact.

The common currency for these inferences is the *effect size*, an index of the magnitude and direction of treatment effects. In group comparison studies, the effect size (ES) for any specific outcome measure is the posttreatment difference between the mean for that measure in the treatment group and the mean in the control group, divided by the standard deviation of the measure (for different ways of doing this computation, see Cohen, 1988; Weisz, Weiss et al., 1995c). Figure 1.1 is a guide to interpreting ES values. As the figure shows, positive ES values indicate treatment benefit, zero indicates no effect, and negative values indicate a harmful effect. As is also shown in the figure, each ES value corresponds to a percentile standing of the average treated child on the outcome measure if that child were placed in the control group after treatment; for example, an ES of 0.90 indicates that the average treated child scored better after treatment than 82% of the

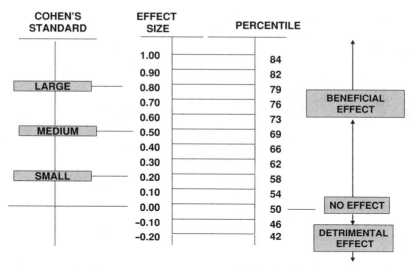

FIGURE 1.1. Guide to interpreting effect size statistics. Each effect size value corresponds to a particular posttreatment percentile for the average treated individual relative to the control group. From Weisz, J. R., Donenberg, G. R., Han, S. S., & Weiss, B. (1995). Bridging the gap between laboratory and clinic in child and adolescent psychotherapy. *Journal of Consulting and Clinical Psychology, 63,* 688–701. Copyright 1995 by the American Psychological Association. Reprinted with permission.

control group. Finally, as an aid to interpretation, many researchers follow Cohen's (1988) guidelines suggesting that an ES of 0.20 may be considered a small effect, 0.50 a medium effect, and 0.80 a large effect.

Effect size values are the building blocks of a technique called *meta-analysis*, which is used to pool the findings of multiple studies and thus gauge the average impact of treatment. The meta-analyst first computes an effect size for each relevant outcome measure used in a study, then averages them all to compute a single mean effect size for the study, then does the same for all other studies in the collection. This makes it possible to compute an overall effect size mean for the entire collection of studies (Mann, 1990; Smith et al., 1980) or to compare subgroups of studies that differ in potentially important ways.

How Well Does Psychotherapy Work with Children and Adolescents?

The effect size metric is sometimes used to address a rather global question: How well does psychotherapy work with children and adolescents? The question is clearly too broad to be answered in a fully satisfying way. So many different forms of therapy are provided, at such varying duration, by so many different therapists, and for such a broad array of problems, among youth who differ so widely in age, gender, and sociocultural and personality characteristics, that a single answer to the question of how well therapy works must certainly overlook many important group differences (see Paul, 1967). On the other hand, it seems useful to assess, from time to time, what the average impact of psychotherapy is across variations in treatments, durations, therapists, problems, and treated youth, to assess whether efforts to treat young people are generally helping or not. Here we will use meta-analytic findings to address that general question. We will take two different looks at the evidence base.

Clinically Derived Treatment in Usual Clinical Care. The millions of youth treated with psychotherapy in clinics, schools, and other service settings each year receive a remarkable variety of different treatments. The blend of 551 named treatments and the great variety of eclectic mixtures used by most therapists make it difficult to describe what psychotherapy looks like in usual clinical care. Indeed, the wide array of treatments across therapists and treated youngsters may be about as numerous as the number of youths who receive treatment in a year. However, the mix of treatment procedures often includes some relatively common elements, such as (a) talking or playing with the child, and talking with the parent; (b) establishing a warm, accepting relationship in which the child is encouraged to express thoughts and feelings; (c) listening reflectively and being empathic; and (d) responding to the issues the child brings to each session. Of course, any list of content and procedural examples will miss what many therapists do in their practice since the range is potentially infinite. A common denominator of many procedures used in usual clinical care is that they are fashioned by individual therapists based on their clinical training, supervision, experience, and judgment, and usually not based primarily on the findings of research.

The general approach outlined here and the four illustrative features have considerable intuitive appeal. Indeed, they are quite close to what I and many others were taught to do in our graduate and professional training. These elements certainly may contribute to a good relationship and a strong working alliance with children and parents, especially when used by empathic, charismatic practitioners. A key question is whether approaches that are primarily clinically guided are sufficient to generate significant measurable benefit, on average, when applied by a variety of clinicians across a variety of practice settings. Answering that question is rather difficult, because there has been so little research on clinically derived usual care as provided in clinical service settings and programs. Some relevant research can be found, however, and we turn to it now.

Effects of Child and Adolescent Psychotherapy: I. Tests of Clinically Guided Care in Usual Practice. My research team has searched for studies that fairly represent usual clinical care of children and teens. We have looked for studies that involved (1) clinically referred youngsters (not re-cruited analog cases); (2) treatment in service-oriented clinics, schools, or programs (not university labs); (3) treatment by practicing clinicians (not researchers or research assistants); (4) intervention procedures that were part of the usual services of the clinic, program, or practitioner; and (5) study designs in which a group receiving the usual care procedures was compared to a group receiving some form of placebo, waitlist, minimal-treatment or no-treatment condition. Thus far, we have found 14 group comparisons (in 13 published articles) that appear to satisfy these criteria. The comparisons span a broad range of methodological rigor; for example, only six involved random assignment of youngsters to usual care versus control conditions. The effect size estimates for each of the 14 compar-isons are shown in Figure 1.2. The horizontal arrow in the figure shows that the mean effect size, averaging across all 14 comparisons, was slightly below 0, indicating no effect. The exact mean was −0.03; means for the nonrandom studies (−0.4) and the random assignment studies (−0.08) were not significantly different (p = 0.44). As the figure shows, the state of the evidence on clinically guided usual care is not very encouraging. It is certainly possible that more favorable evidence will emerge in the future; however, the studies we have found thus far provide little evidence of ben-efit from usual care in the forms and contexts in which it has been tested to date.

Do the effects of usual care improve if multiple treatments are used con-currently? With this idea in mind, some have linked individual forms of clinically guided care together into what are called systems of care, some-times providing a menu of mental health services and a case manager to help connect children to the various services (see Stroul & Friedman, 1986). The evidence to date is generally not very encouraging on this front either. In one assessment (Bickman, 1996; Bickman et al., 1995), the U.S. Army spent $80 million to provide an extensive continuum of mental health care for children in the Fort Bragg (North Carolina) catchment area, and to test its cost effectiveness relative to the more typical fragmented services in a matched comparison site. The Fort Bragg program apparently did produce well-integrated services. It was judged by the American Psychological As-sociation's section on Child Clinical Psychology and the Division of Child, Youth, and Family Services Joint Task Force to be "the most comprehen-sive program to date, integrating many of the approaches demonstrated by other service programs . . . flexibly constructed, yet comprehensive, [with] services available to be adapted to meet the needs of children and their fam-ilies rather than a simplistic application of a single approach . . ." (Roberts, 1994, p. 215). The program was expensive, but it did produce better access to treatment and higher levels of client satisfaction than the comparison site (Bickman et al., 1995). Unfortunately, though, children's mental health and everyday functioning at home and school did not improve any more at Fort Bragg than at the comparison site.

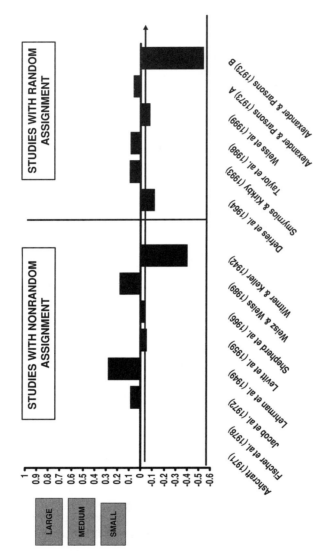

FIGURE 1.2. Clinically derived treatment studies. Estimated effect sizes for 14 comparisons of clinically derived child and adolescent treatment with control conditions. Horizontal arrow shows mean effect size averaging across the comparisons.

In a study with stronger experimental design (including random assignment of children to system-of-care vs. control group), Bickman, Summerfelt et al. (1997) and Bickman et al. (1999) found a pattern very similar to the Fort Bragg results. Studying a mature system of care in Stark County, Ohio, over a two-year period, the Bickman group again found that assignment to the system produced better access to care and larger doses of intervention. However, as in the case of Fort Bragg, there were no reliable differences between system-of-care youth and control group youth in either mental health outcomes or daily functioning at home and school.

Similar discouraging findings have emerged from other studies designed to combine usual clinical services and improve their delivery (Evans et al., 1994; Lehman et al., 1994; Weisz, Walter et al., 1990). Certainly, a number of alternative interpretations of these null findings may be plausible, but one interpretation that must be considered is this: The various treatments that are linked and coordinated within these continua of care simply may not be very effective, individually or in combination (Weisz, Han, & Valeri, 1997). There is no indication that the individual interventions that were combined in these studies had previously been tested and shown to work. Thus, it is possible that the various interventions are simply not effective. It is possible that organizing interventions into coordinated systems is a good idea in principle, but that it may work well only if the specific interventions that are organized and coordinated have beneficial effects.

To summarize findings on clinically guided treatment of youth in usual clinical care: (1) most available evidence on these treatments does not show beneficial effects, and (2) studies on the effects of integrating usual care procedures into systems of care also show little evidence of benefit. To be clear, it seems quite likely that there are individual therapists who use their own distinctive treatment procedures to good effect, and that there are treatment settings and programs where the prevailing forms of care do help children.[1] Moreover, organizing individual services into systems of care may be a good idea in principle, but the impact of any given system

---

[1] As one possible example, a recent article by Angold, Costello, Burns, Erkanli, and Farmer (2000) reported that naturally occurring outpatient mental health care in one region of North Carolina showed a positive dose-effect relationship (i.e., more sessions associated with greater symptom reduction), and apparently greater symptom reduction overall for treated youth than for a control group. However, the finding is difficult to interpret with confidence because (a) the interventions used included medication; (b) the control group consisted of youths from the community who had not been identified as needing treatment, had not been referred, and showed significantly lower symptom and impairment levels at the time of their first assessment than treated youth; and (c) real improvement was not seen in the treated youth who had fewer than eight sessions – our experience suggests that this tends to be a high percentage of treated youth in most outpatient settings. Moreover, the dose-effect finding reported by Angold et al. conflicts with Salzer, Bickman, and Lambert's (1999) findings of a null relationship between dose and effect with children, and Salzer et al. may have done a more thorough job of controlling for factors that could produce a spurious dose-effect association.

may depend on the effectiveness of its individual services. The question of interest here is how well clinically guided youth treatment in usual care seems to work, whether the treatments are provided one at a time or combined into systems. Most evidence to date has not been very encouraging.

Effects of Child and Adolescent Psychotherapy: II. Broad-Based Meta-Analyses. Now we take a different look at the effects of youth psychotherapy as found in the broader research literature not confined to studies of usual care. That broader literature appears to include more than 1,500 group comparison studies (Durlak et al., 1995; Kazdin, 2000a), and more than 350 of these have met methodological requirements for inclusion in major meta-analyses. The treatments employed in these studies differ from one another in many ways, but some relatively common characteristics can be identified. First, the vast majority of the treatments tested in these studies do not represent the usual procedures of clinical practice settings. Most follow rather structured procedures with a specific agenda for the therapy process; therapists are usually guided by treatment manuals or procedural outlines that direct and constrain their actions to some degree. The treatments frequently involve training youngsters in specific skills for coping with their problems, procedures such as systematic problem solving, muscle relaxation, or thought monitoring. In addition, homework or practice assignments are frequently given to treated youngsters and/or their parents. In general, the procedures are structured in orderly ways consistent with what one might expect of researchers planning to submit their studies for peer review. An interesting possibility to consider is that such structure and orderliness may actually enhance the impact of treatment.

For a look at the state of the evidence on these treatments, we will focus on four published meta-analyses that have been particularly broad in their inclusion criteria, encompassing studies of diverse youth problems and disorders, and a variety of different treatments. These four meta-analyses appear to provide a particularly representative cross section of youth treatment outcome research. First we describe the procedures and the findings.

In the earliest of these meta-analyses, Casey and Berman (1985) surveyed outcome studies published between 1952 and 1983. The focus was on child samples – that is, studies whose samples averaged 12 years of age or younger. The mean effect size, averaging across the multiple outcome measures used in the various treatment-control comparisons, was 0.71; the average treated child scored better after treatment than 76% of control group children.

In a second meta-analysis, Weisz, Weiss et al. (1987) included outcome studies published between 1952 and 1983. Mean ages of the samples in these studies ranged from age 4 to 18. The mean effect size was 0.79; following treatment, the average treated child was at the 79th percentile of control group peers.

In the third meta-analysis, Kazdin, Bass et al. (1990b) included studies published between 1970 and 1988. Mean ages across the studies ranged from 4 to 18 years. For the subset of studies that compared treatment groups and no-treatment control groups, the mean effect size was 0.88; the average treated child scored better after treatment than 81% of the no-treatment comparison group. For studies in the Kazdin et al. collection that involved comparison of treatment groups to active control groups (e.g., those receiving a placebo treatment not expected to be effective), the mean effect size was somewhat lower, at 0.77; the average treated child was functioning better after treatment than 78% of the control group.

The fourth meta-analysis, carried out by Weisz, Weiss et al. (1995c), included studies published between 1967 and 1993. Mean ages of the samples ranged from 2 to 18 years. Weisz et al. reported a mean ES of 0.71; after treatment, the average treated child was functioning better than 76% of control group children.

The findings of these four broad meta-analyses are shown graphically in Figure 1.3. For comparison, the two bars at the left of the figure show

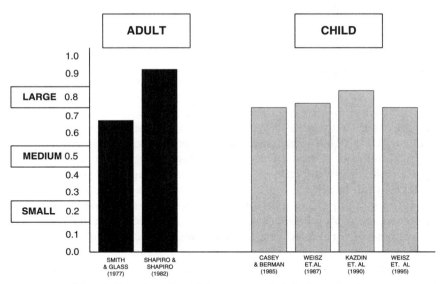

FIGURE 1.3. Mean effect sizes found in meta-analyses of psychotherapy outcome studies in the predominantly adult meta-analysis by Smith and Glass (1977), in the exclusively adult meta-analysis by Shapiro and Shapiro (1982), and in four broad-based meta-analyses of psychotherapy outcome studies with children and adolescents. [From Weisz, J. R., Donenberg, G. R., Han, S. S., & Weiss, B. (1995). Bridging the gap between laboratory and clinic in child and adolescent psychotherapy. *Journal of Consulting and Clinical Psychology, 63*, 688–701. Copyright 1995 by the American Psychological Association. Reprinted with permission.]

the mean effect sizes found in two widely cited meta-analyses with older groups. One is Smith and Glass's (1977) analysis of primarily adult psychotherapy outcome studies; the other is Shapiro and Shapiro's (1982) analysis of exclusively adult outcome studies. The four bars at the right show effect size means from the four child and adolescent meta-analyses just described (Casey & Berman, 1985; Kazdin et al., 1990b; Weisz et al., 1987, 1995b). As the figure shows, mean effect size values were quite consistent from one child-adolescent meta-analysis to the next, and quite positive; means ranged from 0.71 to 0.84 (0.84 is an estimated overall mean for Kazdin et al., 1990b), near the threshold of 0.80 sometimes used to indicate a large effect (see Cohen, 1988). The means fell within the range shown for adult studies, suggesting that the effects of youth treatment may not differ much from the effects of adult treatment.

Two other meta-analytic findings warrant attention. First, we have found (in Weisz et al., 1987 and 1995b) that effects measured immediately after treatment are quite similar to effects measured at follow-up assessments, which average five to six months after treatment termination. Thus, treatment benefits appear to be durable, at least within typical follow-up time frames, and in studies whose authors were thorough enough to include follow-up assessments.

A second finding (Weisz et al., 1995b) concerns the specificity of treatment effects. Frank (1973) and others have proposed that psychotherapy has general, nonspecific effects, helping people with diverse problems in such broad, general ways as promoting a feeling of being understood or inducing an expectancy of relief. An alternative view is that therapies help in specific ways, having their strongest influence on the specific problems they are designed to address. Prompted by this debate, we tested (in Weisz et al., 1995b) whether effect sizes were larger for the specific problem domains targeted by a treatment than for other, more incidental domains; for example, did treatments for anxiety produce bigger changes in anxiety levels than in related but more peripheral problems such as depression? Across multiple comparisons like these, analyses showed that effect size means were about twice as large for the specific problems addressed in treatment as for related problems that were not specifically addressed (Weisz et al., 1995c, p. 460). This suggests that these tested psychotherapies do not merely produce global, nonspecific good feelings that influenced diverse outcomes equally, but instead, that the treatments had rather precise, focused effects consistent with the specific aims of the therapy.

Complementing the broad-based analyses just described, some meta-analysts have addressed rather specific questions by focusing on select subsets of outcome studies. Meta-analyses focused specifically on cognitive-behavioral therapy (CBT) (described later in this book) have found substantial positive effects on impulsivity (Baer & Nietzel, 1991), on depression (Lewinsohn & Clarke, 1999; Reinecke et al., 1998a,b), and across a heterogeneous array of target problems (Durlak et al., 1991). Dush et al. (1989) found positive effects associated with a specific cognitive-behavioral technique that involves training youngsters to change the self-statements they make when confronting problems. Two teams (Hazelrigg et al., 1987; Shadish et al., 1993) have found respectable mean effects of family therapy somewhat higher for measures of individual family members' behavior than for family interaction measures. Beneficial effects have also been found for interventions used to prepare children for medical and dental procedures (Saile et al., 1988), and for psychotherapies administered in school settings (Prout & DeMartino, 1986).

Summing Up: Effects of Child and Adolescent Psychotherapy and Some Caveats

Our survey shows a positive picture of youth treatment outcomes in the broad research literature on youth psychotherapy, but a disappointing picture of the outcomes of usual clinical care. Mean effect sizes in the youth psychotherapy literature have averaged somewhere between medium (0.5) and large (.8), whereas means in the usual care studies have averaged near zero. Three caveats warrant attention. First, the small number of empirical tests of usual clinical care can only provide a rough estimate of treatment effects, an estimate that may change as new research is completed. Second, the conditions in which usual care is provided differ in multiple ways from the conditions in clinical trials, and the latter may be more amenable to favorable findings than the former. Third, the positive effects shown in Figure 1.3 may overestimate true population effects to some degree. Analyses in Weisz et al. (1995b) suggest that, with weighting to adjust for sample size and heterogeneity of variance, effect size means may be closer to medium than large. Moreover, the meta-analyses have emphasized published articles; publication bias may inflate our picture of the mean impact of treatment with studies that show positive outcomes more likely to be submitted and accepted for publication than studies that show poor outcomes (see McLeod & Weisz, in press). Of course, publication bias and unadjusted effect sizes may have influenced our estimates of the effects of clinically guided care in usual practice as well.

What seems clear is that the available evidence needs to be interpreted cautiously. Moreover, the fact that research continues to accumulate means that any summary or meta-analysis will inevitably provide a still photo of a moving target. However, that said, the most current still photo we have does suggest two significant points: (1) usual clinical care for children and adolescents, in the forms studied thus far, may not work very well; and (2) meta-analyses of the broader research base suggest that youth psychotherapy, in the relatively structured forms most often tested to date, can be beneficial.

Task Force Findings: Identifying Specific Evidence-Based Treatments. This is an encouraging conclusion, but it lacks specificity. While meta-analyses are useful in characterizing treatment effects averaged across groups of studies, they do not tell us much about the individual treatments that generate the average effects. One way to address this limitation is to carry out focused reviews searching for specific treatments that have empirical support. The American Academy of Pediatrics (e.g., 2000) has developed practice guidelines for specific conditions constructed partly from evidence on treatment outcome. The American Academy of Child and Adolescent Psychiatry (e.g., 1997) has developed Practice Parameters. Another approach, taken by task forces within the American Psychological Association (e.g., Chambless et al., 1998; Lonigan et al., 1998; Task Force, 1995) has been to focus exclusively on the outcome evidence in order to identify specific psychotherapies that meet criteria for respectable levels of research support.

The most widely used set of criteria was originally developed by a Task Force of the Society of Clinical Psychology, a division of the American Psychological Association (see Task Force, 1995). Within this system, beneficial treatments are classified as either *well established* or *probably efficacious*. Well-established treatments are those supported by either group comparison studies, within-group studies, or single-case studies. If group design studies, then there must be two such studies demonstrating efficacy by showing that the treatment is superior to medication, a psychological placebo condition, or an alternate treatment, or by showing that the treatment is equivalent to an already established treatment. Treatments may also be classified as well-established based on at least nine well-designed within-group or single-case experiments comparing the target treatment to an alternative treatment. If a treatment is supported by the requisite number of studies, it may qualify as well established only if it also (1) uses a manual, (2) clearly specifies the sample used, and (3) is supported by at least two different investigators or research teams.

To qualify as probably efficacious, a treatment must be supported by either (1) two group comparison studies showing the treatment to be more effective than a waitlist control group, (2) at least one experiment meeting most of the well-established treatment criteria, or (3) at least three within-group or single case design experiments. This category also requires treatment manuals and clear descriptions of client samples, but it does not require independent replication by different investigators. It also does not require that the target treatment be shown to be superior to an alternative treatment or even an active control condition; superiority to waitlist is sufficient if demonstrated in at least two studies.

Using these criteria, a child specialist task force (Lonigan et al., 1998) identified well-established and probably efficacious treatments for the four broad clusters of problems and diagnoses that will be addressed in this book: *fears and anxiety* (Ollendick & King, 1998), *depression* (Kaslow &

Thompson, 1998), *ADHD* (Pelham et al., 1998), and *conduct-related problems and disorders* (Brestan & Eyberg, 1998). The specific review procedures used in each case and descriptions of the treatments and the evidence are detailed in the task force articles. Of course, it is possible to question whether the two-category system is the best way to characterize levels of empirical support, whether the criteria used to evaluate the evidence are the most appropriate, or whether the Task Force procedures were sufficiently rigorous. Critiques have been offered and alternative approaches proposed (see e.g., Chambless & Hollon, 1998; Chorpita et al., 2002; Weisz & Hawley, 1998). Clearly, review procedures will evolve over time, as do most scientific processes, and the list of specific treatments will change over time, as more studies are completed. However, the task force report (Lonigan et al., 1998) represents a thoughtful approach applied by distinguished experts, and it was an important starting point in determining which treatments to include in this book.

Identifying Evidence-Based Treatments for This Book. This book focuses on evidence-based treatments, treatments that have been tested empirically and shown to have beneficial effects. In identifying the treatments for description and analysis in this book, certain inclusion criteria were applied to the lists. Treatments were selected for emphasis that (1) were designated as either well-established or probably efficacious in the child and adolescent expert Task Force report (Lonigan et al., 1998); (2) address psychological dysfunction that has already developed (i.e., not preventive interventions for at-risk youth); (3) treat specific problems rather than exposure to harm and trauma (which may lead to quite different problems in different youngsters, and thus require thorough assessment to identify proper treatment goals); (4) focus on primary behavioral and mental health problems rather than problems related to medical-physical conditions (e.g., obesity, headaches; for reviews in that area, see Spirito [1999] and a series of 1999 articles in the *Journal of Pediatric Psychology*); and (5) are supported by replicated evidence (i.e., two or more studies). Throughout the book, treatments are described in as generic a way as the evidence warrants. Thus, descriptions focus on one particular "brand name" treatment with its one specific manual if the evidence is that specific, but we describe generic approaches (e.g., behavioral parent training for youth with conduct problems, CBT for child depression) if multiple manuals or versions have been tested and shown to be beneficial.

Organization of the Book: The Chapters on Evidence-Based Treatments

In all the chapters of this book except the first and last, I examine particular evidence-based treatments – their conceptual-theoretical basis, their procedures, the evidence bearing on their effects with children and adolescents, and their readiness for clinical use. The chapters are grouped into four sections, encompassing treatments for the four broad clusters of problems and disorders discussed earlier: *fears and anxiety, depression, ADHD,* and *conduct problems and conduct disorder*. Each section begins with an introduction describing the cluster of problems and disorders and illustrating that cluster with a case example (altered for confidentiality). The cases will look familiar; they are Sean (anxiety), Megan (depression), Kevin (ADHD), and Sal (conduct problems and conduct disorder), each introduced at the beginning of this chapter.

We return to the case example each time a new treatment is discussed, describing how that particular child and family would be treated within the framework of that particular treatment. These case illustrations of the treatments follow a mastery model in which the treatments succeed in most respects. My intent is to show how the treatments operate when youths and parents are responsive and the procedures work as intended. However, because even the best of treatments can encounter rough sledding with some youths and families, each treatment illustration is followed by a *troubleshooting* section noting common problems that can arise, and effective solutions to those problems recommended by experts who have applied the treatments in practice.

In addition to describing treatment principles, procedures, and evidence, and illustrating the treatment with a case example, I cast a critical eye on each treatment wearing two hats. Donning my researcher hat, I discuss scientific issues that remain salient for each treatment approach, identifying questions that remain unanswered, and suggesting directions and strategies for further research. For example, in discussing each treatment I comment on what we know about (1) which youth characteristics may moderate treatment impact, and (2) change processes that may explain why the treatment works. Then, wearing my clinician hat, I discuss clinical practice issues relevant to each treatment approach – issues for practitioners and policy makers who may want to consider making the treatment a part of their own clinical practice or mental health service program.

The treatments reviewed in this book are both science-based and intervention-focused. Because science and intervention practice evolve continually, each of the treatments reviewed in this book is best viewed as a work in progress. I want to contribute to the evolution by suggesting ways to enrich our scientific understanding of the treatments and how they work, and ways to make the treatments more accessible to dedicated clinicians working on the front lines who want their practice to be guided by evidence.

At the end of each chapter, several resources are listed for those who want to learn more about the topic of the chapter. This first chapter is no exception. Noted in the next section are several references to articles and books about evidence-based treatments. The list of resources may prompt a reasonable question: Given what has already been written, why do we need another book on this topic? The answer, in my view, is complementarity. Extant offerings thus far tend to be either conceptual and empirical analyses of the field or edited collections of chapters about various treatments, written by the treatment developers themselves. Books of both types are valuable. This book complements both by applying exactly the same descriptive, analytic, and case illustrative framework to each treatment program, all from the perspective of an informed observer intent on being dispassionate and objective. My goal is to improve prospects for evidence-based practice by improving communication between clinical scientists and practitioners. My hope is that the book will contribute to that process, adding usefully to an already rich collection of resources on evidence-based treatment for children and adolescents.

How to Find Out More about Evidence-Based Treatments for Youth

Increasing interest in evidence-based mental health care has led to a growing library of resources for those who want to know more. Alan Kazdin's (2000b) *Psychotherapy for Children and Adolescents: Directions for Research and Practice* (Oxford University Press) provides a thoughtful analysis of numerous issues related to the quality and utility of psychotherapy research with young people. Alan Kazdin and I (Kazdin & Weisz, 2003) have also edited a volume, *Evidence-Based Psychotherapies for Children and Adolescents* (Guilford Press), in which leading youth treatment researchers describe their treatment programs and other leaders of the field comment on critical issues such as the challenge of creating evidence-based practice. A forthcoming volume, *Psychosocial Treatments for Child and Adolescent Disorders: Empirically-based approaches* (2nd edition, American Psychological Association), edited by Euthymia Hibbs and Peter Jensen (Hibbs & Jensen, in press) will also bring together various treatment developers who describe their treatments and the evidence bearing on them.

TREATMENTS FOR FEARS AND ANXIETY

Introduction to Section B

The Case of Sean and Treatments for Fears and Anxiety

Sean

Nine-year-old Sean has been a worrier since early childhood, but his worries have caused increasing problems the older he has gotten. In the preschool years, he was afraid of the dark and afraid to be left alone in his room, so fearful of monsters under the bed and in his closet that bedtime was a major ordeal. Dropoffs at preschool were painful scenes, with Sean in tears, clinging to his mom, preschool staff cajoling, and forced separation followed by anguished protests.

Now a fourth grader, Sean is markedly different from most of his classmates – shy and withdrawn at recess, continually worried that he will do something "dumb" in front of his peers and suffer ridicule, or make a mistake in his schoolwork and be criticized by his teacher. He is mortified at the thought of answering a question aloud in class. Last month, when the teacher assigned an oral book report, she precipitated a crisis at home: Each night for a week before the deadline, Sean was tearful and terrified of certain failure – sure that he would make a fool of himself in front of the class, and so paralyzed by fear that he couldn't concentrate on preparing the report. By D-Day, Sean was near collapse, complained of a stomachache, and begged his mother not to make him go to school. Forced to go, he delivered his report in a barely audible voice, with hands and knees trembling; he made no eye contact with the class, forgot his main points, and sat down looking pale, faint, and mortified.

Social interaction is almost as frightening for Sean as class reports. Play dates with peers are a rarity, because Sean is certain that other kids see him as "weird," or "a loser." And sleepovers, common among nine-year-olds, never happen for Sean. He is too afraid of separation to be away from home overnight, and too afraid of rejection to risk inviting a peer. Recently, Sean has developed a fear of eating in the school cafeteria; he says his hands tremble when he is nervous, and he is afraid other kids will see the trembling and make fun of him. He has taken to eating in empty classrooms, hidden from view. Although his mother worries about his social and school problems, she is quite anxious herself, and some of her interactions with Sean seem to reinforce his worries.

Maladaptive fears in young people have been a focus of study and treatment since the very beginning of formal psychological theory and intervention. One of Sigmund Freud's (1909/1955) most famous early cases was that of 5-year-old Little Hans and his 'horse phobia;' applying psychoanalytic theory, Freud interpreted Hans's behavior and ideas as evidence of the Oedipal complex and an intense fear of Hans's father.

Watson and Rayner (1920), in a famous experiment that would never clear a university human subjects committee today, used classical conditioning principles to make little Albert, an 11-month-old boy, fear a white rat. The experimenters struck an iron bar with a hammer to create a loud noise and startle Albert every time he reached for the rat; eventually, the infant feared not only the white rat but other furry objects as well, including a Santa Claus mask and even Watson's hair. Watson and Rayner's behavioral ideas for removing children's fears were put to the test by clinical researcher Mary Cover Jones (1924) who treated Peter, a 2-year-old afraid of a white rabbit. By combining gradual exposure to the rabbit with modeling by other children who liked and petted the rabbit, Jones replaced Peter's fear with a real affection for the rabbit.

In the eight or nine decades since Freud and the behaviorists launched their treatments for fearful children, an enormous number of theorists, investigators, and therapists have addressed fears and anxieties in young people. The result is massive literature on the nature and treatment of anxiety in youth, rivaling the literature on any other childhood condition.

The heavy historical emphasis on anxiety is appropriate, given the high prevalence in our population. Anxiety disorders are the most common class of psychiatric disorders among children and adolescents (see Albano et al., 1996; Bernstein et al., 1996). Silverman and Ginsburg's (1995) review of ten epidemiologic studies led them to estimate the prevalence of "any anxiety disorder" at 6–18% among youth in the general population. Severe anxiety can be highly debilitating, undermining a youngster's adaptation and development in numerous ways. As the case of Sean illustrates, development of peer relationships can be hampered, school performance may suffer, efforts to learn new skills may be thwarted, and normative challenges (e.g., presenting an oral report, meeting a new person) may become major life crises.

Given the adverse impact of anxiety on social relationships, learning, and development, there is a clear need for beneficial treatments. Treatment developers have responded with a broad array of interventions. Freud's (1909–1955) psychoanalytic approach evolved over time into a variety of psychodynamic treatments, some involving play. However, most of the literature bearing on the outcome of such treatments involves case reports. In keeping with our emphasis on strong empirical support, we will focus in this chapter on only those treatment procedures supported in experimental tests (see review by Ollendick & King, 1998). Those tests have been focused on treatments that have grown out of the more behavioral tradition, traceable to the early work of Watson and Rayner (1920) and Jones (1924), as discussed earlier. For example, Jones' procedure of gradually bringing Peter into ever-closer proximity to the rabbit, while Peter ate food that he liked is a sort of template for a cluster of *exposure* procedures that are now a common part of behavioral treatment for fear and anxiety. And Jones's efforts to have Peter observe other children interacting happily with the rabbit form a template for anxiety treatments that involve modeling or observational learning.

As will soon become clear, exposure and modeling are mainstays of most of the empirically supported treatments for anxiety in youth. In this section, we will focus on those treatments, beginning with interventions for specific fears and ending with treatment programs for the more complex combinations of symptoms that form the DSM anxiety disorders. In the first anxiety chapter, we will survey four classic treatment approaches for specific fears: (1) *modeling or observational learning*, in which nonanxious responses are modeled for the fearful youth by others; (2) *systematic desensitization*, in which youngsters are exposed to fear-producing objects or situations while they are very relaxed (or in some other fear-incompatible state); (3) *reinforced exposure*, in which youngsters are rewarded for showing nonfearful behavior; and (4) *cognitive-behavioral treatment*, in which self-talk and other ways of linking thoughts and behavior are brought to bear on the object of the child's fear. In the second anxiety chapter, we will turn to more complex multicomponent cognitive-behavioral treatment programs, applied to full-fledged anxiety disorders.

2

Four Classic Treatments for Fears

Modeling, Systemic Desensitization, Reinforced Exposure, and Self-Talk

For many children and adolescents, fears seem to develop one at a time. One child is frightened by a dog's loud bark and fears dogs thereafter. Another is afraid to be alone in the dark. Another won't take swimming lessons for fear of the water. Even for children like Sean, introduced at the beginning of this section, a cluster of fears that coexist at one point in time may actually have developed in serial fashion. For the focused treatment of specific fears, whether they occur solo or within a complex tapestry, four tested treatment approaches have evolved out of four somewhat different theoretical traditions. We focus on these four treatments in this chapter. First we consider how fears and avoidance take shape and become entrenched.

Across some rather different theoretical perspectives, one can piece together an account of how fears and the avoidance of feared objects and situations come to be such a potent force in the lives of many boys and girls (see e.g., Bandura, 1971; Ollendick & Cerny, 1981). Here is part of the thinking in some accounts: Through a combination of biological vulnerability and learning experiences, the fearful child comes to anticipate that carrying out certain actions (e.g., approaching a dog) or being exposed to certain situations (e.g., being in the dark alone) will lead to frightening consequences (e.g., being attacked by the dog, or grabbed by a monster in the dark). The prospect of engaging in the behavior or being in the feared situation stimulates aversive physiological arousal in the child, in such forms as increased heart rate, tense muscles, a tight feeling in the stomach, or various other bodily changes. Avoiding the feared behavior or situation reduces the aversive arousal, and also brings relief by appearing to prevent the frightening consequence the child has imagined. Avoiding is thus doubly rewarded – through reduced arousal and through perceived prevention of feared outcomes. This double dose of reward increases the likelihood that the cycle will be repeated in the future, culminating in more avoidance of the feared object or situation. How can a therapist break into this cycle, reducing the avoidance and helping fearful boys and girls confront what they fear? Decades of treatment research offer at least four answers to this question.

One of the answers is a set of treatments involving *modeling*. Modeling treatments are built on the potency and efficiency of observational learning. The approach involves exposing children to a model who engages in the activities they fear, but who encounters none of the adverse consequences the children are afraid of. For many fearful children, the message sinks in quickly. The efficiency of the modeling approach is underscored by the remarkable brevity of the interventions. As we will see, there are multiple ways to arrange for modeling – live, symbolic, and with guided participation – and these may differ from one another in their potency and efficiency.

A second approach, *systematic desensitization*, involves more complex procedures. Children are first trained to relax. Then, once in a relaxed state, they are asked to imagine increasingly intense exposures to the objects, situations, or actions they fear. Some believe that the procedures work because a relaxed state is incompatible with a fearful state. Others offer a more complex interpretation of treatment success built on the classical conditioning tradition. Whatever the mechanism, evidence shows that systematic desensitization can be effective in reducing fear and fearful behavior.

A third approach to specific fears falls within the operant conditioning tradition; it is called *reinforced exposure*. Here children are induced to try successive approximations to the activities they fear, and rewarded for doing so, sometimes with praise and sometimes in more tangible ways. The goal is to catch the children showing the desired behavior (i.e., acting in spite of their fear) and to reinforce the behavior so that it is likely to be repeated. Note that in this approach children are neither taught to relax (as in systematic desensitization) nor encouraged by means of a model (as in observational learning methods); instead, they are simply rewarded for behavior that runs counter to their fears.

A fourth approach to treating fears in boy and girls is *self-talk*, a method developed within the cognitive-behavioral tradition. In this approach, children are taught cognitions in the form of self-statements (e.g., "I am brave, and I can do it!") to help them confront what they fear. Successful confrontations are then rewarded. As will be evident in Chapter 3, the cognitive-behavioral approach has been expanded into manualized treatments for use with more complex anxiety disorders – thought and action complexes that go beyond simple solo fears. In this chapter though we focus on simpler versions used to treat one specific fear at a time.

For each of the four treatment approaches discussed in this chapter, we will describe the procedures used, summarize relevant outcome studies, and illustrate the treatment by noting how it could be used with Sean, the youngster described at the beginning of this section. We will also offer some thoughts on research issues for future study, and on clinical practice issues for clinicians who may want to incorporate some of these approaches into their work.

Modeling Treatments: Conceptual Basis and Procedural Overview

For fearful boys and girls, the sequence of feared object → anxious thoughts → aversive arousal → avoidance → relief → reward can be potent and self-sustaining. Intruding into and altering the sequence is not an easy task, as many parents and many therapists have learned. One way the sequence *can* be interrupted is by exposing fearful youths to a model who violates the assumptions underlying the fear. The model engages in the feared behavior, thus demonstrating that it can be done and showing how; and the model does not experience the adverse consequences the child has feared – indeed, the model may even enjoy the behavior. When the treatment works, the observing child emulates the behavior of the model, then learns, in the peaceful aftermath, that this can be done with impunity. In one influential view (Bandura, 1977, 1986), learning nonfearful behavior is mediated, at least in part, by development of perceived self-efficacy, that is, "people's judgments of their capabilities to organize and execute courses of action required to attain designated types of performances" (Bandura, 1986, p. 391).

Whatever the mediating mechanisms, multiple treatment studies have shown beneficial effects of modeling interventions in the treatment of children's fears. Three general forms of modeling have been supported in outcome studies thus far:

- *Live modeling* involves in-person observation of the models' nonfearful behavior.
- *Symbolic modeling* employs video or other representations of models showing nonfearful behavior.
- *Participant modeling* pairs the fearful youngster with a model who encourages shared involvement in the feared activity.

For reasons that are not immediately evident, the current zeitgeist in youth anxiety treatment does not emphasize modeling approaches, even though the evidence suggests that this family of treatments can be quite helpful, and even though the focus and brevity of the treatments is consistent with current pressures for efficiency and cost effectiveness. Because so much of the evidence supporting the modeling approaches was generated through studies published in the 1960s and 1970s, some of the trappings of successful current treatments are missing. Perhaps most important to readers of this book will be the fact that detailed treatment manuals and related materials are hard to find. On the other hand, the relative simplicity of these treatments means that, for some of them, the descriptions provided in the original published articles may provide sufficient guidance for clinical use.

Modeling Treatments: In Brief

Designed for . . . . Specific fears (e.g., dogs, swimming) in children ages 3–12
Number of sessions . . . . Range: 1–8
Session length . . . . Range: 8–35 minutes
Session participants . . . . Therapist, live or video model, children (individually or in small groups)
Theoretical orientation . . . . Observational learning

Treatment steps:

1. Assess fear levels in child who is to be treated.
2. Arrange for child to observe live or video model performing feared activity, with level or intensity increasing over time (e.g., observing dog, then approaching, then petting).
3. Invite child to engage in the activity, initially at low level, then increasing intensity.
4. [optional] Arrange positive consequence for successful imitation of the model.

Treatments classified by Treatment Task Force as . . . Probably Efficacious for live and video modeling, Well-Established for participant modeling (Ollendick & King, 1998).
Key resource for potential users: Ollendick, T. H., & King, N. J. (1998). Empirically supported treatments for children with phobic and anxiety disorders: Current status. *Journal of Clinical Child Psychology, 27*, 156–167. Manuals are not available for the specific treatments reviewed in this chapter, but intervention procedures are described in the relevant journal articles as cited in the chapter.

Live Modeling: Treatment Procedures

In *live modeling*, the fearful child observes a model (perhaps a peer, perhaps the therapist), in person, engaging in the feared behavior, usually by exposing himself or herself to an object or situation the child fears. In some variants of this approach, the model is relatively fearless throughout the process. In other variants, the model appears fearful or reluctant at the outset and at first shows only tentative attempts to carry out the feared behavior, but then increases the intensity or strength of the behavior across successive trials. Across the exposures, even when they involve increased intensity, the model experiences no adverse consequences and often appears to enjoy the experience.

After the child has observed the model's behavior directly, the therapist invites the child to do what the model did. A common practice is to start the child at a low level of intensity (e.g., sitting at a distance from the feared object) and add increments (e.g., moving closer, touching the object, picking it up) following each successful exposure. Optionally, the therapist may praise or reward the child for successes. Specific forms of the live modeling approach have varied from study to study, as will be illustrated in the following study descriptions.

Live Modeling: Outcome Studies Testing the Effects

Live modeling has been used to address several specific fears in children. We will focus here on two research examples targeting animal-related fears.

Using live modeling to help children overcome fear of nonpoisonous snakes. Murphy and Bootzin (1973) used one approach to live modeling with children who were afraid of nonpoisonous snakes. Children were selected who both reported such a fear and proved unable to touch a snake for 10 seconds during a behavioral approach test. The participants included 67 fearful children from first to third grades (age, gender, and ethnicity not reported). The youngsters were randomly assigned (within various fear levels) to *active*, *passive*, and *control* conditions, which are described next.

Children in the active and passive conditions were seen individually; they sat in a chair 15 feet from an adult who was holding a 28-inch boa constrictor. The adult spent two minutes interacting with the snake while relating facts about this particular boa, and commenting that he or she would not pick up an unfamiliar snake, which might be harmful. After the two minutes of modeling, the child was asked to try a graduated series of several types of contact with the snake – ranging from standing near it, to touching it briefly, to holding it with both hands for 10 seconds, to sitting with the snake in the child's lap. In the *active* condition, each child was asked to perform each step after the experimenter modeled it. In the *passive* condition, the children remained stationary while the experimenter approached them with the snake and manipulated the snake's body so that it touched the child. Each live modeling session, in both conditions, lasted eight minutes or less, and no child received more than four sessions. Children in the *control* condition received no intervention, only assessments.

Despite their brevity and simplicity, both live modeling interventions were very effective. Of the 45 fearful children who received intervention, 39 completed even the most difficult step – that is, holding the snake in their laps for 15 seconds with their hands touching it. Only 5 of the 22 untreated fearful children could do that. Moreover, the treatment was remarkably efficient. Treated children passed the snake-holding test in an average of 1.9 treatment sessions, for an average of about 15 minutes of modeling per child.

Using live modeling to help preschoolers overcome fear of dogs. In a somewhat more elaborate intervention, Bandura et al. (1967b) treated nursery school children who showed inappropriate fear of dogs. The 48 children, half boys and half girls, ranged in age from 3 to 5 (mean age and sample ethnicity not reported). All were rated by parents as being fearful of dogs. The young participants were assigned randomly to one of four conditions; two conditions involved modeling.

The two modeling conditions each entailed eight 10-minute sessions, spread over four consecutive days, with groups of four children at a time. In these sessions a four-year-old boy served as model, playing with a brown cocker spaniel in the same room as the fearful children. The boy carried out a preplanned series of interactions with the spaniel, lasting about three minutes. The intensity of the interactions increased from the first session to the last. At the beginning, the boy only talked to the spaniel (e.g., "Hi Chloe.") and occasionally petted it while the dog remained in a playpen; but by the end, the boy was in the playpen with Chloe, petting her with his hands and feet, feeding her wieners and milk from a baby bottle. (Bandura and his colleagues found that this gradual increase in intensity was necessary, because interactions that were too intense in the early stages made children avoid looking, which interfered with learning the fearless responses.)

In one of the modeling conditions, called *positive context,* treatment sessions occurred in the midst of a lively party, with colored hats, cookies, and prizes. In the other modeling condition, *neutral context,* there was no party, and children merely sat at a table while the model went through the steps with Chloe. The two modeling treatment conditions were compared to two control conditions, that is, "exposure-positive context," in which there were parties and a dog nearby, but no model, and "positive context," in which there were parties but no dog and no model.

The day after the eighth session, the children were given behavioral tests with both Chloe and another dog (a white mongrel) they had not seen before. An adult took each child individually into a room containing the dog in the playpen, then asked the child to go through a series that began with walking up to the pen and touching the dog's fur, and ended with climbing into the playpen, scratching the dog's stomach, and remaining alone with the dog. Children who had seen the model interacting with Chloe did very well on the test; 67% were able to complete the final step, remaining alone with the dog in the pen, compared to only 33% of control group children who had not observed the model. The control condition in which children were repeatedly exposed to the dog but without the model was designed to test whether exposure alone might be sufficient to eliminate the children's fears; it was not. The fact that fears persisted, despite repeated exposure to the dog (both in and out of the playpen), indicated that the beneficial effects derived specifically from having children observe the fearless model. By the way, pairing the eight modeling sessions with lively parties did not enhance the impact of the modeling. Modeling worked just as well without the party.

Symbolic Modeling: Treatment Procedures

A particularly efficient treatment approach is *symbolic* modeling. Here, video or other media are used to present models to anxious youngsters. This approach has obvious advantages. For one, once a video has been produced and found to be effective, it can be reused repeatedly with no worry that the models' behavior may change in some way. For another, the availability of a video that has already been shown to work greatly reduces the complexity of the therapist's job.

Beyond the fact that the modeling is virtual, the procedures for symbolic modeling need not differ much from those of live modeling. As in live modeling, the video approach can involve progressive exposure; multiple brief videos can be shown across several days, depicting increasingly close and intense approaches to the feared object. To enhance generalization, the videos may be designed to show progressive exposure by several different child models, and to several different exemplars of the same class of feared objects (e.g., dogs differing in species and size). Where a particular skill is involved – say, swimming – videos can also be produced to illustrate skill development over time; video models who are just beginning to learn the skill may even make mildly fearful comments (e.g., "I'm a little afraid, but I will try this anyway") to help the fearful child identify with the models.

Symbolic Modeling: Outcome Studies Testing the Effects

Research on symbolic modeling is illustrated here via two outcome studies, one involving fear of dogs, the other fear of water that interfered with learning to swim.

Treating children's fear of dogs by means of symbolic modeling. In one example of this approach, Bandura and Menlove (1968) used a video approach to treating children's fears of dogs. As in the live modeling study with Chloe (Bandura et al., 1967b), the investigators focused on preschoolers who were afraid of dogs. There were 32 girls and 16 boys, ages 3–5 (ethnicity not reported). Children were randomly assigned to three groups, two involving symbolic or video modeling, and the third a control condition.

In all three groups, children watched a total of eight different three-minute videos, two per day, on four different days. Each video session was attended by three to four children. In the *single-model* condition, Bandura and Menlove (1968) showed the children the same fearless 5-year-old modeling progressively more courageous interactions with the same cocker spaniel. In the *multiple model* condition, the children saw *various* boys and girls modeling increasingly courageous interactions with *various* dogs that were increasingly large and fearsome over time. A posttreatment task tested children's ability to approach and interact with a dog. Both symbolic modeling groups showed marked increases in fearless behavior, while control group children, who had seen only Disneyland and Marineland movies, showed no change.

Of the two active treatments, the multiple-model approach worked better, showing stronger holding power than the single-model approach over the following month. In fact, the single model on video was less helpful in reducing children's dog avoidance than was the live single model approach used by Bandura et al. (1967b) in the Chloe study described previously. The limitations of a filmed approach (e.g., not as "real" as a live model) seemed to be offset by the use of varied models and targets (i.e., various children and different dogs); children in the multiple-model condition not only showed high rates of improvement right after treatment, but they also actually improved further during the following month.

Symbolic modeling can also work well beyond the preschool years. As one example, Bandura et al. (1969) used a film showing people handling snakes to reduce fear of snakes in individuals ages 13 to 59.

Using symbolic modeling to treat water fears in elementary-aged children. In a rather different application of video modeling, Lewis (1974) treated water fears in 5–12-year-olds. Their sample included 40 African-American boys, all attending a summer camp, and all referred to the study because they had shown fear of water during camp swimming tests.

The 40 were randomly assigned to either a control condition watching cartoons, then playing checkers with the experimenter, or three active treatment conditions. The treatment condition of interest here involved viewing an eight-minute film that showed three African-American boys ages 7, 10, and 11, engaging in various swimming activities, graduated in difficulty. Early tasks included climbing up the ladder, entering the pool, and letting go of the side of the pool, and later tasks included sinking into the water and floating face down, six feet from the side of the pool. The three were all coping models; that is, they all appeared fearful and hesitant at the beginning, but they grew more confident and competent over time. Their comments during the film mirrored this shift, with early comments such as "I am a little afraid, but I will try this anyway," and later comments expressing pride in mastering the tasks. After watching the video, each boy played checkers with the experimenter, as in the control condition.

Prior to the intervention or control condition, and then again the next day, each child was given a graded performance test in a pool. Boys who had seen the modeling video showed marked improvements, doing much more challenging water activities than in the pretest; boys in the control group showed little change.

Participant Modeling: Treatment Procedures

The Lewis (1974) study of water fears also tested another variant of the modeling approach, *participant modeling*, in which the model carries out the feared activity with the fearful person. As in the other forms of modeling, the participant approach often involves graduated exposure, beginning with low levels that arouse only modest worry and advancing to more proximal and intense contact with the feared object or situation.

In participant modeling, the therapist often serves as the model *and* the child's partner, performing the feared activity and nudging the child into joining the action, while providing a comforting presence. Across the different modeling methods, the participant approach appears to be the most potent, perhaps in part because it combines the power of observational learning with the added security of a competent partner and the added impetus of persuasion to try the exposure.

Participant Modeling: Outcome Studies Testing the Effects

To illustrate research findings on participant modeling, we return to the study of water fears at summer camp, and we describe a study with children who feared snakes.

Using participant modeling to treat fear of water. In the Lewis (1974) study of water fears, there were two participant modeling conditions in addition to the video modeling and control conditions previously discussed. One of the participant modeling conditions was paired with the modeling video described earlier; the other was paired with the neutral video consisting of cartoons. Following their respective video presentations, youngsters in both participant modeling groups were taken to the pool individually by the experimenter, who served as the model. The experimenter entered the pool with each boy and spent ten minutes encouraging him to try the graduated steps of water activity, physically assisting him as needed, and praising him for any activities tried and completed.

Individual assessments of each boy's water activities the next day showed substantial effects of this brief procedure. Boys who had done participant modeling following the neutral cartoons showed more improvement than youngsters in the modeling video condition described earlier. Those who had done participant modeling following the modeling video were more improved than any other treatment group. In other words, participant modeling alone outperformed symbolic (i.e., video) modeling alone, and symbolic plus participant modeling was the most powerful intervention of all.

Treating fear of snakes using participant modeling. In another test, Ritter (1968) used participant modeling with 5–11-year-olds who were afraid of nonpoisonous snakes. Her sample included 28 girls and 16 boys (mean age and ethnicity not reported), all of whom had shown significant fear in a pretest with a harmless four-foot-long gopher snake. Specifically, each child had been unable to hold the snake, within a cage, with a gloved hand for five seconds. The 44 children were randomly assigned to either a control condition (pre- and postassessment, with no treatment in between) or one of two modeling conditions, each involving two 35-minute treatment sessions spaced a week apart.

In Ritter's *participant modeling* condition, children in groups of seven or eight sat in a circle around the cage, and watched an adult take the gopher snake ("Posie") out of the cage, sit with her, and pet her. The adult eventually identified a child who seemed boldest and most interested, had the child put on a glove, and encouraged the child to stroke Posie, first with the gloved hand, and then with the bare hand. Gradually, the adult moved around the circle, sitting near each child, and encouraging each child to join in petting and stroking Posie. With hesitant children, the adult began by placing the child's hand on the adult's hand, and petting Posie. Over time, the children were encouraged to try increasingly direct and close interactions with Posie, including taking the snake out of the cage alone with bare hands, and sitting in a chair with Posie in their lap for 30 seconds. By contrast, children in a *vicarious* condition sat around the cage in groups of seven or eight and merely observed the experimenter and five peer models engaging in the graduated activities with Posie.

On the day after the final treatment session, just as before treatment, children's snake fears and avoidance were assessed using a 29-item snake activity test. Those who had been in the participant modeling condition were the most successful of the three groups. Some 80% of these children completed all 29 items, including the final step: sitting in a chair with arms at their sides while Posie rested in their lap for 30 seconds. None of the children in the no-treatment control group were able to complete all the steps. The vicarious group, who had only watched others play with Posie, fell in between; 53% of this group passed all the steps of the test. The findings are consistent with other evidence (see Ollendick & King, 1998) showing that modeling works, and showing that participant modeling works better than other, more passive forms.

What about Sean? Applying the Three Modeling Approaches

Returning to the case of Sean, introduced at the beginning of this section, let us consider how live, symbolic, and participant modeling interventions might be used. Some tailoring will be needed, because most modeling studies have focused on fairly simple challenges, such as holding a snake. Most of Sean's problems involve more complex, multicomponent tasks, such as presenting an oral report in front of his class, or developing a relationship with a peer. However, to the extent that some of Sean's challenges can be simplified, by focusing on one fear at a time, modeling interventions may be helpful.

As an example, suppose that Sean's teacher allows class reports to be read to the class. This makes it possible to have Sean prepare his report in the exact words he wants to use, while he is at home away from the feared situation. Sean's therapist then arranges a live modeling experience in which Sean sits in his "family audience" with seating arranged like a classroom, while his brother reads Sean's report to the family. The therapist also arranges with Sean's teacher to identify others in Sean's class who are planning to read their report and to have some of those students precede Sean, so he can benefit from their live modeling of appropriate behavior.

The therapist also arranges for symbolic modeling. The teacher has offered to videotape the class presentations, and she privately contacts a few of the parents, asking if their child's tape may be shared with another child who would like to use the tapes for "practice." Sean views the borrowed tapes in the therapist's office, and talks to the therapist about the various styles of presenting.

In addition, the therapist arranges for participant modeling by enlisting an ally, Sean's brother Max. At home, Max stands with Sean in front of the "family audience" and alternates reading duties with Sean (i.e., first Max reads the brief introduction to Sean's report, then Sean follows suit, then Max reads the next section, then Sean, and so forth). Because most evidence suggests that participant modeling is the most helpful of the three approaches, the therapist puts special emphasis on these family audience readings, especially at the beginning of Sean's treatment; then she gradually fades Max's role out as Sean becomes more comfortable. The idea is to get Sean ready for his big moment at school when Max won't be there to help.

On the day of the class presentation, Sean is nervous. He feels flushed and can hear his heart beating as he sits at his desk waiting to be called on. However, when the teacher calls on him, and he walks to the front of the class with his note cards, the situation seems more familiar and more comfortable than he had expected, thanks to all his modeling experiences. When he starts his report, his voice trembles a bit, and he loses his place in the note cards twice, but he shows fairly good eye contact with the class, and he is able to read his way through the report without the panic he had feared. When he returns to his seat, he knows he did a fairly good job, and he feels proud.

Troubleshooting: Common Treatment Problems and Recommended Solutions. Modeling worked well for Sean as it does for many children. However, there can be problems in implementing the methods and fitting them to particular youngsters. Here are a few common difficulties and some solutions suggested by experts.

- *Low credibility of the model.* Sometimes the model being used is not believable enough to the youth to inspire emulation. In such cases, effective therapists figure out why credibility is low, and proceed accordingly. If, for example, the model is not enough like the child (e.g., the adult therapist serves as the model), the challenge is to increase similarity, perhaps by engaging a sibling or one of the child's peers as the model. Alternatively, credibility may be low because the model does the behavior so easily that the child thinks, "I could never do that." In such cases, what may be needed is a coping modeling approach, one in which the model shows initial fear but overcomes it.
- *Failure to repeat the model's behavior.* Sometimes the model seems credible, but the fearful child simply can't work up the nerve to try the model's behavior. When this happens, several adjustments may be helpful. One is to downgrade the intensity of the modeled behavior, selecting an activity that is less frightening and thus easier to imitate. Another is to add incentives (e.g., "After you do it, we'll get some ice cream.") to increase motivation to follow the model's lead. A third is to strengthen the physical connection between youth and model during the activity. As an example, the therapists may say "OK, stand behind me and hold my shirtsleeve while I touch this trash can" (for children with contamination fears), then "Stand beside me," and then "Stand in front of me."
- *Excessive dependence on the model.* Children can be *too* connected to their model. Some, for example, won't repeat the target behavior except in the presence of the model. Therapists can address the problem through fading: the child does the exposure activity with a model every time at first, then every other time, then every third time, and so forth. Other children may be overly connected in that they can only perform the model's exact behavior (e.g., they can start a conversation but only by using the exact wording the model used every time). Here the therapist may need to be clear about the goal (e.g., "I want you to say something different from what I said"). Therapist and child can play the novelty game, the object of which is to do or say something different from the original. Novelty can also be paired with rewards to increase the child's motivation to be original.

Systematic Desensitization: Conceptual Basis and Procedural Overview

One of the earliest and most enduring behavioral approaches to treating fears and anxiety is systematic desensitization (SD). Developed by Wolpe (1958), SD builds on the notion that fears develop through classical conditioning (pairing of a fear-provoking stimulus with a neutral stimulus can empower the neutral stimulus to generate fear as well). From this assumption, it follows that fears may be *un*done through *counterconditioning*, or *reciprocal inhibition*. The core idea is that fear-inducing stimuli (e.g., dogs or darkness) are presented together with other stimuli that provoke responses not compatible with fear – most often relaxation. The objective is to arrange the learning experience in such a way that the desired response, such as relaxation, becomes strong enough to replace the undesired response of fear.

Three steps are used to make this happen. First, a fear hierarchy is created with specific feared stimuli ordered from least to most frightening. Second, the fearful youngster is taught to relax, often through highly structured exercises involving tensing and releasing of various muscle groups. Sometimes pleasant imagery is used to enhance the relaxation. Third, items from the fear hierarchy are presented gradually (often through imagination only) while the child maintains a relaxed state. If the youngster is able to remain relaxed during even those items highest in the fear hierarchy, and across repeated exposures, then a key goal has been attained because a person cannot be both relaxed and fearful at the same time.

Systematic Desensitization: In Brief

Designed for . . Specific fears of objects (e.g., dogs) or situations (e.g., tests) in children ages 6–15
Number of sessions . . . . Range: 5–24
Session length . . . . Range: 50 minutes–1 hour
Session participants . . . . Therapist and children
(individually or in small groups)
Theoretical orientation . . . . Classical
(respondent) conditioning

Treatment elements:

1. Assess fear levels in child who is to be treated.
2. Establish fear hierarchy with feared stimuli arranged from least to most anxiety-provoking.
3. Train child to relax, often using muscle tensing/relaxing plus pleasant imagery.
4. Expose child (in vivo or in imagination) to items in the hierarchy, moving from least to most anxiety-provoking.
5. Whenever child signals uncomfortable anxiety (e.g., by raising a hand), revert to items lower in the hierarchy and/or restate relaxation instructions.
6. When child remains relaxed through the full hierarchy, repeat the process in one or more review sessions.

Treatment classified by Treatment Task Force as . . . . . Probably Efficacious (Ollendick & King, 1998).
Key resource for potential users . . . . Ollendick, T. H., & King, N. J. (1998).
Empirically supported treatments for children with phobic and anxiety
disorders: Current status. *Journal of Clinical Child Psychology, 27,* 156–
167. Manuals are not available for the specific treatments reviewed in
this chapter, but intervention procedures are reasonably well described
in the specific articles reviewed here.

Systematic Desensitization: Treatment Procedures

The specific procedures used in SD differ somewhat across therapists, but
there is a common core that resembles the original procedures used by
Wolpe (1958). The first two steps include establishing a detailed fear hierarchy and teaching the child procedures for getting relaxed. The fear hierarchy lists specific circumstances within the target fear domain that provoke
anxiety, with the items ranked from least to most anxiety-provoking. As an
example, if the fear being treated is test anxiety, items low in the hierarchy
might include *getting in the car with your parent to drive to school*. Items near
the middle of the hierarchy might include *having your parent remind you
that you have a test today* or *arriving at school and having two classmates tell you
they are in a panic over today's test*. Items high in the hierarchy might include
seeing that the test the teacher has just given out looks really hard.

The relaxation training can take a number of forms, but the common
core includes a relaxed position (e.g., sitting with both feet on the floor, or
lying down), slow breathing and attending to one's breathing, and progressive tensing and relaxing of muscle groups. The muscle relaxation training
may begin with clenching and unclenching fists, then tensing and relaxing arms and shoulders, neck and face, trunk, upper and lower legs, then
feet. In some techniques, the therapist asks the child, before beginning the
relaxation instructions, to describe a scene that he or she will find relaxing
(e.g., lying on the warm sand of a beach with the sound of the surf in the
background), and this scene is introduced once muscle relaxation and calm
breathing have been well established.

The art of SD comes next. The therapist's task is to gradually introduce
items in the fear hierarchy, working from least to most anxiety-provoking,
while ensuring that the child sustains a relaxed state throughout. In most
cases, the items are introduced via imagination, but some therapists use
in vivo exposure. For the school performance anxiety example given earlier,
the therapist might first ensure that the child is relaxed, then begin exposure
by asking the child, "OK, close your eyes, and imagine that you are getting
in the car with your dad and thinking about what school will be like today."
Later in the process, the therapist might say, "OK, now imagine that you
pass two friends in the hall, and they are in a panic because of the exam

you will all have next period." The child's instruction is to raise a hand if feelings of fear or tension get to be uncomfortable. When this happens, the therapist asks the child to shift to an image lower in the hierarchy, and may also repeat relaxation/breathing instructions. The idea is to have the child eventually work through the full hierarchy without uncomfortable anxiety.

When the youngster is able to get through the full hierarchy across multiple sessions without much anxiety, the time has come for a transition to real-life exposure, to assess whether the desensitization training effects generalize outside the treatment setting.

Systematic Desensitization: Outcome Studies Testing the Effects

Does such generalization occur? Does desensitization reduce anxiety in children's real-life exposures outside therapy? We now review studies investigating this question.

Using systematic desensitization to treat school children's performance anxiety. In apparently the first published study of SD with children and adolescents, Kondas (1967) worked with 23 Czech youths who experienced anxiety over exams, answering teachers' questions in front of peers, and other kinds of school performance. The 23 were 11–15-year-olds (mean age: 13) from grades 5–9 (gender and ethnicity not reported). Four groups were formed via random assignment: (1) relaxation only, (2) SD, (3) fear hierarchy exposure only, and (4) no-treatment control group.

The *relaxation-only* condition ran for ten weekly sessions; children were seated in comfortable armchairs, taken through exercises in relaxed breathing, and led through progressive relaxation of right hand, left hand, legs, abdomen, and chest muscles. (Children were also asked to practice relaxation at home and in school.) The SD group had seven sessions of this relaxation training, then five additional sessions of imaginal desensitization; therapists led the children through a 10-item fear hierarchy, beginning with "Going to school in the morning – you think that you may be asked to give reports," and ending with "Answering questions in front of the class while the school director is present." While the children were in a relaxed state, they were asked to close their eyes, then to imagine items from the fear hierarchy, in a sequence that moved from lower-fear to higher-fear items, and with two to three items covered in each treatment session. Desensitization sessions were spaced about one week apart. In the *fear hierarchy exposure only* condition, children were asked to close their eyes and imagine the items in the hierarchy, with two to three items presented per session; but these children received no relaxation training or instructions.

The SD treatment produced sharp decreases in self-reported performance anxiety, and these reports were paralleled by changes in palmar perspiration in a school examination situation. The changes also held up well in a follow-up assessment five months after treatment had ended. Effects of the SD intervention were amplified by comparison with the other conditions in the study. Neither hierarchy exposure alone nor the no-treatment control condition produced any significant anxiety reduction. Relaxation training alone did produce anxiety reduction immediately after the end of treatment, but the effect disappeared after five months. For lasting anxiety reduction, the findings suggested that the full SD package (i.e., relaxation training combined with hierarchy exposure) was required.

Treating junior high test anxiety with vicarious and direct individual and group desensitization. In a rather unusual study, Mann and Rosenthal (1969) created a horse race comparing five different ways of doing desensitization. The treatments were administered to 50 seventh graders (ages 12–13, 27 girls, 23 boys, ethnicity not reported), all referred by school counselors for test anxiety. An additional 21 test-anxious eighth graders (ages 13–14, 12 girls, 9 boys, ethnicity not reported) served as untreated controls.

The 50 seventh graders were randomly assigned to one of the following procedures: (1) *individual direct desensitization*, with one-on-one relaxation training and imaginal fear hierarchy exposure; (2) *individual vicarious desensitization*, with the individual child observing another individual child in condition *a* while that child underwent the training; (3) *group direct desensitization*, with groups of five children receiving the relaxation training and imaginal fear hierarchy exposure together; (4) *vicarious group desensitization*, with children in groups observing the groups in condition *c* as they underwent training, and (5) *vicarious group desensitization-individual model*, with children in groups observing individual desensitization of a single peer model. Outcomes were assessed using a self-report measure of test anxiety and a reading test designed to be sensitive to effects of anxiety. Analyses revealed essentially no differences in outcome across the various active treatment conditions, all of which outperformed no-treatment. The general pattern of results suggested that all the different ways of delivering desensitization produced similar levels of anxiety relief.

Comparing systematic desensitization to psychodynamic therapy in treatment of diverse child and teen fears. In a particularly stringent comparison involving fearful 6–15-year-olds, Miller et al. (1972) pitted SD against a combination of psychodynamic and behavioral psychotherapy. A nice feature of the study was that participating children were solicited through letters to social agencies, physicians, and schools, and through newspaper ads in an effort to focus on referred youngsters representing clinical-level fears. The 67 youngsters thus identified (55% male, 96% Caucasian, 4% African American, mean age not reported) were referred for diverse fears, with the most common involving school, sleeping or being alone, being in the dark, separation, and dogs; 61% of the children had multiple fears.

Children were randomly assigned to a waitlist control condition or to one of two active treatments, each individually administered and involving about 24 one-hour sessions. One treatment was SD, focused on the specific fear that was most disabling to the child. The SD procedure began with parent relaxation training, so the parent could model relaxation for the child in the first session. Four sessions were devoted to relaxation training and to construction of a fear hierarchy and identification of a pleasant scene that aroused little anxiety. In subsequent sessions, the child was asked to imagine the hierarchy items, working from least to most fear-provoking, and to use the pleasant scene as a replacement whenever one of the fear items produced uncomfortable anxiety.

The alternate treatment was a form of psychotherapy that blended a psychodynamic emphasis "on the child's 'inner experience,' his hopes and fears, particularly his aggressive and sexual fears and dependent needs," and a more behavioral emphasis on formulating "behavioral strategies for coping" (p. 271). Younger children (ages 6–10) had play therapy in a playroom, whereas older children (ages 11–15) had either play therapy or talk therapy, depending on which seemed more appropriate for the child. In both forms, the psychodynamic treatment involved encouraging the child to act out or 'talk out' his feelings, and an emphasis was placed on affective expression and intellectual awareness as steps toward developing healthy ways to cope with fears.

At the end of the treatment phase, outcomes were assessed in multiple ways, including parent ratings of child fears and of child behavior problems, and performance ratings given by the study's primary evaluator based on how well the child handled previously anxiety-provoking situations. The performance ratings actually showed no statistically significant effect of either active treatment relative to the waitlist. Parent ratings did show more anxiety reduction for the two treated groups than for the waitlist group, but even parent ratings failed to show either active treatment superior to the other. Thus, this intriguing study showed only partial support for systematic desensitization, and it showed no evidence that this treatment was superior to a more traditional, partially psychodynamic alternative treatment. One possible reason for this similarity in outcomes across the two treatments is that therapists' work with family members and the child's significant others outside the family was quite similar, and quite behavioral, across the two active treatment conditions. This may have made the overall treatments more similar to one another than intended.

What about Sean? Applying Systematic Desensitization

Sean, the youngster who was introduced at the beginning of the anxiety section, may be a viable candidate for SD. That is, Sean evinces a number of fears that could be broken down into rather specific elements to form fear hierarchies, ranked from least to most frightening. For example, it is easy to imagine Sean and his therapist organizing Sean's fears of performance situations in class into a fear hierarchy like the one used in the Kondas (1967) study just reviewed; waking on a school day and thinking of getting called on in class ranks lower in Sean's hierarchy than actually giving an oral report to his class. Let's imagine what an SD experience might be for Sean.

Although some time in the first four treatment sessions is devoted to constructing the hierarchy, most of the time in each of these sessions goes into relaxation training for Sean. He learns how to achieve relatively complete muscle relaxation by breathing slowly and calmly while attending to his breathing, alternately tensing and releasing serial muscle groups (hands, arms, shoulders, neck, face, trunk, legs, feet), and imagining a very pleasant scene. Sean's preferred scene has him lying in a field of cool grass under a shade tree, with a brook running nearby. The relaxation phase of treatment alone seems to help, empowering Sean to master some of the physiological arousal that accompanies his anxiety.

By the beginning of session five, Sean has become an expert at relaxation, and his therapist moves him to the imaginal exposure phase of SD. While Sean is in a relaxed state, the therapist asks him to close his eyes and imagine waking in the morning and thinking about getting called on in class. Then the therapist moves to the next item up the hierarchy, and so forth. Sean's job is to maintain his relaxed state as long as possible, and to signal with a raised hand should any image make him feel uncomfortably anxious. Each time a hand is raised, Sean's therapist takes him back to an item lower in the hierarchy and reiterates relaxation instructions until Sean appears relaxed again. By the end of the twelfth session, the therapist is able to lead Sean through the full hierarchy with no raised hand; in fact, Sean covers the full hierarchy three times in session 12 alone. Sean also tells his therapist that he is less nervous in real class situations now, that he has answered some questions when called on without shaking or sounding scared, and that once this week he even raised his hand to volunteer an answer in class – something he had not done during the entire school year.

Troubleshooting: Common Treatment Problems and Recommended Solutions. Sean seemed to make real progress using systematic desensitization, but some children and some therapists encounter problems with this technique. Here we note two of the most common problems, and recommended solutions to each.

- *Therapist difficulty in conveying a vivid image for imaginal exposure.* Sometimes the therapist's description of the feared object or situation just doesn't generate real fear during the imaginal exposure. In these cases, therapists may need to work on the imaginal script with the youth, sharpening its image potential prior to the exercise; or therapists may even have the youngster write the script alone, requiring that the script include such key words as "worried" and "afraid." If that approach fails, vivid drawings, pictures in books, or even movie clips may be needed to generate a sufficiently vivid image to provoke real fear and thus set the stage for SD.

- *Youth difficulty in imagining and in mental elaboration.* Some youths seem to lack skill in holding an image in mind and elaborating it. Therapists can often help such youngsters develop and sharpen this skill by guiding them through pleasant imagery at first and then moving to unpleasant images. To further prompt skill development, therapists can probe for details: "OK, now what color is the dog's fur? Is his mouth open or closed? Is he growling or barking? What does he smell like?" And naturally, therapists need to make sure the setting is designed for relaxation and imagination (e.g., with soft comfortable furniture, lights dimmed, and outside sounds muffled).

Reinforced Exposure: Conceptual Basis and Procedural Overview

The next form of treatment we consider grows out of the operant model of learning and implicitly poses an intriguing question: What if we do not try to make anxious people relax, and what if we do not provide models for fearless behavior. Might we still be able to treat fear and anxiety successfully? The answer, it turns out, is yes. Treatments involving *reinforced exposure* do not employ models, do not include relaxation, and do not even assume that fears need to be reduced before people can do the things they fear. Instead, reinforced exposure focuses on the *consequences* that follow behavior. In the basic procedure, the therapist (often in collaboration with the child) designs graduated steps of exposure, and the fearful child is rewarded for accomplishing the steps, which involve doing ever more challenging levels of what the child has been afraid to do.

Why does this procedure work? One influential view is that reinforced exposure is a form of contingency management (see King & Ollendick, 1997), the same general procedure that works so well in treating children's conduct problems (see Chapter 9). In essence, the procedure is seen as altering behavior by changing its consequences (see Ollendick & King, 1998), for example, arranging contingencies so that approaching a previously feared object or situation leads to reward in some form. Viewed this way, treatment benefit is explained partly by reference to the venerable *law of effect.*

Reinforced Exposure: In Brief

Designed for . . . . Specific fears (e.g., dogs, dark, water sports) in children ages 3–12

Number of sessions . . . . Range: 3–10

Session length . . . . Range: 20 min–5 hours

Session participants . . . . Therapist and child (usually seen individually)

Theoretical orientation . . . . Operant conditioning (contingency management)

Treatment elements:

1. Identify feared objects/situations, and arrange a way for graduated exposure to occur.
2. Present child with situation and response options, noting reward for increased exposures.
3. Upon exposure, give child feedback (e.g., on duration); reward and praise increments.
4. Continue until child reaches preestablished criterion for success.

Treatments classified by Treatment Task Force as . . . Well-Established (Ollendick & King, 1998). Key resource for potential users . . . . Ollendick, T. H., & King, N. J. (1998). Empirically supported treatments for children with phobic and anxiety disorders: Current status. *Journal of Clinical Child Psychology, 27,* 156–167. Manuals are not available for the specific treatments reviewed in this chapter, but intervention procedures are described in the relevant journal articles, as cited in the chapter.

Reinforced Exposure: Treatment Procedures

Procedures for reinforced exposure tend to be less complex than for some of the other anxiety treatments. Once the target fear has been identified, a primary task for the therapist is to design graduated steps of exposure. For fear of some situations, such as darkness, the graduating procedure may be as simple as increasing the time the child is asked to remain in a darkened room. For other fears, say, those involving animals or other concrete objects, graduation may consist of increasingly lifelike and direct exposures (e.g., photo of a dog, a dog at a distance, a dog close up but with therapist in between child and dog, a dog close to child with no therapist in between). Appealing rewards are made contingent on passage through the graduated steps, and the child is apprised of the contingencies. Each new step of self-exposure is greeted with reward, and frequently with feedback (e.g., a chart showing how long the child stayed in the dark alone this time, compared to previous times) and praise. The process continues until the child reaches a predetermined criterion for overcoming the fear.

Reinforced Exposure: Outcome Studies Testing the Effects

How well does reinforced exposure work? Here we consider four illustrative studies addressing this question.

Treating children's fear of dogs and public buses by reinforced practice. In an early illustration of the procedure, Obler and Terwilliger (1970) worked with children who were diagnosed as having "minimal brain dysfunction," but who also had specific fears of either dogs or riding on public buses, according to parent reports. The sample ranged from 7 to 12 years of age, and from 50 to 146 in IQ (age mean, gender, and ethnic composition not reported). The 15 randomly selected treatment group children were matched to the 15 control group children on age, gender, IQ, and phobia type (dogs or buses).

The 15 treatment group children were seen individually by 15 different "therapists" (college graduates with no prior clinical experience, who had ten hours of training for their role). Fearful children who were randomly assigned to the reinforced exposure treatment were neither asked to develop a fear hierarchy nor trained to relax, as would have been the case in SD (see earlier discussion), nor were the children asked to report on whether their anxiety was lowered. Instead, they were merely rewarded for participating in progressively more realistic and intense exposures. The exposures began with pictures (of either dogs or buses) and progressed to *in vivo* encounters, such as staying in a room alone with a dog, or standing in the bus talking to the bus driver and putting coins in the fare box. As children completed the exposure steps, they were immediately rewarded with treats they had selected in an earlier session (e.g., toys, books, candy, even pets). The process involved ten weekly sessions of five hours, an unusually lengthy process.

At the end of the study, parent reports of children's real-life behavior indicated that all the children in the reinforced exposure treatment had overcome their avoidance to some extent, either touching a dog or riding on a bus, and that more than half the treated children were able to carry out the exposure alone. By contrast, only one-fifth of the untreated children had overcome their avoidance, and none were able to do their exposure (touch a dog or ride a bus) alone.

Using reinforced exposure to help young children overcome fear of darkness. A few years later, Leitenberg and Callahan (1973) achieved similar results treating nursery school and kindergarten children who were afraid of the dark. Children with such fears had been identified by parents on a study questionnaire and in a follow-up interview, and they performed poorly on a behavioral test of darkness tolerance. Some 14 of these children were formed into pairs, matched for their performance on the behavioral test; pair members were randomly assigned to treatment or control conditions. The eight girls and six boys averaged 5.7 years of age (ethnicity not reported).

Children in the treatment condition were asked to go into a dark room, close the door, and remain there until they were afraid and wanted to come out; they were told they could choose a prize each time they remained in the room longer than before. Children were also praised each time they stayed longer than before. This simple intervention lasted a maximum of eight sessions, two per week, with each session involving no more than five trials in the dark room. By the end, more than half the treated children stayed in the dark room for the maximum period of five minutes, whereas the longest time spent by any child in the no-treatment group was 100 seconds.

Using reinforced exposure and verbal coping skills, solo and combined, to treat preschoolers' fear of darkness. A decade later, Sheslow et al. (1983) treated preschool children's fear of the dark using three approaches, two involving reinforced exposure. The sample included 32 4- and 5-year-olds whose parents' reports and behavioral avoidance tests showed-intense fear of being in the dark. The 32 children (half boys, half girls; ethnicity not reported) were randomly assigned to a contact control group (they recited nursery rhymes) or to one of three treatment conditions. Across all conditions, children were seen individually for a maximum of three 20–30-minute sessions, on three consecutive school days.

In one treatment, *graduated exposure*, the children confronted up to nine steps of increasing darkness, created with a rheostat; as the room was darkened, children signaled their anxiety either verbally or with a bicycle horn. In a second treatment approach, *verbal coping skills*, children were given statements ("special words") to help them cope with the steps of increasing darkness (e.g., "If I think I see things in the dark, I know they are just shadows," and "I can always turn the lights on."). In the third active treatment, *coping skills/graduated exposure*, children repeated their coping statements at each downward step of the rheostat.

Outcome measures included the length of time children tolerated being in the dark, and children's own self-reports of anxiety made on a "fear thermometer." Interestingly, children's self-reports did not show significant group differences, but the behavioral measure did. Children in both exposure groups showed markedly increased tolerance of darkness, significantly outperforming both the coping statement group and contact control group. In other words, exposure worked with or without coping statements.

Using in vivo and vicarious exposure to reduce fear of water activities. A more recent study by Menzies and Clarke (1993) provides further support for reinforced exposure. This study focused on 3–8-year-olds who were afraid to try water activities in a swimming pool, according to parent and child report as well as a behavioral test. The 48 children (mean age 5.5 years, 65% boys, ethnicity not reported) were randomly assigned to either a no-treatment control condition or one of three individually administered, active treatment conditions. Each treatment involved three weekly sessions lasting a half-hour each.

In the *in vivo exposure* condition, children were encouraged to enter the water and progressively increase their water-based activity (e.g., knee depth, waist depth, neck depth, head under water), and they were rewarded each time by praise from the therapist. In the *vicarious exposure* condition, each child watched a live model (the therapist) engage in the water activities. In the *in vivo exposure plus vicarious exposure* condition, each session involved 15 minutes observing the model doing water activities followed by 15 minutes of *in vivo* graduated exposure.

The *in vivo* exposure procedure – with or without vicarious exposure added – produced marked increases in children's water activity, and the procedure was significantly more effective than vicarious exposure, in which the therapist modeled water activity for children. In fact, vicarious modeling was no more effective than the no-treatment control condition, and adding modeling did not even enhance the impact of the reinforced exposure condition. It is possible that modeling by a peer might have been more effective than modeling by the adult therapist. All we know from this study is that reinforced exposure worked quite well. The technique appears to be as powerful as it is procedurally simple.

What about Sean? Applying Reinforced Exposure

Returning to the case of Sean, one can imagine his therapist finding reinforced exposure useful, though perhaps not ideal, given the fact that his most significant fears (e.g., of performance situations in school) cannot be directly confronted in therapy sessions. We can imagine ways the technique might be adapted to fit Sean. As a first step, suppose the therapist works with Sean to identify the kinds of exposure he finds most difficult. These are then broken into steps and ordered from least to most frightening. As one example, when Sean and his therapist focus on speaking up in class, the hierarchy has giving one-word answers aloud at the low end, wordier answers in the middle, and a full-length oral report at the top.

Of course, the therapist cannot lead Sean through *in vivo* exposure at his school, so the two of them try to create a mock classroom setup in the therapy room. Here the therapist encourages Sean to go through the steps of the hierarchy while imagining he is in class. Movement up the hierarchy in the therapist's office is rewarded with praise. In addition, the therapist arranges for more substantial rewards for Sean at various milestones of real-life exposure. When Sean reports having given his first one-word answer in math class, the therapist rewards him with praise and with extra time in the game room. A longer comment in a lit class discussion earns a snack break, with the therapist buying Sean a soda and his choice of snack from the vending machine down the hall. And when Sean proudly tells about giving an oral report in class, the therapist high-fives him and pulls two movie passes out of his pocket. Sean is learning that making himself act in spite of his fear pays off, not only in praise and rewards from his therapist, but also in his own self-confidence.

Troubleshooting: Common Treatment Problems and Recommended Solutions. Reinforced exposure seemed to help Sean. Sean is in good company. This treatment approach works well for many fearful youngsters. However, the approach is not without challenges, some of which we consider now, together with techniques therapists have used to address the challenges.

- *Exposure task too easy or too hard.* As noted earlier, one of the therapist's challenges in reinforced exposure is calibrating the exposures. What the child is asked to do must be frightening enough to represent a true challenge and thus promote real growth, but not so frightening that the child refuses to do it. What if all the tasks discussed with the youngster seem to fall into one category or the other? When this happens, it is time to elaborate the fear hierarchy, identifying additional kinds of exposure in the mid-range of difficulty for the child. What if the exposure hierarchy seems well elaborated, but the youngster still won't try the exposures? When this happens, thoughtful therapists often work on the reward hierarchy. For some youngsters, social rewards (e.g., profuse encouragement, praise for small steps) may make a difference; for others, enriching the material rewards or privileges that can be earned through exposures may tip the balance in favor of taking the plunge.
- *Rewards not rewarding enough.* To tip that balance, and nudge the child into trying a scary exposure, may require quite potent rewards. Such rewards may be hard to identify solely by talking to the child or parent. In such cases, therapists may find home observations helpful. In general, the kinds of activities the child chooses spontaneously and invests significant time in are, almost by definition, highly rewarding. By making such activities (e.g., TV watching, video games, time on the phone with friends) contingent on the completion of exposure tasks, therapist and parents may greatly increase the odds of cooperation.

Self-Talk: Conceptual Basis and Procedural Overview

Another form of treatment for specific fears entails adjusting the ways children think about the objects or situations they fear, or about themselves in relation to their fears. Evidence (e.g., King, Meitz, Tinney, &

Ollendick, 1995) does suggest that anxious youngsters usually have mal-adaptive cognitions about the situations they fear, and about themselves when they are in such situations. Thus, therapists have devised ways to help children alter their cognitions. One approach involves teaching children to make self-statements that embody either constructive coping, positive self-evaluation, or a positive reframing of feared situations.

A core notion underlying these procedures is that, because behavior is often guided by cognitions, altering cognitions can change behavior. Under this assumption, the challenge is to identify those specific cognitive adjustments that can actually lead to more adaptive behavior. The two published studies discussed next illustrate how this challenge has been met by child treatment researchers.

Self-Talk: In Brief

Designed for . . . . Specific fears (e.g., darkness, going to bed) in children ages 5–13
Number of sessions . . . . Range: 1–3
Session length . . . . Range: 30 min.–1 hour
Session participants . . . . Therapist, children (seen individually or in groups), sometimes parents
Theoretical orientation . . . . Cognitive-behavioral

Treatment elements:

1. Identify feared situations and assess baseline fear levels (or have parents do so at home).
2. Identify thoughts child has that makes the situations frightening.
3. Teach child alternative thoughts in the form of coping self-statements (e.g., "I am a brave boy/girl. I can take care of myself in the dark.") and when to use them (i.e., in target fear situations).
4. Observe and record child's degree of tolerance of feared situations when self-talk is being used (or train parents to observe and record at home).
5. Give child feedback on progress (e.g., via a chart or stars) and reward success (e.g., with praise, tokens, prizes, food, gift certificates).
6. Continue until child reaches preestablished criterion for success.

Treatments classified by Treatment Task Force as . . . . . Probably Efficacious (Ollendick & King, 1998).
Key resource for potential users . . . . Ollendick, T. H., & King, N. J. (1998). Empirically supported treatments for children with phobic and anxiety

disorders: Current status. *Journal of Clinical Child Psychology, 27,* 156–167. Manuals are not available for the specific treatments reviewed in this chapter, but intervention procedures are described in the relevant journal articles, as cited in the chapter.

Self-Talk: Treatment Procedures

As with the other fear interventions discussed in this chapter, the use of self-talk procedures begins and ends with assessment of the child's ability to tolerate the feared situation. However, the intervention itself is different, and certainly much simpler than modeling or systematic desensitization. A common beginning for some versions of self-talk treatment involves identifying anxious cognitions. Therapist and child work together to figure out what thoughts the child has that make the feared situation so scary (e.g., "There are monsters in the dark"), and then to replace those maladaptive thoughts with positive coping thoughts. In other versions of self-talk treatment, identification of current cognitions is skipped, and therapist and child move directly to developing coping thoughts. In both versions of this treatment approach, a critical task for the therapist is to identify special words that will inspire the child to venture into feared territory (e.g., darkness). The therapist helps the child memorize the special words, teaches the child to repeat them when feeling anxious, records the child's degree of voluntary exposure to the feared situation before and after the use of self-talk, and provides feedback, praise, and reward for increased exposure.

In some cases, parents play an active role, learning the child's special words, encouraging their use at home, monitoring and recording changes in the child's exposure levels at home, and praising and rewarding success. The fact that children are typically rewarded for tolerating the feared situation does tend to blur the distinction between self-talk on the one hand, and reinforced exposure (reviewed earlier), on the other hand, a point to which we return at the end of this section.

Self-Talk: Outcome Studies Testing the Effects

The two research examples that follow illustrate some of the variability that is possible in the use of self-talk to address child fears.

Using self-talk to help 5- and 6-year-olds tolerate the dark. Kanfer et al. (1975) trained children to use two different types of self-statements to overcome their fear of being alone in the dark. Before the intervention, the 45 5- and 6-year-olds (67% boys, ethnicity not reported) from a Montessori kindergarten had all been unable to remain in the dark alone for three minutes. Each child was assigned to one of three conditions (the article does not state whether assignment was random), each apparently involving only a single individual session with a therapist, and each involving different types of self-statements.

Children in the *competence condition* were given instructions that emphasized their own personal ability to cope with and be confident in the dark. They were told, in part:

> When you are in the dark you know that you can turn on the light when you feel like it. In your room, when it's dark, you know exactly where everything is – your bed, your dressers, your toys . . . . (Kanfer et al., 1975, p. 253).

As a kind of self-talk summary statement, children in this group were told to repeat the following special words to themselves when they were in the dark: **"I am a brave boy [girl]. I can take care of myself in the dark."**

Children in the *stimulus condition* heard instructions designed to reduce the fear-provoking potential of darkness. They were told, in part:

> The dark is the best place to go to sleep and have good dreams. The dark is a special place where you can play games. It is more fun to watch a movie or the TV in the dark because you can see the picture better. (Kanfer et al., 1975, p. 253)

Children in the stimulus condition were told to repeat different special words to themselves when in the dark: **"The dark is a fun place to be. There are many good things in the dark."**

Children in the *neutral condition* (i.e., the control condition) heard the following instructions, in part:

> Mary took a lamb to school with her one morning. That day, when she was finished with school, Mary played with the lamb in the garden behind her house. Mary was very careful and made sure that she fed the lamb every day. (Kanfer et al., 1975, p. 253)

For this group, the designated self-talk was intended to be irrelevant to fear of the dark. Thus, the neutral group's special words were **"Mary had a little lamb. Its fleece was white as snow."**

Treatment effects were assessed by clocking how long children remained in a darkened room after being trained to use their special words. In an additional test, children used a rheostat to adjust room lighting downward "to make the room as dark as you can stay in it for a long time" (Kanfer et al., 1975, p. 254). Results were somewhat different across successive trials for the time in the dark measure versus the rheostat measure. Some findings suggested that both competence self-talk ("I am a brave boy [girl] . . . ") and stimulus self-talk ("The dark is a fun place to be . . .") had beneficial effects compared to the neutral condition. However, the overall pattern of findings suggested that self-talk emphasizing personal competence in coping (i.e., "I am a brave boy [girl]. I can take care of myself in the dark.") worked better than self-talk designed to make darkness less scary. The intervention effects are impressive, given the brevity of the treatment.

Using parents as allies in a self-talk intervention for children with severe fear of the dark. A second self-talk outcome study was built on the Kanfer et al. (1975) work, but focused on children with much more serious and persistent fears of the dark. Children in the Kanfer study had shown low darkness tolerance on a single test (failing to stay in a darkened room for three minutes). By contrast, Graziano and Mooney (1980) identified children (through a newspaper ad) who had shown frequent and highly disruptive nighttime fears for more than two years; in fact, mean duration in the full sample was five years. The families reported crying and severe panic at bedtime; children's demands that bright lights, radios, or televisions be left on in their rooms; battles over going to bed that often lasted beyond midnight; continual frightened cries during late night and early morning hours; and child fatigue and difficulty getting up to go to school in the morning.

The study's 33 highly fearful 6–13-year-olds (mean age = 9 years, 55% boys, ethnicity not reported) were randomly assigned to a waitlist control condition or an active treatment administered to small groups (four to six children). In the active treatment, children were trained to do three things: (1) lie down and relax their muscles; (2) choose and imagine a pleasant scene, such as eating an ice cream cone; and (3) repeat special words adapted from Kanfer et al. (1975): "I am brave. I can take care of myself when I am alone. I can take care of myself when I am in the dark" (p. 209). Children agreed to practice these exercises every night with their parents, and whenever they began to feel afraid. Each night, parents rewarded the children zero to three bravery tokens for their performance on each of the three activities, and an additional zero to three tokens each morning depending on bravery at bedtime and throughout the night. The tokens could be exchanged for a McDonald's hamburger party when the child graduated from the program; graduation took place when the child showed ten consecutive nights of fearless behavior.

Groups of children and parents, seen separately, had three weekly meetings for training and coaching in their respective roles in the treatment. After three weeks of nightly practice at home, the posttreatment results were assessed. The treatment group showed much less fear than the untreated waitlist control group on a parent-report fear strength questionnaire and on nightly parent observation reports of specific fear-related behaviors (e.g., proportion of bedtimes child was afraid, cried, argued, got out of bed; minutes required to get child in bed, minutes until sleep, willingness to go to bed). Among the more striking group differences, (1) untreated children were afraid at 59% of their bedtimes versus 14% for treated children, (2) untreated children required an average of 26 minutes to get to bed versus nine minutes for treated children, and (3) untreated children got back out of bed 44% of the nights versus 7% for the treated group. Phone followups with parents at 2, 6, and 12 months after treatment indicated that the treatment gains not only held up but grew stronger over time, so that by 12 months nearly all of the treatment group children had met the success criterion of ten consecutive "fearless" nights with no behavior problems.

It seems clear from the Graziano and Mooney (1980) study that their intervention worked well, producing quite significant reductions in children's nighttime fears and related behavior problems. What is less clear is the precise mechanism of change, given the fact that the treatment program included multiple components. The self-talk component was certainly a major element, but the intervention also included relaxation with pleasant imagery, as would be used in SD, and reinforced exposure as well, in the form of bravery tokens that were dispensed both for success in practicing designated skills and success in showing fearless exposure to darkness and bedtime. Parents were also trained to provide their children practice in the coping skills taught by the therapists, and trained to dispense the reinforcing tokens in a contingent manner. Thus, while the intervention did appear to alleviate some particularly entrenched fears, the multi-component nature of the treatment makes it difficult to determine the extent to which improvement was caused specifically by the self-talk the children learned.

What about Sean? Applying Self-Talk

Self-talk procedures could certainly be adapted for use with Sean. Because he is a bit older than most of the children in the two studies we reviewed, and because his fears are different in focus, the exact wording of the cognitive instructions and the self-talk suggested to Sean would need to be modified. Indeed, it could be very helpful to develop the self-talk collaboratively with Sean. We can imagine discussions in which Sean is led to examine some of the assumptions underlying his fears, and in which he participates in developing self-talk that is relevant and potent.

When Sean talks to his therapist about his fear of speaking aloud in class, what becomes clear is that his fear is closely connected to his cognitions about the consequences of saying something wrong – for example, that if he makes a mistake or says something wrong, others in the class will think he is a loser and won't have anything to do with him afterward. The therapist works with Sean to test these cognitions and see if more reasonable alternatives can be found. Together, the two of them come up with three alternative thoughts: (1) *others in the class have made mistakes themselves, and they would not see Sean as a loser merely because he too makes mistakes; (2) most of the kids are actually pulling for Sean and hoping he will do well; and (3) the only way to improve is to keep trying, knowing there will be some mistakes along the way.* As Sean buys in to each of these thoughts, he and the therapist write down corresponding self-statements he can use at high-anxiety moments: (1) "Nobody's perfect, we all make mistakes – It's no big deal"; (2) "Most of these kids are pulling for me"; and (3) "I'll get better if I just keep trying."

Taking a page out of Graziano and Mooney's (1980) procedure, Sean's therapist tries to maximize Sean's chances of success by adding other behavioral elements – relaxation training and rewards for progress. With the therapist's help, Sean learns to do an unobservable relaxation routine (e.g., "slow my breathing down, relax my muscles, picture myself on the beach"), then silent self-talk before he speaks up in class, and he also agrees to reward himself with a special treat (30 minutes of video games at home) each day he makes himself speak up.

Sean's parents are also brought into the process, playing a role in tracking Sean's progress and dispensing additional rewards (e.g., TV privileges). The new self-talk procedures, fortified by self-calming and self-rewarding, give Sean a leg up in his efforts to talk in class.

Troubleshooting: Common Treatment Problems and Recommended Solutions. Self-talk intervention does not always go as smoothly as in Sean's case. Here we note three fairly common problems and three solutions recommended by therapists who use self-talk often.

- *The "I don't know" problem.* When asked what thoughts go through their mind when they feel frightened, some children (particularly younger ones) can't think of any. In response, therapists may make a rule: "I don't know" is not an answer; you have to take your best guess. It can help to make the task concrete, by using cartoon thought bubbles on a worksheet, and writing the thoughts within the bubbles. Often it works best to begin with pleasant thoughts, then move to more negative ones. Another approach is to do think-aloud exercises in which children practice saying aloud what they are doing and thinking, beginning with simple nonthreatening tasks and progressing to brief exposure tasks can provide very helpful information. Finally, some youths are more productive when asked, "What would most kids think in this situation?" or "What might I (the therapist) think?" than when asked directly to report their own thoughts.
- *Confusing thoughts with feelings.* Some children respond to questions about their thoughts with answers about their feelings. Conflating thoughts and feelings obviously makes it difficult to identify or modify cognitions. One way to address the problem is to focus children on the concept of *guessing*. Children can be taught that thoughts are guesses. They can also be asked to say what guesses various children might have in various cartoons or pictured scenes, and the therapist can point out that those guesses are thoughts. The transition from discussing another (fictional) youngster's thoughts to discussing one's own thoughts is often quite smooth.

- *Failure of self-talk to generalize.* Sometimes youngsters learn a bit of coping self-talk with the therapist, but then fail to use the talk at any other time. To deal with this problem, therapists can require self-talk during all exposures done in treatment sessions or in all practice outside the session. With older youths, therapists can also stress that self-talk needs to become automatic, and that practice can help make this happen. To illustrate, the therapist can note how hard it is, after years of practice one way, to now cross your arms the "wrong way." With younger children, it often helps to write self-statements down on note cards and encourage or reward their use during session activities and in practice.

Summary of the Outcome Evidence on Four Classic Treatments for Children's Fears

The outcome studies reviewed in this chapter encompass three forms of modeling – live (two studies), symbolic (two studies), and participant (two studies) – as well as systematic desensitization (four studies), reinforced exposure (four studies), and self-talk (two studies). In general, the studies have shown beneficial effects of the various interventions, consistent with the conclusion of the Task Force review by Ollendick and King (1998) that each form of treatment is either "probably efficacious" (live modeling, video modeling, systematic desensitization, and self-talk) or "well established" (participant modeling and reinforced exposure). As with other treatments reviewed in this book, the outcome studies generally show that the various active treatments under study outperform no-treatment and waitlist conditions (but see an exception for *vicarious exposure* in Menzies & Clarke, 1993); in addition, though, we found a surprisingly large number of findings suggesting more potency for the target treatment than active alternatives (see Bandura et al., 1967b; Bandura & Menlove, 1968; Kanfer et al., 1975; Kondas, 1967; Menzies & Clarke, 1993; Ritter, 1968; Sheslow et al., 1983).

Having noted these treatment versus treatment differences, it is also important to note that the various forms of treatment distinguished from one another in this chapter are not always so clearly different from one another in published studies. Note, for example, that the systematic desensitization treatment employed in the Miller et al. (1972) study began by training parents to relax so they could model the procedure for children; thus, the treatment blended desensitization with modeling. And the "psychodynamic" comparison condition in Miller et al. appeared to blend psychodynamic and behavioral procedures, as discussed previously. In another example, Graziano and Mooney (1980) used relaxation and pleasant imagery – elements of SD – to prepare children for their self-talk intervention. Moreover, several studies of treatments other than reinforced exposure have used various forms of reward to reinforce voluntary exposure to feared objects and situations, thus blending their target procedure with a kind of reinforced exposure. Given this blending of treatment elements in the outcome literature on specific fears, it makes sense to include the various approaches in the same chapter, and to consider them something of a family of related and frequently overlapping interventions.

Four Classic Treatments for Children's Fears: Scientific Issues

The evidence reviewed in this chapter shows reasonably consistent support for this family of interventions for children's fears. Perhaps it is the specificity of the target problems that permits the use of rather sharply focused and efficient interventions. On the scientific front, the positive findings are encouraging, but important questions remain for future research.

First, as noted earlier, a number of the studies have blended conceptually distinct treatment elements (e.g., modeling, relaxation training, self-talk, reward for exposure) within the same intervention, and this makes it difficult to interpret positive outcomes with complete clarity. Under such circumstances, although study authors may emphasize one treatment element as key, it is hard to determine whether that element or others may have had the most potent causal role in producing the outcome. Blending elements may serve the goal of strengthening effects, but we may need research in which the treatments are dismantled, with theoretically distinct elements tested separately, if we are to clarify which treatment elements are necessary and which are sufficient to produce the desired effects.

Another concern is that research to date has not taken us very far in understanding the demographic and clinical boundaries within which the treatments are helpful and outside of which they are not. Most of the studies reviewed did not report tests for gender, age group, or ethnic group differences in treatment response; indeed, most failed to even note the ethnicity of their sample. In general, the studies also failed to delve into clinical characteristics of the sample that might have interacted with treatment to account for outcomes. In an interesting exception to these generalizations, Mann and Rosenthal (1969) tested for group differences in the impact of desensitization treatment and found greater fear reduction in girls than boys; further probing showed that this group difference was accounted for by higher initial fear levels in girls. Thus what appeared to be a demographic predictor of outcome turned out to be a clinical predictor. Mann and Rosenthal were able to probe their data in this way in part because they had a relatively large sample ($N = 50$) and an interest in treatment outcome moderators. Their approach bears emulation by investigators in the future.

Another limitation of the research to date is that it has not yet clarified *why* effects are produced when they are. Some intriguing hypotheses have been advanced, such as Bandura's (1977, 1986) notion that fear reduction is mediated by increases in *self-efficacy*, as defined in the introduction to this chapter. Some of the evidence cited by Bandura (e.g., Bandura & Adams, 1977) is in harmony with this notion. In the future, though, it will be useful for researchers to explore this hypothesis and others in the context of treatments for children's fears, and using statistical procedures more recently developed to test for mediation (e.g., Baron & Kenny, 1986).

A final scientific issue concerns the most appropriate general strategy for future research on treatment of children's fears. Experts in the field (e.g., Ollendick & King, 1998) have called for both increased development of multicomponent, high-potency, "total push" interventions, and increased dismantling research designed to identify which specific components are critical in actually reducing fears. Clearly, there is a role for both processes, and the two are potentially complementary, but given limited resources, it may not be possible to give equal emphasis to both. The interpretive difficulties already posed by studies that blend treatment components (see earlier discussion) do raise a concern that beginning with multicomponent treatments could leave us with potent interventions but a weak understanding of how and why they work. Thus, a scientific case could be made for testing relatively focused and precise treatments until their effects are better understood, then beginning to link them together to form more multielement, high-potency approaches. This emphasis will need to be balanced against the clinical need for the most effective treatments possible, as soon as possible, for children whose distress creates an immediate need for help. This brings us to a discussion of clinical issues related to the four classic treatments.

Four Classic Treatments for Children's Fears: Clinical Practice Issues

From a clinical practice perspective, there is much to like about the treatments reviewed in this chapter, but there are potential concerns as well. A major advantage of these treatments, clinically, is the remarkable simplicity and brevity of most, some of which consist of no more than a single session (e.g., Kanfer et al., 1975; Lewis, 1974). This feature is especially valuable in an era of managed care and session limits. A focus on simplicity would argue for modeling, reinforced exposure, and self-talk, which tend to be more time-limited than SD. SD is supported by the bulk of the evidence (see Miller et al. 1972, for an exception), but it is more complex and time consuming than the simpler alternatives reviewed here, and perhaps no more beneficial. Future research may help to clarify whether there are types of children or types of fears for which SD should be the treatment of choice.

To be sure, even some of the briefest procedures discussed here could require effort beyond what practitioners can manage. A clear example is vicarious modeling, which requires videotapes of peer models showing coping behavior very relevant to a treated child's specific fear. Production of such videos, individualized for each new child client, would be beyond the capacity of most clinicians. The good news is that participant modeling may be more beneficial in many circumstances, and it can be done on the spot with the therapist serving as the model.

Another practice-related issue concerns the degree to which the samples and the target problems addressed in the outcome studies are representative of what clinicians actually see in practice. In general, the studies have used children recruited and screened through educational settings and ads, children who had not been referred to a clinic for treatment. One study (Barabasz, 1973) even included all children from the classes participating in the study (and then compared treatment effects for subgroups with high versus low levels of fear). A number of the studies also focused on treatment of fears that are probably developmentally normative in children of the ages treated (e.g., fear of snakes, dogs, and darkness in young children), not fears that are so atypical of their age group as to be likely reasons for referral to a clinic. Indeed, some of the fears (e.g., of an unfamiliar snake) might actually be seen as adaptive.

Two notable exceptions to the concern about nonclinical samples were the SD study by Miller et al. (1972) and the self-talk study by Graziano and Mooney (1980). In both studies the investigators clearly tried to generate a sample that was representative of children referred to clinics for serious and debilitating fears. In the Graziano-Mooney study, for example, children were selected for very long-standing fear of the dark (average: five years) and fear of such unusual severity as to cause major crises at home. From a clinical practice perspective, we need more studies that sample children and problems the way Miller et al. and Graziano and Mooney did.

Clinician training and experience requirements may not pose major obstacles to the clinical use of the modeling, reinforced exposure, or self-talk treatments reviewed here. Most of the procedures involved are straightforward enough to have been carried out by study assistants, and most of these had little or no prior clinical experience. As an example of what may be the high end of training required, Obler and Terwilliger (1970), reported using college graduates with no previous clinical experience to do their successful reinforced exposure treatment. Training for these graduates consisted of two five-hour sessions. SD, by contrast, may require more extensive training, given the inherent complexity of the procedures and the challenge of maintaining a well-calibrated balance of exposure and relaxation throughout the SD sessions. In the Miller et al. (1972) study using SD, for example, the two therapists were the first author, who had 20 years of clinical experience, and the second author, a recent Ph.D. who had completed a study using SD with adults.

As we will discuss in the final section of this chapter, the practitioner who seeks to try any of these four classic treatments will not find a great deal of support in such forms as therapist manuals or training programs. However, most of the procedures are simple and brief enough that the descriptions provided in the published articles may be sufficient to cover the essential ingredients.

How to Find Out More about the Four Classic Treatments

The four treatments discussed in this chapter are called classics, partly because they have been a part of the literature in the field for many years. The downside of this virtue is that all four treatments were developed in an earlier era when manualization of procedures was not standard practice. Some supporting materials were offered by a few of the authors (e.g., Miller et al., 1972), but the passage of time since these articles were published makes such materials less and less available. In general, the best sources of procedural details for the four treatments are the original articles; the Method section in most of these articles provides enough detail to permit a thoughtful reader to approximate the procedures originally used.

Finally, general descriptions of the techniques involved may be found in volumes devoted to those techniques. For example, treatment using modeling procedures was described by Albert Bandura in "Psychotherapy based upon modeling principles," in A. E. Bergin and S. L. Garfield (Eds., 1971), *Handbook of Psychotherapy and Behavior Change* (pp. 653–708, New York: Wiley). Systematic desensitization was described by Joseph Wolpe (1958) in *Psychotherapy by Reciprocal Inhibition* (Stanford, CA: Stanford University Press). Self-talk and reinforced practice procedures are described in a volume edited by Philip C. Kendall (1991) entitled *Child and Adolescent Therapy: Cognitive-Behavioral Procedures* (New York: Guilford).

3

Therapies for Anxiety Disorders

Coping Cat, Coping Koala, and Family Anxiety Management

Most of the evidence-based treatments for youth anxiety are focused interventions targeting specific fears. However, some youngsters develop more complex and pervasive clusters of fears and patterns of avoidance, coalescing in ways that meet all the diagnostic criteria for a formal DSM anxiety disorder. In the disorder called social phobia, for example, youngsters fear embarrassment or humiliation, and they avoid a variety of social or performance situations where they think others will be watching or evaluating them. With social phobia, children may fear speaking in public, playing a team sport, or even eating or writing in school for fear that others will see their hands shake. Separation anxiety disorder involves excessive anxiety from home or from people to whom the child is attached. In generalized anxiety disorder, boys and girls experience excessive anxiety and worry more days than not about multiple events and activities, often related to concerns about their own competence or the quality of their performance (e.g., in schoolwork and social activities).

Building on ideas discussed in the section introduction and in Chapter 2 in relation to specific fears, many in the field also take a multifactor view of anxiety disorder etiology – a view that includes biological, cognitive, and behavioral elements. On the biological front, individuals with anxiety disorders show hypersensitivity to stress and challenge, and a diffuse stress response, probably involving multiple neurobiological systems (see e.g., Albano et al., 1996). The biological stress response is linked to anxiety-elevating cognitions or self-talk (e.g., "I know I'll screw up") and to behavioral avoidance of the stressors. As discussed in Chapter 2, avoidance produces its own reward: deciding to stay away from a scary situation leads to reduced arousal and distress, and thus tends to sustain itself over time. Such a potent reward makes continued avoidance very appealing. So, dysfunctional anxiety becomes a self-perpetuating cycle of elevated biological response to stress, debilitating cognitions, and avoidance of the stressful circumstances.

To disrupt this cycle in youngsters who meet diagnostic criteria for anxiety disorders, treatment researchers have developed a family of cognitive-behavioral techniques. The specific techniques used and the disorders targeted vary somewhat from one research group to another (see e.g., Albano & Barlow, 1996; Barrett et al., 1996; Kendall, 1994; Silverman & Kurtines, 1996a,b). However, two treatment research teams, one in the United States and one in Australia, have produced particularly promising evidence of success (see Ollendick & King, 1998). Both teams have found beneficial effects of an individually administered treatment called Coping Cat in the United States and Coping Koala in Australia; and the Australian team has found that treatment impact can be magnified by adding a Family Anxiety Management (FAM) program. In this chapter, we focus first on Coping Cat/Koala, then on the family program.

The Coping Cat Program: Conceptual Basis and Procedural Overview

The Coping Cat program was developed by Philip Kendall (e.g., 1994) and colleagues for boys and girls who meet criteria for separation anxiety disorder, social phobia (called avoidant disorder in DSM-IIIR), or generalized anxiety disorder (called overanxious disorder in DSM-IIIR). Coping Cat is designed to directly address the interplay of biological arousal, anxious thoughts, and behavioral avoidance discussed at the beginning of this chapter. Biological arousal is a problem in part because children often don't recognize it (they just know that they feel scared) and in part because they don't know how to cope with arousal when they do recognize it. Anxious thoughts are another key problem, because young people often lack skills in identifying those thoughts and in modifying them. Avoidance of feared situations is also harmful because it prevents opportunities to learn that the situations are not actually so bad.

To tackle this triad of arousal, cognition, and avoidance, Coping Cat therapists teach their young clients a cluster of skills. These include (1) recognizing how the body signals anxious arousal; (2) making the body relax when anxious feelings arise; (3) identifying and altering anxious cognitions; (4) planning and doing *exposures* to feared situations; and (5) evaluating one's effort and rewarding oneself for trying hard. Roughly the first half of the treatment is devoted to educating the child about the somatic, cognitive, and behavioral components of anxiety, with particular emphasis on the individual child's distinctive pattern. The second half involves real-world application of what has been learned through a series of personally tailored *in vivo* exercises involving direct exposure to feared situations. Over time in treatment, the situations progress from those that are mildly upsetting to those that evoke major fears. The hope is that by the end of treatment, boys and girls will be able to design and carry out their own exposures, and thus be their own therapists.

The Coping Cat Program: In Brief

Designed for . . . . Youths ages 8–13, diagnosed with Generalized Anxiety Disorder, Separation Anxiety Disorder, and Social Phobia

Number of sessions 16–20

Session length . . . . 50–60 minutes

Session participants . . . . Therapist and youth

Theoretical orientation . . . . Cognitive-behavioral

Treatment steps:

1. Youth identifies situations that make him or her feel anxious, and describes his or her response to those situations.
2. Youth makes a hierarchy of anxiety-provoking situations, ranked from least to most feared.
3. Therapist and youth identify cues (e.g., pounding heart, dry mouth) that signal the onset of anxiety.
4. Therapist trains youth to relax and provides a relaxation audiotape for home use.
5. Therapist and youth identify anxious self-talk (e.g., the thought "If I flunk this test, my teacher will think I'm stupid.").
6. Therapist helps youth identify coping self-talk and other strategies for confronting fears.
7. Youth practices self-evaluation (e.g., of coping efforts) and self-reward.
8. In a series of imaginal, role-play, and *in vivo* experiences, the youth is exposed to various feared situations, starting low in the hierarchy (see #2) and progressing upward.
9. Throughout these exposures, the youth practices the "FEAR steps," that is, identifying physical sensations that signal anxiety ("Feeling frightened") and anxious cognitions ("Expecting bad things to happen"), altering the cognitions and making oneself try the feared activity ("Attitudes and actions that can help"), and evaluating and rewarding one's own coping efforts ("Rate and reward").

Treatment classified by Treatment Task Force as . . . . Probably Efficacious (Ollendick & King, 1998)

Key resource for potential users . . . . Kendall, P. C., Kane, M., Howard, B., & Siqueland, L. (1990). *Cognitive-Behavioral Treatment of Anxious Children: Therapist Manual*. Ardmore, PA: Workbook Publishing.

The Coping Cat Program: Treatment Procedures

The multiple skills embodied in Coping Cat (Kendall et al., 1990) are nicely summarized in an acronym that guides the treatment program. Over the course of the treatment, children learn the **FEAR** steps:

F	Feeling frightened?
E	Expecting bad things to happen?
A	Attitudes and actions that will help.
R	Results and rewards.

To describe these four components of the acronym is to describe the Coping Cat program. We will discuss these four components and how they are brought together to form a four-part coping plan for each treated youngster.

Feeling frightened? An initial step in coping with anxiety is to recognize *when* to cope. Toward this end, anxious youths must learn to identify the situations that make them fearful and to read their own body for signs of anxious arousal, signals that it is time to start coping. Each child (like each adult) has a distinctive signature anxiety pattern, with particular situations more likely than others to spark fears, and with these fears generating a person-specific pattern of physiological arousal. For some, the arousal pattern involves a pounding heart, for others tightness in the throat, for others a flushed face, and for still others a queasy feeling in the stomach. The "Feeling Frightened" component of treatment is aimed at teaching children to recognize their own distinctive pattern. The process is prompted by the therapist who models self-disclosure by discussing some of his or her own anxiety triggers, and the distinctive bodily responses that signal anxious arousal for him or her.

As the child's pattern of anxiety cues and bodily arousal is identified, relaxation training is introduced. The treatment manual (Kendall, Kane, Howard, & Siqueland, 1990) suggests that the therapist discuss with the child the difference between feeling tense and feeling relaxed, and reinforce this notion by having the child clench a fist and then relax it. The idea to get across is that when people feel anxious, parts of their body get tense, and that relaxing the tense parts is a first step toward coping. Relaxation training follows. With the lights lowered, the therapist leads the child through deep breathing exercises, then progressive muscle tensing and relaxing. For children who need a different format, game-like procedures may be used. For example, muscle tensing can be accomplished by asking the child to "walk like a robot." The exercises are audiotaped, and the child takes the tape home for practice.

Expecting bad things to happen? Next, the focus shifts to cognitions and their role in either heightening or reducing anxiety. Using cartoons with empty thought bubbles, children are asked to generate thoughts, or self-talk, likely to accompany various positive and negative events (e.g., opening a birthday gift, having broccoli for dinner), and then asked for thoughts that might connect to various ambiguous events. Ideally, the child reaches a point at which he or she is generating both anxious thoughts and thoughts that might reduce anxiety and promote good coping. One aim is to turn the child into an effective critic of fearful thinking, one who poses and answers questions such as, "Is my scary thought realistic?" Another aim is to build skills in turning anxious self-talk into coping self-talk. This brings us to the third **FEAR** step.

Attitudes and actions that will help. In the next step, the child turns a critical corner, moving from describing fears (in terms of their physiological and cognitive features) to figuring out ways to cope with them. The therapist stresses that the distinctive arousal pattern signaling anxiety can be used as a cue to put relaxation skills into play. In addition, anxious-making cognitions (e.g., "I expect . . . [something bad] . . . to happen." "I am afraid of . . . [something terrible].") can be used as prompts to develop coping self-talk. The idea is to challenge irrational ideas ("Is that scary thought realistic? Is that bad outcome I fear really likely to happen? What else might happen that would be good?"). The basic idea is to reconceptualize the situation as less risky and less frightening. The child workbook provided as a part of the Coping Cat program contains visual aids to help boys and girls think about the impact of thoughts on their feelings. In Figure 3.1, for example,

FIGURE 3.1. Coping Cat workbook exercise illustrating the connection between thoughts and feelings. From P. C. Kendall (1990). *The Coping Cat Workbook*. Philadelphia, PA: Temple University. [Reprinted with permission from Philip C. Kendall.]

two cats have two very different ideas about the same sleeping dog, and the different ideas are apt to have very different emotional consequences for the cats.

With the cognitive reframing accomplished, and fear-provoking attitudes altered, the child's next task is to find ways of reducing the stressfulness of anxiety-provoking situations, by altering the situations. Working with examples of everyday stressors (e.g., "You've lost your shoes somewhere in your house."), therapist and child practice problem solving, and the solution-generation skills are gradually extended to more frightening situations. Nervous about meeting a new kid you don't know? Afraid you won't know what to say? What if you learn a bit about him before you meet so you will know what he is interested in, and then you'll know what to talk about? In this way, the child begins to learn that stressful situations need not be intractable, but that they may be made less stressful through planning and problem solving.

Results and reward. The next step of the program puts the child in charge of evaluating his or her own efforts to cope with frightening situations. Children use a feelings barometer to rate how they feel about their performance. They also learn to allocate rewards to themselves based on their barometer ratings. Rewards may be as simple as writing about the good experience in a diary, or spending time doing a favorite activity. In treatment sessions, rewards can include extra time for a board game with the therapist.

Homework: STIC tasks. Self-evaluation and self-reward are often used in concert with "Show-That-I-Can" (STIC) tasks, assignments in which the child's job is to practice skills taught in the therapy sessions. Toward the end of each treatment session, the child and therapist agree to a STIC task that involves application of skills from that session to a situation tailored to fit the child. Effective tailoring is part of the therapist's art in Coping Cat. The aim is to select STIC tasks that are sufficiently challenging to promote growth, but sufficiently realistic to make success very likely. Experiences of success (not perfection!) are rewarded, first by the therapist, and then (as noted earlier) by the child following self-ratings of performance.

Using the FEAR steps in real life: Role plays, in vivo, and exposure to personal fears. Roughly the second half of the treatment program is devoted to personalized exposure tasks in which the youngster tries to tackle real fears by implementing the FEAR steps. The therapist begins with low-grade stressors, some imaginal and some real, but all very low on the child's anxiety hierarchy. Over successive sessions, the work progresses to fears ranked higher in the hierarchy. The exposure may involve a combination of in-session role plays, *in vivos* in which the child copes with a real-life stressor while being observed or helped by the therapist, and homework in which the child copes without the therapist but describes the experience to the therapist in the next session. In each instance, therapist and child work together to design exposures that are difficult enough to prompt genuine growth in coping skills, but not so difficult as to be out of reach. A key task for the therapist is to help the child frame these experiences in a positive way, after the fact, so that motivation and self-confidence remain high throughout. One goal is for the child to learn that it is possible to go into the feared situation without having the feared outcome happen.

Examples of in vivos and homework assignments: Leslie and Ernesto. To illustrate what an *in vivo* might look like, we focus on Leslie, a child who is fearful of talking to adults, particularly those in authority (e.g., teachers, police, shopkeepers). The therapist and Leslie design an *in vivo* that involves a nearby hotdog vendor. During the treatment session, Leslie and the therapist leave the therapy room and walk outside the building, Leslie walks to the vendor's pushcart while the therapist sits on a park bench within earshot, pretending to read a newspaper. Leslie's job is not only to order a hotdog, but to change her order halfway through, taking the risk of irritating the vendor. The therapist and Leslie have worked out the procedures in advance, using the **FEAR** steps, to make the task as doable as possible for the child. For example:

1. Identifying Leslie's anxious arousal (she will probably feel a choking sensation in her throat when she approaches the vendor's cart), and practicing relaxation that will reduce the arousal (keep shoulders loose, and take long, slow breaths while walking).
2. Reworking her negative cognitions about the experience (e.g., changing from "The vendor will hate me – he'll think I'm just another dumb kid" to "The vendor feeds lots of kids every day, and probably likes kids; that's why he works in this spot where there are lots of kids; and lots of kids change their mind about what they want").
3. Planning actions that can help, such as deciding what Leslie will say to the vendor when she changes her mind, how far away the therapist will be sitting, making sure Leslie has enough money, and planning what Leslie will say if the vendor does look angry. The idea is to do everything possible to help Leslie feel ready to cope.

In some cases, such an *in vivo* might be done cold, without informing the vendor of what is going on; in other cases, the therapist might prepare the vendor before the child arrives for the session, to maximize the chance that the exercise will go well. In either case, after getting the hotdog, Leslie brings it back to the therapist's office and enjoys eating it while debriefing with the therapist, who works to frame the entire experience in a positive light and to praise Leslie's coping success. Finally, Leslie gets a reward for good effort (e.g., time in the game room, shooting pool with the therapist) before the end of the session.

As an example of homework, we focus on Ernesto, a teen whose greatest fear is doing something embarrassing in front of others. His homework assignment is to walk into the staff lobby of his clinic, stumble, and drop an armful of papers on the floor, appearing to do so by accident. Before doing this, the therapist and Ernesto work through the **FEAR** steps.

1. First, they identify the pattern of fearful arousal Ernesto is likely to experience, and they practice doing relaxation exercises to reduce the arousal.
2. Next, they identify any cognitions Ernesto may be carrying around about this experience that make it especially frightening (e.g., "Everyone there will think I'm a loser") and change them to less frightening cognitions (e.g., "Most people have dropped things themselves; they may laugh, but they'll also think it could have been them.").
3. They plan actions Ernesto can take in the situation to help make it less scary (e.g., deciding how many things he will drop (not so many that he will look *too* clumsy!), and planning how he will react when this happens (laughing with the others at his own mistake, to join with them, and to avoid looking embarrassed).
4. Ernesto and his therapist also plan what reward he will give himself for doing this assignment (Jolly Ranchers from a nearby vending machine), so he can look forward to how it will feel (and taste!) to celebrate his success.

In the next session after his homework assignment, the therapist and Ernesto review the experience in detail – how it went, how people reacted (two of them jumped up to help Ernesto rather than laughing at him), how Ernesto felt at various stages of the exercise, how he used relaxation skills and self-talk skills to cope, and how it felt when he had finished and gotten his Jolly Ranchers. The therapist's goal is to maximize what Ernesto learns from his homework assignment and to leave him feeling like a genuine "coping cat."

The Coping Cat Program: Outcome Studies Testing Its Effects

We turn now to empirical evidence on the effects of Coping Cat. Kendall and colleagues have completed multiple studies, and another trial has been reported by an Australian group.

First group comparison test of Coping Cat. Following preliminary support in a within-group multiple baseline study (Kane & Kendall, 1989), an initial group design study was carried out by Kendall (1994), using a sample of 47 9–13-year-olds (60% boys, 76% Caucasian, 24% African American).

All met DSM-IIIR criteria for overanxious disorder, avoidant disorder, or separation anxiety disorder. The youth were randomly assigned to Coping Cat or a waitlist control condition. After treatment, the Coping Cat group showed significantly less anxiety than the waitlist group on most outcome measures, including those derived from parent report, youth report, and researcher-coded observations of youth behavior. After treatment, only 36% of the treated group still met criteria for an anxiety disorder, whereas 95% of the waitlist group still had an anxiety disorder at the end of the waiting period. The Coping Cat group also scored as less anxious than the waitlist group on a number of other posttreatment measures, some based on parent reports, some on child self-reports, and some on child performance (e.g., degree of anxiety displayed during a videotaped task). Followup assessments at one and three years posttreatment (Kendall & Southam-Gerow, 1996) showed good maintenance of gains among the treated youth, although no comparison of treated and untreated youth could be made at followup because the waitlist group had received treatment after their waiting period.

Second group comparison test of Coping Cat. A second group-design outcome study (Kendall, Flannery-Schroeder et al., 1997), using a similar experimental design, also generated supportive findings. The sample included 94 children, ages 9–13 (62% boys, 85% Caucasian, 5% African American, 2% Latino, 2% Asian American, and 5% other). The children were randomized to treatment and waitlist control groups. After treatment, only 47% of the Coping Cat group still qualified for their original primary anxiety disorder; by contrast, 94% of the waitlist control group still had their primary diagnosis (statistics on the percentage who met criteria for any anxiety disorder were not reported by Kendall et al., 1997). A number of other findings showed superior outcomes for the Coping Cat group, findings based on both parent-report and youth self-report measures. Followup assessments pointed to holding power of treatment gains in the Coping Cat group over a one-year period after the end of treatment (there was no comparison with the waitlist group at followup because the waitlist group had been treated at that point).

A third trial comparing individual and group-administered versions of Coping Cat. In a third test, Flannery-Schroeder and Kendall (2000) compared two 18-week versions of Coping Cat, one administered individually and one administered to children meeting in same-gender groups. The 37 participants, ages 8–14 (51% boys, 89% Caucasian) all met criteria for either generalized anxiety disorder, separation anxiety disorder, or social phobia. The youngsters were randomly assigned to an individual treatment, group treatment, or nine-week waitlist condition. At posttreatment, the two treatment groups scored better than the waitlist group on most outcome measures, but some measures suggested somewhat better outcomes for individual than group treatment. As an example, 92% of the waitlist children continued to meet diagnostic criteria for their primary anxiety disorder at the end of the waiting period, versus 50% for the group-treated youngsters and 27% for individually treated youth. Scores on most outcome measures held fairly steady for the two treated groups at a three-month followup. Overall, findings suggested that a group form of Coping Cat may have beneficial effects, albeit not quite as strong as the individually administered form.

The findings of these three outcome studies by Kendall and colleagues are encouraging, and the focus on full anxiety disorders represents a major advance beyond the treatment of simple phobias, which have been the target of most previous work on anxiety. However, interpretation of the Kendall et al. studies is somewhat complicated by an unusual design feature: in both clinical trials, outcome assessment for the treated group took place after 16–18 weeks of treatment, but outcome assessment for the waitlist group took place after only eight or nine weeks on the waitlist. This procedure was designed partly to reduce the risk of differential attrition; that is, the concern was that if the waiting period had been much longer, a high percentage of the waitlist group might have dropped out of the study and sought alternate treatment (see Kendall et al., 1997). This makes sense, but the procedure did not fully control for the passage of time. To the extent that child anxiety symptoms show a natural time course, growing less intense over time following referral (see e.g., Albano et al., 1996; Cantwell & Baker, 1989), there is a risk that differential timing of assessment in the two groups may have favored the Coping Cat youth (whose outcome assessment took place 16–20 weeks after referral) relative to the waitlist youth (whose outcome assessment took place 8–10 weeks after referral). Because the waitlist group received treatment at the end of their waiting period, the one-year and two-year followups (Kendall & Southam-Gerow, 1996) do not address this problem because they include only treated youth. Given this methodological issue, it is helpful to have evidence from an additional clinical trial in which treated and untreated youth were matched for duration of the pre-post interval. Such evidence is found in a study from Australia, to which we now turn.

Australian test of the "Coping Koala" program. In a clinical trial conducted by an Australian team (Barrett et al., 1996), Coping Cat procedures were shortened to 12 sessions and adapted for Australian youth, prompting a new name for the treatment protocol: *Coping Koala.* Barrett et al. compared the Koala program to a 12-week waiting list condition, and to a 12-week. Koala + Family Anxiety Management (FAM) program. In the Koala + FAM condition, children received shortened Coping Koala sessions, followed by family sessions in which the child, parents, and therapist worked together on techniques for anxiety management (see further description of the FAM program later). Therapist contact time was matched (at about 70 minutes per week) across the two active treatments. The sample included 79 children ages 7–14 (57% boys, ethnicity not reported), who met criteria for diagnoses of overanxious disorder, separation anxiety disorder, or social phobia. The children were randomly assigned to Koala, Koala + FAM, or the waitlist condition.

Posttreatment comparisons on multiple outcome measures showed both the Koala and Koala + FAM groups outperforming the waitlist group on mother-report and father-report measures of internalizing symptoms and on reductions in anxiety diagnoses, based on parent-report and youth-report standardized diagnostic interviews. In the Koala group, for example, 57% no longer met criteria for any anxiety disorder at the end of treatment; the figure for the waitlist group was 26%. The percent of the Koala group with no anxiety diagnosis increased to 71% at a six-month followup, and was 70% at 12 months posttreatment. Adding the FAM component enhanced outcomes in several ways, as we will discuss below.

Summary of the outcome evidence on Coping Cat (and Koala). We have reviewed four group comparison studies, three testing the cognitive behavioral Coping Cat program (Flannery-Schroeder & Kendall, 2000; Kendall, 1994; Kendall et al., 1997) and one testing its Australian cousin, Coping Koala (Barrett et al., 1996). All four studies showed substantial positive effects of treatment relative to a waitlist condition. One of the studies (Flannery-Schroeder & Kendall, 2000) showed that a group-administered form of Coping Cat had beneficial effects, less impressive than those of the individually administered form but markedly better than a waitlist control condition. Follow-up assessments (including Kendall & Southam-Gerow, 1996), ranging from three months to three years posttreatment, have shown that posttreatment outcomes hold up over time, although none of these assessments has included a direct comparison to an untreated control group (because control group participants were treated after the waitlist period). Outcome measures showing positive treatment effects have included youth and parent report scales, standardized diagnostic assessments, and youth performance measures (e.g., generating interpretations and coping response plans in response to hypothetical scenarios).

What about Sean? Applying Coping Cat (and Koala) for Youth Anxiety

We return now to the case of Sean, to consider how the Coping Cat program might be applied in his case. Sean's symptom pattern suggests elements of generalized anxiety disorder, social phobia, and separation anxiety disorder, the three target conditions with which Coping Cat has been tested, so he seems an appropriate candidate for the treatment.

After some initial getting-acquainted time, Sean's therapist shows him what she calls "the **FEAR** steps." It is a chart that shows the letters F-E-A-R and some writing beside each letter. She and Sean start with the letter "F," which stands for *Feeling frightened*. The two take turns identifying their bodies' telltale anxiety signals. The therapist normalizes the exercise and models self-disclosure by describing how her face gets flushed and she perspires when she speaks in public. She describes her signals in a smiling "no big deal" kind of way, and she notes that everyone gets nervous sometimes, and everyone's body gives off some signals to tell when they are feeling frightened. "What about you?" she asks Sean. Following the therapist's lead, Sean describes how his heart pounds and his stomach feels tight and queasy when he gets nervous; and he tells her that his hands sometimes tremble, too, which makes him avoid eating in public places such as the school cafeteria.

In another session, Sean and the therapist practice relaxation. The therapist asks Sean to think of a time when he was calm and happy. Sean remembers lying on the warm grass in his back yard last June right after school had ended. The therapist asks him to think about how his body felt then compared to how it feels when he is tense and frightened, and she says they are going to work on ways Sean can create that warm happy feeling of lying in his back yard even when he is not at home and when he is tense. To start the process, she lowers the lights in the office, asks Sean to find a comfortable position, and then has him practice slow, deep breathing, noticing how relaxed his body begins to feel after a few breaths. Next, she has Sean make a very tight fist and hold it while she counts to five; then she asks him to open his fist and notice how warm and relaxed his hand feels. This exercise continues as she leads Sean through tensing and relaxing of several muscle groups – especially those that are known centers of tension for Sean (e.g., his hands, arms, and chest). To help him try it at home, she gives Sean an audiotape of the tensing-releasing session they have just finished. Two days later, when Sean is at home worrying about school, he notices his heart pounding and his stomach tensing, so he lies down on his bed, plays the tape, and does the tensing and releasing exercise. Amazingly, it helps! When the tape has ended, Sean feels pretty good, warm and relaxed.

In a later session, Sean and his therapist move to the letter "E," *Expecting bad things to happen*. Here Sean learns to explicitly identify his anxiety-elevating cognitions (e.g., "Kids will see how scared I am when I talk in front of the class – they'll think I'm an idiot." "When they see my hands shake, they'll laugh out loud."). In the section on *"Attitudes and actions that can help,"* Sean learns to convert negative cognitions into positive, coping self-talk (e.g., "Lots of kids are scared to talk in front of the class; I'm not the only one." "I can get through this if I try."). He also learns to identify various actions that will make the feared situations more manageable and less anxiety-ridden. For example, to get ready for his class presentation, he practices his talk several times in front of family members who try to act like his class members might. He also figures out what props would help soften the edges of the situations he fears. For example, because he especially fears having people look directly at him during a class presentation, he prepares posters and other visual aids that will capture the attention of his audience as he talks; getting them to look at these props instead of him will reduce his sense of being stared at, and also make the talk more interesting to the class. As for meals in the cafeteria, it turns out that trembling hands only really show when Sean uses utensils; he and the therapist figure out that if he only eats finger food (e.g., sandwiches, pizza), no one will see any trembling.

In a later session, Sean and his therapist turn to the letter "R." Sean learns to *Rate and Reward* himself for his efforts and success in various activities. At first, the skill is applied to role-plays that he and his therapist do together in the session. For example, they practice Sean's class presentation with therapist and Sean each playing the role of presenter and audience once; and Sean practices eating a sandwich so trembling hands don't show. In learning how to rate and reward himself, Sean completes the educational phase of Coping Cat, so he is now ready to move to the exposure phase.

Once Sean has mastered the **FEAR** steps, he and his therapist move increasingly into real-life situations to build Sean's skills by arranging exposures to the situations he fears. They do various *in vivos*, practicing the skills in real-world ways but in the context of a treatment session; for example, they prepare visual aids for Sean's class presentation, and they arrange for him to practice his talk in front of a smaller audience of therapists and clients in the clinic, and then to debrief with his therapist about how it felt. Sean also does homework assignments, hatched and planned in the sessions, but actually carried out by Sean on his own time. For example, one homework assignment is to do the practice talk in front of his family members. Another is to take a sandwich and a drink into the school cafeteria and finish both.

The *in vivos* and homework exposures grow increasingly challenging throughout the last half of the treatment program. As the difficulty level escalates, Sean tries some of his most feared situations, including initiating conversation with peers, and even arranging for one play date. Because such tasks touch sensitive areas in which Sean's avoidant style has rendered him ineffective to date, the therapist works hard to arrange exposures that will lead to significant success. For example, in planning for the play date, she works with Sean's mother to identify a peer to invite who is not so popular that he would be likely to turn Sean down, and they select an activity that is fun for almost any 9-year-old boy, even if the conversation level is low (they choose neon bowling). To Sean's mother's surprise, the play date actually works fairly well, and both boys seem to have a good time.

At the end of treatment, Sean makes a video commercial for the Coping Cat program. In it, he says "I liked my therapist, and I learned a lot. I'm still nervous about a lot of things, but I know how to calm down when I need to, and I know how to use my *actions and attitudes that can help*. I also found out that the best way to stop being scared is to do the things I am scared of." That is a beautifully succinct rationale for exposure, a core component of Coping Cat.

Troubleshooting: Common Treatment Problems and Recommended Solutions. Sean responded well to Coping Cat, and the studies we reviewed earlier suggest that children often do. However, some parts of the program can be difficult for some youngsters, and for some therapists. Here we note a few of the problems that can arise, together with suggested strategies for coping.

- *In vivos and STIC tasks that are too easy.* Therapists sometimes fail to create exposures – *in vivos* and STIC tasks – that are challenging enough to promote real growth and change in their young clients. This is especially likely when therapists are drawn into the role of comforter and protector. Some therapists may fear that a really challenging *in vivo* will overwhelm the child, or drive the child out of treatment. In such cases, supervisors need to stress that youngsters must feel genuine anxiety during the task for the exposure to really help. Therapists must thus be willing to allow the child to become anxious, resisting natural tendencies to reassure or protect. As treatment developer Phil Kendall suggests (personal communication, November 2002), exposures can work for both the child and the therapist, teaching that the child both can be resilient and can gain from taking on challenges. Once they have seen children face their fears and do exposures successfully in spite of them, most therapists are better at assigning challenging exposures in future cases.
- *Children who resist exposures.* Of course, some children may respond to exposure tasks by refusing to try them. In such cases, several options are open to therapists. One is to begin with imaginary exposures, mentally walking the child through the full experience in an effort to reduce the fear and facilitate real-life exposure. If that approach fails, the therapist may work with the child to break the task into components, with the child identifying what is troubling about each of the component steps. That information may be used to redesign the exposure, changing

parts of the most worrisome components to achieve a balance between anxiety-provokingness and doability. For example, a presentation in front of a group audience – an exposure task often used in Coping Cat – might be downgraded to a presentation in front of two people, or even in front of a video camera. It is also possible to add twists to the exposure that make it lighter, more fun. For example, the presentation in front of an audience might be done in the style of a favorite comic actor (e.g., Jim Carey, Adam Sandler) or turned into an Academy Award acceptance speech. While the task must be challenging enough to cause genuine anxiety, it can certainly be adapted to ensure that the child will actually go through with it.

- *Anxious cognitions are the only ones the child can think of, or are more believable than the nonanxious ones.* A related problem can arise when the treatment focuses on cognitions that make feared situations scary. Some children find it hard to identify any cognitions about feared situations that are not anxiety-filled. Even when therapist and child do identify alternative thoughts that are not so anxious, the child may still find the anxious cognitions more believable, so that fear is not really reduced. One solution is to have children identify one of their heroes – someone who seems to have mastered fear, and copes successfully. The children are then asked to identify thoughts that their hero might have about the situation the child finds frightening, to think aloud about how it would feel to walk around with those thoughts, and then to act (in the exposure tasks) as if the hero's thoughts were really true.

- *Rigid manual adherence that fails to adapt to child characteristics and contexts.* A more general problem, one that treatment developer Kendall has written about in some detail (see e.g., Kendall et al., 1998), is therapist rigidity in manual use. Excessively strict adherence to manual details and procedures may make the sessions feel wooden or teachy-preachy, may undermine the therapeutic relationship, and may interfere with a therapist's ability to fit treatment to the particular child's style and circumstances. Kendall recommends that therapists read the manual, learn the treatment model, and then work to adapt the specifics to the particular child's personality, sense of humor, and living situation. Especially important, in Kendall's view, is making sure sessions are fun and engaging for the child.

The Family Anxiety Management Program: Conceptual Basis and Procedural Overview

Clinicians and researchers who work with anxious youngsters often note that parents seem to play a central instigating or maintaining role. Consider the following dinner conversation:

> MOTHER: Did you hear about that girl who got kidnapped at the mall?
> CHILD: No.
> MOTHER: Yep. She was about your age. Her parents are worried sick.
> CHILD: A girl from my school?
> MOTHER: No, another town. But it could have been here.
> CHILD: I thought that just happened in movies.
> MOTHER: No, it's very real. Kids get snatched all the time – especially girls your age.

In this instance, the mother instills a new worry in her daughter's mind about risks outside home. In other instances, parents may highlight or amplify worries their children already have by noting new elements of risk or possible disastrous outcomes their children haven't even considered yet. In still other cases, parents may reward children's fearful or avoidant behavior with special attention or unusual levels of nurturance and support. Of course parents of anxious children, who are disproportionately likely to have anxiety disorders themselves (e.g., Last, Hersen et al., 1987), may actively model worry and anxious avoidance for their children. In these and other ways, parents may – intentionally or inadvertently – help to sustain fears and anxious behavior in their children (see Barrett, Rapee et al., 1996).

Given parents' potential impact on their anxious children, it makes a good deal of sense to consider bringing them into the process of child anxiety treatment. Doing so may help reduce the extent to which parents instigate, nurture, or magnify their children's worries, and tolerate or reward their children's avoidance behavior. Moreover, to the extent that the parents' own anxiety generates displays of fear and avoidance for their children to observe, including parents in treatment may provide an opportunity to reduce adverse parental modeling. This is part of the rationale underlying the Family Anxiety Management (FAM) Program.

The program entails 12 sessions, most of which include child, parents, and therapist (sometimes meeting in family groups), and most of which focus on conveying information and skills related to effective coping with anxiety by the child and by the parent. The last few sessions involve only parents and therapist, and these "partner support" sessions emphasize three broad themes. First, parents are taught basic behavioral principles with the aim of creating an environment in which displays of child anxiety are not rewarded and displays of courage are. A second theme of the partner support sessions is how the parents can deal with their own anxiety. Parents are taught to identify the anxious responses they are displaying for their children and to instead model proactive and coping responses. Third, the program includes brief training in communication and problem-solving skills to help the parents work better as a team. In this component, parents are taught skills for reducing their own conflict, particularly over child-rearing issues and the handling of child displays of anxiety, and they are encouraged to have regular discussions, some devoted to solving problems at home, so they can present a unified front to their child.

The Family Anxiety Management (FAM) Program: In Brief

Designed for . . . . Families of 7–14-year-olds diagnosed with Generalized Anxiety Disorder, Separation Anxiety Disorder, and Social Phobia
Number of sessions 12
Session length . . . . 40 minutes to 1.5 hours
Session participants . . . . Primarily therapist with child and family, sometimes in multi-family groups; but last few sessions with parents and therapist only
Theoretical orientation . . . . Cognitive-behavioral

Treatment steps:

1. Talk about how to recognize feelings (e.g., sadness, happiness, anger), the situations that produce the feelings, and how thoughts are connected to feelings.
2. Develop a hierarchy for the child, rank-ordering situations from least to most feared; begin trying low-level exposures to situations low in the hierarchy.
3. Learn how bodies give off hints of fear or worry (e.g., muscle tension), and learn procedures for relaxing the body.
4. Learn how thoughts or self-talk relate to feelings; for example, thinking about bad things that can happen in a situation may cause worried feelings.
5. Practice changing negative, worried self-talk into positive self-talk, or expecting good things to happen.
6. Learn how to praise and reward self for trying to do hard things; extend this concept to self-praise and self-reward for coping with feared situations.
7. Review the **FEAR** plan children have learned for coping with worries; F is for "Feeling Good" (by relaxing and by doing positive activities), E is for "Expecting Good Things to Happen" (using positive self-talk), A is for "Action" (doing things to make a situation less frightening, so as to enter it), R is for "Reward" (praising and rewarding oneself for self-exposure to frightening situations, and for trying to cope).
8. Practice via homework using the **FEAR** plan on real-life frightening situations, and celebrate with a party.

9. Partner Support sessions with parents and therapist only. Parents learn how to react when a problem occurs with the child (e.g., keep voice calm, back up your partner, debrief afterward), how to arrange casual discussions about family matters, and how to have systematic problem-solving discussions to create well thought-out solutions.

Treatment classified by Treatment Task Force as . . . . Probably Efficacious when combined with the Coping Koala individual treatment.

Key resource for potential users . . . . . Barrett, P. (1991). *Management of Childhood Anxiety: A Family Intervention Programme.* Nathan, Australia: Griffith University.

The Family Anxiety Management Program: Treatment Procedures

The FAM program (detailed in Barrett, 1991, and Barrett et al., 1991; originally piloted by Dadds et al., 1992) includes 12 sessions. In most of these, the parent(s) and child meet together with the therapist, and sometimes with other children and their parents, but the last few sessions are partner support meetings designed to help the two parents work in synchrony, solve problems together, and support each other's efforts. The sessions generally involve a mixture of didactic content, discussion, and interactive activities, with homework assigned for the intervening week. Early work focuses on identifying various emotions, how they are displayed on the face and in other parts of the body, and what some of the situations are that lead to positive and negative thoughts and feelings. Then a **FEAR** plan based on the one used in Coping Cat (previous section), but cast in more positive language, is introduced. *F* represents *Feeling good,* and it involves three steps that are to be followed whenever the child is feeling nervous: (1) think positive thoughts, (2) perform a pleasant activity, and (3) relax. As in Coping Cat, bodily signals indicating anxiety are noted, and these are identified as cues signaling a need for the three steps. Exposure tasks begin early in the treatment, with children expected to carry out one activity each day from their previously created fear hierarchy; each exposure lasts as long as it takes for the child's anxiety to be reduced. Parents are enlisted as role models for the child, and as agents of reinforcement who establish reward contingencies for their child's efforts at exposure.

As the exposure tasks are tackled, week by week, other elements of the **FEAR** plan are introduced. *E* is for *Expecting good things to happen.* This is the cognitive focus, aimed at altering anxiety-provoking thoughts. *A* is for *Actions that can help,* things the child can do to make stressful situations less frightening. *R* is for *Rewards,* things the children can do for, or say to, themselves to reinforce their coping efforts. Parents learn **FEAR** with their children, and they learn three additional skills.

One of these skills is reinforcement. Parents learn how to reward their children's courageous behavior with descriptive praise, special privileges, and tangible rewards. In addition, parents learn how to extinguish displays of anxiety and complaining by using planned ignoring. Parents are taught to respond empathically the first time their child complains, but to respond to the second complaint by prompting the child to use one of the coping strategies taught in the treatment sessions, and to respond to further complaints by withdrawing attention until the complaining ceases. These contingency management skills are roleplayed during the sessions, using the parents' own examples of their children's fearful behaviors.

In a second skill component, parents are taught to model effective coping for their children. Parents learn specific strategies for managing their own fears, and they practice ways of openly modeling these strategies when they are with their families.

As a third focus, parents are trained in problem solving and communication to enhance their ability to work as a team and support one another. One focus of training involves situations in which the parents disagree about how to handle a problem with their child. Consider this example involving the parents of Sophie, a child with separation anxiety disorder:

Mother: We are late for school, Sophie. Hurry up!
Sophie: I feel sick. I don't want to go to school.
Mother: You seem fine to me. Come on, you have to go.
Father: If Sophie is sick, she should stay home and rest.
Mother: But she never wants to go to school.
Sophie: (Starts crying and locks herself in her bedroom.)

Here, Sophie's father undermines his wife's efforts to get Sophie to face up to a difficult challenge. In such situations, parents are taught that children need to hear a consistent message from both parents. Now consider a different form of parental mismatch:

Mother: It's time to go to school now, Sophie. Get your books.
Sophie: I don't feel like going to school.
Mother: Come on, it's time to leave.
Sophie: In a little while; I can't go right now.
Mother: Come on, Sophie, we really need to leave now.
Sophie: (Ignores mother)
Father: You heard your mother. Get your books right now, and get in
    the car.
Sophie: (Complies)

Here, father supports mother after a fashion, but the overall pattern established is that Sophie complies with father but ignores mother; thus, mother's authority is undermined, albeit through her own reluctance to follow through. In such cases, it is critical for both parents to follow through with instructions, rather than having one parent rely on the other to be the enforcer. Otherwise, the child will learn to behave one way when the enforcer is present, another when the enforcer is absent.

As these two examples suggest, there are multiple ways that interparent disharmony may undermine parents' ability to help their child stay on track. Other kinds of disharmony addressed in the treatment program are (1) disagreeing over household rules, or consequences for breaking them; (2) arguing in front of the children; and (3) failing to share workloads related to child care or management. To address problems of disharmony, parents are taught six things to do when a problem occurs:

1. Remain calm and speak in a calm voice.
2. Try not to either interfere or come to the rescue when your partner is dealing with the child. The parent who gives instructions should be the one who follows through.
3. Help your partner if you see he or she needs it – for example, if your partner is attending to one child and others begin to misbehave, tend to the others.
4. Back each other up; do not give contradictory instructions to the child.
5. Do not comment on each other's behavior until the problem is resolved, and you are more relaxed. Do not blame or criticize each other.
6. After the problem is over, discuss it together if necessary; arrange a problem-solving discussion.

Parent sessions also stress the value of casual discussions, in which parents review with one another the events of the day, particularly those involving their child. Such discussions may tend to fade out of parents' daily routine, sometimes because days are so hectic that neither wants to review stressful events at the end, sometimes because the discussions rarely seem to change anything, and sometimes because the discussions lead to conflict and unpleasant feelings. The program teaches parents how to bypass such hazards by having discussions in which partners listen to one another and show interest and support, but *do not try to solve serious problems*. When there are such problems, parents taught not to address them at the end of a busy day, but rather to work out a separate time when both can sit down for a problem-solving discussion.

For these problem-solving discussions, parents are given very specific instructions on how to work together:

AGREE on a mutual time and place to discuss the problem, a time and place in which both parents will be calm and will not be interrupted by children.

IDENTIFY the problem in the child's behavior as specifically as possible. Deal with only one problem at a time. Make sure both parents agree on what needs to change.

BRAINSTORM together, writing down as many possible solutions as you can think of.

DISCUSS each possible solution, weighing its pros and cons, its likelihood of success, whether it is practical to use, and any problems that may arise.

CHOOSE the best solution by mutual agreement.

PLAN a strategy for using the solution. Make this very specific, noting exactly what each parent will say and do when the problem arises.

REVIEW how the solution is working; arrange another meeting to discuss this.

To maximize the chance that problem-solving discussions will be productive, parents are also taught how to give feedback to one another (e.g., start with the positive, be specific, describe without judging) and how to receive feedback (e.g., listen to all of it before deciding whether to accept or reject, make sure you understand it rather than just assuming or jumping to conclusions, ask for the feedback you want but don't get).

An overall aim of this program is to recruit the parents as treatment team members and give them the training they need to be effective in that role. This means educating parents about the treatment their child is receiving, enlisting their support in that effort, and providing the training they need to function as a team. Such teamwork requires effective use of behavior management principles, consistency across parents in style and substance of interactions with the child, and clear, supportive communication by the parents with one another to enhance their ability to present a unified front. The evidence thus far suggests that bringing parents into the treatment process does produce notable benefits. We now turn to that evidence.

The Family Anxiety Management Program: Outcome Studies Testing the Effects

Research on family-oriented treatment for youth anxiety has thus far focused only on the *additive* value of a family focus. That is, the two relevant studies published thus far have not tested the family program alone but instead have asked whether *adding* a family component to individual child treatment produces better outcomes than does child treatment alone.

Does adding FAM to the Coping Koala improve outcomes? In the Australian study by Barrett et al. (1996), reviewed earlier, the sample included 79

7–14-year-olds (57% boys, ethnicity not reported), who met criteria for overanxious disorder, separation anxiety disorder, or social phobia. The children were randomly assigned to Koala, Koala + FAM, or a waitlist condition, with all three conditions set at 12 weeks. Barrett et al. found that Koala + FAM not only outperformed the waitlist on most measures but also outperformed the Coping Koala individual treatment on multiple outcome measures, including clinical diagnosis at posttreatment and 12-month followup. As an example, the percent with no anxiety diagnosis at 12-month followup was 70% for the Koala group versus 96% for Koala + FAM, with only a single child in the Koala + FAM group having an anxiety disorder diagnosis a year after treatment. Thus, while the Barrett et al. (1996) study provided independent replication of the beneficial effects of Coping Cat, albeit in a shortened and adapted form, Barrett et al. also found that the addition of family-focused training to basic elements of individual cognitive-behavioral treatment led to better outcomes than individual treatment alone, on some key outcome measures. The combined Koala + FAM procedures proved particularly beneficial for younger children and girls.

Does adding a parent component help more if parents are anxious? In a related study, Cobham et al. (1998) investigated whether adding a parent component to child-focused cognitive-behavioral treatment matters most when parents are anxious. To find out, they assessed both child and parent anxiety in a sample of 67 children, ages 7–14 (51% boys, ethnicity not reported). The child diagnoses included separation anxiety disorder, generalized anxiety disorder, overanxious disorder, simple phobia with severe functional impairment, or social phobia. (Both DSM-IIIR and DSM-IV categories were included because the transition from IIIR to IV took place while the study was being conducted.) Parents of the children also completed standardized self-report anxiety measures for themselves. This made it possible to form two groups of children, those with child anxiety only and those with both child and parent anxiety (i.e., mother, father, or both scored above cutoff on the self-report anxiety scale). Children within each group were then randomly assigned to either individual child treatment based on the Coping Koala program or individual child treatment plus four Parent Anxiety Management sessions, reflecting one component of the Barrett et al. (1996) Family Anxiety Management program.

The content of the parent sessions focused on teaching the etiology of child anxiety disorders, with special emphasis on the role of the family, and teaching cognitive restructuring, relaxation procedures, and contingency management at home. Broadly, the goals were to help parents manage both their child's anxiety responses and their own anxiety so that they could both encourage good coping by their children and model good coping themselves. Findings were not uniform across all measures, but several of the findings did suggest that teaching parents to manage anxiety in the family did the most good for children whose parents were themselves anxious. For example, immediately after treatment had ended, the percentage of children who had shed their anxiety diagnoses was very similar for the individual treatment and the combined treatment groups (82% and 80%, respectively) for those children whose parents were low in anxiety, but for children of anxious parents, the percentages were quite different (i.e., 77% from the combined treatment condition had no anxiety disorder after treatment, compared to only 39% from the individual treatment condition). The pattern was evident, but no longer statistically significant, at 6-month and 12-month followups. Overall, the findings highlight an important possibility, one that may be relevant to a number of child problems and disorders: adding family or parent components to individual youth treatments may not be equally helpful for all youngsters. The impact may depend in part on the characteristics of the parents, and particularly their own patterns of psychological functioning.

Summary of the outcome evidence on family/parent anxiety management. In this section, we reviewed two studies, one focused on the FAM program (Barrett et al., 1996), the other on a shortened version designed to help parents manage both their child's anxiety responses and their own (Cobham et al., 1998). Neither study tested a family-focused program alone; rather, both studies assessed whether adding the family component to individual child treatment would produce measurable gains in outcome. Both studies found some evidence of such gains. In the Barrett et al. study, the Coping Koala + FAM condition outperformed Coping Koala alone on multiple outcome measures including the elimination of anxiety diagnoses. In the Cobham et al. study, adding a parent training component to individual youth treatment improved outcomes on some measures, including anxiety diagnosis, but the gains were found primarily among youth whose parents had shown high levels of anxiety in pretreatment assessments. The superior outcomes of individual + family treatment held up rather well over a 12-month follow-up period in the Barrett et al. study, but not as well in Cobham et al.

What about Sean? Applying Family Anxiety Management Training

The case description of Sean presented in the section introduction indicated that his mother is a worrier herself, and that she may in fact reinforce his anxious avoidance. This suggests that adding a family intervention component to the basic Coping Cat individual treatment might be helpful in Sean's case. So, let us add to our earlier discussion of Sean's Coping Cat treatment by noting how family training might be structured.

The therapist begins by meeting with Sean and his mother and father to explain to them that all family members need to work together as a team, with Sean as the captain, to tackle Sean's problems with worrying and avoiding things that worry him. One of their first team projects is to develop a list of the things Sean is afraid of, ranking them from most feared to least feared. At the low end of Sean's list are looking other kids in the eye and saying "Hi" to them; at the high end, most feared, Sean's list includes answering a question aloud in class and giving an oral report in class. Then the family members talk about how their bodies send them signals when they are starting to get afraid, and Sean says that his body gives him *lots* of signals, such as trembling hands and knees, weak voice, and feeling queasy and faint. They also talk about how thoughts pop into their heads that can make scary things even scarier; and Sean says one of these thoughts for him is, "Other kids will think I'm dumb or 'mental.'"

Next, the therapist starts to introduce what she calls a **FEAR** plan and she gives Sean an assignment one his parents can help with. She says the "F" in **FEAR** stands for *Feeling good*, and it involves three things Sean is to do when he feels nervous: (1) think positive thoughts, (2) do something enjoyable, and (3) relax. Her assignment for Sean is to make himself do something from the low end of his fear list once every day for the next week, and use "F" to help himself do it. Sean chooses to say "Hi" to kids at school, and he accepts the assignment of trying to do this to one kid every school day until the next session. Together, Sean and his parents figure out how to work a, b, and c into his plan for saying "Hi." They figure out that Sean will be more relaxed if he takes four or five deep breaths before he walks into the school building, and that he should try saying "Hi" to someone soon after he walks in each day so there is not much time to worry about it and get more tense. They also figure out that Sean can counter his negative thoughts (e.g., "They will think I'm 'mental.'") by thinking, "Everybody says hi. I'm just being friendly." and "Some kids will like it when I say hi to them." After each success, Sean agrees to say silently to himself, "Good job, Sean!" As for letter b, "Do something enjoyable," the family decides that Sean will be rewarded with special family time each day he succeeds in his assignment. Sean and his parents will start a game of Monopoly at home, and each day that Sean has said "Hi" to someone at school, they will play 15 minutes of the game after dinner to celebrate his progress.

Once this process is underway, the therapist introduces other parts of the **FEAR** plan. E is for *Expecting Good Things to Happen;* the therapist explains that this is just what Sean is doing when he says to himself, "Some kids will like it when I say hi to them." A is for *Action*, doing things to make a situation less scary so it can be faced; the therapist explains that this is what Sean is doing by making sure he says "Hi" as soon as possible each day before he has time to think about it and let it get scary. R is for *Reward*, earned by trying scary things; this is what Sean is doing by cheering himself on ("Good job, Sean!") and what his parents are doing by setting up the Monopoly reward.

After two weeks, Sean reports that saying "Hi" is no big deal for him any longer. This signals that it is time to move further up his fear list, to actions and situations that he listed as scarier than saying "Hi." Sean and his parents work with the therapist to apply the **FEAR** plan to other items on his list, eventually working their way up to the big ticket items involving speaking aloud in class. In each case, they generate some special, positive things Sean can say to himself as he is gearing up for the challenge, other positive things he can say to himself when he has made the attempt, and family-based rewards they can provide for him when he gets home. Not every exposure goes well but some do, and over time Sean grows more confident that he can cope with his fears.

In addition to the family work with Sean, the therapist and parents meet together in partner support sessions to work on skills they will need to support Sean's progress. His parents first learn how to react when Sean gets very upset, as when he panics over an upcoming report at school and tearfully begs them to let him stay home from school. They learn that a critical part of their role is to be a calming influence, not letting their own emotions surface. Sean's mother takes this point seriously, recognizing that her own anxiety has often made her a co-conspirator in Sean's fearfulness. In addition, both parents learn the importance of supporting one another rather than giving contradictory messages to Sean, as they had in the oral report crisis before therapy started. In that crisis, Dad had insisted that Sean must go to school and give his report, but Mom had wanted to write a note saying Sean was sick, and she had made it clear to Sean that his dad was the "heavy." Now she realizes that her behavior gave Sean confusing signals and undermined his commitment to facing his fears. She resolves to work with her husband to present a more unified front when problems arise in the future.

Toward this end, the therapist has mother and father practice holding problem-solving discussions. They identify some specific current problems they are facing with Sean, and these are used as grist for the mill in their practice discussions. For example, Dad thinks it is critical for Sean to have some kind of social interaction with peers outside of school, but Sean is so afraid of rejection that he refuses to invite anyone to his house. To tackle this problem, Mom and Dad are taught that they first need to agree on a time to hold their problem-solving discussion, a time when they can talk calmly and not be interrupted. In the discussion, they learn to clearly identify the specific problem they need to solve – in this case, that Sean needs peer interaction but his fear of rejection prevents him from asking a peer over. They then brainstorm a list of possible solutions, and after the list is produced, they discuss pros and cons of each.

One candidate solution, for example, is to make a reward (e.g., extra time in the family Monopoly game or lunch at a Chinese restaurant) contingent on having Sean invite a peer over. However, they decide that a reward won't be powerful enough to overcome Sean's massive fear of rejection. Reviewing other possible solutions leads them to a more structured plan they think will work. They decide to target Evan, a peer who is low in peer status himself and will thus welcome an invitation; Evan is also so talkative that he will carry most of the burden of conversation, further reducing the pressure on Sean. They also agree to let Sean buy a new video game, so that trying out the game can be the rationale for inviting Evan over. And they agree that if Sean feels unable to extend the first invitation, they will call Evan's parents (who are neighbors they already know) and invite him to join Sean for a video game and a McDonald's meal to get the ball rolling for Sean. Finally, they agree to set aside another time, after the play date, when the two of them can review how it went, and fine-tune planning for further peer interactions.

Another focus of these partner support sessions is the potential value of parental modeling. Sean's mother learns that she can be a potent influence on Sean by demonstrating healthy coping with her own anxiety. She realizes that her collaborative worrying interactions with Sean have likely magnified his anxiety. Working with the therapist and her husband, she practices ways of changing her worried cognitions into more positive ones. She also practices articulating her altered cognitions and actions aloud for Sean's benefit. One evening at dinner, she talks about how she has worried about being called on by her boss at staff meetings. She says she decided to take the lead instead of waiting to be called on, so she volunteered to give a report in an upcoming staff meeting. This gave her a chance to pick a topic she liked, and to plan exactly what she would say and how she would say it rather than waiting to be called on and not knowing what she would be asked about. It also gave her a chance to structure things to make the situation less frightening. As an example, she put together several handouts, partly to ensure that people would be looking at those while she talked rather than staring at her. She reports over dinner, "It worked! They mostly looked at the handouts, and I got through it just fine!" Hearing this, Dad says, "Alright!" and high-fives his wife. From the way Sean looks at his mother, she knows this story has really made an impression.

The therapist is very encouraged by what has happened in the family sessions, the separate parent sessions, and in real life outside therapy. Sean and his parents are clearly learning to work as a team, and the two parents are growing more skilled at supporting one another. There has been obvious growth in family problem-solving skill. And Sean's mother has used her increased skills to cope with her own anxiety, and thus to increase her effectiveness as a coping role model for Sean. So, much of what the FAM program was intended to do is indeed being done, and to the benefit of both Sean and his parents.

Troubleshooting: Common Treatment Problems and Recommended Solutions. The FAM program seemed to fit Sean and his parents rather well. This has been the case with other families obviously. However, problems can certainly arise in the course of family-oriented treatment for youth anxiety disorders. Herewith, some common problems and recommended solutions.

- *Parents' wariness at being "targeted" in treatment.* One of the most common problems is parents' wariness and unease when it becomes clear that their own behavior is a focus of the treatment they had initiated *for their child's benefit.* A frequent inference is that the therapist thinks the parents have an anxiety problem and that they may be to blame for their child's difficulties. The risk of feeling blamed may escalate when the focus turns to the ways parents respond to their child's fears. Experts in family anxiety management suggest that therapists preempt these concerns by the way they present the parent-focused material; one approach is to describe the parent work as an indirect route through which the clinician may help the child, important because the parents spend so much more time with the child than the clinician does. In focusing on parent responses to children's fear displays, it can help to present a list of the top 10 ways most parents respond, and then launch a discussion in which parents help identify advantages and disadvantages of each. With a skillful therapist, this process can lead to identification of particularly effective parental strategies, but it can also highlight the fact that all parents face difficult choices, and that there is no simple answer for any parent.
- *Parental reluctance to grant independence to the child.* Some parents are protective and overly involved with their child in ways that undermine the independence the child needs for effective coping. In treatment sessions, some parents even answer questions for their child; in life outside therapy, parents may protect the child from feared situations rather than encouraging exposure and mastery. In such situations, it is important to identify the reasons the parent finds it difficult to give up control or reduce protection of the child. Perhaps the parent has anxious thoughts about what might happen to the child. If so, the therapist may help the parent identify those cognitions that make letting go so difficult, then gather evidence on how realistic the parent's concerns are, and work to modify the cognitions (just as the therapist would do with an anxious child). Parents may also be given graded exposure tasks focused on granting independence to their child, a little at first, and then in increasing doses. Sometimes a parent's own need for companionship or empathy makes it hard to let go of the child. In such cases, the therapist may initiate a frank discussion about what this costs the child. In more

extreme instances, separate individual therapy for the parent may be warranted.

- *Interparent conflict that undermines child progress.* It is not uncommon for stress related to a child's problems to highlight, or even stimulate, conflict between the parents. Sometimes the conflict relates to disagreements over the best strategies to use in dealing with the child's anxiety; sometimes more basic interparent discord can be expressed in disagreements about the child. When discord undermines the parents' ability to support the child's treatment, the therapist needs to take action. Such action may take the form of separate sessions with parents to focus on their relationship, and sometimes referral to a couples therapist is called for. As an alternative, the therapist may meet with both parents to discuss the concern that their interactions are undermining the child's progress, and to talk about solutions. One possible solution: an agreement that any time a parental disagreement surfaces in a session, the therapist will redirect the discussion to the task at hand, and the parents will cooperate. As a final, less desirable solution, the therapist may occasionally ask that only one parent attend sessions, sometimes with the two parents alternating.
- *Parents can't/won't model exposure for their child.* When parents are asked to develop and model exposures of their own for their child's benefit, the parents often say that they don't have any appropriate anxiety-provoking situations. If discussion in the session doesn't turn up any appropriate target for parent exposure, clever therapists find alternative ways to implement some kind of exposure hierarchy. As one example, most parents can identify some significant task that they have been putting off – painting a room, fixing a dripping shower, building or repairing a fence. By designing and implementing a step-by-step approach to getting the task done, parents can at least model for their children a graduated approach to overcoming problems.

Coping Cat, Coping Koala, and Family Anxiety Management: Scientific Issues

The cognitive-behavioral programs for anxiety disorders are rooted in a rich scientific base. The structure of these programs owes a good deal to earlier work on modification of child cognitions (e.g., Meichenbaum, 1977), reciprocal inhibition and systematic desensitization (e.g., Wolpe, 1958), exposure linked with modeling (e.g., Bandura & Menlove, 1963), and, in the case of the family intervention, behavioral parent training (e.g., Patterson & Forgatch, 1987). Kendall and Barrett and their U.S. and Australian colleagues, respectively, have built nicely on these earlier efforts in designing treatments for youth whose problems with anxiety are pervasive and persistent enough to meet criteria for specific DSM-IIIR or DSM-IV anxiety disorders.

The findings do point to beneficial effects of the individual treatments, alone and in combination with family anxiety management training, and the evidence further suggests that the treatment effects may have considerable holding power beyond termination. However, the evidence could be clearer in some respects. For example, two issues arise from the fact that the standard control group has been on a waitlist. First, none of the studies to date has shown Coping Cat or Koala to be superior to an active alternative treatment; and where the individual youth treatment alone has been compared to the active alternative of youth + family management, the combined treatment has produced better outcomes on several measures, including diagnosis. Second, the understandable need to provide treatment to waitlisted youth without inordinate delay has meant that only the immediate posttreatment assessment involves a comparison of treated and untreated groups. Follow-up assessments by both the American and Australian groups have thus included only treated youth. This procedure, while understandable, does make it difficult to interpret the findings on effect durability given that follow-up assessments do not actually involve any group comparison. Both of the issues noted here are common in the child psychotherapy research literature, but both issues can be addressed via experimental designs that compare the target treatment to active alternative treatments.

Another matter that warrants attention in future research is the unusual timing of outcome assessment in the Coping Cat studies to date. In those studies, posttreatment outcome assessment has been set at 16–20 weeks postintake for the treated youth, but only 8–9 weeks for the waitlisted youth. The procedure was developed partly to reduce delay for families who are randomized to waitlist, and thus to reduce the risk of disproportionate attrition among those families. While it probably does help reduce differential attrition, the unequal timing of outcome assessment in treatment and control groups leaves the natural time course of anxiety uncontrolled, and thus complicates interpretation of the treatment-control comparisons. Because some evidence suggests substantial levels of spontaneous remission of childhood fears and anxiety (though not necessarily anxiety disorders; see Bernstein et al., 1996), it is useful to ensure that treated groups do not have more opportunity than control groups for such remission to occur. Given this concern, it is encouraging that the Barrett et al. (1996) Coping Koala study did find significant treatment effects using a design in which outcome assessment was timed similarly for treated and untreated youth. It may be wise to consider this design feature in future Coping Cat studies.

An important topic that has already received some attention in both the American and Australian research teams is moderation of treatment effects. Because no treatment is likely to be equally effective for all youth, we need to know for each of our treatments the effective range of various youth characteristics within which the treatments work best and outside of which effects are diminished. The studies reviewed here have taken useful initial steps toward exploring the effective range of youth anxiety treatments. For example, Kendall (1994) and Kendall et al. (1997, 2001) have tested whether Coping Cat effects differ by gender, by primary anxiety diagnosis, or by the presence versus absence of comorbid diagnoses; in general, the answer to these questions is no. Barrett et al. (1996) did find that both gender and age predicted the relative impact of Coping Koala alone versus combined with FAM. For younger children (ages 7–10) and girls, including the family management component improved outcomes, whereas older children (11–14) and boys did equally well with Coping Koala alone and with the family component added. Cobham et al. (1998) found that adding family management training improved posttreatment outcomes for children of anxious parents, but not for children whose parents scored low in anxiety; and where effects were found in children of low-anxious parents, they shrank at followup. Race and ethnicity are potentially important moderators that warrant study in future research. Because the proportion of ethnic minority youth, where reported, has been relatively low in the studies published thus far, attention to this issue may need to await new research or pooling of data across studies to generate sufficient power for a fair test.

A particularly positive feature of the Coping Cat research program is the effort to identify mechanisms that may underlie beneficial treatment effects. Kendall and Southam-Gerow (1996) reestablished contact with young Coping Cat participants about three years after treatment, asking them (among other questions) what they recalled about the program, what was important to them about it, and whether they remembered specific core elements such as the **FEAR** steps and doing exposure (STIC) tasks. Of those interviewed, 53% remembered that they had "dealt with fears and problems," 25% remembered learning the FEAR steps, and 25% recalled the exposure *in vivos*. Asked what was most important to them in the treatment, children were most likely to note their relationship with the therapist (44%), dealing with their fears and problems (39%), and "games and activities" (19%). When the authors tested which interview responses were related to outcome, they found that recall of the specific **FEAR** steps and recall of the relaxation exercises both predicted positive change from pretreatment to followup on some outcome measures.

Although these relationships are suggestive, they do not constitute formal evidence that child responses to treatment elements constituted mediators of outcome. For this reason, a study by Treadwell and Kendall (1996) is of special interest because it involved use of one method for specifically testing mediation. The study focused particular attention on whether changes in children's cognitions, or self-talk, might mediate improvement on anxiety measures. Results suggested that reductions in negative self-talk (e.g., "I am going to make a fool of myself."), but not increases in positive self-talk (e.g., "I feel good about myself.") may well have played a mediating role, at least with respect to improvements on child self-report measures (but not on parent- or teacher-report measures). These intriguing findings point to the potential value of further studies on mediation to move us closer to understanding causal processes that underlie treatment effects.

One other challenge for the CBT programs will be to unpack the bundle of intervention techniques that are combined in current treatments in an effort to match treatment components to characteristics of treated youth. At present, the CBT approaches involve relatively uniform combinations of techniques (identifying physiological arousal patterns, changing cognitions, learning to relax, attempting graduated exposure via role plays, in vivos, and homework) applied across all youth within a treatment condition. Future research may reveal more efficient ways of fitting children to components; for example, for some youngsters guided exposure alone may be sufficient without the cognitive training and relaxation instructions. Certainly the strong empirical base now established for CBT approaches provides an excellent launching pad for such new ventures in refining and tailoring treatment.

Coping Cat, Coping Koala, and Family Anxiety Management: Clinical Practice Issues

Several features of the programs suggest their workability in clinical practice. First, a key element of all the cognitive behavioral approaches discussed in this chapter is *individualization*, fitting the treatment to the distinctive characteristics of the child's pattern of fear and avoidance. Within this approach, children are asked to identify the specific situations that trigger anxiety for them, to map their own distinctive pattern of physiological arousal that signals the onset of anxiety, and to note their own personal cognitions that exacerbate the anxiety. Central to the treatments is the development of individually tailored exposure tasks and coping plans, designed to fit the specifics of each child's distinctive fears. Therapists work with children, and sometimes with their parents, to set up encounters with anxiety-arousing events and situations, typically low-grade at first, but eventually progressing to highly anxiety-arousing (e.g., speaking in front of a group). The exposure encounters, or STIC tasks, are planned in advance, with plans that include changes in cognition and in the elements of the situation, changes the child believes will help make the task doable. Thus, the design of Coping Cat seems calculated to foster individual tailoring of procedures to treated children. The program developers continue to discuss new ways of "breathing life into a manual" (see Kendall et al., 1998).

Another strength of the treatments can be found in the nature of the samples used to test their effects. Most of the research support comes from studies with samples severely disturbed enough to warrant formal diagnosis based on standardized assessment procedures. Analyses have also included assessment of clinical significance, and these have shown striking reductions in the percentage of treated youth who qualify for anxiety diagnoses (compared to much more modest reductions in waitlisted youth).

Three additional clinical issues suggest a more mixed picture regarding the ease with which these CBT approaches may be implemented in practice settings. First, the language and illustrations used in the manuals (especially for the FAM program) seem geared more to preadolescent children than to postpubertal youth. In work with older youth, these features will need to be adjusted significantly, and the manuals do not provide extensive guidance as to how this should be done. A second clinical issue is comorbidity. It is certainly a strength of the studies to date that they have included comorbid cases – youngsters who qualify for diagnoses other than the anxiety disorder that is the focus of treatment. This feature speaks to the external validity of the findings with regard to clinically referred youth who tend to show high levels of comorbidity. On the other hand, levels of comorbidity with externalizing, disruptive disorders have tended to be low in the tested samples, ruling out clear assessment of how well the treatments work with highly disruptive children who have difficulty attending. Those particular deficits, which are common in clinically referred youth, might conceivably add to the difficulty of using Coping Cat and Coping Koala procedures, given the cognitive-reflective-hypothetical-advance planning character of those treatments.

Treatment length is another factor that can be seen in both a positive and negative light. On the positive side, it is a plus that these CBT approaches have a relatively fixed duration that is shorter than traditional, long-term treatment approaches. On the negative side, treatments that require 12–20 sessions of 50–90 minutes each exceed what is now typical in community clinic practice and perhaps what is likely to be reimbursable under managed care constraints. Treatment duration and reimbursability may well be regarded as secondary concerns relative to the need to identify treatments that work. Yet, because such practical concerns do enter into real-world clinical practice, they cannot be entirely ignored or summarily dismissed.

How to Find out More about Coping Cat, Coping Koala, and the Family Anxiety Management Program

Procedures for the Coping Cat program are described in *Cognitive-Behavioral Treatment of Anxious Children: Therapist Manual* by P. C. Kendall, M. Kane, B. Howard, and L. Siqueland (1990), available from Workbook Publishing, in Ardmore, PA (phone 610/896-9797). A training video illustrating the treatment program, and a *Coping Cat Workbook* (Kendall, 1990), for use by children during treatment, are also available from Workbook Publishing. The web site www.childanxiety.org provides updates on available Coping Cat materials and training opportunities. The material used for the Australian adaptation of Coping Cat is the *Coping Koala Workbook*, an unpublished manuscript by P. M. Barrett, M. R. Dadds, and R. M. Rapee (1991), and available from Dr. Paula Barrett, School of Applied Psychology, Griffith University, Gold Coast Campus, PMB50 Gold Coast Mall Centre, Queensland, Australia. The manual for the Coping Koala FAM program, *Management of Childhood Anxiety: A Family Intervention Programme*, by P. M. Barrett (1994) is also available from Dr. Barrett. Chapters by Drs. Kendall and Barrett describing their work and its theoretical and clinical context appear in *Evidence-Based Psychotherapies for Children and Adolescents*, edited by A. E. Kazdin and J. R. Weisz, and published in 2003 by Guilford Publications, Inc.

TREATMENTS FOR DEPRESSION

Introduction to Section C

The Case of Megan and Treatments for Depression

Megan

Megan, age 13, seems both miserable and angry. She mopes around the house, complaining that she has no friends, and that other kids are laughing at her behind her back. She is irritable with her parents and she objects bitterly when asked to help with housework. She resents family rules, and she recently told her mother, "When I'm at home, I feel like a prisoner. All I ever do here is work." At meal times, she is sullen and withdrawn, uninterested in communicating with her parents or her younger sister. She has taken to wearing black and using black lipstick, and she has developed an interest in grunge music and reading about Kurt Cobain, the grunge musician who committed suicide in 1996. She listens to his music late into the night, seemingly unable to sleep.

Megan also overeats. She raids the refrigerator late at night, trying to cope with a pervasive empty feeling. The snacking gives her moments of pleasure, but that feeling subsides with the last bite of each snack and is quickly replaced by shame and guilt about the eating and about her noticeable weight gain. In fact, some of Megan's social isolation stems from embarrassment about her appearance. She hates to have peers see how "fat" she is now. She has been skipping PE class because she thinks she looks "disgusting" in her gym outfit – shorts and a T-shirt. Of course, skipping PE means less calorie burning and even more weight gain. Megan is aware of this causal chain, and she sees the situation as "hopeless."

For years, Megan has had an eye for dark clouds rather than silver linings. Her current bout with depression seems to have had a clear starting point. The problem began when a clique Megan had belonged to began to exclude her from their social events. She lost confidence in herself and seemed adrift socially. Her parents sometimes heard her crying behind her locked bedroom door. Once, after dinner, Megan tearfully told her mother, "No one likes me anymore. I'm an outcast."

At home, Megan lacks energy or motivation for schoolwork and she can't muster the concentration needed for studying; her grades have dropped dramatically. A teacher and Megan's school counselor recently contacted her parents to express concern, and her little sister has been asking "What's wrong with Megan?" Her parents are worried sick.

To parents, a child's depression can be both mystifying and terrifying. Unable to get at or fully understand the demons within their child, parents may grope for solutions but find little insight into how they can help. Other parents may be oblivious to their child's depression because so many of its symptoms are locked inside the child, hidden from view. Compounding the problem, depressed youngsters may be silent, withdrawn, or hostile – unwilling to accept help, especially from adults.

About 2% of preadolescents in the general population meet diagnostic criteria for either major depressive disorder or dysthymic disorder, the two most common DSM-IV depressive disorders, and prevalence increases to about 6% in adolescence (Angold et al., 1999; Weisz & Hawley, 2002). Of course, rates of depression are much higher in clinics and other treatment settings for youth than in the general population.

Developmental shifts of several kinds are evident in research on depression. In adolescence gender differences appear, with rates among girls eventually doubling those among boys (Avenevoli & Steinberg, 2001; Birmaher et al., 1996a,b; Holmbeck & Updegrove, 1995). The behavioral expression of depression also changes somewhat in adolescence, with increased hypersomnia, anhedonia, hopelessness, weight loss, substance use, and deliberate self-harm (Avenevoli & Steinberg, 2001; Garber et al., 2002).

The symptoms of depression can be painful and serious in their impact, as in the case of Megan. Depression can cause great distress to the youngsters who experience it and to their family and friends as well. Depression may also undermine social development, learning in school, and other kinds of growth and skill building (e.g., sports and music) that are important to maturation and self-esteem. In addition, of course, depression increases the risk of suicide. Between 6% and 13% of adolescents across surveys report that they have attempted suicide at least once, and suicide is the third most common cause of death among American 15–19-year-olds (Garland & Zigler, 1993). Thus, for many reasons, there is a clear need to develop effective treatments.

As noted earlier, the narrow range of treatment methods used in outcome research does not reflect the broad array of approaches used in clinical practice. For no treatment focus does this statement seem more accurate than depression in young people. While youth depression treatment in private practice and clinic settings reflects diverse theoretical models, and very often emphasizes a psychodynamic perspective, the treatments for which we have the most substantial evidence in clinical trials are cognitive-behavioral (but see recent evidence on interpersonal therapy with teens in

Mufson et al., 1999). On the good news front, however, there are multiple youth treatments that fall within the generic cognitive-behavioral rubric, suggesting that this treatment model is quite robust. Together the various cognitive-behavioral treatments nicely span most of the school-age spectrum. We will cover that spectrum in two chapters, within this section. One chapter is devoted to the elementary school and middle school age range, the other to groups that include high school students.

4

Cognitive-Behavioral Therapies for Child Depression

A well-known hallmark of depression is dysphoric mood, sometimes expressed by children as irritability or anger. Beyond the emotional state, depressed children often show characteristic styles of thinking and behaving. On the thinking front, they may interpret events and conditions in unduly negative ways. Compared to their peers, depressed children may see themselves as less able or worthy and their situations as more hopeless. On the behavioral front, depressed children may be more passive than their peers in situations that need to be changed; they may also show skill deficits that undermine school performance and interfere with peer relationships. Child depression then can involve problems in mood and emotion, problems in cognitive style, and problems in behavior and skill development.

Problems of each type are targeted in cognitive-behavioral treatment (CBT), the focus of this chapter. In CBT, therapists work with depressed children to deal with problems of sadness and irritability, partly by focusing on how the children think, and partly by addressing deficits in behavioral skills. One of the best-known CBT approaches for children is the program developed by Kevin Stark and colleagues (see Stark et al., 1987; Stark, 1990), which addresses mood, cognitions, and behavior, and also teaches children to evaluate and reward themselves for doing difficult tasks well. We will devote most of the chapter to a discussion of the Stark et al. approach. In addition, we will review other CBT treatments used for child depression to illustrate the range of specific approaches included within the CBT rubric. As in the other chapters of this book, we will discuss treatment procedures and outcome studies, illustrate the treatment approach with a case example, then discuss scientific and clinical practice issues.

Stark's Cognitive-Behavioral Therapy for Child Depression: Conceptual Basis and Procedural Overview

As the term *cognitive-behavioral* implies, the CBT model focuses on patterns of thinking and patterns of behavior. The goal is to identify and then modify maladaptive patterns within both domains. These twin foci are nicely illustrated in the CBT program developed by Stark and colleagues (Stark et al., 1987; Starke, 1990; Stark et al., 1991; Starke et al., 1996). Stark et al. construe child depression in terms of symptoms that define the syndrome (e.g., dysphoric mood, guilt, fatigue), cognitive distortions that put a negative spin on events and experiences (e.g., inappropriate self-blame), and deficits in basic skills children need to cope and adapt (e.g., poor social problem solving). These authors have published research on each set of features and have written thoughtful reviews of each body of literature (see e.g., Stark et al., 1990, 1996). Their treatment procedures aim to address each cluster of depression features. Children are taught to identify sad moods when they occur, and to use these moods as cues to try new behavioral skills.

Some of the treatment procedures used by Stark and colleagues were adapted from successful CBTs for adult depression; others are new wrinkles created by the Stark group. Together, the procedures form a sequence of didactic presentations, in-session exercises, and homework assignments, all designed to build specific skills. The program has been used most often in group treatment, but application to individual children is possible as well. Across different versions of the program (see Stark et al., 1987; Stark, 1990), the core skills have included monitoring and increasing rates of pleasant activity and positive self-statements; solving everyday problems by anticipating the consequences of various solutions; replacing negative, unhappy cognitions (e.g., self-blame) with more positive, realistic cognitions; setting realistic standards for self-evaluation; and rewarding oneself for trying and for reaching goals. From its earliest incarnation (Stark et al., 1987) to a later form of the treatment program (Stark, 1990), the number of sessions has roughly doubled and family home visits have been added. To provide the most comprehensive picture, we will focus primarily on the 1990 version; this version is also the most accessible to current practitioners through an available treatment manual (Stark & Kendall, 1996) and child workbook (Stark et al., 1996).

Stark's Cognitive-Behavioral Therapy for Child Depression: In Brief

Designed for . . . . Depression (or elevated depressive symptoms) in children ages 9–13

Number of sessions . . . . 18 with children (12 in Stark et al., 1987), 11 with family

Session length . . . . 50–90 minutes

Session participants . . . Therapist with children (in groups, but individual sessions OK) and parents

Theoretical orientation . . . . Cognitive-behavioral

Treatment elements:

1. Learn labels for various emotions and learn to identify the emotions in self.
2. Learn how emotions are connected to thoughts and behavior – e.g., pleasant events and activities lead to pleasant emotions, positive mood.
3. Identify some pleasant activities; schedule and practice them.
4. Learn problem-solving techniques (identify the problem, think of solutions, evaluate consequences of each, choose one and try it, examine outcome, praise self or try another solution).
5. Apply problem solving to mood disturbance, interpersonal problems, and daily hassles.
6. Learn to catch negative thoughts when they happen and restructure them by thinking about whether they are realistic ("What's the evidence?") and whether there are reasonable alternative interpretations.
7. Learn procedures for self-monitoring, self-talk, self-control, and self-efficacy.

Treatment classified by Treatment Task Force as . . . . Probably Efficacious

Key resources for potential users . . . . . Stark, K. D., & Kendall, P. C. (1996). *Treating Depressed Children: Therapist Manual for "ACTION."* Ardmore, PA: Workbooks Publishing. Stark, K., Kendall, P. C., McCarthy, M., Stafford, M., Barron, R., & Thomeer, M. (1996). *Taking Action: A Workbook for Overcoming Depression.* Ardmore, PA: Workbooks Publishing.

Stark's Cognitive-Behavioral Therapy for Child Depression: Treatment Procedures

The treatment program devised by Stark and colleagues has evolved considerably over the years. The version described most recently (in Stark & Kendall, 1996; Stark et al., 1996) involves a 50% increase in therapist-child contact plus the addition of family sessions, which were not a part of the original treatment program (described in Stark et al., 1987). The more recent version, on which we focus here, begins with an emphasis on helping children understand and influence their own emotional states; teaches them problem-solving skills and has them practice those skills; helps them identify and modify their negative cognitions; and ends with an emphasis on self-improvement. Here we will review the topics separately in the order they are first introduced in the Stark-Kendall (1996) manual. However, the treatment program actually uses a recursive approach, with topics introduced at one point and then revisited in later sessions for application to new problem areas. *Affective education*, for example, begins with exercises to help children identify and label various emotions, later focuses on helping children identify cues that they are feeling particular emotions, and still later addresses ways to cope with those emotions.

Affective Education. A logical first step in coping with depression is learning how to tell when one *is* depressed. To help children do this, the Stark program teaches children to identify their own emotional states. The idea is that if children can recognize when they are depressed, they can know when to use the depression-coping skills they are taught in other aspects of the CBT program. In one early step of affective education, children choose from a set of emotion cards, each showing the name of one emotion. The child's task is to tell group members how the emotion feels and what was happening the last time she or he felt that emotion. Later the child connects emotions to cognitions, describing what a person who feels the emotion might be thinking. In emotion charades, one child acts out an emotion while others guess which one. In emotion statues, a child sculptor shapes another child's face and body to express an emotion, and others guess which emotion it is. The aims of these procedures include teaching children to label their own and others' emotions correctly, and to recognize that emotions exist along a continuum of intensity.

Identifying and Scheduling Pleasant Events. Some depressed children lead sedentary lives. They withdraw from social interactions, shy away from sports, or otherwise deprive themselves of activities that could improve their mood. Thus, it makes sense that the Stark program includes an intentional focus on identifying and scheduling pleasant or goal-directed activities. A first step is to highlight for the child the connection between activities and mood. Any of several approaches may help convey this idea, including developing a graph that plots the child's activities on one axis and mood on another. Once persuaded that activities do indeed influence mood, the child's task becomes that of structuring time to include two types of activities: (1) those the child simply enjoys, and (2) those necessary to adaptive functioning – for example, completing homework or meeting responsibilities to others (such as collecting supplies for a scout camping trip). Child and therapist, working together, create a written activity schedule for days between sessions. As scheduled activities are completed, the child keeps a record of their personal impact, including feelings of mastery or pleasure.

Teaching Children to Solve Problems. Problem-solving training is designed to help children both functionally and cognitively. Functionally, learning to solve problems may reduce the risk of repeated failure that can deepen children's depression. Depressed children may get locked into a few rigid and ineffective coping strategies, and training may help broaden their repertoire. Cognitively, learning to solve problems effectively may help to counter the helplessness and hopelessness that often accompany depression.

Stark and colleagues teach children seven steps of problem solving, building on earlier work by Meichenbaum (1977) and Kendall (e.g., 1981):

Step 1 Define the problem.
Step 2 Brainstorm to generate possible solutions.
Step 3 Focus attention and energy on the task.
Step 4 Imagine the outcome of each potential action.
Step 5 Weigh the consequences of each, and choose one course of action.
Step 6 Evaluate the outcome of the action after trying it.
Step 7 Reward oneself for success, or repeat steps 2–7.

Stark views each step as important in its own way. Even the first step, identifying the problem, may be important to depressed youth who may only recognize that something is wrong or that they do not feel good, but may have only a very fuzzy notion of what is wrong. Brainstorming strategies may be valuable, given the depressed youngster's tendency to focus on a restricted range of solutions, then give up prematurely. The last two steps – evaluation and self-reward – can help consolidate learning from the problem-solving experience, improving the prospects for success in the future. At first the therapist is directive, guiding the child through the problem-solving steps, and looking for opportunities to apply the steps. Over time the therapist asks more questions, provides fewer answers, and nudges the child toward more independent use of the steps. The steps are applied to problems involving mood disturbance, daily hassles, and interpersonal problems, to which we turn next.

Improving Social Skills and Interpersonal Problem Solving. The interpersonal domain gets special emphasis in the Stark program. Depressed children tend to have less satisfying peer relationships than their nondepressed agemates, a problem that can undermine self-esteem and intensify feelings of isolation and loneliness. Some research (e.g., Linn & Stark, 1990) suggests that part of the problem is poorly developed social skills. To combat social skills deficits, therapists in the Stark program shape interventions to fit the nuances of each child's style. Using interactions with the child in sessions, and observations of the child's interactions with peers, the therapist identifies behavioral patterns likely to have adverse social impact – for example, avoidance of eye contact or poor conversation skills. Then the child and therapist role-play social situations, with the therapist first modeling appropriate behavior and the child following suit. Socially effective behavior is refined through coaching and corrective feedback. The training includes a focus on initiating and maintaining interactions as well as resolving conflict.

Altering Maladaptive Thoughts through Cognitive Restructuring. Given its CBT foundation, the program places special emphasis on cognitive change. Several treatment components stress ways to reduce maladaptive, depressive thoughts. A first step is identifying such thoughts (e.g., "No one likes me" or "I'm no good at anything") with active help from the therapist. However, the goal is for children to learn to spot maladaptive thoughts on their own.

Once the offending thoughts are identified, several approaches are used to counter them and alter them. In one approach, *"What's the evidence?"* (adapted from Beck et al., 1979), children practice using evidence about hypothetical other children to reach a verdict about whether those children's thoughts are accurate or not. An example from the Stark program's child workbook is shown in Figure 4.1. As youngsters develop the skill of using evidence to evaluate thoughts, they are asked to apply the skill to themselves. For example, they identify a negative thought of their own, then make a list of supporting and refuting evidence bearing on that thought. For example, one boy believed that his mother was weak and needed his protection. The boy's list did include some supportive evidence drawn from her past harmful relationships with men. However, with the therapist's nudging, the boy noted recent signs that his mother had grown more self-reliant, and thus that he might not have to carry the full burden of protecting her.

Stark et al. also use *alternative interpretations* and *"What if?"* as means of countering maladaptive cognitions. As an example of the former, a child who is demoralized by taunting from peers feels better when the therapist helps him develop a less distressing view of what is happening: the taunting is just an attempt to joke around, it is directed at other kids too, and "you have done it yourself – right?" "What if?" involves identifying exaggerated or otherwise unrealistic perspectives on events that give them undue power to influence mood – for example, "If Carrie and Gretchen aren't my friends, I'll be miserable the rest of my life," or "If I don't make all As in school, I'm a total failure."

Therapists also use action-oriented approaches. For example, therapists *model corrective cognitions* for the children by stating the negative cognitions aloud and then shifting to adaptive, coping-oriented thoughts. In this way, therapists become living illustrations of the kinds of cognition they want their young clients to show. Therapists also make *behavioral*

SLEUTHING FOR THE TRUTH

SUSPECT # 1
Lisa, age 8

Evidence

- lives with her mom and dad
- has one younger sister, age 3
- gets good grades in school
- likes math and reading
- takes piano lessons on the weekend
- has gymnastics on Fridays
- has freckles, blue eyes, and red hair
- likes to swim
- looks like her father, who is very handsome
- best friend Carol spends the night at her house often
- likes to go to the library with her mom and sister

What's your verdict?

The following are some of Lisa's thoughts. Name the evidence that tells you how you know if her thoughts are true or not. Circle the ones that are true and put a line through the ones that aren't true.

"I never get to do anything--I'm always bored."

"I think I am a good reader."

"No one likes me because of my little sister."

"My freckles make me look ugly."

"I am a good friend."

assignments to stimulate cognitive changes. In one illustration (from Stark, 1990), a depressed boy, Jamie, believed he was too "stupid" to complete his homework. The therapist asked Jamie to bring a homework assignment to the session, worked with him to complete the first few questions, then gradually withdrew his help so that the boy succeeded more and more independently. This procedure, plus phone calls to the therapist for occasional homework help, plus tutorials to catch up with a backlog of incomplete work, were all designed to modify Jamie's cognitions about his ability to complete homework and about his intellectual ability more generally.

Stark (1990) emphasizes two key points about efforts to modify maladaptive cognitions. First, a central aim is to identify and alter not just superficial beliefs (e.g., "I can't get my homework done.") but what Stark refers to as core cognitive structures (1990, p. 119 – e.g., "I am stupid"). Second, a critical long-term aim over the course of treatment is to reach a point that children are identifying their own maladaptive cognitions and using the cognitive change procedures to *independently* alter the ways they construe themselves, their world, and their experience. Attaining these two goals can help treatment gains generalize to new life circumstances after the child is no longer in treatment.

Self-Instructional Training: Using Coping Self-Statements. Self-instructional training is used to help children become their own therapists to some degree by using internalized self-statements to guide their own behavior. As an example, children learning the problem-solving steps described earlier may be taught internal prompts such as, "What's the problem?" (for Step 1), "Think of all the possibilities" (for Step 2), and so forth. The typical sequence in self-instructional training involves a demonstration of self-talk (aloud) by the therapist, as the therapist works on a task, followed by the child's trying the same task and modeling the self-talk, followed in turn by whispered self-talk and then silent, covert self-talk. Board games (e.g., Chinese checkers) are used to provide a context for learning these skills, then the skills are transferred to real-life contexts outside the therapy sessions, with subsequent review and feedback during therapy.

Self-Control Procedures. A logical complement to guiding one's behavior through self-talk is evaluating and rewarding the behavior. Several

---

FIGURE 4.1. "Sleuthing for the Truth." An exercise designed to help children learn to ask "What's the evidence?" and thus to evaluate cognitions for accuracy. [From Stark, K. D., Kendall, P. C., McCarthy, M., Stafford, M., Barron, R., and Thomeer, M. (1996). *Action: A workbook for overcoming depression.* Ardmore, PA: Workbooks Publishing. Reprinted by permission of Kevin D. Stark and Philip C. Kendall.]

components of the Stark et al. treatment grow out of Rehm's (1977) notion that depression results from deficits in self-control skills. Training in these skills was made the focus of an entire child depression treatment program by Stark et al. (1987); the most recent version of the Stark program includes self-control training in combination with cognitive-behavioral procedures. Here we note the main self-control components.

Self-monitoring. Rehm (1977) noted that depressed people closely monitor the negative events in their lives while giving shorter shrift to the positive events. Self-monitoring exercises are used by Stark's therapists both to assess the child's tendency to do such biased monitoring, and as a corrective device. For example, a child who tells the therapist that her parents punish her all the time may be assigned the task of monitoring and recording all the times her parents punish her during the next week. Such a record can inform the therapist and the child as to the true frequency of punishment, and the extent to which the child's perception (i.e., "all the time") is realistic.

Children also use self-monitoring to keep track of their *in vivo* use of skills they are learning in treatment and to rate their effectiveness. In another use of self-monitoring, children make diary records of all their pleasant activities (including pleasant thoughts) during the time between treatment sessions. This has two purposes. First, keeping a record of pleasant events counters the tendency of depressed children to notice and recall their negative experiences and overlook or forget the positive ones. Second, by linking these activity records to children's mood ratings, the therapist can help the children recognize the relation between what they do and how they feel. In principle, this promotes self-efficacy as children see concrete evidence that they can control their feelings by choosing activities wisely.

Self-evaluation. A second element of self-control training is teaching children how to evaluate their own performance fairly and accurately. This addresses the tendency of some depressed children to evaluate their performance, possessions, and personal qualities in unduly harsh terms (see Stark, 1990). The training aims to teach youngsters who make overly negative self-assessments to be more realistic – in some cases, simply to apply the same standards to themselves that they apply to others rather than using more stringent standards for themselves.

However, the training process also encourages realistic identification of skill deficits and realistic goal-setting. Suppose a girl believes "I am ugly," and her goal is "to look like Britney Spears." On the goal-setting front, the therapist's role may be to nudge the child toward a more appropriate standard than Britney Spears, by noting for example that the child does not require all her peers to meet this standard. Instead, "looking my best" may be a fairer standard, and applying this fairer standard to oneself may reduce some of the internal pressure that can percolate into depression. In addition, though, on the realistic self-appraisal front, if the girl's self-assessment reflects a genuine skill deficit (e.g., in personal hygiene, grooming, or manner of dress), the therapist may also work with her to build relevant skills. Such skill-building can be facilitated by what the child has learned in other treatment components. For example, the problem-solving steps discussed earlier can be used to develop plans for self-improvement. To increase the likelihood that the plans will work, the therapist can work with the girl to anticipate problems that may interfere and develop strategies for addressing each problem. Self-evaluation training is thus two-pronged: Developing fair standards for self-assessment, and cultivating skills to help the child meet those standards.

Self-reinforcement training. The icing on the cake of self-control training is reward. In the Stark program, children learn to give themselves rewards for the actions they take to build their skills. At first, Stark (1990) notes, "The idea of reinforcing oneself is quite foreign to depressed children" (p. 153). Indeed, at the beginning, it may be difficult to even figure out what the child finds rewarding. To structure this task, the therapist has children list (1) people they would like to spend more time with, (2) places where they would like to spend more time, (3) things they would like to own (e.g., books, CDs), (4) foods and drinks they like best, and (5) activities they would like to do more often. Rewards from this list – at least those that are actually available – are then made contingent on performance of treatment activities. For instance, the girl who took positive steps to improve her appearance through better grooming might reward herself by buying and reading a favorite book. One overall aim here is to boost children's sense of control over their own experience, particularly experience that directly influences their mood. Considerable evidence (e.g., Weisz, Southam-Gerow, & McCarty, 2001; Weisz, Sweeney et al., 1993; Weisz, Weiss, Wasserman, & Rintoul, 1987; Weisz et al., 1989) suggests that depressed youngsters have low levels of perceived control. Placing children in charge of their own rewards helps address a perceived lack of control while also reinforcing children's persistence at skill-building.

Working with the Family. Family work, as an adjunct to child sessions, serves both assessment and treatment purposes. Family sessions at home can reveal parent behavior (e.g., resisting a hug, differential attention to the treated child vs. a favored sibling) or verbalizations (e.g., "The world stinks!" "You can't trust anyone.") that may communicate negative, potentially depressogenic messages to the child. Such sessions can also highlight family processes (e.g., unpredictable punishment, rules against expressing emotion) that make the child vulnerable. Family meetings early in treatment thus help the therapist formulate a treatment plan; later family contacts help refine this plan.

Ideally, the therapist weaves the family into the treatment process in multiple ways. Relatively healthy families are enlisted as allies in the child's treatment. Their help is sought in ensuring that the child completes therapy homework assignments, and they are taught specific content the child is learning so they can reinforce and assist at home. As an example, learning the problem-solving steps listed earlier permits parents to work through the steps with their child when the child comes home from school worried about a problem. In addition, teaching parents how to recognize and combat unrealistically negative thinking positions them to help their child identify and alter such thinking in everyday life.

Unfortunately, many depressed children have parents who themselves have mental health problems, and families whose functioning is less than ideal. In such circumstances, the therapist may encourage troubled parents to seek help for themselves as an adjunct to the child's therapy. Where patterns of family functioning seem to be undermining the child's development and adjustment, the therapist may intervene directly – for example, role-playing conflict reduction strategies with the family, working to help family members learn problem-solving skills, renegotiating maladaptive family rules, and even prescribing specific changes in family members' behavior between sessions. The family treatment component is thus designed to strengthen family support for the child's treatment and minimize deleterious effects of parent or family dysfunction. The ideal is that when the child leaves the therapist's office, the family will be prepared to help the child sustain and apply the skills learned in treatment.

Cognitive-Behavioral Treatment for Child Depression: Outcome Studies Testing the Effects

Several studies have tested the impact of CBT on child depression. Two of these involve Stark's program (the 1987 version in one study, the most recent version in the other). Other tests (see next section) have focused on different CBT programs that are similar to Stark's in several respects.

Initial test by Stark and colleagues: Effects of two treatments involving cognitive and behavioral components. In the first published test of the CBT approach to child depression, Stark et al. (1987) compared two treatments involving cognitive and behavioral elements to a waitlist condition. The two treatments emphasized different components of the list of skills described previously. One of the treatments, *Self-Control Therapy* (12 group sessions), was modeled after an adult depression treatment program by Rehm et al. (1984). It emphasized the self-instructional and self-control skills noted in the latter part of the treatment description. Children were taught to monitor their own activities and self-statements, evaluate their own performance, reward themselves appropriately, and make appropriate causal attributions for good and bad outcomes. The second treatment, *Behavioral Problem-Solving Therapy* (also 12 group sessions), was patterned partly after a CBT program for adult depression developed by Lewinsohn et al. (1980). It blended self-monitoring, affective education, pleasant activity scheduling, and training in problem-solving and social skills. Therapists for the two conditions were a doctoral candidate in psychology and a doctoral-level psychologist.

The sample of 29 fifth and sixth graders from a semirural school were 9–12 years old (mean 11.2); 57% were male; ethnicity was not reported. Children were identified through high scores on a self-report depression questionnaire and on a semistructured clinical interview. The children were randomized to one of the two treatments or to a waitlist condition. Outcomes were assessed at immediate posttreatment for all groups, plus an eight-week followup for the two active treatment groups.

From pre- to posttreatment, the two treatment groups improved significantly on two self-report measures and one interview measure of depressive symptoms, whereas the waitlist group improved significantly only on one of the self-report measures. At posttreatment, with pretreatment scores covaried, the three groups differed significantly only on one of the self-report measures, and only the *Self-Control* group scored significantly lower than the waitlist group when two-group comparisons were carried out. At followup, the two active treatments differed from one another only on the interview measure, which showed the *Self-Control* group to be less depressed than the *Behavioral Problem-Solving* group. Trends for most measures suggested better outcomes for treatment groups than for waitlist, and it seems likely that more group differences would have been significant had the study sample been larger.

Second test: Assessing an expanded CBT program. In a second trial by Stark and his colleagues (Stark, 1990; Stark et al., 1991), an expanded version of the CBT intervention was employed, one that blended elements of both the *Self-Control* and *Behavioral Problem-Solving* treatments from Stark et al. (1987). The program was essentially that described earlier in this chapter, involving 24–26 group sessions at school, plus two to three family sessions at home. Children were taught to identify emotions; to increase self-control through the use of self-monitoring, self-evaluation, and self-reinforcement; to employ realistic, nondepressive cognitions; to use systematic procedures to solve problems; to improve their skills in interactions with peers; and to regularly schedule and engage in pleasant activities. Family sessions were used to teach parents how to (1) support their child's use of the skills taught in treatment, and (2) involve the family in more pleasant activities.

The CBT program was compared to a *traditional counseling* (TC) condition that also entailed 24–26 group sessions at school, plus two to three family sessions at home. TC sessions involved meetings with empathic adults aimed at teaching causes of and remedies for depression. A support group climate was used to facilitate discussion of problems, and to control for attention and expectation of improvement. TC family sessions focused on improving communication and increasing family engagement in pleasant activities. Therapists in both conditions were all doctoral students in school psychology.

Participants were 24 youngsters from the fourth to the seventh grades who met study criteria for elevated depressive symptoms on a self-report questionnaire and a standardized diagnostic interview (age, gender, and ethnicity not reported). Of these, 15 met diagnostic criteria for a depressive disorder. Children were randomly assigned to the CBT or TC groups, and at pretreatment the groups did not differ on self-reported depressive symptoms, structured diagnostic interview scores, or a self-report measure of depressive cognitions and self-esteem. At posttreatment, however, the CBT group scored as significantly less depressed than TC on the diagnostic interview and the measure of depressive cognitions and self-esteem. There were no significant group differences at a seven-month followup, but the authors report that this reflected subject attrition; only seven CBT and five TC children participated in follow-up assessments.

The outcome difference at posttreatment is notable because it reflects a demanding comparison – that is, CBT versus an active alternative treatment, some parts of which seem likely to have had potential therapeutic effects (e.g., teaching children about depression causes and remedies). The strong comparison notwithstanding, the findings would have been strengthened had it been possible to reduce attrition at followup, and thus provide a fair test of the durability of treatment effects. Another concern is that the study has only been described in brief summary form in book chapters, not subjected to journal peer review, and the brief descriptions omit many details needed for thorough evaluation of the findings.

Other CBT programs for children: I. Testing cognitive restructuring and role-playing components of CBT with fifth and sixth graders. The two outcome studies by Stark and colleagues are complemented by studies from other groups, testing other CBT treatment programs with children. In general, these studies show evidence of treatment benefit, although one study (Liddle & Spence, 1990) failed to show significant treatment effects. The first published study in the area was done by Butler and colleagues (1980), seven years before the first study by Stark et al. (1987). Butler et al. tested two different treatments for depression in late elementary school students. Both treatments resembled components that were later combined with other procedures in cognitive-behavioral packages, such as those by Stark and colleagues (this chapter) and Lewinsohn and colleagues (Chapter 5). Each of the treatments and the control condition involved a series of 10 weekly one-hour sessions for groups of six to eight children.

In the Butler et al. (1980) *role-play treatment*, each of the sessions was focused on a particular problem thought to be relevant to depressed children (e.g., acceptance and rejection by peers, self-blame, and loneliness). In a typical session, the problem topic for the day was introduced, the nature of the day's role-play was described to children, the role-play was carried out and then discussed by the group, and successive role-plays used alternate approaches to solving key problems. The aims of each role-play sequence were to (1) make each child aware of his or her own feelings and thoughts in stressful situations, (2) enrich each child's awareness of how others feel, (3) build skills in facilitating social interaction, and (4) teach skills in problem solving, similar to the skills taught in the later Stark program. The Butler et al. *cognitive restructuring treatment* (influenced by Beck, 1967; Beck et al., 1979) was designed to teach children to recognize their own irrational, self-deprecating thoughts, and to replace them with more rational, less personally demeaning thoughts. The intent was to pair this skill with an understanding of how thoughts are connected to feelings. The program also aimed to improve children's listening skills. Each session included group exercises followed by discussions. In the *attention placebo* condition, children were taught to solve problems cooperatively by sharing research information and resource material provided to them by the leaders. Problem topics (e.g., "How did Ernest Hemingway die?") were selected to be engaging but not therapeutic. The study also included a *classroom control* group, who simply remained in their classrooms during the study.

Using teacher judgments and a battery of four child self-report scales (measuring depression and related constructs), Butler et al. (1980) identified 56 fifth and sixth graders (35 boys, 21 girls; age and ethnicity not reported) showing symptoms of depression. These children were randomly assigned to the four conditions: attention placebo, classroom control, role-play treatment, and cognitive restructuring treatment. Outcomes were assessed following the treatment phase, but there was no follow-up assessment.

Butler et al. (1980) did not describe the results in complete detail, but tables in the article provide a partial picture of the outcomes obtained. The role-play program showed the strongest evidence of beneficial effects. Children receiving that program improved significantly from pre- to posttest on self-report measures of depressive symptoms, self-esteem, locus of control, and depressive cognition. By contrast, children in the cognitive restructuring group improved significantly on only the depression and self-esteem measures. Tempering these within-group effects somewhat was the fact that significant between-group effects were found at posttest on only two measures – depressive symptoms and locus of control. Although these overall group effects were not broken down into two-group comparisons in the article, Butler et al. concluded that the role-play approach showed promise and could be recommended for use with depressed preadolescents. Inspection of the data does suggest that the role-play group may have fared better than the other groups, but no significance tests were reported to support that impression.

Other CBT programs for children: II. Primary and Secondary Control Enhancement Training (PASCET) for 8–12-year-olds. Another CBT program with elements resembling those of Butler et al. (1980) and Stark et al. (1990, 1991) has close connections to the literature on perceived control and child depression (see e.g., Weisz, 1990; Weisz, Sweeney et al., 1993). It is based on the two-process model of control (Rothbaum et al., 1982; Weisz, Rothbaum, & Blackburn, 1984a,b). In that model, *primary control* involves enhancing reward or reducing punishment by making objective conditions (e.g., the outcome of a test, one's standing or acceptance in a group) conform to one's wishes. In contrast, *secondary control* involves enhancing reward or reducing punishment by adjusting oneself (e.g., one's beliefs, interpretations, expectations, or wishes) to objective conditions that are hard to change, so as to control their subjective, personal impact.

How might this model apply to depression? One idea is that successful coping with depression may require (1) learning to apply primary control to distressing conditions that are modifiable, and (2) learning to apply secondary control to distressing conditions that are not. In fact, some of the most relevant forms of primary and secondary control may be techniques that have already been linked to the treatment of depression. For example, relevant primary control techniques might include (1) building specific skills and competencies so as to reach one's goals and influence objective outcomes in social, academic, or athletic spheres; and (2) identifying and engaging in pleasant activities. Relevant secondary control techniques might include (1) identifying and altering unrealistically negative cognitions; (2) learning cognitive techniques for mood enhancement (e.g., reinterpreting, selectively focusing on positive events); and (3) learning relaxation and positive imagery to alleviate the tension and anxiety that are frequently a part of depression.

These two primary control components and three secondary control components were integrated to form the PASCET CBT program (Weisz et al., 1997). The eight sessions included group meetings devoted to the specific skills described in the preceding paragraph, plus some individual child-therapist contact to fit the lessons of treatment to the individual child's personal situation. A therapists' treatment manual guided in-session activities (e.g., role-play games, video), and weekly homework for children was guided partly by a practice book designed to provide concrete illustrations and reminders of key points.

The sample was drawn from schools; subject selection and outcome assessment involved a widely used child self-report depression questionnaire and a standardized clinical interview. The 48 children who participated included 26 boys and 22 girls, from the third to the sixth grades (mean age 9.6 years); 30 were Caucasian, and most of the 18 minority youth were African American. The children were randomly assigned to the PASCET program or to a no-treatment control group, and those in the PASCET condition were formed into small groups (3 to 5), meeting once weekly with two cotherapists. The pool of therapists included one Ph.D. clinical psychologist and three graduate students in clinical psychology.

Outcomes were assessed immediately after treatment, and then again at a nine-month followup. At both assessment points, the treatment group showed greater reductions than the control group in depressive symptomatology on both the depression interview and the self-report questionnaire. Posttreatment and followup between-group comparisons both showed significantly less depression on the self-report questionnaire for the treated children than the untreated children, and trends in the same direction (ps = 0.18 at posttreatment, 0.15 at followup) on the clinical interview measure. Clinical significance of group differences was supported by the fact that treated children more than controls shifted from above to within the normal range on both measures. Group differences were significant at posttreatment for the questionnaire measure (50% vs. 16%), and at followup for both the questionnaire measure (62% vs. 31%) and the interview measure (69% vs. 24%). This is the briefest treatment for child depression that has yet been shown to have significant beneficial effects.

Other CBT programs for children: III. CBT versus relaxation and self-modeling treatments for 10–14-year-olds. Kahn et al. (1990), focusing on middle-school children, developed and tested three different intervention programs for depression. One of these was a conventional CBT package; the others were simpler, single-skill-oriented interventions – that is, *relaxation training* and an unusual *self-modeling treatment* that had been shown to reduce depression in adults but had not yet been tried with children or teens. The group CBT treatment was patterned largely after an early version of the Adolescent Coping with Depression course (see Chapter 5, and see Clarke & Lewinsohn, 1984), with additional components reflecting Rehm's (1981) self-control model of depression treatment. The treatment focused on development of specific skills for coping with depression (e.g., pinpointing and solving problems, identifying antecedents and consequences of one's moods, identifying and modifying depressogenic thoughts, setting appropriate goals, scheduling pleasant events, learning communication and social skills, and learning to reward oneself appropriately).

The group relaxation training program included initial training in the connections among anxiety-arousing situations, stress and tension, and depression, together with identification of specific stress-generating situations. This was followed by basic training in progressive muscle relaxation, and then training in alternate ways to achieve relaxation (e.g., counting, controlled breathing, pleasant mental imagery). In the self-modeling treatment, Kahn et al. (1990) used videorecording procedures to train children to display behaviors incompatible with depression – behaviors such as appropriate eye contact, smiling, upbeat tone of voice, gesturing, and positive statements about self and others. Children, seen in individual sessions, were coached and then "interviewed" on videotape (e.g., ". . . tell us what fun things you like to do in your free time . . . tell us who some of your friends are and what you guys like to do together . . . "). The video-tape was edited to (1) eliminate any inadvertent depressed behavior, and (2) limit the length to three minutes. After this, 10–12-minute "treatment sessions" were held twice weekly; in these, the child was merely instructed to watch the tape.

The sample for the Kahn et al. (1990) study included 33 boys and 35 girls, drawn from the sixth, seventh, and eighth grades (age and ethnicity not reported). The 33 were identified through three stages of assessment: (1) school-wide screening with two self-report depression measures, (2) readministration of the same two measures after a one-month interval to rule out youngsters whose depressive symptoms were transitory, and (3) a structured clinical interview. The 33 were then randomly assigned to one of the three active treatments or a waitlist control group. Those assigned to either the CBT or the relaxation training condition were seen in small groups ($N = 2$–5); those in the self-modeling treatment were seen indi-vidually. All three treatment conditions involved 12 sessions, spread over six to eight weeks. Assessments involved both self-report and interview measures of depression and self-esteem immediately after treatment, and again after one month.

Analyses showed greater within-group reductions in depressive symp-toms, and larger increases in self-esteem among the treated children than the waitlist group; and this pattern appears to have held at the one-month followup. Improvement appeared most pronounced in the CBT group, but the other two active treatments also showed effects in comparison to the waitlist condition. A strength of the data analytic procedure was assess-ment of clinical significance, defined as the extent to which treatment was associated with movement from the clinical to nonclinical range on the various measures. Importantly, while less than 20% of the waitlist group showed such movement at posttest or followup, a clear majority of the CBT and relaxation training groups' subjects did so, and the figures for the self-modeling group were almost as good. Moreover, after the waitlist subjects received treatment, they too showed high rates of change from clinical to nonclinical levels.

In two respects, the Kahn et al. (1990) findings are reminiscent of the Stark et al. (1987) findings. First, although the various treatment groups outperformed the waitlist condition, the different active treatments gen-erated fairly similar effects with few significant differences across the out-come measures. Second, as in Stark et al., the parent-report measures ob-tained by Kahn et al. did not show the significant treatment effects the child self-report measures showed.

Summary of the outcome evidence on CBT for child depression. This re-view has summarized five studies pointing to positive effects of CBT on depressive symptoms and related outcomes (e.g., self-esteem, negative cognitions), and one study was noted that used a very brief CBT treatment and did not show beneficial effects (i.e., Liddle & Spence, 1990). The five studies with positive outcomes generally concur in the finding that CBT is superior to a waitlist or no-treatment comparison condition, and one study reported that CBT was superior to traditional counseling (see Stark et al., 1991, 1996). However, the findings do not show that CBT dramatically outperforms other structured, manualized treatments for child depression (e.g., relaxation training, self-modeling, in Kahn et al., 1990), or that different combinations of CBT elements (e.g., the two treatments used in Stark et al., 1987) are markedly different in their effects. A particularly interesting aspect of the findings – especially those by Kahn et al. (1990) – is the impressive outcome associated with relatively simple intervention procedures. In the Kahn et al. study, learning to relax and repeatedly viewing a three-minute video of oneself behaving in a nondepressed way produced reductions in depressive symptomatology that rivaled those of a more complex package of CBT techniques. We will return to this point at the end of the chapter (and revisit the point when we consider treatment of adolescent depression in the next chapter).

What about Megan? Applying Cognitive-Behavioral Therapy for Child Depression

Thirteen-year-old Megan, discussed at the beginning of the depression section, hovers in the limbo between childhood and adolescence; her feelings and behavior show some childlike characteristics and some features more often seen in the teen years. This makes it possible to use her case to illustrate CBT for child depression in this chapter and CBT for adolescent depression in the next chapter. Two characteristics make Megan and CBT a good match: she shows unduly negative cognitions and she shows vegetative features suggesting a need for behavioral activation. The fact that she faces significant social stressors and family issues, and that she sees her situation as hopeless, may make the Stark CBT program especially appropriate.

Let us suppose that Megan works with a therapist who uses the Stark CBT program. Megan joins a group of depressed youngsters of similar age, and after some initial get-acquainted exercises, they talk about how various emotions such as anger, sadness, and happiness feel, and what was happening to each of the participants the last time they felt each emotion. They also play emotion charades in which each child acts out an emotion, and others guess what it is. Because the children are all 12 or 13, they have few problems identifying basic emotions. However, subtle shades of emotion (e.g., guilt vs. shame) are trickier; and the group discusses emotion mingling, as when feelings of sadness or humiliation after a bad day at school get transformed into anger at home. This point hits home for Megan, although she doesn't tell the group.

In a later session, the group discusses where emotions come from, and they focus especially on the connection between activities and emotion. The leader has all the group members make a graph showing their activities on a vertical axis and their mood ratings on the horizontal. Megan notices that listening to music, reading, talking to a friend on the phone, and physical exercise (when she gets around to doing it) all show pretty good mood ratings on her graph. When the leader asks group members to select activities they will commit to doing each day, Megan picks reading, but she also begins at least to *think* about walking or jogging after school.

The group focuses next on problems and how to solve them. Group members learn a seven-step plan. Then each child's job is to apply the plan to a specific problem in his or her everyday life. Megan chooses the problem she is having getting her homework done. She applies the seven steps in this way: (1) *define the problem* – "I can't concentrate enough to get my homework done;" (2) *brainstorm solutions* – "Try harder to concentrate," "Quit trying – just blow the homework off," and "Do the homework in 15-minute spurts, with breaks in between"; (3–5) *focus attention on the task, imagine outcomes, choose one solution* – "Trying harder probably won't work – I've already done that; blowing off homework would mean terrible grades, and then I'd feel even worse; but breaking homework into 15-minute blocks might help, since I *can* concentrate for that long"; (6) *evaluate the outcome* – By breaking homework into little blocks, Megan does complete more of it; (7) *reward success* – So, she secretly says, "Good girl – you're a winner" to herself, and she rewards herself with little reading and music breaks in between her study times, and with a star-shaped pin that she puts on her school backpack. Building on this success, Megan begins thinking about other problems (perceived rejection by her clique at school, conflict with parents over housework) with an eye toward how those problems might be solved. Just thinking that there *might* be a solution makes her feel a bit better, a little less hopeless.

Next the group leader talks about how unrealistic negative thoughts can bring on sad feelings, and group members list some of their own negative thoughts. One of Megan's is, "No one likes me." The leader suggests doing a "What's the evidence?" exercise with this thought. On the blackboard, with Megan's help, group members list the evidence for the thought (e.g., Megan's old clique has begun excluding her) and against the thought (e.g., several other kids are friendly to her at school, kids call her at home, she's been invited to two parties this month, her parents and sister love her). Two kids in the group add that they like Megan, too. The group agrees that there is more evidence against Megan's negative thought than for it. Stretching a bit further, the leader and kids look for other forms the negative thought may take, such as "I can't live without my clique," and they discuss how realistic such a thought is. Clearly, Megan can live without her clique. A more realistic version of the thought – and a less depressing version, as well – may be, "I am very sad to be losing my clique, but I can go on living, and I can probably find other friends to be happy with." Using exercises like these, Megan and her group work on catching and critiquing their negative thoughts when they happen. The goal is to stop and examine such thoughts on the spot with two key questions in mind: (1) Is this thought realistic? and (2) Is there an alternative thought that is more realistic and will make me feel better?

Keeping track of one's own thoughts is what the group leader calls self-monitoring, a term that has several applications in Megan's life during therapy. As one example, one of Megan's thoughts about home life, repeated aloud for her group, is "When I'm at home, I feel like a prisoner. All I ever do there is work." The group leader encourages Megan to monitor her activities at home to find out whether her thought is accurate. So for one week she keeps a chart of the activities she does and how much time she spends at each. High in the chart are activities like listening to music and reading. One of the least frequent activities in her chart is work. What work there is is mostly school homework; there is almost no housework, almost nothing to help the family. The chart is an epiphany for Megan. It shows her something important about how her depression is distorting her perceptions and making her rather self-absorbed to boot.

Megan also learns to put herself in control of some of the rewards in her life. Like the others in her group, she makes a list of people she would like to spend more time with, places she'd like to be, activities she'd enjoy, and things she'd like to have. From this list, she picks out rewards that are the most accessible to her. She learns in her treatment sessions to dole out the rewards to herself depending on the effort she puts into meeting her goals. Some of the goals involve practicing skills she learns in the treatment – skills such as applying the seven steps of problem solving to real problems in her life. Other goals are more personal. For example, she has worried about her weight for some time, but now she resolves to take serious action, developing a plan for avoiding high-fat foods and for exercising regularly. To support this plan, she decides to give herself special rewards – time listening to music and reading – only on days when she has followed her diet and exercise plan.

In another important part of treatment, Megan's therapist reaches out to her parents, bringing them and Megan together to review some of the most important skills Megan is learning. Megan even tells her parents about her self-monitoring experiment, the one that showed how wrong she was to think, "all I ever do at home is work." One of the skills all the family members agree would be useful to apply to their lives together is problem solving. In fact, they practice doing this by applying the steps to a recurrent problem at home: meal times when Megan refuses to leave her room. Together, they actually do identify several solutions and pick one out to try the next time the problem arises. Of course, no one in the family believes Megan's struggle with depression is over for good. However, Megan and her parents agree that she now has some potent new skills to bring to the struggle.

Troubleshooting: Common Treatment Problems and Recommended Solutions. Unlike Megan, some children encounter rough spots going through the steps of CBT for depression. Here are a few common problems and some recommended solutions.

- *Homework not done.* One of the most common rough spots is a failure to complete the between-session homework assignments. Treatment developer Kevin Stark recommends that therapists address the problem via incentives and parent involvement. Stark teaches therapists to offer children rewards from one of two bags. Youngsters who come to the session without having completed their homework choose from a bag containing rewards that are just okay. Youngsters who come with homework completed get to choose from a second bag containing much more desirable rewards. In his own clinical practice, Stark sometimes holds separate sessions with parents to discuss the importance of their child's homework and to encourage parents to incentivize the process by offering small rewards to the child at home for completing the work. He reminds parents that the cost of a few child rewards will be noticeably lower than the cost of extra parent sessions with the therapist that are needed when homework is not done.
- *Cognitive focus seen as criticism of the child.* Another potential problem in CBT is that youngsters may view their therapist's efforts at cognitive restructuring as a personal criticism. They may believe the therapist is suggesting that they are wrong and cannot think properly. Stark recommends addressing the issue directly, telling children that (1) the negative thoughts are caused by the depression, not the child, and (2) the child and therapist are working together as partners to identify those thoughts and change them.
- *Mismatch between coping skill and child's developmental level.* A third potential problem is developmental in nature. Therapists may select coping skills for the child to work on that are developmentally inappropriate for the child (e.g., some forms of complex cognitive monitoring are beyond the reach of some third graders). In such cases, repeated efforts by the therapist may fail to get the skill across. For the frustrated therapist, reviewing session notes or tapes with a colleague or supervisor may clarify what the problem is, and the remedy may well consist of a change in the therapist's perceptions of what the child is ready

for, and of appropriate adjustments in the therapist's objectives and methods.

- *Child's pessimism and hopelessness may undermine efforts to cope.* Finally, the pessimism and hopelessness that so often characterize depression can leave some children disinclined to try the coping skills, or quite ready to give up after minimal effort. In such cases, Stark recommends that therapists work with parents to institute a reward system that will support perseverance by the child. If therapists persist and remain vigilant, he counsels, they will eventually see moments when the child's nascent coping skills pay off. Those moments should become grist for the mill, used as opportunities for the therapist to help the child see how the coping skill worked, and how it could benefit the child to use that same skill again.

Stark's Cognitive-Behavioral Therapy for Child Depression: Scientific Issues

The work of Stark et al. provides a good illustration of theoretically and empirically grounded, multicomponent cognitive-behavioral treatment. Stark and colleagues have drawn from empirical findings on child depression and translated techniques previously used with adults into language and procedures geared to children. They have also provided initial empirical evidence on the efficacy of their procedures. Their pioneering work has set the stage for and pointed the way to a second generation of research on child depression and its treatment. Here we will consider what some of the second-generation agenda might include.

First, and simplest, replication should be on the agenda. The literature on the Stark program illustrates how treatments evolve over time, a process that is quite common in treatment research. Investigators learn lessons from one clinical trial that are incorporated into the next trial, and some of those lessons involve the treatment procedures themselves. This very understandable process does pose certain problems for outcome evaluation, particularly for efforts to replicate treatment effects. In the case of Stark's program, the 1990 version is twice as long as the 1987 version, and the more recent version combines elements of two separate 1987 treatments and adds home visits and family treatment sessions. Thus, the 1990–91 treatment outcome study by Stark et al. could not technically be described as a replication of the Stark et al. 1987 findings. This means that we lack two separate studies testing the effects of the same treatment program. Of course, the outcome findings with three other CBT programs for child depression also reviewed in this chapter do add support for the generic CBT approach.

Further trials with the Stark program could also address certain limitations of the first two trials. In Stark et al. (1987), the small sample made it difficult to identify significant treatment effects. It is true that the two active treatments in that trial were associated with significant symptom reduction, whereas the waitlist condition was not. However, at posttreatment, only the self-control treatment (i.e., not the behavioral problem-solving treatment) was significantly superior to the waitlist condition, and it was superior on only the self-report depression questionnaire, not on other measures. The second outcome study by the Stark group, which focused on the expanded version of their treatment program, was reported only briefly and only in chapters in edited books (see Stark, 1990, and Stark et al., 1991); thus, it may not have been subjected to the level of scrutiny applied in typical journal peer review. The brevity of the two chapter presentations fell short of the level of detail needed for the most precise understanding and fairest interpretation of findings. Beyond larger samples and more detailed reporting, future studies might also be strengthened by efforts to reduce attrition at follow-up assessments so as to generate fairer tests of treatment holding power, and by assessment of functional outcomes (e.g., school performance, peer and family functioning) in addition to the kinds of symptom and diagnosis measures emphasized thus far. Moderator tests would also be helpful. Potential users will need to know what age, gender, ethnicity, or other interaction effects may place limits on the effective range of the treatment program.

Another potentially useful direction for the future is dismantling research. The Stark program has evolved toward increased sessions and increased coverage of various information and skills with elements of the earlier self-control and problem-solving treatments combined, new means of emotion education introduced, and family outreach and home visits added. With expansion of the treatment there is increased need to ask whether all the current treatment components are critical to treatment success, or whether some may be expendable.

Efforts to identify necessary and sufficient ingredients of the treatment program may also be informed by studies testing for mediating effects of various change components. Does change in children's emotion understanding actually mediate depression reduction? What about change in children's problem-solving skills or social skills, or reductions in unrealistic negative cognitions? Each skill emphasized in the Stark program has considerable intuitive appeal. Eventually we will need empirical tests of mediation effects to determine which kinds of change are actually needed for depression relief to occur.

Stark's Cognitive-Behavioral Therapy for Child Depression: Clinical Practice Issues

Clinicians and clinic administrators who consider adopting Stark's treatment program will find a substantial number of pros but a few cons as well. On the pro side, the program is designed to be child-friendly, and a number of the elements seem well suited to the group format in which the treatment is most often delivered. Procedures such as emotion charades, emotion statues, and the coping counters diary are cleverly designed to keep children active and engaged, conveying information through game-like interactions and interesting individual assignments. Another pro is the well-organized and detailed therapist manual, complemented by a visually attractive child practice book, materials that provide ample guidance to the motivated therapist and the motivated child.

One potential challenge of the program is that several features appear to require tailoring to fit the style, circumstances, and situation of the individual child, yet the treatment is primarily delivered in a group format, which can work against individualizing. Perhaps some of the personal tailoring can take place within the family contact that can be included in the program at the therapist's discretion. However, more guidance might be provided to the clinician regarding how to carry out individualizing in the child group sessions without sacrificing the interest and investment of the treatment group as a whole.

One potential limitation, from a clinician's perspective, is that the evidence base supporting the Stark program comes from samples screened from school classrooms, not from children who had been referred for clinical care. Although all the children showed elevated depressive symptoms, not all met formal diagnostic criteria for a depressive disorder. In addition, all three studies of other CBT programs for child depression that were reviewed in this chapter focused on children identified through school screening, not through clinic referral. For clinicians who focus on intervention in school settings, this may not be a concern; but for clinicians who treat children in mental health clinics or private practice offices, the most relevant form of empirical support might be that drawn from samples of clinically referred youngsters.

Other clinical practice issues concern treatment duration and family involvement. The most recent version of the Stark treatment program involves more than two dozen child sessions plus monthly family meetings. Stark notes difficulty in obtaining satisfactory parent involvement, and even if parents do participate actively, the combined number of treatment sessions may exceed what is possible in some clinical settings. Certainly the Stark program's movement toward increased sessions and outreach to families bucks current practice trends, which favor cost-cutting and session limits, even though the Stark approach may have real clinical advantages.

Although the written reports do not detail the level of training and supervision required for therapists to become proficient in the treatment program, Stark et al. (1996) note that effective use of the program "takes a thorough understanding of the treatment program and of the theory that underlies it . . ." (p. 237). Such understanding would likely require considerable pretreatment training and considerable supervision during treatment, at least at the beginning of a therapist's work with the program, and the challenge of finding funds and hours for both would need to be met by the clinical agency or provider seeking to incorporate the Stark approach into routine practice.

How to Find Out More about Cognitive-Behavioral Therapy for Depressed Children

For some of the treatments described in this chapter, the best description available is that found in the published articles cited herein. More detailed accounts are available from some authors, as specified in footnotes to the articles. Details and treatment procedures used in the Kahn et al. (1990) study can be obtained by contacting the first author, James S. Kahn, University of Utah Neuropsychological Institute, 501 Chipeta Way, Salt Lake City, UT 84108. Weisz and colleagues (2003) have presented an extended description of the PASCET youth depression treatment program in the book, *Evidence-Based Psychotherapies for Children and Adolescents*, edited by A. E. Kazdin and J. R. Weisz (New York: Guilford). Stark and colleagues (1996) have offered an extended description of their treatment procedures in the book *Psychosocial Treatments for Child and Adolescent Disorders: Empirically Based Strategies for Clinical Practice*, edited by E. D. Hibbs and P. S. Jensen (Washington, DC: American Psychological Asssociation). Stark and colleagues have prepared a therapist manual and child workbook for their cognitive-behavioral program, which is now called *Action*. The manual and workbook can be obtained from Workbooks Publishing, 208 Llanfair Road, Ardmore, PA 19003.

5

Cognitive-Behavioral Therapies
for Adolescent Depression

Although depression can be a very serious problem before puberty, the prevalence of depressive symptoms and disorders increases sharply in adolescence (Angold et al., 1999; Avenevoli & Steinberg, 2001; Birmaher et al., 1996; Holmbeck & Updegrove, 1995). Adolescence is also marked by the appearance of gender differences in prevalence, with rates among girls doubling those among boys (Avenevoli & Steinberg, 2001). During adolescence, the behavioral expression of depression also changes, with increased hypersomnia, anhedonia, hopelessness, weight loss, substance use, and suicide attempts (Avenevoli & Steinberg, 2001; Garber et al., 2002). Indeed, between 6% and 13% of adolescents across surveys report that they have attempted suicide at least once, and suicide is the third most common cause of death among American 15–19-year-olds (Garland & Zigler, 1993). Given the serious risks, the challenge of treating depression takes on a special urgency in adolescence.

Despite the risks and the urgency, treating teen depression has not had particularly high priority in the treatment literature. In a recent review of published outcome research with adolescents (Weisz & Hawley, 2002), only 9% of the studies identified had investigated treatments for depression. Represented in those studies were several different theoretical approaches to treatment, including family systems (Brent et al., 1997) and interpersonal psychotherapy (Mufson et al., 1999). However, the most fully tested approach with depressed teens has been CBT. Other treatment approaches are gaining support; interpersonal therapy, for example (Mufson & Dorta, 2003), may well appear on future lists of evidence-based treatments. However, given the frequency with which CBT has been supported in the literature thus far, it is an especially appropriate focus for this chapter.

Most of the descriptive part of the chapter is devoted to the specific CBT program developed and tested by Lewinsohn and colleagues (1990), given its replicated research support. However, we will also briefly review other

130 Psychotherapy for Children and Adolescents

CBT programs for teen depression to clarify the range of approaches used within the CBT rubric, and we will note the evidence on those programs. As in other chapters of this book, we will illustrate the treatment approach with a case application, and then discuss scientific and clinical practice issues.

The Coping with Depression Course for Adolescents: Conceptual Basis and Procedural Overview

The adolescent CBT program first tested by Lewinsohn et al. (1990) had its origins in a treatment program for adults, the Coping with Depression (CWD) course (Lewinsohn et al., 1984). Clarke and colleagues (1990a,b) modified the CWD to fit adolescents, thus creating the CWD-A. In keeping with the treatment's cognitive-behavioral pedigree, its creators conceive of depression primarily as a matter of skill deficits, be they cognitive (e.g., pessimistic or irrational thought patterns), behavioral (e.g., poor social skills, insufficient engagement in pleasurable activities), or affective (e.g., unawareness of one's mood). In addressing these deficits, Clarke et al. draw on a number of related cognitive and behavioral treatment methods. These methods all share a key assumption: "the depressed patient has *acquired* maladaptive reaction patterns that can be *unlearned*" (Clarke et al., 1990a, p. 43). Accordingly, the symptoms of depression (e.g., dysphoric mood, fatigue, suicidal thoughts) are viewed as themselves the proper targets for amelioration, as opposed to underlying conflicts, or general personality dysfunction. The treatment addresses the symptoms of depression through the teaching of appropriate coping skills.

Like its adult counterpart, the CWD-A (Clarke et al., 1990a) stresses affective education and skills training in a group environment. However, several steps have been taken to make the program user-friendly to teens. Homework is kept to five or ten minutes and (in contrast to the adult course) involves no reading assignments; instead, it stresses generalizing the skills learned in the course by practicing them in outside situations. Humorous cartoons (e.g., Garfield, Bloom County, Cathy) are used to illustrate various maladaptive behaviors. In general, the course is designed to have a "classroom" rather than a "clinical" feel, reflecting the authors' goal of providing a nonstigmatizing, psychoeducational experience.

Each teen participant is given a *Student Workbook* (Clarke et al., 1990b), which contains the material to be covered, organized session by session. A *Leader's Manual* (Clarke et al., 1990a) guides the work of the therapists. Teaching methods include lectures, discussions, role-plays, and homework assignments. Major subjects covered are improving social skills, decreasing anxiety, changing unpleasant cognitions, resolving conflicts, and planning for the future. A protocol for booster sessions has also been developed. While designed for use with groups of four to ten adolescents, CWD-A can be used in individual therapy. However, the authors stress that the emphasis on role-play and group discussion makes the group format more appropriate.

A parallel component for parents assumes the parents' centrality both to adolescent development in general and to the experience of adolescent depression in particular. The parent component has two aims: (1) to familiarize parents with what their children are learning so they can buttress the adolescents' new skills; and (2) to teach the parents themselves the same skills.

The Coping with Depression Course for Adolescents: In Brief

Designed for . . . . Depression (or elevated depressive symptoms) in adolescents ages 14–18
Number of sessions . . . . 16 with adolescents, optional 7 with parents
Session length . . . . Two hours (for adolescents and for parents)
Session participants . . . . Therapist with groups of teens, therapist with parent groups
Theoretical orientation . . . . Cognitive-behavioral

Treatment elements:

1. Learn how emotions are related to thoughts and actions; practice monitoring own mood.
2. Learn social skills, such as how to start a conversation, listen actively, and show understanding.
3. Identify pleasant activities and arrange schedule to increase their frequency.
4. Develop and carry out a personal plan for change including setting goals and working toward them.
5. Identify negative thoughts and their cause; learn to use realistic, positive counterthoughts.
6. Learn to deal with stress by using two relaxation methods (deep muscle, quiet breathing).
7. Learn ways to interrupt negative thoughts (thought-stopping, rubber band, worry time).
8. Learn problem-solving and negotiation skills for dealing with interpersonal conflict.

9. Discuss how to maintain gains by overcoming fears and obstacles; advance planning for coping with future stressors.

Treatment classified by Task Force as ... Probably Efficacious (Kaslow & Thompson, 1998). Key resources for potential users . . . . . Clarke, G., Lewinsohn, P., & Hops, H. (1990). *Leader's Manual for Adolescent Groups: Adolescent Coping with Depression Course.* Eugene, OR: Castalia Publishing Company. Clarke, G., Lewinsohn, P., & Hops, H. (1990). *Student Workbook: Adolescent Coping with Depression Course.* Eugene, OR: Castalia Publishing Company.

The Coping with Depression Course for Adolescents: Treatment Procedures

The CWD-A program is called a course and presented in the manner of a very interactive seminar. The participants are called students, and the therapist is called a group leader. The sequence of topics is arranged so that subjects covered in the early sessions (e.g., social skills, mood monitoring, pleasant activities) are tied together as a coherent basis for more challenging material later in the course (e.g., constructive thinking, negotiation and problem solving, and maintaining gains). To keep early lessons fresh in the students' minds, key points are reviewed repeatedly and incorporated into new material. Here we survey primary themes addressed in the protocol.

Increasing Social Skills. On the premise that deficient social skills are common in teen depression, the authors have built training in basic social skills into the first eight sessions. "Friendly skills," conversation techniques, and ways to read cues and meet new people are interwoven with other material in the first three sessions. For example, if someone makes eye contact, it may be appropriate to respond with a friendly comment; but if the person looks angry, it may not. The leader demonstrates, then the teens role-play, various appropriate and inappropriate ways of beginning and conducting conversations. Later sessions include lessons on maintaining social relationships by planning shared activities and eliminating such problematic behavior as complaining, being critical, and so forth. These basic lessons built a foundation for more advanced material covered later in the course such as communication and social problem solving.

Mood Monitoring. As with poor social skills, the inability to observe and control one's own affective state is a frequent correlate of adolescent depression. So, from the very first session, students are introduced to several practices designed to help them monitor and control their moods. They fill out a mood questionnaire, practice identifying positive and negative (depressogenic) thoughts, and learn that their actions and thoughts can change how they feel by creating "upward spirals" or "downward spirals" of interlocking cognitions, behaviors, and moods. The leader reads examples of such spirals featuring an adolescent who first creates a downward spiral after doing poorly in school and then reverses it by resuming a social activity (jamming with some musician friends) that he had abandoned. Finally, the students learn how to fill out the mood diary that they will keep throughout the course. Like the other material the students will need, forms for the mood diary are in the *Workbook*.

Scheduling Pleasant Activities. Evidence suggests that failure to engage in enjoyable activities is a precursor of depression (Lewinsohn et al., 1976) and that doing enjoyable things can help elevate mood (Lewinsohn et al., 1996). Building on this notion, students are taught to focus on pleasant activities using a Pleasant Events Schedule (PES), a comprehensive list of 320 usually enjoyable activities. Examples include *meeting someone new; going to a sports event; going to a very fun party; watching television; making snacks.* Participants rate each activity in two ways: how often they do it and how much they enjoy it. Students learn to use the PES for baselining, which means using a frequency count to heighten awareness of their specific behaviors and set goals for change.

To support this process, students are presented with an illustrative chart taken from an imaginary student's mood diary. The chart, shown in Figure 5.1, illustrates how daily totals of pleasant activities are linked, roughly, to daily mood ratings; students are prompted to conclude that the two are causally related. Homework includes filling out a record of pleasant activities and a personal mood diary. Students learn to set goals for increasing pleasant activities, and they complete graphs correlating their own activity counts with the record of their moods. They are reminded that change may be slow and that their goals for change should be realistic and reflect small, incremental increases, not large jumps. Increasing pleasant events is thus offered as one early step toward learning to control behavior and mood.

Relaxation Training. The CWD-A course also incorporates relaxation techniques aimed at decreasing tension and anxiety. In the *Jacobsen* procedure, taught in the third session, major muscle groups are alternately tensed and relaxed. In the *Benson* method, taught later, the person rests calmly while focusing on breathing. A special advantage of the Benson method is that it is a less conspicuous and therefore more portable way of reducing tension. For tense situations that come up without warning

EXAMPLE. Mary collected data on her pleasant activities and mood for two weeks. She found that her mood and the number of pleasant activities she did were closely related.

A. One day when Mary did seven pleasant activities, her mood level was at 7, which was its highest point during the two-week period.
B. On another day, Mary did one pleasant activity and her mood rating was 2. Her mood level was below 4 only three days out of the two-week period.
C. On those days when Mary's mood rating fell below 4, she did three or fewer pleasant activities.
D. Her average daily number of pleasant activities was five.

Mary's Goals

What would be a good minimum *mood* goal? _____

What would be a good goal for *average* daily number of pleasant activities? _____

What would be a good goal for *minimum* level of pleasant activities? _____

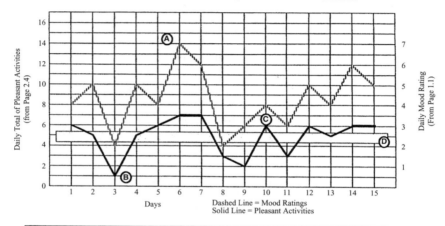

Now look at your own data. What would be some good goals for you?

My goal for minimum level of pleasant activities is _____.

My goal for average daily number of pleasant activities is _____.

FIGURE 5.1. Chart for Mary, showing the association between number of pleasant activities she engaged in and her mood ratings over a two-week period. [From Clarke, G., Lewinsohn, P., & Hops, H. (1990). *Student workbook: Adolescent coping with depression course.* Eugene, OR: Castalia Publishing Company. Reprinted with permission of Gregory Clarke.]

and catch the students off guard, they are taught "the quick Benson." This method, shown in the box that follows, requires only that the students have a personal relaxation word (such as "calm," "easy," or "cool") and that they have a ready-to-use image of a favorite calming place or situation (such as lying on a warm beach).

The Quick Benson

To Calm Down Quickly When You Are Caught Off Guard by a Tense Situation . . . .

1. Check the tension level in the area where you hold tension (for example, your neck or back). Try to relax those muscles.
2. Take a deep breath and let it out slowly, while repeating your relaxation word to yourself.
3. Picture yourself relaxing in your favorite calming place.

Constructive Thinking. By session five, most of the course's basic skills have been introduced, and the students move on to more sophisticated techniques that build on and reinforce what they have learned so far. The first of these, constructive thinking, is taught in sessions five through ten. These *cognitive* sessions draw on the notion that negative or irrational cognitions can both cause and perpetuate depression; the program uses adaptations of techniques proposed by Beck et al. (1979), Ellis and Harper (1961), and others for identifying and challenging such thoughts.

Negative thoughts. A first step is identifying negative thoughts, a task made easier by contrasting them with positive ones. The workbook thus lists examples of negative and positive thoughts – for example, *"There is no love in the world," "I'm ugly,"* or *"I am worthless"* as opposed to *"I feel really great," "I can find a solution to most problems that come up,"* or *"I often receive compliments for doing something well."* Students are asked to check each example that applies to them, then mark the thoughts they have frequently. They also scan the list to see which thoughts are mainly self-referent, or personal. The students also identify negative thoughts in humorous cartoons, and find the activating event that brings on each thought. Once familiar with the concepts of positive and negative thoughts, the students practice coming up with positive thoughts to replace the negative ones. Homework includes taking a baseline of negative thoughts, and signing a contract to change negative thoughts to positive ones with a self-selected reward stipulated for fulfilling the contract.

Later, students learn three techniques for interrupting negative thoughts. The first is the most direct: simply shouting "Stop" whenever they find themselves thinking negatively. In public, where this approach may not be appropriate, students change the shout to a forceful thought. A second technique involves wearing a rubber band around the wrist and snapping it when the negative thought occurs. A third entails scheduling a designated worry time to which all negative thoughts are assigned when they occur.

Irrational thoughts. An important step on the cognitive front is narrowing the focus from *all* negative thoughts to a specific emphasis on negative thoughts that are *unrealistic* or *irrational*. Students are encouraged to challenge such thoughts – to argue with them. For example, a student who thinks, "If I can't get a date on Friday night, I'm a total failure forever," might challenge the thought by asking, "Is this really true? Am I really a failure in *everything* if I can't get a date on one particular night? Is it possible that I might get a date at some time in the future? Even if I *never* got a date, would that make me a failure in *everything?*" Irrational thoughts of this sort are divided into *overreactions, exaggerations, unreasonable expectations,* and *jumping to conclusions*. Students also learn to identify and challenge complex groups of related responses that make up "whole thoughts" (Leader's Manual, p. 166). Such responses may include "disguised personal beliefs" in which a nonpersonal negative thought ("School sucks") actually hides a personal belief ("I got poor grades, so therefore I must be stupid."). The students also practice the C-A-B method, in which the *Consequence* (depression) leads to an examination of the *Activating event* (e.g., a bad grade) and then a reassessment of the *Belief* (e.g., a shift from "School sucks" or "I'm a loser" to "I let that test slide – better study harder next time."). If the belief can be changed to a positive one, then the consequences may be more positive as well.

Communication, Negotiation, and Problem Solving. Training in communication begins near the middle of the program as an extension of earlier lessons in friendly skills, conducting conversations, and saying positive things to others. The training stresses active listening and positive interaction, for example, through eye contact, responding by paraphrasing the other's message, and avoiding negative behaviors such as accusations, interruptions, and put-downs. In later sessions, these skills are applied to negotiation and conflict resolution as the students learn how to define the problem without criticizing the other party, generate alternative solutions to problems, identify mutually acceptable solutions, and decide how the agreement is to be carried out. These communication and negotiation techniques are rooted in skills found effective by other researchers (Forgatch & Patterson, 1989; Gottman et al., 1976; and Robin, 1981).

Communication. The first thing the students are taught about communication is that it is not merely a passive experience, but that it requires an active listener if it is to happen at all. Three rules for active listening are couched in terms of sending and receiving messages:

1. Restate the sender's message in your own words.
2. Begin your statement with phrases like "You feel...," "You think...," or "Let me see if I understand what you're saying."
3. Don't show approval or disapproval of the sender's message.

In-class exercises give several examples of conversational situations, and the students select the appropriate response from among several possibilities. The students also select common mistakes made by listeners from a list of possibilities (such as "thinking about your replies instead of paying attention to the sender" or "not giving the sender your undivided attention"). The concepts of nonverbal communication (body language, facial expressions) and communication breakdown (when the sender's message is misunderstood) are also introduced. Role-play and team activities reinforce these distinctions as the students model such communication errors as *partial listening, making irrelevant responses*, and *judgmental listening,* contrasting the results with those produced by appropriate active listening.

Students also learn to state their positive feelings to others (making helpful self-disclosures) and to state negative feelings in a constructive way. The authors connect these skills explicitly to earlier explanatory concepts, specifically the C-A-B structure discussed earlier. Students also learn that stating their feelings effectively can have at least two positive effects: (1) it can get others to change their behavior, and (2) it can help you cope with your own feelings by increasing your awareness of them. Thus, students are encouraged to put their statements in personal form, stressing their own feelings rather than criticizing others. Saying "It was rude of you to go to the movies without inviting me" may generate an angry or defensive response; saying "I feel bad that you went to the movies and didn't invite me" may be more effective (*Workbook*, p. 10.3). Students also take part in role-plays to explore communication problems in situations they themselves devise.

Negotiation and problem solving. Students also bring their communication skills to bear on resolving direct, issue-laden conflicts with others. As a first step, students are urged to use assertive imagery, in which they visualize both their own disclosure and the other person's likely reaction to it. Again, students use role-play to practice assertive imagery with each other.

Next, the scene for conflict is shifted to the family environment, and students learn strategies for dealing constructively with conflict between them and their parents. After listing some potential problems that might come up between friends (e.g., over what to do and where to go, or things that have been borrowed), the leader contrasts such situations with those that come up at home. Issues at home might include: what constitutes appropriate or inappropriate behavior or clothing; where you can go and what you can do with friends; what time you have to be home; your chores; and who your friends are, and how much time you get to spend with them. As with the potential conflicts between them and their friends, students are encouraged to come up with other issues that may cause problems with their parents. The leader then presents some basic rules for settling disagreements: first, the person with the complaint has a right to be heard; and second, in giving that person a hearing you are not implying agreement or disagreement, but simply trying to understand the complaint. Students are then prompted to suggest which earlier skills (e.g., self-disclosure statements, active listening) might be applied to such conflicts.

A critical skill emphasized in the program is defining problems in conflicts with others. The leader presents the "Eight Rules for Defining a Problem"):

(1) Begin with something positive.
(2) Be specific.
(3) Describe what the other person is doing or saying.
(4) Don't do name-calling.
(5) Express your feelings.
(6) Admit your contribution to the problem.
(7) Don't accuse.
(8) Be brief.

Students practice applying these rules in role-play in which they take the parts of both teens and parents.

Later sessions focus on using the students' newly acquired problem-solving skills to reach negotiated solutions to particularly tough interpersonal conflicts. Students first learn to generate a variety of solutions by following the four rules of brainstorming: (1) list as many solutions as you can; (2) don't criticize, all ideas are allowed; (3) be creative; and (4) begin by offering to change one of your own behaviors. Then they use a problem-solving worksheet to practice narrowing the list of solutions down to a single mutually acceptable choice. Suppose, for example, that Mom is bothered by her teenager's messy bedroom, which embarrasses her when friends visit. Proposed solutions from both sides include: hire a maid (the teen's solution); withhold allowance until the room is cleaned up (Mom); close the bedroom door when company comes (teen); pay $5 for cleaning the room by a certain time (Mom). After discussing each solution, Mother and teen settle on the last one, the cash payment plan. Using examples like this, students are shown how to identify a mutually acceptable solution, and then write a contract spelling out how the solution will be implemented. Typically, the contract specifies what each party will do, when they will do it, and consequences for noncompliance. By the end of the training, ideally, students can combine all the steps they have learned for problem solving and negotiation:

(1) Define the problem.
(2) Brainstorm solutions.
(3) Evaluate the solutions.
(4) Pick a mutually agreeable solution (often a compromise).
(5) Write a contract.

For these skills, as for others, role-play and group discussion reinforce the lessons by giving students a chance to act them out. Students are also guided in how to teach these skills to their parents.

Maintenance of Gains. The final sessions in the program focus on con-solidating skills already learned so they can be used confidently in the real world after graduation from the program. Students discuss their ex-perience in using the negotiation techniques with their parents. Students also develop a life plan, a set of long-term goals in regard to *friends, school, job plans, recreation, home and family, romantic relationships, and spir-itual and religious matters.* Students pair up to discuss and review each other's life plans, and the leader talks with them about how to pursue such plans by breaking long-term goals into manageable steps. Included in the life plan are ideas about how to cope if feelings of depression return in the future.

Parent Participation. A parallel course has been developed for the parents of depressed adolescents (Lewinsohn et al., 1991). In it, parents are apprised of the basic skills their teens are learning, and are actually taught the more advanced skills (i.e., communication and problem solving). Parents receive a workbook and meet with the therapist weekly in two-hour sessions over seven to nine weeks of the adolescent course; two joint sessions can be included as well, with the parents and adolescents meeting together to practice their communication skills.

   The parent program is optional. It is based on the notion that parent-adolescent relationships may be central not just to the development of the adolescent's identity but to onset, perpetuation of, and recovery from depression. In principle, parent participation can support the adolescent's learning and provide a model for healthy family dynamics in the future. However, as we shall see later, the evidence to date shows that adding the parent component to the basic CWD-A program has only a very modest effect.

Booster Sessions. Another supplement to the CWD-A program is a series of booster sessions, designed to address the risk of relapse in treated teens. The booster program is based on the literature on both depression (e.g., Wilson, 1992) and relapse in addictive disorders (e.g., Marlatt & Gordon, 1985). That literature suggests "that three factors affect the maintenance of treatment gains: (a) the continued self-monitoring of behaviors and of situations that may affect this maintenance; (b) relatively pervasive and persistent lifestyle changes designed to cope with future stressful events; and (c) level of social support" (Lewinsohn et al., 1994, p. 120).

   Because individual needs vary, booster sessions are more loosely struc-tured than the course itself. Boosters are offered at four-month intervals over a two-year period, with each booster comprising up to two weekly two-hour sessions. Before the first session, participants complete a ques-tionnaire on their current affective state and their psychosocial functioning before the session; questions also assess how much of the original course the participants remember. Although specific booster content varies across participants, most sessions include review of current problem areas and a focus on how to apply coping skills from the program to those problem areas. As in the main CWD-A program, homework assignments are used to provide real-world practice in applying the coping skills. In the following section, we consider evidence on the effects of these booster sessions.

Outcome Studies Testing the Effects of the Coping with Depression Course and Other Cognitive-Behavioral Therapies for Adolescent Depression

The authors of the CWD-A program have published two trials of their program. In addition, other research teams have tested CBT programs that resemble the CWD-A in their main themes. Here we review multiple studies to convey the state of the evidence on CBT for depressed adolescents.

Initial test of the CWD-A with and without a parent component. In the first published test of the CWD-A, Lewinsohn et al. (1990) compared the effects of two versions, one treating adolescents only, the other involving both adolescents and their parents. Participants were recruited via letters and announcements to health professionals, school counselors, and the media, then screened by phone. Subsequent intake interviews involved 10 depression-related measures, including a structured diagnostic interview. The resulting sample included 69 high school students (grades 9–12), ages 14–18. The 59 who actually completed the study included 36 girls and 23 boys, averaging 16 years of age (ethnicity not reported). All participants met diagnostic criteria for either major depressive disorder (49%), minor depression (7%), or intermittent depression (44%), and 40% had attempted suicide previously.

Participants were assigned randomly to either adolescent-only treatment, adolescent-and-parent treatment, or a waitlist control condition. Therapists for the two treatment conditions were graduate students in social work and in clinical, counseling, and educational psychology. All were trained in an eight-week seminar and given ongoing supervision throughout the treatment phase. The adolescent-only treatment closely resembled the adolescent CWD-A course described earlier in this chapter. The adolescent-and-parent treatment added seven separate two-hour parent sessions covering the skills and techniques that were being taught to the adolescents, with the goal of promoting parental acceptance and reinforcement of the expected changes in their children. Parents were also taught coping skills to address family problems without arguments or fights. Assessments were carried out at pretreatment and posttreatment for all groups; follow-up assessments were done at 1, 6, 12, and 24 months posttreatment for the two active treatment groups. These included the structured diagnostic interview used at the outset, as well as multiple youth-report and parent-report measures of depression and other emotional and behavioral problems.

The findings were encouraging, at least with regard to active treatment versus placement on a waitlist. Compared to the waitlist group, both treatment groups were less depressed on most key measures at posttreatment. Diagnostic interviews with the teens and their parents showed that, after treatment, only 57% of the adolescent-only group and 52% of the adolescent-and-parent group still met criteria for a depression diagnosis, whereas 95% of the waitlist group were still depressed. Youth self-report measures also showed significantly less depression in the two treated groups than in the waitlist group; but parent-report measures did not show significant treatment effects. In general, treatment group gains appeared to hold over the successive follow-up assessments, but the waitlist group began treatment after the initial posttreatment assessment, and thus could not be included in follow-up comparisons. There were trends toward more improvement in the adolescent-and-parent group than in the adolescent-only group, at posttreatment and followup, but only one such trend was statistically significant. So, the value of an added parent component was suggested by the trends but not clearly established.

Second test of CWD-A: adolescent-only and adolescent-and-parent versions, with and without booster sessions. In the second published test of the CWD-A, Clarke et al. (1999) replicated the design of their first study, but added a second phase testing whether booster sessions actually boosted treatment impact. Participants were recruited via letters and announcements to health professionals, school counselors, and the media, plus newspaper and radio advertisements. Subsequent phone screening was followed by intake interviews involving multiple depression measures, including a structured diagnostic interview. The resulting sample initially included 123 14–18-year-olds, but attrition reduced the sample to 96 treatment completers. These included 73 diagnosed with major depressive disorder, 12 with dysthymia, and 11 with both disorders. Mean age was 16, and 71% of the sample were girls (sample ethnicity not reported). The 16 therapists for the treatment groups included advanced graduate students in psychology and social work, and masters- and doctoral-level clinicians; they were provided 40 hours of training in the study treatment methods, plus weekly supervision meetings.

Participants were assigned randomly to a waitlist condition or to adolescent-only or adolescent-and-parent conditions, with both active treatments closely resembling those used in the first CWD-A clinical trial (Lewinsohn et al., 1990). The additional twist used in this 1999 study involved variations in what happened after the replication of previous treatments was completed. Following that replication, called the acute treatment phase, those who had completed the adolescent-only and adolescent-and-parent treatments were again randomly assigned to one of three conditions over a 24-month follow-up period: assessments plus booster sessions every four months, assessments every four months without booster sessions, and assessments every 12 months without booster sessions. As described earlier, the booster sessions focused on how specific skills learned in the CWD-A course could be used to cope with specific problems the youngsters had faced since the end of the acute phase.

Outcome assessment include a structured diagnostic interview with parents and with youth as well as youth self-report and parent-report measures of depression and other problems. At the end of the acute phase, diagnostic interviews showed recovery from depressive disorder by 67% of the treated teens (averaging across the adolescent-only and adolescent-plus-parent conditions) versus only 48% of untreated teens. Among youths in the treatment conditions, those who had attended more sessions showed higher rates of recovery than those who had attended fewer sessions. However, two null findings closely resembled those of the first clinical trial (Lewinsohn et al., 1990): (1) adding a parent treatment component did not lead to significantly better outcomes than treating adolescents only; and (2) measures based solely on parent report did not produce significant treatment effects.

Analyses after the follow-up phase focused mainly on the impact of booster sessions. The sessions did not reduce relapse rates among those who had recovered from depression during the standard course (i.e., the acute phase). However, there was some evidence that boosters helped youngsters who had remained depressed after acute treatment, at least over the first year posttreatment. By the end of that first year, among those who had continued to meet criteria for a depressive disorder at the end of the acute phase, 100% (i.e., 5 out of 5) of the booster session adolescents had recovered, versus only half (i.e., 6 out of 12) of the assessment-only adolescents. However, at two years' posttreatment, the groups had converged, with 100% of booster session youth recovered, and 90% of assessment-only youth recovered. An interesting finding showed that mean time to recovery was 23.5 weeks for the booster session group and 67.1 weeks for the assessment-only group. In other words, booster sessions seemed to hasten recovery in youngsters who had not recovered during the standard course of acute treatment.

Other CBT programs for adolescents: I. CBT versus relaxation. Four years before the first published test of the CWD-A program, Reynolds and Coats (1986) published an intriguing comparison of CBT and a much simpler intervention: relaxation training alone. At the outset, the investigators anticipated that adolescents who received relaxation training would show greater relief from depressive symptomatology than would a waitlist control group, but they also expected that CBT would outperform relaxation training. The investigators were in for a surprise.

The Reynolds and Coats CBT program resembled the later CWD-A (Clarke & Lewinsohn, 1991). Like the CWD-A, it drew heavily from an early version of Lewinsohn's Coping with Depression course for adults; it also included self-control elements (derived from Rehm's [1977] self-control depression model), similar to self-control components in the Stark et al. (1987) CBT program, described in Chapter 4 of this book. Sessions emphasized understanding the relation between activities and mood, noting and altering faulty beliefs, developing a self-change plan (including setting goals, contracting, and identifying rewards for goal striving), and achieving self-control over thoughts, activities, and consequences by using self-monitoring and self-evaluation.

The relaxation program began with discussion of how stress, muscle tension, and depression are related, and how learning to relax can help. Next, participants learned and practiced progressive muscle relaxation by tensing and relaxing of various major muscle groups; the procedures were similar to those later used in the CWD-A. As the skills were developed, participants were helped to apply them to known tension producers in their own lives.

The authors used self-report measures and a depression symptom interview to identify a sample of 30 ninth through twelfth graders who showed significant depressive symptomatology (depressive disorder diagnoses were not required). There were 11 boys and 19 girls, with a mean age of 16, and all were Caucasian. Participants were randomized to a waitlist control group or to one of two active treatments, CBT or relaxation training. Each treatment involved ten 50-minute group sessions spread over five weeks. The therapist for all sessions of both treatments was the study's second author, a behaviorally oriented doctoral-level school psychology graduate student who had previously worked as a school psychologist for four years (specific training for this study was not reported).

Outcomes were assessed immediately after treatment and again five weeks later. Both assessments suggested that, despite striking differences in the content of the two treatments, the two were about equally helpful. On all three of the study's depression measures, posttreatment scores were lower for the two treatment groups than the waitlist group, but differences between the treatment groups were not significant. Results were similar at the five-week followup. Youngsters in the two treatment groups showed much more dramatic rates of movement into the normal range than the waitlisted youth showed. For example, on one widely used self-report depression measure, 83% of the CBT group and 75% of the relaxation group scored in the normal range at posttreatment, whereas no subjects in the waitlist group did so. These analyses, like the mean comparisons noted earlier, showed similar outcomes for the two active treatment conditions.

Reynolds and Coats (1986) offer two possible explanations for the fact that CBT was not reliably more effective than relaxation training. First, both treatments may have enhanced coping skills and increased subjects' sense of personal mastery. Second, relaxation training may have had biological effects, directly influencing brain catecholamines and the action of biogenic amines on depression. Whatever the explanation, it is true that other studies of depression treatment described in this chapter and in the previous chapter have also failed to find striking outcome differences between various active treatments, even in cases where the different treatments significantly outperform control conditions.

Other CBT programs for adolescents: II. Further comparison of CBT and relaxation training. The plot thickens with another study comparing CBT and relaxation training carried out by Wood et al. (1996) with 9- to 17-year-olds in the United Kingdom. The Wood et al. study differs from its predecessors (Kahn et al., 1990 – see Chapter 4; Reynolds & Coats, 1986) in some potentially important respects. First, the participants in Wood et al., unlike those in the prior studies, were all outpatients who had been referred to a clinic specializing in treatment of depression, and all met diagnostic criteria for either DSM-IIIR major depression or minor depression. Second, treatment was administered individually, not to groups as in Reynolds and Coats (1986; and Kahn et al., 1990, for two treatment conditions – see Chapter 4). Third, Wood et al. construed their relaxation training program as a control condition, not as an active treatment. The authors recognized that relaxation training had been found helpful with nonclinical levels of adolescent depression (in Reynolds & Coats, 1986), but they did not think it would be very effective with clinically diagnosed cases, in part because relaxation training ". . . mainly targets symptoms that are not part of the DSM criteria for MDD . . ." (Wood et al., 1996, p. 738).

The Wood et al. CBT program combined elements used in the other CBT treatments described in this chapter and the previous one. Across five to eight sessions, therapists and their clients covered identification and modification of depressogenic cognitions, skills in social problem solving (including goal setting, generating alternatives for action, trying the alternatives, and measuring the results), and symptom focus (addressing symptoms such as poor sleep hygiene and poor activity scheduling). The relaxation training procedures are not described in detail, but the authors do note that the procedures were spread across five to eight sessions, like the CBT program, and that they involved progressive relaxation training steps.

A sample of 53 youngsters entered the study; 48 completed treatment. The 48 included 33 girls and 15 boys, averaging 14 years of age (ethnicity not reported); 44 met criteria for major depressive disorder. Participants were randomly assigned to the two treatment conditions. Treatments were delivered by two therapists, both reported to have "a minimum of three years experience in child psychiatry" (Wood et al., 1996, p. 738), but not identified in the report as to professional discipline or level of professional training/credentials. The therapists met weekly throughout the trial for supervision; the report does not specify who supervised the therapists or whether each therapist participated in both treatments.

Outcomes were assessed via the same structured diagnostic interview used to select the sample, plus multiple self-report and parent-report questionnaire measures, assessing depression and related constructs (e.g., self-image), as well as conduct problems and global functioning. Posttreatment assessments did show a significant advantage for CBT over relaxation on measures of depressed mood, self-image, and global functioning, and rates of remission from a depression diagnosis were higher in the CBT group. However, differences between the CBT and relaxation groups diminished somewhat by the three-month followup, and ". . . by six months, the groups were very similar" (Wood et al., 1996, p. 743). So, the study is a third instance in which the effects of relaxation training alone rivaled those of a fuller CBT program. CBT did seem to produce faster improvement, but the effects of relaxation training eventually caught up.

Other CBT programs for adolescents: III. CBT versus non-focused intervention for teens and children. In another study from the United Kingdom, Vostanis et al. (1996a,b) compared CBT to a non-focused intervention intended to control for time spent with the therapist. A standardized interview was used to find clinic-referred youths who met DSM-IIIR criteria for a depressive disorder. Some 57 who satisfied this and other study criteria, and who completed at least two treatment sessions, formed the sample. Ages ranged from 8–17 years (mean age 13), and 32 were girls; 50 were Caucasian, 5 Asian, and 2 Afro-Carribean. Some 30% met criteria for major depression, 54% minor depression, and 16% dysthymia. Within each of the four participating clinic sites, "subjects were allocated alternatively to CBT or control treatment" (Vostanis et al., 1996b, p. 106).

Both CBT and the nonstructured control treatment were designed to include nine individual sessions, one every two weeks. The CBT program included three main themes: recognizing and labeling emotions, enhancing social skills including problem solving, and restructuring negative thoughts. The nonstructured intervention was described in one part of Vostanis et al. (1996a) as a "review of mental state and of social activities . . ." (p. 203), in another part as "brief 'supportive' therapy" (p. 205), and in Vostanis et al. (1996b) as a procedure in which therapists "showed an interest in the child's problems and showed encouragement through verbal ('you are doing very well' or 'keep up the good work') or nonverbal means (e.g., nodding or smiling)" (p. 109).

Both treatments were delivered by the same three therapists, child and adolescent psychiatrists, two of whom "had piloted the research manual for one year before the trial" (Vostanis et al., 1996b, p. 109). Across the sample of 57 youngsters, 3 were seen by one therapist, 14 by the second, and 40 by the third. Outcomes were assessed via a structured diagnostic interview, a structured social adjustment interview, and youth self-report and parent-report questionnaires. CBT did produce a slightly higher rate of recovery from depression than did the nonfocused intervention (87% vs. 75%), but there was no significant treatment effect on any of the outcome measures, at immediate posttreatment or at the nine-month followup. The null findings are difficult to interpret with confidence. The high success rate of the nonfocused intervention suggests that it may have created a supportive relationship of therapist with youth that had genuine therapeutic benefits. It is also possible that the CBT intervention was not an adequate dose. It was designed to involve nine sessions over a maximum of six months, a rather small dose at best; but the mean number of CBT sessions actually completed by participants was only six (range: 2–9), over an average of only three months. Many consider cognitive restructuring to be the heart of CBT for depression. However, cognitive restructuring came last in the treatment manual, and it was omitted entirely for half the CBT sample (Feehan & Vostanis, 1996). So, the CBT actually delivered in this study appears weaker than that employed in other studies of CBT for youth depression, and the control condition may have been more therapeutic than the authors intended. In addition, the fact that 70% of the sample, across conditions, were seen by the same therapist raises the possibility that results may have been influenced disproportionately by that one individual's characteristics and style. However, taken at face value, the findings of Vostanis and colleagues do not support the efficacy of CBT.

Other CBT programs for adolescents: IV. CBT versus family therapy and nondirective supportive therapy for depressed adolescents. The final chapter in our brief saga of CBT versus alternatives is a study by Brent et al. (1997) in which a CBT approach was compared to *family therapy* and *nondirective supportive therapy*. Diagnostically, the study was the most stringent depression trial to date, requiring that all participants meet DSM-IIIR criteria for *major depressive disorder*, based on structured diagnostic interviews. Participants were assigned to one of three treatments, each designed to consist of 12–16 weekly sessions (this was called acute treatment), followed by two to four weekly booster sessions.

The individually administered *CBT program* emphasized monitoring and modification of automatic thoughts, assumptions, and beliefs, and it included training in problem solving, emotion identification and regulation, and social skills. In addition, the treatment addressed issues of autonomy and trust, and examined mood shifts that occurred during sessions. The *family therapy* intervention involved two phases. In the first, the therapist clarified the concerns that brought the family into treatment and helped family members identify dysfunctional behavior patterns. In the second phase, family members focused on communication and problem-solving skills and worked toward altering family interaction patterns. These approaches were linked to education about depression and parenting practices at home.

The *nondirective supportive* condition was mainly designed to control for such nonspecific aspects of treatment as passage of time, contact with a therapist, and empathic support. Therapists saw their clients individually and sought to build rapport, provide support, and help their clients identify and express feelings. The therapists used reflective listening and empathy and engaged in discussion of client-initiated ideas for addressing personal problems, but they were instructed to refrain from giving advice, teaching specific skills, or setting limits. These features, Brent et al. (1996) suggest, may make this form of treatment well suited to adolescents, who often value autonomy and control.

Participants were recruited from among normal referrals to a university-based clinic for mood and anxiety disorders (about two-thirds of the sample) and through advertisements (the other third). The 107 who met study criteria and entered the sample included 81 girls and 26 boys; ages ranged from 13–18, with a mean age of 16; and 83% were Caucasian (specific minority group ethnicities not reported). Each youth was assigned randomly to one of the three treatments, delivered by three teams of four therapists. The 12 therapists all had master's degrees, and the group averaged 10 years of clinical experience. All the therapists had six months of intensive training in their treatment program, and all were required to treat two cases, showing adherence to their treatment model before becoming a study therapist. Supervisors, master's-level therapists expert in the relevant treatment model, provided one hour of group and one hour of individual supervision per week for all protocol therapists. Thus, therapist training and supervision were especially ample in this study, and equally so across all three conditions.

Outcomes were assessed via a structured diagnostic interview, an interviewer-completed global assessment reflecting life functioning, and measures of depression-related constructs (e.g., cognitions) at the sixth session, at the end of treatment, and then at 3-, 6-, 9-, 12-, and 24-month followups. In addition, a self-report depression questionnaire was administered after each treatment session. Importantly, the investigators conducted *intent-to-treat* analyses of outcome, including all participants originally assigned to study conditions, regardless of whether they had completed their treatment protocol. (But when the authors re-did the analyses including only those youths who had completed their full treatment protocol, the findings changed very little.)

Outcomes after acute treatment. Diagnostic assessments immediately after acute treatment showed significantly lower rates of major depressive disorder in the CBT group than the supportive group, and youngsters in the CBT group showed more rapid treatment response on the self-report questionnaire and the diagnostic interview than those in either the family or the supportive condition. A key measure in this study was *remission*, defined as the absence of a major depressive disorder diagnosis and three consecutive low-level self-report depression scores, sustained through all remaining sessions. Pairwise comparisons showed significantly higher rates of remission in the CBT group (65%) than in either family therapy (38%) or supportive therapy (39%). Weighing all their evidence at the post-acute-treatment time point, the authors concluded that "CBT is more efficacious than structural behavioral family therapy or nondirective supportive therapy for adolescent major depressive disorder in clinical settings, resulting in more rapid and complete treatment response" (Brent et al., 1997, p. 877).

Brent and colleagues (Brent et al., 1998) also investigated predictors of treatment outcome in their study. They found a better treatment response in youngsters who had been recruited through advertisements than those who had been referred for treatment through normal clinical channels; and teens showing high initial levels of self-reported depression were the most likely to achieve remission. Poor treatment response was predicted by comorbid anxiety disorders, higher levels of cognitive distortion, and more hopelessness, prior to treatment. However, even in the presence of the adverse predictors noted here (e.g., comorbid anxiety disorder, clinical referral), CBT continued to outperform the other two treatments.

Outcomes at two-year followup. In contrast to the post-acute-treatment group differences, after two years of followup the three treatment groups had converged to the point that there were no significant group differences on the outcome measures (Birmaher et al., 2000). Most participants (80%) had recovered, but 30% had had at least one recurrence at some time during the study. As in two other studies we have reviewed in this chapter, CBT appeared to hasten improvement and remission during the acute treatment phase, relative to the other two treatments, but youngsters in the other two treatments caught up with the CBT group over the two years following acute treatment.

Using the data from the end of acute treatment through the end of the two-year followup, Kolko et al. (2000) tested for possible differences in specific outcomes of the different treatments and sought to identify moderators and mediators of treatment outcome. At the end of the acute treatment phase, CBT had produced (as anticipated) greater reduction in negative cognitive distortions than had the other two treatments, but the group difference faded somewhat over the two-year follow-up period. There was no evidence that distorted cognitions at the beginning of treatment moderated outcomes, and no evidence that outcomes had been mediated by changes in cognition. Similarly, there was no evidence that family dysfunction at the outset moderated treatment outcome, or that changes in family functioning mediated outcomes. Thus, while the study yielded a number of useful findings, there was little payoff in regard to an understanding of the types of youth with whom treatment was most and least effective or the change processes associated with treatment benefit.

The Brent et al. (1998) study is interesting not only because of its substantive findings, but also because of its structure and design. In some respects, it can be construed as a middle ground between efficacy and effectiveness research. Its sample included a mixture of two-thirds clinic-referred youth and one-third ad-recruited youth. Treatment took place in a clinic setting, but under conditions that departed in several ways from usual clinic operations. For example, each therapist received six months of intensive training in the treatment he or she would deliver, treated at least two cases within the protocol before becoming a study therapist, and received two hours of supervision per week for a caseload of only four cases. Clients had special incentives to participate, including free treatment and payment for assessment interviews. Despite these features, this study comes closer than most in the child and adolescent depression area to testing treatment in a clinical practice context, and the youngsters treated were likely the most seriously depressed of any youth depression treatment trial to date.

The study by Brent and colleagues has numerous notable strengths. Among them are careful and intensive assessment (including weekly self-report depression questionnaires); an exclusive focus on treatment cases showing the most severe form of depression (i.e., major depressive disorder); ample and uniform training and supervision of therapists across all three conditions; care in assessing protocol adherence by the therapists; thoughtful balancing of experimental rigor with the need to attend to clinical realities (e.g., procedures for removing nonresponding youths and suicide attempters from the protocol); the use of intent-to-treat analyses in outcome assessment; and innovative ways of gauging outcome (e.g., the clinical remission index). In a number of ways, Brent and colleagues offer a model to be emulated in other outcome research in clinical settings.

Summary of the Outcome Evidence on CBT for Adolescent Depression. We have reviewed six treatment outcome studies testing CBT in comparison to various control conditions and alternative treatments. CBT consistently outperformed waitlist conditions, but findings were more variable when CBT was compared to active alternative treatments. CBT produced greater depression relief than alternative treatments in some studies (e.g., Brent et al., 1997; Wood et al., 1996) but not others (e.g., Reynolds & Coats, 1986; Vostanis et al., 1996). In some cases (Birmaher et al., 2000; Brent et al., 1997; Wood et al., 1996), an initial advantage for CBT at posttreatment gave way to similar outcomes for CBT and alternative treatments at follow-up assessments, suggesting that a primary strength of CBT may be to hasten improvement and recovery in youngsters who may eventually respond well to other treatments. The evidence that rival treatments – such as relaxation and systemic family therapy – may outperform control conditions and may eventually approximate CBT effects suggests that there are some promising alternatives to CBT for depressed teens. On the other hand, if we quantify empirical support in terms of the sheer number of supportive studies, CBT clearly has the most extensive support of all the available psychotherapies for depression in adolescence.

What about Megan? Applying CBT for Adolescent Depression

We now return to Megan, the depressed 13-year-old introduced at the beginning of the depression section. In the previous chapter, we discussed what Megan's experience might be like in a child-oriented CBT program. Now we take Megan through a CBT intervention designed for adolescents, using the Clarke et al. (1990) CWD-A program as our exemplar.

Nudged by her worried parents, Megan enrolls in a program to help teens improve their coping skills. Held at the local university, the program is ordinarily reserved for 14–18-year-olds; Megan gets in because her 14th birthday is just weeks away. She learns that the program will last eight weeks, with a two-hour teen group meeting every Tuesday and Friday night. Her parents sign up for separate parent group meetings on seven of these nights.

In her first meeting, Megan meets her group leader, Claire, and five 14- and 15-year-olds from different schools than hers who will be in her group for the duration. She is also given a *Student Workbook* with a bright yellow-orange-gold cover, and cartoons, charts, and quizzes inside. She is surprised to see, on the inside title page, that the book is for the "Adolescent Coping with Depression Course"; she had thought of herself as angry, and maybe lonely, but not depressed! Still, Claire seems nice, and Megan is curious to see what the other kids in the group are like and what they have to say. So she stays put.

Assessing Mood and Establishing Group Rules. From the very first meeting on, the group feels more like a school class than therapy. There is a blackboard, and Claire has already written an agenda on it. After brief introductions, Megan and the other group members go to the first agenda item: "I. MOOD QUESTIONNAIRE." They all turn to the appendix of their Workbook, and rate their feelings during the past week. Some of the items (e.g., "During the past week, I felt that everything I did was an effort," and "...I could not 'get going.'") hit close to home for Megan. If these are signs of depression, she thinks, then maybe I *am* depressed. The second agenda item is "GUIDELINES FOR THIS CLASS (10 min.)." Three of the four guidelines are predictable: confidentiality, equal talking time for each person, and being constructive and supportive (not critical or sarcastic) with one another. However, Megan is surprised by the first guideline: "AVOID DEPRESSIVE TALK." The purpose of the group meetings, she learns, is not to talk about feeling down or depressed but rather to talk about positive changes. "Well, there goes most of what *I* usually talk about," she thinks.

Friendly Skills and the Thought-Action-Feeling Connection. In a get-acquainted exercise, the kids pair up and take turns telling about themselves and listening to their partner; Claire coaches them to use "friendly skills" – that is, "Make eye contact, smile, say positive things, tell about yourself." Then Claire gives a little lecture. She draws a triangle on the blackboard; at the three corners she writes, "Feelings and Emotions," "Thoughts," and "Actions." She explains that the three are closely connected, that each one affects the other two. When people feel depressed, she says, they often try to "feel better," but that may be a mistake because feelings are the hardest part of the triangle to change. A better approach is to change *thoughts* or *actions* first; that can lead to changes in feelings. The group then discusses examples of the feelings-thoughts-action connection and how it can cause *downward spirals* into depression, and *upward spirals* out of depression. In one example, a 16-year-old starts telling himself that he is a failure and will never do well in school; these thoughts lead him to withdraw from pleasant activities and from friends and spend more time alone; he grows unhappy and confused. In a counterexample, the same youngster decides to replace some of his negative thoughts with positive ones, makes himself get back to playing guitar with friends, and finds that his mood begins spiraling upward.

To help them think about what they discussed in the meeting, Megan and the others get a two-part homework assignment: (1) practice their "friendly skills" and check off in their workbook the skills they have practiced; and (2) fill in a mood diary every day until the next group meeting. As if homework weren't enough, the last school-like part of the meeting is a written quiz, with questions like, "Name the four things we said a friendly person does." Megan learns that quizzes and homework will be a regular part of the program. Although she isn't looking to add to her workload, she does admit that both of these school-like features will probably help her learn and remember.

Conversation Skills and Pleasant Activities. At the beginning of the second session the main ideas of the first session and the homework get reviewed, and the postsession quiz from that session is readministered orally, as a memory refresher. This is the standard routine for later sessions as well. Next, the group goes beyond the basic "friendly skills" of Session 1 to learn and practice something more complicated: how to start a conversation. One of the skills Megan had not thought much about was sizing up whether the time is right for a conversation by reading the other person's cues – if he makes eye contact and says "Hi," then conversation may be appropriate, but if he looks busy, preoccupied, or angry, it may be a bad time to start talking. Megan realizes that she is often so caught up in her own mood that she fails to read other people's cues; she can remember times this happened, how her efforts at conversation flopped, and how bad she felt afterward. She decides to work on this skill.

Later in the session, there are group exercises to show that doing pleasant activities makes people feel good. "Well, duuuuh!" Megan thinks; but she admits that she does spend a lot of her time locked in her room at home, shutting off activities that would almost certainly lift her mood – especially social activities. All the group members make a list of personally enjoyable activities, and Megan notes that most of hers are activities she can't do while shut up in her room. Megan's homework assignment for the week is perfect: (1) start two conversations using the skills learned in the session, and (2) keep a daily tally of which enjoyable activities on her list she actually does.

Relief from Tension Through Relaxation Training. In their third meeting, the group talks about tension and how it can get in the way of doing things to overcome depression – things like meeting new people or starting a conversation. Megan knows this is a problem for her; it's one reason she shuts out the world so much by hiding at home. So she takes it seriously when Claire leads the group through the Jacobsen relaxation technique. Some of the group members giggle a bit as Claire has the group members tape a mini-thermometer to their fingers, and then tense and relax various muscle groups – first the hands and arms, then the face and head, and so on – and finally imagine having all the tension glide out from the tips of their toes. At the end of the exercise, when she opens her eyes, Megan sees that her finger thermometer shows an increase in temperature. Claire explains that this shows relaxation; the blood vessels have expanded, which makes fingers warmer. Megan actually looks forward to doing her homework – that is, practicing Jacobsen three times before the next session.

Goal-Setting and Self-Reward. In the next session, the group works with charts they have been keeping, relating the number of pleasant activities they do each day to their mood at the end of the day. The evidence is pretty clear that, for most of them, moods get better as pleasant activities increase. This leads into a goal-setting process. Like the others, Megan sets a goal to modestly increase her rate of pleasant activities, and she writes a personal contract specifying what reward she will give herself for reaching her goal. Part of her homework is living up to her contract. That's fine with Megan; she doesn't mind doing more activities she likes, and then giving herself a reward!

Identifying and Modifying Negative Thoughts. In the fifth meeting, the focus broadens to include not just how the group members act and feel, but how they *think* as well. The students write down their most frequent positive and negative thoughts and then total the two sets. Megan finds it easy to list the negative ones – for instance, "No one likes me," "At home I feel like a prisoner," and "School sucks." However, she struggles to come up with positives. When she computes the totals, she finds that negatives outnumber positives by 4 to 1. No wonder she feels so gloomy most of the time! Her homework assignment is to write down her *worst* negative thought each day, write down the event or situation that caused it, and try to come up with a positive thought to replace it. That last part proves to be a tough assignment for Megan.

Lucky for Megan, much of the next session focuses on ways to increase positive thinking. In one exercise, each group member writes down a positive thought about each member; as the others read their thoughts about Megan, she writes them in her Workbook, thus preserving a collection of positive ideas about herself. In another exercise, students use various methods to generate positive counterthoughts in response to their negative thoughts. For example, a student who feels that "bad things are always happening to me" is encouraged to compare himself to others who face such major adversity as homelessness or loss of limbs, and realize how lucky he is in comparison.

A third approach is to look for irrational elements of negative thoughts, and revise accordingly. An example: "If I don't have a date this weekend, I'm a total failure *forever*." A possible challenge to this thought: "Is this really true? Am I a failure in *everything* if I don't get a date on one particular weekend? Is it possible that I might get a date some other night? Suppose I didn't get a date for a whole month, would that really make me a total failure in *everything*?" The exercises hit home with Megan. She realizes that she tends to exaggerate how negative things are. For example, one of her thoughts was "When I'm at home, all I ever do is work," but in truth, she realizes, she does very little work at home. Another of her thoughts has been "I'm a social outcast at school." However, the truth is that her only rejection is from some kids in her former clique; several other kids have made overtures, but Megan hasn't responded. So her social isolation is really *self*-imposed. Changing how we think is hard to do, but the exercises do make Megan more conscious of how tilted her thinking can be. She now realizes that her distortions actually make her feel worse.

Using the C-A-B Method to Understand How Events and Beliefs Lead to Mood. In the seventh session, the group learns to use the C-A-B method to connect the dots between sad feelings and their antecedents. The basic model is that sad moods are a Consequence of Activating events (e.g., bad grade) and Beliefs (e.g., "This shows I am stupid."). A key point Claire stresses is that the same activating event may cause sadness in one person and happiness in another, depending on the belief the two apply to the event. For example, Bill and Steve both look outside and see rain; Bill feels sad, but Steve feels happy. Why? Because Bill thinks, "Oh man, rain in October means summer is really over, no more leaves on the trees, and four months of gloomy winter." On the other hand, Steve thinks, "Alright! Rain down here means it's snowing in the mountains – I'll be skiing soon!" The take-home message for Megan is that her mood doesn't have to be controlled by events. Instead, how she feels in response to events can be shaped partly by the beliefs or thoughts she applies to those events. To get specific, a major activating event for Megan was her ousting from a school clique. The belief she applied to that event was, "This means no one likes me; I'm an outcast," and that made her feel rotten. What if she tried a different belief, such as, "Those girls are sort of snobby; maybe I'd be better off with other friends"? Might this belief lift Megan's mood a bit? Maybe, she thinks.

Refining and Polishing Skills. Over the next several sessions, Megan builds on skills she started to develop in the first seven meetings. For example, she learns two quicker, less conspicuous, and more portable ways to relax than the Jacobsen deep muscle procedure; in one, she checks her muscle tension, breathes deeply, and exhales slowly, while silently saying "calm," and thinking about lying on a beach. This way of calming down will be really useful in public places – for example, just before she takes a test, or tries to start a conversation with someone she doesn't know well. As a complement to coming up with positive counterthoughts, Megan learns ways to simply stop her negative thinking – for example, popping her wrist with a rubber band when she catches herself thinking negatively, or reserving a special "worry time" to contain her negative thoughts. And Megan picks up several new pointers on good social communication, such as avoiding judgmental responses that imply disapproval, and building a close relationship through appropriate self-disclosure. These are helpful hints to Megan, who realizes that she needs to break out of her cocoon and forge some new social connections.

Negotiation and Problem-Solving Skills: Peer and Parent Work. In Sessions 11 and 12, Megan and her group tackle negotiation and problem solving, with a particular emphasis on social problems. They learn some basic rules for defining a problem (e.g., be specific, admit your own contribution, don't accuse) and for brainstorming solutions (e.g., list as many solutions as you can, begin by offering to change one of your own behaviors). They also learn to evaluate possible solutions, choose one, and make a written contract stating exactly what each person will do as part of the solution. Megan and the others break into imaginary "families" and role-play problem solving with parents. Then they actually bring the parents in, teach them the procedures, and work on solving family problems together. This sequence helps Megan in two ways. First, playing a mother in the family role-play with group members gives Megan at least a glimmer of what it must feel like to be the mom of a depressed teen. Second, when she and her parents do the exercise, they focus on the problem of work distribution at home, a sore point for Megan. Although they reject one of Megan's proposed solutions ("Hire a maid."), they make some real progress toward a fair compromise: parents write down specific duties for Megan and her sister, and then no complaining allowed about undone jobs that are *not* on the list.

Preparing for the Future. In the final sessions, Claire leads the group through some life-planning work. Everyone fills in a chart listing long-term goals concerning friends, education, jobs, home and family, and so forth. For each category, they note potential obstacles and plans for overcoming obstacles. An additional exercise that Megan finds helpful is listing everyday hassles (e.g., with family, with friends, with school, with romantic relationships) and how to cope with them. She can think of several very predictable problems, such as running into girls from the clique that rejected her, and not knowing how to act; now that she has built some trust in the other kids in her group, she really values their ideas about how to cope. And it makes her feel good and useful to others to give them suggestions on how *they* can cope with *their* everyday hassles.

Throughout the process Megan has gone through, she has compared notes with her parents. She has learned that the parent groups discuss many of the same concepts and skills the teens are covering. Apparently, parents get a heavy dose of communication skills training and practice, with an emphasis on good communication in the family. The training may have paid off, because Megan now finds it easier to talk to her parents without having things escalate into shouting. Whether this is due to improved parental skills, improvements in Megan, or both, is not clear. The fact remains that home life is calmer, and Megan is less withdrawn, gloomy, and gothic, which brings genuine relief to everyone in the family.

Troubleshooting: Common Treatment Problems and Recommended Solutions. Although Megan responded well to CBT, therapists often encounter challenges in using this approach with depressed adolescents. CWD-A experts note the following common problems and offer the following suggested solutions.

- *No-showing for sessions, particularly at the beginning.* When a young person fails to attend a group session, the group leader calls immediately after the session to say that the youth was missed and to inquire about what the problem was. Ideally, problem solving follows, addressing specific reasons for missing the session (e.g., transportation problem, conflict with other activities, social anxiety). The leader tries to get the teen (and parents) to commit to four sessions – otherwise, the leader notes, there is no way the teen can make a truly informed decision. The leader stresses that the CWD-A program is not like "treatment" the teen may have experienced or seen on TV. If the youth wants to drop out after four or more sessions, the leader usually accepts the decision and offers to arrange a referral. Most youths who commit to the four-session plan end up staying for the duration.

- *Co-occurring disorders, problems, life events, and family pathologies.* Many depressed teens meet criteria for other disorders (e.g., in the anxiety or conduct spectrum), a number have experienced sexual abuse, and a significant proportion have parents who struggle with their own mental disorders; none of these important problems is explicitly addressed in the CWD-A program. Therapists who encounter such challenges but who want to rely on evidence-based procedures have at least two options. One is to add empirically tested procedures from other treatment programs that are designed to tackle such challenges. School refusal, for example, a common co-occurring problem, can be effectively addressed via recently developed CBT procedures growing out of the work of Albano and Barlow (1996). Another approach is to use standard CWD-A content for non-depression-related problems. As an example, cognitive restructuring can be applied to anxious thoughts as well as to depressive thoughts.

- *Insufficient time for relationship-building.* Sometimes the CWD-A protocol gets into the skill-building work so quickly that trust- and relationship-building gets rather short shrift. For some depressed youngsters (e.g., those who are very compliant or perfectionistic) this is not a major problem. For other teens (e.g., those who are hostile, sullen, resentful), working on trust and the relationship between therapist and youth may be crucial. This is difficult in the traditional CWD-A group format. In the individual treatment format that is now increasingly used with CWD-A, therapists often set aside the initial session for relationship-building and to encourage teen choice as to which therapy approach (cognitive or behavioral) to try first.

- *Perceived uniqueness and pessimism – "My problems are worse than other kids' problems, so the program won't work for me."* Some teens accept that the program has worked for others their age but believe their own problems are unique and more severe than those of other kids, such that the program won't really help in their own case. In the face of such pessimism, therapists do well to acknowledge the concerns and encourage the teen to approach the program as an experiment, trying the skills to see if any of them work. Therapists may also stress that not every skill is useful to every depressed youngster, but that virtually everyone seems to find at least one of the skills helpful. In general, therapists are encouraged to be cheerleaders, not debaters; so, rather than argue with teens about these issues, therapists work to praise and reward the youths who use and practice the skills, and simply give less attention to the youths who do not.

- *Not doing the homework.* CWD-A therapists give out small rewards (e.g., little pieces of candy) and praise to group members who have done their homework, and the group format can make praise quite rewarding. When homework is not done, the best therapists become detectives, working with the youth to discern the reason, be it not caring, not understanding the assignment, forgetting to do it, or losing the form. For each reason there is an appropriate problem-solving response. Youths are also given opportunities to do their homework in session for partial credit, or to tell how they did the homework without writing it down. Finally, observant therapists try to catch group members doing their homework without realizing it. For example, in a week when pleasant activities are assigned, most members will have done *some* pleasant activity and experienced *some* mood elevation, even if they were not intentionally doing their homework. Clever therapists take advantage of such inadvertent homework to score key conceptual points. After all, helping group members see that *their own behavior in everyday life shows how well the coping skills work* is more important than technical completion of a specific homework assignment.

CBT for Adolescent Depression: Scientific Issues. Methodologically speaking, some of the best treatment research in the field has been done with adolescent depression. The studies by Brent and colleagues (e.g., Brent et al., 1997) and the Oregon group (e.g., Clarke et al., 1999; Lewinsohn et al., 1990) represent the Lexus of youth depression treatment research. The work is methodologically sophisticated, with demanding subject selection criteria and rigorous methodology, including high standards for therapist training, treatment protocol adherence, and outcome assessment. The work also addresses important questions relevant to treatment of depression and many other child and adolescent conditions – for example, (1) Does it help to include parents in the treatment process? (2) Do booster sessions improve outcomes or reduce relapse? (3) Can we identify moderators and mediators of treatment outcome? The studies by Brent et al. (1997), Wood et al. (1996), and Vostanis et al. (1996) deserve special credit for comparing CBT to a strong alternative condition rather than a no-treatment waitlist.

The studies by the Oregon group also represent a rare instance in which virtually the same treatment manual and procedures have been tested in two successive clinical trials (more than 90% of the protocol content was identical in the two studies), thus providing a genuine replication. The series of two CWD-A treatment trials raises intriguing questions. Why did all groups in the more recent study – including the waitlist group – show higher rates of recovery from depression than the corresponding groups in the initial clinical trial? And why was the treatment effect size in the second study only about two-thirds as large as that in the first study, even though initial depression severity was very similar in both study samples? Definitive answers may prove elusive. Treatment studies can differ from one another in diverse unmeasured ways, including sample characteristics, family patterns, therapist abilities, and numerous other factors that are difficult to control or even detect. Given such differences, clinical trials involving very similar treatment manuals may well show substantial study-to-study variation in effects. All this underscores the need for replication, and for research on moderators and mediators of change, topics to which we now turn our attention.

Moderators of Treatment Outcome. CBT findings to date offer hints about factors that may moderate treatment outcome. For example, in both trials of CWD-A, a positive treatment response was predicted by lower initial levels of depression, greater frequency and enjoyment of pleasant activities, and more frequent endorsement of rational thoughts (Clarke et al., 1992; Lewinsohn et al., 1996). Other potential moderators have been identified by Brent et al. (1998), who found that teens who showed high levels of hopelessness and those diagnosed with comorbid anxiety disorders prior to treatment showed relatively poor treatment response. Brent et al. (1998) also found that depressed teens recruited through ads fared better in treatment than those who had been referred through normal clinical channels; this appeared to be due in part to higher levels of hopelessness in the referred youth. And Wood et al. (1996) found that treatment response was moderated by psychosocial adversity: the more adversity faced by treated youth, the worse the treatment response.

The moderator findings are not completely consistent across studies or even across different waves of analyses in the same study. For example, in apparent contrast to Clarke et al. (1992), Brent et al. (1998) found that clinical remission was predicted by initially *higher* levels of self-reported depression. And whereas Brent et al. (1998) had found that poor treatment response in the acute phase of their study was predicted by higher levels of pretreatment cognitive distortion, Kolko et al. (2000), who focused on measurement through the two-year followup in the same study, found no evidence that distorted cognitions moderated outcomes. The failure of findings to converge neatly suggests that much work lies ahead in the search for outcome moderators; but the good news is that the search has begun in earnest.

Mediators of Change. A few researchers have also begun to search for change processes that can explain why teens improve when CBT is successful. In their initial clinical trial of the CWD-A program, Lewinsohn et al. (1990) showed that teens in the program did show the intended reductions in anxiety and depressogenic cognitions and increases in pleasant activities over the course of treatment. A logical next step is to test whether such changes account for reduced depression in treated youth. Kolko et al. (2000) did examine that question with regard to cognitive changes in the Brent et al. (1997) clinical trial, but found no evidence that depression relief was associated with reduced depressogenic cognitions. Clearly we are at an early stage in the quest to understand change processes that underlie treatment effects; but at least the quest is underway.

Impact of Treatment Add-Ons: Parent Involvement and Booster Sessions. The outcome research has included tests of two intuitively appealing ideas: adding parent involvement and booster sessions to basic CBT. Results in both cases have been disappointing. Two trials by the CWD-A research team indicated that adding a parent component did not significantly improve outcomes with teens alone. This is roughly consistent with findings by Brent et al. (1997) that even a full course of family therapy did not outperform the effects of individual CBT with teens; acute effects of family therapy in the Brent et al. study were more modest on important outcome measures than the effects achieved through solo CBT.

What about follow-up booster sessions? These were tested with the CWD-A program by Clarke et al. (1999). The sessions did appear to hasten improvement in those who had not recovered from depression in the acute phase of treatment, but they did not reduce relapse as had been expected. This may have been the case because attendance at CWD-A booster sessions was poor. Poor attendance, in turn, may have resulted in part from the absence of peer contact in booster sessions, because peer contact in the acute phase appeared to keep some reluctant teens engaged and attending. Alternative approaches that boost attendance may yet prove effective in reducing relapse, and that is a worthwhile goal. We should not minimize the one benefit that did derive from the CWD-A boosters. Accelerating recovery among youngsters who do not improve during the acute phase of treatment means reducing the duration of the distress and dysfunction associated with depression, and that is no trivial contribution.

To keep the findings on treatment add-ons in perspective, it is important to note that there are numerous alternative ways to structure family involvement and booster sessions, and some alternatives may work well. In addition, though, the findings to date can serve to remind us that treatment components that seem intuitively and clinically compelling may not all be beneficial, and that we need empirical tests to distinguish between those that help and those that do not.

CBT versus Other Active Treatments. It is clear from the findings that CBT can outperform a waitlist condition (see e.g., Clarke et al., 1999; Lewinsohn et al., 1990; Reynolds & Coats, 1986). Moreover, if we focus on the sheer number of supportive studies, CBT is unquestionably superior to other treatments for teen depression. On the other hand, in head-to-head comparisons of CBT with other active treatments (as in treatment vs. treatment comparisons in the youth literature generally), the evidence has been mixed. A few studies have found at least some evidence that CBT outperforms alternative treatments (Brent et al., 1997; Kahn et al., 1990; Wood et al., 1996). However, in two of these studies (Birmaher et al., 2000; Wood et al., 1996), follow-up assessments showed most differences between treatments fading to nonsignificance over time. In these instances, the CBT advantage lay in faster relief from depression, but apparently not more lasting relief. Note that faster relief is not a trivial advantage, given the debilitating nature of depression; but it will be important to understand why the advantage for CBT fades over time, in cases where the fadeout occurs.

What Works Best: Complex and Comprehensive or Simple and Focused? One subset of the findings regarding CBT versus active alternatives highlights an intriguing question about psychosocial intervention in general: Is it better to fashion comprehensive treatments that address many components of dysfunction (e.g., low rates of pleasant events, weak social skills, cognitive distortion) in a single program, or is it better to keep interventions focused on one or a small number of key skills? In the case of depression, complex intervention packages such as CBT programs tend to address multiple aspects of the condition, but they may conceivably be hard for some participants to learn and to remember when they feel stressed or depressed outside the treatment setting. More narrowly focused interventions, such as relaxation training, may lack the conceptual richness of CBT, but may offer the advantage that they are simple enough to promote genuine learning and ready accessibility in times of real-life stress.

In this context, it is intriguing to note that such a conceptually simple treatment as learning to relax has proven to be *as* efficacious (in Reynolds & Coats, 1986), *nearly* as efficacious (in Kahn et al., 1990), or *eventually* as efficacious (in Wood et al., 1996) as the multi-component CBT packages to which it was compared. It is possible that some complex treatment packages may risk overloading children and youth, teaching more facts and coping skills than they can really master. By contrast, treatments that involve repetition of a simple exercise (e.g., relaxing muscles, controlling breathing) until the skills involved have been truly mastered may work well because they generate relatively high levels of actual competence in the targeted skills, and because this translates into increased likelihood that the skills will be used in real life outside the treatment session. The tension between comprehensive coverage and focused simplicity will continue to confront treatment developers and investigators for years into the future. So will the more general question of whether CBT can outperform other forms of active intervention for youth depression. Given the complexity and expense of CBT training and treatment, it will certainly be important to focus future research on the question of when the full package is needed and when simpler procedures, such as relaxation training alone, may suffice.

CBT for Adolescent Depression: Clinical Practice Issues

In this final section, we consider CBT from a clinical perspective. We weigh issues of special relevance to practitioners who may be considering CBT for the depressed teens in their own practice.

Clinical Representativeness of the Studies. First we consider the degree to which the evidence supporting CBT comes from samples and treatment conditions like those of real-world clinical practice. On this issue, the studies covered in this chapter span a broad continuum. Of course, the participants and conditions in a study need not necessarily look exactly like those of clinical practice to provide useful information. There are many depressed youngsters in school settings who might never be referred to a clinician but who could profit from a depression treatment program administered at school by group leaders who are not full-time clinicians. Thus, research involving treatment of nonreferred but symptomatic youth who are identified and treated in school by nonpractitioners may be worthwhile. However, because most youth treatment occurs in a clinical service context, we pay special attention in this book to the degree to which treatment studies approximate the clientele and conditions of that context.

Focusing first on the clientele, the range across adolescent depression treatment studies extends from nonreferred teens screened and recruited entirely through schools (Reynolds & Coats, 1986) to youngsters referred for treatment through normal clinical channels (e.g., Brent et al., 1997 [two-thirds of the sample]; Vostanis et al., 1996; Wood et al., 1996). Severity and diagnosability of samples also ranges widely, from youngsters who showed elevated depressive symptoms (Reynolds & Coats, 1986) to youngsters who qualified for various depressive diagnoses (i.e., major depressive disorder, dysthymia, and minor depression – e.g., Clarke et al., 1999; Lewinsohn et al., 1990) to a sample all of whom met criteria for major depressive disorder (Brent et al., 1997). That sample characteristics and sources may really matter is suggested by the finding that teens who had come into the Brent et al. (1998) study through normal clinical referral channels fared significantly worse in treatment than teens recruited into the study through ads.

Sample characteristics aside, how representative were the treatment settings and therapists in the teen depression studies? Settings ranged, across studies, from schools (Reynolds & Coats, 1986) to service clinics (e.g., Brent et al., 1997; Wood et al., 1996), although the clinic settings were generally linked to universities and research programs, which may make them rather different from most service clinics. Therapist training and professional degree are noted in several of the studies, but whether the therapists were primarily practitioners is not clear from most descriptions. Frequently the therapists were study authors or their research employees, although in some cases, the research employees who served as therapists may have been professional clinicians. A primary reason for attending to study settings and therapists is to explore the extent to which the treatments will lend themselves to use by practitioners in clinical service contexts, and that issue brings us to the question of implementability of the treatments.

Implementability of the Treatment Programs. The well-replicated empirical support for CBT with depressed adolescents certainly warrants the attention of practitioners who want to do evidence-based practice. In addition, the engaging conceptual content and visually attractive, well-organized written materials available for some of the programs (e.g., Clarke et al., 1990b) seem likely to appeal to adolescents and their parents. On the other hand, practitioners will need to weigh the potential costs of using CBT. The most thoroughly studied CBT treatment for teens, the CWD-A, involves 16 two-hour sessions, more than some clinics may permit and more than some managed care companies may reimburse. In the most recent test of the CWD-A (Clarke et al., 1999), for example, therapists received 40 hours of pretherapy training plus weekly supervision meetings throughout the treatment process. Replicating all this training and supervision may be difficult in many clinical settings. However, it is not clear that such extensive training and supervision are absolutely essential for clinical use, and the fact that treated youth can be seen in groups adds efficiency to the CWD-A. Similar issues concerning treatment duration, training time, and supervision requirements arise for other CBT treatment programs reviewed here, including the program by Brent et al. (1997).

Practitioners committed to doing evidence-based practice may well decide that these issues are worth tackling, given the substantial base of evidence on the benefits of CBT for depressed teens. Once this decision is made, the question of how to obtain appropriate training and supervision will surface. Training programs are sometimes offered for the CWD-A program, but these are not widespread. Training in the other CBT programs discussed here will prove even more difficult to find. Yet, training in the most common core elements of CBT for depression is a part of numerous continuing education programs, and a great deal has been written on the topic. In addition, at least one set of self-guiding treatment materials can be obtained directly from the publisher, and from the internet, as noted in the next section.

How to Find Out More about CBT for Depressed Adolescents

Descriptions of the CWD-A program and the Brent et al. (1997) program, their empirical basis, their evolution, and the outcome evidence on each, can be found in separate chapters in *Evidence-Based Psychotherapies for Children and Adolescents*, edited by Alan Kazdin and John Weisz (2003, Guilford – see chapters by Clarke, DeBar, and Lewinsohn, 2003, and Weersing and Brent, 2003). For a much more detailed presentation of the CWD-A program, see the *Leader's Manual for Adolescent Groups: Adolescent Coping with Depression Course* and the *Student Workbook: Adolescent Coping with Depression Course*, both by Gregory Clarke, Peter Lewinsohn, and Hyman Hops (1990, Castalia Publishing Company, Eugene, Oregon). Clarke and colleagues have built on their experience in treating diagnosed depression with the CWD-A to develop an adolescent depression prevention program. That program is described in *Adolescent Depression Health Class Curriculum* (Clarke, 1991) and a *Leader Manual* (Clarke & Lewinsohn, 1991), together with supporting videotape material for adolescent groups. The prevention program has been described, and outcome findings reported, in Clarke, Hawkins, Murphy, and Sheeber (1993) and Clarke et al. (1995). Finally, the CWD-A authors have generously made free copies of their treatment and prevention programs available through the Internet, at http://www.kpchr.org/acwd/acwd.html. They have also made available an interactive depression self-help program at http://www.feelbetter.org.

TREATMENTS FOR ATTENTION DEFICIT/HYPERACTIVITY DISORDER

Introduction to Section D

The Case of Kevin and Treatments for Attention Deficit/Hyperactivity Disorder

Kevin

Eleven-year-old Kevin is a human tornado. He moves through his house following an unpredictable course and leaving a path of destruction in his wake. Kevin is not malicious, but he is nearly always in motion, and he is so spacey and impulsive that each day is a series of collisions, spills, scars on the wall, and broken objects. Because his attention waxes and wanes, and shifts its focus so easily, Kevin is accident prone. Walking one way while looking another has led to a painful collection of bruises and broken glass; spilled drinks at mealtime are commonplace. Even simple daily routines, such as teeth brushing and hair care, seem to elude him unless his parents remind him and check up afterward; he still has to show his teeth for inspection before going out; he flunks half the inspections, and then needs to rebrush, sometimes more than once. He has major difficulty following directions and rarely finishes what he starts.

Kevin's inattentive, disorganized style makes even basic household chores a challenge. Asked to take his clothes to the hamper after his shower, Kevin is frequently halted by some interesting distraction along the way and, more often than not, fails to make it to the hamper. When his parents ask him to clean his room, Kevin starts, but when they check in later, they are apt to find the room still a mess, and Kevin caught up in playing with an old toy found under the bed, or pretending his bedspread is a tent. For Kevin's parents, the difficulty does not end at bedtime because Kevin's sleep pattern is erratic; they frequently wake up in the wee hours of the morning to the sound of Kevin wandering through the house and finding things to do.

At school, Kevin's inattentive and impulsive behavior has caused problems both academically and behaviorally. He has a great deal of trouble following his teacher's lesson or the class discussion for more than a few minutes, he fidgets incessantly at his desk, and he rarely comments appropriately on the topic of the moment. Instead, he is prone to blurt out answers impulsively without raising his hand, or to make comments he thinks are funny (others rarely think so). So while others in class are

167

learning, Kevin misses most of the class content. Kevin's desk at school is a random jumble of books, papers, pencils, erasers, kids' magazines, and candy wrappers; his backpack looks the same. Both desk and backpack reflect the disorganized state of Kevin's academic life. Working with his parents at home might help, but Kevin rarely remembers what his homework assignment was. When a homework handout does make it home, he is as likely as not to have left the appropriate books at school. Even when homework is done on time, there is a fair chance that Kevin will forget to turn it in when he gets to school, so he also loses points for homework he has done on time but turned in late, or failed to turn in altogether.

The impact of Kevin's impulsivity and poor attentional control reaches beyond home and school, and into his relationships with peers. He has trouble listening carefully enough to discern the general direction of a discussion, and thus he has trouble participating appropriately. In a recent conversation during a school lunch break, when a group of peers was discussing a favorite TV show, Kevin blurted out "I'm getting a new bike for my birthday!" Two of the kids rolled their eyes, and the others smiled knowingly. Kevin has gotten into several scuffles with peers, sometimes sparked by his out-of-control mouth (e.g., "That's a stupid-looking shirt!" "You look like a monkey."), sometimes by Kevin's combative reactions to peer's insults ("Hey, space cadet."), and sometimes by Kevin's impulsive behavior on the playground (e.g., throwing a soccer ball at another boy's head).

Hoping to find a positive outlet for Kevin's energy, his parents have gotten him into Little League, but his attentional and behavioral problems spill over onto the baseball field. In the outfield, while others are watching the batter and planning where to throw the ball if it is hit to them, Kevin is as likely to be staring into space or watching that shiny new car driving into the parking lot. When the ball does come to him, Kevin may not be watching, or if he catches it, he may have no plan for where to throw it; indeed, he rarely even knows how many outs there are. Other kids on the team, like his peers at school, say Kevin is "mental," that he is "from outer space," and they show little interest in socializing with him. He is rarely invited for play dates or birthday parties, and when he wants to invite a friend over, there is usually no one who wants to come.

Problems like Kevin's have been around for centuries, but they probably came into sharper focus with the advent of compulsory schooling, which requires sustained self-control in group settings (see Hinshaw, 1994). Sustained self-control is a critical skill for school-aged youngsters, and deficits in this skill pose major problems. In the late 1950s, professional and research attention was focused mainly on the unusual level of physical activity involved, and terms such as *hyperkinesis* and *the hyperactive child syndrome* were used to identify children like Kevin. By the 1970s, Douglas (e.g., 1972) and others made a persuasive case that problems in attention and impulse control were at least as important as problems in motor activity. This notion – that there is a syndrome that includes hyperactivity, impulsivity, and poor attentional control – is reflected in the current diagnostic term,

Attention Deficit/Hyperactivity Disorder (ADHD), used in DSM-IV (American Psychiatric Association, 1994). The closest counterpart among the empirically derived syndromes of the Child Behavior Checklist (Achenbach, 1991) is the Attention Problems syndrome, which encompasses such problems as "Can't concentrate," "Can't sit still," "Confused or seems to be in a fog," "Impulsive," and "Poorly coordinated or clumsy."

The best estimates currently available suggest that 3–5% of all school-aged youth meet the diagnostic criteria for ADHD; this translates into about one child per classroom, and well over two million individuals in North America (Mash & Wolfe, 2002; Szatmari, 1992). The diagnosis is about three times as common in boys as in girls. ADHD is one of the most common diagnoses associated with clinic referral; a third to a half of all clinic-referred children show ADHD characteristics, either alone or together with other disorders (Barkley, 1990).

In the typical developmental course, hyperactivity and impulsivity appear earliest, often by age 3 or 4, and attentional problems emerge in the early school years, about ages 5 to 7. While the hyperactivity and impulsivity may fade somewhat during the primary school years, the poor attention control remains relatively stable up to adolescence. All three clusters of symptoms decline somewhat in adolescence, and 25–50% will lose the diagnosis by adolescence or young adulthood (or learn to cope well), but most children diagnosed with ADHD will have some related problems throughout their lives, even as adults.

As Kevin's story illustrates, the behavioral patterns associated with ADHD provoke all sorts of problems, across multiple settings. Life at home can be difficult for the child, and perhaps even tougher for others in the family, who must cope with the chaos, clutter, forgetfulness, unfinished jobs, spills, property destruction, and sleeplessness. At school, poor attending and impulsivity can be a toxic combination, poisoning the child's relationship with the teacher, undermining academic performance, and leading to conduct problems borne not so much of ill will as of impulses the child's will can't curb. Among peers, the child with ADHD may well be a misfit and an outcast, as poor attention control makes conversations directionless, play activities frustrating, and performance in sports erratic. Given all these forms of impact, it is clear that attentional problems, overactivity, and ADHD warrant treatment, but what forms of treatment?

Treatment decisions in the ADHD area are enriched, but also complicated, by the existence of empirically supported interventions in both psychological and pharmacologic forms. Numerous studies have demonstrated the benefits of stimulant medication in reducing the intensity of ADHD symptoms (see Barkley, 1998; Weisz & Jensen, 1999). A recent study (MTA Cooperative Group, 1999) provides particularly strong evidence that stimulant medication, if properly monitored, can have potent effects on core ADHD symptoms, at least in the short run. However, some 20–30%

of ADHD youngsters show either no response or an adverse response to stimulant medication (Swanson et al., 1995), and thus need some alternative treatment. Even those youngsters who are helped by stimulant medication may experience unwanted side effects, especially insomnia (usually mild) and appetite reduction, as well as temporary growth suppression, and this may make nonmedical alternatives appealing to some youth and parents. Beyond these matters, some parents may not want to see their children depend on drugs for acceptable social and school behavior. Thus, the search for effective psychological interventions has continued for many years.

That search has led to tests of a number of psychological-behavioral treatments. Because diagnostic categories and criteria have changed over the years, much of the most relevant research did not employ samples selected to fit the most recent criteria, in DSM-IV (APA, 1994). However, intervention research has, for at least two decades, tested treatments aimed at the prevailing diagnostic counterparts of DSM-IV ADHD. And for more than 30 years, treatments have been tested that address core symptoms now associated with the ADHD diagnosis (e.g., disruptive behavior, overactivity, impulsivity, poor attentional control). So, for simplicity of presentation, we will be using the term ADHD to refer to the problems addressed by these treatments.

The three decades of treatment development research have been marked by a number of blind alleys and a few successes. An emerging etiologic model may help explain both the disappointments and the successes. As Barkley (1998) puts it, advances in research and theory increasingly indicate that ADHD is "... a developmental disorder of probable neurogenetic origins in which some unique environmental factors play a role in expression of the disorder, though a far smaller role than genetic ones do" (p. 69).

According to this model, ADHD does not result from deficits in skill, knowledge, or information, and thus it will not be very responsive "to interventions emphasizing the transfer of knowledge or skills" (Barkley, 1998, p. 69). This might explain why some of the treatments tested in years past, such as cognitive and cognitive-behavioral approaches, have produced such modest effects that they are now considered to have very limited clinical value (see Baer & Nietzel, 1991; Bloomquist et al., 1991; Dush et al., 1989; Pelham et al., 1998).

An increasingly accepted view is that ADHD is a *disorder of performance* (Barkley, 1998). That is, individuals with ADHD may well know what they should do, but often do not do those things when they should. From this perspective, the treatments most likely to help will be those that assist the youngster in performing the appropriate behaviors at the precise times when those behaviors are needed. That is, interventions need to be in effect at *points of performance* – that is, at those times and in those situations where success depends on overcoming the deficits, for example, by paying attention and managing behavior. Following this logic, it makes sense that the most successful psychosocial treatments for ADHD children are those involving *environmental* intervention or specific adjustments in the contingencies that prevail in children's social settings. Two of these environmentally focused approaches have such strong empirical support that they have been identified as "well-established" in the review carried out by Pelham et al. (1998) as part of the expert task force review discussed in Chapter 1 (see Lonigan et al., 1998). These two are *behavioral parent training* and *behavioral interventions in the classroom* (broadly construed to include camp settings). These two approaches are the focus of this section of the book.

Many of the core principles and procedures of generic behavioral parent training are similar across a number of different studies, and the same is true of generic behavioral intervention in classroom and camp settings. It is worth noting, though, that the particulars (and the specific manuals used) do differ from one treatment and study to the next. Thus, the two chapters that follow are designed to provide a picture of some common elements within each of these two generic categories, while also noting some of the specific features of particular treatment protocols. In an effort to span the general and the specific, we will first review common features of the generic approach (i.e., either behavioral parent training or behavioral classroom intervention), then provide details from specific treatment manuals, then illustrate how the treatment procedures might be applied to the case of Kevin, and finally present information on the variety of manuals, materials, and training opportunities available to readers who want to learn more. Each chapter ends with a summary evaluation, focusing on research issues and clinical practice issues relevant to the treatments.

6

Using Behavioral Parent Training to Treat ADHD

Because children with ADHD often have difficulty monitoring and managing their own behavior and following through with plans, a series of one-hour visits with a psychotherapist may not be so helpful to them. Insights gained and skills practiced with the therapist may be forgotten soon after the child returns to real life. Even if the insights are recalled, their power to govern behavior may be swamped by the force of impulses and distracting events. As noted in the introduction to this section, ADHD may not involve deficits in insight and understanding so much as deficits in performance that have their impact on child functioning in important life settings. What may be needed to address these performance deficits for the ADHD child is intervention that is located in those life settings, present on a daily basis, and monitored and managed by significant others in the setting. In one of the most extensively studied approaches to treatment, those significant others are the child's parents, and the setting is home.

Most approaches to behavioral parent training involve helping parents learn to design and implement contingency management programs. A number of such programs have been used with parents of youths diagnosed with ADHD. A common sequence is that parents are assigned readings on behavioral principles, they have a series of group sessions to learn and practice standard behavioral procedures, and they apply the procedures with their child and receive corrective feedback until the child's behavior shows desired change. In this chapter, we will discuss some of the conceptual principles and procedural commonalities of the parent training programs, and then we will turn to a specific exemplar of that approach, a protocol developed by Barkley (1997b). We will discuss how parent training procedures might be used to help Kevin. We will also discuss research and clinical practice issues that arise in regard to parent training for youngsters affected by ADHD.

Behavioral Parent Training for ADHD: Conceptual Basis and Procedural Overview

The literature on ADHD is rich in parent training programs, but the programs used most often were not designed exclusively for ADHD. In fact, two of the programs most widely used for ADHD are described in chapters of this book dealing with conduct problems and oppositional behavior – that is, Behavioral Parent Training and Family Treatment based on Patterson's work (Chapter 9) and Help for the Noncompliant Child (Chapter 10). Both of these treatment programs were first developed to address child conduct problems, but their use was later extended to ADHD youth. Of course, even in the early studies applying these treatments to conduct problems, it is likely that a substantial proportion of the children whose parents were trained would actually have met today's criteria for ADHD (Pelham et al., 1998). Later in the book, we consider the conceptual basis for those two treatment programs in relation to conduct problems and noncompliance. Here we focus on the rationale for applying parent training to ADHD in particular. In much of this chapter, we will concentrate on a parent training program developed by Barkley (1997b) for difficult or "defiant" children, a program that is very often used with parents of ADHD youth.

One of the most important reasons for using parent training with ADHD youth is the *points of performance* notion, discussed in the introduction to this section. If youngsters with ADHD do in fact suffer from performance deficits rather than deficits in understanding (i.e., if they know what they should do, but often can't make themselves do it – see Barkley, 1998), then the most effective interventions may need to be located precisely within the performance contexts where the deficits show up and cause problems. According to this reasoning, what may be needed is a set of environmental contingencies that reinforce the kinds of adaptive behavior the child finds difficult to perform independently – e.g., paying attention, planning, and thinking before speaking or acting. If contingencies are to be altered in this way, there need to be people in the child's world who can maintain the contingencies by systematically rewarding appropriate behavior and not rewarding inappropriate behavior. This is where parents come in.

The evidence suggests that training parents in behavior management skills can be very helpful with ADHD children; but this is not to say that ADHD is caused by poor parenting. Three lines of evidence argue against parent blaming. First, poor child management skills are more closely associated with the child conduct problems in oppositional defiant disorder than with ADHD itself (Barkley, Anastopoulos et al., 1992; Fletcher et al., 1996). Second, research suggests that negative and controlling behavior directed by parents toward their ADHD children is more a *reaction to* their children's problem behavior than a cause of it (Danforth et al., 1991). Third, parent training does not normalize ADHD children, nor do parent training benefits generalize well to nontreatment settings such as school classrooms where child problems may be quite significant. Thus, behavioral training for parents of ADHD children should not be seen as implying that parents caused the ADHD, nor should the training be expected to cure ADHD.

In.,tead, parent training is best seen as an environmental way to help the child cope with self-regulation deficits that are genetically influenced, neurologically based, and quite enduring (see Barkley, 1997a; Pennington & Ozonoff, 1996; Quay, 1997). Numerous studies of ADHD youth point to diminished nervous system arousal or arousability, an underactive behavioral inhibition system, and to abnormalities in brain structure (e.g., smaller than normal corpus callosum, atypical prefrontal cortex and basal ganglia). At present, we have no way to repair or reverse the biological abnormalities, but parent training may at least help children show improved behavioral control by infusing the environment with structure and consistency.

A two-part rationale for parent training with ADHD has been described by Russell Barkley (1997a, 1998), whose own parent program (Barkley, 1997b) is the primary focus of this chapter. First, Barkley proposes that ADHD youngsters' biological abnormalities may produce a specific deficit in rule-governed behavior – that is, a reduced capacity to adjust behavior in response to commands, rules, and self-directed speech. Parent programs address this reduced child responsiveness by training parents to (1) use especially explicit, systematic, and compelling methods of presenting rules and instructions, and (2) provide clear, consistent, and powerful consequences for compliance and noncompliance with the rules and instructions. The idea is that a parentally organized environment that is rich in appropriate cues and contingencies can help children stay on track for appropriate behavior (e.g., attending, thinking before acting, persisting at tasks) and avoid inappropriate behavior (e.g., carelessness, impulsivity, hyperactivity) in spite of their relatively enduring biological deficits.

A second part of the rationale for parent training is the well-documented fact that ADHD is often accompanied by serious conduct problems and a diagnosis of oppositional defiant disorder, and that children who show this combination tend to have particularly poor adolescent and adult outcomes (see Hinshaw, 1987; Paternite & Loney, 1980; Weiss & Hechtman, 1993). Thus, it is important to address oppositional and defiant behavior and other conduct problems in any treatment for ADHD youth. The most thoroughly tested and well-supported approach for addressing such problems is behavioral parent training.

When parents of ADHD youth receive behavioral training, the typical format includes assigned readings on the use of behavioral principles with children, and a series of 8 to 20 weekly group sessions held in a clinic. The sessions focus on learning and applying behavioral principles and methods with the individual children involved (Pelham et al., 1998). Coverage usually includes such core behavioral notions as maximizing parental attention (and praise) in response to appropriate child behavior, withholding attention (and praise) when behavior is inappropriate, developing reward and incentive systems (e.g., charts, points, tokens) to encourage desired behavior, and effective use of time-out for noncompliance. In the discussion that follows, we will focus primarily on the widely used parent training program developed by Russell Barkley (1997b).

Behavioral Parent Training for Defiant Children: In Brief

Designed for . . . . Defiant and ADHD children, ages 2–12
Number of sessions . . . . 10, plus booster session and follow-up meetings
Session length . . . . 1 hour for individual families, 2 hours for groups of families
Session participants . . . Therapist with parents, child included for parts of individual family sessions
Theoretical orientation . . . . Behavioral
Treatment steps:

1. Therapist leads parents through a review of information on nature, etiologies, developmental course, and prognosis of ADHD; may include video illustrations and reading material.
2. Therapist and parents discuss and practice procedures for attending to appropriate child behavior; procedures include close visual attending, narrative descriptions, and praise. Procedures implemented in daily "special time" at home.
3. Parents learn how to give effective commands to child, and how to respond immediately with positive attention when the child complies.
4. Parents learn how to make reinforcement concrete and external by establishing a token economy at home.
5. Parents learn to use consequences for noncompliant and inappropriate behavior. Such consequences include loss of points or chips in the token economy, and time-out.
6. Parents and therapist fine-tune the time-out procedure, discussing problems in implementation at home, and new applications that can be tried.
7. Parents learn procedures for managing noncompliance and inappropriate behavior in public places.
8. Parents learn procedures for improving the child's school behavior – coordinating communication with school personnel via the daily school behavior report card.

9. Parents and therapist discuss future problems that may arise, and how the skills learned may be applied.
10. Booster session, one month after end of Step 9, to review the main ideas of Steps 1–9, and to plan solutions to problems that have arisen during the month.

Behavioral parent training programs for ADHD, in general, classified by Treatment Task Force as . . . . Well-Established*

Key resource for potential users . . . . Barkley, R. A. (1997b). *Defiant Children: A Clinician's Manual for Assessment and Parent Training*, 2nd edition. New York: Guilford.

*Note: The Task Force report on ADHD (Pelham et al., 1998) concluded that two generic forms of treatment, *behavioral parent training* and *behavioral interventions in the classroom*, met criteria as "well-established"; individual treatment programs (such as the Barkley parent training program) were not classified separately. We focus on the Barkley program here because it is very widely used, and because other programs most often used to train parents of ADHD children have been described elsewhere in the book (see Chapter 9 on behavioral parent training based on Patterson's work, and Chapter 10 on the Help for the Noncompliant Child Program).

Barkley's Defiant Children Program: Treatment Procedures

An overall aim of Barkley's (1997b) Defiant Children Program (DCP) is to give parents the skills they need to help their children adapt in spite of biologically based deficits in self-control and attention. In essence, the DCP aims to compensate for the child's deficits in internal control by increasing the level of external control implemented by parents. Working toward this end, DCP therapists first teach parents about the nature and causes of ADHD, disobedience, and defiance, then teach and supervise practice in the use of core principles for management of child behavior at home, and then work on ways to apply the principles at school and other out-of-home settings where problems may arise. The program is most often carried out with groups of parents because this format is as effective as treating one parent or one couple at a time (personal communication, Russell Barkley, March 1, 2000), and it is obviously less expensive. However, for parents who are not high school graduates, who have significant psychological problems of their own, or who for other reasons seem likely to be slow to learn the skills, Barkley recommends working with the individual parent or couple.

Value of a Socratic Approach. The DCP involves nine steps, which can often but not always be completed in nine sessions, plus a booster review meeting held about one month after step nine has been completed. Sometimes the DCP therapist sees a single family at a time; in these cases, sessions last about an hour. The program can also be used with groups of families, and in these cases the sessions run about two hours. In both individual family and family group formats, DCP therapists strive to avoid lecturing to parents, aiming instead for a Socratic style, with therapists posing questions and leading parents through steps of reasoning that culminate in sound conclusions. The idea is to leave parents feeling that they played an active role in coming up with plans and conclusions.

Barkley (1997b) argues that the Socratic approach is both more respectful of parents and more interesting to them than being lectured to. It has the added advantage of reducing the risk of parental dependence on the therapist. That is, if nearly all the good ideas in therapy have come from the therapist, the risk is that parents will bring every new problem to "the expert." Since the expert will not be available after therapy ends, the goal must be to have parents reach the point that they can reason independently through challenges posed by their child's behavior. For this to be possible, parents need to understand not a series of specific procedures and solutions the therapist has devised, but rather the principles and concepts that guide procedures and solutions. This kind of understanding is enhanced by the Socratic process, and by periodic assessments by the therapist to ensure that parents understand key concepts, and that parents can apply the concepts to new problems.

Key Concepts in Child Management Training. Several concepts are central to child management training, in the DCP and other programs. Some of these have to do with optimum arrangement of consequences for child behavior, and some have to do with a particular perspective on family interactions. Across the various sessions, the DCP therapist tries to ensure that these key concepts are understood by parents.

Making consequences immediate, specific, and consistent. Key to the success of the DCP and other child management programs is ensuring that desirable and undesirable child behaviors are followed by appropriate consequences. If the consequences are to have maximum impact, they need to (1) follow immediately after the child behavior, (2) include explicit information as to what behavior is being rewarded or punished, and (3) be applied consistently across all episodes of the behavior. As for item 3, three kinds of consistency require attention. Consistency *across settings* means the rules that prevail at home should also be in effect in settings outside home; if the rules are allowed to slide outside home – say, in public places – children quickly learn where it is safe to misbehave. Consistency *over time* means that parental standards and consequences should not vary greatly from one moment to the next; they should remain stable because they are logically appropriate, and thus they should not depend on whether the parent had a good day or is in a good or bad mood, or on other factors that can fluctuate across time. Consistency *between parents* is critical as well; when mother and father have different rules, or apply consequences differently despite the same ostensible rules, children soon learn where the soft spots are in the system, and adaptive behavior change is undermined.

Establishing incentives before punishments. The DCP teaches parents that punishment for unwanted behavior should not even be introduced at home until the parents have set up a specific plan for rewarding appropriate and wanted behavior. Because most parents who refer their children for treatment have concerns about unwanted behavior, it is quite natural for them to focus on the negatives in their child. This focus can lead to complaints about what behaviors need to be *stopped*, and a corresponding emphasis on the use of punishment to make them stop. A heavily punitive climate, with low levels of incentives to do well, is not conducive to effective learning by the child. So, the DCP therapist works with parents to convert their complaints about their child into positive terms that describe the appropriate behavior they would like to see (e.g., working on your homework, being kind to your sister).

Anticipating misbehavior and planning for it. Some parents may be as impulsive in their reactions to child misbehavior as their children are in reacting to events in their own lives. Such parents may spend a great deal of time coping with child misbehavior after it has occurred, and relatively little time examining, anticipating, and preventing the situations in which child problems are most likely to occur. The DCP therapist tries to help parents understand enough about the most common problem situations to operate proactively, eliminating some of the stress of responding to child misbehavior by reducing the frequency with which the misbehavior occurs in the first place.

Recognizing that child behavior is overdetermined, and that family interactions are reciprocal. It is not unusual for parents of ADHD children to enter treatment with a rather unidirectional causal model in mind – that is, the view that they themselves are the cause of their child's problem, or that the "fault" lies with their child. In these cases, the DCP therapist works to enrich the parents' causal account by emphasizing that (1) causal processes in ADHD tend to be quite complex; (2) biology plays an important role; and (3) family interactions are richly reciprocal, with child behavior influencing how parents behave toward the child, and parent behavior influencing how the child acts. Given this causal richness, it makes little sense to parse blame for the child's problems, and DCP therapists actively avoid any effort to do so. Instead, the DCP perspective is that all parties to problematic interactions bear some responsibility for resolving the problems. Of course, given the relative strengths and deficits of parents and ADHD children, the parents are given more responsibility for structuring environmental controls to help their child improve, but this has nothing to do with *causal* responsibility, and efforts to assign blame may actually undermine constructive problem solving.

Overview of the Program, Order of Steps, Skipping Steps as an Option. The steps of the DCP (listed in the In Brief box) cover (1) information on the nature and causes of ADHD and misbehavior; (2) procedures for maintaining appropriate child behavior (e.g., parental attention, praise, and concrete reinforcers); (3) procedures for responding to misbehavior (e.g., time-out, fines within a token economy system); (4) ways of preventing misbehavior; and (5) ways of applying behavior management in settings outside home (e.g., shopping mall, school) and with new problems that may arise in the future. The order of the steps has been derived from considerable research and clinical experience. As an example, Barkley (1997b) suggests that presenting time-out and punishment procedures first has been shown to lead to a parental overemphasis on negative consequences, which is less effective than initially establishing a home environment that is rich in positive incentives for appropriate behavior.

So, Barkley (1997b) strongly recommends that the DCP steps be presented in the prescribed order, in most cases. However, when child noncompliance is mild, a therapist may choose to train parents only in the use of praise for acceptable behavior, then skip over the home token economy system, moving directly to the use of time-out procedures for occasional child noncompliance. The general principle is that the intervention's intensity can be calibrated to fit the severity of child problems. Such calibrations should not alter the order of events in the program – for example, positive procedures for encouraging appropriate behavior should always be learned before more negative procedures (e.g., time-out and punishment) for discouraging inappropriate behavior.

Structure of the Separate Sessions, and the Issue of Homework Compliance. Except for the beginning of treatment, devoted to information on ADHD and noncompliance, all the sessions with parents follow a predictable sequence. First, and very important, homework from the previous session is reviewed, together with any information the parents want to share about events in the family since the previous session. Failure to complete the homework is discussed, with the aim of designing a solution so that homework will always be done. If the therapist is seeing the family individually, the same homework is reassigned, and no new material is discussed until that homework has been completed. In a family group format, the therapist schedules a separate session with those parents who did not complete the homework to determine whether the problem can be resolved, and thus whether the family can continue in treatment. The DCP program is firm about the importance of parental homework; parents who persistently fail to complete the assignments are excluded from further treatment until homework completion can be assured.

After homework review, the therapist introduces the rationale for the skill that will be taught in the session, leads a discussion with parents related to that particular skill, and then distributes a handout (included in the DCP manual) that summarizes the main ideas. After discussing with parents their thoughts about the skill, and their reactions to the ideas in the handout, the therapist models the skill for the parents. In a single family format, the parents practice the skill in interactions with their child, and the therapist provides coaching and feedback through a bug-in-the-ear or some related procedure (see examples in Chapter 10). In the family group format, group discussion is used instead of actual practice, and parents are encouraged to identify problems they might encounter in applying the skill at home.

Toward the end of the session, homework is assigned, and any questions about the homework are discussed. Throughout the session, the therapist uses attention, encouragement, and praise to support the parents' efforts to learn the new skills, participate in discussions, complete the homework, and actively engage in the program.

Session Content. In this section, we survey some of the specific contents of the treatment steps (each step roughly corresponding to a separate session). For each step, we will note the main goals, procedures, and a typical homework assignment for the parents.

Step 1: Learning why children misbehave. In the first step, the therapist talks with the parents about some common causes of child defiant behavior, works with the parents to identify any of those causes that may apply to their own family, and begins focusing on remedies. After an open discussion with parents about their own views on causes of child disruptive and defiant behavior, the therapist shares some of what the research has shown, noting and building on the parents' ideas where relevant. As an example, parents may mention "getting attention" or "poor parenting" as causes; the therapist can build on these general notions, adding specific information on how attentional processes and parental behavior play roles in the process, and noting other factors that may help mitigate child-blaming and self-blaming by parents. As in each treatment step, the therapist gives the parent a handout (provided in the manual, and available in Spanish). The handout and the discussion present a model of child misbehavior that entails four causal components.

    a. *Child characteristics.* First, child characteristics, many largely inborn, give some youngsters a predilection for disruptive behavior. Such characteristics may include attentional problems, impulsivity, or irritability that shows up as early as infancy in the form of difficult temperament. Beyond these factors, children born with a predisposition to developmental delay or even thought disorder may also have difficulty complying with parental directives. In the session, parents fill in a portion of the Step 1 handout, listing which child characteristics within the various dimensions they think may contribute to their child's behavioral difficulties.

b. *Parent characteristics.* A second cluster of potential causal factors resides in the parents. Like their children, parents may have temperamental characteristics, difficulties with attention span or impulse control, or propensities toward patterns of personality or psychopathology that contribute to their child's difficulties. Using the Step 1 handout, parents note any of their own characteristics that may be relevant.

c. *Situational factors, environmental contingencies.* Child behavior does not occur in a vacuum, but rather as a response to specific situational demands, constraints, and contingencies. Children may misbehave in order to escape from unpleasant conditions or demands. For example, when assigned to do chores that are boring, require extended effort, or interfere with continuing an enjoyable activity, children may experiment with ways of avoiding the chores – dawdling, whining, or outright refusal, for example. The child's noncompliance may be followed by repeats of the parental command, further noncompliance by parental threats, and still further noncompliance by eventual parental acquiescence, or even by parental aggression toward the child; both parental responses are damaging, and both are targets of intervention in the DCP.

d. *Family stressors.* The fourth causal cluster consists of stressors impinging on the family – for example, parents' personal problems, financial difficulties, marital distress, job tensions, difficulties with relatives and friends, and problems created by the child's siblings. Such stressors can influence child behavior in a variety of ways. Stress may directly affect child behavior, making a youngster more negative, moody, or oppositional. Stress may also impinge on parents' perceptions of their children, leading to exaggerated views of how difficult or deviant the child's behavior is. In addition, stress can distract parents or deplete their emotional reserves, hampering their ability to respond effectively and consistently to child misbehavior, or leading them to overreact, with increased demands or harsh punishment. Inertia can be a problem, as parents grow accustomed to the stressors and implicitly decide to simply live with them. The NCP therapist attacks the inertia, encouraging parents to identify specific family stressors that are causing problems, and to develop plans for reducing their impact.

The impact of these four causal clusters is magnified by their interactions with one another. For example, a serious mental health problem in one of the parents can interfere with job performance, contribute to financial stress, and generate marital discord, spilling over onto child behavior and undermining parents' ability to respond appropriately and consistently to child disobedience. The therapist talks with parents about the potential for cascading of causal factors, and the need for parents to take three key steps at the outset of treatment: (a) identify their child's risk factors, and begin planning ways to alter them or cope with them; (b) recognize their own parental risk factors and begin planning ways to eliminate them or reduce their impact on the child; and (c) identify situational contingencies that support, maintain, or exacerbate defiant child behavior in their home, and begin planning for appropriate changes. Parents are told that their motivation is critical to success – that no matter how successful this program has been with other parents in the past, benefits for their child will depend on how conscientious they are in learning the skills, doing the homework, and following through at home. This view is contrasted with a Jiffy Lube approach, in which parents drop their child off to be "fixed" by the therapist while the parents sit in the waiting room. For homework during the following week, parents are asked to complete a Family Problems Inventory (part of the parent handout), noting specific problems in eight domains (e.g., marital, occupational, other) and proposing solutions to each. Because research shows elevated risk of accidents and property damage among oppositional children, especially those with ADHD, parents are also asked to childproof their home, room by room, finding ways to reduce the risk of harm to the child or to valued property.

Step 2: Teaching parents how to pay attention. In the second step of DCP, typically covered in the second session, the therapist teaches parents how to pay attention. The basic idea is that the way parents allocate their attention when they interact with their children has a powerful impact – for good or ill – on subsequent child behavior. Barkley (1997) suggests starting by asking parents to list characteristics of the worst job supervisor and the best supervisor they have ever worked with. After discussing the specifics with parents, the therapist asks them which of the two supervisors they are most similar to in their own interactions with their behavior problem child. Most parents, Barkley notes, report that they are more like the worst supervisor than the best, and this can launch a discussion of how children, like employees, can go "on strike" or stage a "work slowdown" in response to problems in the relationship with their parental "supervisor."

One goal of the session is to improve that relationship by teaching parents a way to interact with their child that resembles the child-directed interaction of Parent-Child Interaction Therapy (see Chapter 10). Parents are encouraged to set aside 15–20 minutes per day as "special time" to be with the child alone to engage in an activity of the child's choosing, and to use the time to attend totally to the child's activity – watching it, appreciating it, and occasionally narrating and praising it, while avoiding questions, commands, criticism, or control of the child. The therapist models the appropriate style of interaction for parents, coaches as the parents try it, and works with parents to nail down the details of how and when the "special time" will happen at home. The week's homework assignment is to do the special time activity every day and to record a few sentences in a notebook about what the parent and child did each time, and how the child reacted. As in Parent-Child Interaction Therapy (Chapter 10) and the Help for the Noncompliant Child program (Chapter 10), the goal of these child-focused interactions is to increase the attractiveness of parents as people with whom to interact, and thus make their attention and approval more valuable to the problem child. This will set the stage for the strategic use of attention, taught in Step 3.

Step 3: Increasing compliance and appropriate independent play using parental attention and monitoring. In the third step, the therapist and parents work on using parental attending skills to increase child compliance with parents' instructions. A key idea is for parents to "catch the child being good," and respond with attention and praise. Parents are told to be especially watchful when they give directives to their child, to remain in the area where compliance is expected to happen (not leave after telling the child what to do, a common practice in families with noncompliant children), and to offer specifically labeled praise when the child complies – for example, "Great job cleaning up!" or "I really like it when you pick up your toys." According to the DCP, the likelihood of compliance increases if parents follow certain guidelines:

a. Be sure you really mean it, and thus are willing to see the task through to completion; don't give commands that won't be followed up.
b. Present the command as a direct statement, not as a question or as a favor you are asking.
c. Keep the commands simple; complex, multiple commands may be difficult for the child to process or remember.
d. Make eye contact with the child while issuing the command.
e. Reduce distractions (e.g., turn down the radio or TV) before stating the command; remember, ADHD youngsters tend to be distractible.
f. When in doubt, have the child repeat the instruction, to ensure that it was understood.
g. Finally, for extended tasks and those that involve several steps, it may help to set a time limit (use a kitchen timer) and to give the child a "chore card" listing each of the steps in order (this makes it easier to comply and eliminates arguments about what all the task components were).

During this part of the treatment program, the therapist tells parents they should increase their rate of commands to the child, and models doing do (e.g., "Come here so I can tuck your shirt in," "Hand me that magazine," "Please get me the salt shaker"); this will increase opportunities for the child to comply and thus to receive attention and praise. Ideally, the increased commands will be timed to maximize the chances of comp-liance – for example, during lulls or transitions between activities.

In Step 3, parents learn more about why disruptive behavior occurs and what they can do in response. Consider a common problem faced by parents of ADHD children: difficulty carrying on a phone conversatiion because of continual interruptions. Asked how often they have stopped such a conversation to tell the child to stop interrupting, most parents say they've often done so; but asked by the DCP therapist how often they have stopped a phone conversation to praise their child for being quiet and not interrupting, most will admit that they rarely do so. From the child's perspective, then, the contingencies are clear – play quietly and independently, and I get no attention, but interrupt Mom or Dad and I get a lot. With reasoning like this, the therapist encourages parents to use attention and praise for such positive behavior as appropriate independent activity. In Step 3, parents also begin learning to increase their monitoring of the child's behavior, interrupting their own activities from time to time to check in and observe the child's activities, ideally when the child is not expecting to be observed. Each time the child is found doing something appropriate, praise or reward should follow; and each time the child is found to be misbehaving, a fitting punishment should be meted out swiftly. The idea is for the parent to establish good monitoring patterns as early as possible, to reduce the risk of noncompliant, aggressive, and clandestine delinquent behavior, all of which have been linked to inadequate parental monitoring (see, e.g., Loeber, 1990).

Step 4: A token economy at home. The changes in parental behavior growing out of Steps 1–3 may produce noticeable change in child behavior at home, but more striking transformations in child behavior are likely to follow Step 4, introduction of a token economy. In fact, Barkley (1997) notes that more than half the families treated with the program will report a near-complete remission of the child's behavior problems when the concrete reward system of Step 4 is in place. The system involves awarding the child tangible tokens for appropriate behavior, with tokens exchangeable for privileges and concrete rewards. Some evidence suggests that children with ADHD may be less sensitive than their peers to attention and praise, and that more powerful, tangible consequences are needed to engage them and prompt significant behavioral change.

In harmony with this idea, a token system draws on the power of con-crete, attention-getting consequences that are relatively easy for parents to dispense. Chips or points can be taken anywhere and awarded at any time, and they can be linked to almost any kind of privilege or concrete reward the child wants and the parent thinks appropriate. Token rewards have the added advantage of durable impact. That is, unlike specific rewards such as food, which may fade over time in their attractiveness to the child, tokens can be linked to an ever-changing array of specific rewards, such that the subjective exchange value of the tokens remains high for the child. Another attraction is that token systems can be made systematic and fair, with clear rules that place control over consequences in the child's hands – rather than, say, leaving rewards contingent on what kind of mood the parent happens to be in. Two other advantages are significant. Token systems force parents to pay close, consistent attention to the child's appropriate behavior, and they teach children a fundamental societal concept – that is, that most of the things we desire in life have to be earned through our behavior.

Several steps are involved in setting up a token system.

a. *Selecting the token.* First, parents need to decide what form of token will work best for their child. For children younger than 8, concrete tokens such as poker chips are recommended; for older children, parents award points using a chart or notebook.

b. *Explaining the program to the child.* The key here is a positive tone. Much better that a parent should present the system as a way of making sure the child is rewarded for showing good behavior than to say the system is needed because the behavior has been so bad.

c. *Designing a way to bank tokens.* Success of the system may depend partly on how salient the accumulation (or loss) of tokens is to the child. For children under 8, salience is enhanced by designing a container for the tokens (e.g., a decorated jar or shoe box); for older children points are recorded in checkbook balancing fashion, with columns for date, behavior performed, points added or subtracted, and current balance.

d. *Selecting rewards and privileges.* Of course, the true value of the tokens resides in what they can buy for the child, so it is crucial to develop a list of attractive rewards and privileges (e.g., extra TV or video game time, renting a movie, meal at a favorite fast-food place). Barkley advises that the list should include no less than 10 items, with some easily awarded short-term items (e.g., TV time) and some weightier, longer-term items (e.g., a fishing trip) that will require greater earnings (see next section).

e. *Selecting the behavior that will earn tokens.* Another focus of parent-child discussion is identification of the specific behaviors that will earn tokens. The list should include jobs that support the family (e.g., setting the table), self-care duties the child has not performed well thus far (e.g., bathing, independently dressing for school), and appropriate social behaviors the parent wants to target for change (e.g., saying nice things to a sibling). For negatives that the parent wants to discourage – such as not stealing, swearing, or arguing – the tokens can be made contingent on a time period during which the negative behavior is absent. As an example, the child might earn three points if there is no arguing between lunch and dinner on Saturday.

   f. *Bonus tokens for "attitude."* Because it is possible for children to earn tokens while still being unpleasant about it, parents may find it useful to add the option of bonus tokens, to be awarded at the parent's discretion when the child shows a positive attitude.

   g. *Establishing exchange values.* Parents and child need to work out what earnings will accrue for each of the targeted behaviors, and what each of the rewards and privileges will cost in tokens. A rule of thumb is that the tokens earned through an average day of completing most routine jobs should generate enough tokens to buy the rewards and privileges the child might reasonably want, with about one-third of the day's earnings left over as "savings." The exchange values should be written down, and for young children, supplemented with pictures (e.g., magazine cutouts showing the reward item or privilege paired with a drawing of the poker chips needed).

The main homework assignment for parents is establishing the token system. In addition to covering the steps outlined here, parents are given several bits of advice based on prior experience with the system. First, in the early days of the system, there should be no penalties. Tokens should be awarded for the designated appropriate behaviors but not withdrawn for inappropriate behavior. Although penalties will be introduced eventually, using them in the early stages can cause children to lose interest in the program. So, the initial goal should be to reward children liberally, to give them a taste of the "good life" they can achieve through good behavior. Parents are also cautioned not to give tokens in anticipation of a job but rather only after completion of the job, and to keep chips out of reach of children who are known to steal. Another important note: tokens should be awarded with a pleasant, upbeat tone, with praise, and with a clear message about exactly what behavior is being rewarded. The specific list of behaviors to be rewarded and rewards to be earned is open to review every few weeks, as behavioral targets change and as children's interests evolve.

Step 5: Time-out and other means of discipline. In the ideal world, using praise and rewards for desirable behavior would be all parents need to make their children model citizens. In the real world, children misbehave in ways that require consequences. Step 5 focuses on two such consequences: (a) fines within the token economy, and (b) time-out. Parents are warned in this step that this is apt to be the most difficult week in the program, generating very negative child reactions, and that the parents will need to be very consistent if the transition to these new disciplinary procedures is to work well.

Once the positives of the token economy have been made salient for the child by a week of tokens and rewards, it is time to introduce the idea that tokens may also be withdrawn in response to inappropriate behavior. The rule of thumb is that the same number of tokens that can be earned for completing an assigned task (e.g., making up the bed, getting dressed for school) should be withdrawn if the child fails to complete the task. In addition, parent and child may draw up a list of fines that will be levied for specific unacceptable behaviors – for example, arguing, swearing, property destruction, lying, and stealing. Parents need to be cautioned about the risk of *punishment spiral*. As an example, suppose the child commits one fineable offense (e.g., arguing), is fined, then reacts to the fine by swearing, which generates more swearing and verbal abuse of the parent, followed by another fine, then a glass is smashed, and another fine levied. At some point in this process, the child may have lost more points than could be re-earned in weeks, and all motivation to participate in the token system is wiped out. To prevent such punishment spirals, the therapist teaches parents a simple rule: fine the child once through the token system, and if this generates further unacceptable behavior, send the child to time-out.

At this point, parents are taught specific procedures for effective time-outs. A first principle is that parents should not give their child a command unless they are prepared to back it up with a properly administered time-out. If they are not willing to do this, then the command should not be issued in the first place. If the command is important enough to be backed up, then the parent should state it only once, then use the following steps. After stating the command, the parent counts backward, aloud, from five to one, thus signaling to the child that compliance is expected right away. After the five-second countdown, the parent gives a warning: "If you don't do as I say, you are going to sit in that chair!" Another five-second countdown follows. If the child still has not complied, the parent says, "You did not do as I said; now you are going to the chair!" The parent takes the child firmly by the arm and escorts the child quickly to the time-out chair, saying, "You stay there until I say you can get up!" The procedure sounds simple, but several questions arise:

a. *What kind of chair, and where should it be located?* The time-out chair should be in a place that is easy for the parent to observe, so the child in time-out remains in view while the parent goes about normal household activities. It should be a normal, straight-backed chair, and it should be placed far enough from the wall that the child cannot kick the wall without leaving the chair.

b. *How long should the child stay in time-out, and what must happen for time-out to be ended?* The DCP calls for a "minimum sentence" of one to two minutes per year of the child's age. Although the child may protest or make noise during some parts of the time-out, about 30 seconds of silence is required before the time-out can end. So, near the end of the minimum period, the parent is to say something like, "I'm not coming back to the chair until you are quiet." If the child does not comply, the time-out may last as long as an hour or two in the early stages, but most children quickly learn that silence gets results. Finally, to get out of time-out, the child must agree to rectify the problem that originally led to time-out. If the problem was refusal to comply with Mom's request to set the table, the child must agree to set the table; if the problem was swearing, the child must agree not to swear again.

c. *What if the child leaves the chair without permission?* If the child gets up from the chair before time-out has ended, the parent provides a warning: "If you get out of the chair again, I am going to send you to your bed." If the child refuses to return to the chair, or gets up again without permission, the parent takes the child directly to the bed, stripped of all diverting stuffed animals, toys, or games, and time-out takes place there, with the bedroom door open. Parents who do not wish to use the bed in this way, have the option of fining the child (tokens) for failure to comply, or threatening the removal of a privilege (e.g., TV after dinner).

d. *What if the child asks to use the bathroom?* The time-out must be completed before permission is granted. Barkley (1997) notes that in 20 years of experience, he has seen only two children have "accidents" while in time-out, and both cases were obvious intentional acts by the children. In both cases, by the way, the children were required to remain in time-out until the standard conditions were met, and had to clean up the area and change clothes afterward.

e. *What if the child says he or she will not love the parent anymore?* This is a predictable form of manipulation, and parents should show no outward reaction.

f. *What if the child refuses to leave time-out?* This is typically a bid by the child to control the episode. Parents should reply that since the child has refused to obey the parent's request (i.e., to leave the chair), he or she must now do another time-out, and an additional minimum sentence is levied, with the same rules as before.

g. *What if the child is assaultive?* In a few cases, the child is so violent that a mother (usually not a father) fears physical violence if she uses time-out. In these cases, the DCP recommends that mothers only use time-out when father is in the home to provide backup. After weeks of success with father present, mother may experiment with assigning time-out when father is absent. If this fails, inpatient, residential, or day treatment may need to be considered.

To ensure understanding, the time-out procedures are modeled in the session. If only parents and therapist are in the room, the therapist may play the role of parent while the parent plays a child, and then the roles can be reversed. If the child is present during the session, the therapist can play the role of parent acting out a time-out with the child, and then the child's parent can take a crack at it. As an alternative, or complement, there may be a genuine *in vivo*, with the parent and child in a playroom, the parent issuing various commands until one is disobeyed, and then trying a time-out while the therapist observes; afterward, in the child's absence, the therapist provides feedback to the parent. Homework for the following week is for parents to try the time-out procedure, but only a few times; for each episode, parents are asked to keep a written record of what the child did to provoke the time-out, how long the time-out episode lasted, and how well the parents felt the procedure was implemented. This written record will be a focus of discussion in the next session. Before leaving this session, to make things concrete, parents are asked to identify (a) the location in the home where the time-out chair will be placed, and (b) the specific problem behaviors for which time-out will be used during the week.

Step 6: Refining and extending the use of time-out. In Step 6, the therapist and parents review the parents' homework records and discuss how each time-out episode went. Fair game for the discussion are any problems the parent may have encountered, and even the parents' feelings about using time-out. In some cases, considerable discussion and even new practice may be needed to iron out problems. If all has gone well, only minor procedural fine-tuning may be needed, and the session may be brief. At the end, therapist and parents identify two new problem behaviors to which time-out will be applied as homework for the next week.

Step 7: Managing child behavior in public places. Public places give children an opportunity to test limits in ways they might not try at home. Thus, parents need special skills for coping when they take their children to restaurants, shopping malls, the homes of friends, and other settings outside home. Step 7 is devoted to building those skills, essentially by adapting the child management methods already learned.

Parents are taught a four-step "think aloud – think ahead" approach to anticipating and reducing public misbehavior. First, before entering any public place with the child, the parent needs to establish the rules the child is expected to follow – for example, stand close, don't touch, and don't beg. To ensure understanding, the parent should require the child to repeat the rules before entering the place. Next, the parent should establish an incentive for compliance – for example, extra tokens within the token economy, treats the parent has brought along as rewards, or perhaps a purchase at the end of the trip. Third, of course, a clear consequence for noncompliance needs to be identified for the child, again before entering the place. Fourth, the child needs to be given some special responsibility to occupy attention during the trip – such as, helping Mom find three articles in the store, helping her carry purchases, or carrying the shopping list and checking off items as they are purchased. This reduces the risk of misbehavior stirred up by simply not having anything to do.

Throughout the trip, parents should praise their child for following the rules, and periodically adding tokens to the child's 'bank account' may help to keep the good behavior rolling. If the child slips and breaks one of the rules, time-out should be enforced in the setting. The alert parent will have scanned the place upon entry, to identify an appropriate spot – a dull time-out corner – just in case. The child will need to spend about 30 seconds facing the time-out corner for each year of age, and must follow the same rules used at home (see previous section) to terminate time-out after the "minimum sentence" has expired.

What if there is simply no good place for a time-out corner – for example, in a cluttered grocery store? The child may be taken outside the store and require to face an outside wall; or the time-out can be carried out in the back seat of the family car in the parking lot. In some cases, parents may simply record the offense and the "sentence" in a small notebook, show it to the child, and delay implementation of time-out until the family has returned home, but this delayed approach is not ideal.

The four-step "think aloud – think ahead" program can be generalized to other situations in which the risk of misbehavior is elevated. In such situations – for example, a shift from play time to homework, transition from TV to bedtime, the arrival of a friend for a play date – parents can reduce the risk by explaining the rules to the child at the outset, and then following the other three steps of the plan, much as would be done in a shopping mall. Homework for this week includes two trips to public places, each designed to practice the skills in the four-step plan.

Step 8: Using the daily school behavior report card. Problem behavior at school – both in class and between classes – is, of course, common among ADHD youngsters. While parents may not be there to deal with school behavior, they can establish a presence via their relationship with the child's teachers. In Step 8, parents learn to do this by means of a school behavior report card that is filled in by teachers and brought home by the child each day. The DCP manual provides sample report cards the therapist can photocopy for parents. Two of these are shown in Figure 6.1. As these illustrate, parents will need one card focused on time in the classroom and another focused on such nonclass periods as recess and lunch.

Early in the session, the therapist and parents identify the primary problems the child has been having at school, and determine whether the standard cards shown in Figure 6.1 are appropriate, or whether a more individually tailored card is needed. Procedures for use of the card will need emphasis. Each school day, new cards are to be filled in and initialed by teachers, with ratings for each category ranging from one (excellent) to five

DAILY SCHOOL BEHAVIOR REPORT CARD

Child's name_____ Date_____

Teachers:

Please rate this child's behavior today in the areas listed below. Use a separate column for each subject or class period. Use the following ratings: 1 = excellent, 2 = good, 3 = fair, 4 = poor, and 5 = very poor. Then initial the box at the bottom of your column. Add any comments about the child's behavior today on the back of this card.

Behaviors to be rated:	Class periods/subjects						
	1	2	3	4	5	6	7
Class participation							
Performance of class work							
Follows classroom rules							
Gets along well with other children							
Quality of homework, if any given							
Teacher's initials							

Place comments on back of card

-------------------------- Cut here after photocopying ---------------------------

DAILY RECESS AND FREE TIME BEHAVIOR REPORT CARD

Child's name_____ Date_____

Teachers:

Please rate this child's behavior today during recess or other free time periods in the areas listed below. Use a separate column for each recess/free time period. Use the following ratings: 1 = excellent, 2 = good, 3 = fair, 4 = poor, and 5 = very poor. Then initial at the bottom of the column. Add any comments on the back.

Behaviors to be rated:	Recess and free time periods				
	1	2	3	4	5
Keeps hands to self; does not push, shove					
Does not tease others; no taunting/put-downs					
Follows recess/free time rules					
Gets along well with other children					
Does not fight or hit; no kicking or punching					
Teacher's initials					

Place comments on back of card

FIGURE 6.1. School behavior report cards used in the *Defiant Children Program* (DCP) to provide feedback to parents on how their child behaves at school. One card is used for classroom behavior, the other for behavior during free time. [From Barkley, R. A. (1997). *Defiant Children: A Clinician's Manual for Assessment and Parent Training.* New York: Guilford. Reprinted by permission from Russell A. Barkley and Guilford.]

(very poor). In addition, if homework compliance has been a problem, the child may be required to write the day's homework on the back of the card and have the teacher initial this as well. At home, after school, parents review the card with their child, beginning with praise for good ratings, then moving to the more negative ratings. For each negative rating (e.g., four or five), the child is asked to describe what behavior contributed, and to say what can be done the next day to prevent that same behavior from recurring. Just before leaving for school the next day, the child is reminded of the discussion, and of the plan for change.

Each day's ratings fit into the family's token economy, with tokens awarded for good ratings and fines levied for poor ratings. Every few weeks, parents meet with the teachers to review all the report cards, discuss strategies for dealing with persistent problems, and identify any report card forgeries by the child. Parental homework includes establishing the report card system and bringing all the report cards to the next session for review with the therapist.

Step 9: Handling future behavior problems. In the ninth step, the therapist reviews with parents the procedures they have learned, the ways they have been applied, and the ways they may continue to be used for future problems. Especially emphasized is a coping strategy for new behavior problems that develop. Parents are to record, for a week or so, what the child is doing wrong and what the parent is doing about it; then parents are to assess whether they have returned to older, less effective ways of responding – for example, repeating commands too often, not rewarding appropriate behavior with attention and labeled praise, stopping the special time spent with the child. In addition to correcting any slippage in their own behavior, parents may need to set up a special procedure for the new problem, applying skills learned in previous sessions. As an example, if the problem seems to occur in one particular place or situation, the four-step plan taught in Step 7 (anticipate the problem, review the rules just before entering the new situation, review the incentives for good behavior, review the consequences for inappropriate behavior) may need to be applied.

A goal of this session is to begin weaning parents away from dependence on the therapist as their problem solver. Toward this end, the therapist will begin challenging parents with hypothetical child problems and asking them to explain how they would address the problems using the skills learned in previous sessions. No homework is assigned at the end, but a one-month booster session is scheduled.

Step 10: Booster session and follow-up meetings. In the booster session (and any subsequent meetings deemed necessary), therapist and parents review the general principles taught in the DCP, the parents' experience implementing them, and any problems or questions that have arisen since the last meeting. In addition, if the child's behavior is relatively problem-free at this point, the important process of fading out the home token economy and the daily report card can begin. The home token system first drops formal recordkeeping and eventually progresses to a stage in which the child has automatic access to privileges in the absence of misbehavior. The daily report card fades to Wednesdays and Fridays only, and then is dropped altogether after the child has two successive weeks with no ratings of four or five. There may also be a need in this final session to discuss the pros and cons of stimulant medication for the child. Some therapists and families schedule a longer-term follow-up meeting, three to six months down the road, to review maintenance of the child's behavior and to address any new problems that may have arisen in the interim.

The Defiant Children Program and Other Behavioral Parent Training Programs Used for ADHD and Related Problems: Outcome Studies Testing the Effects

Behavioral intervention with parents of ADHD youth has a rather long history, although earlier work used diagnostic terminology reflecting the times, with terms like *hyperkinetic* used to describe these children and diagnostic criteria that overlapped but did not match precisely those used currently. To convey a bit of the historical flavor and the diversity of parent training approaches, we begin with a parent training study done in the mid-1970s, and we then turn to later research using the DCP program as well as some other behavioral parent training interventions.

Early test of parent training to improve school performance. An early study by O'Leary et al. (1976) included 17 "hyperkinetic" children who had high scores on a standardized teacher-report measure of hyperactivity (mean age 10 years, all of average intelligence, all in grades 3–5 of an elementary school in a lower middle-class neighborhood; no other demographic data provided). Parents of the children were randomly assigned to receive a ten-session parent training intervention ($N = 9$) or to have no treatment during the period of the study ($N = 8$). The program designed by O'Leary et al. bore some resemblance to the content of Step 8 in the DCP (see previous section). Steps of the O'Leary et al. program included (1) specifying the child's daily classroom goals; (2) praising the child for trying to achieve the goals; (3) end-of-the-day evaluation of child's behavior relevant to the goals; (4) daily school behavior report card completed by the teacher, covering both academic and social behavior; and (5) parents rewarding the child for progress toward the goals. Treatment outcome was measured via the teacher report measure noted earlier, and also by individualized ratings by teachers of the specific problems/goals most relevant to each individual child. At posttreatment, both measures showed more improvement in treated than untreated children.

Multiple baseline test of an early version of the DCP. In the early 1980s, Pollard et al. (1983) tested a parent training program involving eight two-hour sessions, derived from Barkley (1981) and from the Help for the Noncompliant Child Program (Forehand & McMahon, 1981; see Chapter 10). The program included teaching mothers ways to attend to their child's play, compliance, and independent activity while using time-out for noncompliant and disruptive behavior. Pollard et al. treated three boys, ages 6–7 (ethnicity not reported), all diagnosed with attention deficit disorder with hyperactivity (ADDH). The study design involved staggering the onset of parent training, and varying the presence/absence of stimulant medication. Parent ratings of child behavior at home, plus structured observations of videotaped parent-child interactions, provided the outcome evidence. The measures suggested that both parent training alone and medication alone were associated with reduced maternal commands and reduced reports of child problem behavior at home, and variable improvement in child compliance to commands in the observed interactions; there was no evidence that effects were improved by combining medication with parent training.

Two group design studies of parent training program based partially on the DCP. Pisterman and colleagues (1989, 1992a,b) developed another parent program based on principles from Barkley (1981) and the Forehand-McMahon (1981) Helping the Noncompliant Child program reviewed later in this book (see Chapter 10). The Pisterman et al. (1989) version involved 12 weekly sessions, ten in parent groups and two individual sessions in the clinic with the child. The content showed heavy overlap with the DCP program described earlier (Barkley, 1997). Included in the session coverage were information about the etiology, course, and treatment of ADHD; practical issues such as childproofing the home and developing support networks; and use of didactics, modeling, and role-playing to teach differential attention for appropriate behavior, appropriate parental commands, and how to use time-out for noncompliance. The final session was a review, with guidelines for managing future problems.

The sample for one study using this program (Pisterman et al., 1989) included 46 preschoolers (mean age 4, 37 boys, 39 from two-parent homes, 25 target parents without postsecondary education; ethnicity not reported), who were diagnosed with what was then called attention deficit disorder with hyperactivity (ADDH). All were randomly assigned to immediate treatment or waitlist. Outcome measures included a parent-report checklist, a child compliance task, and direct observations of parent-child interaction. A beneficial treatment effect was found on measures of parental interaction style, child management skills, and child compliance, and the effects held up at a three-month followup. On the downside, the study failed to find evidence that effects generalized to core behaviors of ADHD that were not targeted in treatment, such as inattention.

In a second study, Pisterman et al. (1992b) used another version of the 12-session parent training program in an effort to target attentional problems by rewarding children's on-task behavior, praising sustained attention to tasks, neatness, and accuracy. Participants included 45 youngsters (mean age 12, 41 boys, 7 single-parent families, mean parent education 13 years; ethnicity not reported). The children, all diagnosed with ADDH, were assigned randomly to a treatment or waitlist condition. As in Pisterman et al. (1989), the investigators found that the treatment was associated with improvements in parental behavior (fewer directive statements, more praise for compliance by the child) and child compliance, but not with improved attention allocation in the children – this despite a heavy emphasis on attention training in the revised program. Pisterman et al. speculate that the attentional problems in these youngsters may have such a powerful biological basis that psychological interventions will have very limited impact even though such interventions may work well in reducing noncompliance, which is less biologically driven.

In a third report, Pisterman et al. (1992a) reported beneficial effects of parent training on parents' psychological state. Compared to waitlisted groups, treated parents in the two studies just described reported greater reductions in parenting stress and greater increases in self-perceptions of competence. Interestingly, though, these positive changes were uncorrelated with measured improvements in actual parent and child behavior observed more objectively by the researchers.

Testing for independent and additive effects of parent training and self-control therapy. Horn et al. (1990, 1991) assembled another 12-session parent training program, this one derived from a combination of the Barkley DCP manual, Forehand and McMahon's (1981) parent program, and Patterson's (1976) parent program, *Living with Children.* The combined program appears to have included most of the elements of Barkley (1997), as described earlier, although the specific form of some of the training may have differed. An alternative treatment tested by Horn et al. was a cognitive-behavioral self-control program, derived from the work of Camp and Bash (1981), Kendall and Braswell (1985), and Meichenbaum (1977). The program used didactic instruction, modeling by therapists, guided practice, and role-plays to teach children to deal with problems by using a six-step plan: self-calming, identifying the problem, generating possible solutions, examining pros and cons of each, selecting one and trying it, and assessing how well it worked.

The sample included 34 boys and 8 girls who had been diagnosed with ADHD; average age was 9 years (range 7–11), mean IQ was slightly above average, mean family income was about $30,000 per year, and 36 of the children were Caucasian, 4 African American, 1 Hispanic, and 1 Asian. The youngsters were randomly assigned to either parent training or self-control, or a combination of the two programs. In general, results showed significant improvement in all three groups on both parent-report and teacher-report measures of child problem behavior, although only the two conditions that involved parent training showed effects on parent ratings of hyperactivity. There was a slight advantage for the combined treatment over the two individual treatments in the proportion of youngsters showing clinically significant improvement on parent-reported externalizing problems and on self-reported self-concept. However, the overall pattern of findings here, as in a similar earlier study by Horn, Ialongo et al. (1987), showed similar outcomes for the different treatments, and thus little evidence that combining parent training and self-control therapy generated more improvement than relying on either treatment alone. The inferential power of these studies was limited by the absence of a randomly assigned control condition.

Child and parent change following Barkley's Defiant Children Program. Two group-design studies have used the Barkley DCP specifically, without adding other treatment elements. In one of these, Anastopoulos et al. (1993) focused on children ages 6–11 (mean = 8), all meeting DSM III-R criteria for ADHD. The 25 boys and 9 girls were predominantly Caucasian, their families were predominantly middle class, and all but six came from two-parent families. Youngsters were assigned to immediate treatment or waitlist conditions "depending on clinic caseload limitations at the time they entered the project" (Anastopoulos et al., 1993, p. 586); if this means that children were not randomly assigned to groups, then interpretation of findings needs to be tempered. After treatment, the DCP group scored better than the waitlist group on parent-reported ADHD symptoms and on parents' reports of their own parenting stress and parental self-esteem. Clinically significant change was also more evident in these domains for the DCP group than the waitlist group.

Applying the Defiant Children Program, problem-solving and communication training, and structural family therapy to adolescents with ADHD. In a second study using the DCP, Barkley, Guevremont et al. (1992) compared program effects to the effects of two other treatment approaches. One of these, problem-solving and communication training (Robin & Foster, 1989), addresses parent-youth conflict by teaching problem-solving skills, effective communication among family members, and the identification and modification of irrational thoughts. The other treatment approach, structural family therapy, was intended to help families identify and alter maladaptive family systems (e.g., transgenerational coalitions) and interaction processes (e.g., scapegoating). The sample included 61 adolescents, ages 12–17 (mean = 14), 56 boys and 5 girls, all Caucasian, predominantly middle class, and all diagnosed with ADHD and having symptom duration of at least one year.

Cases were assigned randomly (within gender) to one of the three treatments, with no control group included in the study. In tests of both statistical and clinical significance, the three treatment conditions showed very similar patterns of change, with improvements from pretreatment to posttreatment and followup on measures of parent-adolescent communication, number of conflicts, and anger intensity as reported separately by parents and teens. Parent-reported school adjustment, parent- and youth-reported internalizing and externalizing problems, and even parent self-reports of depression all showed improvements over time as well. As in Horn et al. (1990), the absence of a no-treatment or waitlist condition in this study imposes some limits on what can be inferred about how much treatment effects surpass spontaneous improvement over time. Another concern is the modest percentage of the sample showing clinically significant change; across groups and measures, only 5–30% moved into the normal range on outcome measures by the end of treatment. Writing about these findings, Anastopoulos et al. (1996) suggest that adolescents with ADHD may be a particularly difficult group, and "may require more intensive intervention than that afforded by short-term, psychologically based, single treatment approaches" (p. 278).

Summary of the outcome evidence on behavioral parent training for ADHD. We have reviewed seven outcome studies in this chapter, one multiple baseline assessment involving three children (Pollard et al., 1983) and six group design clinical trials. The early study by O'Leary et al. (1976) helped establish the feasibility of treating child problem behavior by training parents in behavioral methods and linking parents to teachers via a daily behavioral report card. In the multiple baseline study, Pollard et al. (1983) used a parent training program based on both Barkley (1981) and Forehand and McMahon (1981), adding an emphasis on parental attending to the child's play activity and training in the use of time-out. The studies by Pisterman and colleagues (1989, 1992a,b) and Horn et al. (1990, 1991) also combined ideas from Barkley (1981) and other behavioral treatment developers (Forehand & McMahon, 1981; Patterson, 1976), producing a treatment package that resembled Barkley's (1997) most current version of the DCP in many respects. Anastopoulos et al. (1993) and Barkley et al. (1992) used the DCP manual only.

Taken together, the findings suggest that behavioral parent training can be helpful in improving parent behavior (e.g., increasing appropriate attending and rewarding), reducing parent stress, improving parents' self-esteem, increasing child compliance, and reducing adult-reports of child problem behavior. However, Pisterman et al. (1989, 1992b) found that such core symptoms of ADHD as inattention were not altered by parent training, and other studies have not offered evidence to the contrary. This is consistent with Barkley's (1997) comment that for children who have very significant ADHD symptoms before treatment, the attitude taken in DCP "...is one of training parents to 'cope' with the child's problems rather than 'cure' them" (p. 5). Another caveat offered by Barkley (1997) is that "children who are older than 12 years of age or those who are seriously aggressive and assaultive with others should not be considered candidates for this program" (p. 5). This is consistent with the relatively weak pre-to-post and follow-up findings reported with adolescents (Barkley et al., 1992). Most of the positive findings, found primarily with preschool through preadolescent samples, rest on adult-report measures rather than direct observations of child and parent behavior; and interpretation of some findings (e.g., Barkley et al., 1992; Horn et al., 1990, 1991) is complicated by the absence of a no-treatment control group, which leaves the natural time course of problems unexamined and uncontrolled. In these no-control studies, findings have generally shown similar changes in child and parent behavior across various approaches to treatment, ranging from behavioral parent training to structural family therapy to problem-solving and communication training. Looking across the various studies, the findings point to some beneficial effects of behavioral parent training but do not provide strong evidence that such training in particular produces measurably stronger effects than other approaches to treating families.

What about Kevin? Applying the Defiant Children Program

The description of Kevin, provided at the beginning of the section on ADHD, includes a number of problems that the DCP and other parent training programs are designed to address. Applying parent training to Kevin's case is a relatively straightforward process, so it is easy to imagine a therapist using the DCP with Kevin's parents.

In the first step the therapist focuses on reasons why children misbehave. Asked for their thoughts, Kevin's parents say that they feel responsible for Kevin's problems because they think "poor parenting" is a major cause of noncompliance. The therapist tries to broaden this picture, noting that misbehavior can be caused partly by child characteristics (e.g., distractibility, limited attention span, limited responsiveness to social feedback from others), partly by parent characteristics (e.g., temperament, level of patience), partly by situational factors (e.g., chores the child considers boring and wants to avoid), partly by specific stressful events (e.g., tension brought on by a hard school year or a loss of friends), and partly by interactions among these factors (e.g., mismatch between child and parent temperament combined with a stressful day at school).

One goal of the parent program is to engineer a best fit among all the different potential causal processes to reduce the probability of child misbehavior. As first steps toward this goal, the therapist works with Kevin's parents to identify specific risk factors in Kevin, the parents themselves, situational factors at home and school, and stressful events in their lives that might conspire to cause problems, and they begin thinking about changes that could reduce the impact of those risk factors. One of the first changes is embodied in the parents' first homework assignment: childproofing their home by placing toxic materials out of Kevin's reach, limiting his access to risky machines, and putting valuable, breakable family property in safe places. This concrete first step signals to Kevin's parents that this treatment program is going to address practical problems in concrete ways, not just through "talk therapy."

In the second session, the therapist focuses attention on the parents' limited success in changing Kevin's behavior through the use of approval and disapproval. Guided by the therapist, the parents write down characteristics of their best and worst job supervisors, and then discuss ways in which their relationship with Kevin resembles their best and worst supervisors' relationships with them. The parents are quick to note more similarities to their worst supervisory relationship than to their best. The therapist notes that the relationship between parent and child can influence the child's behavior in much the same ways that the relationship between supervisor and employee can influence the employee's work behavior.

To begin strengthening and warming the parent-child connection, the therapist teaches Kevin's parents to carve out a special time with him on a regular basis, for example 15–20 minutes per evening, during which Kevin takes the lead in selecting play activities and Mom and Dad attend fully while narrating what Kevin is doing, something like the way a sportscaster announces a game, and praising where appropriate. Kevin is near the top of the recommended age range for the DCP, but if all goes well, these child-focused special times will enhance the attractiveness of interactions with Mom and Dad, and thus magnify the impact of their attention, approval, and praise on Kevin's behavior.

In the third step of treatment, Kevin's parents learn to use the power of parental attention and praise to increase his appropriate behavior. One strategy is to "catch Kevin being good," and respond with positive attention and encouragement, labeled to make it clear what, specifically, they like about Kevin's behavior. They also learn that after giving Kevin instructions to carry out some activity, they should remain in the area where the activity is supposed to happen, so they can catch Kevin complying, and respond with comments such as "I really like the way you are cleaning up your room." To maximize the chance that compliance will happen, Kevin's parents also learn how to give appropriate commands (e.g., reduce distractions by turning off the TV; use simple, direct statements; make eye contact when stating the command), and ask Kevin to repeat the command to make sure he understood and remembers. Perhaps the most important part of the session is what Kevin's Mom and Dad discover about the contingencies of attention in their home. Prompted by the therapist, both parents realize that they've been paying much more attention to Kevin's inappropriate behavior than to his positive, appropriate behavior, and this may help to explain why there is so much of the inappropriate behavior. They resolve to change the pattern so that Kevin is more likely to receive attention for doing what he should do rather than for doing what he shouldn't.

The fourth step is development of a family token economy. Kevin is a bit too old for poker chips, so his parents decide to use a point system, with points recorded on a chart kept on the refrigerator. To frame the system positively, they tell Kevin that they want to make sure he gets rewarded for all of his good behavior, so they are going to give him points for such behavior, and that the points can be exchanged for special treats or privileges. The three of them work together to compile a reward list, with some items that can be awarded instantly (e.g., extra video game time) and some that require more advance planning (e.g., renting a movie, lunch at McDonald's, a fishing trip with Dad). Together, they also make a list of appropriate behavior for which Kevin will earn points, and they assign a point value to each. Some of these are positive behaviors that involve self-care or helping the family – for example, making the bed without being told (one point), setting the table before dinner (two points), helping Kevin's little sister with her second-grade homework (three points), mowing the front lawn (five points). Others involve the *absence* of negative behaviors – for example, no swearing or lying all day (one point for each day), no arguing with little sister all weekend (three points). To help Kevin work on his tendency to be sullen and irritable, they also add the option of a bonus point whenever they notice that he is showing a particularly positive attitude. In the first two weeks of the token economy, Mom and Dad emphasize giving out points for good behavior, and they do so liberally enough that Kevin earns more video game time than usual, gets two McDonald's lunches, and is well on his way to earning a fishing trip to a favorite spot with Dad. Kevin is in heaven, and his behavior at home has improved markedly.

After the first two weeks, Mom and Dad introduce the idea of penalties for inappropriate behavior. Points are subtracted from Kevin's running total for specific targeted misbehaviors that have been a problem in the past – disobeying, arguing with parents, and swearing (which Kevin sometimes does when he gets angry). Occasionally, Kevin's parents find that his problem behavior cascades – for example, with disobeying followed by arguing, which escalates into swearing. To prevent situations in which Kevin loses massive points in a single episode of this sort, the therapist teaches Mom and Dad to use a single fine per episode, and if the misbehavior continues, to use time-out. So, a typical sequence of consequences for Kevin might look like this: Mom tells Kevin to set the table for dinner and Kevin refuses, so Mom levies a two-point fine, noting it on his chart on the refrigerator; then she repeats the command, counting aloud from five down to one; at one, if Kevin has not begun to comply, she says, "If you don't clear the dishes, you are going to sit in that chair!" (pointing to the time-out chair), and she repeats the countdown from five to one; if he still has not complied, then she says, "You didn't clear the dishes like I asked; so, now you are going to the chair," and she directs him to the chair, taking him by the arm if necessary to lead him there. Time-out is quite aversive for Kevin, so she limits each time-out to 1 minute per year of age, thus 11 minutes, which to Kevin feels like eternity. At the end of the 11 minutes, Kevin must agree to set the table before he can leave time-out.

In the next session, Mom and Dad talk to the therapist about how difficult the transition to fines and time-out has been for everyone in the family, and they adjust the procedures to keep difficulties to a minimum. Kevin has been saying he needs to go to the bathroom in the middle of his time-outs; the therapist assures them that an 11-year-old should be able to hold on without accidents for a period of 11 minutes, and that they should not give in. Once during the week, Kevin simply refused to stay in time-out for the full 11 minutes, so Mom and Dad consult with the therapist on how to handle such a refusal. They agree that threatening the loss of TV privileges for the night should get Kevin's attention. Indeed, when they try this the following week, Kevin quickly returns to time-out to finish his 11 minutes rather than risk having no TV for the night.

In the seventh step of treatment, the therapist works with Kevin's parents on how to deal with his misbehavior in public places. Both parents want to be able to shop and eat out with the family, but Kevin's unruly behavior has spoiled many such outings. The therapist teaches Mom and Dad a four-step "think aloud – think ahead" strategy. First, before entering the store or restaurant, they are to state the rules Kevin is to follow (e.g., no arguing, no loud voice, no touching objects that are for sale) and have Kevin repeat the rules back to them. Second, they establish an incentive for Kevin's compliance – for example, extra points he will earn, or the privilege of a dessert in the restaurant. Third, the parents need to specify consequences for noncompliance – for example, loss of points, loss of dessert, time-out (which may take place in an unused corner of the public place, or perhaps in the car in the parking lot). Fourth, in each public place they enter, Kevin needs to be given some special responsibility, such as finding milk, salt, and a loaf of bread and bringing them to the shopping cart, or helping his little sister read the menu and decide what to order in the restaurant. This helps prevent boredom and inactivity, which can sometimes lead to bad behavior.

In the eighth treatment step, the parents and therapist make plans for the all-important connection with Kevin's school. They identify three problems that have gotten Kevin in trouble in the classroom: making inappropriate comments, blurting out answers without raising his hand, and not turning in homework. These are worded in a positive direction for entry on a Daily School Behavior Report Card. Thus, on the card, Kevin's teacher is asked to rate on a five-point scale (1 = excellent, 5 = very poor) the following: "Makes appropriate comments in class," "Raises hand before speaking," and "Turns in homework." After every school day, Kevin's parents review the card with him, first praising him for his good ratings, then discussing any negative ratings and what can be done to improve them. Points are added and subtracted for the good and bad ratings, respectively, and these changes are noted on the refrigerator chart.

In Step 9, the therapist works with Kevin's parents to identify problems likely to arise in the future, and places increasing responsibility on them for coming up with their own adjustments to the family behavioral program in response to changes in Kevin's behavior. The idea is to make them increasingly able to engineer their own solutions to problems, and less and less dependent on the therapist, who, after all, won't be working with them much longer. In a final booster session one month later, Kevin continues to have attentional problems, but his behavior is much improved both at home and at school. The improvements are marked enough that Mom, Dad, and the therapist work out a plan for gradually fading out both the daily school behavior report card and the home token economy. In addition, the persistence of Kevin's attention problems despite an otherwise successful behavioral program suggests that a possible biologically based difficulty with attention deployment and regulation may need to be addressed with stimulant medication. Kevin's parents and their therapist discuss pros and cons of medication, and the therapist offers to provide a referral to a medical specialist.

Troubleshooting: Common Treatment Problems and Recommended Solutions. Behavioral parent training can work very well, but it does not always go as smoothly as with Kevin's parents. Here are some common problems that can arise, and some useful coping strategies developed by experts.

- *Parents who miss sessions.* Sometimes parents fail to appear for appointments. To address this risk in advance, therapists are encouraged (by Barkley and others) to assess motivation and readiness for change in their initial encounter with parents, and to stress the importance of regular attendance and investment of time and energy in the training. Parents should be told that no matter how effective the program has been for others, its effectiveness with their own family will depend on how much the parents attend, practice the skills, and implement the procedures. Finally, Barkley (1997) recommends firmness. For parents in a group training program, one missed session is permitted, but only if parents have a separate makeup meeting with the therapist. After a second missed meeting, parents are discontinued from the group program and offered individual training.
- *Parents who attend but don't do the parental homework: the "breakage fee."* As discussed earlier, a failure to complete parental homework or to otherwise follow program procedures may reflect low parent motivation or low readiness for change, but a variety of other forces may be

at play as well. Therapists are encouraged to inquire until they understand the underlying reasons. Is there a time management problem requiring a reminder system? Is there marital discord requiring a very different problem-solving strategy? In addition to detective work and problem solving, therapists are encouraged by Barkley (1997) to institute a "breakage fee" (Patterson, 1982): parents leave a fixed sum of money with the therapist, and a portion of this is mailed to the parents' most hated organization each time an appointment is missed.

- *Parents who attempt the homework, but don't do it properly.* Parents who attempt the homework but do it incorrectly may do so for diverse reasons. Some parents may be too quick to assume that they understand, and thus overlook critical details. For example, in program Step 2 (discussed earlier), parents are asked to set aside 15–20 minutes per day as special time to be with the child alone and attend totally to the child's activity; parents often comment that this will be simple, since they have lots of experience playing with their child. In truth, the specifics (total attentiveness, narration and praise, avoiding questions, commands, criticism, or control) are quite exacting, and thus easy for parents to carry out incompletely. Role-plays with the therapist can help nail down the details. Another common problem arises when parents haven't yet bought the rationale behind the procedures. For example, the token system the therapist has been describing may be seen as bribery by some parents, or as unfair because it gives one child something the siblings don't get. For each of these parental concerns, Barkley has developed ways of making the case for the intervention, and these are described in the manual (Barkley, 1997). Barkley notes, for instance, that bribery is actually the offer of an incentive for an immoral or illegal act, not desirable behavior, which is what the parent is encouraging in this program. For concerns about inequity among siblings, he draws an analogy between a physical handicap requiring a prosthetic device and a behavioral handicap in the child with ADHD, which may require the behavioral prosthetic of a token system.

Behavioral Parent Training for ADHD: Scientific Issues

As the research descriptions presented earlier in this chapter suggest, the outcome studies testing effects of behavioral parent training for ADHD youngsters have a number of strengths, but also some limitations that will need attention in future research. The specific combinations of treatment elements tested have differed somewhat across the various treatment outcome studies. Barkley's DCP has been used alone (Anastopoulos et al., 1993; Barkley et al., 1992), and most of the treatment programs tested resemble the DCP in key respects; but in most of the outcome studies, authors have created their own new combination of manuals and treatment components (with elements of the DCP, Forehand & McMahon [1981] and Patterson [1976] included), thus introducing study-to-study differences in the specific parent training program being tested (see e.g., Horn et al., 1990, 1991; Pisterman et al., 1989, 1992a,b; Pollard et al., 1983). The published empirical evidence available thus far is best construed as supporting generic behavioral parent training more than any specific 'name brand' treatment program.

In general, sample sizes in the studies have been relatively small, posing a risk of somewhat unreliable effects and making it difficult to provide information of several types that will ultimately be needed to fully understand treatment effects and the types of children for whom the treatment is best suited (see next section). In addition, in some of the studies, comparisons showing negligible differences between various family-based treatments, and lacking any control group, do not provide much information on effects associated with behavioral parent training in particular. Finally, the fact that outcome measures showing treatment effects have not often included such symptoms as attentional problems, hyperactivity, and impulsivity (for exceptions, see Dubey et al., 1983; O'Leary et al., 1976), suggests that parent training, while useful in changing parent behavior (e.g., increasing alpha commands, differential attention to appropriate vs. inappropriate child behavior, and appropriate labeled praise and rewarding) and child behavior (increasing compliance with parental commands, reducing specifically targeted behavior problems), and possibly enhancing parents' self-confidence, stress-resistance, and emotional state, may not address all the core symptoms at the heart of ADHD. Research is needed to determine whether significant change in such core symptoms requires the use of stimulant medication, and whether parent training can add to the effects of medication on core symptoms (see Ialongo et al., 1993; MTA Cooperative Group, 1999; Pisterman et al., 1992b). We turn now to other issues that warrant special attention in future research.

Moderators of Outcome. Research on behavioral training for parents of youths with ADHD has not focused on moderators of outcome, but this will be an important agenda item for the future. One reason is that findings (e.g., Anastopoulos et al., 1992; Barkley et al., 1992) show that half or more of treated youngsters may fail to show reliable or clinically significant change on key outcome measures. With such a substantial number of treatment nonresponders, it is important to identify factors associated with good versus bad outcome; findings of such research can guide the search for alternative interventions for those groups who are unlikely to respond to behavioral parent training.

One potential moderator that clearly needs attention is age. Most of the parent training research has focused on the preschool through preadolescent age range. The modest results obtained in treatment of adolescents (see Barkley et al., 1992) has led some (e.g., Anastopoulos et al., 1996; Barkley,

1997b) to suggest that behavioral parent training may not work so well with parents of adolescents. One can imagine a number of reasons why this may be the case, including the fact that adolescents spend less time than younger children in their parents' sphere of influence, and may be heavily influenced by peers. Gender needs attention as a possible moderator of effects. Most of the studies to date have included girls, albeit in smaller numbers than boys, but authors have not yet compared effect magnitude for boys versus girls. Most of the studies have also included small numbers of ethnic minority youth and families. As these numbers increase, it will be increasingly possible, and important, to assess whether behavioral parent training produces different effects for different ethnic groups, as one might expect given cultural differences in values and ideas regarding appropriate parenting and ideal parent-child relationships. It is also possible, as suggested by Barkley (1997), that multiple parental characteristics (including temperament, SES, education and intelligence) predict the degree to which behavioral training will be assimilated and implemented as taught in the DCP, and even the extent to which training may need to be done with individual couples versus groups of parents.

Findings from the recent Multimodal Treatment Study of Children with ADHD (MTA study; MTA Cooperative Group, 1999), another moderator of behavioral treatment effects was identified: comorbidity. Among children with comorbid anxiety disorders, but not among those without comorbid anxiety, behavioral treatment yielded effects equal to those of stimulant medication and significantly better than usual community care. Because the behavioral intervention in the MTA study combined parent, child, and school components, the finding may or may not pertain to behavioral parent training alone; and of course any finding of a single study warrants replication before much is made of it. Still, the MTA moderator finding does highlight the need to include patterns of comorbidity among the moderators assessed in the future, especially given the high rate of companion disorders associated with ADHD.

Mediators of Change. The search for processes that may mediate change with treatment has not been a focus of much ADHD research yet. However, some potential mediators are so consistent with the logic of parent training as to cry out for assessment. Certainly, one would want to know whether changes in parent behavior (e.g., increased alpha commands and decreased beta commands, better differential attention deployment to appropriate vs. inappropriate child behavior) that are intended to result in child improvement are in fact associated with such improvements. Because the methods and outcome measures featured in much of the ADHD treatment research so closely resemble those of other parent training approaches used for conduct problems and noncompliance (as discussed in Chapters 9, 10, and 11), some of the findings suggesting possible mediators for those treatments may be relevant here. For example, Eddy and

Chamberlain (1999) did find evidence that child behavioral improvements were linked to gains in parental management skills. Research investigating the potential mediating role of parental skill acquisition and other processes proposed as causes of improvement could add significantly to the treatment literature on ADHD.

Improved Outcome Assessment: Direct Observations Needed. Outcome assessment in the ADHD research to date has relied heavily on adult reports, especially the reports of parents, who are of course not blind to treatment condition. Because parents are so actively involved in the particular form of treatment discussed in this chapter, it may be difficult for them to perceive or report no change in either their child's behavior or their own. The field needs more assessment like that carried out by Pisterman et al. (1989, 1992b) in which actual parent-child interactions are coded by trained observers, generating measures of child and parent behavior and of interaction quality (e.g., cooperation). It would also be helpful to have measures of such functional outcomes as school report card grades and whether children were placed in regular or special classes, and such service use outcomes as whether parent training reduces the likelihood of stimulant medication use. Finally, there is value in learning how enduring treatment effects are, and that question is difficult to answer with the two- to three-month follow-up assessments that have been typical in the field; moreover, when waitlisted control groups begin treatment before the follow-up period has ended (as in Anastopoulos et al., 1993), it becomes difficult to distinguish between true holding power of treatment effects and simple recovery time course that might be seen in untreated youth. Thus, there are several aspects of outcome assessment that might profitably be addressed in future investigations.

Behavioral Parent Training for ADHD: Clinical Practice Issues

Finally, we focus on issues of particular relevance to practitioners who may want to consider using behavioral training for parents of ADHD children in their own practice. A first concern is that the treatment needs to be applied within the appropriate age range; for the DCP, this means children ages 2–12 years, or children of equivalent mental abilities. Other issues relevant to practice include the following.

Clinical Representativeness of the Outcome Studies to Date. Treatment studies in the ADHD area are stronger in external validity than are studies in several of the other problem domains reviewed in this book. Although some of the studies (e.g., O'Leary et al. [1976]) used recruited samples, a much more common pattern has been for investigations to rely on referrals to clinics specializing exclusively or partly in the treatment of attentional difficulties, hyperactivity, or ADHD, and located in universities (e.g., Anastopoulos et al., 1993; Barkley et al., 1992; Horn et al., 1990) or hospitals (e.g., Pisterman, 1989, 1992a,b). Of course, the youngsters referred to such research-focused specialty clinics may differ in important ways from those who show up at community mental health clinics, the therapists are more likely to be research-oriented and familiar with manualized treatment, and the conditions under which treatment is provided tend to be arranged to facilitate research to a greater degree than in the service-oriented clinics. Nonetheless, the practice-relevance of the referred youth and the treatment conditions are certainly apt to be greater than in a typical efficacy study, and the outcome findings thus potentially more relevant to what might be seen with referred youngsters in clinical practice.

Accessibility and User-Friendliness of the Treatment Procedures. A strength of the DCP is the well-organized, clearly written treatment manual by Barkley (1997). The manual reflects 20 years of experience with the DCP in various incarnations, and it is full of practical advice on how to respond to problems and glitches as they arise. The manual comes complete with all the questionnaires, rating forms, and other measures Barkley recommends using in treatment, and also with parent handouts for each of the sessions. The handouts, also available in Spanish, serve to guide some of the sessions and to summarize the main points of all the sessions. Another advantage of the handouts is that they support treatment fidelity across families and therapists by conveying a consistent message about the main points, regardless of how the DCP material has been presented in the session.

It is not clear how much training is required for therapists to be proficient in DCP, but the clarity of the manual should help make training more efficient than for the average empirically tested treatment program. In addition, for therapists who want to become competent in DCP, Barkley and his colleagues offer training programs in locations around North America. A variety of supporting materials, including videotapes (*Understanding the Defiant Child* and *Managing the Defiant Child*), are available from Barkley for use by therapists seeking to learn the program, or as aids in providing the behavioral training to parents.

Cost. In the current climate of cost-conscious behavioral health care, the relative brevity of the program may be seen as a significant plus. With nine weekly sessions plus a possible booster and optional followup, the DCP ranks as one of the more focused and efficient of empirically tested treatments. Adding to the cost-saving possibilities is the option of carrying out the program with groups of parents rather than couples. Evidence suggests that the group format for parent training is five to six times as cost-effective as seeing individual families (Cunningham et al., 1995;

Webster-Stratton, 1984). Most evidence from parent programs in general also indicates that families are similarly satisfied with, and derive similar levels of benefit from, behaviorally oriented treatment in individual family and family group formats (see Adesso & Lipson, 1981; Christensen et al., 1980; Cunningham et al., 1995; Webster-Stratton, 1984; Webster-Stratton, Kolpacoff, & Hollinsworth, 1985; but see conflicting findings by Eyberg & Matarazzo, 1980). For these reasons, Barkley and colleagues use parent groups as the default format, moving to treatment of individual parents or couples only when this seems necessary to ensure adequate comprehension of treatment principles. Thus the program can usually be carried out efficiently and at relatively low cost.

How to Find Out More about Behavioral Parent Training for ADHD. The treatment manual for DCP is Barkley's (1997), *Defiant Children: A Clinician's Manual for Assessment and Parent Training* (2nd ed.; Guilford). A broader reference on the topic is Barkley's (1990) book, *Attention-Deficit Hyperactivity Disorder: A Handbook for Diagnosis and Treatment* (Guilford). Barkley (1995) has also written a book for parents: *Taking Charge of ADHD: The Complete, Authoritative Guide for Parents* (Guilford), and several videotapes that could be used to enhance therapist learning and enrich parent training. Among these are: (1) *Understanding the Defiant Child* (Guilford), and (2) *Managing the Defiant Child: A Guide to Parent Training* (Guilford).

7

Behavioral Programs for ADHD in Classroom and Camp Settings

As we noted in Chapter 6, many experts believe that psychosocial treatment for ADHD needs to be located not in a therapist's office but in the settings where the affected youngsters live their lives, and where their performance deficits cause problems. Training parents to implement behavioral programs at home is one way to locate treatment in real-life settings (see Chapter 6), but behavioral programs have also been placed in settings where children are learning skills in the company of peers; such settings include school classrooms, summer camps, and weekend day programs – collectively labeled "classroom and camp" programs for the purposes of this chapter.

Behavioral classroom and camp programs aim for such goals as (1) improving attention to assigned tasks; (2) reducing overactive and impulsive behavior; (3) reducing disobedience and behavior problems at school; and (4) improving learning. The programs rely heavily on basic reinforcement principles. Typically, specific behavioral goals and objectives are identified for the child, a procedure is set up to monitor target behaviors, rewards are made contingent on the desired behaviors, and unattractive consequences are attached to unwanted behaviors such as disobeying, drifting off-task, or disrupting class. These consequences may be loss of points or chips in a token economy, loss of privileges (e.g., no outdoor time during recess), or brief time-outs. A number of creative approaches have been developed. For example, Rapport et al. (1982) found that salient cues were effective. They placed a small display counter (which teachers could access by remote control) on top of the desks of overactive children. During times when the children worked on-task, teachers added points to their counter. When the children drifted off-task, teachers activated a small light on the counter and removed points – visible reminders to the children to get back to work.

This is but one example of a broad array of behavioral approaches to classroom and camp intervention that have been shown to work.

Assembling the evidence across the various approaches for their task force review of ADHD treatment studies, Pelham et al. (1998) identified 23 studies supporting the efficacy of behavioral classroom and camp programs, and they classified this general approach to ADHD treatment as well-established. In the same year, a meta-analysis of ADHD treatment outcome research (Dupaul & Eckert, 1997) identified 26 studies of school-based intervention and calculated very respectable mean effect sizes of .60 for the between-group design studies and about 1.0 for the within-group studies.

In this chapter, we will discuss some conceptual principles and procedural commonalities of school classroom and camp programs, and then we will turn to a specific exemplar of that approach, the one that is guided by the most fully developed manual – a summer camp program developed by Pelham and his colleagues (Pelham, Greiner, & Gnagy, 1998). We will discuss how such a program might be used to help Kevin, the youngster described at the beginning of this section. And we will discuss research and clinical practice issues that arise in regard to behavioral classroom and camp interventions for ADHD.

Pelham's Summer Treatment Program and Other Behavioral Programs for Classroom and Camp Settings: Conceptual Basis and Procedural Overview

The conceptual basis for classroom and camp intervention with ADHD is closely linked to the *points of performance* notion discussed in the section introduction (Chapter 6). The idea is that youngsters with ADHD suffer from performance deficits more than comprehension deficits – that is, they know what they ought to do, but often can't make themselves do it (see Barkley, 1998). Barkley (1997a, 1998) proposes that ADHD youngsters' biological abnormalities may produce a specific deficit in the ability to adjust behavior in response to commands, rules, and self-directed speech. Addressing such biologically based deficits may require putting interventions into the contexts where the most significant problems arise for the child. Prominent among such contexts are group learning situations, including classrooms, camps, and other contexts where the goal is to convey information and skills in the company of peers.

A second part of the rationale for placing interventions in group learning situations is that ADHD is often accompanied by serious conduct problems and peer relationship difficulties, both of which are often displayed in those situations, and both of which are associated with poor long-term outcomes (see Hinshaw, 1987; Pelham & Milich, 1984; Weiss & Hechtman, 1993). Because office visits with outpatient therapists have not proven very effective with such conduct and social problems, many experts favor interventions placed in the social settings where the problems arise. In such settings, contingencies can be arranged to reinforce obedience and specific solutions to social problems. Without those contingencies, ADHD children may not be able to attend closely, follow instructions, or inhibit impulsive and aggressive behavior that can cause serious problems with teachers and peers.

For the ADHD child, making adaptive and appropriate behavior possible on a regular basis may require both reminders and rewards. The classroom or camp environment can be altered to include salient cues for appropriate behavior, and to ensure that rewarding consequences follow such behavior. In addition, there may need to be adverse consequences for failing to show the appropriate behavior. Evidence suggests that such consequences, called *response cost*, improve child behavior beyond the effects of reward alone (e.g., Pffifner & O'Leary, 1993; Pfiffner et al., 1985). Each of these features – salience, reward, and response cost – can be incorporated into classroom and camp settings and coordinated by teachers, counselors, or staff. In addition, some means of providing a daily report to parents as discussed in Chapter 6 may be used to link the child's behavior in the group situation to consequences at home, thus magnifying the strength of the intervention by arranging for continuity across settings.

The majority of studies testing classroom, camp, and other group setting intervention have used some but not all of the features outlined in the previous paragraph, and most have used small samples. In this chapter, to provide a particularly complete illustration of this form of intervention, we focus on a very comprehensive program that has been used and refined over a period of two decades, and described in what is very likely the most thorough and detailed treatment manual available for behavioral intervention in group settings. The Children's Summer Treatment Program (STP), developed by William Pelham and his colleagues (1998), was based at Florida State University from 1980 to 1986, moved to Western Psychiatric Institute and Clinic of the University of Pittsburgh from 1987 through 1996, and is currently based at the State University of New York at Buffalo. For several years, the program has been replicated in other locations – the medical schools of Emory University and Vanderbilt University, and a private psychiatric hospital in Houston, Texas. In 1993, the STP was named a "Model Program for Service Delivery for Child and Family Mental Health," by the Section on Clinical Child Psychology and the Division of Child, Youth, and Family Services of the American Psychological Association (see Pelham, Greiner et al., 1996). The STP will be described here in some detail, together with treatment outcome studies addressing this program and related interventions.

Pelham's Summer Treatment Program for ADHD: In Brief

Designed for . . . . ADHD children, ages 5–15

Duration of the program . . . . 360 hours over 8 weeks of summer; parent training, Saturday treatment, and/or school followup may be added

Session length . . . . 8:00 A.M. to 5:00 P.M., every weekday, for 8 weeks

Participants . . . . Children in age-matched groups of 12, each group has 5 clinical staff

Theoretical orientation . . . . Social learning theory, operant, cognitive-behavioral

Treatment components:

1. Daily schedule for children that includes training in social skills, cooperative projects, academic subjects, arts and crafts, sports, and computer use.
2. Token economy with points/chips awarded for appropriate behavior and withdrawn for inappropriate behavior throughout the day, to be exchanged for privileges (e.g., field trips).
3. Use of appropriate commands (e.g., brief, specific) with generous reinforcement for compliance – i.e., points/chips, liberal praise by staff, public recognition, parental rewards.
4. Use of time-out and loss of privileges as consequences for specific prohibited behaviors.
5. One hour per day in a school-like classroom learning academic subjects, with token economy and consequences to support appropriate behavior and learning.
6. Peer relationship training, with daily group sessions to learn specific skills, daily cooperative group task, group problem-solving training, and buddy system to learn dyadic/friend skills.
7. Sports training, three hours/day, to learn rule-following, improve motor coordination, skill in the sport, thus to improve self-esteem and self-efficacy and reduce risk of rejection by peers.
8. Parent involvement: Weekly behavioral training sessions, near-daily parent contact with camp staff, daily report cards, with home token economy, praise, and privileges as reward.
9. Trials to assess whether stimulant medication improves child behavior beyond effects of other camp components.
10. Follow-up treatment options including Saturday treatment program, intervention in schools to which children return, and parent booster sessions.

> Classroom behavioral interventions for ADHD, in general, classified by
> Treatment Task Force as . . . . Well-established*
> Key resource for potential users . . . . Pelham, W. E., Greiner, A. R., &
> Gnagy, E. M. (1998). *Children's Summer Treatment Program Manual.*
> Buffalo: State University of New York at Buffalo.
>
> * Note: The Task Force report on ADHD (Pelham et al., 1998) concluded that two generic
>   forms of treatment, *behavioral parent training* and *behavioral interventions in the class-
>   room* (i.e., including summer camp), met criteria as well-established; individual treat-
>   ment programs (such as the Pelham Summer Treatment Program) were not classified
>   separately.

We focus on the Pelham STP here for several reasons: (1) it is unusually comprehensive, illustrating numerous specific behavioral interventions used
in classroom, camp, and other group settings; (2) it is the most thoroughly
described in an easily accessible manual (see Pelham et al., 1998); and
(3) it may be the most widely used program of its type, employed in multiple settings and over a period of two decades.

Pelham's Summer Treatment Program for ADHD: Treatment Procedures

The STP is designed for ADHD youngsters ages 5–15. Both boys and girls
are included, but given gender differences in population base rates of
ADHD, boys greatly outnumber girls in every camp. The camps are staffed
primarily by undergraduate and graduate students, supervised by a small
number of permanent staff, some at the doctoral level. In addition, developmental and educational specialists teach academic subjects, and medical
specialists consult on stimulant medication. Because the STP requires classroom space, sports fields, and play areas, the physical layout of schools is
ideal; thus, the STP rents space at schools that are on summer break to
house its activities.

The STP is viewed as "an intensive beginning to what needs to be a long-
term intervention for ADHD" (Pelham et al., 1998). Primary goals of this
intensive beginning are to improve children's peer relationships, their interactions with adults, their academic performance, and their self-efficacy.
To accomplish these goals, the STP uses an unusually full array of specific
interventions that have been found to be helpful in studies over the years.
Some 360 hours of structured child training in camp is complemented by
behavioral parent training and regular parent contact, as well as medication evaluations when needed. At the end of the camp, follow-up treatment
options include a Saturday treatment program for the children, intervention in the classrooms to which the children return, and behavioral parent

TABLE 7.1. *Illustrative Daily Schedule for One Child in the Summer Treatment Program*

Time	Activity
7:30–8:00 A.M.	Arrive at camp, greeted by counselor, backpack checked
8:00–9:00	Baseball skills training
9:00–9:15	Transition
9:15–10:15	Baseball game
10:15–10:30	Transition
10:30–11:30	Academic subject in the Learning Center
11:30–11:45	Transition
11:45–12:00 noon	Lunch
12:00–12:15 P.M.	Recess
12:15–1:15	Soccer game
1:15–1:30	Transition
1:30–2:15	Art and craft activity in the Learning Center
2:15–2:30	Cooperative task
2:30–2:45	Transition
2:45–3:45	Swimming
3:45–4:00	Transition
4:00–5:00	Computer learning center
5:00–5:30	Pick-up and departure

training booster sessions. Here we provide further details about several of the most important treatment components.

Daily Schedule, Arrival Procedures. Holding ADHD children's interest for nine consecutive hours over five successive weekdays is not an easy task. To accomplish it, the STP creates a variegated mix of activities, alternating physical exertion through team sports with academics and arts in classrooms. A typical daily schedule is shown in Table 7.1. Although the numerous activities and transitions serve to keep children engaged, each of the activities has a more substantive purpose, addressing specific problems associated with ADHD, and maximizing the likelihood of successes for the children. Even the time when children arrive for camp at the beginning of each day is carefully planned with several goals in mind. To counter negative expectations the children may bring from previous adverse group, educational, and camp experiences, staff members are trained to be friendly, enthusiastic, and energetic when greeting the children each day, and to arrange for arrival period activities that children can easily join (and thus not be rejected from) when they first get to camp (e.g., passing a soccer ball, playing catch). Staff members also check backpacks at the start of each day, to find any notes from parents, parent ratings of child behavior overnight, or cards reporting medication use. To reduce the risk of serious discipline problems, counselors also remove from the backpacks any prohibited items, for example, pocket knives or matches.

Role of Counselors: Appropriate Commands, Abundant Contingencies, Maximizing Environment. The camp experience is designed to maximize opportunities for children to succeed by following instructions, learning new skills, and being amply rewarded for their accomplishments. Counselors are key elements in the formula. Each group of 12 children is assigned a team of five counselors. The counselors receive intensive training in how to relate to the children, give instructions, and respond to appropriate and inappropriate behavior. To maximize the likelihood that instructions will be followed, the staff are trained to give commands that have characteristics such as specificity and brevity, and that have been shown to enhance child comprehension and compliance (McMahon & Forehand, 2003; see Chapter 10). To make compliance and skill learning rewarding, staff are trained to provide immediate consequences for appropriate and inappropriate behavior. Positive consequences for appropriate behavior include:

- Points or chips that are used in the camp token economy (see following paragraph)
- Positive daily report cards that are sent home to parents
- Privileges and tangible rewards, such as computer time, swim time, and field trips
- Abundant and ubiquitous social reinforcement in the form of praise and public recognition, in such forms as stickers, buttons, posted charts).

Negative consequences for inappropriate behavior include:

- Loss of points or chips
- Unfavorable report cards
- Time-out
- Loss of privileges and tangible rewards.

Some of these positive and negative consequences warrant a more detailed discussion, as follows.

Earning (and losing) points in the camp token economy. The camp token economy is in effect all day every day, so children are earning points (or chips, for ages 5–6) for their appropriate behavior and losing points for their inappropriate behavior in every activity. Some of the behaviors that earn and lose points are shown in Table 7.2. Within every team of five counselors, one is always standing to the side of the group activity with a clipboard and a point sheet, recording the points awarded to and withdrawn from each child by the other counselors. From time to time, counselors review point totals with the children to keep them apprised of the accumulating consequences of their behavior. Points earned can be exchanged for privileges

TABLE 7.2. *How to Earn Points and Lose Points within the Summer Treatment Program Token Economy*

Behaviors That Earn Points	Behaviors That Lose Points
Following rules	Violating rules
Good sportsmanship	Poor sportsmanship
Answering attention questions correctly	Answering attention questions incorrectly
Complying with requests and commands	Not complying with commands
Helping a peer	Stealing
Sharing with a peer	Interrupting
Contributing positively to group discussions	Complaining or whining
Ignoring provocations, teasing, or insults	Verbally abusing staff or peers
Bonus points for not showing negative behaviors	Cursing
	Leaving activity area without permission

(e.g., weekly field trips), public honors ("High Point Kid" status), and rewards from parents at home.

Daily report cards. As standard practice in the STP, all children receive a daily report card, a concept developed by O'Leary and colleagues in the 1970s (see e.g., O'Leary et al., 1976). Three to six specific target behaviors are identified for each individual child. Examples might be "Complains fewer than four times" and "Encourages or compliments another camper at least two times." The behaviors are listed on a card, with space arranged for the staff to rate each behavior (yes, no, or NA) for the morning and again for the afternoon. At day's end, the completed cards are sent home, where parents review the ratings and provide appropriate consequences to the child. These daily report cards serve at least three purposes:

- Providing concise daily feedback to children about their performance in the STP
- Maintaining daily communication with parents about their child's behavior and progress
- Providing a way for parents to systematically reward their children for improved behavior.

Time-out. Time-out is used for three categories of behavior: *intentional aggression*, *intentional property destruction*, and *repeated noncompliance*. Because of the unique camp situation and the absence of parents, instructions to staff are quite detailed, requiring 41 single-spaced pages in the STP manual (Pelham et al., 1998), and covering a variety of potential problem situations. What, for example, should be done if a child is stung by a bee or approached by a snarling dog during a time-out? In such instances, the child may make the sign of a T, requesting "time-out from time-out" until the problem has been solved. In addition to such details, some distinctive twists have taken shape over years of camp experience to improve compliance. As one example, the initial time-outs assigned to the children are relatively long (e.g., 20 minutes), but children are told that they can earn a 50% reduction for good behavior. The idea is to put the children in an earning situation even while they are being punished, and the result appears to be improved compliance with the rules of time-out. Even the rules for *ending* a time-out require considerable study before most staff master them. Here is one example from the manual illustrating the use of point penalties and a "sit-out" (i.e., additional time to cool down) for a child who is obviously not quite ready to leave time-out:

COUNSELOR: Doug, your time-out is finished.

CHILD: It's about f—ing time!

COUNSELOR: Doug, you lose 20 points for Verbal Abuse to Staff and 20 points for Violating Activity Rules. You're not ready to rejoin the group now so I'll come back in two minutes.

[Two minutes later . . . . .]

COUNSELOR: Doug, your two minute sit-out is over, and there are no more sit-outs. Why did you have a time-out?

CHILD: Because I ripped my homework to bits before class.

COUNSELOR: That's correct, Doug, now go stand behind Joey in the dugout.

CHILD: (Appropriately stands in line.)

COUNSELOR: Doug, you earn 10 points for Compliance. (Pelham et al., 1998, p. 149)

Payday Friday. Fridays are special in the STP program. On Friday morning, counselors announce the consequences of the children's point earnings and daily report card ratings. Children with 75% positive daily report card ratings plus cumulative weekly point totals greater than zero (i.e., earned more points than they lost) are at Level I or II, which means that they win special Friday afternoon activities, typically field trips. These may include a trip to the zoo or the city's Science Center, or a pizza lunch plus a movie. Children with more middling performance on points or daily report cards are at Level III or IV, which entitles them to a relatively normal afternoon of games and skill drills, much like what they do on Monday through Thursday. Children whose behavior during the week falls well below expectations are placed at Levels V or VI, which means they are required to do chores or other remedial activities. The stark difference between these three categories of Friday activities is quite intentional. The idea is to convey to children that their behavior has cumulative consequences, and that good behavior leads to very clearly desirable consequences. An additional aim is to help children think in terms of the midterm effects of their behavior, not just the immediate consequences within a particular situation.

Honor Roll Program. Token economies like the structured STP point system have a long history, and the evidence indicates that they generally succeed in shaping and maintaining appropriate child behavior, at least while the economies are in place (Kazdin & Bootzin, 1972). However, most intervention programs, including the STP, aim to produce behavior changes that will generalize to new situations and hold up over time after the token systems are dismantled. With this goal in view, Pelham and his colleagues (1998) devised a program called Honor Roll that encourages transition to self-maintenance of improved behavior.

Youngsters qualify for Honor Roll status by showing high levels of appropriate behavior within the standard point system, in the classroom-like Learning Centers (see next section), and on Daily Report Cards. Once in the Honor Roll program, children are given special privileges and responsibilities designed to make the Honor Roll appealing and to enhance independent behavior management. Privileges include public recognition, such as wearing an honor roll symbol on clothing, use of a personal locker, automatic 20% bonus points added to the child's earnings, private (rather than public) feedback on rule violations, a chance to help peers earn points by reporting their positive behaviors to counselors, and nine other specific perks.

Responsibilities include maintaining a high level of compliance with STP rules and standards for positive behavior, avoidance of any instance of specially targeted negative behaviors (e.g., stealing, lying, intentional aggression, or property destruction), and the particularly important task of self-monitoring. For this task, children use Honor Roll recording cards to keep track of their positive behaviors such as following activity rules, showing good sportsmanship, and finishing assignments accurately in the learning centers, and their negative behaviors such as violating rules, getting bad marks on the Daily Report Card, and lying. A key goal in this recordkeeping is to match the ratings the counselor has made for the child; so, after each activity period, the counselor and Honor Roll child meet to compare their ratings.

Youngsters whose ratings match the counselors' ratings for them across 80% of the activity periods, for two consecutive days, are elevated to a special status called "Honor Roll Star." Stars receive extra status plus daily point bonuses, and their meetings with counselors to compare ratings are stretched from 12 per day to only one at the end of each day. The clear intent of the Honor Roll and Star procedures is to reduce dependence on external, environmental structure and expand children's use of accurate self-monitoring and self-control. A transition from external to internal control should improve prospects for maintenance of behavioral gains after the STP has ended.

Social Skills Training. Peer relationship problems are prevalent and pronounced among ADHD children (Milich & Landau, 1982), and may be among the strongest predictors of long-term outcome (Pelham & Milich, 1984). Thus, peer relationships receive special attention in the STP, and in several forms. Training focuses on four core social skills emphasized by Oden and Asher (1977):

- *Communication* (e.g., talking to others about interesting things, listening to others, keeping eye contact when listening and talking)
- *Cooperation* (e.g., sharing, taking turns, being a good sport whether you win or lose)
- *Validation* (e.g., being supportive, offering help, smiling and being friendly)
- *Participation* (e.g., getting involved in group activities and paying attention, being interested in the activity, not quitting).

A 10–15-minute portion of every morning is devoted to social skills training within each group of 12 youngsters. Each of the four core skills is the primary focus on one day of each week. In a typical sequence, counselors introduce the core skill for the day, define it, lead a discussion on why it is important, and model both positive and negative examples of the skill. Then children role-play the skill, and counselors remind them of ways to earn points by showing the skill in camp, such as by sharing or taking turns appropriately.

Throughout the day, counselors watch for both positive and negative examples of the core social skills, offering praise and rewards within the token system for the positive examples, and explicitly labeling what is being praised or rewarded. In addition, counselors prompt self-evaluation by children, asking such questions as, "Were you showing good cooperation just now? How?" and "You just refused to play the game. Should you get points for participation?" Counselors also encourage peer social reinforcement, inviting individuals or the group as a whole to praise a group member for displaying one of the skills.

Daily cooperative group task. Efforts to build social skills also include a daily cooperative group task designed to teach children to work together toward common goals, and group training in problem-solving skills, based on Spivak et al. (1976) and resembling the problem-solving steps discussed in Chapters 4 and 12. When counselors identify a problem in the group that seems solvable, that problem becomes grist for the mill in a meeting. Such problems might include repeated arguing or fighting between two group members, dissatisfaction over poor quality baseball equipment, or disagreement over plans for a field trip.

Members work together to identify the problem, brainstorm possible solutions, select one of them, and then write a contract specifying (1) what the problem is, (2) what the individual group members agree to do to solve the problem, (3) what the specific consequences will be for children who do what has been agreed to, and for those who do not, and (4) a date and time for a future group meeting to evaluate how successful the solution plan has been. A special case of group problem solving occurs in cases of stealing or intentional property destruction. In these instances, the group must decide what reparation will be required of the offending child. If Max stole and ate cookies from Gretchen's backpack, the group might decide that his reparation is to apologize publicly to Gretchen and bring her extra cookies the next day.

Training in basic friendship skills. In a particular interesting wrinkle, boys and girls get practice in dyadic relationships by being assigned a buddy. They are assigned the goal of developing a close friendship with their buddy. Buddies get together regularly, pair up for organized camp activities, and meet from time to time with adult buddy coaches who help them work out any relationship problems that may develop. The idea is to teach children who may have had real difficulty maintaining friendships just what such a relationship is like, how it ebbs and flows, how to resolve interpersonal problems rather than give up on the friendship, and how to find pleasure in getting to know a peer very well. The hope is that increased skill in nurturing relationships will help the children address problems of unpopularity and loneliness that are so often the fate of youths with ADHD (Furman & Gavin, 1989).

Individualized training. Social skills training may also be individualized to fit specific vulnerabilities of individual children or groups in the camp. As one example, some children find it very hard to ignore teasing, and are frequently provoked into impulsive responses involving verbal aggression, confrontation, or fights. For such children, the STP uses a teasing module developed by Hinshaw, Henker, and Whalen (1984), and resembling some of the procedures discussed in Chapter 8 on anger control. Children first learn to identify the signs that show they are beginning to get mad (e.g., face feeling flushed, or thinking "I'm going to get him."); then they learn to use those cues as signals to catch themselves and use a self-control plan before they get so angry they can't control themselves. Each child develops his own self-control plan, helped by options suggested by counselors. For example, the counselor might suggest that a young child look away and sit on his hands, and that an older child silently count to ten, read a book, or use his self-talk. Counselors role-play provocation situations, with one taunting another (e.g., "Dumb play, meathead.") and the other "thinking aloud" so as to model the angry feelings and thoughts (e.g., "That stupid idiot – I hate his guts! I'll get him!") and the self-control plan ("OK, I better cool it, or I'll get in trouble. I'll just ignore him and read this book. Hey, it's working – I'm staying cool. Great job!"). Then the children practice their self-control plans in role-plays with one another, and these may continue from time to time throughout the STP. Counselors also look for opportunities to praise and reward children in their groups for showing the self-control skills in everyday interactions at camp, ultimately a much truer test of whether the skills have been mastered.

Classrooms and Academic Skills Training. About three hours of every camp day is spent in classrooms called learning centers. These are staffed by special education teachers and aides and designed to mimic what the children experience at school. In one classroom, for two hours, children work on academic tasks. These are individualized to fit ability level and needs, but a typical array for one hour will include three assignments – for example, silent reading for comprehension, basic math computations in multiplication and division, and language skills such as punctuation and alphabetical order. In the same hour, children do peer tutoring in reading, working on such skills as getting the main idea and predicting future outcomes. In a second hour, children work with computers, using academic software geared to their particular learning needs. In a third hour, in another classroom, the campers work on art projects such as drawing, painting, and sculpting.

While in these learning centers, children are not subject to the complex STP point system described earlier, but instead use a simpler program, more workable in a school context (patterned after Carlson, Pelham, Milich, & Dixon, 1992) in which they earn points for assignment completion and work accuracy, and lose points for violating class rules. The rules are fairly standard; examples include *work quietly, raise hand to speak or ask for help, stay on task,* and *remain in your assigned seat or area.* Learning center staff also dispense public recognition and praise to children who reach designated thresholds for total points each day.

For adolescents in the STP (through age 15), the learning centers are modeled after middle school classrooms, and the specific academic subjects are complemented by training in skills especially needed by teens in school. Examples include note-taking during lectures and strategies for effective test-taking.

Sports Skills Training. ADHD is associated with three kinds of deficits in sports: poor motor skills, poor understanding of rules, and poor rule-following (Pelham, McBurnett et al., 1990). These deficits hamper children's ability to make friends and undermine their social standing and self-esteem (Pelham & Bender, 1982). One "bonehead play" that causes the team to lose a game can damage a child's standing with peers and make the child feel worthless. Because sports skills are complex, their development requires intensive coaching and extensive practice, neither of which is feasible within an office visit model of treatment. However, a summer camp program is an ideal context for both, and both figure prominently in the STP. Of course, sports is supposed to be a part of most summer camp experiences, but the STP structures and uses sports in a very different way than other camps, since the purpose in STP is remedial and therapeutic. The orientation inclines away from a *professional model* in which the primary goal is winning, and toward a *developmental model* in which athletics is a medium for teaching children important life values, such as good sportsmanship, self-confidence, discipline, cooperation, and skill-building through practice (see Smoll & Smith, 1987).

Three hours of each camp day are devoted to sports. In one of the hours, children receive small-group skills training in an age-appropriate sport – such as teeball and dodgeball for 5–6-year-olds, soccer and basketball for ages 7 and up. Camp staff evaluate each child's specific skills, such as dribbling the basketball with the right hand, then the left, dribbling while running, shooting free throws, passing, and shooting layups. They then conduct drills to refine the skills through structured practice.

In the other two hours, children play the sports under close supervision from counselors and in conjunction with the point system and social skills training program (described earlier). For example, before the game begins, counselors hold a discussion with the children, covering the main rules for the sport they are about to play and the specific social skill that is the focus of the day, as well as ways that skill can be used in the upcoming game. For example, if the skill is validation (e.g., through being supportive), it can be practiced during the game by encouraging teammates who are about to shoot free throws, praising or high-fiving them after they make a shot or a good pass, and showing optimism during time-out coaching sessions. At the end of each game, counselors lead another discussion, reviewing progress the children made, problems that occurred during the game, ways the children used their sports skills and social skills, ways they earned and lost points by their conduct in the game, and sports skills the children need to practice in the future. Thus, recreational activities become the context for learning not only specific sports skills, but also important social and self-regulation skills.

Medication Assessment. As noted earlier, numerous studies have documented the beneficial effects of stimulant medication with ADHD youngsters. However, there is also evidence that everyday prescribing patterns do not include adequate assessment of need or monitoring of response (Gadow, 1986; Pelham, 1993; Sloan, Jensen, & Kettle, 1999). Because stimulants are an important part of the treatment package for so many ADHD youngsters, the STP is set up to address gaps in assessment and monitoring.

Medication protocols are tried with children for whom parents, staff, and the child's physician agree that problem severity warrants a stimulant trial, and there are no physical conditions that may contraindicate stimulant medication.

The procedures are used in the last six weeks of the program. The first two weeks are used to acclimate children to the camp, to establish behavioral baselines, and even to train children who do not know how to swallow pills. Training involves praising successive approximations, starting with chugs of water, then tiny candy decors, and up to larger candies, then pills. In the last six weeks, those children whose parents, staff, and physician agree that they should be medication candidates are taken through evaluation protocols that involve some days on active medication and some days on a placebo. Neither children, staff members, or parents know which days are which. Data that are routinely collected through the point system, the daily report cards, and learning center performance evaluations (e.g., assignment completion) fit perfectly into the evaluation protocol. At the end of the STP, clinical staff members meet and evaluate all this information, comparing each child's behavior on versus off meds. If a child is found to have substantially better behavior when medicated, and there have been no adverse effects, then the staff may recommend that medication be included as part of that child's continued treatment.

In past STPs (as reported by Pelham et al., 1998), just under 88% of campers have been judged appropriate candidates for medication assessments. Of the assessments that were done, about 70% led to staff recommendations for continued medication; for an additional 11%, the staff recommended medication only if behavioral interventions at home and school proved insufficient.

Parent Training. Parents participate in the STP in several ways that have already been noted. For instance, they review daily report cards and dispense rewards at home, and they talk with or send notes to counselors at the beginning of camp days. Parents also attend weekly training sessions on how to implement behavior modification programs at home. The training involves procedures similar to those used in programs by Barkley (see Chapter 6), Patterson (Chapter 9), and Forehand and McMahon (Chapter 10). While parents take part in these sessions, campers remain on site at the STP, and child care is provided for siblings. Pelham et al. (1998) report that attendance at the parent sessions runs close to 100%.

Follow-Up Treatment Options. Most experts view ADHD as a chronic, long-term condition, one that will not be "cured" by short-term intervention. Pelham and colleagues take this view as well, and they view the STP as an intensive beginning to what should be a very long-term course of treatment. They tell parents of STP children quite directly that, unless they continue treatment, the gains their children have made in the program will soon slip away. Parents are invited to consider several options for continued treatment, including (1) continued parent training; (2) interventions in the classrooms children will enter after summer vacation; (3) medication, as noted earlier; and (4) continued direct work with the children including Saturday treatment programs.

Continuing parent training is usually scheduled biweekly or monthly, ideally for a full year beyond completion of the STP. The focus is on continuing, refining, and adjusting to problems in the home-based behavioral programs parents developed during the STP. School interventions are typically designed through collaboration among the STP specialists and the children's school teachers, with input from parents. Ideally, the interventions are planned prior to the beginning of school so they can be implemented from the child's first school day. School programs address such diverse factors as classroom structure (such as location of the child's desk), assignment structure (such as assigning work in brief chunks), teacher's attention allocation (such as praising appropriate behavior and ignoring minor inappropriate behavior), daily report cards, and reward versus response-cost programs. In locations where a biweekly Saturday treatment program is available during the school year, the emphasis is primarily on maintaining learning children have done in the summer program, so the structure and activities resemble those of the STP. This includes the use of field trips as rewards; but field trip destinations include locations where the children tend to have behavioral problems. Why? To give the parents practice in using the child management skills they have learned.

Pelham's Summer Treatment Program and Other Behavioral Programs for Classroom and Camp Settings: Outcome Studies Testing the Effects

The STP is an excellent focal example for this chapter because of its long history, its extensive documentation in a detailed and clearly written treatment manual, and its use of so many different specific behavioral interventions. However, there is limited research testing the full STP. Instead, most of the relevant evidence consists of studies testing various specific interventions that have been incorporated into the STP. So, the review that follows will focus mainly on tests of these interventions. We will end, though, with a recent study of the full STP package.

Using tokens and points to improve behavior and academic performance. Extensive research has documented the beneficial effects of reward in changing children's behavior, and many of the studies involved have included children who would very likely be labeled ADHD today. Here, we note two examples of this research. In the first of these, Ayllon et al. (1975) used a multiple baseline design to assess changes in three children (a girl age 8, boys ages 9 and 10; ethnicity not reported), all in a special education class, all "diagnosed as chronically hyperactive," and all taking methylphenidate "to control their hyperactivity" (p. 139). The procedure involved two baselines, one while the children were on medication, one while they were off. Baseline periods were compared to periods on a token reinforcement system in which the teacher awarded checks on an index card for correct academic responses. The checks could be exchanged later in the day for rewards, ranging from candy and school supplies to free time and picnics in the park. During the baseline periods and during intervention, trained observers used time sampling to code the level of hyperactivity shown by the children during reading and math classes, and daily records were kept of the children's academic performance in those two subjects. Comparing baseline data on and off medication and data from the token reward system showed several interesting findings: (1) discontinuing medication was followed by a roughly fourfold increase in hyperactivity and a slight increase in reading and math performance; (2) after the reward program was introduced, hyperactivity dropped to the level achieved with medication; and (3) the reward program produced dramatic gains in reading and math performance. The authors concluded that, with the reward system, "each child performed behaviorally and academically in an optimal manner" (p. 137), and that "contingency management techniques provide a feasible alternative to medication" (p. 137).

Bowers et al. (1985) used a similar point system with six elementary school boys in a resource specialist program of a suburban public elementary school (ages 8–11, lower-middle to middle-income families; ethnicity not reported). All the boys had average to above-average IQs, but all were functioning at least one year below grade level, and all had been diagnosed with a learning disability that included attention deficit. As in the Ayllon et al. (1975) study, each child was awarded points in the form of check marks on an index card, on the child's desk. During reading class, the teacher awarded a check mark each time she looked at one of the children and saw him attending to his work. The accumulated check marks were later exchanged for money. Target outcomes included children's attention to task (coded by trained observers stationed in the classroom) and accuracy in reading assignments (correct answers to daily multiple-choice tests on the reading assignment). Both target outcomes showed significant improvements over baseline as a function of the teacher-administered point system. The study included one additional treatment condition, child self-reinforcement, quite relevant to the STP. We discuss this aspect of the study later.

Using response cost to improve behavior and school performance. Numerous studies over the past two decades have focused on the logical complement to a reward: response cost. Here we survey some representative studies of what happens when negative consequences follow inappropriate behavior.

In the most recent of these studies, Carlson and Tamm (2000) compared the effects of receiving versus losing money. The sample included 22 children diagnosed with ADHD. The youths were from middle- to lower-middle socioeconomic status, had IQ scores slightly above average, and averaged 9.7 years of age. Some 73% were male, with 68% Caucasian, 18% Latino, 5% African American, and 5% Asian. The youngsters played two video game problem-solving tasks under three conditions. In the reward condition, children were given a dime for each problem completed correctly; perfect performance earned $4.00. In the response cost condition, children started with $4.00 and lost dimes for each problem not solved correctly or not attempted during the time limit. In the no contingency condition, children neither earned nor lost dimes. Across the two tasks, both reward and cost procedures led to more correct solutions, relative to the no contingency condition. Response cost actually led to fewer errors than the reward procedure. In fact, on measures of the percent correct and number incorrect, ADHD children in the response cost condition were not reliably different from a demographically matched control group of non-ADHD elementary schoolers who did the same video tasks. On the downside, losing dimes did appear to generate lower self-rated motivation than winning dimes, at least on the less interesting of the two video tasks. The results suggest that cost is a potentially important complement to reward, but that the two types of contingency may have somewhat different specific effects, and properly calibrating the two may require considerable care.

Another way to operationally define response cost is illustrated in two reports by Rapport and colleagues (1980, 1982) and one by DuPaul et al. (1982); these investigators used a visual display (flip chart or electronic counter) of the maximum number of minutes (i.e., 20–30) the children could obtain by staying on task during academic desk-work periods. At any time the teacher observed a child not working on task, the teacher subtracted one minute from the visual display. Rapport et al. (1980) used the procedure with a 7-year-old boy and an 8-year-old girl (ethnicity not reported), both diagnosed as hyperkinetic and both treated with methylphenidate prior to the application of the behavioral procedures. In this study, varying the timing of intervention onset and offset indicated that both response cost alone and response cost plus medication increased both on-task behavior and academic performance in reading, writing, arithmetic, and spelling; medication alone was not very effective, particularly in enhancing academic performance.

This conclusion was reinforced by similar findings of another study, in which Rapport et al. (1982) used the response cost procedures with 7- and 8-year-old boys (one of low socioeconomic status, one middle socioeconomic status; ethnicity not reported), both assessed as having average intelligence, but both showing poor attention and performance in class, and both meeting DSM-III criteria for attention deficit disorder with hyperactivity. For one of the boys Rapport et al. developed an electronic counter with a small digital display, so the boy could observe numbers increasing and decreasing in response to on-task and off-task behavior. Seeing off-task behavior, the teacher cued the counter with a handheld remote, which reduced the display by one number and illuminated a red light on the counter for 15 seconds, signaling to the boy that off-task behavior had cost him a point. Using this procedure and the more manual approach, Rapport et al. (1992) found, once again, that response cost was superior to stimulant medication in raising levels of on-task behavior and improving academic performance (on phonics and arithmetic). DuPaul et al. (1992) independently replicated the beneficial effects of the electronic response-cost device used by Rapport et al. (1992); DuPaul et al. found improvements in attention to task and academic productivity, and reduced ADHD symptoms (e.g., fidgeting and vocalizing), in two ADHD boys treated in a school setting.

Effects of verbal reprimands. The most common form of discipline in most classrooms may well be the verbal reprimand. Some research has found rates of reprimands from teachers at about one every two minutes (Heller & White, 1975; White, 1975). Thus, it is very appropriate for researchers to investigate whether reprimands actually help; and many researchers have done so. As one example, Abramowitz et al. (1987) studied reprimand effects among 16 children (ages 7–9, of average intelligence, all from a middle-class suburban area, ethnicity not reported), all of whom scored high on a teacher measure of ADHD symptoms or showed significant academic deficits. The experimental manipulation took place in reading groups. Teachers scanned the class seven times per session and varied their response to off-task behavior across the various days, to create three different conditions: *no feedback* (teacher said nothing to children who were off-task), *encouragement* (teacher said something encouraging [e.g., "Try your best." "I know you can do it."] to each child who was off-task), and *reprimand* (teacher reprimanded each child who was off-task). Observers behind a one-way glass coded children's behavior as on- or off-task, and the children's accuracy on worksheets was also recorded.

Abramowitz et al. (1987) found that reprimands produced lower rates of off-task behavior and higher productivity on the worksheets than either encouragement or no feedback. In other studies, researchers have found that reprimands work best when they involve eye contact and close proximity (Van Houten et al., 1982), intensity (McAllister et al., 1969), consistency (e.g., continuous vs. intermittent; Pfiffner et al., 1985; Van Houten, 1983), brevity (Abramowitz et al., 1988) and immediacy (Abramowitz & O'Leary, 1990). In general, results of multiple studies suggest that some degree of negative consequences for inappropriate behavior is a necessary element in effective classroom management (see Rosen et al., 1984).

Effects of social skills training: a group design study. Social adjustment is complex, involving subtle skills that can be difficult to teach children. Some investigators have achieved moderate success, albeit with very limited generalization to nontreatment settings (Hinshaw, Henker, & Whalen, 1984a,b; Horn et al., 1987; Pelham & Bender, 1982). However, a recent program that resembles STP social skills training in several respects has produced rather encouraging findings. In this program, Pfiffner and McBurnett (1997) used skills-training modules focused on *good sportsmanship* (following directions and rules, taking turns, participating in games and not quitting, sharing, and saying nice things to peers), *accepting consequences* (showing a good attitude when experiencing a negative outcome), *assertiveness* (showing assertive communication rather than passivity or aggression), *ignoring provocation* (inhibiting verbal and nonverbal responses when teased or taunted), *recognizing and dealing with feelings* (including coping with anger), and *problem solving* (using a five-step procedure to work through alternative solutions and choose the best one).

Children met in groups for eight weekly sessions; in each, therapists presented the target skill dramatically, modeled it extensively, led a discussion on why and how to use the skill, and coordinated role-plays of the skill by participant children. During postsession games, children were prompted to use the targeted skills and were given token rewards ("good sports bucks") when they did so. Some of the children had the added component of a parallel parent training program in which parents were taught what their children were learning and how to support acquisition and use of the skills at home.

Pfiffner and McBurnett (1997) tested both versions of the program (children alone and children-plus-parents) with a sample of 27 ADHD children (70% boys, 96% Caucasian, ages 8–10, 70% meeting DSM-IIIR criteria for oppositional defiant disorder, all middle- to upper-middle socioeconomic status, all in regular school classrooms, 93% from two-parent families). In addition to meeting DSM-IIIR diagnostic criteria for ADHD or undifferentiated attention deficit disorder (and various comorbid conditions), the children all had very high scores on a parent rating scale for ADHD symptoms, and all were reported by parents to have disturbed peer relations. The children were assigned randomly (within gender) to receive treatment in child groups only, to have child groups supplemented by parent training, or to be in a waitlist control group.

Afterward, group comparisons showed markedly better scores for treated than control children on parent-report measures of social skills and problem behavior, and on a test of children's social skill knowledge; the effects on parent measures were clinically significant, in that they surpassed what could be explained by measurement error (Jacobson & Truax, 1991), and they represented much more movement of treated than control children into the normal range. Teacher-report measures, interpreted as an index of generalization to the school setting, showed weaker effects; but some measures of clinical significance showed significant differences favoring the treated youngsters. Interestingly, there was little evidence that adding the parent training component boosted effects beyond those produced by child training alone. Overall, the findings support the value of a social skills training program that bears numerous similarities to the one used in the STP, but the findings underscore how hard it can be to produce large effects generalizing beyond the treatment setting.

Connecting school and home via the daily report card. In Chapter 6, we reviewed a study by O'Leary et al. (1976) showing beneficial effects of a daily school behavior report card, sent from teachers to parents, combined with a full program of behavioral parent training (see also McCain & Kelley, 1993). Other research has reported beneficial effects of daily report cards in combination with both behavioral protocols and medication, in the context of the full STP program discussed earlier (see Hoza et al., 1992). How effective is the daily report card procedure when used without much other intervention? A report by Kelley and McCain (1995) sheds some light on this question. These authors worked with five elementary school children, ages 6–9, all scoring at least one SD above the mean on a parent rating scale for hyperactivity, two on stimulant medication, all referred by parents or teachers for psychological services due to problem behavior in the classroom, and all showing off-task behavior at least 35% of the time in baseline observations by researcher-trained observers.

The intervention for all five children involved notes placed on the students' desks, listing the target behaviors, "Completed Classwork Satisfactorily" and "Uses Classtime Well." The teacher rated each student on both behaviors at the end of each morning session, using ratings of "yes," "so-so," or "no," and parents delivered consequences at home each day (e.g., special snacks, Nintendo time), depending on the contract arranged with the child. As an example, one child's contract specified that reward would be earned for a minimum of one "yes" and one "so-so" rating. The study included one additional wrinkle: for randomly selected morning sessions, a response-cost component was added to the teacher ratings, in that the note on the desk contained five smiley faces linked to the "Used Classtime Well" target behavior, and a face was crossed off each time the teacher observed the child behaving inappropriately. On such occasions, the teacher would comment orally – for example, "Maria, you are not working on math. Cross off a face and begin working." On response-cost days, a number of uncrossed smiley faces were included in the contract requirements for reward at home.

Rather than pair the report card procedure with extensive parent training, Kelley and McCain (1995) explained the full system, including home consequences, in a one-hour training session with parents, children, and teachers. Effects were assessed by examining the trained observers' time-sampling records of on-task behavior as well as the percentage of classwork completed, on days when the report card was in effect and days when it was not. Both measures showed marked differences favoring report card days; three of the children showed more on-task behavior on response-cost days than other days, whereas two showed no clear difference. In general, the findings suggest beneficial effects of a daily report card procedure on hyperactive and disruptive children's classroom behavior and productivity, even with very modest parent and teacher training.

Teaching children self-evaluation: the match-the-teacher task (Drabman, Spitalnik, & O'Leary, 1973; Turkewitz, O'Leary, & Ironsmith, 1975). Studies of daily report cards and other behavioral interventions involving external evaluations and contingencies have shown changes in child behavior while the interventions are in effect; but the behavior changes often do not generalize to other life contexts, where no behavioral program exists. It is partly to address this problem of generalization that the STP includes an honor roll system in which children learn to evaluate their own behavior by trying to match their teachers' ratings. This matching procedure, like other elements of the STP, has its roots in research findings on classroom intervention. The aim, in the research and in STP, is to make gains last after structured behavioral programs (e.g., token economies) have ended by teaching children to self-evaluate rather than rely on external feedback from powerful others. Early efforts to try this with emotionally disturbed youngsters shifted from external evaluation to uncontrolled self-evaluation quite abruptly, and found that children soon (e.g., within four days) began behaving disruptively while simultaneously giving themselves high ratings (see Kaufman & O'Leary, 1972, and Santogrossi et al., 1973). Drabman et al. (1973) used a more gradual transition and had better success.

Drabman et al. worked with eight 9–10-year-old boys who were members of "Adjustment classes" for students with academic and emotional problems, all viewed as "very disruptive even in their small Adjustment classes" (p. 11), and all lagging at least one year behind in reading skills (no other demographic or clinical information on participants was provided). The procedure was carried out on late afternoons during one-hour work periods in a university lab school, by two student teachers. After 11 days of baseline observation in the setting, children were introduced to a token system in which the teachers awarded them up to five points for "good behavior" and up to five points for "completion of assignments" during 15-minute work periods. The accumulated points could be exchanged at the end of each day for fruits, cakes, candies, or money. After this system was in place and understood, children were asked to assign points to themselves, and given bonus points for matching or approximating the ratings their teachers had given them for the same 15-minute period. Once in place, this system was faded in stages, by randomly reducing the extent to which the matching process took place in the 15-minute periods.

Throughout the matching phase, the researchers interspersed control periods with no matching, to assess whether matching made a difference. For the last 12 days of the study, children continued to do self-ratings, but all comparison between teacher ratings and child ratings was discontinued; thus points were awarded based on children's self-ratings and on teacher ratings, but the two were not compared. This permitted an assessment of how well any improved behavior would hold up when matching was no longer used.

The results were encouraging. During the baseline period, the children averaged 0.86 disruptive behaviors per 20 seconds, and 83 correct answers on their academic worksheets. During the token reinforcement period (points awarded by teachers only) disruptive behavior dropped to 0.28 per 20 seconds, and correct answers rose to 130. During the matching phase, both disruptive behavior and correct answers remained better than baseline, but both were notably better in the matching periods than the control periods when no matching was done. Finally, in the 12-day self-evaluation period, when there was no advantage to matching the teacher ratings, disruptive behavior averaged less than 0.20 per 20 seconds, and the mean number of correct answers rose to 158. In other words, the matching program appeared to have helped students maintain appropriate behavior even after all checking of student self-evaluations was discontinued.

In a closely related study, Turkewitz et al. (1975) used a similar matching-plus-fading procedure with eight disruptive 7–11-year-olds (5 girls, 3 boys) attending transitional adjustment classes for students with academic and social problems (p. 578). The setting and time of day were the same as in Drabman et al. (1973), and again two student teachers carried out the procedures. The results were similar to those described in the previous paragraph. However, Turkewitz et al. also assessed whether effects generalized to the children's regular classrooms, and they found relatively little evidence that this had occurred. This highlights the challenge faced by many behavioral programs in generating change that will persist in settings, and under contingencies, that are very different from those associated with intervention.

Testing multicomponent behavioral programs using group-design studies. We turn now from tests of specific individual interventions to tests of more comprehensive multicomponent behavioral programs. The studies involved each employed group-design methods. Note that, while the programs tested in these studies have all emphasized classroom and camplike intervention, each one has included parent training and parent involvement as well. So the effects are best interpreted as reflecting the impact of training and contingencies set up in school or camp settings bolstered by additional support from parents at home.

In one of the studies, Abikoff and Gittelman (1984) (using a sample overlapping with Gittelman et al., 1980, discussed next) tested a multicomponent behavioral treatment program with 28 hyperactive 6–12-year-olds (average range IQs, low-middle socioeconomic status; majority Caucasian, but exact numbers not reported), all having elevated teacher ratings on a standard hyperactivity rating scale, and all reported by parents to have long-standing problems indicating hyperactivity. The intervention was an eight-week operant program implemented at school and in the home. Across multiple meetings with teachers and with parents, therapists explained and illustrated principles of learning theory as applied to school and home settings, including reinforcement and the use of time-out, and both teachers and therapists were provided with readings on behavioral principles and their application to children. Behavioral contracts were developed for school and home, specifying what behaviors were acceptable and unacceptable, and with rewards (e.g., special treats, money, privileges, time with a parent) in both settings made contingent on acceptable behavior. The intervention also included psychosocial counseling dealing with interpersonal and familial problems.

After the program began, trained observers watched the children in multiple 16-minute observation periods during structured academic work at school. The observers noted 14 specific types of behavior (e.g., off-task, minor motor movements, gross motor movements), and rated the children on two behavior rating scales. The study design paired each hyperactive child with a gender-matched, nonhyperactive child from the same classroom, to provide an assessment of whether behavioral training "normalized" the hyperactive youngsters – that is, whether the behavior levels of the two groups fell within predetermined thresholds for similarity. Observers made all the same observations and ratings for all the children but were not informed as to which group (hyperactive or not) any child belonged.

Findings showed that one target category of behavior – aggression – was "consistently and fully normalized" (Abikoff & Gittelman, 1984, p. 449) during the behavioral program. Noncompliance and minor motor movements showed normalization at some measurement occasions but not others, and observations of hyperactivity showed improvement. On the other hand, most of the 22 observational measures of behavior showed little or no evidence of normalization during the eight-week intervention. Of course, one might argue that normalization of aggressive behavior and measurable improvement in noncompliance, minor motor movements, and hyperactivity is not a trivial treatment benefit, and that normalization of most or all deviant behavior is too demanding a goal for an eight-week treatment of extremely hyperactive children. It is also possible that a larger dose of intervention could produce more substantial changes on more target behaviors.

Findings supporting this view come from Pelham et al. (1988) in a test of a multicomponent behavioral program lasting five months (i.e., about 2.5 times the duration of the Abikoff-Gittelman program). Pelham et al.

found more substantial evidence of behavior change in treated youngsters. In the Pelham et al. study, 22 children who showed attention deficits and hyperactivity (19 boys, 3 girls; age range 5–9, median 7; all IQs greater than 85; ethnicity not reported) received treatment involving school and home intervention with teacher and parent training, a program that was similar in several respects to Abikoff and Gittelman's, and derived from a similar research base. To assess outcomes, Pelham et al. used parent and teacher ratings and classroom observations by trained observers. The researchers also used peer nominations, asking the children to name three children they liked and three children they didn't like. Like Abikoff and Gittelman (1984), Pelham et al. (1988) found relatively little evidence of normalization in their sample; very few of the target children had posttreatment scores on the outcome measures that were "within a 'normal' range of functioning" (p. 42). Unlike Abikoff, Gittelman, and their colleagues (Abikoff & Gittelman, 1984; Gittelman et al., 1980), Pelham et al. reported that the "children who received standard, clinical behavior therapy showed statistically and clinically significant improvement on all measures" (p. 41). Thus, with an intervention more than double the duration of Abikoff and Gittelman's, Pelham and colleagues saw an apparently substantial increase in measured benefit.

By logical extension, it is possible that outcomes could be improved further via interventions that are even more encompassing than those used by Abikoff, Gittelman, Pelham, and their colleagues in their studies in the 1980s. One such approach involves immersing children in settings specially designed to maximize cues and rewards for self-control and appropriate behavior. The best example of this approach is Pelham's STP, which was tested in the final study to be reviewed in this section.

Group-design test of the full STP: comparison to medication effects (Pelham et al., 2000). The most complete test of the STP program to date was recently completed by Pelham et al. (2000). The study grew out of the Multimodal Treatment Study of Children with ADHD (MTA; see MTA Cooperative Group, 1999, discussed in the introduction to this section). Pelham et al. compared participants treated with the STP and no medication to participants who received both the STP and stimulant medication. The sample included 94 boys and 23 girls, ages 7–9 (68% Caucasian, 19% African American, 3% Latino, 11% other; mean IQ 101, median family income $40–50,000). All met formal DSM-IV criteria for ADHD. Participants all took part in an STP program at one of three large universities participating in the MTA project. All were randomly assigned to receive either behavioral treatment only or a combined treatment involving the behavioral intervention plus carefully monitored stimulant medication. The STP program followed the manualized procedures summarized earlier in this chapter. Children attended the camp weekdays from 8:00 A.M. to 5:00 P.M. for eight weeks, going through camp activities in age-matched groups of 12.

The most striking message of the study was that adding medication had relatively little incremental effect on most outcome measures. The children who received STP throughout the summer performed about as well as those who got medication plus STP, on 25 of the 30 outcome domains used in the study. In fact, if specific measures are counted, the figure is 81 of 87. There were numerous significant effects of time, indicating improvement over the successive weeks. There were almost no interactions of time by group, indicating that the two groups showed similar gains, especially on the most objective measures, such as earnings and penalties in the point system, academic productivity, and daily report cards.

The authors interpret these findings as evidence for the efficacy of the STP as a whole. The reasoning runs like this: As discussed earlier in this section of the book, extensive evidence shows that stimulant medication is a potent treatment for ADHD, and most direct comparisons in the past have shown that stimulants outperform psychological treatments. In the MTA study, the potency of medication should have been maximized, because of unusually careful monitoring and prescribing procedures and unusually large doses. This being the case, it is notable that the behavioral improvements seen with STP were not generally enhanced by the addition of a stimulant regimen. Instead, the results point to a general similarity of STP alone and STP plus the best-established treatment for ADHD, that is, stimulant medication. In this interpretation, the findings are consistent with the view that STP produces beneficial effects.

Summary of the outcome evidence on school classroom and camp-based behavioral interventions. We have reviewed a number of outcome studies in this chapter, most involving single-subject or within-group designs, a few involving group-design approaches. The participants have spanned ages 5–12, with boys predominating but girls often included. The studies provide evidence bearing on the effects of several specific components of the STP and behavioral classroom and camp intervention in general: token economies/point systems, response-cost procedures, verbal reprimands, social skills training, daily report card, and teaching children accurate self-evaluation via the match-the-teacher/counselor task. In addition, we included two studies of more comprehensive multicomponent behavioral programs, and a study testing the full STP program alone versus the STP plus stimulant medication.

The evidence reviewed provides support for acute effects of several of the specific procedures most often associated with classroom and camp-based behavioral intervention, and more comprehensive multicomponent programs. Findings of Abikoff and Gittelman's (1984) eight-week program versus Pelham et al.'s (1988) 20-week program suggest the hypothesis that effects will be more pronounced as multicomponent programs are applied for longer periods of time. And the recent findings by Pelham et al. (2002) on the STP program show at least one instance in which behavioral treatment that involves nine-hour days of environmental immersion appears to have produced effects substantial enough that not even heavy doses of stimulant medication could improve on most of them. Treatment effects have been found on measures including parent and teacher reports, peer nominations, and direct observation by trained observers stationed in classroom settings. In general, the findings offer support for acute effects, while the behavioral interventions are in effect, but there is relatively little evidence pointing to effects that last well beyond intervention termination or generalize to settings very different from those where treatment is carried out. We will return to these and other scientific and clinical issues at the end of the chapter.

What about Kevin? Applying Camp and Classroom Behavioral Training

Kevin, the 11-year-old described at the beginning of our section on ADHD, has an array of problems associated with the diagnosis and characteristics of the youngsters typically referred to the STP. Here we will assume that he lives in the vicinity of an STP program, and that his parents have been referred to the program by their pediatrician. Assessment by the STP staff shows that Kevin fits the age range and problem profile of youngsters typically seen in the program, so he is accepted for treatment.

Arriving at the school grounds where the STP will be based, Kevin and his parents see other youngsters across a broad age range, from kinder-garteners to teens who are already in high school. They learn that Kevin will spend most of his time with a group of twelve 10–12-year-olds, "the Trekkies." They also meet five counselors, most of them college students on summer break, who will work only with the Trekkies during most camp activities. Exceptions are the three hours that the Trekkies will spend in classrooms, doing reading and math, and learning to make sculptures. Kevin and his parents meet the special education teachers and their aides who will be supervising the classroom work.

Learning the point system and the daily report card. Kevin quickly figures out that doing well in camp, and getting to do special activities like field trips, requires earning points; so he sets about learning how to do that. It turns out that most points are earned by following rules and doing as the counselors say. He notices that the counselors help by saying things more simply and clearly than his parents do; whereas, his parents might say something like, "Kevin, do me a favor and put down the basketball, and come over here where I am, because we have company coming over, and I need to talk to you for a minute," his counselors would be more likely to say, "Kevin, put the ball down, and come here." When he does do what the counselors say, they almost always say something friendly, like "Good job, Kevin," and they add points to his total. Kevin has had trouble obeying his parents, but the simple wording and the chance to earn points helps him obey more often. In addition, when Kevin remembers to follow camp rules, such as waiting his turn, he gets more points. He gets still more points for showing positive behaviors, such as being a good sport and congratulating his opponents when he loses a sports event. Before the summer program, Kevin has had trouble keeping calm when he is upset over losing, and it is still hard for him; but the chance to earn points, and thus special privileges, helps him to keep his temper in check. The encouragement and praise from the counselors when he does obey, follow rules, and behave like a good sport make him feel proud of himself, too.

Of course, Kevin doesn't follow every rule, and sometimes he disobeys the counselors. On these occasions, he loses points. Sometimes he has time-outs, most often for lashing out at other Trekkies, who have learned how to push his buttons. He really hates it when they call him "mental," and his instant reaction is to lash out aggressively, but the time-outs are good reminders to get himself under control. Even the way time-outs are done at camp help him to gain control. The counselors always give him a chance to reduce the time by half if he goes straight to time-out and behaves while there.

Consequences for Kevin's behavior – good or bad – accrue both in camp and at home. For the home part, he gets a daily report card to take to his parents at the end of every camp day. The card lists four behaviors his parents and counselors agree that he should show more of, with a goal set for each: (1) obeys at least 80% of adults' instructions, (2) completes three assignments at 80% accuracy, (3) helps or compliments another camper at least two times, and (4) argues fewer than four times. Every morning and again every afternoon, counselors and teachers put "yes," "no," or NA beside the items. When Kevin gets home, his parents check the report card and give him rewards according to a menu worked out with Kevin and the counselors. For example, three "yes" ratings earn Kevin his choice of dessert after dinner, and eight "yes" ratings earn him an hour of TV time. This helps Kevin stay motivated to do well because he can earn rewards every day. It also helps Kevin's mom and dad find out how he did each day of camp.

At camp, the payoff for good behavior comes on Friday mornings, when counselors announce all the kids' point earnings and daily report card rating totals. On weeks when Kevin earns more points than he loses and gets 75% positive report card ratings, he gets to go on Friday afternoon field trips. His favorite so far has been the pizza lunch followed by a trip to the aquarium. On the downside, he still remembers his second week at camp, when his points and report card ratings were so bad that he spent Friday afternoon picking up trash from the playground while other kids went to a movie. He doesn't want that to happen again. His goal now is not only to get field trips every Friday, but to do so well that he is on the

Honor Roll. That way, he can get his picture on the Honor Roll board, wear an honor roll decal, have a personal locker for his stuff, and get extra point bonuses. One of the other Trekkies just got promoted to Honor Roll Star, by filling in ratings for his own behavior that came close to the counselor ratings for two days in a row, and he now gets more point bonuses and some other privileges. Kevin thinks this is pretty cool, and he hopes to be a Star before long.

Learning to get along with peers, and to make and keep a friend. One of Kevin's big problems has been peer relationships. He doesn't always pay close attention to conversations and thus may say inappropriate things. He also says things that offend others without realizing the impact. For example, he said to Bill, another Trekkie, "That's a stupid-looking shirt." He also has a short fuse when teased or taunted, and he gets testy and sullen when things aren't going well for him in a game. Not surprisingly, Kevin has real trouble making and keeping friends. The STP has several procedures for helping Kevin tackle his social problems.

The most pervasive way of addressing social problems in the STP is the intensive, ongoing interaction among members of the small peer group, in Kevin's case, the Trekkies. The Trekkies' counselors are continually on the lookout for appropriate social behaviors to reward with praise and points, and inappropriate behaviors to note verbally and penalize with point loss. In addition, every morning the Trekkies have a 15-minute social skills training session, in which they learn about a specific skill and role-play both positive and negative examples. Then, for the rest of the day, the counselors watch for positive and negative examples to note for the youngsters in their everyday interactions. Especially relevant to Kevin is the skill called *communication*, which includes talking to other kids about interesting things and listening carefully when others are speaking. At lunch, on the day communication was discussed and role-played, Kevin blurts out, "I'm going to Raging Waters this weekend," in the middle of a group conversation about who will play what positions in the upcoming baseball game. The counselor sees other Trekkies rolling their eyes, and comments, "Kevin, was that good communication – talking about Raging Waters when the other kids are planning the ball game?" Another social skill very relevant to Kevin is called *participation*. It involves getting in-volved in games, paying close attention to them, being interested in them, and not quitting when the going gets tough. Like communication, partici-pation is discussed in the Trekkies' group meeting, practiced in role-plays, and then noted by counselors during social activities later in the day.

For Kevin's difficulties involving peer conflict, the counselors look for incidents they can turn into group exercises in problem solving. Two boys in the Trekkies have found ways to irritate Kevin, especially with com-ments about his being "weird" and with body language suggesting he is undesirable. Kevin's characteristic response has been physical aggression.

The Trekkies meet to discuss the problem and what can be done to solve it. Together they brainstorm possible solutions, select one, and write up a contract that Kevin, Jake, and Leshawn all agree to, and sign. It calls for Jake and Leshawn to apologize to Kevin for saying disrespectful things to him, for Kevin to apologize for hitting them, and for all to shake hands. In addition, the contract calls for each boy to bring peace offerings the next day – one cookie each from Jake and Leshawn to Kevin, and one from Kevin for each of his adversaries.

For more generic help with Kevin's sensitivity, the Trekkies go through what the STP labels the teasing module. Counselors teach and role-play the skills of recognizing when teasing is making you mad, then finding a personally effective means of self-control (e.g., ignoring, counting to ten, looking away). The Trekkies break into small groups of three or four, and rehearse teasing and responding, with the help of counselors. Then the full group reassembles, and Kevin (like the other children, in turn) describes his personal plan for avoiding anger, and for dealing with the anger if it arises anyway. After hearing his self-control plan, the Trekkies help Kevin practice, by teasing him. The counselors monitor the teasing carefully to make sure it is moderate, they work with Kevin to help him think through the implementation of the plan during the teasing, and they debrief with the Trekkies afterward, to make sure everyone understands the purpose of the exercise and there are no hurt feelings.

In another part of the social skills training that Kevin's parents really like, he is paired with a "buddy," Max. Both buddies are told that their job is to learn to be friends. Max and Kevin often sit together at lunch, work together on camp projects, and sometimes help each other out during sports events (e.g., passing off to one another for layups in basketball games). Occasionally they have disagreements. When these flare up, they meet with their "buddy coach," a Trekkies counselor named Megan, who helps them talk through their issues and reach a resolution. The experience is helping Kevin to see that friendship has ups and downs, but that staying in the relationship through good times and bad is part of what it means to be a friend.

Working on academic skills. During his three hours in a classroom each day, Kevin works on math computation, language skills such as punctuation, and reading for comprehension. He also has a computer class involving video-guided activities designed to help him pay attention. And he gets to express himself in the form of sculpture. The point system is different and simpler here than in the rest of the STP. Here he earns points for completing his work assignments, and still more points for doing them correctly, and he loses points for violating class rules, such as failing to raise his hand and be recognized before speaking.

Working on sports skills. Three more hours of each day involve sports. In baseball, for example, the coaching involves identifying Kevin's specific skill deficits – such as poor batting and difficulty catching grounders – and drilling to correct them. Kevin is showing genuine improvement in his game, and his parents are persuaded that this will improve his peer status when he returns to school in the fall. In addition, the STP staff treat sports as a medium for learning life values, such as good sportsmanship, cooperation in pursuit of a team goal, and backing up a teammate. All the Trekkies' sports activities are closely monitored by counselors, who continually dispense points for displays of healthy values – such as being a good sport about losing – and positive behaviors such as validation of peers by supporting and encouraging them.

Medication evaluation. Kevin's parents have wondered for years whether he needs Ritalin, but they have never followed through. Thus, they are pleased to learn that Kevin can be in an evaluation protocol at the STP. The protocol involves having some days on active medication and other days on placebo pills, with neither Kevin, his parents, or the counselors informed as to which days are true medication days. At the end of the STP, the staff compile Kevin's records (points, report card ratings, etc.) for the various days, and discover that his point totals and ratings are markedly better on medication than off, and the records show no evidence of adverse reactions on drug days. So, the staff recommend that the parents consider medication as a part of Kevin's continued regimen after the end of STP, and they provide a referral to a local pediatrician.

Parent training and follow-up options. Throughout the STP program, Kevin's mother and father have attended weekly sessions to learn how to use behavioral procedures. They have found the sessions helpful, both in understanding how the STP works and in improving their effectiveness with Kevin at home. They decide to enroll for another year of biweekly parent sessions. In addition, they take advantage of the STP staff's offer to work out a plan with Kevin's teacher at school. In meetings with the teacher before school begins, they work out a plan for the placement of Kevin's desk (near the teacher), homework monitoring (to be sure he has the assignment written down correctly), and a daily report card she will send home (identifying three key behaviors to be rated at the end of each day). Mom and Dad work out with Kevin the menu of options they will use to reward good teacher ratings on the report card. To help ensure that Kevin retains skills he has learned in the STP, his parents also enroll him in the Saturday treatment program. This way he will get a sort of STP booster session every other week throughout the school year.

Troubleshooting: Common Treatment Problems and Recommended Solutions. Kevin's case provides an example of one child's response to a structured, camp-based, behavioral program. However, every child's response is distinctive, and some problems are virtually inevitable. Here are two common difficulties, and some solutions suggested by experts in the program. In addition, we note a problem of access that arises because of the complexity and cost of the STP program.

- *Child comorbidity and severity.* An array of problems can arise because so many children with ADHD have co-occurring disorders and problems. Children with serious conduct problems, including aggressive behavior, are more likely to require rather different intervention strategies and goals than children whose ADHD involves primarily inattention combined with depression or anxiety. To address the diverse combinations of disorders and problems, the STP manual stresses individualizing each child's treatment based on functional analysis of the child's behavior. The daily report card (DRC; see earlier discussion) offers a particularly flexible way to tailor treatment to the child's individual problem areas; items can be added to the DRC targeting depression, anxiety, or other difficulties not addressed by the standard treatment. The STP protocol also calls for adding empirically supported treatment components for comorbid conditions that are not responding to the standard treatment – increasing pleasant activities to combat depression, for example (as discussed in Chapters 4 and 5).
- *Failure by parents and teachers to follow maintenance/generalization procedures.* As noted previously, the STP includes several procedures designed to help sustain children's gains in settings outside the camp – notably home and school. Failure by parents or teachers to implement these procedures correctly can mean that gains made in summer camp will fade quickly at home or in school. When this occurs, STP experts recommend a family-based and/or school-based functional analysis to identify the contingencies that make it more rewarding for parents or teachers *not* to follow the program procedures than to follow them, followed by an effort to adjust the contingencies accordingly. Sometimes the interference is rooted in deeper problems that require their own attention in treatment, as when a parent's depression makes it hard to focus on implementing behavioral procedures; in such cases, therapists may help the adults involved connect with treatment for their own concerns and conditions.
- *Limited accessibility of treatment.* Programs like the STP are quite resource-rich and expensive, requiring ample space, skilled personnel, and substantial energy and effort at the organizational level. As a consequence, most regions have no STP, and thus most youths with ADHD will not have access to this form of treatment. Of course, this concern applies to most of the treatments described in this book, but it is particularly acute for programs like STP that require so much more to implement than therapist training and supervision alone. To address the problem, STP experts are now working with clinical service centers to help them

implement the program within their own service configurations. Building on the stability and financial base of such centers (e.g., community mental clinics), and their commitment to community-based care, may be a sound approach to outreach.

Behavioral Programs in Classroom and Camp Settings: Scientific Issues

The outcome studies reviewed in this chapter provide evidence that classroom and camp-based behavioral programs can improve the behavior of children with attention deficits and hyperactivity, many of whom qualify for a formal diagnosis of ADHD. This encouraging conclusion grows out of three decades of research, much of it by Susan and Daniel O'Leary, their students at the State University of New York at Stony Brook, and the impressive diaspora of former Stony Brook students. One of those former students, William Pelham, synthesized a variety of specific behavioral interventions, creating an intensive ADHD summer treatment program and, in the process, a distinctive model of treatment delivery quite different from the traditional office visit approach. Recent evidence on effects of the total summer package (Pelham et al., 2000) suggests that changes in child behavior over the course of the program are substantial, such that most are not significantly improved by large doses of stimulant medication.

In addition to beneficial effects, a survey of the research reveals some limitations that warrant attention in future studies. Overall, the ADHD literature on treatment in classroom and camp settings involves primarily single-subject, small sample, within-group designs that, in my view, are weaker inferentially than group-design studies involving random assignment. Where randomized group-design studies have been used, as in Pelham et al. (2002), they might have been designed in ways that support more direct inference about benefit; for example, it would have been useful if Pelham et al. could have included a direct comparison of STP youngsters to an untreated group or a usual community care group, to assess whether STP "beats" available alternatives ADHD children are most likely to receive in the absence of the program. The findings presented are consistent with that inference, but somewhat indirectly so.

Returning to the earlier studies noted in this chapter, the very reversal design of those supportive single-subject and within-group studies highlights a limitation. When studies show beneficial effects by demonstrating appropriate behavior while an intervention is in effect (e.g., reward, response cost) but a return to baseline behavior when the intervention is withdrawn, the findings are also showing that effects dissipate after treatment ends – that is, that they lack staying power. In general, the evidence does point to beneficial *acute* effects of behavioral treatments for ADHD youth, but not to effects that (1) endure over time after the intervention is terminated, or (2) generalize to settings different from the treatment context.

This limitation is acknowledged by leading ADHD researchers. It may reflect the rather intransigent biological basis of ADHD. Pelham and colleagues are quite explicit about this in discussions with parents of potential STP campers (e.g., Pelham et al., 1998). As they put it, "The STP is viewed as an intensive beginning to what needs to be a long-term intervention for ADHD. Thus, parents of potential participants are instructed that without continued treatment, the gains their children have made in the STP will be short-lived" (p. 11). Of course, practical constraints limit the extent to which treatment can be prolonged, and most STP graduates will eventually reach an age and life stage at which such behavioral treatment is no longer an option. So the challenge of making effects last and making them generalize (e.g., to new classrooms, groups of non-STP peers, and work environments) ranks as one of the most important in the field. The agenda for future research on ADHD needs to reflect this long-term objective. We turn now to some other elements of that agenda.

Moderators of Outcome. Much of the research on behavioral treatment of ADHD has focused on demonstrating effects of various interventions, and testing their relative impact (e.g., reward vs. response cost, which approach to reprimands works best). For this reason, and because a number of the studies used single-subject designs or very small groups, there has been relatively little attention thus far to the question of what child and family characteristics moderate treatment effects. Where participant characteristics have been examined in relation to outcome (e.g., Pelham et al., 2002; Pelham & Hoza, 1996), tests have shown few differences as a function of child age, presence of comorbid externalizing problems (i.e., aggression, diagnoses of oppositional defiant disorder, or conduct disorder), or family structure (i.e., single-parent vs. two-parent). It seems unlikely, though, that behavioral interventions – done singly or in combination as in the STP – have precisely equivalent effects across all child and family characteristics. Such child characteristics as gender, race or ethnicity, and intelligence may matter; and symptom pattern or subtype of ADHD – for example, whether the child is predominantly inattentive or is highly impulsive and overactive – may relate to the need for and likely benefits of various component behavioral interventions. Such possibilities remain largely open for study, to date. Researchers could contribute significantly in the future by progressively clarifying the boundary conditions within which the various treatments are most beneficial and outside of which treatment refinements or alternatives may be needed.

A related challenge for research on ADHD will be to identify predictors of response to medication in relation to behavioral treatment. Even in cases where medication does not add markedly to the impact of behavioral treatment across study groups (e.g., Pelham et al., 2002), it is possible that subsets of children may differ markedly in their response to stimulants, with some helped substantially, some unaffected, and some actually hampered in their ability to respond to the behavioral treatment by deleterious effects of medication. Pelham et al. (1998) have reported that only 50 – 67% of ADHD children have a positive response, and that of the 88% of STP youngsters who have undergone the program's medication assessments, stimulants were recommended for only 70%. All this suggests that another goal of moderator-focused research should be to identify child (and possibly family) factors that predict whether stimulant medication will enhance or weaken the impact of behavioral intervention.

Mediators of Change. The research reviewed in this chapter has not featured a systematic search for causal processes that mediate change. Implicit within much of the research, though, are various implicit candidates. For example, the use of reward and response cost may well work by changing the child's motivation for self-control and appropriate behavior, but this notion has not been tested directly. Various competence-building procedures, such as social skills training, may work by sharpening knowledge of what to do, and how to do it, in various interpersonal contexts; but we lack strong evidence thus far. Indeed, for each of the behavioral methods noted in the chapter there is likely to be an implicit change model. In the next generation of research, it will be important for treatment researchers to make these models explicit and to provide empirically sound tests (see Kazdin & Weisz, 1998, 2003; Weersing & Weisz, 2002; Weisz & Jensen, 1999).

Given the multicomponent nature of the most comprehensive classroom- and camp-based behavioral programs for ADHD, and the concomitant emphasis on teaching children a variety of skills (e.g., academic, sports, social, problem solving), another kind of mediation research may ultimately be valuable. Over time, research on such programs as the STP might include assessment of the mediational role of specific kinds of skill acquisition in relation to specific program outcomes. It seems possible, for example, that social skills acquisition mediates peer acceptance and peer status, but perhaps not academic outcomes. Outcomes in the academic sphere might be mediated by study skill changes seen in conjunction with the classroom training component (and its connection to the daily report card), but not by skills of other kinds acquired in other program components. Addressing mediation in such skill-specific and outcome-specific ways may be a complex task, but taking it on will ultimately contribute to the capacity to match child needs to program components in the most efficient way.

Improved Outcome Assessment: Need for More Extended Assessment Across More Domains. Another area warranting increased attention is outcome assessment. Given the numerous ways ADHD adversely affects children's lives, a rich array of dependent variables seems appropriate for most studies. Relevant domains include such defining symptoms as inattentiveness, impulsivity, and hyperactivity, but extend readily to disobedience at home and school, aggression toward peers and siblings, and peer rejection and failure to make or maintain friendships. To promote the fullest possible understanding of which deficits are responsive to which treatments, we need a generation of research that routinely assesses outcomes across multiple domains (see also Hoagwood, Jensen, & Petti, 1996). The recent MTA study (see MTA Cooperative Group, 1999) and associated STP assessment by Pelham et al. (2000) are particularly impressive examples of rich and variegated outcome assessment. That research was costly, and certainly not replicable in full by most researchers. Still, most investigators can find ways to diversify their assessment, attending to plausible candidate outcomes as their resources permit. Movement in this direction could be very good for the field, sharpening our picture of where treatment does and does not have an impact.

In addition to diversifying outcome assessment, researchers would do well to extend assessment across time. As noted earlier, leading ADHD researchers (e.g., Barkley, 1997; Pelham et al., 1998) agree that, although behavioral interventions in classroom, camp, and home settings can produce measurable acute effects, the evidence on holding power of effects after treatment ends is not impressive. The same researchers caution parents, at the outset of treatment, that they are embarking on a lengthy process, one that could take many years, and even extend in many cases into the adult lives of their children. This dose of reality seems important; parents need to enter the process with appropriate expectations. A useful complement to such grounding, though, would be information on the likely time course of various core problems under various treatment options. Our capacity to offer such information to parents obviously depends on substantial increases in the duration of outcome assessment beyond what has been done to date, and on the kind of multidomain assessment discussed in the previous paragraph. In the interim, it could be useful heuristically for researchers to track individuals who have passed through various treatment combinations on their path into adulthood, and for whom data on childhood functioning are available (e.g., children from early years of the STP, for whom extensive assessment data were collected upon entry) to compare outcomes across multiple domains. Longitudinal comparison of youngsters whose 'treatment careers' differed in significant ways (e.g., high vs. low medication use crossed with high vs. low reliance on behavioral treatments), with early symptom patterns controlled statistically might yield important hypotheses for study in more controlled research.

Behavioral Programs in Classroom and Camp Settings: Clinical Practice Issues

Placing behavioral interventions in classrooms makes excellent sense in a number of ways. It is in these settings that children undergo much of their basic training in paying attention, following instructions, learning, and getting along with peers. Interventions that can support acquisition and exercise of these skills have obvious value for ADHD youngsters, and placing the interventions in the classroom has self-evident ecological validity. Extending the use of behavioral treatment into summer camp settings is an innovative complement to classroom intervention. It provides an opportunity to address the most pressing deficits associated with ADHD in a single intervention, by immersing the child in an environment designed to maximize motivation and opportunity for growth and skill development. The STP is a particularly fine example of such multimodality intervention given its strong empirical base; indeed, the program is essentially a tapestry that weaves together empirically tested behavioral procedures culled from 30 years of research. Summer camp for youth is a rich tradition in many countries, and the STP pairs that tradition with intervention goals and procedures that appear to engage both children and parents. With these thoughts as a backdrop, let us turn to issues bearing on clinical implementation of classroom and camp programs.

Clinical Representativeness of the Evidence. First, we consider the extent to which the clients, settings, and interveners in the treatment outcome studies reviewed earlier are representative of real-world community interventions. As for the clients, the youngsters treated in the studies reviewed here have included some who appear to have been genuinely clinically referred (e.g., Rapport et al., 1980), others who were recruited specifically for intervention research (e.g., Abramowitz et al., 1987), and still others who were not referred for treatment but appear to have been relevant candidates because of prior placement in special classes or programs for hyperactive or inattentive children (e.g., Rosen et al., 1984); substantial numbers of the children sampled do appear to have shown problems significant enough to fairly represent referred children, and others certainly might represent the kinds of children teachers raise concerns about in parent-teacher conferences. Because the diagnostic criteria and terminology have changed so over the years, it is not clear how many of the children treated in the early studies of the 1970s and 1980s would have met DSM-IV diagnostic criteria for ADHD, but most of the youngsters were reported to show inattention and/or impulsivity, typically combined with disruptive or disobedient behavior, suggesting the presence of at least some core symptoms of ADHD.

Setting issues are more complex. A major purpose of the STP has been precisely to create a new kind of treatment setting, one in which a combination of interventions can be brought to bear concurrently. Thus, the issue of setting representativeness may be rather orthogonal to intervention research in the STP. The issue is more relevant to the many studies of specific behavioral procedures used in classroom situations, where the settings have included self-contained special education classrooms (e.g., in Ayllon et al., 1975; DuPaul et al., 1992), resource specialist programs (e.g., Bowers et al., 1985), a laboratory school for hyperactive children (Abramowitz et al., 1988), a regular classroom in a private school (e.g., Rapport et al., 1980), and a remedial summer program (less comprehensive than Pelham's STP) to which children were recruited through an ad (Abramowitz et al., 1987). Most of the settings seem appropriately representative of contexts in which real-world intervention might occur independently of research.

The issue of clinical representativeness does arise, to some degree, when we consider who the interveners have been in the classroom studies. In general, the interventions have been designed by university faculty members and their graduate students and implemented by the graduate or undergraduate students and children's teachers, often working in concert. The format for classroom interventions that seems most likely to fit into current clinical practice models is one in which the therapist works primarily with parents, ideally with some consultation with the target child's teachers, to design a behavioral procedure, and the parents are primarily responsible for working out implementation with the teacher. This particular model has not been tested well in most of the classroom research to date.

Cost and Feasibility of Deploying STP and Classroom Interventions. Perhaps the most obvious impediment to widespread use of programs like STP is their size and complexity. Large teams and extensive person-power are required. It may also appear that the cost lies beyond the reach of most communities. However, estimates from Pelham et al. (2000) are that the cost of offering an STP is about $2,500 per child – less than $6 per child per hour (see also Pelham, 1999). The per-child costs of the STP are in fact comparable to the annual cost of usual services per ADHD child in Western Pennsylvania (see Kelleher, 1998; Pelham et al., 2000). The costs, in some cases, are borne by direct and third-party payments. Past experience has shown that community demand grows quickly once such programs are established, so the cost side of the process may not be a significant obstacle.

More significant than the financial challenge may be the sheer complexity of the task faced by anyone seeking to mount a program as ambitious and comprehensive as the STP. Consulting help is available from those closely connected to the STP. Nonetheless, the individuals most responsible for establishing an STP-lookalike in a new location would face an enormous organizational task and would need to make major time commitments. As noted earlier, STP sites have been set up in other U.S. locations, so it is clear that some have exported the Pelham model. In the future, it will be useful to have data on the number of hours required to launch and run these programs, the extent to which the programs have replicated key features of the STP, and the degree to which the child outcomes generated by start-up programs resemble those of the parent STP.

Compared to replicating the STP, developing specific classroom-based interventions for ADHD youngsters – for example, reward systems with response cost and daily report cards – seems a much less daunting challenge, one that many clinicians should be able to manage as part of their usual clinical practice. For some, learning the behavioral principles and methods may require additional training, but developing a plan that links parents, teachers, and children together to support appropriate child behavior should come very naturally to many practitioners. A potential challenge here may be that of identifying teachers who are willing to buy in and faithfully implement behavioral programs for individual children when doing so adds to their workload and offers them little or no external incentive for all the effort.

Accessibility of Procedural Information and Training. Practitioners who want to use some of the methods described in this chapter will find considerable support. Although separate formal manuals are not available for most of the specific classroom procedures tested in the 1970s and 1980s, the procedures are generally described clearly in the published articles cited here, and those articles are available in most university libraries. For the most part, the procedures were designed with simplicity as a goal, to ensure that busy teachers could execute them correctly in the midst of their other activities, and that children could detect the contingencies involved. Their simplicity should make most of the procedures readily applicable to classrooms of today, provided teachers are willing. Finally, although manuals for the various classroom procedures are not available from the authors of the original studies, many of the procedures are described in detail in the unusually thorough program manual developed for the STP (Pelham et al., 1998), to which we now turn.

The most comprehensive and fully researched ADHD program using the day camp format is Pelham's STP, and the manual detailing STP procedures (Pelham et al., 1998) is impressively detailed. In 429 pages, written with impressive clarity and packed with vivid and detailed examples from past STPs, the manual guides readers through the specific procedures used in each treatment component (point system, time-out, peer interventions, daily report cards, classroom learning centers, etc.), ways to individualize programs to fit specific children, steps used for medication assessment, methods for training STP staff and allocating staff responsibilities, and administrative procedures used in coordinating the camp. The manual clearly reflects enormous and sustained effort. Indeed, the 1998 version is the twelfth revision since the original in 1985. It will be a valuable resource for professionals who want to consider developing summer treatment programs in their own area.

The STP manual and the method descriptions in published articles can be complemented by training programs offered in various locations by William Pelham and colleagues (see next section). Some of the specific classroom-based procedures (e.g., daily report card) are discussed in other workshops on behavioral intervention with ADHD and disruptive children, led by other experts (e.g., Russell Barkley, as discussed in Chapter 6). Thus, considerable support is available, in both written and workshop form, for professionals who want to learn more about the methods described in this chapter.

How to Learn More about Behavioral Programs in Classroom and Camp Settings. How-to descriptions of many of the specific classroom procedures discussed in the chapter are presented briefly and clearly in Linda Pfiffner's book for teachers on the front line, *All About ADHD: The Complete Practical Guide for Teachers* (Scholastic Professional Books, 1996). Further information can be found in George DuPaul and G. Stoner's, *ADHD in the Schools: Assessment and Intervention Strategies* (Guilford, 1994). For an overview of the STP (including typical daily schedule and main treatment components), measures used to assess its effects, and preliminary findings with those measures, see William Pelham and Betsy Hoza's chapter entitled, "Intensive Treatment: A Summer Treatment Program for Children with ADHD," in the book, *Psychosocial Treatments for Child and Adolescent Disorders: Empirically Based Strategies for Clinical Practice* (1996, American Psychological Association, edited by Euthymia D. Hibbs and Peter S. Jensen). For a detailed picture of the full STP, including not only program details but also procedures for training staff and administering the program, see the richly detailed *Children's Summer Treatment Program Manual*, by William Pelham, Andrew Greiner, and Elizabeth Gnagy (1998), published by William Pelham at the Department of Psychology, State University of New York at Buffalo. The program manual, as well as information on STP training programs and on summer program availability, for potential staff members and for potential campers and their families, can now be found at http://wings.buffalo.edu/psychology/adhd).

TREATMENTS FOR CONDUCT PROBLEMS AND CONDUCT DISORDER

Introduction to Section E

The Case of Sal and Treatments for Conduct Problems and Conduct Disorder

Sal

Sal, age 13, has a reputation to protect – his own, as a bad dude. He gets in trouble at school almost every week, sometimes for disobeying a school rule, sometimes for blurting out provocative comments in class, and frequently for getting into shoving matches or outright fights with other kids. He has been suspended three times, once for stealing money from another child's backpack, once for hitting another child with a stick and drawing blood, and once for shouting profanity at a teacher who was disciplining him.

One of Sal's problems is his very short fuse. He is quick to take offense, quick to assume that others mean him harm, and quick to interpret ambiguous events in a negative light. Recently, when another boy accidentally collided with him on the school playground, Sal's first response was a punch in the face and a kick in the ribs when the boy fell to the ground. Understandably, most of Sal's peers at school actively avoid him, and his only "friends" are other youngsters with conduct problems like his own; two of the youth in this deviant peer group have already been arrested once, and both are suspected of being gang members.

Sal's problems at school are paralleled by disobedient, disruptive behavior at home, which dates all the way back to the preschool years. At home he is difficult to manage and full of attitude, particularly with his mother, with whom he has never developed a close relationship. He insults her cooking, mocks what he calls her "lesbian friends," ignores her requests to clean his room and help with chores, stays out as late as he wants, and generally does what he chooses. His mother's repeated requests for better behavior take the form of nagging, and often shouting when she loses her temper, but all this is mere background noise to Sal. On the rare occasions when Sal is cooperative, she holds her breath and avoids commenting on his good behavior, for fear of breaking the spell. Sal's father is uninvolved; he watches television, drinks a lot of beer, orders Sal's mother around, and has a sort of mutual ignoring relationship with his son. In this climate, Sal is increasingly out of control, dabbling in progressively riskier behavior with his delinquent peers, and neighbors suspect that he is on his way to a criminal career.

Conduct problems – aggression toward peers, disobedience and disruptive behavior at home and school, and defiance of authority – are currently a source of great concern in western societies, and the prevalence of such problems appears to be increasing (Achenbach & Howell, 1993). Indeed, in the United States, rates of aggression, assault, and even homicide by children and adolescents have mushroomed (Richters, 1993), and rates of incarceration are climbing (Hinshaw & Anderson, 1996). Such shocks as the murders of students and teachers by armed youths in schools in Colorado, Arkansas, and elsewhere in the United States in the late 1990s (see Gibbs, 1999), served as wake-up calls to the populace, a reminder of the extremes to which aggressive tendencies can be taken if they are not curbed successfully in childhood.

Conduct problems are the most common reason for child clinical referrals in North America (Hinshaw & Anderson, 1996; Weisz, Suwanlert, Chaiyasit, & Walter, 1987). Of course, this is partly due to the high prevalence of such problems. Formal diagnoses of conduct disorder are found in 2–6% of school-aged youth in community samples (see Hinshaw & Anderson, 1996; Zoccolillo, 1993); rates of oppositional defiant disorder are found to be uniformly higher, with estimates ranging from 10–22% in the general population (Nottelman & Jensen, 1995). However, other evidence (Weisz & Weiss, 1991) indicates that even when problem prevalence in the general population is controlled, conduct problems are much more likely than most other problems to be the reason children are taken to American clinics for treatment. This fact, together with the obviously high stakes for society, may help account for the high activity level among researchers in developing treatments for conduct problems.

One of the most consistent findings of research on conduct problems is that such problems are depressingly persistent across developmental periods (see Eyberg, Edwards, Boggs, & Foote, 1998). Even children as young as 2–3 years old who show high levels of behavior problems across different settings are at risk for continued behavior problems (Campbell & Ewing, 1990; Egeland, Kalkoske, Gottesman, & Erickson, 1990). And conduct problems that are stable by the time of school entry are likely to persist into adolescence. The bad news, overall, is that conduct problems in early life predict subsequent delinquency and criminal behavior, underscoring the need for treatments that work with children.

The challenge of understanding and treating conduct problems is complicated by the heterogeneity of such problems and the youth who display them, and by the fact that multiple causes (biological, cognitive, interpersonal, sociological) interact to produce the problems (see Frick, 1998). A particularly worrisome trend is the developmental progression of conduct problems from childhood through adolescence, with early oppositional behavior presaging later more sinister forms, including fighting and vandalism at the intermediate level, and stealing and mugging at the high end (see Lahey & Loeber, 1994).

Many experts agree that any search for a simple causal explanation is doomed from the outset. Similarly, any search for a single magic bullet, one treatment that can address all forms of disruptive and deviant conduct, may be a frustrating process. It is quite possible that various treatment approaches differ in their impact on different subsets of youth, depending in part on which factors converge to maintain the various youngsters' conduct problems. Thus, it may be quite fortunate that the treatments developed and tested thus far are such a remarkably variegated collection, focused on various target problems and addressing various hypothesized causal and maintaining factors.

Given their diversity of forms and likely origins, it certainly is not surprising that problems of conduct have been construed and studied in diverse ways by various investigators. Some have focused on simple descriptive distinctions, such as verbal versus physical aggression, while others have distinguished between more subtle but theoretically significant subforms – for example, instrumental versus hostile (e.g., Feshbach, 1970), overt versus covert (e.g., Loeber, 1990), direct versus indirect (Bjorkqvist, Osterman, & Kaukiainen, 1992), reactive versus proactive (e.g., Dodge & Coie, 1987). Conduct problems have also been conceptualized rather differently within different psychopathology taxonomies. In one popular dimensional taxonomy problematic conduct has been located within narrowband Aggression and Delinquency syndrome scales derived from the Child Behavior Checklist (see Achenbach, 1991). In the categorical approach represented by the DSM-IV, conduct problems in youth have been organized into formal diagnostic categories, most notably Oppositional Defiant Disorder (a pattern of persistently negative, hostile, and defiant behavior) and Conduct Disorder (a persistent pattern of behavior violating the rights of others or major age-appropriate societal norms). As will be described in this section of the book, treatment approaches for conduct problems have been organized around diverse ways construing and classifying conduct problems. Because the DSM-IV was only published in 1994, most of the treatment research we will review, which began prior to that year, was not organized around that particular way of classifying problems.

The treatments, as will soon be evident, range from very focused efforts to teach anger control, to broad efforts to revamp the family and social ecology of the errant child's life. In Chapter 8, we consider an approach that focuses on treating youths directly. Chapter 9, Chapter 10, and Chapter 11 deal with approaches that emphasize parent training. In Chapter 12, we examine a program that combines youth-focused and parent-focused treatments. In Chapter 13, we discuss a treatment approach that intervenes within multiple systems that touch the youth's life. By the end of this section, it should be quite clear that the domain of conduct problems and conduct disorder offers an unusually rich array of evidence-based treatment options spanning a broad developmental range.

8

Treating Conduct Problems by Teaching Anger Control

Conduct problems have many causes, but it is often possible to spot flash points at which behavior gets out of control. One of the most common is the burst of anger, during which rational problem solving and self-control are abandoned, and aggressive behavior erupts. The case of Sal illustrates how this works. Quick to assume that others mean him harm, he explodes in a fury at the slightest evidence of disrespect, or at an ambiguous encounter with a peer. One way to treat conduct problems like Sal's is to defuse the explosives before they ignite.

A tendency to give in to angry impulses has been the target of considerable clinical research on aggressive behavior. Rule and Nesdale (1976) reported that anger arousal operated as a mediator of aggressive behavior, and Bandura (1973) and Camp (1977) offered evidence that poor verbal skills for coping with stress, and insufficient cognitive processing of stressful events, may lead to anger and aggression. Building on such notions, investigators have developed two partially overlapping treatment programs intended to reduce aggression by helping young people overcome their tendency toward angry outbursts. Here we describe the two programs and the evidence on their effects.

Anger Control Training with Stress Inoculation: Conceptual Basis and Procedural Overview

The first of the two programs, Anger Control Training with Stress Inoculation (Feindler et al., 1984; Schlichter & Horan, 1981), appears to be built on an important two-part assumption – the idea that an explosive style can arise in part because of deficits in youngsters' understanding of the factors that spark their angry arousal, and in part because of a failure to learn coping skills – or at least a failure to establish the skills firmly enough to withstand the force of real-life challenges. The treatment program is designed to fill these gaps.

Toward this end, therapists first try to help youngsters understand the nature, causes, and consequences of anger, especially their own. Then therapy builds on the notion of stress inoculation (see Meichenbaum, 1977; Novaco, 1975); young people are exposed to manageable doses of provocation, in response to which they practice their coping skills, guided by the therapists. The program is designed to reduce angry, explosive behavior by increasing understanding of the behavior and by providing practice in the use of tailor-made coping skills. This approach was initially applied to delinquent adolescent boys by Schlichter and Horan (1981), and later adapted for use with disruptive junior high students by Feindler et al. (1984; following a dissertation by Feindler, 1979).

In the original program design, assembled by Schlichter and Horan (1981), there are three phases, presumably intended to address deficits among anger-prone groups. An educational phase teaches clients about the causes and consequences of anger, and about alternative methods of control. This is followed by training in specific coping skills, and then by role-play exercises to provide practice in those skills.

Anger Control Training with Stress Inoculation: In Brief

Designed for . . . . Delinquent, disruptive adolescents
 ages 12–18
Number of sessions . . . . 10 (range: 20–25)
Session length . . . . 50–60 minutes
Session participants . . . . Therapist with youth,
 individually or in small groups
Theoretical orientation . . . . Cognitive-behavioral

Treatment steps:

1. Therapist teaches youth about the nature of anger by analyzing recent episodes of client's anger – noting causes, nature of specific angry behaviors, and consequences to youth.
2. Youth self-monitors anger episodes and constructs "anger hierarchy."
3. Youth learns multiple methods for reducing angry arousal – e.g., count backward, induce relaxation, use positive imagery, repeat self-instructions not to explode, use assertiveness.
4. Therapist models techniques for youth in role-plays.
5. Youth practices techniques in role-plays, using increasingly potent anger triggers from hierarchy (see Step 2).

Treatment classified by Treatment Task Force as . . . . Probably Efficacious (Brestan & Eyberg, 1998)

Key resources for potential users . . . . Feindler, E. L., & Guttman, J. (1994). Cognitive-behavioral anger control training for groups of adolescents: A treatment manual. In C. W. LeCroy (Ed.), *Handbook of Child and Adolescent Treatment Manuals.* New York: Lexington Books.

Feindler, E. L., & Ovens, D. (1998). *Cognitive-Behavioral Group Anger Management for Youth.* Unpublished treatment manual (can be ordered from Psychological Services Center, LIU/C.W. Post Campus, 720 Northern Boulevard – Post Hall, Brookville, New York 11548-1300.

Anger Control Training with Stress Inoculation: Treatment Procedures

The treatment approach has evolved to some degree across the studies testing it. In the first variant of the program, tested by Schlichter and Horan (1981), youngsters are seen individually, in one-hour sessions, twice weekly for five weeks. Early sessions focus on teaching about the nature of anger by analyzing actual recent episodes. The youngsters talk about times they got angry, identify causes of the anger, note the specifics of their own angry responses, and discuss consequences to which their anger led. These personal accounts are complemented by construction of a six-item anger hierarchy, which is used later to design role-play practice sessions.

Participants are taught multiple coping strategies for reducing angry arousal – for example, backward counting when provoked, use of relaxation and pleasant imagery, and self-instructions aimed at guiding both overt and covert behavior in appropriate (i.e., non-explosive) directions. Another part of coping training focuses on how to be assertive without being aggressive – that is, ways to directly state one's wishes so as to be heard, without giving way to anger and without displaying aggression. Participants are also taught to reward themselves for use of the program elements.

Therapists model the techniques for their young clients, and learning is reinforced by role-plays, intended partly to serve as stress inoculation. Clients first play the role of provoker, with therapists demonstrating how to use various coping methods for dealing with provocation. Then roles are reversed. Therapists provide feedback and coaching during the role-plays. This training format is first applied to items low in the individual's anger hierarchy, then to progressively more stressful items, up to the most potent anger triggers in the hierarchy.

Building on the work of Schlichter and Horan (1981), Feindler et al. (1984) developed a group form of the stress inoculation program, designed for groups of up to six students led by two cotherapists. The program involves ten biweekly 50-minute sessions. Students are taught general self-control strategies, and they develop additional strategies specific to their own aggressive encounters. The initial treatment phase focuses on immediate suppression of both verbal and nonverbal aggressive responses to provocation. As in Schlichter and Horan (1981), participants are taught to do self-monitoring in which they identify components of provocation cycles – that is, anger cue → aggressive response → consequent events. Each youngster keeps a personal log of provocation episodes and their components, and these logs are used to track changes in their own ways of responding.

To generate early improvements, therapists begin by teaching two simple time-out responses to provocation: (1) insert a time delay between the provoking stimulus and the response, and (2) ignore the provoking stimulus for a few seconds. Then youngsters are taught to insert brief relaxation and deep breaths into the time delay to reduce arousal. Instruction and practice also focus on replacing aggression with appropriate nonverbal and verbal assertive responses, so as to obtain desired outcomes in interpersonal interactions. Assertiveness training includes replacing such aggressive responses as staring, making demands and threatening gestures, and using harsh tones, with such specific alternatives as using nonthreatening direct eye contact, requesting a change in the other person's behavior, using appropriate gestures, and using a modulated tone of voice.

The training also includes problem-solving techniques derived from Shure and Spivack (1972). These include specifying exactly what the problem is, generating alternative solutions, listing the possible consequences of each alternative, trying out the alternatives, and evaluating how each one that was tried actually worked (as described in Chapter 12). These steps are rehearsed in the sessions, and applied whenever possible to typical school and home conflict situations.

A third cluster of skills entails cognitive controls. Four techniques are involved.

1. *Self-instructions*, regarding how to behave – for example, "I'm gonna ignore this guy and keep cool."
2. *Covert modication of cognitions*, designed to reframe anger-arousing situations – for example, "This kid is just jealous because I did well on my test."
3. *Self-evaluation* of performance during conflict situations – for example, "How did I handle myself? How did things turn out?"
4. *Think ahead*, anticipating upcoming situations that might prompt angry arousal, and planning appropriate self-control behaviors – for example, "If he insults me, I'll walk away from it."

As in Shlichter and Horan (1981), the sessions involve didactic presentation of the coping skills, followed by modeling of those skills by the therapists, and then structured behavioral rehearsal with active participation by the youngsters themselves. The conflict situations used for these role-plays are taken from information provided by the youths about their own real-life conflicts.

Therapists also use the barb technique (Kaufman & Wagner, 1976), in which they gradually increase the intensity of specific provocations, and gradually decrease prompts to prepare for the provocations. The idea is to firm up each youngster's ability to use the anger coping skills when there is no therapist handy to provide instructions, and to strengthen the skills enough so that they will work with even the most incendiary provocations. Transfer of learned skills is further encouraged through homework assignments in which youngsters apply their self-control skills in real-life problem situations outside therapy, and document their behavior and its consequences for discussion in later sessions.

Anger Control Training with Stress Inoculation: Outcome Studies Testing the Effects

Here we review three studies testing the impact of anger control training with stress inoculation.

Testing the individually administered program with incarcerated delinquent youth. In the first published study of the anger control treatment, Schlichter and Horan (1981) focused on a particularly appropriate target group: adjudicated delinquent boys, ages 13–18 (ethnicity not reported), who had been committed to a correctional facility, had preinstitutional histories of verbal and/or physical aggression, and had been nominated by two independent youth workers as exhibiting significant anger control problems within their institution. The 40 youths identified as the most difficult in the institution were invited to participate in the study; the 38 who agreed to do so were randomly assigned to receive (1) the full stress inoculation treatment program (see previous section); (2) an attenuated "treatment elements" version that included relaxation as the only coping skill taught, and used abbreviated role-plays without modeling by therapists; or (3) no treatment.

After treatment, the youngsters who had received the full treatment program scored better than untreated youths on three self-report anger and aggression scales and on verbal aggression in laboratory role-played provocations. Interestingly, the attenuated version of treatment showed effects similar to those of the full treatment; both active treatments outperformed the no treatment control condition on self-report measures, but on the role-played provocation test it was only the full stress inoculation program that significantly outperformed the no treatment control condition. On the downside, treatment effects did not show up in behavior ratings made by the institutional staff. The authors attribute this fact to the social milieu of the institution, with staff who were minimally cooperative at best, who appeared to make arbitrary ratings, and who frequently encouraged and modeled angry responses to frustration that conflicted directly with what was taught in the stress inoculation program.

Testing a group version of the program with delinquent junior high students. Feindler et al. (1984) tested their group version of the program with a group of delinquent junior high students, ages 12–16 (gender and ethnicity not reported). All were in a specialized school program for disruptive youth, all had high rates of classroom and/or community disruption, all had been suspended at least twice during the previous school year, and 40% had police records.

Although the 36 youngsters were randomly assigned to treatment and no treatment groups, there were some unintended pretreatment differences between the groups that complicated interpretation of findings and may have been partially responsible for a failure to detect treatment-control differences on some of the outcome measures used. However, there were differences favoring the treatment group on a measure of problem-solving ability and on teacher-reported self-control, and these were paralleled by relatively greater treatment group reductions over time in rates of school fines for severe disruptive and aggressive behavior. Thus, although not all outcome measures showed the treated group outpacing the no treatment control group, some particularly significant measures did show such group differences. On balance, the evidence does suggest that the intervention had beneficial effects on actual school behavior, on teacher perceptions of self-control, and on ability to apply problem-solving skills on a test.

Testing the group program with adolescent psychiatric inpatients. In another test of the group version, Feindler et al. (1986) used it with teenage boys in a psychiatric institution for behaviorally and emotionally disturbed youth, all of whom were judged by the staff to be in need of anger control. The 22 participants averaged about 16 years of age (range 13–18); 14 boys were Caucasian, 7 were African American, and 1 was Latino. Ten boys from one unit served at the treatment group, and 11 from another unit served as the waitlist control group. This nonrandom approach to group assignment was associated with some significant differences; for example, the treatment group was somewhat younger and less mature interpersonally than the control group.

The core treatment was similar to that used in Feindler et al. (1984), but the content of behavioral rehearsal activities and homework assignments was adapted to fit the inpatient hospital setting. For example, video-guided role-play activities featured hospital staff members and hospital situations. At the end of the intervention period, the treatment group had shown more improvement than the waitlist group on some measures – rule violations in the hospital, for example. In this and other respects, the findings did tend to support the efficacy of the treatment program. However, the fact that groups had not been randomly assigned, and the evidence that the groups did differ at pretreatment in potentially important ways, complicates interpretation of the findings.

Summary of the outcome evidence on anger control training with stress inoculation. The published group-comparison studies of this treatment approach have focused on delinquent teens and psychiatric inpatient teens (see also a single case report by McCullough et al., 1977, and a report on four cases by Feindler, 1979). None of the studies showed treatment effects on all outcome measures used, but this is not unusual in the treatment outcome literature. All three studies did appear to show beneficial effects of treatment not only on informant-report measures but also on performance measures (e.g., responses to role-played provocations, in Schlichter & Horan, 1981; problem-solving assessment and rates of school fines, in Feindler et al., 1984; hospital rule violations in Feindler et al., 1986). So, although more consistent evidence from a larger body of research would be very helpful, there is some initial evidence and some replication suggesting that anger control training with stress inoculation can be helpful with adolescents who have problems with anger and self-control.

What about Sal? Applying Anger Control Training with Stress Inoculation

This anger control program could certainly be used with Sal, the youngster discussed at the beginning of this section. Sal has a short fuse. He is prone to jump to conclusions, to assume that ambiguous actions by others reflect hostile intent, and then to explode in an aggressive outburst. The stress inoculation program would likely begin with information gathering by the therapist, which could be tough going at first. Sal is not an easy youngster to work with, and he really doesn't want to talk about times when he has gotten in trouble. In fact, he walks in to his first meeting with the therapist full of attitude, saying "What the hell is this all about? I'm not talking to some shrink." He slouches into a chair and sits in sullen silence for several minutes. The therapist breaks the ice a bit by saying, "I'd feel the same way if I were you. I mean, we don't know each other at all." Then the therapist continues, "But since we are here anyway, let me see if I understand why you ended up being sent to me." The therapist then recounts a bit of what the referral noted about Sal's fighting, adds that this doesn't tell anything about Sal's point of view, and asks if Sal can tell how *he* thinks the fights usually happen. Very slowly, and very reluctantly, Sal begins to fill in details of a typical provocation cycle, which looks like this: Someone says or does something that Sal considers an affront or an attack (e.g., another boy says, "Hey punk!" when he passes Sal at school, or someone collides with him in a basketball game), Sal responds with an insult or a physical attack, and various consequences ensue. The consequences may include a brawl, injuries, intervention by the assistant principal, and suspension from school.

The therapist asks Sal to construct a personal anger hierarchy, a list of "things that make you mad," rank-ordered for their power to upset him. Sal says that number one on his list is "Coming to this chicken-shit therapy." The therapist takes this in stride with a smile, saying "Good hit. Now, how about outside of therapy, in school?" This good-humored reply evokes a hint of a smile from Sal, who then actually begins listing everyday anger triggers. Taunts from peers rank highest. Criticism from teachers is almost as high on the scale; he hates it when "teachers get in my face, disrespect me," especially when this happens in front of Sal's peers. Third on his list is when other kids bump or run into him, even in a sports event; he thinks they usually mean to do it. The therapist asks Sal to keep a personal log of anger episodes in his daily life, noting in each case (1) what situation or event made him mad, (2) what his own behavior was after he got mad, and (3) what the consequences of his angry behavior were.

In treatment sessions, these anger episodes become grist for Sal's mill, in two respects. First, Sal and his therapist discuss the episodes to expand Sal's understanding of how anger happens and how it harms him. Second, Sal and his therapist use the anger episodes as the plots of role-plays in which Sal tries out new coping skills. The two take turns, with Sal playing provocateur and the therapist playing Sal, and then reversing the roles. One of the first coping skills Sal learns is the simplest: "time out." The basic idea is that Sal inserts a time delay between the anger trigger (e.g., "Hey punk!") and his response. Time alone may reduce the intensity of his response, but the time delay can also be used to insert special techniques to reduce arousal; three techniques that seem to help Sal are (1) silently counting backward, (2) taking five deep breaths, and (3) doing covert relaxation procedures.

The therapist also works with Sal on cognitive reframing. For Sal, two kinds of reframing turn out to be especially helpful. Given his tendency to jump to negative conclusions, Sal finds that it helps for him to stop and think, immediately after a provocation, asking himself, "Is it cool?" (i.e., is there an innocent explanation for what just happened)? Perhaps, for example, the playground collision with that other boy was a pure accident, and the boy is already sorry about it. In cases where a peer's intent is clearly negative, as when 12-year-old Max called Sal "a retard," Sal's task is tougher: the therapist pushes him to search for a deeper understanding of the event. For example, Sal knows that Max's father is a heavy drinker and abusive, that he sometimes beats Max. Perhaps Max is feeling down and angry at the world because of problems he is having at home, so he says things he shouldn't to other kids at school. It is a struggle for Sal to make allowance for Max in this way, but the therapist perseveres, hoping for at least a modest epiphany in his young client. The hope is that fuller and more sympathetic interpretations of peer behavior can serve to reduce Sal's angry arousal by making the provocations feel less personal.

Once time-out has been introduced, and a provocation has been reinterpreted, it is time to try problem solving and perhaps to apply skills in assertiveness. As part of the problem-solving training, Sal and his therapist review the anger episodes Sal has described in his personal log, trying to identify and describe the specific problem that needed to be solved to prevent the angry outburst. For each such problem, they list various alternative responses Sal might have tried, and write down the pros and cons of each alternative. Using the lists of pros and cons, Sal picks out the most promising of the alternative responses, and he and his therapist try this out in role-plays.

In some cases, the ideal response involves assertive but nonaggressive responding. As an example, in the episode when Max called Sal a retard, and a fight ensued, Sal identified "the problem" in this way: "He was disrespecting me in front of other kids, and I couldn't let him do that." Among the alternative responses Sal and his therapist discuss is an assertive one: Instead of hitting Max, Sal could make eye contact with Max, and say in a modulated tone, "I know you are feeling bad, man, but I need you not to talk to me that way. Let's respect each other, OK?" The basic idea is to make a clear and direct request for behavior change, and to do so in a way that does not escalate arousal or spark further aggression. The in-session role-play of this strategy starts with Sal playing the role of Max, and the therapist playing Sal; then the roles reverse. Over time, and across sessions, Sal and his therapist apply such problem-solving-plus-role-play exercises to several of the anger episodes in Sal's log.

A key to the stress inoculation part of the treatment program is the use of repeated trial runs of the coping skills Sal is learning, in response to increasingly potent anger triggers. Toward this end, the therapist uses the barb technique, role-playing with Sal the various provocations listed in Sal's hierarchy. As Sal and the therapist work their way from the weakest to the strongest provocation in the hierarchy, they continue to play alternating roles, with the therapist also serving as coach and cheerleader, praising Sal for his successes. Early on in these role-plays, the therapist inserts numerous prompts, reminding Sal when to use his time-outs, deep breaths, relaxation, reframing, problem solving, and assertive responses. Over time, these prompts grow less frequent and less detailed; the goal is to build Sal's skills in generating his own nonaggressive responses to events that have made him angry in the past.

To be sure, anger control training with stress inoculation does not address all of Sal's difficulties. His poor schoolwork and his poorly functioning parents, for example, might remain relatively untouched by this particular treatment. On the other hand, Sal's explosive responses to provocation, even very minor ones, have gotten him into lots of trouble, and are arguably the major cause of his problems with peers and school staff. If he can learn to manage his anger and curb his aggression toward peers and teachers, Sal will be taking a major step.

Troubleshooting: Common Treatment Problems and Recommended Solutions. Anger control training with stress inoculation addresses behavior that is often quite entrenched, so the path to improvement is not always smooth. This is also true of the Anger Coping Program, which we consider next. Because the two programs can present similar problems, we will save our discussion of common problems and recommended solutions until we have covered both anger programs.

Anger Coping Program: Conceptual Basis and Procedural Overview

The Anger Coping Program, developed by Lochman and colleagues (Lochman et al., 1981, 1984, 1989), is similar to Anger Control Training with Stress Inoculation in its emphasis on teaching self-control and problem-solving skills. The two approaches differ somewhat in their theoretical underpinnings, and Anger Coping puts more emphasis on live and video modeling, on immersion in problem-solving skills, and on weekly experience in setting specific behavioral goals and monitoring whether they are attained. Anger Coping has also been used primarily with children ages 9–13, in contrast to the junior high and high school-aged youth treated with the Stress Inoculation approach.

The Anger Coping Program is based on a social-cognitive model of anger arousal and aggressive behavior. Elements in the process of angry arousal and aggressive responding, as construed by Lochman et al. (1991), are shown in Figure 8.1. The individual youth encounters a potentially anger-arousing stimulus event, but the youth's emotional and physiological response is due to the youth's perception of the event, not to the event itself. The perception, accurate or inaccurate, is derived from such sources as the youth's learning history and selective attention to specific aspects of the event. The way these factors converge helps set the stage for the youth's response to provocation. The behavioral response that results is followed by some consequence – for the aggressive youth, often an undesirable consequence.

The social-cognitive model, as elaborated by Lochman et al. (1989), posits multiple deficits that make aggressive youth prone to maladaptive behavioral responses in the sequence shown in Figure 8.1. Five deficits are prominent in the model:

1. *Attributional biases.* Aggressive youth tend to overperceive hostile intentions by others (see Dodge, 1986; Dodge et al., 1990).

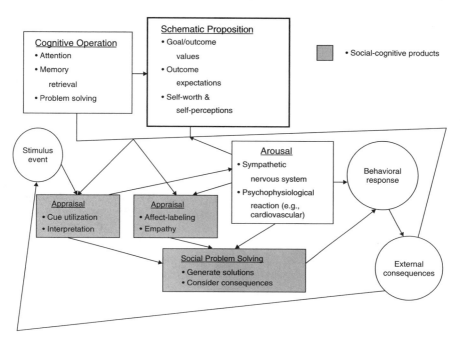

FIGURE 8.1. Anger arousal in the context of a social-cognitive model. [Adapted from Lochman, J. E., White, K. J., & Wayland, K. (1991). Cognitive behavioral assessment and treatment with aggressive children. In P. C. Kendall (Ed.), *Cognitive behavioral therapy with children and adolescents*. New York: Guilford Press. Reprinted with permission from Guilford Press.]

2. *Distorted perceptions of interpersonal interactions.* When conflict occurs, aggressive youth underestimate their own aggressiveness and overestimate others' responsibility for the conflict (see Lochman, 1987).

3. *Faulty emotion identification.* Aggressive youth tend to mislabel affective arousal as anger (see Garrison & Stolberg, 1983).

4. *Restricted range of social problem-solving strategies.* Aggressive youth rely heavily on direct action in nonverbal forms, such as hitting, and are not skilled at verbal approaches to problem solving (see Lochman & Lampron, 1986).

5. *Maladaptive expectancies.* Aggressive youth have low-level expectancies that problems can be resolved through nonaggressive means (see Perry et al., 1986).

Lochman and colleagues developed their Anger Coping Program to confront these five deficits, with a special emphasis on social problem-solving skills (deficit #4). Youngsters meet in groups for a series of exercises designed to counter their reflexive responses to perceived threat. Three steps are considered critical. Therapists teach the children (1) to inhibit their initial angry and aggressive reactions, (2) to cognitively relabel stimuli perceived as threatening, and (3) to solve problems by generating alternative coping responses and choosing adaptive, nonaggressive alternatives. An overall aim is to enhance children's cognitive processing of their stressful encounters and strengthen their ability to plan effective and adaptive responses. In addition, as the program has evolved, an emphasis on learning to set and achieve specific behavioral goals has become quite central as well.

Anger Coping Program: In Brief

Designed for . . . . Aggressive children ages 9–12
Number of sessions 12–18
Session length . . . . 40–60 minutes
Session participants . . . . Therapist with youths in
   small groups
Theoretical orientation . . . . Cognitive-behavioral
Treatment steps:

1. Discuss group goal of learning about members' similarities and differences; take pictures of each group member with instant camera; use visual exercises (e.g., face/vase) to illustrate how different people can have different perceptions of the same thing.
2. Exercises and discussion to explore children's reactions to cooperating with, being controlled by, and being distracted by peers, for example, building domino towers while peers try to verbally distract.
3. Use stories and role-plays to practice identifying the problem – that is, which specific aspect(s) of an interpersonal situation create a problem and lead to anger.
4. Use cartoon sequences and role-plays to practice generating alternative solutions to problems.
5. Use cartoon sequences and role-plays to practice evaluating pros and cons of various alternative solutions to problems.
6. Use modeling videotape to learn to identify bodily cues that signal angry arousal, and to identify negative and positive thoughts (or self-statements) that can increase or diminish angry arousal.
7. Use other modeling videotapes to practice integrating (1) physiological awareness of angry arousal, (2) self-talk (e.g., "Stop! Think! What should I do?"), and (3) social problem solving, to resolve interpersonal problems without aggression.
8. Use role-plays to continue practicing physiological awareness + self-talk + interpersonal problem solving. Videotape the role-plays and discuss them. Plan for extending anger control skills to future situations at school and home.

9. Practice setting specific behavioral goals – for example, no arguments with teacher, achieving them and being rewarded for doing so; this component may be introduced at any point in treatment, and may operate concurrently with other treatment components.

Treatment classified by Treatment Task Force as . . . . Probably Efficacious (Brestan & Eyberg, 1998)
Key resources for potential users . . . . Lochman, J. E., Nelson, W. M., III, and Sims, J. P. (1981). A cognitive behavioral program for use with aggressive children. *Journal of Clinical Child Psychology, 10,* 146–148. Lochman, J. E., Fitzgerald, D. P., & Whidby, J. M. (1999). Anger management with aggressive children. In C. Schaefer (Ed.), Short-term psychotherapy groups for children (pp. 301–349). Northvale, NJ: Jason Aronson. Lochman, J. E., Lampron, L. B., Genner, T. C., & Harris, S. R. (1987). Anger coping intervention with aggressive children: A guide to implementation in school settings. In P. A. Keller & S. R. Heyman (Eds.), *Innovations in Clinical Practice: A Source Book,* Vol. 6. Sarasota, FL: Professional Resource Exchange.

Anger Coping Program: Treatment Procedures

The Anger Coping Program comes in a core form (described in Lochman et al., 1981) and an enhanced form (described in Lochman, 1985, and Lochman et al., 1984).

The core Anger Coping Program. The original core program involved 12 biweekly group sessions. In this core program, participants begin group meetings with get-acquainted exercises (e.g., instant photos of each participant, body tracings on large pieces of paper), and then explore one another's reactions to cooperating with, being controlled by, and being distracted by peers. Activities include acting like pairs of robots and building domino towers while being verbally distracted by peers. A third session focuses on problem identification. Participants review brief stories and carry out role-plays, with the aim of figuring out which specific aspects of situations create problems and lead to anger and aggression.

In session four, group members learn to generate alternative solutions to problem situations; cartoon sequences and role-plays among the members provide the problem contexts for which alternative solutions are devised. Sessions five and six involve evaluation of alternative solutions. Here again, cartoons and role-plays provide the raw material, with exercises devoted to noting pros and cons of various alternative solutions, and culminating in decisions about the relative value of the alternatives.

Beginning with Session 7, video material is brought into the process and used to convey important lessons to the group. In Session 7, group members are taught how to identify angry arousal, how to use arousal as a cue for problem solving, and how to use positive self-statements when provoked. In an illustrative videotape, a boy tells an off-screen narrator how he felt physically when his mother reprimanded him for failing to do homework. The boy noted his own negative self-statements (e.g., "I want to get back at my mother and teacher for making me miss a television show."), as well as positive statements he could use to decrease his angry arousal (e.g., "If I stick to the homework rules, I can watch TV sooner.").

Session 8 emphasizes integration of physiological awareness, self-talk, and constructive problem solving, together with the use of covert inhibitory speech (e.g., "Stop! Think! What should I do?") to forestall immediate reflexive reactions to stressful encounters. The session employs three additional videotapes, portraying children reacting angrily to (1) being punished by a teacher for something they did not do, (2) being teased by a peer, and (3) being ignored by peers. After each video, group members are encouraged to generate alternative solutions and to evaluate the pros and cons of each one. In the remaining sessions, children continue to practice integrating the techniques for inhibiting impulsive responding and for blending positive self-talk with problem solving. This practice involves both role-playing and production of group videotapes (filmed by the children themselves) showing the youngsters applying their new skills to problem situations. Finally, participants discuss the use of anger control procedures at home and in school, looking to the future and anticipating what new problems may arise, and thinking about how they will fit their skills to the problems.

The enhanced Anger Control Program, with goal setting added. In a later innovation, Lochman et al. (1984) and Lochman (1985) developed a Goal-Setting Program that can be combined with the basic Anger Control Program. In the Goal-Setting intervention, children in the groups develop specific, weekly goals for themselves, stated in terms of observable behavior. "Being good in class" would not be acceptable, because it is not stated in terms of clear, observable behaviors, but "Not talking back to my teacher" is both behavioral and observable, so it works well as a goal. Pursuit of the goals is monitored by each child's teacher, using a form like that shown in Table 8.1.

When a youngster does meet a goal, a reward that was negotiated prior to the five-day test period is provided, together with ample praise for success. Other members of the group play a role throughout the process – helping each individual youth to formulate appropriate, attainable goals that are similar in difficulty level to the goals of others in the group, helping to monitor levels of success attained, and celebrating when the youngsters meet their goals and win rewards.

TABLE 8.1. *Goal sheet similar to that used in the Anger Coping Program*

My Goal Sheet

Name:_____   Today's Date:_____

My goal is:_____

. . . . .for at least _____ out of five school days this week.

Group Member's Signature:_____ Group Leader's Signature:_____

My teacher will write "Yes" if I met my goal for the day, or "No" if I did not meet
   my goal.

	Day 1	Day 2	Day 3	Day 4	Day 5
Yes/No	_____	_____	_____	_____	_____
Teacher's Initials	_____	_____	_____	_____	_____
Was my weekly goal met? (Circle One)	Yes!	Not Yet		Date: _____	

Anger Coping Program: Outcome Studies Testing the Effects

Goal-setting and attainment skills have now become central to the Anger
Coping Program; we will review here the evidence on both the core program and the version that includes a goal focus.

Preliminary test of the core Anger Coping Program. The core program was
first tested in a preliminary way using a within-group design. Lochman
et al. (1981) carried out the program with two groups of aggressive and disruptive children (group $Ns = 5$ and 7) from two regular elementary school
classrooms (ages 7–10, all African American, 1 girl and 11 boys). After
treatment, the children showed marginally significant reductions in acting out behaviors on a standardized teacher-report problem checklist. The
five children in one of the treatment groups were rated by teachers daily,
for aggressiveness and off-task behavior. Both ratings showed significant
improvement over time in the program, suggesting that the intervention
might warrant further testing.

Testing the Anger Coping Program with and without Goal Setting. Such further testing took the form of a group comparison study by Lochman et al.
(1984) with 9–12-year-old boys (53% African American, 47% Caucasian)
who had been rated by their teachers as high in aggression. The boys were
assigned to four different experimental groups, on a rotating basis (see
Lochman et al., 1984): the core Anger Coping Program, the Anger Coping
Plus Goal Setting Program, Goal Setting alone (construed as a minimal
treatment condition), and no treatment. Compared to Goal Setting alone

and no treatment, the two Anger Coping conditions produced significantly greater reductions over time in disruptive and aggressive off-task behavior in the classroom, as rated by trained observers, blind to treatment condition of the children, and using time-sampling methods. This is an important finding, in that it comes from direct observation of the youngsters' behavior by presumably unbiased raters.

In addition, the two Anger Coping conditions led to lower parent ratings of aggression at home, on a standardized checklist, than did the no-treatment and minimal-treatment conditions. There was some evidence that adding Goal Setting may have enhanced the effects of the core Anger Coping Program on observed behavior in the classroom. The program did not produce benefits on all outcome measures employed in the study, and one nonfinding may be especially important: The two Anger Coping conditions did not produce significant effects on peer and teacher perceptions of the boys in the study. This is consistent with the notion that reputation may linger among peers and teachers, even after actual behavior has changed.

Testing a lengthened version of the program, including goal setting. Lochman (1985) used a quasi-experimental design to assess whether lengthening the Anger Coping Plus Goal Setting Program might produce more dramatic effects. In the school year following completion of the four-group study just described (Lochman et al., 1984), Lochman (1985) selected an additional sample of boys identified by their fourth, fifth, or sixth grade teachers as the most aggressive and disruptive in their classrooms. The 22 boys thus identified (55% African American, 45% Caucasian) ranged from 9 to 12 years of age. All were treated with an expanded, 18-session version of the full program that provided additional role-playing experience and more discussion of the boys' real-life anger-arousing experiences. At the end of the treatment program, outcomes for this new group were compared to outcomes in the four groups treated the previous year in the Lochman et al. (1984) study. The comparison showed beneficial effects of the 18-session program that resembled, in several respects, the effects seen with the 12-session version used by Lochman et al. (1984), both with and without the goal-setting component. For example, the 18-session treatment produced a reduction in observer-rated disruptive-aggressive off-task behavior that was similar to that produced by the 12-session versions tested in the earlier study (Lochman et al., 1984), thus replicating an important effect. In addition, though, the 18-session version did a better job than the 12-session versions of increasing on-task classroom behavior and reducing passive off-task behavior. These findings suggested the potential value of a more traditional experimental test of the 18-session version.

A stronger test of the longer version of Anger Coping Plus Goal Setting. Precisely such a test was carried out by Lochman et al. (1989), with 32 boys identified by their teachers as the most aggressive and disruptive in their fourth, fifth, and sixth grade classrooms. The boys ranged in age from 9 through 13; 22 were Caucasian, 10 African American. The study compared a no-treatment condition to the 18-session Anger Coping Plus Goal Setting Program, provided with and without adjunctive teacher consultation. (Teacher consultation was assigned on an alternating basis to the different schools, and boys were assigned on an odd/even basis to treatment or a no-treatment control condition.)

In the treatment-plus-teacher condition, two leaders of the boys' treatment groups met with teachers for six hours, focusing on (1) helping teachers find ways to support the boys' problem-solving skill development in class, and thus enhance generalization of treatment lessons; (2) enhancing the teachers' own problem-solving skills in their efforts to help students deal with problems; and (3) helping teachers develop consistent expectations and contingencies for their students' behavior, including contingency contracting (see Lochman & Breyer, 1977) when needed.

The results actually showed no evidence that teacher consultation enhanced treatment effects. However, compared to the no-treatment control group, both of the 18-session Anger Coping Plus Goal Setting groups (i.e., with and without teacher consultation) produced more marked reductions in observer-rated disruptive-aggressive off-task behavior in the classroom, greater increases in self-rated social competence, and marginally greater reductions in teacher-rated aggressiveness.

Identifying the youngsters who profit most (Lochman et al., 1985). In another report, Lochman et al. (1985) carried out a secondary analysis of data from a previous intervention study (Lochman, 1984), with the goal of identifying characteristics of the youth who profited most from the treatment program. They used a sample of 76 boys who had been identified as aggressive and disruptive at the time of the previous study. The boys ranged from 9 to 12 years of age, and 53% were African American, 47% Caucasian.

Two predictors of treatment gains held up for both versions of the Anger Coping program, that is, with and without Goal Setting: (1) low pretreatment social problem-solving skills, and (2) high pretreatment levels of disruptive-aggressive off-task behavior in class. At first glance, these findings may seem to suggest simply that the most extreme cases regressed toward the mean of their group over time; but that interpretation alone does not fit the full pattern of findings, because results were different with untreated children. In fact, improvement in untreated children was predicted by initially *higher* level skills in social problem solving. Taken together the findings suggest that those youngsters who had the weakest skills initially were able to make the best use of treatment and to manifest the most marked improvement. In later analyses, Lochman and colleagues (1999) have broadened the answer to the question of who benefits from the program. They report that aggressive youngsters who benefit most tend to be those who (1) show poorer initial social problem-solving ability, (2) are less prone to perceive hostility in others, (3) are more rejected by peers, (4) accept more personal responsibility for the outcomes they experience, and (5) manifest more anxiety symptoms and somatic complaints.

Long-term effects of the intervention. In an interesting follow-up report, Lochman (1992) presented findings from assessments carried out three years after completion of the Anger Coping Program by 31 boys, all treated in the fourth, fifth, and sixth grades (in studies by Lochman, 1985; Lochman et al., 1984; and Lochman & Curry, 1986). These boys were compared with both untreated aggressive boys (N = 52) and nonaggressive boys (N = 62; age and ethnicity of the three samples was not reported). A notable finding was that, three years after their treatment, boys who had received the Anger Coping Program showed lower rates of drug and alcohol involvement, higher levels of social problem-solving skill, and higher self-esteem than the untreated aggressive boys. In fact, the treated boys were not significantly different from the originally nonaggressive boys on any of these variables. Thus, the evidence suggests that the Anger Coping Program may have both short-term benefits and long-term preventive effects.

Summary of the outcome evidence on the Anger Coping Program. We have reviewed six published studies of the Anger Coping Program. One group-design study supported the efficacy of the early core version without goal setting (Lochman et al., 1981), and two others supported the efficacy of the full complement including goal setting (Lochman et al., 1984, 1989). In addition, Lochman (1985) found that lengthening the full treatment program from 12 to 18 sessions appeared to improve some of the treatment outcomes; and Lochman et al. (1985) found that it was those boys who showed the poorest problem-solving skill and the worst disruptive and aggressive off-task behavior who profited most from the treatment program. The measures showing improvement as a function of treatment have included not only informant reports but also direct observations by trained observers, not likely to have been biased by a knowledge of the youngsters' treatment condition. Finally, Lochman (1992) provided follow-up evidence on boys three years posttreatment, and the evidence suggested rather enduring improvements on social problem solving and self-esteem as well as reduced risk of drug and alcohol involvement.

What about Sal? Applying the Anger Coping Program

As the Anger Coping Program has evolved, the goal setting aspect has become quite central and is now introduced at a relatively early stage in the treatment sequence (see description in Lochman et al., 1987). Our discussion of Sal's case will reflect this more recent incarnation of the treatment program.

Because of Sal's record of angry outbursts and conduct problems at school and home, he is nominated by his teachers to participate in anger management groups held at a nearby school. Sal's mother agrees that he needs this help, and she readily gives her consent. Of course, getting her son to go is a major struggle, but she is as adamant as she has ever been with him, and despite his protests ("I'm not talking to some damn shrink!"), she drags him to the first meeting. Walking into that meeting, Sal sees five other boys and two group leaders. He rolls his eyes and says, under his breath, "Geez – losers and geeks!" He slumps into a chair and avoids eye contact with others in the group while the leaders discuss basic rules for the meetings (e.g., no physical contact, confidentiality of what the boys say in the group). Then the leaders have the boys play a "pass the ball" game in which they must correctly name the boy on their right before they can pass the ball on to him. At the beginning, Sal says "Oh, can we play Ring Around the Rosie next?" When it is his turn to pass the ball, he introduces the boy on his right as "Larry Loser," which leads to a shove from Larry and a tussle, broken up by the leaders. When tempers have cooled, the leaders review group rules for how the boys are to talk to one another (no "dissing" unless the boys are told to, as part of a group activity), and they present a final warning regarding consequences for rule-breaking. Perhaps because of the warning, or perhaps because he has expressed his views, Sal drops the insults, and takes part (half-heartedly) in the group activities.

In another version of the get-acquainted game, each boy must state some way that he is similar to and some way that he is different from the boy on his right, before he is allowed to pass the ball. Then the boys are all shown a complicated picture of a group of kids involved in some activity, but one that is not clearly identifiable. Each boy is taken from the room to state on a tape recorder what he saw in the picture. After all boys have made their statement, the tape is played for the entire group, and everyone is amazed at how different the statements are. The basic take-home message: different kids have different points of view; the same situation may look different to one kid than to another; and there is often no single right way to see a situation. Sal gets the point, but only in its narrowest form; he doesn't yet see how this relates to his conflict with others.

In the second meeting, the group talks about goals. The leaders tell the boys that each of them will be writing down one personal goal for each week, and that the goal needs to be something related to self-control or coping with anger in school. The boys are told they can win small prizes each week if their teacher says they have met their goal. Sal says his goal is "Be good in class." The leaders press him to get specific – that is, "Be good . . . ." by doing what? Sal thinks for a minute, then says, "OK, by not talking back to the teacher." Sal and the leaders agree that the teacher will need to check "yes" on her report form three out of the next five school days for Sal to have reached this goal. If that happens, Sal will win a small individual prize (sugarless gum), and he will contribute one point toward a group prize (watching a funny video of basketball bloopers together). Each of the other boys selects a personal goal as well, and then the boys all "vote" on the goals, to make sure all are about equally challenging – for example, that no one has picked one that's too easy. The boys are all given a form (see previous paragraph) with their goal written down, and with space for the teacher to check for each of the next five school days. Sal takes the form, and starts thinking about how he is going to manage to keep his mouth shut when the teacher makes him mad.

The third meeting begins with a group review of each boy's success in meeting his goal. Boys who did succeed are asked to relate what they did that helped them reach their goal. Sal can only report that he got his teacher's signature on two days, not the three required for his goal. Jaron, a boy in the group who had a goal similar to Sal's, did succeed, and he says he did it by imagining his mouth was zipped, and counting to five before saying anything in class. Sal decides to try the counting approach for the next week. Next, the leaders tell the boys to get a puppet from a pile in the center of the room; but there is one puppet fewer than the number of boys. When the dust has settled, the leaders review with the boys, (1) what the problem was with the puppets, (2) what problem-solving method (if any) the boys used to deal with the problem, (3) how well this worked, and (4) whether they could have done anything different. Sal later learns that this was a first dose of practice using a special method for solving problems. In the remainder of the second session, the boys use the puppets in a taunting game. Each boy's puppet takes turns receiving and responding to taunts from the rest of the group. Each episode lasts about thirty seconds. After each, the boys discuss how the targeted puppet feels. The leader models self-talk the puppets can use to show self-control and avoid getting mad when taunted – for example, "OK, I'm starting to get mad; I need to be careful not to blow up; I'll ask them to stop, and see if that works;" or "I better stay cool, or I'll get in trouble."

When the boys come back for meeting 4, they again review their success in meeting their personal goals, and they do more practice of self-control strategies in the taunting game. In this meeting, though, the taunting escalates to personal comments directed at the boys themselves, not their puppets, and the boys all talk about how this resembles things that happen to them in real life. Sal, who is one of the oldest boys in the group, had thought the puppets were beneath him – toys for younger kids, really – and he hadn't actually felt angry during those exercises but the personal taunts in this session do start to get to him. They generate some of the same feelings that have gotten him in trouble at school. During the taunting game, one boy, Alex, said "Your momma!" and Sal had the impulse to punch him in the face. Fortunately, the leaders had the boys well separated; although Sal did clinch his fist, he caught himself and held back. After this experience, Sal could see how the bad feelings come up, and also how it might help him to learn some ways to get control.

The fifth and sixth meetings focus mainly on helping the boys understand that the same situation can look very different to different people, and that how a situation looks to one person can influence that person's thoughts and feelings. Using pictures, stories, and role-plays based on the boys' own real-life experiences, the leaders get each boy to take the perspective of various people in the picture or story and describe how things look and feel from the different perspectives. One point Sal takes away from the meeting is that two boys may have an argument because each one sees things from his own viewpoint, and thinks the other boy is wrong, or unfair. In fact, he remembers a fight he got in when another boy kept saying it was Sal's fault. Sal didn't think so at the time, but looking back on it, he can see how he did things that made the other boy mad.

Getting mad is, in fact, the main topic in meeting 7. The boys discuss how they can tell when they are starting to get angry, especially how their bodies feel; Sal says he can feel his muscles get tight and his heart beats faster. The boys watch a videotape showing what happens to the body when we get angry. Then the discussion shifts to anger and self-statements. The boys talk about statements in their heads that go along with angry feelings. Sal says that when another kid crosses him, he thinks, "You asshole! You're dead meat." The leaders guide the discussion to positive self-talk, things kids can say to themselves to reduce their angry feelings and boost self-control. Sal has no ideas on this front. However, another boy, Mauricio, remembers the discussion about different points of view, and suggests, "How does it look to the other guy?" Alex says, "How about saying, 'Uh oh! My heart's pounding. I better count to three.'"

Meetings 8–18, the remainder of the program, are devoted primarily to building and reinforcing skills in thoughtful problem solving. In the eighth session, the boys recount various problem situations they have confronted in the past. They describe what actions they took in response to the problems, and what consequences followed. Sal tells about an argument when he hit another kid with a stick because the kid wouldn't give him a soccer ball he wanted, and about a time when his teacher disciplined him and Sal called her "Bitch!" The consequence in both cases was suspension from school. The leaders then ask the boys to generate several alternative solutions to the two problem situations, and to predict what consequences each solution would produce. Although Sal is pretty defensive during this discussion, maintaining that he was in the right both times, he does grudgingly admit that there were smarter things he could have done than hitting and swearing.

Building on this exercise, and adding a videotaped illustration of a boy who gets blamed by his teacher for something he did not do, the leaders guide the boys through practice in the full problem-solving sequence they want to instill. To guide the discussion and practice, one leader writes the following questions on the blackboard:

1. What is the problem?
2. What are my feelings?
3. What are my choices?
4. What will happen? (. . . if I make choice #1, #2, and so forth)

Once the boys are able to easily remember this sequence, and apply it to various problem situations, they work together to produce their own videotape illustrating the sequence. Together they select a problem situation involving anger, and they write a script to illustrate the problem-solving steps. Then they make an actual videotape. The tape begins with a presentation of the problem situation, which the boys have decided will be one in which two boys collide with each other in a busy school hallway. This scene is followed by several different takes, each one illustrating actions the boys might take in response to the collision, and a consequence that follows from those actions. In one take, the boys each see the collision as a deliberate provocation by the other, angry words and insults follow, then a fight; the principal appears, and both boys are suspended from school. In another take, the boys are angry at first, but then one defuses the situation by saying, "Sorry, man, my fault – I should look where I'm going. You OK?" The other boy visibly calms when he hears this, then smiles and says, "Yeah – I'm OK – how about you?" Sal gets to play the role of the boy who says "Sorry, man . . ." This makes a real impression on him. It helps him see that apologizing may not be a sign of weakness but that in fact it can show how strong you are. Of course, it can also help you stay out of trouble.

In the last two sessions, the boys watch their completed video production and talk about it. They also review the problem-solving steps and what they have learned about their own anger and how to control it, and they talk about future situations in which they are especially likely to need to use their anger control skills. In Sal's case, he is most worried about confrontations with his school's assistant principal, who tends to make insulting comments to the kids he doesn't like, including Sal. The other boys pitch in to help Sal generate alternative solutions to that specific problem. Sal especially likes two of the ideas: (1) having a heart-to-heart with the assistant principal before anything bad has happened, apologizing for past times he has gotten in trouble, and asking if he is willing to say things to Sal in a way that will help Sal avoid getting mad; and (2) if another incident with the assistant principal arises anyway, using the internal self-talk, "Stay cool, like I did in the video."

Sal has made some progress. This shows up in his weekly goal-setting reports; he has met his personal self-control goal in three of the past four weeks. Sal's future certainly will not be problem-free; his short fuse may well ignite again when he faces new provocations. However, the Anger Coping Program has given Sal some useful basic skills to take back with him – that is, a better understanding of what happens that causes him to get so angry, an ability to recognize the physical signs that tell him he is getting mad, an ability to use self-talk to soften his angry thoughts and feelings, and a more systematic approach to solving problems, one designed to generate nonaggressive alternatives to the aggressive and violent solutions he has used in the past.

Troubleshooting: Common Treatment Problems and Recommended Solutions. Although anger control programs can work, even with boys like Sal, therapists who use the programs with such short-tempered youngsters who have such well-entrenched styles may be in for some challenging moments. Here are a few common problems and some recommended solutions.

- *Low motivation to change.* Referrals to anger management programs often come because others are distressed, not because the anger-prone youth is eager to change. Some referred youngsters are not motivated for treatment because they believe their angry, aggressive responses to peers are justified (e.g., because "the other kids start it"), or their angry responses are effective ways to get results. Therapists who try to attack such core beliefs directly may not be so effective. An alternative approach is to focus on specific instances in which the costs of angry outbursts outweighed the benefits – as when a fight at school leads to a 10-day suspension and grounding at home. Most youngsters can acknowledge that anger management would be useful to them in at least some situations. Those situations can provide the therapist with a foot in the door to begin skills training.
- *Overarousal and anger discharge in role-plays.* Both anger management programs reviewed in this chapter use role-playing, with taunts and other provocations, to simulate the interactions that lead to explosions in real life. Sometimes these role-plays become so realistic that real fury bubbles up, verbal exchanges escalate, and even physical contact can follow. To reduce the risk that role-plays will get out of hand, experts in anger management have developed a set of protective procedures. The role-plays can begin with leaders modeling the taunts, the self-control strategies, and the appropriate responses. When the youngsters themselves do the role-plays, a therapist, or a peer buddy can serve as coach standing beside the youths during the role-plays and reminding them what to do. Therapists and youngsters can also identify and disallow specific taunts that are most likely to trigger anger, and even reduce the length of time role-playing continues. Finally, having a youth face away from the taunters, or even face a wall, can reduce the feeling of

being directly threatened, and thus reduce the potential for an angry outburst.

- *Lack of engagement in problem solving.* Both of this chapter's anger management programs emphasize teaching youngsters to do systematic problem solving. The problem-solving steps may seem rather abstract to some youths, and perhaps not so relevant to their lives. Clever therapists look for ways to make the learning process engaging, and to show the personal relevance of the skills. As we have seen, the Anger Coping Program puts boys to work writing scripts and making videos, which are used in part to portray problem situations and alternative solutions. To increase personal relevance of the skills, observant therapists look for real-life teaching moments – times when a genuine problem has surfaced for one of the youngsters. At such moments – when one of the group is upset over a fight with a peer, conflict with a teacher, or a blowup at home – the full group can be engaged in thinking through what happened and generating alternative solutions. The process can tie problem solving to real life while also building group solidarity.

Programs to Enhance Anger Control: Scientific Issues

The two anger control programs reviewed here differ noticeably in the nature and extent of their scientific support. The Anger Control with Stress Inoculation Program has support from only two published group design studies (plus two within-subject comparisons), but the fact that these were from different investigative teams supports the case for robust effects of the core program. The limited research base does not, however, provide information on moderators or mediators of treatment effects, the holding power of effects over time, or the impact of variations in methods of treatment delivery. These remain as topics for future research on this particular intervention program.

In contrast, the Anger Coping Program has been more thoroughly examined, in a series of studies by the same core research team, holding multiple factors constant (e.g., methods of selecting subjects, methods of assessing outcomes – e.g., with blind trained observers using the same observational measure), while varying factors of special interest in specific studies. As a result of the decade and a half of research by Lochman and colleagues, a story has begun to take shape with regard to the impact of variations in treatment delivery and treatment supplements; the findings to date suggest, for example, that 18 sessions are better than 12 in some respects, adding goal setting helps, and adding teacher consultation does not help, at least in the form tried by Lochman et al. (1989). A three-year follow-up study (Lochman, 1992) suggests long-term benefits of the program in the form of reduced drug and alcohol involvement, and improved self-esteem and social problem-solving skills. In addition, we have evidence (from Lochman et al., 1985, 1999) on which kinds of youth profit most from this treatment. That evidence suggests that treatment benefits are greatest for youngsters who, at the time treatment begins, show *lower* levels of social problem-solving skill and perceived hostility in others, and *higher* levels of anxiety symptoms, somatic complaints, peer rejection, aggressive-disruptive off-task classroom behavior, and perceived personal responsibility for the outcomes they encounter.

Despite the significant strengths of the research base, there are important gaps that warrant attention in future studies, for both anger control programs reviewed here. The search for treatment moderators, though it has certainly begun in the case of Anger Coping, could be broadened substantially. Both treatment programs have been tested either exclusively or predominantly with boys, and each program has been tested with a relatively narrow age range. It is quite possible that both the triggers and the dynamics of angry arousal and aggression are different for girls than for boys, and it thus remains unclear whether the Stress Inoculation approach or the Anger Coping approach would be successful with girls, if delivered in their current forms. Given the restrictive age ranges within which the two programs have been tested, current evidence also does not permit any conclusion as to whether Stress Inoculation would work, in its current incarnation, with preadolescents, or whether Anger Coping could succeed with adolescents.

Finally, a concern common to most treatments at this stage of the field is that mediators of treatment-related change remain to be clearly established. Some thoughtful speculation has been advanced regarding the cognitive changes that may make treatment effective (see e.g., Lochman [1992] on the importance of increasing logical mean-ends reasoning). With recent advances in quantitative methods for assessing mediation (see e.g., Baron & Kenney, 1986; Holmbeck, 1997), this question seems ready for close attention. As we learn more about the change processes that are responsible for treatment gains, and as dismantling research clarifies those treatment components that are and are not needed to initiate those change processes, it will be increasingly possible to separate wheat from chaff in the design of treatments that are both beneficial and efficient.

Programs to Enhance Anger Control: Clinical Practice Issues

Both anger control programs have considerable intuitive appeal. Both seem to address a critical flash point for many incidents of youth antisocial behavior. Both also do so in a way that seems likely to engage the interest and attention of young people. Moreover, the research teams working with both programs have provided guides to the clinical use of the treatments (see e.g., Lochman et al., 1987), including case examples (e.g., Ecton & Feindler, 1990; Feindler, 1995).

However, several clinical practice issues arise. Some are closely related to the scientific issues noted earlier. For example, limited moderator assessment, associated with the narrow range of youth characteristics sampled in the research to date, leaves it unclear what the effective range of these treatments may be, demographically and clinically. Will these treatments work well with girls, despite the dearth of research with girls? Will there be treatment benefits outside the narrow age ranges employed in studies of the two treatments? And will the treatments be beneficial for youngsters whose problems are not so severe as those employed in the research to date? The treatments appear promising, but clinicians who want to try them with girls, or with moderately aggressive first graders, will be stepping outside the range of what has been directly tested thus far. A related issue for the Anger Coping Program is that the tested procedure relies heavily on interaction among youngsters in group sessions; it is not clear from research to date how much of the essence of the program can be captured in the context of individual treatment, which is still the most common modality for young people.

Another issue concerns treatment trappings that may not be readily available to most practitioners. The Anger Coping Program, for example, involves considerable use of specific videotapes showing anger episodes. Will unavailability of those particular videotapes undermine treatment effects in clinical practice, or might the treatment work just as well with, say, movie or television clips that illustrate interpersonal provocation and anger? And if a practitioner does not have an office VCR and monitor, might role-plays illustrate key points as well as videos? The last third of the 18-session Anger Coping Program involves production and review of a video by the treated boys; for clinicians who are not able to replicate that aspect of the program, considerable creativity may be required. Of course, to the extent that clinicians are creative and depart from the tested procedures, they are also departing from the base of evidence on what works. One would like to think that the treatment effects demonstrated in the research are not so fragile as to be lost with any departure from the standardized treatment format and materials. However, practitioners who do depart will be testing this notion one client (or treatment group) at a time.

Returning to a recurring theme of this book, we must note that all the research on both of the anger control programs reviewed here involves conditions that are rather different from those of most clinical practice. For example, sampling for the studies entailed screening and recruitment of participants from school or institutional settings, not naturally occurring clinical referrals; and treatment took place in those same settings, wherein treated youngsters were captive participants to a large extent. To be sure, the youths sampled did appear to have had significant behavioral problems; and the youngsters used by Schlichter and Horan (1981) were "clinical" in the sense that they had been placed in an institution for delinquents. Moreover, placing treatment for anger management in school settings may make very good sense outside of research, and rather detailed guidance has been provided to those who may want to base anger management treatment in such settings (see e.g., Larson & Lochman, 2002; Lochman et al., 1987).

However, it is true that all the studies supporting both treatment programs were done in school or institutional contexts, and the emphasis was on behavior in those contexts, although some assessment included parent reports of home behavior. This leaves unanswered the question of how well the treatments would fare in an outpatient practice context where children are referred by parents and treated by clinical staff, where attendance may not be consistent, and where the most important reference contact is the home, not the school.

Under these circumstances, it is possible that the low level of parental involvement called for in either of these anger control programs could prove to be a disadvantage. The treatments certainly do not draw substantially from the literature on parent training, the most time-honored approach to externalizing child behavior problems (see Chapters 9, 10, 11, and 12). On the other hand, because parent commitment and involvement often cannot be achieved, there may be real value in programs that focus on what young people can achieve independently of parent involvement. It would certainly be bad for the field, and bad for clinical practice, if all the evidence-based intervention programs for aggressive youth required active involvement of parents. From this perspective, these youth-focused approaches to anger control may be seen as important additions to the practitioner's armamentarium.

How to Find Out More about Anger Control Training with Stress Inoculation and the Anger Coping Program

Anger Control Training with Stress Inoculation is described and discussed in a variety of materials available from the Psychological Services Center, Long Island University, C.W. Post Campus, 720 Northern Boulevard – Post Hall, Brookville, NY 11548–1300. These include two treatment manuals (Feindler, E. L., & Guttman, J. [1994]. Cognitive-behavioral anger control training for groups of adolescents: A treatment manual. In C. W. LeCroy [Ed.], *Handbook of Child and Adolescent Treatment Manuals*. New York: Lexington Books. Feindler, E. L., & Ovens, D. [1998]. *Cognitive-Behavioral Group Anger Management for Youth*. Unpublished treatment manual), plus reprints of case illustrations, outcome studies, and literature reviews.

The Anger Coping Program is described in its earliest published form in Lochman, J. E., Nelson, W. M. III, and Sims, J. P. (1981). A cognitive behavioral program for use with aggressive children. *Journal of Clinical*

Child Psychology, 10, 146–48. Descriptions of more recent modifications can be found in two sources: Lochman, J. E., Fitzgerald, D. P., & Whidby, J. M. (1999). Anger management with aggressive children. In C. Schaefer (Ed.), Short-term psychotherapy groups for children (pp. 301–49). Northvale, NJ: Jason Aronson. And Larson, J., & Lochman, J. E. 2002. A review of relevant research is provided by Lochman et al. (2003). *Cognitive-Behavioral Intervention for Aggressive Children in the School Setting.* New York: Guilford. A training video for the Anger Coping Program, including segments for use in the treatment sessions, can be obtained from Jim Larson, Ph.D., at the University of Wisconsin-Whitewater (larsonj@uwwvax.uww.edu). Requests for training in the program can be addressed to John Lochman, Ph.D., at the University of Alabama (jlochman@gp.as.ua.edu).

9

Behavioral Parent Training and Family Treatment for Conduct Problems

In the 1950s, a young psychologist named Gerald Patterson worked in a residential treatment program for children and adolescents. He saw many youngsters improve their behavior in the structured, institutional environment. However, many reverted to their old ways when they returned home. To understand such relapses, Patterson and his colleagues began observing parents and children in their everyday interactions at home. Lessons learned from these observations were translated into hypotheses about causes of conduct problems, and eventually into intervention procedures for parents (see Forgatch & Martinez, 1999). The behavioral parent training approach that emerged from this process, and others like it, is now almost certainly the most venerable and thoroughly studied approach to addressing child conduct problems.

The general approach to intervention involves essentially *re-engineering* the family by teaching parents how to develop and maintain a social environment that supports appropriate child behavior and discourages inappropriate behavior. As we will see later, such an emphasis certainly fits the case of Sal, described in the section introduction, whose father is uninvolved and whose mother has failed to establish consistent contingencies at home.

Although many in the field have contributed to an understanding of parent-child interaction and to the development of parent training procedures, the Patterson group has been particularly influential. In the 1960s and beyond, this group's research has enriched our understanding of family interaction patterns associated with child conduct problems, and of how parents can be taught to alter those patterns and improve child behavior. In general, findings have supported the notion that much of a child's behavior can be understood by assessing the environmental pushes and pulls that influence both child and parents. Indeed, the Patterson group's *Coercion Model*, which emerged in the 1970s, described family patterns that are both maladaptive and rewarding for both children and parents, making the patterns especially hard to stop.

Parent training programs a la Patterson are designed to alter the consequences for children, and for parents, so that rewards are produced by appropriate, not inappropriate behavior. In some cases, the reward at issue may be as simple as attention from parents. If unwanted child behavior is being rewarded with attention (even in the form of nagging, scolding, or yelling), the therapist may work with parents to get their attention focused on desirable child behavior instead. Most often, though, the problem – and thus the treatment – is more complex than this.

Many of the earliest and most basic ideas in the Patterson tradition are described in Patterson and Gullion's (1968) landmark book, *Living with Children* (now in a revised edition – Patterson, 1976). The book, which still sells briskly, is a programmed text – a series of statements and questions, with an answer key – on child management techniques. The book reflects social learning theory and research findings from the Patterson group. More recent popular books by Patterson and Forgatch (e.g., 1987) encompass the coercion model (discussed later in this chapter) and focus specifically on adolescents. In this chapter we will cover some of the models and some of the treatment programs growing out of the work by Patterson and colleagues.

Behavioral Parent Training for Youth Conduct Problems: Conceptual Basis and Procedural Overview

Patterson and colleagues (e.g., Patterson, 1982; Patterson, Littman, & Bricker, 1967; Patterson & Reid, 1970) have argued that much of child behavior, both good and bad, can be explained by the consequences to which the behavior leads. In this view, even unwanted behavior – say, aggression or defiance – happens because it produces rewarding consequences. Indeed, by blending social learning theory (a la Bandura & Walters, 1963) with an operant model of behavior (a la Skinner, 1953), and then moving beyond the operant model, Patterson and colleagues offer intriguing ideas about how parents and others may actually come to support and maintain the very deviant child behavior about which they complain. A key idea is that both child and parents are often both architects and victims of their relationship. Some of the parent-child exchanges involved are included within the umbrella term, *coercive processes.*

Coercive Processes. These processes involve coercive child behaviors (e.g., demanding, shouting, hitting) and coercive parent behaviors (e.g., criticizing, humiliating, harsh discipline). A number of patterns described by the Patterson group help fill in the picture. Consider the following examples.

Negative reinforcement. A child is demanding and loud at home, and his parents repeatedly give in to his demands. Why does this pattern recur so often? Perhaps because it is rewarding to all concerned. The child's reward is that he gets his way. The parents' reward is that giving in makes the demanding and shouting stop. Mom and Dad gain peace and quiet, an end to an unpleasant situation, at least in the short run. This is a form of what behaviorists call *negative reinforcement*, that is, reward in the form of reducing or escaping from an aversive condition. Of course, the parents' reward is short-lived; giving in to the child increases the likelihood that the child's coercive behaviors will be repeated in the future. However, the short-term gain of negative reinforcement may be sufficient to sustain the coercive cycle. Similarly, a child may lie that her homework is finished, to shut down the aversive condition of a nagging parent; she will later be caught in the lie, but the short-term negative reinforcement is too appealing to resist.

Negative reciprocity. In another kind of coercive process, one person says or does something angry or aggressive, and the other reciprocates, setting a cycle in motion. Mom comes home after a stressful workday, finds that her daughter has made a snack and left the kitchen a wreck, and says, "Look at this mess. You do this all the time. You are so inconsiderate." Daughter replies, "All you ever do is criticize me. I hate you," and runs to her room, slamming the door. Both are now upset, and the mess in the kitchen remains (see Forgatch & Martinez, 1999).

Escalation. Sometimes reciprocity leads to a coercive process called *escalation*. Shouting leads to insulting, and this in turn leads to hitting. Some research (e.g., Snyder et al., 1994) suggests that such escalation can also be explained behaviorally. The reward for escalation is that when retaliation ratchets up to intense levels, one participant often withdraws, ending the bout of anger or aggression. Of course, escalation is also a sign of a very distressed relationship, one in which neither parent-child relationships nor child behavior is likely to improve.

Within the family context, there are diverse ways parents may fall prey to coercive cycles that maintain disruptive and aggressive child behavior. Patterson et al. (1973) offered examples. They referred, for instance, to *diffusion parents,* those who are inattentive to steps in the coercive cycle, and who use counterproductive management methods, such as nagging, yelling, or hitting, all of which are likely to increase rather than decrease rates of aversive child behavior. *Selective diffusion parents* apply contingencies unevenly, due to certain distorted beliefs. For example, parents may tolerate maladaptive behavior in a child who is seriously ill, or sickly, or who was once sickly. Or parents beliefs about children (e.g., "Boys will be boys.") may lead them to select certain children for poor contingency management. Parents who perform the *sadomasochistic Arabesque,* Patterson's colorful term, engage in a dance in which only one parent is able to control the child effectively, and only when that parent is physically present. So, one parent plays the heavy, while the other parent tries to compensate for the severity of the other by being noncontingently warm and accepting. As a consequence, the child is well-behaved when the disciplinarian is present, and out of control at other times.

The Matching Principle. Patterson's ideas have evolved in a direction that departs somewhat from the traditional operant model. An especially important development in the late 1970s was the *Matching Principle*, intended to account for the role of negative reinforcement in social exchanges. The principle begins with the idea that a broad array of behaviors, both coercive (e.g., disapproving, shaming, threatening, hitting) and constructive (e.g., acknowledging, asking questions, giving information), can be used to respond to aversive behavior by another person. The probability that any one of these behaviors will be used by a particular person during conflict depends on the degree to which that behavior, relative to the other behaviors, has been associated with an end of conflict in the past. In support of this general idea, Patterson and colleagues (see Snyder, Stoolmiller, & Patterson, in press) have shown that the degree to which specific parent and child behaviors have succeeded in ending conflict in the past is an excellent predictor of how often those same behaviors will be used in future parent-child interactions.

Building on their evolving ideas and growing evidence base, Patterson and his colleagues developed methods for training parents to manage their children's problem behavior by identifying and breaking down coercive patterns, by arranging contingencies to make appropriate behavior more rewarding than inappropriate behavior, and by getting parents to work together rather than at cross-purposes. Other treatment development teams adapted parts of the Patterson approach and created their own parent- and family-focused treatments. There are differences in the specific training procedures developed by different treatment research teams, and there are differences in the kinds of youth to whom the procedures have been applied. However, all the treatments covered in this chapter address undercontrolled or externalizing behavior, and all use some combination of at least three elements: (1) teaching parents basic behavioral principles; (2) teaching parents to define, pinpoint, and count the frequency of their child's target behaviors, both antisocial and prosocial; and (3) helping parents design and implement behavior modification programs.

Behavioral Parent Training for Youth Conduct Problems: In Brief

Designed for . . . . youths who show aggression and conduct problems; ages 5–13, in the original work by Patterson et al.; adaptations by others have extended range to ages 3–17

Number of sessions . . . . Highly variable; originally, typical treatment duration was 30–35 hours, spanning 3–4 months; more recent versions may be as brief as 8–12 weekly sessions

Session length . . . . Variable within and across types of sessions; e.g., in multiparent-multitherapist groups, each therapist-parent group describes their plan for 30 minutes, and discussion follows

Session participants . . . . . . Therapist with parents, therapist with parent groups, therapist with family

Theoretical orientation . . . . Social learning theory, operant conditioning, coercion model

Treatment steps:

1. Therapist works with parents to identify problem behaviors that cause concern.
2. Therapist learns (e.g., via office discussion or direct observation) about family interaction patterns, looking for those that may explain child misbehavior.
3. Parents learn (via assigned readings or discussions with therapist) social learning principles and discuss them in relation to their family.
4. Parents work with therapist to identify specific child behaviors they want to change, then learn to observe the behaviors systematically and track their frequency.
5. Parents and therapist develop behavior management plans to change targeted child behaviors, then practice applying the plans via role-plays.
6. Parents implement the plans at home, sometimes supported via phone calls with therapist.
7. Parents and therapist discuss changes in frequency of targeted behaviors, week to week, and discuss and role-play changes in the behavior management plan as needed.
8. Review and wrap-up; stability of child's behavior change monitored by parent via behavior frequency counts at home.

Treatment classified by Treatment Task Force as . . . . Well Established (Brestan & Eyberg, 1998; this classification was applied generically to behavioral parent training programs derived from Patterson and Gulion's book, *Living with Children*).

Key resource for potential users . . . . Patterson, G. R. (1976). *Living with Children*, revised. Champaign, IL: Research Press. (This is a revised edition of the original programmed text of the same name, by G. R. Patterson and M. E. Guillion [1968].) Patterson, G. R., Reid, J. B., & Dishion, T. J. (1992). *A Social Learning Approach*. Vol. 4. *Antisocial boys*. Eugene, OR: Castalia.

Behavioral Parent Training for Youth Conduct Problems: Treatment Procedures

In surveying exemplars of the many different behavioral parent training programs that have been developed for youth conduct problems, it is appropriate to stress the particularly influential ideas and treatment procedures of the Patterson group (e.g., Patterson, Cobb, & Ray, 1973; Patterson et al., 1992). As we turn to the outcome evidence, we will broaden our focus and consider complementary treatment approaches built by others on the foundation laid by Patterson and colleagues.

Through a series of pilot and research efforts in the late 1960s and early 1970s (e.g., Patterson, McNeal et al., 1967; Patterson & Reid, 1970), Patterson and his group developed a sequential approach to parent training that involves at least three components: (1) parents learn basic behavioral principles relevant to child rearing (Originally, parents were required to study a text such as *Living with Children*, but as work extended to parents who did not read, videos were used, or discussion in the therapist's office.); (2) parents learn how to define, track, and record rates of the deviant and prosocial behaviors they want to target; and (3) parents are helped to design, role-play, carry out, and refine behavior modification programs, while continuing to record rates of target behavior, to assess intervention impact. At times, before or after Steps 1–3, therapists or others may observe families at home to assess base rates of antisocial and prosocial child behaviors, and patterns of parent reinforcement of the behavior. The procedures were originally administered to individual parents and couples, one at a time, but in an effort to increase efficiency, group-administered procedures were also developed (see Patterson et al., 1973).

Studying principles of behavior management. To prepare parents for the changes they will need to make at home, therapists have them learn some basic behavioral principles relevant to rearing children and managing child behavior. A core idea conveyed to most parents is that most children act the way they do in large part because they have learned to act that way; much of that learning involves identifying what behaviors are rewarded in their environment, and doing more of those behaviors. So, for instance, most children show some generous, prosocial behavior, but if that behavior is not noticed, praised, or rewarded, it is apt to decline in frequency over time. And most children show some aggressive, antisocial behavior at some times; if that behavior is rewarded, it is likely to increase in frequency. A particularly common reward for such unwanted child behavior is attention. Parent-to-child eye contact, a raised voice, nagging complaints about the child's behavior – these may not seem like rewards at first blush, but against a backdrop of being ignored even negative attention may be quite reinforcing.

Pinpointing, observing, and counting behavior. In another aspect of the program, the therapist tries to turn parents into skilled identifiers and observers of their child's behavior. Parents are asked to identify a specific child behavior or two that they want to target for change, and then to record the frequency of the behavior at home. Identifying the problem behaviors may sound easy. It isn't. Parents may be concerned that their child "is disrespectful," "only thinks of himself," or "shows attitude," but those concerns may be too vague or general for the child to understand or for the parent to observe reliably; if that is the case, then it will be very difficult to even determine whether the problem has changed as a function of parent training. In fact, problem identification is a complex and important part of the parent training process. Parents are taught five guidelines for judicious problem selection (see Patterson & Forgatch, 1987):

1. **Be specific.** For the reasons just noted, parents are taught to be specific about their child's target behaviors. Saying that the child "is disrespectful" is being too general. Disrespect needs to be operationally defined by pinpointing the specific behaviors that need changing. Examples might be smirking, sighing, or rolling eyes when a parent is talking.

2. **Start with fairly neutral behaviors.** Parents should avoid starting with problems that make them very upset (e.g., something insulting the child says repeatedly) or issues that are very emotional for their child (peers the parent does not approve of). High levels of emotional arousal, or loss of control, by parent or child, can interfere with good behavior management.

3. **Begin with problems you can see.** Much of what worries some parents is what they suspect their child may be doing when they aren't around – for example, swearing, smoking, or vandalism with peers. Although the worry may often be justified, problems that cannot be seen cannot be counted reliably, and thus change in the problems cannot be easily assessed. For parent training purposes, it only makes sense to focus on directly observable problems.

4. **Select behaviors that occur at least two or three times per day.** Focusing on frequently occurring behaviors increases the chance that parents will notice the behaviors when they occur, and the high initial frequency helps make it possible to see change when it occurs.

5. **Choose behaviors for which clear alternatives can be identified.** For each problem identified, parents need to be able to specify what the child should do instead. So, for example, instead of smirking and rolling his eyes, parents might expect their child to maintain eye contact and show a respectful facial expression.

Once one or two target problems have been identified, parents are asked to record their frequency every day for a specified baseline period, perhaps three to five days. If there are two parents at home, both are asked to do so,

Behaviors	Monday	Tuesday	Wednesday	Thursday	Friday	Saturday	Sunday
Disobeying...............	III	IIII	II	III	II	IIII	IIII
Disrespect (smirk, sigh, roll eyes).........	II	III	I	II	I	III	II

FIGURE 9.1. A simple chart for parents to use in tallying frequencies of specific child problem behaviors for the Patterson parent training program.

and separately, so their reliability can be checked. The recording process need not be fancy. It can involve simple tallies on a chart, like that shown in Figure 9.1.

At times, the Patterson system has called for parents to be contacted by phone at prearranged times throughout the baseline data collection period. Calls might begin with parents reporting the tally for the day as well as any difficulties they experienced in determining whether the target problem occurred. These calls help remind parents to do their job, and they also provide an opportunity to fine-tune parents' understanding of the details that are so crucial to the success of the training. For parents who have done their tallies, therapists ask for information about the situations or events that preceded the problem and the consequences that followed the child's behavior, thus beginning to size up contingencies surrounding the target behavior. For parents who have not done their tallies when the therapist calls, the conversation may end quickly with a request to be ready at the time of the next call; in this way, therapists may use differential reinforcement to encourage parents to show the desired behavior as well.

Changing youth behavior by changing parent behavior. Once parents have successfully recorded problem behaviors for the designated baseline period, they are ready to begin the centerpiece of the training program: changing their own behavior in ways that will create changes in child behavior. In some cases, this is done in individual work involving a therapist and one set of parents; in other cases, up to five sets of parents and therapists may meet together to present and discuss their work and give feedback to one another (see Patterson et al., 1973). In either format, two sets of procedures are developed: one set to reduce the strength of unwanted child behaviors, the other set to increase the strength of desired behaviors. Therapists and parents may be creative in designing both types of procedures, but we will illustrate with one of the most common forms of each.

To *reduce the frequency of unwanted behaviors,* parents are often taught to use *time-out.* Every time parents see the target behavior occurring, they are to place the child in a location with light and a chair but no interesting objects or activities, for an age-appropriate period of time. Parents role-play with the therapist the skills of calmly sending their child to time-out, with no discussion and no debate before, during, or after, and of calmly increasing the allotted time if the child resists or misbehaves while in time-out. Phone contacts may continue through this period as well, so the therapist can help parents iron out problems and refine techniques on the spot.

To *increase the frequency of desired behaviors*, parents are taught to increase the rewarding consequences that follow such behaviors. In some cases, increased social reinforcement in the form of praise may be helpful. However, Patterson and colleagues see several limitations to the exclusive use of social reinforcement, including some evidence that particularly deviant children may not find praise from adults to be all that rewarding! So the Pattersonian therapist is likely to emphasize *token or point systems that lead to tangible rewards*, administered by parents. A common procedure is to develop a contract to which both parents and child agree. The contract specifies which behavior the child is to be rewarded for, how many points (or stars, tokens, etc.) she or he is to receive each time that behavior happens, what rewards the points/starts/tokens can be exchanged for, and what the exchange rate is to be – that is, how many points are required for each reward. The rewards may include a small amount of money, a special dessert, or extra TV time. Contract terms can also be lengthened, with more substantial rewards for more substantial good behavior – a bowling or fishing trip, for example, or a "kids' menu night" in which the child chooses all the foods the family will have for dinner.

The contract, signed by all in the family, can be attached to the point chart, which is in turn fastened to the wall or the fridge. That way, the child can track progress toward the reward, and can check details of the contract when in doubt. Children are often delighted at the whole idea – the power to negotiate a contract, the visible reminder of progress toward a goal, and of course the reward at the end. One particularly good effect of the contract process can be that both child and parent learn to be very clear about which behaviors are wanted, and what the consequences of each will be. In this way, contracts can make the interactions between parents and child more predictable for everyone, and that alone can serve to reduce tensions at home.

As the initial one or two problems are reduced through the use of time-out, point systems, or other changes in the contingencies at home, parents and therapist usually broaden the agenda by tackling other child problems. Some parents may eventually work on as many as four or five problems at a time. As planned changes in contingencies are implemented, the impact of the changes is assessed by having parents continue to count and chart the child behaviors they have targeted for change, and sometimes by means of the parent daily report; in this report, a youth behavior checklist is read to parents over the phone, and parents indicate which of the behaviors their youngster has shown over the previous 24 hours.

Reducing or eliminating coercive exchanges. More recent versions of the Patterson approach include an emphasis on identifying and eliminating (or reducing) coercive exchanges between parents and children. For example, the pattern known as *reciprocity* (see earlier discussion) may be addressed by helping parents identify and avoid the coercive parenting techniques they employ that spark retaliation by their child. In some cases, parents say things that hurt the child's feelings, and the child replies in anger; learning to avoid hurtful statements could prevent some of the angry replies that cause such stress in the home. As another example, the coercive pattern known as *escalation* (see earlier discussion) may be addressed by helping parents learn to respond firmly but calmly to their child's aversive behavior – for example, when Renee is listening to loud rock music instead of doing her homework, parents who would typically say, "Renee, you're wasting time again. Turn that crap off, and get your homework done" might learn to say, "OK, honey, it's time to do your homework." Addressing coercive exchanges is a feature of some current approaches, but it was not central to much of the early behavioral parent training we will review next.

Extending behavior management to out-of-home settings, such as classrooms. Often the youngster's problem behaviors extend to settings outside home – school, for example. In these cases, the therapist and parents work to extend the behavioral intervention into these settings. In the case of school, if the teacher is willing, a school card can be used to provide a daily report to parents (see Chamberlain, 1994, and see Chapters 6 and 7). The card is designed to be easy for the teacher but to cover the issues most important to the parents: Was all the day's homework turned in? (yes/no) Did the child arrive in class on time? (yes/no) Did the child stay on task in class? [rate 0, 1, or 2] Did the child have positive interactions with peers? [rate 0, 1, or 2]. Here, as with the parent observations that started the training process, the goal is to be quite specific about what the teacher is asked to observe and record. Feedback from the school card can be incorporated into the contract and point system described earlier. Each element of the teacher's report can be assigned a point value, and these points too can be used to earn privileges and tangible rewards.

Wrapping up. Ideally, it gradually becomes clear to parents and the therapist that parents have the hang of it, and that most newly arising problems can be handled within the skill set the parents have developed. Eight to twelve training sessions with the therapist, or with the multiparent/multitherapist groups, is often enough to reach threshold for ending the training. As a final step, in some cases, parents may do behavior frequency counts as they did at the outset, to reassess rates of deviant and prosocial behaviors, and thus gauge the holding power of treatment effects.

Behavioral Parent Training and Family Treatment for Youth Conduct Problems: Outcome Studies Testing the Effects

The intervention procedures described here evolved initially through careful work with single cases. The procedures were then tested in within-group studies, using groups of increasing size. Eventually the procedures were examined in between-group clinical trials, carried out by investigators inside and outside the Patterson group. Here we review an illustrative sample of the within-group and between-group studies.

Early within-group tests of the Patterson approach. The initial studies of the Patterson procedure involved small groups of aggressive boys, all of whom received treatment (i.e., there was no control group). In the first of these within-group studies, Patterson, Ray, and Shaw (1968) worked with parents of five aggressive boys (age and ethnicity not noted) who were consecutive clinic referrals. After a mean of 22.8 hours of professional intervention per family, deviant child behavior seen by trained observers in the home was reduced by 62–75%. Follow-up data were available on four of the families, and in three of these training effects held up over time. A second within-group report, by Patterson et al. (1973), consisted of 13 consecutive referrals, all boys, ages 6–13 (12 Caucasian, 1 Asian American), and all highly aggressive. In this project, parent training occurred in weekly group sessions, over 8–12 weeks, and the amount of professional time involved averaged 25.7 hours per family. At termination, 9 of the 13 boys showed at least 30% reductions in deviant behaviors. Nine of the families were available for 6–12-month followups, and eight of these showed maintenance of gains, or improvement.

In a third early within-group study, Patterson and Reid (1973) reported on work with families of 11 highly aggressive boys, ages 5–12 (all Caucasian), who were consecutive clinic referrals. Rates of deviant behavior dropped noticeably after parents merely read *Living with Children* (Patterson & Gullion, 1968), the programmed text on child behavior management. However, the rates dropped more sharply after the full intervention (totaling a mean of 31.7 hours of professional time per family), with an average reduction in aggressive behavior of 61%, compared to the pretreatment baseline. These changes were paralleled by improvements in parents' reports of their children's behavior problems, and by improvements in mothers' global perceptions of change.

Illustrative between-group studies of the Patterson program. Other studies testing the Patterson approach have used more rigorous, between-groups comparisons to assess outcome. In one of these studies, Wiltz and Patterson (1974) included 12 boys (mean age 9 years, age range and ethnicity not reported) referred by juvenile court, school counselors, and mental health specialists for treatment of their aggressive behavior. Six boys were assigned to a treatment group; another six, matched to the treatment group boys for age, socioeconomic status, and level of aggression, were assigned to a control group. The treatment group parents read *Living with Children*, identified individual child behaviors they would target for change, set up procedures for tracking and recording those behaviors, worked with a therapist to set up contingencies to modify the target behaviors, and met with other parents and their therapists for five weeks, to compare notes and discuss questions about the parents' behavior modification plans. The intervention apparently worked. In-home observations by trained observers showed significant declines over the five weeks in the targeted aggressive behaviors of the treatment group; target behaviors of the control group held steady over the same five weeks.

In another between-group comparison study, Firestone et al. (1980) tested the efficacy of the Patterson parent training approach with families referred to a hospital outpatient clinic. The test involved an adaptation of the Patterson program scaled down to fit the resources and procedures common in most clinics. Thus, instead of the labor-intensive home visits used in the original Patterson work, the hospital staff provided all parent training in the hospital during regular weekly appointments. Participants were parents of 18 boys ages 3–11 (ethnicity not reported), all referred to a children's hospital by physicians, who had reported such behavior problems as aggression, noncompliance, and temper tantrums. Parents were assigned sequentially to three different groups: for the first six families referred, each child's mother and father went through the behavioral training together; for the next six, only mothers received the behavioral training; the next six formed the no-treatment control group. The first two groups were constituted to address the question of whether fathers are really necessary for effective parent training. The question is important because fathers are often much less likely to participate than are mothers.

Parents in the treatment groups all read a Patterson book on behavioral principles in family life, and they all took a test to ensure that they had learned the key points. In addition, they all pinpointed one or two target problems in their children (most often noncompliance and aggression), charted the frequency of these problems daily, identified rewards and punishments appropriate for their child, and worked out behavioral contracts involving contingencies for acceptable and unacceptable behavior. Parent group discussions focused on adjustments in the contracts and procedures needed to make them work well; and some of the parents extended what they had learned into the school setting, working with teachers to use behavioral charts and contracting to improve their children's behavior. The full treatment lasted an average of 11.5 hours per family.

At the end of the program, a parent-report checklist showed significantly lower levels of problem behavior in the children of both treatment groups than in the control group children. One analysis showed a slight advantage for the two-parent groups, but the overall pattern of findings suggested that father involvement added little to what could be achieved by training mothers only. On the negative side, no significant treatment effects were evident in analyses of teacher-report data from schools, but schools had not been targeted by most of the participants. So, one interpretation of the teacher data is that one cannot simply assume that home-based effects will automatically generalize to school.

Comparison to alternate treatments: I. Behavioral parent training versus client-centered counseling. In a different approach, Bernal et al. (1980) compared the Patterson approach to another active treatment for conduct problems in 5–12-year-old boys and girls. Some 36 children (86% male, ethnicity not reported) were recruited through ads and professional referrals to a project clinic "specializing in the treatment and evaluation of conduct problem children" (p. 679). Children brought to the clinic were randomly assigned to either behavioral parent training following the Patterson model or client-centered parent counseling in which therapists helped parents explore their ideas about discipline, their roles as parents, the meanings conveyed by child behavior, and communication patterns among family members. A waitlist control group was assigned nonrandomly, based on therapist availability. At the end of the eight-week training program, parent-report measures and paper and pencil tests of child deviance showed superior outcomes for the behavioral parent training group, relative to both the client-centered group and the no-treatment control group, which did not differ in outcome. However, direct observations of child behavior at home did not show either treatment group to be superior to the control group. Follow-up assessment, at six months and one year posttreatment, involved telephone-administered parent-report measures administered to the two treatment groups, but not the waitlist group. These follow-up assessments showed some significant improvement from posttreatment to followup in the two treated groups, but no significant difference between the groups. Overall, the Bernal et al. study provided some support for the efficacy of the Patterson parent-training approach, but there were caveats: (1) participants had not been assigned to groups randomly, (2) the important home observational measures did not show treatment benefit, and (3) the parent self-report measures did not show the Patterson approach to be superior to client-centered counseling at followup.

Comparison to alternate treatments: II. Behavioral parent and youth training versus client-centered family groups versus psychodynamic family treatment: the beginning of Functional Family Therapy. In a more complex design than that of Bernal et al. (1980), Alexander and Parsons (1973) compared three approaches to treating delinquent 13–16-year-old boys and girls, all referred from juvenile court after offenses. The 86 youths (56% girls, ethnicity not reported) and families who were included in the study analyses were assigned randomly to one of four conditions ("minor exceptions" to random assignment occurred "caused by program availability," see Alexander & Parsons, 1973, p. 220). The target treatment approach was *short-term behavioral family intervention*; the program was quite Patterson-like (including use of a modification of Patterson and Gullion's [1968] *Living with Children*), but it included such additional elements as (1) family sessions designed to improve communication and increase family reciprocity, and (2) encouragment of negotiation among family members with each member receiving a privilege for each responsibility assumed. One of the alternative treatments, *client-centered family groups*, entailed "didactic group discussion... focusing on attitudes and feelings about family relationships and adolescent problems based on the client-centered model" (p. 221). This intervention was designed to be representative of the treatments provided in many juvenile centers. The second alternative treatment was a Mormon Church-sponsored *psychodynamic family counseling program* that was commonly used in Utah, where the study took place; the program was described as insight-oriented and based on an eclectic psychodynamic model. One additional group of families was randomly assigned to receive no treatment.

Alexander and Parsons measured outcomes by assessing patterns of family interaction in a series of three tasks (e.g., discussing changes various family members should make in their behavior), and by examining juvenile court records to assess recidivism of the adolescents, that is, re-referral for behavioral offenses. Both sets of measures showed effects favoring the behavioral parent training group. The three primary measures of family interaction quality – that is, balanced talk time among family members, silence, and interruptions – all showed better posttreatment scores for the behavioral group than the other groups. And recidivism rates over the 6–18-month follow-up interval posttreatment were lowest for youth in the behavioral parent training group at 26%, compared to 47% for the client-centered group, 50% for the no-treatment controls, and 73% for the eclectic psychodynamic group; the usual countywide recidivism rate was 51%. These results are particularly useful because they involve comparisons of a structured behavioral family program with two less structured alternative treatments, both reportedly quite representative of the usual interventions provided in the study location; the evidence showed that the structured treatment was not only superior to no treatment, but also to active alternative treatments that the youngsters would have been likely to receive in the absence of the study.

In an interesting followup to this study, Klein et al. (1977) studied whether the four treatment conditions were related to rates of subsequent court referral in the siblings of targeted youth. The idea was that if treatment improves parenting skill and family functioning, the beneficial effects might well spread beyond the single youth in the family who had originally been referred. Examining juvenile court records 2.5 to 3.5 years beyond the study interventions, Klein et al. did find evidence of sibling benefit in the behavioral parent training group. Only 20% of the families in this treatment condition had subsequent court contact for siblings, compared to 40% for the no-treatment controls, 59% for the client-centered group, and 63% for the psychodynamic group.

The evolution of Functional Family Therapy. The short-term behavioral family intervention tested by Alexander and Parsons (1973) has been tested in other studies (e.g., Alexander et al., 1976), and has evolved sufficiently to be given its own name, Functional Family Therapy (see Alexander & Parsons, 1982; Barton & Alexander, 1980). Investigators have built a body of research support for Functional Family Therapy, including extension to new populations and settings (see Barton et al., 1985) and tests showing long-term effects so robust that they held up even as treated adolescents matured into adulthood (see Gordon et al., 1995).

Using behavioral parent training to improve foster care. In a valuable extension of behavioral parent training, Chamberlain (1996) has focused on enhancing foster care for youngsters who are placed outside their families' homes because of their serious delinquent behavior. Every year in the United States, large numbers of delinquent youth are removed from their homes because of conduct problems so severe that the family cannot handle them, and because courts judge that society needs protection from the youngsters' illegal and often violent acts. A particularly common out-of-home placement for such youth is the group home, staffed by a combination of residential staff and mental health professionals. Concerns have arisen about both the effectiveness and the cost of group home care. An alternative approach developed by Chamberlain and her colleagues is *Multidimensional Treatment Foster Care* (MTFC). In this program, Chamberlain and her colleagues train foster parents to cope with the difficulties that arise when they try to manage the behavior of court-referred, severely antisocial teens.

The first challenge of the Chamberlain program is recruiting and training foster parents for this challenging task. Through clever ads like those shown in Figure 9.2, community families are drawn into telephone screening, which is followed by completion of a written application, a home visit by MTFC staff, and a 20-hour preservice training program. For candidate foster families who persevere through this sequence, supervision is provided weekly through foster parent group meetings run by project case managers, and through daily phone calls covering the youth's progress and problems during the previous 24 hours.

The core of the MTFC program is closely linked to the Patterson principles and procedures, as discussed earlier. Chamberlain's experience with these unusually difficult court-referred youths has led to innovations and supplemental procedures as well. For example, in the most recent version of the program:

EUGENE/EUGENE

NON-VACATION PACKAGE

NO TRAVEL

182 DAYS

182 NIGHTS

$640 PER MONTH FOR YOU

OSLC is looking for skilled, dedicated parents to
provide 6 months (182 days) foster care for
mildly delinquent boy.
We provide training, lots of support, and stipend
in sunny Eugene.

Call OSLC, Kathy R., for info. 485-2711

SUMMER HOME
Needed now for cute, mild
mannered 14 year old boy.
Comes from abuse background.
Prefer experienced parents or
singles willing to provide foster
home for 6 months. Training,
support and $540 a month. Call
Kathy, Oregon Social Learning
Center, 485-2711

HUCK·FINN
12 year old boy with troubled
background needs stable foster
home with older or no children.
Mental health background or
like experience preferred.
Training support and $700 per
month. Call Kathy, Oregon Social Learning Center, 485-2711

Gain 130 lbs.

14-year-old boy needs foster home. Oregon Social Learning Center is
looking for skilled, dedicated parent(s) for 6 months care for troubled
youth. We train, provide support, $640/month. Call Kathy R., 485-2711.

COUPLE or single parent with older or no children wanted for 13
old twin boy who needs a
HOME FOR
CHRISTMAS
He's very likeable but from a troubled background. Comes with
parakeet companion. $540
month for 3 months. Call Kathy,
weekdays, Oregon Social Learning Center, 485-2711.

Couples with
EMPTY NEST

We are looking for dedicated and skilled parents to provide 6 months of
foster care to a teenage boy from a troubled background.
We provide training, lots of support, and $600 per month
Call Oregon Social Learning Center, 485-2711, and ask for Kathy.

FIGURE 9.2. Newspaper ads used to recruit parents for Chamberlain's Multidimensional Treatment Foster Care program. Reprinted with the permission of Patricia Chamberlain.

- Each youth receives weekly individual therapy focused on skill building in problem solving, taking the perspective of others, and nonaggressive methods of self-expression.
- Each youth's biological family (or other source of social relationships to which the boy will return after the court-mandated program ends) receives weekly family sessions involving training in the use of behavior

management principles (supervision, encouragement, discipline, constructive problem solving).

- Each youth's school participates in behavioral management as well; for example, participating youths all carry a card to each class, on which teachers sign off on attendance, homework completion, and attitude. Such teacher feedback generates consequences for each youth, such as point and privilege gains and losses, and even – for serious infractions – brief stays in detention.
- Each youth is monitored closely throughout each day, with close attention to how each waking moment is spent and with which peers. Contact with peers known to be delinquent is simply prohibited.
- Case managers are on call 24 hours, seven days per week, providing ongoing consultation to the treatment foster parents.

The average foster placement in the program lasts about six months. Treatment foster parents are paid $800–$1,000 per month. A recurrent challenge in mounting the program is that of training and certifying sufficient numbers of foster parents to accommodate youths who need care. Various states differ markedly in laws and certification requirements bearing on the program. Where regulations slow the flow of trained and certified foster parents, referral agencies may lose patience and turn elsewhere for care of their most difficult foster children. Although such practical difficulties pose real challenges, the evidence we will now review suggests that MTFC has the potential to make a real difference in foster care outcomes.

Testing the impact of behavioral training for foster parents. Four studies have tested the feasibility and effects of the MTFC program (Chamberlain, 1990; Chamberlain, Moreland, & Reid, 1992; Chamberlain & Reid, 1991, 1998), but the most recent of these is the most complete randomized trial, so we focus on that study here. Chamberlain and Reid (1998) compared outcomes of the MTFC program to outcomes achieved through placement in community group care settings. The study focused on 79 boys, ages 12–17 (85% Caucasian, 6% African American, 6% Latino, and 3% Native American), who may have represented one of the most severely antisocial samples in the youth treatment literature. All the boys had been judged so severely delinquent and so hard to control that juvenile authorities had required separation from their biological families. The boys averaged 14 prior criminal referrals, with more than four felonies. All had been detained in the year prior to the study, with a mean of 76 days in detention. All had previously been placed out of home at least once.

These seriously delinquent boys were randomly assigned to either the MTFC program or to one of 11 community-based group care programs that had from 6–15 youths in residence at a time. The group care programs had varying treatment philosophies, but most often followed a "positive peer culture" approach (Vorath & Brendtro, 1985), with group work in which the teen participants were expected to establish prosocial norms, confront one another about norm violations, and participate in decision making and disciplinary actions.

Evidence collected after the end of treatment indicated that youngsters assigned to MTFC fared much better than youngsters in group care. Compared to group care boys, the boys in MTFC were about half as likely to run away during the treatment period (31% vs. 58%), were twice as likely to complete their treatment program (73% vs. 36%), and spent 60% fewer days in detention facilities (means of 53 days vs. 129 days). In the year following treatment termination, the MTFC boys were able to spend about twice as much time as group care boys living with parents or relatives, and the MTFC group showed about half as many documented referrals for criminal activity, and fewer than half as many self-reported delinquent offenses.

The evidence strongly suggests that the MTFC program developed by Chamberlain and her colleagues can produce beneficial effects that outpace effects of conventional community-based group care for delinquent youth placed out of home. The encouraging evidence is consistent with the growing popularity of treatment foster care programs that reflect the principles of MTFC, programs now promoted by the Foster Family-Based Treatment Association, in 44 states and four Canadian provinces (see Chamberlain, 1996). The demonstrated benefits of the program, and the extent to which it is being emulated around North America, illustrate the potential of those basic principles articulated and tested so many years ago by Patterson and colleagues.

Summary of the outcome evidence on behavioral parent training. We have reviewed eight studies, selected to illustrate both the origins of parent training and a few of the ways it has evolved. We noted the important pioneering work of Patterson and his colleagues in developing and testing parent training procedures, using both within-group studies (Patterson et al., 1968; Patterson et al., 1973; Patterson & Reid, 1973) and between-group designs (e.g., Wiltz & Patterson, 1974). We summarized two group-comparison tests of Patterson-derived parent training procedures by other investigative teams (e.g., Bernal et al., 1980; Firestone et al., 1980). We also reported on illustrative tests of expanded versions of parent training, encompassing family sessions (e.g., Alexander & Parsons, 1973) and training of foster parents for delinquent youth (e.g., Chamberlain, 1996; Chamberlain & Reid, 1998). Outcome assessment across the various studies has encompassed informant reports (especially from parents), direct observations of youth behavior, and such real-life outcomes as runaways, arrests, court contacts, and days spent in detention facilities. In general, findings have shown that behaviorally oriented parent training produces greater reductions in youth problem behavior than no-treatment or waitlist control conditions and, in the main, than alternative treatments (but see Bernal et al., 1980). In addition, to the extent that follow-up assessments have been conducted, most have pointed to holding power of parent-training effects after the end of treatment.

What about Sal? Applying Behavioral Parent Training and Family Treatment

In Sal's family, it is easy to spot ways in which his misbehavior is being inadvertently rewarded. Sal's mother responds to his aversive behavior with nagging and yelling, both of which are not just ineffective but counterproductive, because they are rewarding his unwanted behavior with attention; attention is a valuable commodity in this chaotic home. She also rewards Sal's willful behavior (e.g., staying out late at night) by giving in. The picture involves what Patterson and colleagues call a *coercive process*. Giving in to Sal provides negative reinforcement to Mom: when Sal gets his way his behavior is less aversive, and when he is away from home, the stress level at home drops sharply. And when Sal shows desirable behavior, such as helping his mother bring in groceries, telling her an interesting story about his day at school, or sharing a laugh with her, she often fails to even comment on it (or reward it in more subtle ways), fearing that she may break the spell. So, Sal's undesirable behavior is being rewarded with attention and compliance, and his more positive behavior is not being rewarded. With these contingencies in effect, Sal's conduct problems would come as no surprise to a behavioral therapist. Let us suppose that Sal's mother is referred by the school counselor to a therapist who specializes in behavioral parent training. Here is the sequence that might unfold.

The process begins with an intake interview in which Sal's mother describes her reasons for seeking help. The therapist asks her for details – what specifically does Sal do and say that worries her most? What are the situations where he most often does and says these things? And how do she and Sal's father respond at these times? It soon becomes clear that Sal's father is primarily trying to avoid the stress of dealing with Sal, and that he is not very likely to participate in the treatment process. The therapist knows about research (Firestone et al., 1980; Martin, 1977) showing that parent training can work even if only the mother takes part, but he does want to ensure that Sal's father won't try to oppose or undo what she learns to do. He wants to avoid the situation Patterson et al. (1973) labeled the "sadomasochistic Arabesque," in which one parent's effective approach is undermined by another parent's inept or hostile counteractions.

The therapist judges that this is indeed a situation in which behavioral parent training can make a difference, and in which Sal's father is too passive to put much energy into opposing his wife. The therapist doesn't always ask parents to read before he begins treatment, but Sal's mother is so motivated and so eager to do all she can that he decides to lend her a programmed text, *Living with Children*. Later, at home, as she reads through the text and answers the questions inserted within each point, Sal's mother begins to realize that she has not been very organized in dealing with Sal's behavior. For example:

- On page 63 she reads, ". . . before you begin to change a defined behavior, you must first observe and _____ [count] it." She realizes that she has had a general sense that Sal is disrespectful and difficult, but that she has not actually stopped to identify his specific behaviors that trouble her, or to count how often they happen.
- On the same page she reads, "Then, carefully plan the manner in which you can weaken the undesirable behavior, and the steps you can take in _____ [strengthening or reinforcing] a competing, desirable one." She realizes that she has often complained to Sal about his behavior, but that she has not actually planned specific steps to make his bad behavior less rewarding to him, or to make better behavior more rewarding!

By the time Sal's mother has finished the book, she has learned a number of important concepts she will need in the upcoming training program with the therapist. For example, she has learned what *reinforcers* are and how they can be used to strengthen or weaken behavior. She has learned how important it is to be specific about behaviors she wants to see changed, and how important it is to count those behaviors carefully, to see if they are changing when she changes reinforcement patterns at home. She has also learned that one of the best ways to weaken unwanted behavior is to increase rewards for positive alternative behavior. She is so anxious to help Sal that she studies the book as if for an exam at school. Her study at home is complemented by some video viewing; her therapist uses videos of common parent-child interactions to illustrate core behavioral principles, such as how reinforcement works.

After the reading and videos, it is time to get to work, focusing on Sal. One of the first tasks Mom works on with the therapist is identifying just one or two of Sal's behaviors that will be targeted for change. Trying to change too many things at once is a prescription for confusion and failure. In any event, what the therapist wants to do is not to oversee a complete revamping of her son but rather to improve her skill in identifying, observing, and changing specific behaviors, so that she can take charge. One of the first crucial steps is judicious problem selection. The therapist gives Mom five guidelines (drawn from Patterson & Forgatch, 1987):

1. **Be specific.** Mom needs to be specific about Sal's target behaviors. For example, saying that Sal is "rude" is being too general. The therapist helps her sharpen the focus a bit, to "saying insulting things to Mom." One example: Insulting his mother's cooking. They also focus on disobeying Mom, as we discuss under guideline #4.

2. **Begin with problems you can see.** Much of what worries Mom is what she suspects Sal is doing when she can't see him – for example, truancy, threatening others, delinquent acts with peers. Instead of those suspected behaviors, the therapist asks her to focus on behavior she can observe and record at home. This way, she can tell whether the procedures she works out with her therapist are helping.

3. **Start with fairly neutral behaviors.** The therapist insists that Mom not start off with problems that make her furious, or issues that will be highly upsetting to Sal. Because Sal's comments about her "lesbian friends" is so upsetting to her, she and the therapist decide to save that problem for later, so she can remain calm when enforcing the first contingencies.

4. **Select behaviors that occur at least two or three times per day.** The therapist presses Mom to identify fairly high-frequency behaviors. This, he says, will increase the chance that she will notice the behaviors when they occur, and the high starting rate will make it possible to detect change when it occurs. Together they select "disobeying Mom" as the target problem they will work on first. That problem is guaranteed to happen frequently!

5. **Say what replacement behaviors are needed.** The therapist notes that rather than specify only what Sal should not do, it is useful to clarify what behavior he should replace the unwanted behavior with. As an easy example, instead of disobeying, Sal should obey. As another, for use later in treatment, when talking about his Mom's friends, Sal should refer to them only as her "friends."

The next task for Mom and her therapist is to develop a consistent set of contingencies for Sal; there need to be no positive consequences (and perhaps some negative consequences) when the unwanted behaviors happen, and positive consequences when the desirable replacement behaviors happen. Given Sal's age, time-out procedures may not work well. So the therapist and Mom decide to work with Sal to develop a behavior contract. It spells out what behaviors are expected of Sal, what benefits will accrue if he meets those expectations, and what costs there will be if he fails to meet them.

The first contract they hammer out is a very simple one. It focuses only on the issue of obeying Mom. The deal is that each time Sal obeys, Mom will write "M" (for Mom) on a chart they keep on the kitchen wall. Each M signifies one point. Ten points will be worth any one of a set of rewards Sal and Mom have agreed on – including a half-hour of TV or video game time, or an extra helping of dessert at dinner – Sal's choice. Larger point totals are worth larger rewards, all identified by Sal and approved by Mom. On the first day she tries the contract, Sal is not interested in obeying. When she mentions the contract he says, "Screw your contract," and slams the door to his room. Later, a major conflict ensues, with shouts and threats from Sal, when Mom holds to the contract, and refuses to let Sal have video time or extra dessert. With the help of the therapist (during a phone check-in), Mom sticks to her guns and rides out the conflict without giving in to Sal's pressure.

Gradually, much to Mom's surprise, Sal begins to obey more than before, glancing at the chart frequently to make sure he gets the credit. He even seems to get into the challenge of earning points. By the end of the first week, he has obeyed her more than in any week in recent memory. Progress continues during the second week. Occasionally there is a glitch, or a dispute over how much Sal must do to qualify as truly obeying, and occasionally the therapist's input during phone check-ins is needed for problem solving. Overall, though, the trajectory on obeying Mom looks quite good by the end of week two.

Building on this success, Sal, his mother, and the therapist work on an expanded contract, adding new target behaviors and point values for each, and enriching the reward options available. Negative behaviors are also added, with point penalties for each. For example, "insulting Mom" is added to the contract, with each insult costing Sal five points. After three weeks of gradual improvement, this more complex contract seems to have produced further gains in Sal's appropriate behavior and reductions in his inappropriate behavior.

With these gains in place, the agenda expands further, encompassing some of Sal's behavior that worries his mother but is not directly observable by her. Sal's behavior at school has already gotten him into serious trouble. Research findings (e.g., Firestone et al., 1980) suggest that parent training intervention effects evident in youths' behavior at home do not necessarily generalize to school when no special outreach to school personnel is employed. It is important, then, to work out a behavioral system that involves school staff and places them in regular contact with Sal's mother. The therapist recommends a daily school card.

To develop the card, Mom and therapist meet with Sal's teachers to decide together what Sal's most pressing problems are at school. At the top of the consensus list are: *getting off-task, conflict with peers,* and *disrespectful behavior toward teachers.* The teachers agree to give Sal a daily rating on these three items if Sal brings a rating card to their desk at the end of each period – classes, lunch, and recess. The three scales are:

- Stays on task. 0 1 2
- Gets along with other kids. 0 1 2
- Respectful to teachers. 0 1 2

Sal's job each day is to bring the card to each teacher at the end of each period. The teacher ratings are reviewed by Mom when Sal gets home each school day. These ratings are incorporated into a daily schedule point

Sal's Point Chart for School Days			
Behavior	Description	Deadline	Points
Up on time	Out of bed	7:00 A.M.	+10
Ready for day	Breakfast eaten, teeth brushed, hair combed, dressed, backpack ready	7:30 A.M.	+10
Morning duties	Bed made, dirty clothes put away, room neat, towel & wash cloth put away	7:45 A.M.	+10
Teacher ratings	Have each teacher rate & sign card; bring home	3:45 P.M.	+0 -6 per teacher
	[10 bonus points for each full day with all "2"s from all teachers!]		
Daily chores	Listed each day; each one is 10-15 min.	by 6:00 P.M.	+10
Homework	50 minutes	7:00 -7:50 P.M.	+20
Volunteering	Volunteering to do extra jobs		+2-10
In bed	On time and lights out	9:00 P.M.	+10
Disobeying Mom		at any time	-10
Disrespecting Mom or her friends		at any time	-10

Some of the Items On Sal's Privilege List		
Privilege	Description	Cost in Points
Basics	Listen to radio or CD in your room; 9:30 bedtime	20
TV	Watch TV *with permission* if studying, reading, & chores are done	25
Other	Talk to friends on phone, use game room supplies	10
Late bedtime	11:00 P.M. --Friday, Saturday, and nights before holidays	30
Note: **Basics** must be purchased before you are eligible for other privileges.		

FIGURE 9.3. Sal's point chart and some of the items on his privilege list.

chart that encompasses Sal's full day, at school as well as home. Sal and his mom also develop a privilege list, to show what can be purchased with the points he earns. Sal's point chart and some of the entries in his privilege list (adapted from Chamberlain, 1994) are shown in Figure 9.3.

Sal's mother and the therapist have now expanded their focus to include both home and school. One other theme needs coverage. The growing influence of peers on Sal's behavior makes it clear that monitoring and limiting his peer contact will be critical to success. With help from school personnel,

Mom identifies two peers with whom all contact needs to be terminated, and others with whom Sal should only associate under close adult supervision. Enforcing such limits, the therapist explains, is an effective way to reduce the opportunity for Sal to be rewarded for antisocial behavior by the approval and encouragement of deviant, antisocial peers. Controlling peer contact is a major element of some of the most successful behavioral programs for delinquent youth (see e.g., Chamberlain, 1996), and it clearly needs to be a part of Sal's program.

Given the severity of Sal's behavior problems, and the fact that risks increase as he matures, Sal may need to be monitored throughout his day, so that Mom will know where he is and what he is doing at virtually all times. The steps she and the therapist have taken thus far are useful, but it is possible that the full plan will be too complex for her to manage. Moreover, as Sal grows bigger and stronger, he may be too difficult for her to control effectively, particularly since she lacks support from her husband. If Sal's behavior does get out of control, and especially if it leads to juvenile justice involvement, a program such as Multidimensional Treatment Foster Care (Chamberlain, 1996; Chamberlain & Reid, 1998) may be needed to achieve the close management Sal needs. In this program, behaviorally trained foster parents use contingency management and close monitoring of school behavior and peer contact to help delinquent youths keep their behavior under control. If all goes well at home, such a program may not be necessary for Sal; but if his difficulties swamp his mother's ability to help, behaviorally oriented foster care may be an appropriate next step.

Troubleshooting: Common Treatment Problems and Recommended Solutions. For problems like Sal's, behavioral parent training (including multidimensional treatment foster care) and family treatment can make a real difference, but not all parents are as conscientious as Sal's mother, and even highly motivated parents may find some of the procedures difficult. Problems that arise in working with parents have been discussed in detail by Patterson, Forgatch, Chamberlain, and their colleagues over the years (e.g., Patterson & Chamberlain, 1992; Patterson & Forgatch, 1985), and some of the most common have been given the following labels by Marian Forgatch (personal communication, January 2003).

- *"I can't."* Some parents – particularly those who are depressed, stressed out, or overwhelmed in the role of single parent – may regard the behavioral procedures suggested by the therapist as too difficult for them to manage, or requiring too much effort. A common response by therapists is to try to convince parents that they can. Big mistake. This sets in motion an unproductive dance in which parents try to prove they can't, and the therapist tries to prove they can. A more effective approach is for the therapist to sidestep the dance by becoming very interested in the circumstances that make it impossible for the parents, and very sympathetic about those circumstances. In fact, the therapist may even assume a defeated posture and agree: yes, it *is* too much to ask. At this point, the debate is over; therapist and parent are in total agreement. So a serious discussion can begin about this impossible task and what can be done about it. Among the therapist's options: (1) break the task into small steps and plan how to take the first Step; (2) offer to support the parents' efforts in various ways, including phone calls during the week to provide on-the-spot consultation; and even (3) give the parents a "vacation," a week with no home practice assignment. A key here is to accept enough of the parents' perspective to create a collaborative relationship, one that is focused on problem solving rather than nagging or debating.

- *"I won't."* Few among us like being told what to do. Parents of disobedient, disruptive children can be especially sensitive in this regard. Even when they appear to be seeking the therapist's advice, that advice may be met with "I'm not doing that," "That would never work," or "You gotta be kidding." An observant therapist will detect the pattern quickly: therapist proposes; parents reject. One possible response is for the therapist to propose more and more plans; the outcome of that approach is predictable. A more effective strategy is to shift roles, with the therapist noting a goal the parents have identified, and the parents brainstorming ideas for reaching that goal. The therapist's role then becomes that of facilitator, writing the ideas down, framing and reframing them, constructively examining the pros and cons together with the parents, and guiding the process to a final plan that all agree might work. In this way, the plan belongs to the parents, not the therapist, so it is much less likely to be resisted and rejected.

- *"I didn't."* Many parent sessions begin with a review of the previous week's home practice assignment. Parents sometimes respond that they didn't do it – they forgot, they were sick, the child was suddenly and unexpectedly out of town, or aliens from outer space interfered. Even when the reasons make good sense, a series of practice assignments not done and not debriefed is a major impediment to parent skill building. Some reasons for noncompletion may be addressed through joint problem solving; forgetful parents, for example, may get reminder phone calls during the week. Clever therapists may also find ways to squeeze simulated practice and constructive debriefing out of the parents' everyday experience during the week. Let's illustrate. After weeks of "I didn't," a clever therapist avoids hitting further brick walls, by steering clear of questions such as, "Did you do your assignment?" or "How did the home practice go this week?" Instead, the therapist opens the session by saying things like, "For this past week, you were going to try some new ways to get Sal to obey – like getting his attention first, making eye contact, standing next to him, and using a pleasant but firm tone of voice." (This reminds parents what the assignment was.) "These changes could be hard for many parents." (This acknowledges the difficulty.) "Which of these strategies was easiest for you?" (This establishes the assumption that the practice was tried.) If the parents start to say they didn't do any of the strategies, the therapist might reply, "Well, chances are you asked Sal to do *something* during the week – right? (Parent nods.) "OK, did you make eye contact with Sal when you did?" At this point, the same discussion (i.e., using eye contact to evoke compliance) can take place that would occur if the parents had intentionally done the home practice assignment.

Behavioral Parent Training and Family Treatment: Scientific Issues

The science of behavioral parent training research is generally strong. Over four decades, methods have progressed from single case studies to within-group assessments of improvement over time, to between-group clinical trials. Much of the research is marked by unusual care, caution in interpreting findings, and an admirably programmatic, cumulative process of knowledge building. The evidence strongly supports the premise that when parents change the consequences of their children's behavior, the behavior of their children changes. Much of the research has focused on the questions of what kinds of changes in consequences actually work best, and how best to teach parents to make those changes. Over the past four decades, behavioral researchers have substantially expanded our ability to answer both questions.

Replication of treatment effects across laboratories was considered an important factor in assessing the empirical status of treatments, by the original APA Division 12 Task Force (see Chambless et al., 1995, 1998) and by the task force of child specialists (see Lonigan et al., 1998). On this respect, behavioral parent training and family treatment must be regarded as particularly strong empirically. As discussed elsewhere (see Kazdin & Weisz, 1998), at least five independent labs have produced evidence in support of the benefits of this form of treatment. While the research on behavioral parent training and family intervention has been impressive in many ways, a number of challenges remain.

One significant challenge involves objective assessment of treatment impact. A laudable strength of much of the Patterson work has been its reliance on direct *in-home* observation of behavior in its natural context. In contrast, a number of studies of parent training (e.g., Firestone et al., 1980) have relied only on parent-report and teacher-report measures, and have not employed any direct observation. An advantage of this latter approach is that it does reflect what is likely to be possible in most practice settings. However, findings by Bernal et al. (1980) illustrated that parent-report measures can make parent training effects look quite good even when direct observations do not show such effects. This suggests a genuine need for direct observation. Because parent training requires such a large investment of parents' time and energy, there is a possibility that the demand characteristics of self-report are very significant; not only do the parents know they received the intervention, but their great investment in the process might make it very difficult for them to report that their child is no better, despite all the effort. Thus, it seems that some form of observational assessment by experimentally naïve observers will continue to be a mainstay of research on this particular form of treatment.

Even the most beneficial of treatments is likely to work well only within a certain range of human characteristics. Thus, it is important to understand as much as possible about factors that moderate treatment impact. In the behavioral parent training domain, age may well be a moderator. Although this chapter has sampled studies across the child-adolescent spectrum, it is fair to say that behavioral parent training has been applied primarily to preschoolers through preadolescents, and it is within this age range that the evidence of treatment benefit is strongest. Treatment impact has been found to be more modest with adolescents (see e.g., Dishion & Patterson, 1992; see also Barkley, 1997), who also tend to be more severely and chronically impaired than preschoolers and preadolescents.

Gender and ethnicity also warrant attention as moderators. The research on behavioral parent training a la Patterson has emphasized boys, in part because they are more likely than girls to be referred for aggression and other conduct problems. Also, largely Caucasian samples have predominated in the research base. Thus, relatively little attention has been given, to date, to whether gender or ethnicity may be related to intervention effects, or whether variations in intervention methods might boost effects for girls or non-Caucasian ethnic groups. These questions need to be a part of the agenda for future research.

A particularly important challenge for research on behavioral parent training and family treatment is identification of those processes that mediate change. To illustrate the need, consider the behaviorally oriented Multidimensional Treatment Foster Care Program, developed by Chamberlain and colleagues (Chamberlain, 1996; Chamberlain & Reid, 1998). The evidence thus far suggests that it works well. But why does it work? Through what kind of change processes does improvement in youth functioning actually come about? To state the case in the extreme, it is possible in principle that foster parents' increases in behavioral skills are not actually responsible for treatment success. Instead, perhaps the program works only because the intervention leaders select unusually strong, resilient adults with superior parenting skills to serve as foster parents; perhaps these adults would produce excellent outcomes even if they received none of the training and monitoring provided by the Chamberlain program.

Given that hypothetical possibility, it is very helpful to have evidence from a particularly important study by Eddy and Chamberlain (2000), using rigorous analytic procedures (Baron & Kenny, 1986) to identify two true mediators of their treatment program's impact: (1) foster parents' family management skills, and (2) youths' associations with deviant peers. Such evidence on mediation is sorely needed to help identify the processes that matter in treatment and to help us understand why treatment works when it does. This study by Eddy and Chamberlain (2000) sets an admirable standard for other researchers in the area of behavioral parent training and family intervention.

A final issue has to do with maintenance of effects over time. Although some studies show effects lasting more than five years (Gordon et al., 1995; Long et al., 1994), such studies are not common in the literature. A recent review concluded that evidence for long-term maintenance of gains is limited and quite mixed (Eyberg et al., 1998). In the future, the agenda for research in this area must certainly include more follow-up studies, and more effort to increase the generalization and staying power of treatment gains – strategies such as training in ways of preventing relapse, and scheduling of refreshers or booster sessions at intervals after treatment has formally ended.

Behavioral Parent Training and Family Treatment: Clinical Practice Issues

From a clinical practice perspective, behavioral parent training offers a number of advantages and poses a number of challenges. Among the advantages is an unusually rich record of scientific support, showing that behavioral parent training can work with a variety of externalizing youth. Clinicians who develop expertise in behavioral parent training are adding a potent skill to their repertoire, one that will serve them well with precisely the kinds of cases that are most often referred for treatment. Another advantage is that behavioral parent and family experts have been quite prolific in describing their procedures and generating supporting materials for use with parents. Such readable best-sellers as *Living with Children* (Patterson, 1976) and *Parents and Adolescents Living Together: The Basics* (Patterson & Forgatch, 1987) are complemented by a variety of other books and videotapes that therapists can use as adjuncts to their one-on-one time in parent training sessions. Another plus for the clinician is face validity. Thanks to widespread dissemination and acceptance of some basic ideas of behavioral intervention, such concepts as "time-out" and "consequences" are familiar to many parents, even if the details and nuances are not fully understood by them. Thus, a general acceptance of behavioral parent training within our culture helps make the ground fertile for intervention by experts in behavioral work with parents.

However, this approach to intervention does face challenges. For participating parents, the workload can be heavy, with significant amounts of study to master basic behavioral principles, and a great deal of energy needed to maintain vigilance and consistency in contingency management at home. Because many youngsters are referred in part because of school problems, additional time may be required for the parent to design and coordinate intervention procedures with school staff, some of whom may not be such willing participants. The time and effort required for all these components will certainly exceed the motivation or capacity of some parents. As an example, when Firestone et al. (1980) offered the treatment to 25 families, nine refused outright, and another four dropped out within three sessions; and this was a truncated treatment with fewer time demands than the original Patterson approach.

Practitioners who consider using a behavioral parent and family approach will also need to consider the demands such an approach will place on their own time, some of which may not be reimbursable, and some of which will come at the cost of time with additional clients. Another issue for practitioners who are not trained in these methods will be the accessibility of learning opportunities and help with implementation. Although parent training may sound simple, some of its component procedures can be quite subtle and difficult to calibrate effectively; these procedures include selecting and sequencing a youth's problems for contingency adjustment (which problems to attend to first, when to add new problems), correctly discerning the youth's reinforcer hierarchy, developing contracts and point systems that will be understandable and motivating, and addressing breakdowns skillfully. Hands-on training in the complexities of behavioral parent training is not readily available in most locations. On the other hand, there are numerous handbooks, texts, and manuals that provide detailed descriptions (e.g., Chamberlain, 1994; Forehand & McMahon, 1981; Patterson & Forgatch, 1987; Patterson & Gullion, 1968, 1968), sample materials (e.g., point systems, behavioral charts), and troubleshooting guides. A particularly valuable resource is a well-researched program of parent training videotapes, developed by Webster-Stratton and colleagues (see e.g., Webster-Stratton, 1996), discussed in detail in Chapter 11.

Even if demands on the therapist's time can be reduced, as in Firestone et al. (1980), or through the use of parent-training videos to replace some of the hands-on parent training, a question remains as to whether behavioral parent training and family work can improve on the alternative care that youth with conduct problems would otherwise receive. Several studies in this area suggest that the answer is yes. Studies comparing behavioral parent and family approaches derived from Patterson have shown that these approaches produce better youth outcomes than a variety of commonly available alternatives, including usual community care (Patterson,

Chamberlain, & Reid, 1983), client-centered and psychodynamic family treatments (Alexander & Parsons, 1973; see mixed evidence in Bernal et al., 1980), court-mandated intensive family treatment (90-minute sessions weekly; Bank et al., 1991), and community-based residential group care (Chamberlain & Reid, 1998). The collective force of these and other comparative findings suggests that the time demands of the behavioral parent and family approach are justified by the outcomes produced.

Another notable strength of the evidence base, from a clinical practice perspective, is the severity of the cases for whom beneficial effects have been demonstrated. The youths targeted in some of these intervention studies (e.g., Chamberlain & Reid, 1998) represent some of the most difficult and dangerous treated in all the youth psychotherapy literature. The fact that so many of the youngsters treated were community-referred and seriously antisocial underscores the relevance of this treatment approach to the real world of clinical practice, both in the therapist's office and in such outreach settings as social service systems and foster care programs.

How to Find Out More about Behavioral Parent Training and Family Treatment

Descriptions of the basic Patterson concepts and parent training procedures can be found in a number of chapters (e.g., Patterson, Cobb, & Ray, 1973) and books (e.g., Patterson, Reid, & Dishion, 1992; Patterson, Reid, Jones, & Conger, 1975). *Living with Children*, Patterson's famous programmed text for parents, is available in revised form (Patterson, 1976). A nonprogrammed and highly readable series by Patterson and Forgatch (e.g., 1987), focused on parent-adolescent relationships, and a set of audiocassettes for parents (Patterson & Forgatch, 1975) rounds out the available support for skill-building. Functional family therapy and its effects are described by Alexander and Parsons (1982) and Alexander, Waldron, Newberry, and Liddle (1990). Multidimensional treatment foster care is described, and its effects reported, by Chamberlain (1994, 1996), Chamberlain and Reid (1998), and Chamberlain and Smith (2003).

10

Parent-Child Interaction Treatments
for Child Noncompliance

Most treatments addressing conduct problems in youth emphasize corrective action aimed at the offending behavior. In the most common of these approaches, therapists work with parents on discipline skills, trying to restructure contingencies so as to stop the undesirable behavior (see Chapters 8, 9, 11, and 12). Readers who are most familiar with traditional child therapy may wonder what has happened to the venerable tradition of working with the child through the medium of play, letting the child take the lead, commenting on the child's activity and building a positive relationship with the child (see e.g., Bromfield, 1992; Russ, 1998; Tuma & Sobotka, 1983). Some of these traditional elements do survive within the evidence-based treatments, but in a modified way, in a two-stage treatment approach based on the work of Hanf (1969, 1970; Hanf & Kling, 1974). The Hanf approach was originally developed for work with physically handicapped children, but applications soon evolved for use with noncompliance in general. A core assumption underlying the Hanf approach is that a parent's efforts to influence a child's behavior will gain potency in the context of a positive parent-child connection, partly because a positive relationship enhances the child's attentiveness to, and motivation to cooperate with, the parent.

In the Hanf model, the therapist works directly with the parent, serving as both teacher and coach, as the parent engages in a series of playlike interactions with the child. In the first phase of the process, labeled "Child's game" by Hanf, the child chooses the play activities; as the child takes the lead, the parent learns to attend closely, comment descriptively, and praise and reward the child liberally. In a second phase, called "Parent's game," the parent takes the lead in play activities, and the coaching and training focus on evoking child compliance, dealing with noncompliance (e.g., via time-out procedures), and generally establishing effective management of child behavior. In this therapeutic two-step process, some of the same goals and methods we discussed in Chapter 9 as a part of behavioral parent training, are combined with some of the relationship-building goals and methods used in play therapy. Can this marriage of two such different traditions actually work? The evidence thus far suggests that it can; in this chapter, we review that evidence, provide treatment descriptions, and discuss related conceptual issues.

In the chapter, we distinguish between two somewhat different incarnations of the Hanf model: (1) the Helping the Noncompliant Child Program (HNCP) (Forehand & McMahon, 1981; McMahon & Forehand, 2003; Peed et al., 1977; Wells & Egan, 1988); and (2) Parent-Child Interaction Therapy (Eyberg, 1988; Foote, Eyberg, & Schuhmann, 1998). There is evidence that both approaches have beneficial effects, both on the parent-child relationship and on child behavior. Because the Helping the Noncompliant Child Program (e.g., Forehand & King, 1974; Peed et al., 1977) was developed and tested first, and because it is perhaps a bit closer to the original Hanf conception, we will begin with it. Then we will consider Parent-Child Interaction Therapy (e.g., Eyberg, 1988).

Helping the Noncompliant Child Program: Conceptual Basis and Procedural Overview

The HNCP (described by Peed et al., 1997; Forehand & King, 1974, 1977; Forehand & McMahon, 1981; McMahon & Forehand, 2003) involves the two phases originally outlined by Hanf and colleagues (Hanf, 1969, 1970; Hanf & Kling, 1974). Phase 1, which Hanf called the "Child's game," which Peed et al. (1977) labeled the "reinforcement phase" (p. 335), and which Forehand and McMahon (1981) labeled the "Differential Attention" phase, involves free play during which the child controls the interaction and the parent practices attending and rewarding. In Phase 2, which Hanf called the "Parent's game," and which Forehand and McMahon (1981) labeled "Compliance Training," parents are taught to give direct, concise commands to reward compliance; and to use a warning-and-time-out procedure to decrease noncompliance. Throughout these two phases, therapists stationed behind one-way observation windows use a bug-in-the-ear device to coach parents in appropriate behavior. Parents do additional interaction exercises with their children at home, to practice the skills they are learning. The rate at which parents pass through the different steps and phases of treatment depends on how quickly the parents can show that they have learned the skills, by attaining specific behavioral criteria.

At the foundation of HNCP is the notion that noncompliance is the keystone of conduct problems, that is, the foundation out of which other conduct problems develop (see Loeber & Schmalling, 1985; Patterson, 1982), and that it thus warrants focused and early attention. Forehand and

McMahon (1981) review evidence supporting this notion and suggest that when noncompliance is treated successfully other conduct problems are also alleviated, without being treated directly. HNCP is rooted in social learning theory (see Forehand & McMahon, 1981; McMahon & Forehand, 2003), and the terminology in a number of the outcome studies draws concepts from multiple models of learning. Peed et al. (1977), for example, describe their approach in this way: "Using modeling, role-playing, and direct communication with the parent while he or she interacts with the child, the therapist attempts to shape certain behaviors on the part of the parent that will result in increased compliance by the child" (p. 324). The relationship-building phase of treatment was described by Forehand and King (1977) as aimed in part at "training the mother to be a more effective reinforcing agent . . ." (p. 98). Elaborating on this notion, Forehand and McMahon (1981) stress that Differential Attention interactions in the first phase of treatment are intended to improve the parent-child relationship by helping the dyads break out of coercive cycles of interaction and thereby establishing a context of warmth and positivity. The hope is that this will increase the child's motivation to comply with the parent's directives.

The second broad phase of treatment, Compliance Training, builds on the improved parent-child connection by training the parent to provide clearly divergent consequences for child compliance and for child noncompliance. In these and other ways, the conceptual basis for the treatment approach fits mainstream models of social learning theory, drawing some concepts from operant and observational learning models.

Helping the Noncompliant Child Program: In Brief

Designed for . . . . Noncompliant children ages 3–8
Number of sessions . . . . 10 (range: 5–15)
Session length . . . . 60–90 minutes
Session participants . . . . Parent-child dyads, therapist
Theoretical orientation . . . . Behavioral, social learning theory

Treatment steps:

1. Therapist observes parent-child interactions, identifies problems, sets goals.
2. Differential attention sessions: child leads play activity, parent attends, describes, and rewards appropriate behavior, ignores inappropriate behavior.

---

3. Compliance Training sessions: parent leads play activity, gives directives, sets limits, learns to reward compliance and appropriate behavior and use time-out for noncompliance.
4. Therapist observes parent-child interactions to assess parent learning, child compliance.

Treatment classified by Treatment Task Force as . . . . Probably Efficacious (Brestan & Eyberg, 1998)

Key resource for potential users . . . . Robert J. McMahon and Rex L. Forehand (2003). *Helping the Noncompliant Child: Family-Based Treatment for Oppositional Behavior* (2nd ed.). New York: Guilford.

Helping the Noncompliant Child Program: Treatment Procedures

The specific procedures used by HNCP therapists are quite structured in setting, content, and sequence of events. Treatment is designed to take place in a play room that can be viewed from outside, either through one-way glass or using a videocamera; but a low-tech approach, with the therapist in the same room, is also workable. The play room contains a table, chairs, and age-appropriate toys. Treatment sessions last 60–90 minutes, and there are usually about 10 sessions. Treatment can be focused on a single parent-child dyad, but both parents are included in treatment whenever possible. Each HNCP session follows this six-step format:

1. Parent plays with child for five minutes while therapist observes and gathers data.
2. Therapist and parent discuss the parent's behavior with the child during the preceding observation period and at home.
3. Therapist models a specific parenting skill for the parent.
4. Therapist and parent role-play the specific skill, with therapist playing the role of the child.
5. Therapist and parents explain the new skill to the child, then model it for the child; parent and child then role-play the skill.
6. Parent practices the skill with the child while the therapist (usually stationed behind a one-way window) provides feedback (usually via a bug in the ear).
7. Parent plays with child for five minutes, while therapist observes and gathers data.

These six steps are followed in the sessions of both major phases of treatment ("Differential Attention" and "Compliance Training" – see next section). Within both phases, movement from one type of skill training to the next is determined by the therapist, based on whether the parent-child interactions observed in Steps 1 and 6 meet specific criteria; if the interactions show that skill A has been learned, the teaching and coaching shift to skill B. Between sessions, parents do assigned activities with their child at home, practicing the skills taught in the session; each home practice experience is discussed with the therapist at the beginning of the next treatment session, to identify and address problems in real-world application of the target skills.

Phase 1: Differential Attention. The first of the two broad phases of treatment is designed to increase parents' effectiveness as agents of reinforcement. Three parental skills are targeted in this differential attention phase: attending, rewarding, and ignoring. Each of these skills is the focus of a specific portion of the training, each is taught in conjunction with specific guidelines from the therapist, and each is trained through a combination of didactics, discussion, and therapist feedback during ongoing parent-child interactions.

Attending. As a part of learning to attend, parents are taught to observe the child's behavior closely, and to describe the behavior in narrative form (e.g., "Now you're collecting the blocks . . . and now you're putting them away . . ."). As a part of learning the skill of attending, parents are taught to increase the rate and range of the positive comments they direct to their child. They are also taught to avoid certain kinds of verbal behavior that are statistically associated with child misbehavior, for example, parental commands, questions, and criticism. Mastery of the specific attending skills is assessed by the therapist during the five-minute observations of parent-child interaction that are a part of every session (see previous section). For example, one criterion used to gauge mastery of the attending skills is four descriptions of child activity per minute, combined with four or less commands plus questions per minute, assessed in the initial five-minute observational period (see Step 1).

Rewarding. After mastering the attending skills, the parent is taught how to use contingent rewards to increase the rate of desirable child behaviors. Parents are taught to distinguish among three kinds of reward: *physical* (e.g., hugging, kissing, patting on the back), *unlabeled verbal* (i.e., praise that does not identify what is being praised – e.g., "Terrific!" or "I like that."), and *labeled verbal* (i.e., praise that specifically identifies what the child did that was good – e.g., "Good boy! You're putting away the blocks."). This third type of reward is especially valuable, because it tells children what they are being rewarded for, and thus what behaviors may pay off for them in the future. Most parents dispense the first two types of rewards often, but many parents show low levels of labeled praise. It is this third category that is most heavily emphasized in HNCP. Using the bug-in-the-ear method, HNCP therapists teach and coach parents to dispense labeled praise contingent on child behaviors the parent wants to see increased.

Forehand and McMahon (1981) offer four general guidelines for the effective use of reward (of all three types) in HNCP: (1) Rewards should immediately follow the desired behavior; (2) rewards should be specific, clearly recognizable by the child as a consequence following from a particular action on the child's part; (3) when the child is first learning a particular behavior, rewards for that behavior should be used consistently, such that the behavior can be counted on by the child to reliably generate a good consequence; and (4) rewards may be intermittently administered after the desired behavior has been learned. Ideally, the HNCP therapist will also teach parents to be enthusiastic and sincere in dispensing rewards to their children, and in making sure that the rewards selected are indeed reinforcing to the children. Rewarding, by the way, is not intended as a replacement for attending; instead, the two parental skills ideally operate in tandem, with attending serving to bolster the salience and impact of rewards. In addition, attending is viewed by HNCP theorists as a more versatile technique, one that can be used in a broad variety of situations, even those in which overt rewarding might be inappropriate.

In this part of training, as in others, HNCP therapists use the five-minute observation periods in each session to apply very specific criteria for parental mastery, thus to determine whether parents are ready to move to the next step in training. For example, a mastery criterion suggested by Forehand and McMahon (1981) is the parent's use of at least four rewards plus attends per minute, with at least two rewards per minute and an average of no more than 0.4 commands plus questions per minute.

Ignoring. A third focus of training in the Differential Attention phase is an effective alternative to punishment, but an alternative that is not often used well by parents: ignoring. One of the most basic principles of social learning is that behavior tends to decrease in frequency when it is not rewarded with attention. Although many parents agree with this general principle, many also report that they have tried ignoring but that it did not work. The treatment developers who created HNCP believe this is because most parents are not using ignoring with the precision and comprehensiveness required for effectiveness. Thus, HNCP includes some very explicit instructions. Parents are taught to ignore inappropriate child behavior by (1) physically turning away from the child (90–180 degrees), (2) avoiding all eye contact, (3) avoiding all verbal contact, and (4) avoiding physical contact (even if this requires leaving the room). For ignoring to be maximally effective, the ignoring must end as soon as the child's inappropriate behavior has ended. One downside of ignoring is that it cannot be used when the child's behavior is physically damaging to property or potentially dangerous to the child or others, but in most situations, ignoring is a potent parental tool. As evidence of mastery, Forehand and McMahon (1981) suggested at least one five-minute parent-child observation period in which the parent successfully ignores at least 70% of the child's inappropriate behavior.

Homework assignments for the parent. As the skills are learned in the therapy sessions, the parent takes the show on the road, trying the Differential Attention skills at home. Each parent is asked to devote 10–15 minutes per day to a Child's Game type of interaction with the child, and to record the time, day, and child's response, on a standard form, given as a handout. This helps to ensure quality time for parent and child, it gives the parent repeated practice of the Phase 1 skills, and it generates a written record that parent and therapist can discuss at each subsequent treatment session. In another type of homework assignment, parents are asked to identify three specific behaviors they would like to see more of in their children. The parent challenge is then set: increasing those three specific target behaviors, by using the Differential Attention skills learned in Phase 1. In addition to firming up the real-life application of Phase 1 skills, this assignment also conveys the important notion that child noncompliance can be construed as a series of specific behaviors that can each be targeted for change and altered by consistent use of differential attention skills.

Phase 2: Compliance Training. Once the parent has met the mastery criteria for Phase 1, the second broad phase begins. In this, the Compliance Training phase, parent and child play, with the parent directing the interaction. During this phase, the therapist uses instruction, role-play, and modeling to teach parents two kinds of skills: (1) giving clear instructions or commands, and (2) providing consequences for compliance and noncompliance.

Learning to give effective directives: alpha versus beta commands. The emphasis on clear instructions grows out of a thoughtful analysis of noncompliance and its context. As Forehand and McMahon (1981, p. 73) note, most parent training programs have focused on changing the consequences of such unwanted child behavior as noncompliance, with relatively little attention paid to the antecedents. A particularly common antecedent of child noncompliance is the parental command, and close attention to parents' styles of giving commands may reveal problems that go a long way toward explaining the noncompliance.

Of special interest in the HNCP are *beta commands* (a term first used by Peed et al., 1977), instructions that are unclear, overly complex, or otherwise structured in ways that reduce the likelihood of compliance. Forehand and McMahon (1981) identify five different types of beta commands:

1. *Chain commands,* serial instructions strung together, often involving behaviors that are not inherently or logically related, and thus producing information overload. An example: "Pick up these blocks, put them in the box, then pick up all your dirty clothes and put

them in the hamper." Even a child who wants to comply may have difficulty remembering the full chain.

2. *Vague commands,* which do not tell the child what specific behaviors to carry out. Examples: "Be a good boy," and "Be careful." Even a child who wants to comply may not know what specific actions to perform.

3. *Question commands,* which leave it unclear whether the child is being asked to comply or to provide information. An example: "Will you color these trees brown?" Thinking the parent is merely seeking information, a child might reasonably answer, "No," without any intention of disobeying.

4. *"Let's..." commands,* which seem to imply joint action with the parent. An example: "Let's clean up this mess." The wording implies that the child may wait for the parent to join in the cleanup; but if the parent really intends for the child to clean up his own mess alone, then the wording is misleading.

5. *Commands followed by a rationale or other wording.* An example: "Clean up your room, because we are having company tonight, and I want the house to look nice for our visitors." In such a command, the trailer can obscure the instruction, distracting the child from the initial behavioral directive. For this reason, a rationale for a command should be given before the command.

In HNCP, such beta commands are contrasted with *alpha commands* (Peed et al., 1977), instructions that are clear and unambiguous, maximizing the child's ability to comply if he or she wants to do so. Alpha commands have three characteristics that are stressed in HNCP:

1. *Specificity and directness.* The parent should first get the child's attention, then call the child by name and wait until eye contact is established, then state with slightly raised volume (to cue the child that a command is being given), and in language the child can understand, what the child should do. "Do" commands are much preferred over "Don't" or "Stop" commands, because they convey information about what specific behavior is expected.

2. *Focused on one behavior at a time.* If the parent wants the child to complete multiple tasks, each task should be treated as a separate command (thus avoiding "chain commands," as described earlier).

3. *Followed by a five-second wait.* There should be no additional directives during the five-second delay. This gives the child time to comply, or, alternatively, the parent time to fairly conclude that noncompliance has occurred. The HNCP specifies what parental procedures should follow compliance and noncompliance.

Successful completion of this command segment of Phase 2 is defined as at least one five-minute observation of Compliance Training in which

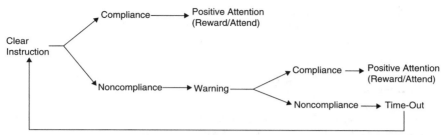

FIGURE 10.1. Flow chart of the clear instructions sequence. From McMahon, R. J., & Forehand, R. L. (2003). *Helping the noncompliant child: Family-based treatment for oppositional behavior (2nd ed.)*. New York: Guilford Press. Figure 7.1. Reprinted with the permission of Robert J. McMahon and Guilford Press.

the parent produces an average of two alpha commands per minute and in which no more than 25% of the total commands fall into the beta category.

Training in consequences for compliance and noncompliance. The second part of the Compliance Training phase of HNCP focuses on what to do when the child complies, and when the child does not comply. If the child begins to comply within the five-second waiting period after a command, or even after a warning, the parent is instructed to use the attending and rewarding skills, especially the labeled verbal rewards, taught in the first part of the treatment program. Attending is particularly valuable as a means of maintaining compliance with tasks that take considerable time to complete – for example, cleaning a room, picking up toys. Labeled verbal rewards are especially useful at the beginning of compliance and at completion of the task.

Noncompliance evokes a very different set of parental actions, within HNCP. Failure to comply within the five-second waiting period triggers a specific warning-then-time-out procedure, described by Forehand and King (1974) and further detailed by Forehand and McMahon (1981) and McMahon and Forehand (2003). The procedure is depicted in Figure 10.1, adapted from one of the handouts HNCP therapists provide to parents in treatment.

Here are the steps in the procedure:

(1) child is warned that continued noncompliance will lead to a time-out;
(2) if child has not complied by five seconds after the warning, he or she is placed in a time-out chair in the corner of the room;
(3) if child leaves the chair, the parent places her or him back in it, and warns child that there will be a punishment (e.g., placed in a separate "time-out room") if he or she leaves the chair again;
(4) if child leaves the chair again, punishment follows, after which child is returned to the chair;

(5) this cycle is repeated until child remains quietly on the chair for three minutes;

(6) child is then returned to the uncompleted task and given the original command;

(7) compliance leads to contingent attention from the parent;

(8) noncompliance leads to a repeat of the time-out procedure.

Two elements of this sequence warrant special comment. First, Steps 6–8 are important because the purpose of the time-out procedure is to generate compliance with the original command. Some children would much rather spend three minutes in time-out than clean their room; such a preference should not be rewarded. Second, the use of spanking in step 4 is a good example of how treatment programs evolve with changing cultural perspectives, and with accumulating evidence. Personal communication (December 23, 1999) with program codeveloper Robert McMahon (see Forehand & McMahon, 1981; McMahon & Forehand, 2003) indicates that spanking, though included in the HNCP, has never actually been used very much, even in the 1970s and 1980s, because the other parental procedures so often lead to compliance. Moreover, spanking is no longer recommended in the most recent version of HNCP, as presented in the recent book by McMahon and Forehand (2003).

Taken together, the time-out steps present a significant learning challenge, and parents often need considerable practice. Moreover, the steps may need adapting to various situational constraints. Recognizing this possibility, therapists ask parents to list nonclinic situations in which the child frequently disobeys or misbehaves, and the HNCP therapist works with them to plan the use of time-out procedures in each of those situations. The most consistently applied mastery criterion for ending Phase 2 of treatment is a specific child compliance rate. For example, Forehand and McMahon (1981) require at least one five-minute Compliance Training observation period with (1) a 75% child compliance/parental command ratio, and (2) a 60% parental reward + attending/child compliance ratio.

Deciding when to give commands. One other aspect of the Compliance Training phase of treatment deserves attention here. In addition to being taught how to elicit compliance with their commands, parents are taught to be thoughtful about when they need to issue commands. Indiscriminate commanding may reflect an authoritarian style that can undermine the positive parent-child relationship. The use of commands that the parent does not have the energy or motivation to follow through on can encourage a habit of noncompliance in the child. Thus, the HNCP therapist encourages the parent to be selective, identifying the specific areas that are important enough to warrant true commands, and then issuing only those directives that the parent is willing to see through to compliance, regardless of how long it takes.

Standing rules. What should a parent do about child misbehavior that occurs repeatedly but unpredictably, and that cannot be ignored because it causes genuine harm – for example, hitting siblings or peers? In such cases, a specific parental command may only be possible after the harm is done. To address such problems, the HNCP therapist works with the parent, late in the treatment program, to develop *standing rules* – i.e., specific "if ... then" statements that are to be explained to the child and then remain permanently in effect. An example: "If you hit your sister, then you must go to time-out."

Helping the Noncompliant Child Program: Outcome Studies Testing the Effects

HNCP has been evaluated in a series of studies with noncompliant children and their parents, conducted primarily at the University of Georgia. In some of the studies, treatment was given to all the referred children and parents, and analyses focused on pre-post changes in the full sample. In two studies, the design involved treatment-control comparisons.

Initial test using a pre-post design. In the first published test, Forehand and King (1974) used HNCP with eight mother-child pairs. The five boys and three girls ranging from 3–6 years old (ethnicity not reported), were referred for treatment because of noncompliance; fighting, disruption, and disobedience were reported by most of the parents. Treatment was brief, averaging only six sessions per dyad, and all eight dyads were treated. Analyses focused on changes in parent and child behavior during the two phases of treatment, then called Child's Game and Parent's Game. During the Child's Game phase, parents showed significant increases in their rate of rewarding and significant decreases in their rates of commands and questions. During the Parent's Game or "time-out phase," parents showed significantly increased rates of rewarding, and children showed increased rates of compliance with parental commands.

Replication test, with pre-post design and three-month followup. In a second published test of the HNCP, Forehand and King (1977) sought to replicate and extend the findings of this first study. The sample included 11 mother-child pairs, with 10 boys and 1 girl, and the children ranged in age from 3 to 7 (ethnicity not reported). The parents ranged from upper-middle-class business executives and university professors to welfare recipients. All had been referred to clinics at the University of Georgia or Emory University. The primary complaint for all the children was "noncompliance to parental commands" (p. 95), but there were also frequent reports of temper tantrums and inappropriate attention-seeking behavior. Procedures were similar to those of Forehand and King (1974), but the mean number of treatment sessions was a bit higher, at nine. Significant changes during treatment mirrored those reported in the earlier Forehand and King

(1977) study: Parental rewarding increased, and commands and questions decreased, during the reinforcement phase; and rates of child compliance increased during the time-out phase. These changes were maintained at a three-month followup. In addition to these behavioral changes, the investigators found that parents' responses to a parental attitude test showed that mothers perceived their children as better adjusted after treatment.

Treatment-control comparison, and test of generalization to home. In the first treatment-control comparison test of HNCP, Peed et al. (1977) worked with a sample of 12 mother-child pairs, all of whom came in response to an announcement about the treatment program or were referred by professionals in the community. The eight boys and four girls ranged in age from 3–8 (ethnicity not reported). All showed multiple behavior problems involving noncompliance. As parents called, they were asked their child's age and sex, and also asked for information relevant to their social class. "Based on this information, subjects were assigned to either the treatment or control group" (Peed et al., p. 327). Thus, rather than using random assignment, the authors apparently tried to form groups that were similar demographically; the groups were, in fact, similar in age and socioeconomic status, and matched in gender composition. In addition, the two groups did not differ significantly at the outset on most of the measures used to assess treatment outcome.

The treatment group received the standard HNCP intervention, averaging 9.5 sessions, and in no case exceeding 12 sessions. Outcomes were assessed not only in the lab setting, where treatment had occurred, but also during home visits by trained observers. Treatment effects were evident in numerous significant treatment control differences in both settings, and in both parent and child behavior. During the Child's Game phase in the lab, treatment group parents showed higher rates of attending and rewarding than control group parents did. During the Parent's Game phase, treated parents showed more contingent attention to child behavior than did control parents, and treated children showed higher rates of compliance than control children. And during the home visits, the treatment group proved superior on rates of parent attending, parent rewarding, parent contingent attention, and child compliance to parental commands. Parents in the treatment and control groups had given their children similar ratings on adjustment prior to the intervention, but after treatment the treatment group parents gave significantly higher child adjustment ratings than control group parents. So, the evidence suggested that treatment effects generalized to the home and extended to parents' perceptions of their children's overall adjustment. Subsequent findings suggested that clinic to home generalization occurred across a range of family socioeconomic status levels (Rogers et al., 1981) and across a range of child ages from 3–8 years (McMahon et al., 1985).

Testing the holding power of home effects. In a related study, Forehand et al. (1979) followed up 10 mother-child pairs at 6 and 12 months following the completion of HNCP, to assess the holding power of treatment effects on home behavior. Focusing on the measures used in Peed et al. (1977), Forehand et al. found that improvements were maintained at both follow-up points, on nearly all the measures, including positive maternal attitudes toward the children.

Testing very long-term holding power. Three studies have reported evidence on the holding power of HNCP effects that extends well beyond the period studied by Forehand et al. (1979). Baum and Forehand (1981) collected parent-report data and home observations with 34 mother-child pairs who had been treated with HNCP one to four years previously. The 22 boys and 12 girls ranged in age from 4–12 years of age (ethnicity not reported). The families spanned a broad socioeconomic status range, with both professionals and welfare recipients included. Both observed child behavior and parent-reported child adjustment held at the positive levels that had been found immediately after treatment had ended. Moreover, no significant differences were found between subgroups assessed at different follow-up time periods, suggesting that changes over time may be relatively stable from one to four years.

Forehand and Long (1988) managed to trump even these impressive findings, showing holding power of treatment effects over periods ranging from 4 to 10 years after HNCP, for a sample of 21 families. The 14 boys and 7 girls (ethnicity not reported) had ranged from 2 to 7 years of age at the time of treatment, and were 11 to 14 years old at the time of the follow-up assessment. As in previous studies by this group, the families spanned a broad socioeconomic status range, such that the sample included both professionals and welfare recipients. An interesting feature of the Forehand and Long study is their finding that HNCP-treated youngsters, assessed at followup, did not differ reliably, on most outcome measures, from an age- and gender-matched comparison group of presumably normally functioning youngsters who had never been referred for treatment.

In a later article, Long et al. (1994) reported on 26 former HNCP clients, 14 years after the end of their treatment. At the time of the followup, the 26 were all late adolescents or young adults, age 17 and older. All had been treated between the ages of 2 and 7, all for noncompliance, but with an array of secondary problems, ranging from aggression to fire-setting. There were 17 males, 9 females, all Caucasian, with middle-class to lower-middle-class families predominating, but with a broad range of socioeconomic status represented. A matched, nondeviant community comparison group was identified for this study. It consisted of 26 individuals who had participated in previous research by the authors, and who were matched to the individuals in the HNCP treatment group for age, gender, ethnicity, and socioeconomic status. For both groups, the authors obtained measures of delinquency, emotional adjustment, academic progress, and relationships with parents. None of these measures showed reliable differences between the two groups. From this evidence, the authors concluded that "noncompliant children who participated in parent training during their early years are functioning as well as nonclinic individuals as they move into adulthood" (Long et al., 1994, p. 101).

Each of these long-term follow-up studies has certain methodological limitations (e.g., understandably, they lack a prospective design with treatment and control groups assigned prior to treatment – see Scientific Issues). Still, the findings are intriguing, and they involve assessment over what appear to be the longest-term follow-up periods employed for any child or adolescent treatment to date.

HNCP versus systems family therapy. More than ten years after the Peed et al. (1977) study was published, Wells and Egan (1988) published a particularly stringent test of the effects of HNCP. These authors pitted HNCP against a popular alternative treatment, Systems Family Therapy. The Systems approach was patterned after the work of Minuchin (1974) and Haley (1976). It involved looking for evidence of, and treating, potentially damaging structures or processes within the family, such as maladaptive relationships (e.g., covert coalitions of family members undermining another member), harmful and repetitive behavior sequences, or unproductive conflict-avoidance tactics. In the Wells-Egan study, when such problems were identified and seen as causes of the child's problems, the Systems therapist intervened to alter the harmful processes or reinterpret ongoing patterns.

The sample for this treatment versus treatment comparison included 19 families who had been routinely referred to an outpatient child psychiatry clinic in a large urban children's hospital. The target children were all 3–8 years old (gender and ethnicity not reported), all were diagnosed with Oppositional Disorder (according to DSM-III, the system in use at the time of the study), all showed less than 50% compliance with parental commands in a 15-minute observational assessment, and all their parents had expressed interest in family treatment. Children meeting these criteria were randomly assigned to either the HNCP or the Systems treatment. Each treatment lasted 8–12 sessions.

At the end of treatment the two groups were compared on measures of parent adjustment and symptomatology, parent behavior toward their children, and child compliance. Posttreatment scores on the parent adjustment and symptom measures – assessing anxiety, depression, and marital adjustment – did not differ between the two groups. But the HNCP group of parents showed better attending to and rewarding of child behavior, and higher rates of attention that was contingent on acceptable child behavior. Most importantly, rates of appropriate child compliance were markedly higher in the HNCP group than in the Systems group.

Do HNCP effects generalize to school? Because children who misbehave at home often do so at school as well, it would be very helpful if the HNCP effects seen in clinic and home observations generalized to the school setting. Unfortunately, two studies that have probed for such generalization have failed to find it. In both studies (Breiner & Forehand, 1981; Forehand et al., 1979), pretreatment versus posttreatment comparisons showed increased child compliance and decreased problem behavior at home, but not at school.

Summary of the Outcome Evidence on HNCP. Multiple studies have suggested beneficial effects of HNCP. Four studies reviewed here (Breiner & Forehand, 1981; Forehand & King, 1974, 1977; Forehand et al., 1979) showed within-group improvements over time, in samples all of whom received HNCP. One study (Peed et al., 1977) showed evidence of beneficial effects in an experimentally stronger treatment-control comparison. Another study (Wells & Egan, 1988), using a particularly stringent treatment versus treatment design, showed that HNCP outperformed Systems Family Therapy in altering parents' behavior toward their children and in increasing rates of child compliance. Studies (see previous discussion and see McMahon & Forehand, 1984) have also shown evidence that treatment effects generalize from the clinic to the home setting (e.g., Peed et al., 1997; Rogers et al., 1981), that parents' behavior changes in response to HNCP generalize to the parents' behavior toward their untreated children (Humphreys et al., 1978), and that those untreated siblings show increased compliance as well (Humphreys et al., 1978). Thus, there is some evidence that treatment effects may ripple through the family, benefiting even those who were not directly treated. Less encouraging has been the evidence suggesting poor generalization of treatment effects to child behavior in school (see McMahon & Davies, 1980). A notable aspect of the outcome literature on HNCP is the series of studies (Baum & Forehand, 1981; Forehand & Long, 1988; Long et al., 1994) suggesting that effects on child behavior and on parent perceptions of child adjustment may last as long as 4–14 years posttreatment.

Parent-Child Interaction Therapy: Conceptual Basis and Procedural Overview

A second adaptation of the Hanf approach is Parent-Child Interaction Therapy (PCIT), developed by Eyberg and colleagues (e.g., Eyberg, 1988; Eyberg & Calzada, 1998; Eyberg & Robinson, 1982). A principal difference between PCIT and other Hanfian approaches is that PCIT, significantly influenced by attachment theory, emphasizes teaching parents the relationship-enhancing skills espoused in the play therapy literature, particularly the work of Axline (1969). Within the play therapy model, the therapist's job includes listening to the child with undivided attention, following the child's lead in play, verbalizing the child's play activities and behavior to clarify and encourage elaboration, offering opportunities for the child to express thoughts and feelings in a safe and noncritical atmosphere, communicating the belief that the child's productions are important, and conveying empathy and acceptance (see Axline, 1969; and see also Bromfield, 1992; Russ, 1998; Tuma & Sobotka, 1983). So, although both HNCP and PCIT emphasize improving the parent-child relationship via child-focused play, the means employed in PCIT involve more of an emphasis on teaching parents "child therapist" skills.

Why work on the parent-child relationship? The reasons given in published accounts of PCIT (see Eyberg, 1988; Eyberg, Boggs, & Algina, 1995) are embedded within two key assumptions: (1) many of the behavioral problems shown by young children develop in the context of their earliest interactions with their parents, and (2) parents' efforts to discourage misbehavior will work best in the context of a generally positive parent-child bond, a relationship in which the child perceives the parent as attentive, involved, and supportive (see also Campbell, 1990). In PCIT, an emphasis on strengthening the parent-child bond is complemented by the goal of establishing parental control over disruptive behavior. If all goes well, training in relationship building and in parental control will combine to inculcate in parents what Baumrind (1967) labeled the authoritative parenting style.

Like HNCP, PCIT is aimed at parents of preschoolers, to get an early start on the relationship-building process, and to catch conduct problems before they escalate to very serious levels. The treatment techniques involve both teaching and coaching. Parents are taught ways to interact with their child, and they try their hand at these methods, in parent-child interactions that are observed in real time by the therapist. On the spot, the therapist models, coaches, corrects, and encourages, until parents have mastered the skills.

As in Hanf's original approach and in HNCP, the PCIT intervention is organized into two distinct phases. In the first phase, *child-directed interaction* (CDI; adapted from Hanf's "Child's Game"), parents interact with their children in ways that resemble the play therapy used in more traditional child treatment (see e.g., Bromfield, 1992; Tuma & Sobotka, 1983); children take the lead, and parents are attentive and responsive. Expressly forbidden during this CDI phase are such controlling parental behaviors as giving commands, asking questions, and criticizing.

In the second phase, *parent-directed interaction* (PDI; adapted from Hanf's "Parent's Game"), parents lead the activity and use operant procedures reminiscent of the Patterson-like methods discussed in Chapter 9 to encourage appropriate behavior and discourage specific problem behavior.

Parent-Child Interaction Therapy: In Brief

Designed for . . . . Oppositional children ages 2–6 (but clinical trials have included 8-year-olds)
Number of sessions . . . . 13 (range: 9–16)
Session length . . . . 60 minutes
Session participants . . . . Parent-child dyads, therapist
Theoretical orientation . . . . Behavioral, psychodynamic, attachment

Treatment steps:

1. Therapist observes parent-child interactions, identifies problems, sets goals.
2. Child-Directed Interaction sessions: child leads play activity, parent follows child's lead, using praise, reflection, imitation, description, and enthusiasm (PRIDE).
3. Parent-Directed Interaction sessions: parent leads play activity, gives directives, sets limits, learns to use time-out for noncompliance, learns to reward compliance and appropriate behavior.
4. Therapist observes parent-child interactions to assess parent learning, child disruptive behavior.

Treatment classified by Treatment Task Force as . . . . Probably Efficacious (Brestan & Eyberg, 1998)
Key resources for potential users . . . . Sheila M. Eyberg and Esther Calzada. (1998). *Parent-Child Interaction Therapy: Procedures Manual.* Gainesville, FL: University of Florida. Cheryl B. McNeil and Toni Hembree-Kigin (1995). *Parent-Child Interaction Therapy.* New York: Plenum.

Parent-Child Interaction Therapy: Treatment Procedures

As Eyberg and colleagues note (e.g., in Eyberg, 1988; Eyberg & Robinson, 1982), the overall format of PCIT was strongly influenced by, and resembles, the two-phase model introduced by Hanf (1969, 1970; Hanf & Kling, 1974). In this respect, PCIT is similar to HNCP, just reviewed. PCIT can be distinguished from HNCP by the heavier emphasis in PCIT on teaching parents the therapist-like, play therapy-based, relationship-enhancement skills espoused by Axline (1969). Other differences between the models are discussed elsewhere (e.g., Foote et al., 1998).

What happens in typical sessions. Each of the two phases of PCIT begins with a didactic session that the child does not attend. In these didactic sessions, the PCIT therapist directly teaches parents the rules of each phase (see next section), presents the rationale for each rule, and then role-plays the parent-child interactions with each parent. When possible, both mother and father are involved in this process and in later sessions. Parents are given a handout describing rules and procedures, for their review at home.

In each of the two phases, the didactic session is followed by sessions that include the child. In these sessions, the child plays with each parent in turn, while the spouse and PCIT therapist observe from a corner of the room or from behind a one-way mirror. The therapist uses the Dyadic Parent-Child Interaction Coding System-II (DPICS-II; Eyberg et al., 1994) to code behavior during the initial five-minute observation period, and the resulting data are used to determine the areas in which the parent needs to be coached during the session.

After the observation period comes the coaching period. Parents wear a bug-in-the-ear device, as in HNCP, or (if the equipment or one-way mirror is not available) the therapist sits nearby and coaches the parent through the ongoing parent-child interaction. Although corrective feedback (e.g., "Try doing it this way, instead . . . .") may be used, PCIT therapists try to emphasize positive comments on what the parent has done correctly (e.g., "Nice labeled praise!" or "Good comment – that sounded very genuine."). Coaching typically includes a mixture of labeled praise for the parents, gentle correctives, straightforward directives, and observations on the interaction process or the child's reaction. Some examples of common CDI coaching statements in each of these categories are presented in Table 10.1.

After the coaching period, therapist and parent(s) discuss the interaction. To guide the discussion, they review the DPICS data from the current session and each previous one. This helps parents see what progress they are making over time, and it helps identify areas where problems remain. These problem areas then become a focus of both home-based practice and future sessions. Parents are assigned homework in the form of one five-minute interaction with their child each day, after which they record information about the interaction on a homework sheet.

This account describes the flow of events during a typical session. The actual content and style of the sessions is quite different during the two broad phases of treatment, so we consider those two phases in more detail.

First phase: child-directed interaction (CDI). In the first phase of PCIT, CDI (adapted from Hanf's "Child's Game"), children run the show. As in Hanf's "Child's Game," the child is left completely free to choose the play activities, and to make decisions about these activities. The most basic rule of CDI is that the parent must follow the child's lead. Beyond

TABLE 10.1. *Examples of CDI Coaching Statements of Four Types Used in Parent-Child Interaction Therapy*

	Labeled Praise	
Good ignoring.	Good job imitating her play.	Nice eye contact.
Nice timing giving back your attention.	Good example of gentle play.	Terrific enthusiasm!
	Gentle Correctives	
Sounds a little critical.	You're getting a little ahead of him.	Might be better to say . . .
Careful not to frown here.	Did you catch her question?	A little leading.
	Directives	
Try to label it.	Show more enthusiasm!	Try holding it for her.
How about a hug with that praise?	Say, "Nice manners!"	Praise him for sharing.
	Observations	
She's enjoying playing with you.	He talks more when you reflect.	
He slows down when you do.	You seem happier with him today.	He loves your praise.

this, the parent is taught to behave in some of the ways a traditional child therapist might, describing what the child is doing, sometimes imitating or replicating the child's actions, reflecting what the child says during play (i.e., by repeating it or using synonymous wording), and finding positive aspects of the child's play-related actions so that these can be noted and praised. The character and content of the CDI phase is nicely captured by Eyberg's (1988) *Dos* and *Don'ts* of CDI. Nearly all of these *Dos* and *Don'ts* are paralleled by training procedures used in HNCP, underscoring the procedural similarity of the two Hanf-derived approaches, despite some differences in their conceptual and theoretical basis.

Do's and Don'ts of Child-Directed Interaction (from Eyberg, 1988). *Do describe.* Parents are taught to describe the child's activities aloud, sometimes in the form of a running commentary – for example, "You're stacking those blocks really high; now you're putting the yellow one on top; that makes four blocks in the tower!" This kind of ongoing description is intended to keep the parent involved even as the child leads. It also shows the child that the parent is attending, encourages the child to elaborate on play activity, and may even teach the child new concepts, such as "stacking," and "on top."

Do imitate. Parents learn to replicate the child's activity. For example, if the child is making a design with tiles, the parent may add tiles or make a similar design beside the child's. This is intended to communicate to the child that the parent is interested and values the child's activity. If all goes well, the parent's imitative behavior will draw the child into a pattern of cooperative play that can generalize to peer interactions.

Do reflect. Reflecting the child's play activity orally may involve near-repetition of what the child has said, as when the child says, "That car is slow," and the parent replies, "Yes, that car is really slow." Such reflection serves to demonstrate that the parent understands and accepts what the child says. Eyberg and colleagues also believe that such reflective statements, by showing children they were heard, prevent escalation to repetition and whining.

Do praise. Praising children's play activities and productions conveys appreciation and valuing, and may thus enhance self-esteem. Eyberg and colleagues are particularly keen on labeled praise, such as "It's nice of you to say 'thank you' like that," or "I'm proud of you for playing so quietly today." Labeling in this way conveys to the child what aspect of their activity is being singled out for positive attention, and thus clarifies for the child what can be done to earn further praise.

Do ignore inappropriate behavior. Inappropriate behavior that would ordinarily be dealt with directly by parents of young children is to be ignored during CDI, unless it is dangerous or destructive. This means, for example, that whining, yelling, acting bossy, or saying disrespectful things to a parent must all be consistently ignored and unacknowledged during CDI; the goal is to make the interaction as pleasant for the child as possible, and to keep the child in control of the flow of events.

Don't command. Parental commands or instructions do exactly the opposite of what one wants in the CDI phase – that is, they take the lead away from the child. This would violate a cardinal rule of CDI. Moreover, parental commands can be followed by noncompliance and other oppositional behavior by the child, leading to disagreement or tension between parent and child, further undermining the main purpose of CDI, which is to create a warm, supportive interactive atmosphere.

Don't ask questions. Some questions are actually commands, for example, "How about putting away the toys?" Other questions can serve to undermine the child's role as leader of the interaction – for example, "Want to play with the blocks?" Still other questions subtly take control of the verbal interaction (e.g., "What do you want for your birthday?"), or carry an implied criticism (e.g., "Why did you put the toy there?"), or risk unintentionally bringing up painful memories or bad feelings (e.g., "What happened at preschool today?"). Given the multiple risks, and the fact that questions communicate little information to the child, the PCIT therapist cautions parents to simply avoid questions altogether during CDI.

Don't criticize. Even a mildly worded criticism of the child's activity, style, or work products (e.g., "That drawing is a little messy.") can be painful to the child, and may also lead to negative behavior, or even a counterattack. Such adverse effects would undermine the positive relationship CDI is intended to create. Thus, parental criticism is strictly verboten during CDI.

Second phase: parent-directed interaction (PDI). In the second phase of PCIT, PDI (adapted from Hanf's "Parent's Game"), parents take the lead. Parents continue to describe, reflect, and praise appropriate play and to ignore such inappropriate behaviors as whining, bossing, and saying disrespectful things to parents, but parents lead the activity by giving specific directions to the child, and by consistently enforcing consequences for compliance and noncompliance.

A goal in PDI is to maximize predictability for the child, making it clear at each point how rewards can be obtained and punishment avoided. Thus, as in HNCP (Forehand & McMahon, 1981; McMahon & Forehand, 2003), parents are taught to use alpha commands, instructions that are direct, clear, and very difficult for a child to misinterpret. Also in harmony with HNCP, alpha commands are contrasted with beta commands, instructions that are indirect, unclear, or otherwise susceptible to misinterpretation. As in HNCP, parents are encouraged to (1) tell children what to do, not what *not* to do (e.g., instead of, "Stop throwing toys," the parent should say "Put your hands in your lap."); (2) be developmentally appropriate (in both the language employed and the behavior requested – e.g., a parent should not tell a 3-year-old to tie her shoes); and (3) ask for only one behavior at a time (avoiding what Eyberg calls *sequential* commands [cf. and McMahon's (1981) *chain commands*], and also avoiding *global commands*, which appear to ask for only one act, but which actually call for multiple acts, often carried out in a specific order). Eyberg noted that global commands, such as "Clean up the playroom," may be particularly troublesome because of their hidden complexity; multiple steps are involved, such that child and parent may interpret the commands differently, and noncompliance with the parent's expectations may result, even if the child is trying to comply.

After mastering the first step of PDI, giving appropriate commands, parents move to the second step – that is, giving labeled praise. Such praise (e.g., "I like it when you come so quickly," "That's very nice of you to share.") communicates the parents' approval and makes clear what specifically the child has done that the parent is so pleased with. All things being equal, this should maximize the chance that the same behavior will be repeated in the future. Here is an example (from Eyberg & Robinson, 1982, p. 134) illustrating how parents can blend issuing commands, ignoring inappropriate behaviors, and giving labeled praise, all in the same brief interaction:

Mary: (pounding hammer on wall while walking toward mother.)	[inappropriate behavior]
Mother: "Please come here."	[command]
Mary: (comes)	[obeys]
Mother: "I like it when you do what I ask so quickly."	[labeled praise]
Mary: "You're no fun."	[inappropriate behavior]
Mother: "Give me the hammer."	[command, ignores inappropriate behavior]
Mary: (smashes the hammer into the table and gives it to mother)	[inappropriate behavior, obeys]
Mother: "Thank you for giving me the hammer."	[praises compliance; ignores inappropriate behavior]

The third step in PDI is learning to use time-out when the child is non-compliant. Why use time-out rather than simply ignoring? According to Eyberg and colleagues (e.g., Eyberg, 1988), noncompliance is one behavior that does not fade away if it is ignored, presumably because avoiding an unwanted task is inherently reinforcing. The time-out procedure used in PCIT is modeled after Hanf's (1969) description. It entails an initial warning, a three-minute time-out in a corner, and – in the original version – a back-up spank if necessary, to enforce staying on the time-out chair. As in the case of HNCP, the spank has been dropped in the most recent refinement of PCIT (see Eyberg & Calzada, 1998).

Parents first practice PDI skills with their child in the clinic, under therapist coaching and supervision. Parents are cautioned not to practice the PDI elements at home until they are confident that they can use the skills well – that is, appropriate commands, praise for compliance, and time-out – when the therapist is not nearby to help.

During the in-clinic sessions, when the child is showing good compliance, parents begin to work with their therapist on giving commands directly geared to the presenting problems. If overactivity is a problem, a parental command might be, "Sit in this chair while you draw," and relevant labeled praise might be, "I like it when you sit still." If academic performance is an issue, a relevant command might be "Copy this letter 'B' " and the labeled praise might be "That's a really good 'B'!" For any skill parents want to teach their child, the task is to break the skill down into component steps, beginning with an early step the child already knows how to do, and progressing through increasing difficulty levels, using labeled praise to shore up each new component skill. As in the CDI phase, these in-session activities are complemented by brief (usually five minutes), daily PDI practice sessions at home.

Houserules. As in HNCP, PCIT therapist complements training in commands and consequences with development of procedures for handling behavior that occurs persistently but without warning, and cannot be ignored because of its significant consequences. These procedures involve what are called *houserules.* Houserules are introduced during the last few PDI sessions, because they involve a special application of PDI skills. The steps include (1) selecting the behavior that must be stopped (e.g., strangling the cat), (2) choosing words for the behavior that the child will understand (e.g., "hurting Snowflake"), and (3) explaining the houserule to the child (e.g., "I like it when you are nice to Snowflake. But whenever you hurt Snowflake, you will have to go to the chair."). After the child has learned to obey one houserule, another may be introduced; but parents are cautioned to introduce the rules sequentially, not concurrently, to avoid risking disobedience caused by confusion or memory overload.

Most parents complete both the CDI phase and the PDI phase within 9–16 sessions. Afterward, the evidence suggests that both the parent-child relationship and child behavior will have improved. We now consider that evidence.

Outcome Studies Testing the Effects of Parent-Child Interaction Therapy

PCIT has been tested in a series of studies, most from Eyberg and her colleagues, but one from an independent investigator. As in the case of HNCP, the treated children have ranged in age from 2–8 years, and primary presenting concerns have been conduct problems of various kinds, including noncompliance.

Early test using a pre-post design, and comparison with siblings. In an early published test of PCIT, Eyberg and Robinson (1982) used PCIT with seven families, all having children between the ages of 2 and 7 years (ethnicity not reported). The six boys and one girl were all referred for active behavior problems in the home, in such forms as disobedience, aggression, destructiveness, hyperactivity, or temper tantrums. An additional inclusion criterion was that all the children were required to have a sibling between the ages of 2 and 10 years; those siblings remained untreated during the study. Treatment for the target siblings averaged about nine sessions.

Analysis of pre-post differences for the CDI phase of treatment showed significant decreases in mothers' use of commands and questions, and significant increases in the use of both labeled and unlabeled praise. Pre-post analyses for the PDI phase showed significant decreases in critical statements, and significant increases in clear and direct commands, opportunities to comply with commands, labeled and unlabeled praise. Especially important was the fact that target children showed significant declines in deviant behavior, and increases in compliance. Interestingly, target children's siblings also showed behavioral improvements even though they had not been included in treatment, suggesting that PCIT training effects generalized usefully at home. Changes in parent and child behavior were accompanied by reductions in parents' reports of anxiety and pessimism, and increases in parents' reports of involvement with others, and perceived internal control.

PCIT versus nonrandom comparison groups. The pre-post analyses of Eyberg and Robinson (1982) were suggestive but not definitive, given the absence of an equivalent comparison group that did not receive PCIT. A study by McNeil et al. (1991) took a step in the direction of a more definitive procedure, comparing 10 children treated with PCIT to 10 comparison children labeled "untreated deviant classroom controls" (McNeil et al., 1991, p. 141) and 10 comparison children labeled "normal classroom controls" (p. 141). Nonrandom procedures were used for group assignment, and the two groups having problems were not screened and selected in the same way, so the study presents some interpretive limitations.

The treated children were all boys, nine Caucasian and one African American, ages 2–7 years. Their referral problems were serious and long-lasting (i.e., at least six months in duration), including noncompliance, temper tantrums, serious aggression resulting in injury to others (e.g., broken bones, stab wounds), fire-setting, cruelty toward animals (including killing them), chronic stealing, and vandalism. Diagnostic interviews based on DSM-IIIR criteria showed that all of the treated children qualified for a diagnosis of oppositional defiant disorder, conduct disorder, and/or ADHD. All treated families received 14 weekly sessions of PCIT. For each treated child, one untreated deviant child and one untreated normal child were selected from the treated child's classroom. The untreated deviant group were youngsters selected by staff from the same school as being those who demonstrated behavior problems in the classroom. The group ranged from 2–7 years of age, included seven boys and three girls; six of the children were Caucasian, three African American, and one Hispanic. The untreated normal group was selected by school staff as showing "average behavior" in the classroom. This group ranged from 2–6 years of age, included six boys and four girls, and had eight Caucasian and two African American children.

Comparison of pre- and posttreatment observations and parent reports for the treated children showed substantial reductions in problem behavior at home, reductions to within the normal range of child behavior. Comparable analyses showed similar improvements in school behavior. The analyses also showed significantly more behavioral improvement among the treated children than the two control groups, and most of the gains remained significant when pretreatment scores were controlled.

In one respect, these results are encouraging. Previous findings had suggested that parent-focused intervention was effective in improving child behavior at home, but that such effects were not likely to generalize to child behavior in school (see e.g., Breiner & Forehand, 1981; Horn, Ialongo, Popovich, & Peradotto, 1987; Patterson, Cobb, & Ray, 1973). In contrast, the McNeil et al. (1991) findings appeared to show generalization to the school setting. However, because the three groups in the study were not randomly assigned, and the treatment group showed markedly higher levels of problem behavior than the two control groups at the outset of the study, the results are difficult to interpret, and the covariance procedures used by the authors to control for pre-treatment group differences do not completely solve the problem. There remains a possibility that the results reflect regression artifacts more than true treatment effects (see Hsu, 1989). So, further evidence is needed beyond McNeil et al. to provide a more definitive test of PCIT.

A random assignment study. One step in this direction can be found in a study by Zangwill (1984), who used a Hanfian treatment method based on PCIT. The study focused on 11 families of 2–8-year-olds, 10 boys and 1 girl (ethnicity not reported). The referral problems all involved high rates of unruly conduct in such forms as physical aggression, noncompliance, and temper tantrums. Families were randomly assigned to either the two-phase treatment offered immediately (N = 5) or a waiting list (N = 6). All families were seen by two-person therapist teams, for 10 one-hour treatment sessions, half devoted to CDI and half to PDI.

After treatment, comparison of the treatment and waitlist groups showed significantly greater increases among the treated parents in their rates of reinforcement, and significantly greater decreases in their rates of punishment. Treated parents reported fewer child problems and less aggression posttreatment than did waitlist parents. Observational assessments showed that children in the treatment group, compared to the waitlist, were more compliant with parental commands, in both the clinic assessments and home observations; although generalization of the effects to home behavior was only modest. Unfortunately, Zangwill (1983) also found no significant differences between treated and waitlist youngsters in observed deviant behavior, either in the clinic or at home. Group differences on both parent-report and observational measures generally pointed in the direction of beneficial treatment effects, and the limited support generated in terms of statistically significant differences may have resulted from very low statistical power, due in part to the very small sample employed by Zangwill. The small sample size also limits generalizability of the positive findings.

Random assignment test with oppositional defiant children. In the most sophisticated test of PCIT, to date, Shuhmann et al. (1998) studied a substantial sample, 64 youngsters ages 3–6; 81% were boys, and ethnically the sample was 77% Caucasian, 14% African American, and 9% Hispanic, Asian, or mixed. All the children were noncompliant and oppositional, and all met diagnostic criteria for oppositional defiant disorder (in DSM-IIIR);

66% also met criteria for ADHD, and 22% also met criteria for conduct disorder. Families were randomly assigned to either a waitlist (N = 27) or an immediate treatment condition (N = 37) in which they received an average of 13 sessions of PCIT. About two-thirds of the cases involved two-parent families, and in these cases both mothers and fathers were trained.

At completion of PCIT, the immediate treatment group looked significantly better than the waitlist group on both parent-report and direct observation measures. Treated parents reported lower levels of problem behavior in their children, lower levels of parenting stress, and higher scores on a parenting locus of control measure. Direct observations showed that treated parents were more praising and less critical of their children (as a percentage of total parent talk) than were waitlisted parents. Child compliance with parent commands increased markedly from pre- to posttreatment in the treated families (from 23% to 47% with mothers, 27% to 45% with fathers), whereas compliance remained virtually unchanged in the waitlisted families.

Follow-up assessment at four months posttreatment did not involve treatment versus waitlist comparison, because the waitlist group had received treatment at that point, but gains in the immediate treatment group did hold steady over the four-month period. A number of the analyses showed improvement from pre- to posttreatment that involved movement from the clinical range to the normal range on various measures (including parent ratings of child problem behavior and parenting stress). Overall, the results pointed to substantial positive changes in parents' styles of interacting with their oppositional children, and parallel changes in child problem behavior, changes that were in some cases both statistically and clinically significant.

Does it help to have CDI before PDI? One other study by the Eyberg group warrants attention here because it tested a basic Hanfian assumption. According to Hanf's model, the child-directed (Child's Game) phase of treatment needs to take place before the parent-directed (Parent's Game) phase, because it is the strengthened relationship between parent and child, produced in the child-directed phase that empowers the parents to control the child's disruptive behavior in the later parent-directed phase and after treatment ends. It follows from this reasoning that reductions in child compliance should be greater in PCIT when PDI is preceded by CDI than when CDI has not come first. To investigate whether this is, in fact, the case, Eisenstadt et al. (1993) arranged an interesting experimental procedure. They randomly assigned a sample of 24 2–7-year-olds who had severe, long-term conduct problems to one of two treatment groups: CDI first versus PDI first. All children met formal DSM-IIIR criteria for diagnoses of either oppositional defiant disorder, conduct disorder, or ADHD. Some 92% of the children were boys, and 88% were Caucasian (race/ethnicity of the remainder not reported). The families covered a range of socioeconomic status levels, with welfare funds the sole source of income for 33%; 46% of the children were from father-absent families.

Both groups in the study received both CDI and PDI, with groups differing only in the order of the two phases. The authors' prediction, based on the Hanf model, was that at the end of treatment, there would be more behavioral improvement by children (and more improvement in appropriate parent behavior) in those families receiving CDI first than in families receiving PDI first. The results did not support this prediction. Few significant differences were found between the two groups in outcomes at posttreatment, but where there were significant differences, they favored the PDI-first group. In the PDI-first families, mothers reported more substantial improvements in their children's behavior and more satisfaction with therapy; PDI-first families were also less likely than CDI-first families to return for follow-up assessments, and there was some evidence that this may have resulted from less perceived need for further help on the part of PDI families. The findings raise a question as to the validity of the Hanfian assumption that child-directed relationship building is needed to make parental discipline and limit setting effective. We return to this issue at the end of the chapter.

Summary of the Outcome Evidence on PCIT. In this section, we reviewed five outcome studies testing PCIT. The studies generally show improved parent behavior, improved child compliance, and reduced child behavior problems coincident with delivery of the treatment program. However, only two of the studies (Shuhmann, 1998; Zangwill, 1984) involved comparison of randomly assigned treatment and no-treatment groups, and one of these studies (Zangwill, 1984) employed a very small sample and found relatively few significant group differences. Thus, there is promising support for PCIT, but there is also room for improvement in experimental design and thus strength of the supporting evidence.

What about Sal? Applying the Parent-Child Interaction Approach

We return now to the case of Sal, described at the beginning of the section on conduct problems. Sal's case is a good fit, because a core problem seems to be his failure to have developed a warm, respectful, affectionate relationship with his mother (or his father, for that matter), and because the poor relationship may well be a cause of his noncompliant behavior and other conduct problems. This is precisely the combination of problems the two-phase parent-child treatments are designed to tackle; their most distinctive feature is an effort to shore up the parent-child relationship and thus to empower the parent as a limit-setter and disciplinarian, thereby reducing the frequency of conduct problems.

Because Sal is older than most children treated by HNCP and PCIT, we need to imagine what he would have been like in his preschool and early elementary school years, in order to describe how the two-phase parent-child treatment model might have been applied to his case. In making this leap, it is helpful to draw specifics from a case illustration ("John M") provided by Forehand and King (1977, pp. 101–2), from treatment segments quoted by Eyberg and Robinson (1982, p. 134), and from treatment manuals provided by Eyberg and Calzada (1998) and Forehand and McMahon (1981). From what we know of Sal's family situation, it seems likely that his conduct problems did not arrive out of the blue in his adolescent years; instead, it is likely that Sal showed significant levels of noncompliance and misbehavior as early as his preschool and/or early elementary years. We know that his relationship with his mother, who is his primary caregiver, has been troubled for some time. These characteristics suggest that he might well have been a good candidate for one of the Hanfian treatment programs in his preschool or early elementary years. Let us picture what such a program might have looked like in Sal's case.

First, if we assume that Sal's father would not invest the time and energy required of parents in these two-phase treatments, treatment would most likely involve only Sal and his mother. A focus on only the mother-child dyad is consistent with the procedure followed with many of the families in the studies described earlier, and, the studies suggest, should be sufficient to produce beneficial effects in most cases.

The initial step in the treatment process (for both HNCP and PCIT) is an assessment process, involving reports from Sal's mother of the behavior she sees him presenting, combined with direct observation of Sal-Mom interactions. The observations are coded for behavioral categories of interest, with respect to both Sal (e.g., obeying, disobeying, hitting) and his mother (e.g., praising Sal, criticizing Sal, issuing commands). The idea is to determine the baseline rates of both desirable and undesirable behavior, by both Sal *and* his mother, thus to provide benchmarks for assessing treatment gains.

After assessment, Sal and his mother take part in 9–12 treatment sessions. Roughly the first half of the treatment involves parent-child interactions in which Sal takes the lead and Mom is attentive and supportive; the last half involves interactions in which Mom takes the lead in structuring activities, setting limits, and giving and enforcing commands. Each of the sessions begins some initial structured observation of Mom and Sal interacting (about five minutes) and a brief discussion with the therapist in which Mom is taught certain things to do during the session, sometimes observing the therapist's modeling, and sometimes role-playing with the therapist to prepare her for further dyadic interactions with Sal. After these preliminary steps, Mom engages in a lengthier interaction with Sal, while she receives instructions, encouragement, and coaching from the therapist;

therapist input comes through a bug-in-the ear device worn by Mom. As an example, when Mom is being taught not to attend to misbehavior, and she slips and responds to Sal's shouting with, "Sal, why can't you ever be quiet?!" the therapist comments, "Why don't you just ignore that behavior." And when Mom later succeeds in intentionally not attending, the therapist says, "Good ignoring!" Once, when Mom is being taught to use a time-out procedure, she tells Sal to do something but then lets Sal get away with disobeying her; at this point, the therapist reminds her, "That was a command you gave. So now give the chair warning." In the last five minutes of each session the therapist observes the interaction between Mom and Sal, without commenting, to take stock of how well Mom has learned the skills emphasized in that session.

First phase: Sal takes the lead. In the first phase of treatment, Sal leads the interactions. The structure of these child-led interactions is similar within the HNCP and the PCIT models. Within both treatment approaches, Mom is taught to (1) attend closely to Sal's behavior while eliminating such unrewarding parental behavior as commands and questions; (2) describe Sal's ongoing behavior aloud in a running commentary (e.g., "You're putting the cars together. Now you're pushing them into the box."); (3) reward Sal's appropriate behavior with praise (e.g., "That's a very tall tower – good work, Sal") and physical contact (e.g., hugs); and (4) respond to inappropriate behavior (unless it is truly harming people or property) by ignoring – that is, no eye contact with Sal (turning 90–180 degrees away from the child), no verbal contact (not even an answer to "Why aren't you looking at me?"), no nonverbal cues (not even brief frowns or smiles), and no physical contact.

Both Mom and Sal have homework assignments. The primary assignment is daily practice of the child-focused activity at home (5–15 minutes each day). Each week, Mom practices with Sal the skills she has learned in previous sessions, and she keeps a written record of what she did and how Sal responded. This record is a focus of discussion with the therapist at the beginning of the next session.

A few differences between the HNCP and PCIT models show up in the child-directed phase of treatment. In HNCP, given its roots in social learning theory, a major goal is to stop coercive interaction sequences, making interactions more positive and rewarding; a primary goal is to empower Mom as an agent of reinforcement so as to strengthen her influence over Sal. In PCIT, by contrast, the therapist presents the interactions to Mom as a form of "play therapy," and as a way to help Sal calm down or become less angry. As a part of the play therapy process, Mom is taught to work at strengthening Sal's connection to her by imitating Sal's behavior in the interactions, and by reflecting Sal's comments, much as a child therapist might do while a child plays. For example, when Sal says, "The house fell down," Mom says, "Yes, the house fell right down." So, while the overall idea in both HNCP and PCIT is for Mom to tune in fully to Sal's behavior and to be highly rewarding to interact with, there is a difference in flavor, reflecting the social behavioral roots of HNCP versus the influence of attachment theory and play therapy theory on PCIT.

Second phase: Mom takes the lead. After Mom demonstrates mastery of the skills taught in the Sal-directed interactions, it is time to begin Phase 2 of treatment, the part in which she takes the lead in interactions with Sal. In these interactions (in both HNCP and PCIT) the therapist teaches Mom to give Sal specific behavioral directives or commands, and then to ensure that Sal experiences specific differential consequences for complying and for not complying. This, of course, goes to the heart of the problems Sal manifests in the case description at the beginning of this section. An important lesson for Mom (one that is featured in both HNCP and PCIT) is the distinction between alpha and beta commands. Mom specializes in beta commands, i.e., poor ones that do not convey clear instructions. Of the five types of beta commands described earlier, Mom especially uses question commands, such as "Are you ready to pick up the blocks now?" (to which Sal's most likely reply is "No."), and "let's" commands, such as "OK, let's pick up the blocks" (which implies incorrectly that Mom will participate with Sal in picking up). Mom is taught to replace these ineffective beta commands with clear, concise alpha commands, that is, appropriate directives that are specific and direct such as, "Sal, put these toys in this box."

Teaching the use of alpha commands helps to solve one potential problem – that is, Sal may disobey, in part, because he fails to understand that he is being given a command. If Sal responds to alpha commands by obeying, the problem may have been solved, and Mom will respond with the attending and rewarding (e.g., with labeled praise, physical contact) she was taught to use during the initial, child-directed phase of treatment. As it turns out, Sal chooses to disobey, even when he is given clear alpha commands. To deal with this problem, Mom needs another skill that is taught within both HNCP and PCIT: time-out. In one of their exchanges, Mom instructs her son, "Sal, put these toys in this box," but Sal continues to play with the toys. Following the HNCP and PCIT models, Mom is taught to (1) wait five seconds for Sal to initiate compliance; (2) after five seconds, warn Sal by saying, "If you don't put the toys in the box, then you will have to sit in this chair" [or "... have to have a time-out"]; (3) wait another five seconds; (4) if noncompliance continues, take Sal by the hand and place him on a chair, saying, in a disapproving but calm voice, "Since you didn't put the toys in the box, you have to sit in this chair until I say you can get up"; (5) keep Sal in the chair for three minutes (ignoring shouts, protests, or tantrums); (6) if Sal gets out of the chair without permission, respond first with a warning, "If you don't stay in the chair, I will take you to the time-out room," as he is returned to the chair; (7) after three minutes have passed, and Sal has been quiet in the chair for

15 consecutive seconds, return Sal to the toy area and repeat the original command; and (8) follow the same sequence of Steps (1, 2, 3, etc.) again until Sal complies as instructed. At any point in the sequence when Sal complies (including compliance following a warning), Mom offers labeled praise at the beginning (e.g., "Good, Sal, you're putting the toys in the box.") and end (e.g., "Good job putting those toys in the box, Sal!"); and she rewards Sal throughout the compliance process by attending closely to his actions. Mom is also taught to give reasons together with praise – for example, "When you put the toys in the box, you made the room look nice and clean!"

As in Phase 1, Mom has homework assignments to carry out with Sal. These include practice (5–15 minutes each day) in the use of alpha commands, rewarding Sal when he complies, and following through with the time-out cycle when he does not. Also following the pattern of Phase 1, Mom uses the records she keeps on a printed form to review how the week's homework assignments went, with the therapist at the beginning of each session. These reviews are used to plan not only the learning tasks of the session at hand, but also to do problem solving for difficulties that have arisen at home. For example, Mom and the therapist discuss what to do with Sal when he refuses to remain quiet in his room during the one-hour quiet time his mother has tried to establish after lunch. The therapist asks her how she might use what she has learned thus far to reach her goal for Sal. She replies that she might try rewarding Sal for short periods in which he remains quiet. The therapist agrees, suggesting that she begin by rewarding Sal with attention and labeled praise for each five-minute block of time spent in quiet activity, then expand the intervals to 10 minutes after a week, and so forth. This works well. By the end of treatment, Sal is quiet throughout the one-hour postlunch period, requiring only one visit for attending and labeled praise from Mom at the half-hour mark each time. This experience goes a long way toward showing Mom that she can effect real change in Sal's behavior, on her own, at home.

Even in this second phase of treatment, which emphasizes interactions controlled by Mom, the therapist (and this is true for both HNCP and PCIT) encourages some continued practice of the child-focused activity. This is seen as a way of continuing to strengthen the positive aspects of the relationship between Sal and his mother, considered crucial to the long-term success of the intervention.

There are some differences between HNCP and PCIT in how Phase 2 would be carried out with Sal. For example, PCIT tends to involve somewhat more nurturant sessions than HNCP, with some alternating interaction sequences in which Mom gives Sal opportunities to set the agenda but inserts her own commands intermittently, thus blending elements of child-directed and parent-directed interchange. HNCP does include child-focused exercises in treatment even after the Phase 2 Compliance Training has begun; but the child-focused exercises are more clearly distinct from the exercises in which parents direct the interaction.

However, the differences between HNCP and PCIT in Phase 1 and Phase 2 are outweighed by the similarities. The goals of the two approaches are certainly quite similar. The most important goals for Mom are that she learn to be consistent in her use of positive and negative consequence for Sal's appropriate and inappropriate behaviors, respectively, that she learn to use clear and effective alpha commands, and that she establish the kind of relationship with Sal that will make him want to cooperate with her and comply with her directives. Key goals for Sal are increased compliance with his mother's requests, and more frequent choice of appropriate behavior in preference to inappropriate options. The outcome evidence reviewed earlier suggests that exposure to HNCP or PCIT in the preschool or early elementary years might have done a good deal to prevent the kind of disobedient and disruptive behavior Sal shows in early adolescence.

Troubleshooting: Common Treatment Problems and Recommended Solutions. Although the parent-child interaction approach to treatment can work well with preschool and early elementary children, therapists can encounter rough spots along the way. A few examples follow, together with solutions the experts have found to be effective.

- *Homework noncompliance.* Some parents fail to do their homework assignments and thus fail to make much progress in skill acquisition between sessions. Effective therapists use both proactive and reactive ways of addressing the problem. To be proactive, therapists can discuss homework with parents at the outset of treatment, even before an assignment has been made. Therapists may stress that even though a few minutes a day for homework may not seem like much, it may actually take a lot of effort to follow through consistently. Before starting, most parents can't imagine that the short homework assignments could be a problem, so many are quick to insist that they will have no trouble with homework. Wise therapists will praise parents for this positive attitude, then ask parents to identify the time of day or night and the exact location where the homework will be done; a concrete plan enhances follow-through. In cases where the preseason peptalk and advance planning do not lead to homework compliance, therapists are encouraged to call parents between sessions to ask how the homework is going and to offer help by phone. Some therapists even use money as an incentive. One approach is to require that parents leave a monetary deposit with the therapist, to be refunded at the end of treatment but with deductions for each missed assignment. Another approach is to pay parents a "parenting salary" – a monetary payment for each assignment completed (see Fleischman, 1979); this may seem an odd concept, but considering the cost of the therapist time needed to make up for undone homework, some clinics and clinicians consider it a reasonable investment.

- *Parental stressors that interfere with child treatment focus.* Another common challenge is that genuine life stressors can intrude into parents' time with the therapist. The opportunity to talk with an empathic, skilled clinician may lead parents to focus session time on their own personal concerns rather than on their relationship and interactions with their child. If the therapist sees such discussions as productive but as distracting attention from the parenting skills focus, one appropriate response is to ask that the discussions be saved, in each session, until after the parent-child interaction coaching has been completed. It is also quite appropriate to tell parents that these concerns are so important that they need special attention outside of the parent-child interaction program, and to make a referral to another therapist.

- *Mismatches between parent style and treatment approach.* At times, parents arrive with a personal style that conflicts with the aims and methods recommended in treatment. The *drill sergeant* parent (McMahon & Forehand, 2003), for example, issues many commands and expects children to fall in line and obey with little or no explanation of the reasons for commands and rules. By contrast, the *afraid-to-confront* parent (McMahon & Forehand, 2003) is uneasy issuing parental commands and prone to accept the child's every excuse for not complying. Understanding the belief system that underlies the style can be a useful first step in treatment. Sometimes, the problem is an incomplete understanding of children's capacities and needs at various developmental levels. The drill sergeant may need to learn that a normal 4-year-old simply cannot process and retain all those commands, and that explaining the reasons for rules can contribute importantly to the child's cognitive development. The afraid-to-confront parent may need to hear that learning to obey is a crucial developmental step for children, best learned through interactions with their parents, and that failing to learn that skill can presage a very troubled developmental course. When therapist and parent cannot achieve a meeting of the minds, another approach is to have the parent agree to suspend disbelief long enough to try the skills being taught. Both HNC and PCIT emphasize collecting evidence on parent behavior and child responses. Sometimes it takes such evidence to persuade skeptical parents that their children actually do respond to the parenting behaviors taught in the program.

Parent-Child Interaction Treatments: Scientific Issues

The rationale for parent-child treatment in early childhood is closely linked to the *developmental progression* model of conduct problems (see Frick, 1998; Lahey & Loeber, 1994), discussed in the section introduction. This model posits a sequence in which children begin showing oppositional and argumentative behavior early in life (e.g., ages 2–8) and progress to increasingly severe conduct problems as they mature. Evidence supports such a pattern in at least a substantial proportion of disruptive and disobedient children (see Frick, 1998; Lahey & Loeber, 1994; Reid, 1993), particularly those exposed to poor parental discipline and aversive parent-child interactions (see Loeber & Dishion, 1983; White et al., 1990). HNCP and PCIT are targeted at the age range in which early disobedience and poor parenting are thought to have a particularly significant and lasting impact; the intent is to cut short the developmental progression of problems while it can still be stopped.

Perhaps some would question whether the evidence thus far shows unequivocally that the two parent-child interaction treatments specifically prevent early childhood discipline problems from escalating into conduct disorder and antisocial behavior in late childhood, adolescence, and adulthood, but the evidence does suggest that the two treatments improve child compliance and reduce a variety of externalizing behaviors (e.g., tantrums, aggression; see Wells et al., 1980). Moreover, a number of the effects on both child and parent behavior that are evident at immediate posttreatment hold up well in follow-up assessments. PCIT effects have been found to persist at one-year followups, and findings on HNCP have shown effects lasting up to 10–14 years after the end of treatment, the most enduring treatment benefits yet identified in the child and adolescent treatment literature. Interpretation of the long-term findings is constrained by methodological issues (as discussed later in this section), but the findings are certainly in harmony with the view that these parent-child interaction treatments may prevent development of increasingly serious conduct problems as children mature.

A particular strength of the evidence on these interactional treatments is that so much of it has come from direct observation of parent and child behavior, coded by trained observers. This reduces the risk of interpretive problems, associated with exclusive use of parent reports. Beyond outcome assessment, both the HNCP and PCIT teams have made direct observation integral to their treatment programs; such observation is used to (1) understand what parent-child interaction is like prior to treatment, and thus plan what skills need to be taught; (2) inform the therapist's use of the bug-in-the-ear method during parent training in the sessions; and (3) determine when the parent has learned a particular target skill, so that the next step of skill training can begin. Thus, the use of direct observation is a notable strength of both the HNCP and PCIT treatment programs and the evidence on their outcomes.

As with some of the other treatment programs discussed in this section, certain limitations are evident in the outcome research literature on HNCP and PCIT. A number of the studies have relied on relatively small samples and on pretreatment versus posttreatment comparisons rather than comparing randomly assigned treatment and control groups. Another methodological limitation is common to numerous other treatments: Although multiple studies report encouraging follow-up data years after treatment termination, the fact that control groups are treated after the posttreatment assessment denies investigators an opportunity to compare prospectively assigned treated and untreated children at followup. This limitation is obviously difficult to avoid; design purity is hardly a sufficient rationale for withholding a beneficial treatment from a control group for 10–14 years! And some of the investigators have taken steps to address the design limitation by identifying useful comparison groups that were not prospectively assigned. This may be the best our researchers can do, given the complex mix of ethical and design issues that arise, but the evidence would be more definitive if researchers could find an acceptable way to experimentally control for the passage of time (and the possibility of naturally occurring developmental gains) in groups that had not received the target treatments.

Another theme that warrants close attention in future research is the identification of factors that moderate treatment effects. A positive aspect of research on both HNCP and PCIT is the rich mix of human and situational variability that characterizes the samples employed in the outcome studies. Samples have included both boys and girls, multiple ethnicities, single-parent and two-parent families, and a broad socioeconomic status range extending from low-income parents receiving public assistance to relatively affluent professionals. Early studies failed to find evidence that treatment effects differed with child age (across a range of 3–8 years; McMahon et al., 1985) or socioeconomic status (Rogers et al., 1981). Such findings do not eliminate the need for research on the boundary conditions (person and situation factors) within which these treatments are most beneficial, and outside of which adjustments or alternative treatments may be needed.

Another useful focus for research in the future will be the question of what specific change processes are actually responsible for the positive effects of the parent-child treatments. In the original Hanf model, a key idea was that favorable changes in the nature of the parent-child relationship fostered increased motivation by the child to comply with the parent's directives, and that compliance was further strengthened by improved consistency in the parent's use of positive and negative reinforcement (e.g., labeled praise, time-out). Assumptions such as these remain to be tested directly. Fortunately, there have been important advances in statistical methods for testing mediational models. These advances make it increasingly possible for investigators to assess, for example, whether improved child behavior is, in fact, mediated by improvements in the relationship (e.g., increases in warmth, affection, positive tone), by improvements in parental management practices (e.g., contingency setting, appropriate ignoring, appropriate consequences), or by other factors related or tangential to the original Hanf model.

Perhaps the most important theory-based scientific issue for HNCP and PCIT is the question of whether the two-phase concept adds significantly to the benefits of treatment for child conduct problems. In Hanf's original conception, the Child's Game phase is needed to strengthen the parent's influence over the child (both in the Parent's Game and after treatment ends). In the HNCP model, the child-focused interactions (Differential Attention) are needed to empower the parent as an agent of reinforcement. In PCIT, the child-focused interactions (CDI) are thought to accomplish for the parent the kind of relationship enhancement that is theoretically associated with therapist effectiveness in play therapy, according to the Axline (1969) model, and this enhanced relationship is needed to make parent-directed interactions work as intended. However, the study by Eisenstadt et al. (1993), reviewed earlier, showed little support for the idea that child-directed interaction, or strengthening of the child-parent relationship via Axline-like play interactions, is needed to make a parent's directiveness and limit setting effective. In fact, in the Eisenstadt et al. study, parents for whom PDI came before CDI actually reported more behavioral improvements in their children, and more satisfaction with treatment, than parents who went through PCIT in the traditional order, with CDI followed by PDI. Such findings raise a basic question about a core assumption of the parent-child treatment models discussed in this chapter.

The findings raise the further possibility that the two-phase treatment approach, emphasizing a period of relationship building through CDI, may not provide substantial benefits beyond what would be obtained through more traditional behavioral parent training, as discussed in Chapter 9. It is possible that behavioral parent training is simply a more direct and efficient path to the same outcomes as HNCP and PCIT. However, what evidence we have relative to efficiency actually suggests that the two-stage parent-child interaction approach may require less therapist time than Pattersonian parent training as described in Chapter 9. For example, Baum and Forehand (1981) reported an average cost of 7.4 hours of professional time per family for the HNCP treatment used in their study, versus 31.4 hours of professional time in the behavioral parent training study reported by Patterson (1974).

The efficiency issue cannot be fully addressed with currently available data, nor can the question of whether the child-focused interactions are really essential for the success of PCIT or HNCP. In Eisenstadt et al. (1993), for example, both treatment groups did in fact receive both CDI and PDI, albeit in two different orders. Thus, that study, like others discussed in this chapter, does not address the question of what effects might result if the child-directed play were omitted altogether. Given the important findings by Eisenstadt et al. (1993), it now seems appropriate to carry out such an experimental test. Research on this theme could also address the question of whether the child-directed play component is differentially useful for different types of children or parents. Robert McMahon (personal communication, December 23, 1999) suggests, for example, that the Child's Game phase, while important for all parents, may be especially crucial for parents who enter treatment simply looking for a bigger stick with which to punish their child; for such parents, McMahon believes, "reorienting them to a more positive approach, as in Phase 1, is really key, I think."

One remaining question spans scientific and clinical issues: whether treatment effects generalize to school settings. Because HNCP and PCIT training is typically done in the clinic office, with additional practice carried out at home but not at school, one might reasonably ask whether the effects generalize to school behavior. The question is important because children who are disobedient and oppositional at home often have very similar problems at school. Evidence on the generalization question is mixed, with some studies showing no evidence of generalization (Breiner & Forehand, 1981; Forehand et al., 1979); some studies suggesting apparent beneficial generalization to school behavior but based on methods that fail to clearly document treatment effects (e.g., Strayhorn & Weidman, 1989), do not include a control group (Sayger & Horne, 1987), or include nonequivalent and nonrandomly assigned control groups (Funderburk et al., 1998). Thus, the question of generalization to school settings has not yet been resolved in an empirically ideal way. To the extent that beneficial effects depend on maintenance of the specific behaviors parents are taught in HNCP and PCIT, it may simply be unreasonable to expect generalization to settings where no adults have been trained in those behaviors. If a referred child has behavioral problems at school, the most reasonable response may be to intervene in the school, rather than to hope for parent training to generalize (see McMahon & Wells, 1998, on this point).

Parent-Child Interaction Treatments: Clinical Practice Issues

HNCP and PCIT have several similar strengths with regard to their clinical utility, and PCIT may have one additional attraction to many practitioners. Among the shared strengths are the fact that both are relatively brief treatments, guided by clear procedural rules, including rules for when parents are ready to transition from one step of skill training to the next, and ready to end treatment. Another strength is that the treatments are focused on goals that are likely to be quite motivating to many parents – that is, reducing parent-child conflict, making interactions more satisfying, and increasing rates of child obedience. Another appealing aspect, from a parent's perspective, is the fact that the treatment begins with positive interactions that focused partly on teaching the parent to appreciate and reward the child for appropriate behavior. More stressful interactions, where the parent exerts control, are saved for the latter half of treatment. Not surprisingly, research on both treatment programs has shown high consumer satisfaction ratings (e.g., McMahon et al., 1984; Schuhmann et al., 1998) suggesting that the treatments are perceived as appropriate and helpful by parents.

HNCP and PCIT may differ slightly from one another in their appeal to different groups of therapists and parents. HNCP may be a bit more appealing to those who prefer highly structured procedures focused on clear-cut behavioral objectives, but without a heavy emphasis on therapist procedures derived from play therapy. PCIT may appeal a bit more to psychodynamic therapists, and to those who favor more traditional notions of how an adult should interact with a child in play therapy (Axline, 1969). Thus, PCIT and its rationale may be particularly attractive to therapists whose own preferred approach involves play therapy and more traditional forms of rapport building and intervention with children.

On the downside, from a clinical perspective, some elements of HNCP and PCIT may not be easy to replicate in a typical clinic that serves diverse clients. One-way glass and a bug-in-the-ear device may not be available in some clinics; alternatives are acceptable, such as having the therapist simply sit near the parent in the same room during parent-child interactions, but these alternatives have not been systematically tested, to date. Also, practitioners may find it difficult to replicate some parts of the observational coding systems that are used in both treatment programs to identify specific parent training needs, and to gauge when parents have learned a particular skill and are ready to progress to the next. Achieving reliable observation of parent-child interaction using standardized procedures may be important to treatment success, and this obviously requires time for observer training. This issue has been addressed by the PCIT group (see Eyberg, Bessmer et al., 1994) through development of the clinic version of the DPICS-II; this system is relatively quick to learn and the only supplies and equipment required are pencil and paper.

Another potential point of concern in clinical practice is that some of the treatment procedures may seem a bit more controlling than some practitioners prefer, with a strong emphasis on parental commands and child obedience. This emphasis was more pronounced in some of the early research on HNCP, which created discipline training opportunities by instructing parents "to give a series of commands designed to evoke noncompliance" (Forehand & King, 1977, p. 100; Peed et al., 1977, p. 336). More recent versions are not geared to creating noncompliance. It is certainly true that, while parents are taught to be in control, they are also taught to attend to and support their children in ways that go well beyond what most parents do.

A general concern is that tests of the HNCP and PCIT model, like most tests of most treatments reviewed in this book, may not have taken place in the most clinically representative circumstances. The children treated in several of the studies were referred for treatment, but typically to university-based programs specializing in HNCP or PCIT, and sometimes in response to advertising and recruitment efforts. In some of the studies it is not clear how much the resulting samples resembled the children and families who are typically referred to service clinics and private practitioners. Some were referred by community sources – for example, pediatricians. Even in these cases, though, it is not clear whether the referring individuals and agencies were spontaneously referring to a pre-existing clinic or responding to a recruitment effort. To the extent that future research tests HNCP and PCIT in clinic settings and under practice conditions, it will be clearer which of the potential challenges noted earlier may warrant serious concern, and whether adaptations will be needed to facilitate everyday use by practitioners.

How to Find Out More about the Parent-Child Interaction Treatments

More about Helping the Noncompliant Child Program. A detailed description of HNCP in its original form was first provided in Forehand and McMahon's (1981) book, *Helping the Noncompliant Child: A Clinician's Guide to Parent Training.* That book has recently gone out of print, replaced by an updated second edition, covering concepts, treatment methods, and outcome findings. The second edition, published in 2003 by Guilford Press, is written by McMahon and Forehand and entitled *Helping the Noncompliant Child: Family-Based Treatment for Oppositional Behavior.* A companion guide for parents is available as well: *Parenting the Strong-Willed Child: The Clinically Proven Five-Week Program for Parents of Two- to Six-Year-Olds* (2nd ed., McGraw-Hill), by Forehand and Long (2002). A training videotape, *Parent Training for the Noncompliant Child: A Guide for Training Therapists,* can be obtained from Child Focus, 17 Harbor Ridge Road, South Burlington, VT 05403 (current cost: $29.95). For additional information on resources and training opportunities, contact either Robert J. McMahon, Ph.D., Department of Psychology, University of Washington, Box 351525, Seattle, WA 98195-1525, or Rex L. Forehand, Department of Psychology, University of Vermont, Burlington, VT 05405.

More about Parent-Child Interaction Therapy. The formal manual for PCIT is Eyberg and Calzada's (1998), *Parent-Child Interaction Therapy: Procedures Manual.* A useful complement to this manual is the book, *Parent-Child*

Interaction Therapy, by McNeil and Hembree-Kigin (1995). Several articles describe the theoretical basis, rationale, and procedural nuances of PCIT (see Eyberg, 1988; Eyberg & Robinson, 1982; Eyberg et al., 1995; Foote et al., 1998). Research support for PCIT is described in a recent review chapter by Brinkmeyer and Eyberg (2003). Additional information on training resources and training opportunities can be obtained from Sheila Eyberg, Ph.D., Department of Clinical and Health Psychology, Health Sciences Center, University of Florida, 1600 SW Archer Road, Gainesville, FL 32610.

11

Parent Training Through Video Modeling and Structured Group Discussion

Behavioral parent training is a potent treatment for child conduct problems, as discussed in Chapters 6, 9, and 10. For some therapists, though, the challenge of becoming a behavioral expert and finding time to structure individual interventions, one family at time, can discourage efforts to try behavioral approaches – particularly under the productivity pressures of managed care. Fortunately, there is a cost-effective approach that relieves therapist burden to some degree, and has unusually strong empirical support. The approach uses videotaped illustrations to convey behavioral principles through observational learning, one of the most efficient ways to build skills.

The most thoroughly tested video modeling approach has been developed by Webster-Stratton (e.g., 1981a,b, 2001) and her colleagues. In the parent component of their Incredible Years Training Series, a therapist shows brief videos of parent-child interactions to groups of mothers and fathers and leads discussions on themes illustrated in the videos. In this chapter, we describe some of the videos, some of the themes, and some of the evidence on treatment effects.

The Incredible Years BASIC Parent Training Program: Conceptual Basis and Procedural Overview

Advantages of teaching parents child behavior management skills were discussed in Chapter 9. Teaching parents via video illustrations may offer further advantages. One is that the video approach employs modeling, a highly efficient form of learning that outpaces, for example, the trial and error process involved in operant conditioning (see e.g., Bandura, 1971, 1986). The video-guided approach is also more engaging for many parents than didactic learning in a classroom format, or being required to read a book and take a test on it. The advantages of a video-guided approach seem obvious for parents who do not read or who may have relatively little formal education. However, the Webster-Stratton program has been found to work well across a broad range of parent education and intelligence. Another strength is that the video material is the same at every presentation, which ensures significant uniformity across therapists and settings. Such uniformity may help limit the impact of variations in therapist training, orientation, style, and skill. Finally, and notably in an era of managed care, video modeling is cost-effective; it limits expensive therapist training time, and therapist intervention time, in ways that cost-conscious mental health administrators will appreciate.

Although observational learning is one part of the conceptual basis for the treatment, other theoretical perspectives have been influential as well. Building on Bandura's (1989) self-efficacy theory, Webster-Stratton trains therapists to work as collaborators with parents, rather than as teachers or dispensers of advice; the collaborative approach is thought to enhance parents' "efficacy expectations" – that is, the conviction that they can successfully change their own and their child's behavior.

Cognitive-behavioral theory is also highly relevant, as therapists work with parents to identify and modify unproductive cognitions (e.g., "I'll never be an effective parent," or "My child is impossible to control.") or to reframe distressing events (e.g., a difficult child's demands can be construed as "testing limits" or "moving toward independence").

In their approach to parent training, Webster-Stratton and her colleagues share basic goals with those who train parents directly through didactics and discussion – that is, to reduce inappropriate child behavior and increase appropriate, prosocial behavior. The skills Webster-Stratton and colleagues try to inculcate in parents are also similar to the skills more traditional parent training approaches aim to teach. However, unlike those who use traditional behavioral parent training, Webster-Stratton capitalizes on the efficiency and other advantages of observational learning, and she combines this with the social support potential of the parent group format. She and her colleagues have developed multiple programs. We will focus here on a particularly well-researched series of 10 videotaped programs in which adults and children act out various interactions in brief vignettes. This series, called The Incredible Years BASIC Parent Training Program includes 250 vignettes, most one to two minutes long, each illustrating a behavioral principle and its implementation in parent-child interaction. The tapes are usually shown to parents of 3–8 year-olds, in groups, for 12 sessions or so, with the vignettes used to both model appropriate parent behavior in response to child problems and to stimulate group discussion.

Webster-Stratton's BASIC program has been applied primarily to youngsters in early childhood through early elementary school. There are both empirical and practical reasons for such a focus. As noted previously, the evidence on developmental pathways (e.g., Loeber, 1991; Patterson, DeBaryshe, & Ramsey, 1989) suggests that "early starters" are the most at risk for serious long-term conduct problems. One popular early starter model involves oppositional and defiant behavior in the preschool years, progressing to aggressive and devious behavior (e.g., lying, stealing) in middle childhood, and leading to property crimes and violence in adolescence (see Lahey, Loeber, Quay, Frick, & Grimm, 1992). Early starters account for a disproportionate share of delinquent acts in adolescence, and some evidence suggests that the primary developmental pathway for serious conduct problems in adolescence and adulthood is laid down during the preschool years (see Campbell & Ewing, 1990; Loeber, 1991).

All this evidence suggests that, if one must make a choice as to what age group to focus on for intervention, the preschool through early elementary years may be a particularly wise choice. Practically speaking, the use of video modeling does require that a choice be made, because the young models must be of some age, and effective observational learning is apt to require similarity between the modeled situation and the situation faced by the learner. Videotapes with young child models probably would not be very useful to parents of disruptive adolescents.

So, the evidence on developmental pathways into serious conduct problems has led to a focus on parents of preschool through early elementary-age children. Observational learning theory and research has led to the idea of video modeling for parents. And self-efficacy theory and cognitive-behavioral principles have informed the particular approach used in working with parents.

In the BASIC program, groups of 10–14 parents meet with a therapist for 13–14 weekly two-hour sessions. Parents view a series of video vignettes showing other parents dealing with their children in a variety of situations, sometimes successfully, sometimes not. These videos are used to stimulate discussion of basic behavioral principles. Parents practice the principles in homework assignments, some of which include tracking their children's behavior to look for changes resulting from new parenting methods. Over the series of sessions, four themes are addressed: constructive use of play, using praise and reward effectively, setting and enforcing limits, and handling misbehavior.

The Incredible Years BASIC Parent Training Program: In Brief

Designed for . . . . Parents of children ages 3–8 who have conduct problems
Number of sessions 12–14
Session length . . . . 2 hours

Session participants . . . . Therapist with groups of 10–14 parents
Theoretical orientation . . . . Observational learning, operant,
cognitive-behavioral, relationship, group support

Treatment steps:

1. *Constructive use of child-directed play.* Therapist uses video vignettes
   and role-plays to focus parent discussion on constructive use of
   child-directed play skills to help build children's self-esteem and
   self-confidence, help children handle boredom, avoid power struggles with peers, improve language skills (including emotion language) and problem solving, and cope with frustration.
2. *Effective use of praise and reward.* Using other videos, role-plays, and
   guided discussion, therapist teaches parents ways to use praise and
   tangible rewards to increase the frequency of specific, desirable child
   behaviors. Parents are helped to generalize principles of praise to
   other relationships such as partners and teachers.
3. *Limit-setting.* With videos, role-plays, and discussion, therapist helps
   parents learn basic rules for effective limit-setting – for example,
   limit commands to the ones that really matter, make them clear and
   concise, fit them to child's maturity level, don't insert a barb, and
   use distraction to enhance compliance.
4. *Handling misbehavior.* Videos, role-plays, and discussion focus on
   dealing with child misbehavior through preventing it, strategic ignoring, time-out, logical and natural consequences, and problem
   solving.

Other features, present throughout the steps . . . . Intervention individualized through parent goal-setting and self-monitoring, solution-
focused assignments with identification of personal barriers, notes
to/from therapist in parent folders, home assignments, and therapist
phone calls to parents at home; peer support comes through a support
group and through "buddy"calls at home.
Classified by Task Force . . . . Well established (See Brestan
& Eyberg, 1998)
Key resources for potential users . . . . Webster-Stratton, C. (2001). *Leader's
Guide, the Parents and Children Series: A Comprehensive Course Divided
into Four Programs.* Seattle, WA: University of Washington. Webster-
Stratton, C., & Reid, M. J. (2003). The Incredible Years Parents, Teach-
ers, and Children's training series: A multifaceted treatment approach
for young children with conduct problems. In A. E. Kazdin & J. R.
Weisz (Eds.), *Evidence-Based Psychotherapies for Children and Adolescents.* New York: Guilford.

Incredible Years BASIC Parent Training Program:
Treatment Procedures

The BASIC program consists of 12–14 weekly sessions, each about two hours long. In each session, the therapist meets with a group of 8–12 parents, shows a series of about 15 one- to two-minute video vignettes, each depicting a parent-child interaction of some kind – typically some problem behavior by the child followed by a parental response. After each vignette, the therapist asks parents for their reactions to the situations and events, including their ideas as to how the problem shown in the vignette should be solved. The therapist's role includes some direct teaching, some reframing and refining of ideas proposed by the parents, and extensive use of role-plays to illustrate points and procedures.

Promoting parent identification with vignette models, individual goal-setting, home assignments. An important goal is to bridge the gap between the specific structure and content of the vignettes, on the one hand, and the often diverse backgrounds, situations, and problems represented by the parent participants, on the other. To assist in this process, the vignettes have been constructed with diversity in mind. The tapes show parents and children of differing ages, cultures, socioeconomic backgrounds, and temperaments. The intent is to help parents perceive at least some of the models as similar to themselves and their own children, thus to promote identification and a perception that the taped material is personally relevant. Beyond the diversity of the tapes, therapists work to help parents make the treatment personally relevant. At the beginning, parents are asked to identify specific goals for themselves and for their child (i.e., behaviors they want to see more of and less of). The therapist works to help each parent move toward these goals and to monitor progress over time. Parents are asked to read portions of the Webster-Stratton book, *The Incredible Years,* and also to apply some of what they are learning to their interactions with their children at home. This is one form of the home assignments parents are given each week; for example, they might be asked to read (or listen to audiotapes) about limit-setting or time-out, and try the procedure with their child.

Promoting communication between therapist and individual parents: folders, weekly evals, phone calls. The therapist takes several steps to promote communication with individual parents as a complement to the group sessions. First, each parent is given a folder, in which the therapist places personal written notes to the parent, including feedback on the previous week's home assignment, plus praise (and sometimes stickers or candy) for achieving a special milestone or accomplishment. Each week, as parents arrive at the group meeting, they place in their folder the written work they have done for the week's home assignment, and they retrieve the therapist's folder entries written for them. Each parent also completes an evaluation form for each session, which gives the therapist a window into how the parent responded, and whether there were problems that warrant a follow-up phone call. The therapist tries to call each parent every other week, to check in, inquire as to how things are going, and nurture the relationship.

Collaborative approach to intervention. Therapists are trained to adopt the role of collaborator with parents rather than expert who tells parents what to do. So, for example, during discussions of vignettes and role-plays, the therapist asks open-ended questions, actively solicits parents' ideas, and tries to facilitate group problem solving. Debate is encouraged, and parents who disagree with the therapist on some point are urged to express their views. When parents' session evaluations suggest a problem, it is the therapist's job to change in response to the feedback. In these ways, and by having parents set and monitor their own goals, procedures are designed to support the development of self-efficacy and discourage excessive dependence on the therapist, who, after all, will not be available for long.

Mutual support by parents. The therapist also engineers mutual parental support as much as possible. Parents are urged to bring a spouse, partner, other family member, or good friend to the sessions, to provide ongoing support. Each parent is also assigned a buddy, a group member who will agree to call during the week to check on how the home assignment went. Buddy assignments shift from time to time, to give parents varied experiences of giving and receiving support. The group as a whole devotes significant time to discussing ways they can be a source of strength and help for individual members, particularly when those members are feeling tired, stressed out, or unable to cope. Finally, the parent groups are encouraged to continue meeting as support groups after the formal treatment program has ended.

Tapes show parents doing it "right" and "wrong." An important aspect of the treatment experience is that the tapes show parent models both *doing it right* and *doing it wrong.* The "wrong" tapes are intended to help stimulate problem solving and discussion by parents in a way that would not be likely if parents were simply shown the right answer. In addition, Webster-Stratton has been influenced by the literature suggesting that coping approaches to modeling – that is, showing models who need to learn how to cope, and illustrating how such learning can happen – are often more beneficial than mastery modeling, in which the models simply do everything right from the outset (see discussion in Webster-Stratton, 1981b).

Do's and don'ts of using the videotapes. Therapists try to pace vignettes evenly throughout the session, and to ensure that a discussion follows each vignette. Key points are highlighted through role-plays, three to four per session. The therapist may do the first role-play, aiming for humor by exaggerating bad parenting behavior, such as yelling orders to a child from behind a closed door (in which case one can't tell whether the child heard, understood, or obeyed), and then asking the group for better ideas. In fact, in the first parent role-play, parents may be told, "OK, do it the worst way possible," to help reduce pressure and add humor to the situation.

Contents of the BASIC Parent Video Program. The BASIC parent program contains 250 vignettes, covering four core parenting skill domains. Content of the first two domains – *play interaction* and *reinforcement skills* – was derived from important work by Hanf (1970) and Robinson and Eyberg (1981) on parent-child interaction. Content of the last two components – *setting limits* and *handling misbehavior*, including the use of effective problem-solving techniques – was derived partly from the family interaction and parent training research of leaders like Patterson (e.g., 1982; see Chapter 9) and Forehand and McMahon (1981; see Chapter 10), and partly from research by D'Zurilla and Nezu (1982) and Spivak, Platt, and Shure, (1976) on enhancing problem-solving skills. Here we summarize the four components.

1. *Play interaction.* The first set of video vignettes (25 vignettes, 36 minutes) focuses on the importance of adult attention during children's play, and on ways parents can use child-directed play to help their children develop imagination and creativity, build self-esteem, handle boredom, and learn to avoid power struggles with peers. A second set (22 vignettes, 35 minutes) illustrates ways of playing and talking with children to promote language development (including feeling or emotion language) and problem-solving skills, help children deal with frustration, and make learning enjoyable through play. One video vignette, for example, shows a parent working on a peg board with her son:

"OK, that's a tough one. You're doing a good job. [Child struggles with the wrong square on the wrong peg.] How about this? Let's find two more pegs. See if it fits here, Darren. [He tries it, as suggested.] How can you make that one fit? Turn it around. Good job. Try it again, it will fit. Good for you, that was a hard one!" (Webster-Stratton, 1989, Play, Part 2: *Helping Children Learn*, p. 24)

2. *Using praise and rewards.* A second set of vignettes teaches parents effective ways of using praise and tangible rewards to enhance child growth and adjustment. As for praise (26 vignettes, 25 minutes), parents are taught to be discriminating and planful, identifying the specific child behaviors they want to see more of (e.g., sharing, complying with requests, doing chores, doing homework, being kind to someone), and praising those specific behaviors. For their homework assignment, parents pick out one such behavior in their child, increase their rate of praise for that behavior, and track changes in the frequency of the behavior. The therapist cautions against common pitfalls, such as saving praise for only perfect behavior, which may send an unfortunate message to the child. Parents are also taught how to give praise – that is, immediately after the desired behavior, with labeling so the child is clear what the praise is for, directly and with

enthusiasm (smile, eye contact, excitement in the voice), combined with pats and hugs, and in front of other people where possible.

On the subject of tangible rewards (15 vignettes, 15 minutes), parents are shown several ways to reinforce desirable behavior in their children. For example, one vignette shows how to use unexpected rewards.

The scene. Luke's mother enters the kitchen as he is putting away the dishes.

MOTHER: Luke, I really appreciate you helping me by putting away the dishes so nicely. Since you've been so helpful, what would you like to have for dessert tonight that's your favorite?
LUKE: (with enthusiasm) Apple pie!
MOTHER: OK.
(Webster-Stratton, 1989, Praise and Rewards Program, Part 2: Tangible Rewards, p. 5)

After viewing the video, parents and therapist discuss the special value of the surprise reward (e.g., very salient for the child), and what is especially effective about the mother's approach (e.g., she combines the reward with praise, and she is very specific about what behavior is being rewarded). Models also illustrate how to set up and use star and chart systems (e.g., start simply, with a single behavior as the focus) and how to design procedures to fit the age and maturity level of the child (e.g., use star charts for younger children, point systems for older ones).

3. *Effective limit-setting.* The limit-setting component comes in three parts. The first is a set of rules for how to set limits (34 vignettes, 30 minutes). One rule is not to overdo; limit-setting commands should be used only for issues that really matter. Having too many rules and commands makes it difficult for children to keep track, and hard for parents to follow through consistently. Videotapes illustrate the problem by showing parents giving unnecessary commands during such activities as board games, coloring, and cookie baking – commands about child behavior that does not matter in the least, such as where to put the cookies on the cookie sheet. The tapes also illustrate the need to be clear and concise in giving commands to children, and to avoid commands that are not appropriate for the maturity level of the child. Consider this example of a mother's comments in a vignette showing milk being spilled by her preschooler:

"Oh, Denise, you're spilling your milk. Oh, my! Well, here, why don't you wipe that up .... Use the towel. [Denise tries, but some milk spills on the floor.] Denise, be careful – you're going to spill that milk. Look what's happening here, Denise. You better watch out!" (Webster-Stratton, 1989, Effective Limit Setting, Part 1: How to Set Limits, p. 13)

Denise tries to comply, but her mother's correcting and criticizing comments lack the specificity Denise needs, and the task itself may simply be beyond a preschooler's capacity in the first place.

Other vignettes focus on the need to give the child alternatives to prohibited actions, rather than just saying "No," and on the need to be aware of which child behaviors are being rewarded by attention. In one scene, for instance, a mother is reading, while her son plays with rubber puppets. Suddenly he bites the mother on the arm with the coyote puppet; here is what happens next:

Mother says, "No, I don't want the coyote to eat me, let the coyote eat some other animals. [Mother turns back to her magazine and reads; the boy takes the puppets and starts biting puppet animals.] (Webster-Stratton, 1989, Effective Limit Setting, Part 1: How to Set Limits, p. 23)

In this vignette, mother gets credit for clarity in limit-setting, and for suggesting a behavioral alternative rather than simply saying "No;" but she rewarded the prohibited behavior with attention, and she ignored her son when he obeyed her. Thus, the vignette shows both pros and cons, which become grist for the mill of parents and therapist in their postvideo discussion.

Parents are also cautioned about the tone of their limit-setting. Commands that include a barb can be counterproductive. "Jake, will you sit still for once in your life," carries a critical implication about Jake's usual behavior. This may make Jake feel incompetent, defensive, or angry, and it may thus make him less likely to obey.

Another set of video clips illustrates ways to help children accept limits (19 vignettes, 15 minutes). One approach is to follow a prohibition with distraction, as in, "OK, turn off the TV ... and let's see what other toys there are here." Other vignettes illustrate ways to avoid arguments about rules and commands; examples include involving the child in joint problem solving (where to park the bike when we put it away) and simply ignoring a child's inappropriate or combative responses.

A third set of vignettes shows ways to deal with noncompliance (9 vignettes, 13 minutes). For example, when Mom asks Max to hang up his coat, and he ignores her, she waits five seconds and then says, "OK, Max, you didn't do what I asked, so you have to go to time-out now." If Max says, "No, I'm hanging it up now," Mom lets him hang it up, but then says, "That's six minutes for arguing."

4. *Handling misbehavior.* The fourth component, handling misbehavior, is also presented in three sets of vignettes. The first set (14 vignettes, 17 minutes) involves avoiding and ignoring misbehavior, and using differential attention. Here is an example of ignoring:

THE SCENE: Dad is making dinner when his 10-year-old son enters.

LUKE: Dad, can I go over to Jimmy's house?

FATHER: Not now, Luke. It's almost time for dinner.

LUKE: But I'm not hungry. Why can't I play with Jimmy? (The father does not respond. Then Luke begins to hang on his father's arm and plead.) Please, please.

FATHER: (continues to ignore Luke's pleading and begging until Luke walks away unhappily) Want to help me decide what to have for dinner?

LUKE: Yeah.

FATHER: How about Swedish pancakes? Mom will love that. (Luke eagerly becomes involved in helping his father plan dinner.)

(Webster-Stratton, 1989, Handling Misbehavior, Part 1: Avoiding and Ignoring Misbehavior, p. 12)

A second series of video clips on handling misbehavior focuses on time-out and other penalties (31 vignettes, 35 minutes). In one clip, 12-year-old Derek refuses to get with the program, but his father clearly knows what to do:

THE SCENE: Derek stubbornly refuses to go to Time Out.

FATHER: Derek, go to Time Out.

DEREK: (angrily) You and your dumb old Time Outs. I'm not going!

FATHER: (calmly) That's six minutes.

DEREK: (sarcastically) Oh . . . where did *you* learn how to count?

FATHER: (calmly) That's seven minutes.

DEREK: (continues to protest) I don't wanna go. I don't have to!

FATHER: Eight minutes. (The father picks up the newspaper and begins to read it. A few minutes later he looks at his watch.) That's 10 minutes now, Derek. If you don't go to Time Out right now, you're going to lose your TV privileges tomorrow, and that means you're not going to be able to watch the big game.

DEREK: (protests) That's not fair.

FATHER: (calmly) Forget the game tomorrow. You've just lost your TV privileges.

DEREK: (starts to go to Time Out) But I was just going to go.

(Webster-Stratton, 1989, Handling Misbehavior, Part 2: Time Out and Other Penalties, pp. 19–20)

Here, father does all the right things, using time-out and backing it up with loss of privileges for arguing. He stays remarkably calm and matter-of-fact throughout the interaction, even when Derek insults him ("Where did you learn how to count?"). The father's calm demeanor deprives Derek of the reinforcement of emotional attention, prevents escalation of Derek's noncompliance into an argument, and adds quiet power to Dad's parental authority.

The final set of video illustrations in this last section of the BASIC program involves handling misbehavior by preventing it in the first place (7 vignettes, 11 minutes). In one scene, an eight-year-old girl runs into the kitchen to tell her mother about her friend Colleen, who is teasing and calling her names. Mom asks, "What do you think you can do about it?" Her daughter mentions hitting Colleen. Mom asks, ". . . will that make things better or worse?" Worse, her daughter admits, because Colleen and her parents will get mad. Then the two discuss tattling on Colleen to her parents, and the daughter agrees that this would not work so well, either. Mom presses on, "So what else could you do? What do you think would be best for you?" Her daughter replies, "Ignore her and play with someone else." Mom says, enthusiastically, "Good idea! Let me know how that all works out." (Webster-Stratton, 1989, Handling Misbehavior, Part 3: Preventive Approaches, pp. 11–13).

The vignettes, and discussions of each, are complemented by parent handouts, and by practice assignments in which parents try the procedures at home, and track the results. Parent groups discuss these take-home assignments and troubleshoot any problems encountered at home. This helps parents fine-tune their learning, and it promotes a climate of group support that is so important to the Incredible Years philosophy. Of course, the process also helps therapists track whether parents have caught the concepts and mastered the skills.

Other Incredible Years Video Programs Developed by the Webster-Stratton Group. The BASIC parent program addresses core parenting skills that are thought to have a major impact on child outcomes, and particularly on whether children develop serious and enduring conduct problems. Additional Incredible Years programs have been developed to attend to other risk factors associated with child problems. For example, the ADVANCE program for parents focuses on such skills as personal self-control (e.g., how parents can control their anger and reduce their depressive, angry, or blaming self-talk), communication skills (e.g., constructive approaches to dealing with spousal conflict), problem-solving skills (esp. for interpersonal problems), and generating personal social support (e.g., how to ask others for support and help). Another series, called SCHOOL, focuses on the things parents can do to enhance their children's development of academic skills (e.g., how to provide homework structure and support, how to use teacher conferences to the best advantage). A Teacher Training Series is designed to help teachers enhance classroom management skills, promote students' social competence, reduce peer aggression, and build parent-teacher partnerships. Finally, the Incredible Years Child Training Series, including the Dina Dinosaur Curriculum, uses videos and exercises to teach children social skills (e.g., friendship, teamwork, helping), problem solving (including anger management), and adaptive classroom behavior (quiet hand up, compliance, concentrating, thinking before acting, cooperating with peers and teachers). These additional programs have been supported in randomized trials (see Webster-Stratton & Hammond, 1997; Webster-Stratton et al., 2001a,b; Webster-Stratton & Reid, 2003), with an emphasis over the past decade on treatment that combines the BASIC and ADVANCE programs. However the most extensive research to date has been devoted to the BASIC parent program. It is to that research that we now turn.

The Incredible Years BASIC Parent Training Program: Outcome Studies Testing the Effects

Webster-Stratton's parent training program is one of the best-researched in the field, with at least seven randomized trials testing its impact. As with virtually all evidence-based treatment programs, Webster-Stratton's has evolved across successive trials; thus, early tests involved somewhat shorter versions of BASIC than later tests. Among the outcomes of interest in these studies have been parental attitudes, parent-child interactions, including parents' use of various disciplinary and behavior management methods, and of course, the frequency of child conduct problems. We turn now to the outcome evidence.

BASIC (short form) versus no treatment. In the initial trial (Webster-Stratton, 1981a,b, 1982a,b), which was focused more on prevention than treatment, 35 mothers of 3–5-year-olds (66% boys; ethnicity not reported, but the article implies exclusively or predominantly Caucasian) were recruited through flyers announcing a parent-training program. The mothers, who averaged 33 years of age and four years of college, were randomly assigned to receive either a four-session (two hours per session, one session per week) version of BASIC or to be waitlisted until two weeks after postintervention data had been collected. The tapes and discussions focused on effective play techniques, limit-setting, ways to handle misbehavior, and communication and feelings.

After the intervention group had finished the program, several outcome measures showed them faring better than the control group. Behavioral observations (30 minutes videotaped in a playroom) indicated that BASIC mothers showed more positive affect and less dominating and nonaccepting behavior toward their children than did parents in the untreated group. Mothers in the intervention group also reported fewer and less intense behavior problems in their children. Children of the BASIC mothers showed correspondingly less negative affect, less submissive behavior, and more positive affect than did children of control group mothers. BASIC and control group mothers showed fewer differences in parental attitudes, although the BASIC group did show a trend toward greater confidence; and on a consumer satisfaction survey, all of the mothers who had received BASIC reported that they were "very positive" about the program and perceived positive changes in themselves and their children. Notably, when the control group mothers were later given the BASIC program, most of the positive changes seen in the original intervention group were replicated; and a follow-up assessment showed that most of the behavioral changes noted for mothers and children in coding of their interactions at posttreatment were either maintained or improved one year later.

BASIC group versus individual one-on-one (nonvideo) therapy. In a second trial, Webster-Stratton (1984) compared the BASIC group approach to a non-video individual treatment approach, with parents of 35 3–8-year-olds (71% boys; 43% having a history of reported abuse; ethnicity not reported) who showed serious oppositional behavior in such forms as chronic defiance, aggression, and tantrums. After recruitment and screening, parents were randomly assigned to (1) a nine-week session (17 hours) version of BASIC, carried out with groups of 8–19 parents; (2) a nine-week session (16 hours) program of individual therapy involving parent, child, and therapist; or (3) a waiting list. The individual therapy program was designed to resemble BASIC in a number of ways. The first four weeks of each were devoted to training in interaction skills, a la Hanf and colleagues (Hanf, 1970; Hanf & Kling, 1973; see Chapter 10), and the last five weeks focused on teaching parents specific techniques for behavior management.

However, the manner of training differed markedly across the two groups. Unlike BASIC, with its combination of videos and group discussion, the individual treatment placed the therapist in sessions with each parent and target child alone. During these sessions, the therapist modeled appropriate parenting skills, then the parent role-played these skills with the child while the therapist, stationed behind a one-way mirror, provided direct supportive and corrective feedback to the parent via a bug-in-the-ear device. A particular advantage of the individual therapy approach was that, in addition to teaching the general skills covered in BASIC, therapists were also able to focus directly on each target child's specific behavior problems and coach each parent via the bug in appropriate responses.

This individual treatment may seem an unusually strong comparison condition to pit against BASIC. Indeed it was! In fact, while the BASIC and individual therapy groups outscored the waitlist group on multiple parent-report and home observation measures of parent and child behavior at posttreatment, none of these measures showed a significant difference between the BASIC and individual therapy group, either at the end of treatment or at a one-year followup.

Does this null finding represent a failure of the BASIC program? No. Remember that BASIC was superior to a waitlist control condition on multiple measures of child and parent behavior; it clearly worked better than no treatment. Remember, also, that individual treatment is much more expensive to deliver than group treatment. Total therapist time was 251 hours for the entire individual therapy group, but only 48 hours for the BASIC video group. Thus, at one-third the cost in therapist time, BASIC produced benefits essentially equivalent to individual therapy. From a cost-effectiveness perspective, this study offers substantial support for the BASIC program.

One other notable feature of this study (Webster-Stratton, 1984) is that it employed a sample that was different from, and arguably more at-risk than, the sample used in the first trial. Parents in that initial trial (Webster-Stratton, 1981a,b, 1982a,b) were college-educated, middle and upper socioeconomic status, mostly married, highly motivated to seek out parent training (75% had done so previously), and nonclinical in the sense that they were recruited through flyers rather than referred to the clinic; and their children evidently did not have very severe behavior problems. Parents in this second clinical trial were generally low in socioeconomic status and educational level and predominantly single parents; they showed a high prevalence of child abuse, and their children's problem levels were above the 95th percentile on national norms. The fact that the BASIC program produced markedly better outcomes than waitlist, on multiple measures, with such a sample, is encouraging evidence that the program benefits can generalize to more at-risk parents and children.

BASIC versus video-only versus group discussion-only. The third clinical trial (Webster-Stratton et al., 1988; Webster-Stratton et al., 1989) was a dismantling study. It tested whether the full BASIC package of videos plus therapist-led group discussion is more efficacious than (1) merely viewing the videotapes, with no therapist and no group discussion, and (2) group discussion covering the BASIC topics and skills, but with no videos. The sample included parents of 114 3–8-year-olds (69% boys; ethnicity not reported), referred because of noncompliance, aggression, and oppositional behavior. Home observations prior to the study showed that the children averaged almost one noncompliant behavior per minute. The parents were a heterogeneous group in socioeconomic status and income level, and they reported high rates of alcoholism or drug use in the immediate (40%) and extended family (61%); 13% of the mothers reported some involvement with Child Protective Services, and 31% reported significant depression (scores above 10 on the Beck Depression Inventory). Some 57% had been referred to the project by professionals, with the remainder self-referred.

Parents were randomly assigned to either a waitlist condition or one of the three alternate treatment approaches. In the video-only treatment, parents came to the clinic weekly for 10–12 self-administered sessions (most lasting about one hour); a secretary set them up with a room and that week's set of videotapes, which parents viewed at their own pace, reviewing tapes if they wished. By the end, the video-only parents had seen the same videos as the BASIC group, but with no input from a therapist and no group discussion. Parents in the group discussion-only treatment came to the clinic weekly for 10–12 two-hour sessions. They met in groups of 10–15 parents, led by a therapist, who directed a group discussion of the same topics and skills featured in the BASIC video series, but without any videos.

Outcome assessment included parent-report measures of child problems, home observations of parent and child behavior conducted by trained observers, teacher reports on the children, and a consumer satisfaction questionnaire. Compared to parents in the waitlist condition, parents in all three treatments reported significantly less spanking by parents, fewer child problems, and more child prosocial behaviors; and home visit observations also showed better mother, father, and child behavior in treated than untreated families. Where there were differences among the three treatments, they generally favored the BASIC group that had received both videos and therapist-led group sessions; for example, the full BASIC program outperformed the single-component treatments in increasing mothers' and fathers' praise to their children, reducing mother's reports of parenting stress, and generating good session attendance, low dropout rates, and consumer satisfaction with treatment.

However, one of the most striking findings was the absence of treatment group differences on most of the outcome measures! These findings held up rather consistently at a one-year follow-up assessment (see Webster-Stratton et al., 1989). Overall, the study results suggest that both components of the BASIC package – that is, the videotapes and the therapist-led group discussions – can be efficacious when used alone, if they cover the same issues and skills addressed in the BASIC program. The full BASIC package, with videos plus group discussion, was somewhat more beneficial than the separate components alone, on a few measures but not on most.

Testing individually administered BASIC videos, with and without therapist consultation. In the dismantling study we just discussed, the least expensive of the three alternative treatment methods was clearly the video-only approach in which parents viewed the videos alone. This approach required only a bit of secretarial time to hand parents the videos and situate them in a viewing room. Across all the outcome measures employed, this simple approach fell short of the full BASIC package (i.e., videos plus therapist-led parent discussion groups) on only a handful of measures. This finding led Webster-Stratton (1990) to explore the possibility of enhancing the impact of this highly cost-effective video-only approach. Her strategy: pairing solo video watching by parents with modest amounts of therapist consultation. In Webster-Stratton (1990), parents who viewed the tapes alone were told they could call the therapist any time they liked over the 10 weeks of video viewing, and they were scheduled for two one-hour individual sessions with the therapist, one midway through the program (after the play, praise, and tangible reward parts) and one at the end (after the limit-setting and discipline parts).

The sample consisted of families of 43 3–8-year-olds (79% boys; ethnicity not reported), all referred for misconduct, in this case misconduct persisting more than six months. Some 26% of the mothers reported experiencing spousal abuse, 42% reported substance abuse in the immediate family, and 14% had had prior involvement with Child Protective Services because of child abuse reports. The participating parents (all 43 mothers and 26 fathers) were randomly assigned to either (1) a video-only condition like that of the Webster-Stratton et al. (1988, 1989) dismantling study described earlier, (2) the video + therapist condition described in the previous paragraph, or (3) a waitlist control condition.

At posttreatment, compared to the waitlist group, mothers in the two treatment groups reported significantly fewer child behavior problems, less use of spanking, and lower parenting stress levels; and home observation data showed that treated mothers showed more positive affect with their children. Comparison of the two treatments showed only two significant differences in outcomes – that is, families in the video plus therapist condition, compared to those in the video-only condition, showed fewer no-opportunity maternal commands (i.e., commands to which the child is given no chance to respond) and less child deviance in home observations. Other measures, even consumer satisfaction, showed no significant difference between the two treatment approaches. So, like the dismantling study discussed earlier, this study found beneficial effects of merely having parents view the tapes alone, plus some modest incremental benefits of adding a small amount of therapist consultation.

Testing BASIC + ADVANCE. In a later study, Webster-Stratton (1994) tested whether adding the ADVANCE program, discussed earlier, might enhance the impact of the BASIC program, by addressing the parents' ways of handling stress. Recall that the ADVANCE program teaches parents to cope with interpersonal stress via improved communication, self-control, and problem-solving skills. The potential value of such adjunctive training was suggested by Webster-Stratton's analysis of her own data from 218 families, showing that the most potent predictors of child deviance at long-term followup were marital distress and lack of a supportive partner. This 1994 study was designed to test whether addressing such stressors through the ADVANCE program would strengthen the impact of the BASIC program.

To structure this test, a sample of 78 3–8-year-olds (74% boys; ethnicity not reported) was assembled; the children in this sample had not only been misbehaving for six months, but all met criteria for a DSM-IIIR diagnosis of oppositional defiant disorder or conduct disorder. The full sample received the standard BASIC program, with the full set of videos and therapist-led discussions. After completing BASIC, half the parents were randomly assigned to the ADVANCE program. When ADVANCE was completed, outcomes were assessed in both the BASIC-only and the BASIC + ADVANCE groups.

Did ADVANCE make a difference? Yes, on some key measures. Families in the combined program showed significant benefits in the areas of parental problem-solving, communication, and collaboration skills, in consumer satisfaction (and treatment attendance), and in the number of prosocial solutions their children proposed on a problem-solving test. However, adding ADVANCE did not enhance parents' self-reports of marital satisfaction, anger, or stress levels, nor did it reduce either parent reports or observer reports of child deviant behavior at home. So, the various outcome measures presented a mixed picture. And those findings that did show beneficial effects of adding ADVANCE may be difficult to interpret, because the add-on study design meant that the combined treatment group received about twice as much treatment time as the BASIC-only group. However, the outcomes that did show benefits of adding ADVANCE were regarded as particularly important by the Webster-Stratton group, and their subsequent research has heavily emphasized combining the two programs.

BASIC versus eclectic mental health center treatment. In a particularly timely study, given current interest in taking evidence-based treatments into practice settings (see Weisz, in press), Taylor et al. (1998) compared the standard BASIC program with the kind of treatment that would otherwise be available in a community clinic. In doing this, they also provided a test of the usability and impact of the video approach in representative clinic practice. Wasn't this done in the clinical trials just reviewed? Perhaps not very fully, at least according to the list of illustrative clinic therapy characteristics discussed by Weisz et al. (1992, 1993, 1995a). As Taylor et al. (1998) note, in those earlier trials, "...the program was offered in a university laboratory, rather than a clinic," "...treatment was delivered to a homogeneous group," "....The therapy was offered by the program developer or by assistants under her direct supervision," and all of them "had small therapy caseloads of [similar] clients" (p. 223). This is certainly not a criticism of those prior studies, because their intent was not to provide a test in a fully representative clinical practice setting. Nonetheless, it is appropriate for clinical practitioners to ask whether the BASIC procedure (and other evidence-based treatments as well) can produce beneficial effects in a representative service-oriented community clinic, with clinic staff therapists leading the groups, and with clientele consisting of families referred to the community clinic. It was this question, in part, to which the Taylor et al. study was directed.

In addition, the study was designed to answer a comparative question: How would the BASIC program fare relative to the usual treatment provided in this community clinic? This question goes to the heart of what many want to know about empirically tested treatments – that is, whether such treatments will lead to better outcomes than those already achieved via current treatment procedures, or usual care. The Taylor et al. study tackled this question as well.

As in the previous clinical trials, the Taylor et al. sample was limited to parents of 3–8-year-olds, parents who had contacted a community clinic regarding child conduct problems or difficulties in parenting. There were 108 children (74% boys; ethnicity not reported), all living in Canada, where the mental health center was located. Families deemed appropriate for waitlist placement were randomly assigned either to a waitlist, to BASIC (with therapist group leaders who had been thoroughly trained, in part by Dr. Webster-Stratton), or to the usual treatment of the clinic, which was an eclectic mixture of approaches including "ecological, solution-focused, cognitive-behavioral, family systems, and popular press parenting approaches" (Taylor et al., 1998, p. 229).

Results showed that both BASIC and usual care generated reports of significantly fewer child problems than the waitlist condition on multiple parent-report measures, although a teacher-report measure and some parent measures did not show such differences. When BASIC and usual care were compared, the two parent-report measures of child problem behavior (of six) that showed a significant difference favored the BASIC program. The BASIC program also generated higher consumer satisfaction ratings.

Interpretation of the findings is complicated somewhat by the fact that the participants were partially recruited through physicians and school principals (i.e., not all spontaneous call-ins), the fact that BASIC parents received a larger average number of therapy contact hours than the usual care parents, and the absence of direct observations of parent or child behavior. Still, the overall pattern of findings is certainly consistent with two important conclusions: (1) the BASIC program does appear to have been useable and effective in a community clinic setting, and (2) BASIC generated better outcomes and higher levels of consumer satisfaction than the usual care provided in that setting, on at least some measures, and none of the measures showed usual care to be superior to BASIC.

British clinic test of BASIC effects. In another application of the treatment program in a clinical practice context, Scott et al. (2001) tested BASIC with parents of children referred to any of four local mental health service programs in England for treatment of antisocial behavior. The children, ages 3–8 and 75% boys (ethnicity not reported) were above the 97th percentile on interview-assessed conduct problems, compared to population norms. At the beginning of the study, children were assigned in blocks (not randomly but using an unbiased assignment strategy) to either a waitlist condition or the BASIC program; videos were dubbed into English accents. Treatment was delivered by therapists of multiple disciplines who held regular jobs in the service settings, and who had received training in the program over a period of three months. After the program, parents in the treatment condition had shown marked improvements in parenting behavior; with the ratio of praise to ineffective commands tripling from pre- to post-treatment. By contrast, parents in the waitlist group showed change in the opposite direction. The children of treated parents also showed marked reductions in conduct problems, falling to within the normal range on the interview assessment, whereas children in the waitlist group showed no improvement.

Summary of the clinical trials evidence. We have reviewed seven outcome studies testing the BASIC program. Together, the studies offer rather consistent evidence of beneficial effects. The BASIC program is associated with improved parent-child interactions, reduced parental reliance on critical and violent forms of discipline, and reduced child conduct problems. The full program, including therapist-led parent discussion groups, has the strongest support, but there is evidence of benefit when parents merely view the videos alone, and when therapist-led discussion groups cover the topics of the BASIC program without any videos involved. When parents view the videos alone, therapist consultation may help a bit; and when BASIC is combined with the ADVANCE program described earlier, there appear to be increments in benefit associated with helping parents address stressors in their lives. Recent evidence from Taylor et al. (1998) and Scott et al. (2001) suggests that the BASIC program can work well when it is taken out of the university and used in community clinic settings by staff therapists.

Research on Webster-Stratton programs other than BASIC. Webster-Stratton and her colleagues have also carried out studies of her programs that complement the BASIC parent training program. Findings on the benefits of multiple-parent programs (BASIC + ADVANCE) have led the Webster-Stratton team to make the combination of BASIC + ADVANCE + SCHOOL (22–24 sessions) their core treatment program for parents of children referred for conduct problems. Studies have also tested the programs for children (see Webster-Stratton & Hammond, 1997; Webster-Stratton et al., 2001) and teachers (see Webster-Stratton & Hammond, 2001), and evidence (reviewed by Webster-Stratton & Reid, 2003) suggests that the child training and teacher training programs may add significantly to the impact of parent training. A case study (Reid & Webster-Stratton, 2001) illustrates ways to combine components of the various programs, a strategy that may be particularly important for children whose problems show up in multiple settings, not just at home.

What about Sal? Applying the Incredible Years BASIC Parent Training Program

Thinking about Webster-Stratton's video modeling approach in light of the case of Sal highlights several issues. First, Sal's age and the severity of his conduct problems place him beyond the usual range of the BASIC program, which is designed for parents of children in elementary school or younger, and for less entrenched and less dangerous behavior than Sal's. The level of difficulty and the intransigence of Sal's current style remind us of the literature on developmental pathways, noted at the beginning of this chapter. Sal's case is consistent with research suggesting that basic building blocks of serious conduct disorder are often in place by early elementary school (see Campbell & Ewing, 1990; Loeber, 1991), and that "early starters" are particularly at risk for serious long-term conduct problems (see e.g., Loeber, 1991; Patterson et al., 1989). Sal has had a poor relationship with his mother since his preschool years, and she is now almost completely ineffective in managing his behavior. Might Sal's mother be more effective with him now if she had had early training via the BASIC program? This seems a real possibility. We will develop the idea here, describing how the BASIC program might have been applied when Sal was a first grader and already showing disobedient and disruptive behavior.

Sal's mother seeks out a therapist when Sal is six, after the first progress report and parent-teacher conference of his first grade year. Learning from Sal's teacher that he is disobedient and disruptive in class, and that he is aggressive toward peers, scares her. The behavior in school sounds a lot like what she has seen at home, and this tells her that Sal's problems are spreading, that they are more than just normal mother-child conflict. The therapist agrees that the problems are significant, and that the time is right for intervention. She invites Sal's mother to join a parent training group that is about to begin, and to bring her husband along as well.

The odds of getting her husband in are slim to none, Mom thinks, but the therapist is very persistent, even going to the extent of calling Dad at home to ask about his perspective on Sal, then calling again to invite him to the first session "just to see if you think it might help." The therapist knows that the BASIC program can be helpful even if only mothers do the program, but that effects show better long-term holding power if fathers (or grandparents, or others in the family who are close to the child) join in (Webster-Stratton, 1985). Together, the therapist and Sal's mother wear Dad down. He grudgingly agrees to come to the first meeting, saying he'd like to find a way "to make the kid less of a pain in the butt." To his surprise, he quickly learns to appreciate the therapist's respectful, collaborative approach. He has never liked having so-called experts tell him what to do, but this therapist doesn't do that. She seeks his opinions, listens closely when he speaks, and follows up with occasional phone calls. Although Dad warms up to the therapist's collaborative approach, he is still not consistent in attending the group meetings. The therapist is ready for this problem. For each session Dad misses, the therapist either schedules a make-up session or sends Mom home with videos covering the key skills, and the job of discussing each vignette with Dad.

In their first meeting with the parent group, Sal's parents get acquainted with nine other parents – four couples and one single mom, all with children ages 5–7. As the other parents describe the difficulties they are having with their children, Sal's mother breathes a sigh of relief. At least she is not the only parent who faces these difficulties, and who feels the need for expert help. After a get-acquainted discussion, the therapist tells the parents that she expects to have 14 weekly meetings, all lasting about two hours. She also explains that the meetings will not be like a class in school, with lots of lecturing and note-taking. Instead, most of each meeting will involve short videotapes of parents and children, followed by discussions. Sal's mom and the other parents like this idea; it sounds more interesting than what they had pictured.

Using Play to Teach Skills and Build a Relationship. The first set of skills the parents learn about are positive skills – ways to encourage their children to do good things. As a first step, the therapist has the parents focus on ways of using play activities to build child skills and self-esteem and strengthen the parent-child relationship. Sal's mother is impressed by the videos that show parents helping their children learn to solve problems that arise in play – from peg board pieces that don't fit to conflict with playmates. She realizes that much of Sal's misbehavior, including his explosive temper, grows out of frustration over problems he can't solve. She also learns, through the videos and discussion, that she can help Sal build problem-solving skills through a gentle, supportive style of play that models patience and encourages creativity and perseverance. The idea that this may also improve her relationship with Sal has a lot of appeal. She knows the relationship needs help.

At home, she tries to use the gentle, narrative style she has seen modeled in the parent meetings. First, because Sal is fascinated by cars, she buys a simple model kit – a plastic car that she and Sal can assemble together. As they work on it and encounter problems, she tries to maintain the patient, encouraging style she has seen modeled in the videos. Here is a sample of their interaction:

SAL: (frustrated) This wheel won't go here!

MOM: Gee, you're right. I thought it would fit, too. Is there a different place for it?

SAL: Well, maybe. But where?

MOM: Maybe it could go here, or here – which one do you think is right?

SAL: I think here. (tries it, and it does fit) Hey – it works!

MOM: Great job, Sal. You figured it out! (high fives)

Through interactions like this, Sal's mom models patient perseverance for her son, she encourages him to try different options when he encounters a problem, she offers guidance but avoids taking over the task, and she praises him when he perseveres and succeeds. In addition to helping Sal build skills, these shared play and problem-solving experiences are also strengthening the mother-son relationship in ways that may pay important dividends, especially as Sal matures and the problems he confronts grow more complex. The therapist has told parents they can think of this as a bank account, one they can build up through positive interactions, and then can withdraw from when problems arise and discipline is needed.

Sal's mom also uses what she learns in the parent group to help Sal deal with a second type of situation that often leads to problems – peer conflict. As an example, when Sal has 6-year-old Evan (the son of Mom's parent group buddy) over for a play date, a shouting match erupts.

SAL: (pushing Evan) Go home. I don't want to play with you.

EVAN: (crying) Me neither. I want to go home.

MOM: Hey guys – what's the problem?

(Both boys shout at once. Sal wants to play outside. Evan wants to play a video game. Neither boy will budge.)

MOM: Well, this sounds like a problem we can solve. If Evan wants a video game, and Sal wants to play outside, what could we do to be fair? (Both boys are silent.) Is there a way for both of you to get some of what you want?

EVAN: (after a long pause) We could do both things?

MOM: What do you think, Sal? How about that idea? Video game for a while, and then play outside for a while?

SAL: (reluctantly) OK.

MOM: Alright, guys – nice work! I think you two have solved the problem. You did such a good job, you get a reward – how about some ice cream while you do the video game?

SAL AND EVAN: (in unison) Yeaaaaah!

Here again, Sal's mom models a calm, problem-solving approach, and she provides the guidance two 6-year-olds need while avoiding the trap of completely taking over. In fact, she coaches the boys from the sideline throughout their play date, using other skills learned in the program. She describes their friendly behaviors such as waiting, taking turns, and helping each other; and she comments on how they are working as a team and on how much they seem to be enjoying being with each other. As in the video example, she praises and rewards the boys for successful problem solving. The praise and reward are crucial, as she has learned in another component of the parent program.

Effective Use of Praise and Reward: Catching Sal Being Good. The parent meetings that focus on praise and reward make a strong impression on Sal's mom. She realizes that her style of parenting has been mostly negative; she has criticized (and sometimes punished) Sal for his misbehavior, but she has been quite passive in response to his good behavior. She has been fairly consistent in criticizing Sal for breaking household rules, but when he has played quietly or done a chore without complaining, she has most often been silent (afraid to break the spell). This style of parenting, the therapist explains in one of the meetings, can lead to increased misbehavior; children learn that they gain little by behaving appropriately, and they gain attention by misbehaving. The way to increase good behavior is to make it rewarding. Prompted by the therapist, Sal's mom decides that a key part of her job description needs to be "catching Sal being good," and then praising and rewarding the good behavior.

The parent meetings make it clear that using praise and reward effectively involves much more than simply dispensing a lot of each. A critical part of the process is deciding what specific kinds of positive behaviors are to be targeted. As an experiment, the therapist asks all the parents to pick one child behavior they would like to see more of, and to increase their rate of praise for that specific behavior. Sal's mom chooses washing hands after using the toilet. She learns that to make her praise most effective, she needs to (1) give it within 5–10 seconds of the desired behavior; (2) label the praise, so Sal will know what he did that made Mom so pleased; (3) be direct and enthusiastic; (4) add pats and hugs; and (5) do the praising in front of others, if possible. She also learns not to reserve praise for only perfect performance, but to look for reasonable approximations, even if they have to be prompted a bit. Clearly, proper praising is more complicated than she ever realized. So, she studies her notes carefully after the parent meeting, and then she waits for the right moment. It comes before dinner the following evening, when the three of them are sitting down at the table. Sal jumps up to run to the bathroom. The toilet flushes, and the door opens immediately.

MOM: Sal, remember what we do after flushing the toilet? (she prompts Sal)

SAL: I did! (Mom looks away from Sal, says nothing) .... Oh yeah – I forgot. Just a minute. (returns to bathroom and washes hands; returns to table)

MOM: Good, Sal. Thank you for washing up (not waiting for perfection, but rewarding a reasonable, prompted washup; giving labeled praise, immediately after the desired behavior). Your dad and I like it when you wash up. (praising in front of a third party)

SAL: (smiles, looks down shyly)

MOM: My smart boy! (enthusiastic, and with direct eye contact; she reaches out and hugs him, magnifying the praise by adding physical affection)... and how nice and clean your hands smell (sniffs the soapy smell)!

SAL: (sniffs his hands, smiles) Yeah – smells good.

Mom briefly considers adding, "Next time, don't make me ask you to wash," but she remembers that the therapist cautioned parents not to mix praise with criticism, even implied criticism. One of the videotapes the parents watched showed how adding a statement such as "Next time, do it this way . . ." can undermine the positive effect of praise. So she decides not to add the "Next time" comment. Instead, she figures she can just watch for a time when Sal washes without a prompt, and then she can give enthusiastic, labeled praise for washing without being asked. Good job, Mom!

As the themes of praise and reward are developed further in the parent sessions, Mom expands her agenda to include more specific positive behaviors by Sal: brushing his teeth before school and before bedtime, putting his dirty clothes in the hamper, and – importantly – obeying parents. To help make these behaviors rewarding for Sal, the therapist suggests the use of a star chart, in addition to the usual procedures for praising good behavior. Each time Sal does one of the desired behaviors on Mom's list, she gives him a star to stick on the chart (labeled "Sal's Stars"). The consequences of good behavior are thus expanded. Whenever Sal has earned seven stars, he gets to choose a prize from a grab bag of small toys and stickers Mom has put together. Each time Sal shows one of the desired behaviors, she looks directly at him, gives him labeled and lively praise, hugs or pats him, and gives him a star to put on his chart. Each time he gets his seventh star, the praise escalates, and the grab bag ceremony is carried out.

With her growing skills in the use of praise and reward, Sal's mom sees a real difference, both in her behavior and in Sal's. She has become much more of a strategist, setting goals for Sal's behavior, and ensuring that he receives positive consequences when he attains those goals. Just as the therapist suggested, when Sal's consequences for good behavior grow more positive, so does the frequency of his good behavior. Not surprisingly, the overall tone of their interactions has grown much more positive and loving. Of course, the specifics of what Mom does will need to evolve over time. The same praising comment will lose some of its sparkle with repeated use, and the grab bag of goodies will be less thrilling with increasing familiarity, and as Sal matures. So, ways of praising Sal will need to change from time to time, and the menu of star rewards will need to be revamped, eventually including certain valued privileges (e.g., TV or video game time). Nonetheless, Sal and his mom both have made real gains, and they have established a relationship in which she has a significant positive impact on his behavior.

Setting Limits and Giving Commands. Although things are better than before, and Sal's mother feels more in control than she has in years, there are still times when she feels she has little leverage with Sal – times when he does what he wants regardless of what she tells him. She has an idea as to why this may be the case. In the parent discussions, and through the video illustrations, she comes to realize that her general lack of confidence spills over into the ways she gives Sal directives and commands. She often gives directives in vague ways that make it hard for Sal to be sure what she wants. As one simple example, she sees Sal and herself illustrated in this video of a son and his father:

> FATHER: Derek, your bike is still in the yard!
> DEREK: (irritated) So?
> FATHER: You know better than that.
> DEREK: (angrily) Better than what?

She has had very similar interactions with Sal, in which she complains to him about what he has done without saying specifically what she wants him to do (e.g., without saying, "Put your bike in the garage."), and in which Sal has grown angry at her, in just the way Derek does in the video. She realizes that she has also weakened her effectiveness with Sal by making two other command errors discussed in the parent group meetings: (1) *"Let's" commands* (e.g., "Let's put the video game away now."), which falsely imply that she is going to help; and (2) *Question commands* (e.g., "Want to put your video game away now?"), which imply that it's up to Sal to decide. She resolves to try to make her commands very clear and direct, to see if this changes Sal's responses. She quickly learns that simple, declarative commands, such as "Sal, put your video game away now," work noticeably better than her old, obfuscating instructions.

Several other tips on effective use of commands also prove helpful. Mom learns not to let her irritation show up in barbed commands, such as "Eat with your mouth closed – not open like a pig." She learns to offer alternative behaviors when forbidding some activity (e.g., telling Sal that he can't watch TV, but he can look at his comic books). She learns to help Sal anticipate good consequences of compliance by using When/Then commands (e.g., "When you put your toys away, then you can go outside."). She learns not to get drawn into the Why game, by letting Sal badger her into justifying every command. She also learns to use her newfound skills in praising and rewarding each time Sal complies with a command. In the past, she had viewed Sal's compliance (when it happened) as the end of the episode; she now realizes that each episode of command-comply should end with a positive consequence for Sal.

Reducing and Responding to Sal's Misbehavior. Even children whose parents are very skilled behaviorally sometimes misbehave. So, all parents need skills in how to respond to misbehavior. Sal's mother finds the skills she learns in the final part of the parent program to be especially useful in dealing with her son, who is widely recognized as a handful.

Strategic ignoring. One of the most useful skills she learns is a deceptively simple one: strategic ignoring, sometimes combined with distraction. Sal sometimes gets it into his head that he simply must have something, such as ice cream. When his mom refuses, he pleads, and the pleas escalate to shouts. In the past, she has responded by explaining her reasons, or bargaining for a compromise, or even crumpling under the pressure and giving in to Sal's demands – all of which helps to explain why his demanding style has gotten out of hand. With the benefit of the parent meetings and the very helpful videos, she adopts a new strategy for dealing with Sal's demands, as reflected in the following episode.

SAL: (after dinner) Hey, Mom, I want some ice cream for dessert.

MOM: (looking directly at Sal) No, Sal. You've had enough sweets today.

SAL: No I haven't. I'm hungry. Give me some ice cream!

MOM: (immediately turns away from Sal and walks to another area of the kitchen)

SAL: (follows Mom, and says with rising volume and pleading tone) I'm really hungry. I've got to have ice cream! (continues pleading, continues following her, grabs her arm and pulls her toward the refrigerator)

MOM: (continues to ignore Sal, busies herself in the kitchen, and then, when Sal has been quiet for a moment, says . . .) "Hey, want to make some popcorn and play checkers?"

SAL: Sure. I bet I'll win!

Here she ignores the unwanted behavior of a very persistent son, then shifts him to another track through the skillful use of distraction. Clearly, Sal's mom is learning some useful skills.

Time-out. Another important skill she hones in the training program is the use of time-out. She has tried time-out prior to the parent program, of course, but she discovers that she has not done it in the best possible way. One problem: she has always presented time-out as punishment, and always when Sal was upset and she was angry with him. The therapist explains to parents that time-out should actually be explained to the child, in a more positive way, and at a time when the child is behaving appropriately. When this happens, the parent should explain that time-out is a way of helping the child learn not to do certain things that are unacceptable; it is also a way to help the parent avoid getting angry and help the child calm down. The parent needs to be clear about what specific behaviors will lead to time-out, where the child will go during the time-out, and how long the time-out will last. Sal's mom decides that (1) hitting and (2) refusing to obey after three requests will both lead to time-out, so she explains this to Sal. She tells him that he will need to go to the time-out chair she will place in the hallway, and that his time-outs will last six minutes (one minute for each year of age, the therapist suggests).

In the parent discussion during this phase of the training program, parents come up with lots of problems they have encountered in using time-outs, and some of these sound familiar to Sal's mom. One is that the child may simply refuse to go to time-out, or may insist on arguing about it. If this happens, the therapist suggests first ignoring the child's protests to see if they subside; if ignoring does not stop the behavior, then the parent should tell the child that one more minute has been added to the time-out. If the refusal or protests continue, parents should add additional minutes, one at a time, until nine minutes has been reached. At that point, parents should tell the child that further refusal will lead to a loss of some valued privilege, such as TV time, or an upcoming play date with a friend.

Sal's mother listens attentively, makes notes on her parent handout, but remains skeptical. However, when Sal comes home from school the next day, she sits down with him before there has been time for any misbehavior. While both are calm and relaxed, she explains the rationale and procedures for time-out. To her surprise, Sal listens attentively. He seems to be interested in hearing about time-out from this new perspective, one that sounds more like solving a problem than it does like punishment. It is three more days before she actually has to use time-out. When she does, she soon discovers that Sal hasn't given up testing limits. The occasion is Sal's refusal to take his plate to the sink after dinner. He refuses twice, his mother reminds him of the time-out rule, but he then refuses a third time. Then the following exchange ensues:

> MOM: OK, Sal, remember what I said about time-out. If you disobey
> me three times, you have to go to time-out. Go to the time-out chair
> now. (pointing to it) You have to stay there six minutes.
> SAL: No! It's not fair, and I'm not going!
> MOM: OK, I'm adding another minute. You now have to stay for
> seven minutes. (Sal stays put.) OK, now it's eight minutes. (Sal puts
> on his angry face, stands fast.) OK, now nine minutes. (Still no
> movement by Sal.) Sal, you now have to stay there for 10 minutes.
> SAL: No way!
> MOM: Sal, if you don't go now for 10 minutes, there's no TV for you
> tonight. Understand? (Sal doesn't budge) . . . . Well, Sal, you've lost
> your TV for tonight.
> SAL: (hangs his head, begins walking to the time-out chair.) OK, but
> it's not fair. (sits down)
> MOM: (ignores his comment and follows through with loss of TV for
> the evening.)

This exchange makes a believer out of Sal's mom. She is amazed to see that the procedures taught in the parent group actually work with Sal, albeit after considerable resistance on his part. Certainly, she is not home free, and there is a good deal more to be learned and done. She needs to work with Sal on developing good problem-solving skills, to prevent his erupting in anger when things don't go his way. She also needs to assess whether Sal's improvement at home is generalizing to his behavior at school. If not, she will need to work out a collaborative plan with Sal's teacher. However, the parent group discussions, the illustrative videos, and the therapist's insights have helped Sal's mother sharpen her parenting skills in some very important ways, and Sal's behavior is already showing encouraging changes.

Of course, all this assumes that the parenting skills taught in the BASIC program, if learned when Sal was a preschooler, might have made a big difference in his behavior as a 13-year-old. We cannot be sure in any specific case, but the evidence reviewed earlier is consistent with this idea. Indeed, Sal's behavior at age 13 might be seen as an illustration of why many in the field favor a "stop it before it multiplies" approach to conduct problems in early development.

Troubleshooting: Common Treatment Problems and Recommended Solutions

The Webster-Stratton program has an impressive track record with families like Sal's, but experts in the program acknowledge that problems can arise, some involving parents' behavior in the group meetings, and some involving the interplay between parents and therapists.

- *Parents who push the therapist's buttons.* Sometimes parents in the groups manage to say and do things that rub their therapist the wrong way. Parents may show a lack of interest in treatment ("I'm only here because I was forced to come."), express skepticism toward the program ("What makes you think that would work with my child?") or the therapist ("You don't understand what it's like because you are not a refugee like I am."), or claim the intervention is nothing new ("I'm already doing all these things . . ." sometimes followed by ". . . and they don't work."). An important part of the therapist's job is to forge a positive connection with each group member – even the more difficult ones – perhaps finding grains of truth in what they say and focusing on those grains, and ideally finding some attributes or accomplishments for which genuine praise can be offered. Where this proves especially difficult for a particular therapist, a cotherapist may do the heavy lifting of relationship building with particular parents.
- *Group process issues.* Because the intervention format is a series of group meetings, process issues familiar to many group therapists are likely to surface. These may include parents who dominate the discussions or keep them focused on their own issues, parents who say things in ways that make the other group members dislike them, and even marital discord that gets expressed in the group context. To address such process issues, therapists need to be confident enough in their group management skills to set clear ground rules and enforce them consistently. Arranging for speaking turns with time limits may make sense when one or two group members are monopolizing air time. A separate discussion with the angry couple may be needed to emphasize that the group needs to focus on parent-child interaction issues, and that couple conflicts need to be dealt with outside the group. The therapist's challenge is to be nice, but not so nice that group management needs are ignored.
- *Therapist discomfort with role-playing and other group leader expectations.* Therapists are expected to make extensive use of role-playing in the parent group meetings, but some are not so comfortable in role-plays. Therapists are expected to model core elements of good parenting that they are helping parents learn – differential attention, and enthusiastic praise, for example – but not all therapists are comfortable doing such things in their interactions with adults. For such therapist difficulties supervision and consultation can be helpful, with session videotapes used to examine trouble spots and the supervisor and therapist brainstorming various solutions together. Perhaps role-plays can be designed in ways that do not make the therapist uneasy, and perhaps the therapist

can find ways to be encouraging and support parents' successes without dispensing praise that seems awkward, infantilizing, or insincere. In general, supervision is intended to bridge the divide between therapist characteristics and capacities, on the one hand, and expectations that go with the therapist's role, on the other.

The Incredible Years BASIC Parent Training Program: Scientific Issues

The work of Webster-Stratton and colleagues builds on the power of modeling in ways that go well beyond most parent training treatments for conduct problems. It is an intriguing application of social learning theory to the challenge of inducing observational learning in parents. Of course, the therapists who work with parent groups also apply operant principles, especially social reinforcement, to enhance learning of new behaviors. The process is intended to help parents, in turn, make effective use of operant principles with their own children to increase prosocial behavior and reduce disobedient, disruptive, and otherwise inappropriate behavior. Do the procedures work? Evidence on the core program, BASIC, is quite positive thus far, and findings on other training programs in the Incredible Years series are also encouraging.

The evidence has rather consistently shown that BASIC produces positive changes in parent behavior and reductions in child conduct problems, both as reported by parents, and (to a somewhat lesser extent) as recorded by trained observers during home visits. This has been especially true in comparisons of BASIC to waitlist control groups but also true to some degree in more challenging treatment versus treatment comparisons. Studies have shown evidence of clinical significance, in that families receiving BASIC, relative to those not receiving BASIC, (1) showed parent reports of more normal range functioning and less clinical range problem scores by children on standardized measures, and (2) were less likely to request additional therapy for child behavior problems at follow-up assessments. Child behavior ratings tended to hold up over time, as assessed at follow-up, but study designs that assign waitlist groups to treatment after the posttreatment assessment do lose the opportunity for clear-cut treatment versus control comparisons at followup.

The overall research portfolio shows an admirable blend of designs and methods, and an interesting variety of control and comparison groups. Control groups have ranged from no-treatment waitlist to individual therapy to usual care in the clinic, the latter a particularly valuable point of comparison. One study (Webster-Stratton, 1984) showed no difference on any outcome measures between BASIC and individual therapy (covering the BASIC topics), but even that finding was impressive in that the cost-effective BASIC program required less than a third of the total therapist time required for individual therapy.

Webster-Stratton and colleagues have endeavored to ensure that the treatment works with a range of client families, from middle-class college grads to low-income, low-education parents. The study array has included add-on designs testing proposed methods of enhancing treatment effects (e.g., by adding the ADVANCE program to BASIC), and a dismantling design in which comparison groups received separate components (i.e., video only, and therapist-led discussions only). The results of the dismantling study (Webster-Stratton et al., 1988, 1989) and its sequel (Webster-Stratton, 1990) raise the intriguing question of whether the full BASIC package, with videos and therapist-led parent group discussions, is actually necessary to generate respectable treatment benefits. While therapist contact added some benefit, on at least some measures, the effects obtained by simply having parents come in and view the tapes were striking, and a bit disquieting from the perspective of one who both does therapy and trains therapists! The findings of these two studies certainly deserve followup in future research; we need to discern the optimal role for therapists in video-guided parent training.

Tests of the BASIC program have encompassed a broad range of parent and child characteristics along such dimensions as socioeconomic status, educational level, presence versus absence of child maltreatment, and severity of child problems. This should make possible a systematic search for predictors of treatment impact, and Webster-Stratton (e.g., 1992a) and colleagues have begun that search, focusing on both posttreatment and follow-up outcomes. In some of the research, children showing the poorest outcomes tended to come from families characterized by marital distress, single-parent status, parental depression, lower socioeconomic status, and higher levels of life stress. Interpreting such findings is complicated by the fact that such factors may also predict poor outcome in untreated families. In the future, applying methods that have been developed specifically for zeroing in on moderators (see e.g., Baron & Kenney, 1986) may add importantly to the knowledge base, helping us discern the boundary conditions within which the intervention can be expected to work well.

Another useful goal for future research is identification of outcome mediators. The suggestion by Webster-Stratton (1994) that "...causal modeling work is needed to explore the direct and indirect links between marital processes, parent's personal adjustment, parenting skills, and child adjustment" (p. 392) suggests that understanding the change processes that account for BASIC treatment effects may be a part of her group's agenda. If so, the information gain could be quite substantial.

Another useful direction for research will be the study of generalization of treatment effects to child behavior in settings outside home, where the contingencies parents have learned to use are not in place. Generalization of benefits to new settings has been a problem for most behavioral child and adolescent treatments. Tests of the BASIC program thus far have made only rather gingerly attempts to assess child behavior in preschool and school settings, and with somewhat mixed results. However, the Webster-Stratton group appears to be taking a different tack than most investigative teams have. Their approach to generalization, which may be very wise, has been to complement parent training with training of teachers and children, as discussed earlier. The idea seems to be that if we want behavioral treatment effects to be evident in out-of-home settings, we need to extend the training to individuals in those settings. Early evidence (e.g., Webster-Stratton & Reid, 1999) suggests that this view may be right on target.

The Incredible Years BASIC Parent Training Program: Clinical Practice Issues

From a clinical practice perspective, major advantages of the Webster-Stratton approach include its readiness for clinical use, its natural appeal to parents, and its very low dropout rate. Because the core content of the treatment program is inherent in the sequence of videos, the program is, to a certain extent, self-teaching; this means that, even though therapist training is certainly needed for optimum use of the BASIC program, the time required to reach proficiency is apt to be less than with most manualized treatments. Training programs are increasingly available for therapists (see next section). The video approach clearly has an inherent appeal to a generation of parents reared on television, and the combination of videos and therapist-guided group discussion has been rated very high on consumer satisfaction measures used by Webster-Stratton and colleagues.

A common practitioner concern is that the samples used in clinical trials do not look like the cases they themselves treat in practice, raising questions about the relevance of the treatment to their usual cases. Such concerns may not be so worrisome in the case of the BASIC program, given the broad array of families seen in the trials to date. Samples have ranged from predominantly middle- and upper-socioeconomic status, college-educated parents whose children showed relatively modest problems (e.g., Webster-Stratton, 1981a,b) to high-risk families with low-socioeconomic status, low-education single parents, high rates of substance use and child abuse, and very serious child conduct problems (e.g., Webster-Stratton, 1984; Webster-Stratton et al., 1988, 1989). Two studies (Scott et al., 2001; Taylor et al., 1998) have included families referred to local community mental health services. The evidence base supporting the BASIC program certainly seems to encompass many of the kinds of families likely to be seen in everyday clinical practice.

Therapist time to administer the full BASIC program appears quite manageable, even in an era of cost cutting. Although the full program can involve up to 14 two-hour sessions, the sessions are for relatively large groups of parents, which creates considerable efficiency in average therapist hours per case. There may be a certain comfort in findings indicating that, in the extreme case, simply having parents view the videotapes alone (with no therapist guidance and no parent group discussions) can be quite helpful (Webster-Stratton et al., 1988, 1989), and that adding just a few hours of therapist consultation can further enhance the benefits of individual parent video-viewing.

The fact that the tapes lend such consistency and structure to the treatment program nicely addresses a major concern that many have about manualized treatments – that is, that differences among various therapists in the ways they administer the treatments will lead to departures from the precise approach that has been tested in clinical trials. In BASIC, the combination of standard videotapes, all shown in a fixed sequence, with manualized discussion questions, prewritten parent handouts, and parent homework assignments, helps to ensure more consistency and standardization than in perhaps any other evidence-based treatment for child problems.

An important boundary condition is that the materials and procedures tested thus far are not designed for parents of youngsters beyond age 10. Omitted from the tapes, for obvious reasons, are such adolescent issues as sexuality, association with dangerous peers, dealing with physically dangerous confrontations, and drug and alcohol use. As originally intended by Webster-Stratton, the objective of the program is to cut short the development of conduct problems early in life. In cases where such problems have developed and extended into the middle school years and beyond, other treatment approaches are likely to be needed.

Webster-Stratton's approach is subject to a constraint that applies to all parent programs: It requires motivated parents who are willing to invest considerable time attending sessions, doing homework, and answering questions over the phone. However, the video and group discussion approach is probably more inherently engaging, and more likely to reach parents regardless of their reading level and despite variations in therapist skill and experience, than a number of alternative parent training approaches. Because the videos and discussions keep things lively and interesting, parents who have only marginal interest may be more likely to continue participating than would otherwise be the case (but see Webster-Stratton, 1984, showing no difference in parent consumer satisfaction between individual parent therapy and the BASIC program).

In this section we have focused on parent and therapist perspectives, but another important perspective in the clinical practice domain is that of those who organize and fund services – clinic administrators, managed care representatives, and payors. For this group of stakeholders, programs like Webster-Stratton's should have genuine appeal, combining cost-effectiveness, measurable client benefit, and a high level of consumer satisfaction.

How to Find Out More about The Incredible Years BASIC Parent Training Program and Other Webster-Stratton Programs

An overview and discussion of BASIC and other video-guided programs for parents, teachers, and children by the Webster-Stratton group can be found in a recent chapter by Webster-Stratton and Reid (2003). A leader's guide to the video course has also been prepared (Webster-Stratton, 2001). Webster-Stratton's (1992b) *The Incredible Years: A Troubleshooting Guide for Parents of Children Ages 3–8 Years* (Toronto: Umbrella Press) serves as a text for the parent program; the book is available in audio form, for nonreaders. The actual video series and a variety of supporting materials can be obtained by contacting The Incredible Years, 1411 8th Avenue West, Seattle, WA 98119 (phone 888-506-3562) or by going to the website, www.incredibleyears.com. The site includes detailed information on available video series and supporting materials (e.g., books, audiotapes, stickers, magnets, puppets), upcoming workshops and other training opportunities in various locations, and certification requirements and procedures for becoming a group leader in the parent, child, and teacher programs.

12

Problem-Solving Skills Training and Parent Management Training for Children with Conduct Disorder

One way to construe aggression and antisocial behavior is that they are ineffective ways of solving problems. Jared pushes Alex in the lunch line. Alex solves this problem by punching Jared in the face. This may seem effective in the short run, but it may also earn Alex an enemy for the rest of the school year, and it may cause some of Alex's peers to avoid him. Most likely it will get Alex into serious trouble at school. If he could suspend time for 15 minutes and think through all this before acting, Alex might come up with some alternative responses that are less risky. Unfortunately, Alex doesn't have 15 minutes to think it over, so he does what comes naturally, and fists fly.

Problem-Solving Skills Training (PSST), the treatment approach we consider in this chapter, is designed to teach aggressive youngsters to use their heads before using their fists. The children first learn basic steps of problem solving in the context of familiar games. The steps include defining the problem, identifying response options, and evaluating them. Then they learn to apply these steps to interpersonal situations, eventually including the kinds of situations that have led to aggressive behavior and prompted referral. If all goes well, the youngsters learn to apply their cognitive training during real-life stressful encounters, identifying and using increasingly prosocial solutions to their interpersonal problems.

PSST relies heavily on children's capacity to learn how to generate their own prosocial solutions to problems, although parents are also trained to help their children use the problem-solving steps. An alternate approach is to pair PSST with behavioral parent training, similar to that described in Chapter 6 and Chapter 9, thus aiming for both internal and external control over child behavior. Both approaches – PSST alone and PSST plus behavioral parent training – have been tested through the programmatic research of Alan Kazdin and his colleagues, in studies at the University of Pittsburgh and Yale University. In this chapter, we review this treatment research and some of the conceptual and theoretical literature related to it.

Problem-Solving Skills Training: Conceptual Basis and Procedural Overview

PSST grows out of a particular model of how antisocial behavior and conduct disorder develop and are maintained (see Kazdin, 1993, 1995b; for a later elaboration, see Kazdin, 1997a). The model focuses on packages of risk factors (biological, social-environmental, and cognitive) that may combine to produce behaviorally toxic outcomes, and on the snowballing of these factors over time. For example, children with initially difficult temperaments who are exposed to ineffective parenting may fail to develop adequate self-control. Disciplinary problems may follow, together with deficient school performance and impulsively aggressive behavior. Aggression, together with other social and academic problems, may lead to social rejection, and then by default to affiliation with deviant peer groups in which antisocial behavior is modeled and reinforced (see Patterson et al., 1989; see also Caspi et al., 1987; Loeber, 1990). Of course, different risk factors and different patterns of snowballing may characterize the evolution of aggressive and antisocial behavior in different youths.

The variety of ways serious conduct problems may evolve makes it virtually impossible to fashion a treatment program that can address all possible risk factors and all possible developmental pathways. Accordingly, what theory-guided treatment developers may need to do is select a treatment focus that encompasses a significant component of their causal model, ensure that the component selected has empirical support as a contributing factor, and ensure that this component can be modified through intervention. Ideally, addressing the component selected as the hub of the intervention will interrupt the developmental progression toward ever more serious conduct problems and antisocial behavior. This, in general, is the approach Kazdin and colleagues have taken in their treatment development work.

One particularly important component of the model used by Kazdin and colleagues is child cognition. Several kinds of cognitive processes have been identified as potential contributors to aggression and other conduct problems (see e.g., Shirk, 1988). A core idea is that aggression is not caused so much by environmental events as by the ways such events are processed and interpreted. As an example of relevant interpretive processes, Dodge and colleagues (e.g., Dodge, Bates et al., 1990; Dodge & Crick, 1990; Dodge, Price et al., 1990) have shown that aggressive youths are more likely than their nonaggressive peers to read ambiguous social encounters as signs of hostile intent by others. These hostile attributions evidently help spark and fuel aggressive responses to such social encounters. For example, when two youngsters collide in a crowded school hallway between classes, the aggressive child is more likely than most to perceive deliberate provocation and to respond accordingly.

Aggression may also reflect a poverty of information processing. Aggressive children often lack the competencies that Spivack et al. (1976) called "Interpersonal Problem-Solving Skills." Their list includes such skills as (1) recognizing that one has a specific interpersonal problem (rather than, say, just getting mad and striking out), (2) thinking of alternative solutions that one might use to address the problem (rather than simply following one's first impulse), (3) thinking through the steps needed to carry out a particular solution, (4) anticipating the likely consequences of various solutions one might try, in terms of their impact on others as well as oneself. Thus, the aggressive child may be one who, in the face of a frustrating social encounter or interpersonal problem, does not generate very many alternative solutions (e.g., can think of only a combative response), does not anticipate the consequences to which the various solutions might lead (e.g., the negative consequences of the combative response), and does not systematically select the best alternative. Deficits in such interpersonal problem-solving skills have been linked to multiple measures of troublesome youth social behavior, particularly aggression (see e.g., Rubin et al., 1991; Spivack & Shure, 1982).

PSST is designed to address such deficits in problem-solving skills. It was originally derived from procedures developed by Spivack et al. (1976) and Shure (see Shure, 1996, 1999), and related procedures described by Kendall and Braswell (1985). The procedures were modified and refined by the Kazdin group to fit the characteristics and problems of antisocial youth in particular. An important element of the Kazdin modification is the extensive use by therapists of applied behavior analysis (see Kazdin, 2001) during sessions. Therapists learn to prompt appropriate behavior, shape it, and deliver broad gradations of verbal and nonverbal reinforcement for appropriate behavior, and they learn ways to extinguish inappropriate behavior. Two central goals of PSST warrant attention here. One is to improve the process by which children reason as they confront various interpersonal problems – for example, to make the process more systematic and less impulsive, and to bring a broader range of solutions into focus for consideration. Another goal is to increase the number of prosocial solutions children consider and ultimately choose to employ.

In PSST, children ages 7–13 take part in about 20 weekly sessions with a therapist. Each session lasts about 40–50 minutes. In these sessions, children are taught five steps they can apply to problems of many different types. The steps range from simply identifying the problem to laying out potential solutions and selecting the most promising of these to try. These problem-solving steps are first practiced in the context of simple games, and then increasingly applied to the kinds of real-life social problems that have caused difficulties for the youngsters in the past. Parents are taught the skills so they can help their children outside the sessions. PSST is sometimes paired with behavioral parent training in child management (see also

Chapters 6 and 9), which is called *Parent Management Training* (PMT) by Kazdin and colleagues. PMT involves about 16 weekly one-hour sessions, most of which include some explanation of behavioral concepts and procedures, some teaching of the relevant skills, some planning of how to apply the skills at home with the child, and some role-playing and rehearsal with the therapist. Parents try the skills with the child at home and use therapy sessions, in part, to troubleshoot and refine their application of PMT skills.

Problem-Solving Skills Training: In Brief

Designed for . . . . Aggressive and antisocial children ages 7–13
Number of sessions . . . . 20 (range: 20–25)
Session length . . . . 40–50 minutes
Session participants . . . . Therapist with child, plus
    parent contact
Theoretical orientation . . . . Behavioral

Treatment steps:

1. Therapist teaches child five problem-solving steps (identify the problem, list possible solutions, evaluate them, choose one, try it and evaluate the outcome).
2. Child practices the steps on various games (e.g., Checkers, Connect Four).
3. Child practices applying the steps to real-life, everyday problems (e.g., peer conflict).
4. Parent learns the steps; learns to prompt and praise child's use of steps with real-life problems (called "supersolvers"), including problems that originally led to referral.
5. Child continues to practice applying steps to real-life situations (e.g., peer taunting, social exclusion, peers encouraging antisocial behavior); solutions re-enacted with therapist.
6. Wrap-up, review of what has been learned, role-reversal in which child teaches the skills to the therapist.

Treatment classified by Treatment Task Force as . . . . Probably
    Efficacious (Brestan & Eyberg, 1998)
Key resource for potential users . . . . . Kazdin, A. E. (2003). Problem-solving skills training and parent management training for conduct disorder. In A. E. Kazdin & J. R. Weisz (Eds.), *Evidence-Based Psychotherapies for Children and Adolescents* (pp. 241–62). New York: Guilford Press.

Problem-Solving Skills Training: Treatment Procedures

PSST is intended to enhance children's skills at solving interpersonal problems and to increase their rates of prosocial behavior when the children are on their own. In pursuing these goals, the PSST therapist places a heavier emphasis on the processes children use in thinking through problems than on making sure children come up with the correct solutions. The process of problem solving taught in PSST is guided by self-talk; that is, children are taught to talk themselves through a prescribed set of problem-solving steps. The therapist plays an active role in this process, modeling the cognitive processes that are being taught, role-playing the use of these processes with the child, and prompting, guiding, praising, and rewarding the child to shape appropriate behavior. The therapist may also discourage inappropriate behavior via mild punishment, usually a loss of tokens (see next section); this can be quite potent in the context of a highly rewarding interaction with the therapist.

The typical case involves about 20 individual weekly sessions, each 40–50 minutes long. The treatment may be expanded, though, with sessions added early on to help children learn the problem-solving steps, or later in treatment to help children apply the steps to actual problem situations in their lives. The core skills of the program are embodied in the five problem-solving steps, cast in terms of five statements the youth is to make when confronting a problem:

1. *What am I supposed to do?* As a first step, the child is taught to clearly identify the problem. This may seem a simple task at first blush, but it may actually be both challenging and informative for some of the most worrisome problems. As an example, some aggressive children may discover that they are responding to a rather diffuse or amorphous sense of frustration. Step 1 can help these children identify the specific problems that make them frustrated, and then begin the task of solving the problems, one at a time. In other cases, children may store up anger from an early offense, let it fester, and then unleash it in response to later, minor offenses by relatively blameless peers. In these displacement situations, Step 1 can increase the chance that the true stimulus for aggression will be accurately identified, and thus that problem-solving steps can be applied where they are most needed.

2. *I have to look at all my possibilities.* The task in this second step is to generate an array of possible solutions to the identified problem. Aggressive children may tend to identify only one, rather impulsively generated solution, or they may think of a restricted range of solutions, all involving hostile or socially unacceptable behavior. The therapist's task is to use Step 2 to help children enrich their universe

of possible solutions and to help ensure that the array of possibilities includes at least some prosocial responses.

3. *I'd better concentrate and focus in.* Step 3 is the evaluation phase, during which children examine the pros and cons of the various solutions they have identified. As a part of the skill of *consequential thinking* (see Spivack & Shure, 1982), children are led through hypothetical reasoning about what the outcome might be if they choose option a, option b, and so forth. Failure to engage in such thinking is thought to be associated with the impulsivity that is often linked to aggressive behavior.

4. *I need to make a choice.* In the fourth step, children use the results of their consequential thinking in Step 3, selecting the solution that seems likely to generate the most favorable outcomes.

5. *I did a good job (or) Oh, I made a mistake.* The fifth step involves the critical skill of self-evaluation. Children are taught to assess whether the solution they chose was indeed the best one available, and whether they followed the problem-solving process correctly in arriving at that solution. If they conclude that their process involved a mistake, or that the solution they chose was not the best, then they begin the problem-solving process again.

Early in the treatment program, these five problem-solving steps are taught in the context of simple games (e.g., Checkers, Connect Four). The games help make the sessions engaging, and they provide a context for learning not to respond impulsively, and for learning the treatment format and the reward and response cost system (see next section) that will be in place throughout treatment. In the usual format, the therapist presents the child with a problem to try, uses modeling to illustrate how the problem-solving steps can be applied, and then role-plays with the child the process of trying out the solution that was selected. As the child then goes through the steps, the therapist prompts appropriate problem-solving behavior as needed and gives the child concrete feedback with extensive use of praise and other forms of social reinforcement such as smiling, applauding, and high fives.

In addition, the therapist uses a token system to enhance learning. At the start of each session, the child has a cache of plastic chips. More chips may be earned for appropriate behavior, and chips may be lost for inappropriate behavior, such as failing to use one of the problem-solving steps. The chips are sometimes used to shore up learning in an area of special focus for a particular child, such as the need to develop a particular type of prosocial solution that has proven difficult for the child. The chips have value to the youngsters because they can be used to purchase prizes in a store at the end of each session.

Therapists use praise and reward following principles spelled out by Kazdin (2001). For example, children's learning is best strengthened by praise and chips that come immediately after the desired behavior, and therapists need to ensure that the specific forms of praise, and the rewards chips can buy, are in fact highly valued by their young charges. Density is also important, and needs to change over the course of learning. That is, praise and chips need to be continuous until a skill has been well learned, but intermittent once the goal is to maintain learned behavior. Clearly, PSST therapists need to be skilled in applying behavioral principles.

Praise and chips continue to be used as the training sessions shift to a focus on real-life problems in the interpersonal domain. A specific problem is identified, such as conflict with a peer at school, and the therapist models applying the problem-solving steps to that problem, generating alternative solutions, and selecting one. The child and therapist act out that solution, to give the child practice in applying it in the safe context of the session before taking it on the road. Next comes a critical aspect of the treatment program – using the problem-solving steps in real life, outside the clinic.

In vivo practice assignments, called *supersolvers*, ask the children to apply the problem-solving skills to specific everyday situations. These supersolver assignments become increasingly challenging over time, and eventually focus on precisely the problem areas that were central to the child's referral in the first place. In the initial phase of treatment, supersolvers are tackled by the child with considerable guidance by the therapist. Then parents are brought into the process to play increasingly central guiding and supporting roles, and to dispense praise for their child's application of the steps. By the last third of treatment, children are rewarded for completing real-life applications of the problem-solving skills on their own, without adult assistance (see Kazdin et al., 1989).

To strengthen their role in supporting the child's learning, parents are taught the same problem-solving sequence their child is learning, and they practice the assignments – especially the supersolvers – with the child at home, until the child reaches the later stages and is carrying out supersolvers independently. Indeed, some of the supersolvers are likely to focus on the home, and on parent-child interpersonal problems. As with the children, therapists use prompting, role-playing, and praise to facilitate effective learning by the parents. Parents are also taught to use praise effectively with their children, to help them learn the skills and continue to apply them.

Parent Management Training. Often, basic PSST is supplemented with rather comprehensive behavioral training of the parents, which is called parent management training (PMT) by Kazdin and colleagues. The rationale for behavioral parent training was described in some detail in Chapters 6 and 9; the need for these procedures is supported, in part, by research findings showing that poor management of contingencies in the home, and resultant coercive exchanges between parents and children, may operate to reinforce disobedient and aggressive child behavior (see e.g., Kazdin, 1995b; Patterson, Littman, & Bricker, 1967; Patterson & Reid, 1970). PMT addresses this state of affairs by teaching parents how to design contingencies under which obedient and prosocial behavior leads to favorable consequences for the child, and disobedient or aggressive behavior leads to adverse consequences. Setting such contingencies and enforcing them consistently can make child behavior manageable, and can promote prosocial behavior.

PMT programs originally drew most heavily from procedures described by Patterson, Reid, Jones, and Conger (1975) and Fleishman and Conger (1978; see also Patterson, Cobb, & Ray, 1973; Patterson & Gullion, 1968; Patterson, McNeal, Hawkins, & Phelps, 1967), but those original procedures evolved in a number of ways as a result of the clinical and research experiences of the Kazdin group. As the name implies, PMT is conducted primarily with parents who are trained to carefully specify and closely observe the child problem behaviors that cause them concern and that they want to target for change. Parents are taught to use positive reinforcement and mild punishment (e.g., time-out, withdrawal of privileges), as well as negotiation and contingency contracting. Sessions are used to teach the skills, practice them via role-plays, and review and troubleshoot efforts to implement child behavior change programs at home. There is an extensive literature demonstrating the efficacy of PMT and related behavioral parent training interventions (see Chapters 6 and 9; see also Kazdin, 1997b; Kazdin & Weisz, 1998; McMahon & Wells, 1998) in modifying adult behavior toward children and reducing child conduct problems.

The basic PMT program used by Kazdin and colleagues involves 16–20 weekly one-hour sessions, with additional sessions added as needed to ensure successful learning of the procedures, or for other purposes such as planning and implementation of specially tailored interventions for specific problems at home. The usual format of the sessions involves (1) some explanation of a particular behavioral concept or procedure (such as reinforcement or time-out), (2) teaching of the relevant skills (e.g., identifying reinforcing consequences and setting criteria for awarding them, or calibrating the length of time-out to fit the child's age and the nature of the offense), and (3) planning how to apply the skills at home with the child, given the characteristics of parent, child, and household, the child's target behaviors, and the reinforcers that are available to the parents.

Teaching parents the relevant skills can represent a large proportion of the session, as therapists teach and model the behavioral technique of the day, then engage the parents in role-playing and rehearsal of that skill. Audiotapes of problem interactions between parents and children may be used to stimulate discussion, provide practice in developing behavioral programs for use in the home, and set up role-play exercises. In such exercises, parent and therapist may alternate roles, with therapist and parent playing parent and child in some of the role-plays, then reversing roles for other role-plays. Switching is valuable, because parents may need to both observe and practice (with feedback) some of the nuanced skills involved in order to really master them. As an example, Kazdin (1996) notes that "delivery of reinforcement (e.g., praise) by the parent is likely to be infrequent, flat, delayed, and connected to parent nagging. Shaping begins with the initial parent repertoire and moves progressively to obtain more consistent, enthusiastic, and immediate praise, reduced nagging, clearer prompts, and so on" (p. 386).

Like the behavioral parent training program developed by Barkley (1997; see Chapter 6), the PMT procedures used by Kazdin and colleagues include a token reinforcement system in the home, to provide a structured way for parents to reward their child's desired behavior. The tokens may include stars, marks on a chart, or simply points, depending on the child's age and other aspects of the situation. Tokens plus praise are made contingent on specific behaviors by the child. Kazdin (1996) sees the tokens as valuable not only for what they convey to the child but also because they prompt the parents to reinforce consistently. In other words, tokens help shape both child and parent behavior. Another advantage of tokens is that they provide a convenient way to track exchanges involving child behavior and parent reinforcement, because it is relatively easy to record the earning and spending of tokens. The record thus generated each week can then be made a focus of discussion (including re-enactment or role-play) at the beginning of each subsequent treatment session.

A key feature of PMT is that it focuses not only on the child's behavior at home but also on performance and conduct at school. The PMT therapist contacts the child's teachers to identify individual problem areas, including conduct, homework compliance, and grades. This information is used to develop a home-based reinforcement system. In a typical system, the child's behavior is monitored at school and communicated to the parents, who, in turn, administer the appropriate consequences at home. Classroom contingencies may also be developed and implemented by some teachers, but not all teachers are willing or able. The PMT therapist keeps track of the child's school behavior through phone contact with school personnel and through discussions in the weekly parent meetings.

Although PMT is adult-focused, the child is kept apprised of the process. Portions of some PMT sessions include the child, in an effort to make sure the child understands the program. In addition, occasional child input can help ensure that the program is, in fact, being implemented at home in the way the parent reports. Session segments that include parent(s) and child are also used to negotiate behavioral contracts with contingencies that all parties can agree to. Where problems have arisen in implementation of a home contingency contract, the child may be brought in to help pinpoint the difficulties, practice the procedures via role-play, modify the contract, or provide the therapist with a chance to give feedback to parents and child jointly. The therapist may also use these occasions to model adjustments in parent behavior toward the child, or changes in child responses to the parents' application of contingencies.

Combining PSST and PMT. In cases where both PSST and PMT are applied to a case, each family has two therapists. This permits the family to make one weekly trip to the clinic, with child receiving PSST while parent(s) receive PMT. As Kazdin (1996) notes, the two treatment programs have a different conceptual basis and address different processes thought to be related to conduct problems, but both pursue the goal of changing how individuals behave in everyday life. PSST focuses on how the child behaves in interpersonal situations involving parents, teachers, siblings, and peers. PMT focuses on parent-child interactions, with an emphasis on what parents can do to reduce inappropriate child behavior and increase prosocial child behavior. Both PSST and PMT emphasize training in specific forms of behavior and the application of that behavior in situations outside the clinic.

In PSST and PMT, treatment is not limited to the weekly sessions held at the clinic. Instead, both treatments include therapist contacts with family members during the week. These contacts provide a way of monitoring the programs at home and school, addressing any crises that have arisen, and fine-tuning planned procedures to adapt to unforeseen difficulties.

Problem-Solving Skills Training and Parent Management Training: Outcome Studies Testing the Effects

Several studies have assessed the effects of PSST, some with PMT added and some without. Most of these studies have been conducted by Kazdin and colleagues, at the University of Pittsburgh and at Yale University. One other study is relevant as well. We review all the studies here.

Initial test: PSST alone versus relationship therapy and therapist contact. In the first published test of PSST, as applied to aggressive youth, Kazdin, Esveldt-Dawson et al. (1987a) compared PSST to nondirective relationship therapy. The children, ages 7–13, had all been referred for treatment because of antisocial behavior (including fighting, stealing, truancy, running away, and being unmanageable at home or school). All in the study had been rated above the 98th percentile on either the Aggression or Delinquency scale of the parent-report Child Behavior Checklist (CBCL; Achenbach & Edelbrock, 1983). Some 70% of the sample received DSM-III diagnoses of conduct disorder. The sample of 56 children included 80% boys; 77% of the children were Caucasian, 23% African American.

Children were randomly assigned to one of three conditions: (1) PSST, (2) relationship therapy, and (3) a contact control condition. Each condition involved 20 sessions; PSST and relationship therapy sessions were 45 minutes long; the contact control sessions were 20 minutes long. The PSST procedures used in this first study were similar to those described earlier in this chapter, but did not include the *in vivo* practice assignments called supersolvers (see previous section); instead the training focused largely on teaching the problem-solving skills through training and practice in the treatment sessions with therapists.

In the relationship therapy condition (patterned after C. Patterson, 1979, and Reisman, 1973), therapists focused on developing a close relationship with the child. They provided "empathy, unconditional positive regard, and warmth" (Kazdin et al., 1987a, p. 79). Like PSST, relationship therapy involved some play activity, a token reinforcement system, and discussion of interpersonal themes and individual problems; but unlike PSST, which focused on developing specific problem-solving skills, relationship therapy focused on establishing a trusting relationship with the therapist and discussing the child's feelings. The treatment contact control condition was designed to control partially for repeated individual contact with a therapist, but not to have significant therapeutic or instructional content; so, in this condition, the child and therapist met individually to discuss routine activities on the unit, with no in-depth discussion of emotionally laden issues and no use of the specific procedures of PSST or relationship therapy.

Treatment outcome was assessed primarily by means of parent-report and teacher-report checklists. According to these measures, PSST was associated with significantly greater decreases in aggressive behavior, externalizing problems, and overall problems, and significantly greater increases in prosocial behavior and overall adjustment, than were relationship therapy and the contact control condition. The effects were seen at posttreatment and again in a one-year followup. There were trends suggesting that relationship therapy may have been somewhat more helpful than contact control, but differences between these two conditions were generally nonsignificant. After treatment and at the one-year followup, a greater proportion of the PSST children than relationship therapy or contact control children had moved into the normal range of prosocial behavior; but a majority of PSST children, and nearly all of the relationship therapy and contact control children, remained outside the normal range on measures of deviant behavior.

Combining PSST with PMT. In the second PSST study by the Kazdin group (Kazdin, Esveldt-Dawson et al., 1987b), PSST was combined with PMT. Children in the study were 7–12-year-olds, all referred to an inpatient psychiatric facility for antisocial behavior, in such forms as fighting and other aggressive acts, stealing, truancy, running away, or being unmanageable at home or school; and all were rated at or above the 98th percentile on either the aggression or delinquency scale of the CBCL. The sample of 40 included 78% boys, and 75% of the sample were Caucasian, with the remaining 25% African American.

In this study, children were randomly assigned to receive either the combination of PSST and PMT or a contact control condition (with 20-minute sessions) like that used by Kazdin (1987a, see previous paragraph), with both children and their parents having regular contact with a therapist, but less lengthy than and much less skill-focused than was true of the PSST plus PMT sessions. In the PSST plus PMT condition, children received the standard Kazdin PSST, as described earlier, but without *in vivo* practice assignments (i.e., "supersolvers") outside the therapist's office; and concurrently, parents received their own sessions of PMT, as described earlier in this chapter.

Treatment outcome was assessed by means of parent-report and teacher-report checklists, as in Kazdin et al. (1987a). The measures indicated that, after treatment, the PSST plus PMT group showed significantly less aggression and externalizing behavior both at home and at school, and more parent-reported prosocial behavior, than did the contact control group. These differences held up at a follow-up assessment, one year after the end of treatment. The authors also assessed the degree to which the treatment and control conditions served to place these initially deviant children within the normal range of functioning on the parent-report and teacher-report measures. Only a small number of significant differences were found, but these did show a higher proportion of PSST plus PMT youth than contact control youth returning to normal levels. Still, as Kazdin et al. (1987b) note, "the majority of treated and control children remained outside of this (normal) range on parent and teacher measures of behavioral problems" (p. 423).

PSST alone versus PSST-Plus-in-Vivo-Practice versus Relationship Therapy. In a third study, Kazdin, Bass et al. (1989) compared two versions of PSST to relationship therapy. Treated youngsters were 7–13-year-olds who had been seen at a diagnostic triage center and then referred for either inpatient or outpatient care. Inclusion criteria were very similar to those employed by Kazdin et al. (1987a,b). For example, all child participants (both outpatient and inpatient) had been referred for treatment of antisocial behavior, including fighting, stealing, truancy, running away, or unmanageability at home or school. And all children had been rated by parents as at or above the 90th percentile on either the aggression or delinquency scale of the CBCL. The sample of 112 included 78% boys; 55% of the sample was Caucasian, with the remaining 46% African American.

Each child was randomly assigned to one of three treatment conditions. In addition to PSST and the form of Relationship Therapy (see C. H. Patterson, 1979) that was used by Kazdin et al. (1987a), Kazdin et al. (1989)

used a third treatment approach – that is, an enhanced version of PSST that included *in vivo* practice, therapeutically planned activities designed to extend the exercise of learned skills to settings outside of treatment. These activities, called supersolvers and described earlier in this chapter, consisted of assignments that were to be completed outside the therapy session. Early in treatment, supersolvers were relatively simple and non-threatening, such as solving math problems. Over time in treatment, the supersolvers grew more challenging, both cognitively and interpersonally, often involving troubling interactions with parents, teachers, peers, and siblings.

Analyses to assess outcome included the parent and teacher checklist measures used in previous research by the Kazdin group, but additional assessment approaches enriched the picture. Of special interest were a parent daily report procedure (see Patterson, 1982), in which parents were called each day and asked to note which, if any, of 23 specific problem behaviors their child had shown during the previous 24 hours. A second measure added to the assessment package was a structured interview with parents, surveying the degree and duration of 30 diverse forms of antisocial behavior, all derived from referral problems reported for conduct-disordered youth.

Assessments at posttreatment and at one-year followup showed significantly more marked improvement in both PSST groups than in the relationship therapy condition on most measures, based on both parents' and teachers' reports, and encompassing both reduced antisocial behavior and increased prosocial behavior. In fact, children in the relationship therapy group tended to remain at their pretreatment levels of functioning on most measures, despite treatment, whereas both PSST groups showed significant improvements on most measures. Among children receiving PSST, adding *in vivo* practice appeared to enhance the initial beneficial effects on teacher-reported school behavior, as measured at immediate posttreatment; but the advantage for the *in vivo* group faded by the one-year followup, at which time none of the measures showed a significant difference between PSST-alone and PSST with *in vivo* practice. As in other research using PSST, there was evidence that more children in the PSST conditions than in relationship therapy moved to within the normal range, at least on overall school behavior at immediate posttreatment; but most of the children, across conditions, remained in the clinical range immediately after treatment and at followup. Thus, while PSST in both the forms tested here seemed to produce genuine benefit, it could not be said to have brought children entirely into the normal range of functioning.

Assessing separate and combined effects of PSST and PMT. In the fourth study, Kazdin, Siegel, and Bass (1992) used a dismantling design to assess the separate and combined effects of PSST and PMT. As in previous studies with these treatments, the target group consisted of youngsters

ages 7–13, who had all displayed severe antisocial behavior. All had been referred for outpatient treatment, and the referral problems noted by Kazdin
et al. (1992) were generally the same as in previous studies by this group –
for example, fighting, stealing, unmanageable behavior at home or at
school – and all the youngsters had received problem ratings by parents
that placed them above the 90th percentile on either the Aggression or
Delinquency scale of the CBCL. The sample of 97 included 78% boys, and
69% Caucasian youngsters, with the remaining 31% African American.

The children were randomly assigned to receive either PSST, PMT, or
PSST plus PMT. Outcomes were assessed primarily through the parent-
report CBCL, the Teacher Report Form (Achenbach & Edelbrock, 1986), a
prosocial behavior measure completed by teachers, and the Parent Daily
Report as discussed earlier. Children also completed self-report measures
of aggressive and delinquent behavior, and parents completed measures
of family environment, parenting stress, and their own symptoms of depression and other forms of psychopathology.

Posttreatment and one-year follow-up assessments showed that the
combination of PSST and PMT generally outperformed either of the treatment components delivered alone, but the results differed across measures. The most consistent findings across the posttreatment and one-year
follow-up assessment points showed PSST plus PMT to be superior to the
two separate treatments on child-report measures of delinquent and antisocial behavior, and on parent-report measures of parenting stress and
parental symptoms of psychopathology. The parent daily report measure
showed this pattern (i.e., superior outcomes of the combined treatments)
only at posttreatment; at one-year followup, both the combined treatment
and PSST only significantly outperformed PMT. Where there were significant outcome differences between the two component treatments alone,
on various measures, they showed superior outcomes for the PSST group
relative to the PMT group.

Clinical significance of the changes in all three groups was evaluated,
as in previous research by this team, through comparisons of participants'
posttreatment and follow-up scores on the CBCL and the Teacher Report
Form, relative to the normal range of scores obtained by nonclinical samples. As shown in Figure 12.1, the mean total behavior problem T-scores
on the CBCL alone were well above the normal range at pretreatment, but
markedly lower at posttreatment; the mean for the PSST plus PMT group
dropped especially sharply, extending well into the normal range by posttreatment and showing further reductions one year later. As the figure
also shows, Teacher Report Form ratings moved from above the normal
range at pretreatment to within the normal range at posttreatment and at
one-year followup, for all three groups. Complementary analyses, focusing
on the proportion of individual children who moved into the normal range
on both measures, showed that combined PSST plus PMT children fared

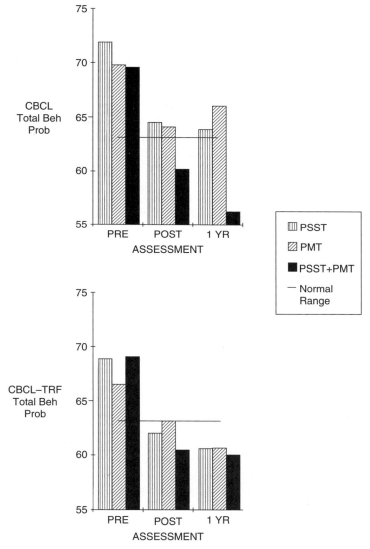

FIGURE 12.1. Group mean scores for Problem Solving Skills Training (PSST), Parent Management Training (PMT), and PSST + PMT combined, on the Total Behavior Problem scale of the parent-report Child Behavior Checklist (CBCL, upper graph) and the teacher-report CBCL-Teacher Report Form (CBCL-TRF, lower graph). Scores above the horizontal line indicate Total Problem levels in the clinical range; scores below the line indicate Total Problem levels in the non-clinical or "normal" range. [From Kazdin, A. E., Siegel, T. C., & Bass, D. (1992). Cognitive problem-solving skills training and parent management training in the treatment of antisocial behavior in children. *Journal of Consulting and Clinical Psychology, 60*, 733–47. Reprinted by permission from Alan E. Kazdin and the American Psychological Association.

significantly better at both posttreatment and one-year followup than children who had received only PSST or only PMT. Overall, the results suggest particularly strong treatment effects for intervention that combines a focus on individual child problem-solving skills (i.e., PSST) with a focus on parental skills in child behavior management (i.e., PMT). These findings are in harmony with findings Webster-Stratton (1996) has reported for her video-guided interventions (described in Chapter 11); she noted that clinical significance tests conducted at one-year followup showed that a combination of parent training plus child training that included a problem-solving component produced more significant improvement in child behavior at a one-year followup than did either parent training or child training alone.

Impact of treatment on parent and family functioning. Although the primary goal of PSST and PMT is to improve child functioning, it seems reasonable to suspect that the treatments might enhance parent and family functioning as well. Kazdin and Wassell (2000) investigated this possibility, focusing on 250 youths and families treated with PSST, PMT, or both. The youngsters ranged in age from 2–14; 76% were boys; and 74% were Caucasian, 18% African American, 4% Latino, and 4% of other or mixed ethnicity. Changes in parents were assessed via self-report questionnaires focusing on depression and other symptoms, and on how stressful the parenting role was for them. Changes in family functioning were assessed via questionnaires asking about such matters as family relationships, social support, how the family deals with conflict, and the quality of the marital (or cohabiting couple's) relationship. For comparison purposes, Kazdin and Wassell also reported on therapeutic change in the children treated, based on parent reports on the CBCL, on an observation measure of home behavior, and on a clinical interview.

In general, the findings showed large changes over the course of therapy in treated youngsters, and smaller but substantial changes in parent and family functioning. Moreover, changes in the children, parents, and families were significantly correlated with one another. The findings suggest that benefits of treating children for conduct problems may be broader and richer than is widely recognized, extending beyond the children to the functioning of their parents and their families.

Predictors of treatment outcome. The research reviewed thus far suggests that PSST and PMT can produce substantial benefit for groups of aggressive antisocial youths and their families. However, no treatment works equally well with all youths, and any treatment will fall short in some cases. This being the case, an important objective for treatment researchers is to identify moderators of treatment outcome, such as child and family factors associated with different levels of benefit. Kazdin and Crowley (1997) took a step toward this goal by testing for predictors of outcome in a sample of 120 children, ages 7–13, all referred for outpatient treatment of aggressive, antisocial, or oppositional behavior. Some 75% were boys, with 64% of the sample Caucasian, 29% African American, and 7% other ethnicities. All received PSST. Degree of improvement was gauged by comparing pretreatment and posttreatment parent reports on the CBCL and teacher reports on the Teacher Report Form (Achenbach & Edelbrock, 1986).

Both child characteristics and parent-family context factors predicted improvement. Among child characteristics, the most consistent findings across the outcome measures were that poorer treatment response was associated with low levels of reading achievement and school performance, and high levels of symptomatology across all diagnoses. In addition, low family income, use of public assistance, and parent history of antisocial behavior and adverse child-rearing practices, were all associated with poorer child outcome; these factors were also associated with the child factors that predicted outcome. Thus, the findings highlighted three useful points: (1) not all children profited equally from PSST, (2) variations in child response were related in orderly ways to particular child characteristics, and (3) variations in child response were also related to family and contextual factors that were themselves associated with the child predictors. The association between high levels of problem severity before treatment and fewer reductions in problems at home and school replicated findings of a previous study by Kazdin (1995a).

Do problem-solving skills transfer to observed school behavior? The studies by Kazdin and colleagues are methodologically strong in many respects, but one limitation that may warrant attention in the future is the absence of outcome assessment via direct observations of child behavior at home or in school. A multiple baseline study by Guevremont and Foster (1993) highlights the potential value of such an assessment strategy. In this study, five aggressive boys, ages 11 and 12, were treated with a problem-solving skills training program that resembled Kazdin's PSST in a number of ways. All the boys were referred to the program by a local school system's special education department because of aggressive and disruptive school behavior. Two of the five were on probation; all five were rated by teachers at or above the 98th percentile on the aggressive scale of the Teacher Report Form (Achenbach & Edelbrock, 1986).

The problem-solving training program involved 18 individual sessions, 40–45 minutes in duration, covering five steps similar to those in the Kazdin program (see previous description). For each skill, the therapist gave a rationale, modeled its use, supervised behavioral rehearsal, and gave feedback to the boy. Vignettes were used to describe situations that were especially problematic for the boy, and these vignettes became the context for modeling and rehearsing. Each skill was introduced only after the child demonstrated mastery of the earlier skills. To support transfer of skills to the classroom, the boys completed daily problem-solving logs, telling whether they had used the skills, in what situation(s), and how well this had worked. Teachers initialed the logs at the end of each day, and therapists praised the boys and gave them stickers for completing the logs. These logs turned out to be closely associated with outcome (see next section).

Changes in each boy's behavior coincident with treatment were assessed in multiple ways. In one approach, boys responded to problem vignettes by saying what the problem was, identifying solutions, noting likely consequences of each, and telling which solution they thought was best. One sign of treatment benefit was that performance on each component skill (e.g., problem identification, generation of alternative solutions, evaluating consequences) was poor until training in that skill had been introduced. In another assessment approach, trained observers watched the boys at six-second intervals, in two different classrooms, recording disruptive and aggressive behavior. These observations showed only modest changes in school behavior. Importantly, the changes that did occur generally did not begin when the boys acquired the problem-solving skills in training, but rather when they started keeping self-report logs. This suggests two possibilities: Perhaps keeping the log reminded the boys to apply the problem-solving skills they had learned; or perhaps, as the authors note, the training had little impact, and keeping the log affected the boys' behavior directly by prompted self-recording and self-evaluation (see e.g., Lochman et al., 1984, and Nelson et al., 1978). What the findings highlight is the need to (1) assess the degree to which children actually learn specific problem-solving skills, (2) carry out observations of actual child behavior in important life settings, and (3) assess the relation between changes in problem-solving skill and changes in child behavior in the settings where they live their lives. We will return to these themes in the Scientific Issues section of this chapter.

Summary of the Outcome Evidence on PSST, PMT, and PSST-plus-PMT.
We have reviewed eight outcome studies in this chapter, four group-design clinical trials by Kazdin and colleagues (1987a,b, 1989, 1992), one study reporting effects of child treatment on parent and family functioning (Kazdin & Wassell, 2000), two studies probing for predictors of treatment outcome (Kazdin, 1995a; Kazdin & Crowley, 1997), and one multiple baseline study by Guevremont and Foster (1993) that included direct observational assessments of outcome. The clinical trials by Kazdin and colleagues give evidence that PSST, both alone and combined with PMT, generates reliable reductions in reports of aggressive and antisocial behavior, and reliable increases in reported prosocial behavior, among children in the 7–13-year age range; several effects show an advantage for the combination of PSST plus PMT, relative to either PSST or PMT alone.

The measures showing improvement in the various trials have included reports of child behavior at home, at school, and in the community, and the effects have been evident not only immediately after treatment, but also at one-year followup. Positive treatment effects have been found in samples of inpatient as well as outpatient youth. And the benefits of treatment have shown up not only on reports of child behavior but also on measures of parenting stress, parental symptoms of psychopathology, and family functioning. The search has begun for predictors of treatment outcome, identifying both child and family contextual factors that predict degree of improvement. The findings by Guevremont and Foster (1993) underscore the need, in future research, to assess children's acquisition of specific problem-solving skills and to include outcome assessments involving direct observations of child behavior.

What about Sal? Applying Problem-Solving Skills Training and PMT

Sal, discussed at the beginning of this section, is at the upper end of the age range with which PSST has been tested. Nonetheless, his problem-solving skills clearly need upgrading, as do his mother's child management skills. Let us imagine that Sal has been referred to the Kazdin et al. Child Conduct Clinic to receive PSST while his mother receives PMT.

Problem-solving skills training for Sal. The PSST portion of the treatment involves about 20 individual sessions with Sal, each lasting about 40–50 minutes. At the beginning of the process, it is no surprise to the therapist that Sal is not thrilled to be sent to a "conduct clinic" to see a therapist. The boy arrives for his first session in a sullen, resentful mood. When the therapist introduces himself and reaches out to shake hands, Sal smirks and looks away. Asked whether he is OK, Sal replies, "You're the shrink; read my mind," but the therapist ignores Sal's negativity and is so positive and enthusiastic that Sal begins to warm up in spite of himself.

Sal's interest grows a bit stronger when he learns that he can win prizes and that much of what they will be doing in the meetings will involve familiar games like checkers and Connect Four. Through these games, Sal soon discovers, he will be learning to stop and think before he acts. The process of stopping and thinking is guided by five specific steps of problem solving that Sal learns and practices, first in the context of checkers: (1) *What am I supposed to do?* ("OK, I need to move forward without getting jumped."); (2) *I have to look at all my possibilities.* ("Here are my four possible moves."); (3) *I had better concentrate and focus in.* ("Let me think what will happen with each move. These three will get me jumped, but this fourth one looks good."); (4) *I need to make a choice.* ("Alright, I'll try this fourth one."); and (5) *I did a good job or Oh, I made a mistake.* ("Great – I did a good job; this move worked.").

Throughout this learning process, Sal is prompted by his therapist to use the five steps (e.g., "OK, what are some moves you might make now . . . and what will happen if you do that?"), and he receives both social and material rewards for appropriate use of the steps. The social rewards come in both verbal forms (e.g., "Alright, Sal! Nice work!") and nonverbal forms (e.g., smiling, nodding, high fives). The material rewards come in the form of a token system; the therapist gives Sal plastic poker chips for appropriate effort and success. Sal knows he can use the chips to buy things from the therapist's store, and he has seen some good stuff in that store, so he guards his growing pile of chips closely.

As Sal masters the problem-solving steps through games, his therapist begins helping him apply the skills to problematic social interactions. Sal has many of these to choose from. His interactions with peers are riddled with conflict, and his style with teachers frequently gets him into trouble. Sal and his therapist begin by focusing on teachers, in part because the therapist judges that teachers may respond more predictably than peers to improvements in Sal's behavior. The focal interaction is one in which a particular teacher, Mr. Blake, criticizes Sal in front of the class, and orders Sal to stop talking to his friend. The combination of public ridicule plus a command pushes Sal's button, and often provokes a disrespectful retort, further conflict with Mr. Blake, and frequently a disciplinary incident. Because this sequence occurs two to four days out of every week, Sal is virtually certain to have an opportunity to use his problem-solving skills with Mr. Blake soon after practicing with his therapist in a session.

The therapist uses a role-play to help Sal prepare. Sal plays Mr. Blake while the therapist plays Sal and models the problem-solving sequence: (1) *What am I supposed to do?* Answer Mr. Blake in a way that won't get me in trouble. (2) *I have to look at all my possibilities.* I could answer with attitude or try to be funny, ignore Mr. Blake and keep doing what I'm doing, or apologize and change what I'm doing. (3) *I had better concentrate and focus in.* Attitude will get me in trouble; ignoring Mr. Blake will get me in trouble; but apologizing and changing my behavior will help me get along with Mr. Blake. (4) *I need to make a choice* . . . . etc. Then the role-playing flips, and Sal plays himself, practicing the problem-solving process with the therapist, who plays Mr. Blake.

All this practice leads to a supersolver assignment in which Sal's job is to apply this problem-solving process in actual interactions with Mr. Blake at school. Later supersolvers involve Sal's interactions with other teachers, with peers, and with his mother at home. In the early supersolver assignments, the task is structured to ensure plenty of therapist guidance for Sal; during the middle third Sal's parents play an increasingly supportive role; and during the last third Sal earns chips for carrying out supersolvers on his own, with minimal adult help. The content of the supersolvers moves steadily toward the concerns that prompted Sal's referral – conflict with peers and teachers, and disobedience and disrespect of his mother.

To reinforce Sal's learning experience in the therapy sessions, his mother is involved in treatment as well. She learns the problem-solving steps and she practices assignments with Sal at home. However, the therapist and

PSST colleagues recognize early on that Sal has little respect for his mother, and that her ability to influence his behavior is modest at best. Thus, the decision is made to pair PSST with PMT for Sal's mother.

Adding parent management training. In PMT, Sal's mother has 16 weekly one-hour sessions with her own therapist. She learns principles of behavior management, and she learns how to apply those principles to her daily interactions with Sal. As an example, she learns that social rewards in the form of praise for good behavior need to be immediate, enthusiastic, and clearly connected to the desirable behaviors she wants to see more of in Sal. She also learns to give praise without attaching nagging or criticism as an add-on. For example, she should say, "Good job, Sal!" rather than "Good job, Sal. Don't be so slow next time." She also learns how to identify reinforcers that Sal values but to which she holds the key (such as special foods, privileges, television time), and how to make these reinforcers uniformly contingent upon Sal's behavior. To shore up her ability to use this learning in real life, Mom and the therapist carry out role-plays, first with Mom playing Sal and the therapist playing Mom, and modeling appropriate parental behavior; then the roles are reversed, to ensure that Mom cannot only recognize the right behavior but perform it as well.

Mom is also taught to use tokens at home, in a manner similar to the way the PSST therapist uses tokens with Sal. Mom gives out tokens plus praise in response to desirable behaviors by Sal. The tokens have symbolic value for Sal, but he can also turn them in for edible treats, small prizes, and privileges. The distribution of tokens is also easy to keep track of, so it provides a record of Sal's behavior and Mom's rewarding, both of which are discussed in each subsequent PMT session with the therapist.

Beyond working with Sal's mother, the therapist connects with personnel in Sal's school. Information is collected on Sal's most significant individual problem areas, including poor conduct and poor grades, in Sal's case. Sal's teachers agree to fill in a brief daily report form regarding his behavior at school, and Sal is required to bring this form home to his mother, who, in turn administers the appropriate consequences at home, using the reinforcement system she and the therapist have constructed. The PMT therapist keeps track of Sal's school behavior by phoning Sal's teachers from time to time, and by reviewing with Sal's mother the teacher daily reports she has received each week.

Although most of the PMT work involves Sal's mother with her therapist, Sal is occasionally brought into the sessions. Early in the process, for example, Sal, his mother, and her PMT therapist work together to hammer out a family contract, specifying what behaviors are expected of Sal, what rewards he will receive, and what role his mother will play in this process. Later, some parts of the contract seem not to be working well; Sal complains that some parts are not fair, and his mother finds some parts too complicated to use consistently in real life. So, the parties reconvene

for a summit conference, to fix the problems. As one part of the conference, the therapist has Sal and his mother role-play interaction sequences
that illustrate problems with the contract; then, in true PSST fashion, the
group discusses various solutions, weighing the pros and cons of each and
selecting solutions that all three can live with. Through this process, the
therapist (1) helps Sal and his mother solve specific problems, (2) demonstrates the usefulness of the PSST steps, and (3) creates an opportunity for
mutual problem solving and cooperation between Sal and his mother. In
this way, and by check-in phone contacts on days between sessions, the
PMT therapist works to strengthen Mom's ability to nudge Sal's behavior
in a positive direction, before it is too late.

Troubleshooting: Common Treatment Problems and Recommended Solutions

The case application to Sal and his mother illustrates how PSST and PMT
can work, but it doesn't convey much about the kinds of challenges that
can arise in the course of treatment. Here we focus on two broad challenges
and ways they can be addressed.

- *Adversity and disadvantage faced by treated youths.* One class of challenges
  relates to the complexity and life circumstances of many youngsters who
  receive PSST. In addition to high levels of co-occurring disorders and behavioral and emotional problems, the youngsters may be embedded in
  quite difficult living situations that include cramped quarters, frequent
  changes in caregiving arrangements, conflict and instability in familial
  relationships, maltreatment or close approximations, and limited financial resources that add uncertainty and stress to daily living, with so
  many difficulties, treatment of the youth's conduct problems may not
  be the highest priority. Under these circumstances, therapists are coun-
  seled to start small and stay focused. The general strategy is to begin
  with specific, modest skills, apply shaping, and to build through extensive practice to problem-solving ability that can be applied more and
  more broadly outside the therapy context, as described in the preceding
  account of PSST.
- *Adversity and disadvantage faced by treated parents.* Another class of challenges relates to the adverse life circumstances that make it hard for
  many parents of conduct-disordered children to benefit fully from PMT.
  Many of the difficulties faced by treated youths (see previous discussion) are both shared and magnified in the lives of their parents and
  other caregivers. As those responsible for the family, parents and caregivers experience financial disadvantage with a special intensity, and the
  difficulties are compounded when adult mental disorders are added to
  the mix. Therapists are encouraged to adopt two approaches to what

can sometimes seem a daunting array of difficulties in the parents' lives. First, it is wise to avoid overwhelming parents with more complexity than can be fitted into their lives; instead, therapists are advised to begin with small behavior management skills, refined through shaping, and practiced to proficiency, so that they may gradually make their way into the parents' daily interactions with their child. Second, PMT therapists are encouraged to focus treatment on the sources of parent stress, with efforts made to increase the time parents have for themselves, enhance development of friendships, and pursue activities they find personally fulfilling. It is possible that a certain threshold of parental well-being may be needed for PMT to take root and thrive.

Problem-Solving Skills Training and Parent Management Training: Scientific Issues

As is evident in the descriptions presented earlier in this chapter, the studies testing PSST alone and PSST in combination with PMT have numerous methodological strengths. Together they form a substantial body of evidence in support of treatment efficacy. Here we focus on issues relevant to further research on these treatments.

Moderators of Outcome. As noted earlier, Kazdin and colleagues have begun the task of identifying moderators by reporting on predictors of treatment outcome. Strictly speaking, identifying moderators requires tests of the interaction between treatment condition and other factors, since predictors of outcome in treated youths might also predict outcome in untreated youths having the same disorder. But finding predictors is a useful first step. Kazdin (1995a) reported that breadth and severity of child impairment, parental stress and psychopathology, and family dysfunction, predicted treatment outcome, with greater deficits in any of these domains associated with poorer response to treatment. In addition, Kazdin and Crowley (1997) found that outcomes were predicted by (1) low levels of child reading achievement and academic and school performance, (2) high levels of child symptomatology across all diagnoses, (3) low family income and use of public assistance, and (4) parent history of antisocial behavior as well as adverse child-rearing practices.

The search for predictors and moderators will certainly continue; it reflects one of the long-term goals of the Kazdin program (see Kazdin, 1996, 2003). In the future, it will be useful to include, within the purview of this search, such demographic characteristics as child age, gender, and race and ethnicity. There are several reasons to suspect that age may matter. As an example, PSST builds on hypothetical reasoning (e.g., about the likely outcomes of various possible problem solution strategies), and the developmental literature suggests that such reasoning grows more potent as children mature through childhood into adolescence (Flavell et al., 1993). Consistent with this developmental trend, at least one meta-analysis (Durlak et al., 1991) found much larger effects of CBT interventions with 11–13-year-olds than with 7–11-year-olds. It is also possible that child age moderates PMT effects, although perhaps in the opposite direction. PMT, like other procedures teaching parents child management skills, seems likely to have a stronger impact when parents have more daily contact, and leverage, with their children, relative to peers and other influences; this ratio obviously changes over the period from 7–13, the target ages for the Kazdin research program.

The roles of gender and race/ethnicity should be addressable, in principle, given that substantial proportions of the Kazdin samples have been girls and African American youngsters. Family structure also seems a potentially important focus for moderator analyses. Given that PMT relies heavily on parent involvement, and PSST includes parents in significant ways, it may matter whether the child comes from a two-parent family with both parents or caregivers involved in treatment, a single-parent family (in which the single parent is apt to have less time and energy to devote to the treatment process than would two parents combined), or a foster care situation without stable caregivers. The work of Kazdin and colleagues (see Kazdin, 1996) has already shown that single parents and minority families are more likely to drop out of treatment. It would be useful to know whether such factors also moderate outcome for those families who remain in treatment.

Mediators of Change. The search for processes that mediate change with treatment has not been a primary focus of research by the PSST group yet, but the question is certainly of great interest to Kazdin and colleagues (see e.g., Kazdin, 2000; Kazdin & Weisz, 1998). On the mediation front, one of the simplest questions may also be one of the most important: Does growth in understanding of problem-solving skills and their application mediate behavioral improvements in PSST? A parallel question for PMT is whether parents' gains in child management skills are associated with behavioral improvements in the children.

To answer such questions, researchers will need to document the degree to which children receiving PSST actually do change their problem-solving skills and their problem-solving behavior, and the degree to which parents receiving PMT change their skills and behavior. Reports of such assessment have not been featured in the work by the Kazdin group thus far. Several research findings from other sources highlight the importance of (1) assessing changes in child problem solving with PSST, (2) assessing changes in parent management practices with PMT, and (3) testing the degree to which both types of change can account for improved child behavior. At least one study that did assess problem-solving skill acquisition (Yu, Harris, Slovitz,

& Franklin, 1986) found that changes in such skills did not correlate with changes in their behavioral adjustment. This result is consistent with findings of a meta-analysis of CBT treatment studies indicating that changes in children's cognitive processes were not significantly related to changes in their behavior (Durlak et al., 1991). Kazdin et al. (1992) also reported that changes in parent behavior were not correlated with changes in child behavior, but more recent findings (Kazdin & Wassell, 2000) show moderate positive correlations between child and parent outcome measures. It is important to note that PSST includes additional components (e.g., token reinforcement of socially appropriate behavior, self-instructional training) that might, in principle, account for behavioral changes independently of the problem-solving training. So, it will be important to assess the degree to which the specific focus on problem-solving skills is the active ingredient that produces changes in children's aggressive and antisocial behavior.

Improved Outcome Assessment: Need for Direct Observations. Another area needing attention in future research is outcome assessment. The studies by the Kazdin group have relied primarily on parent and teacher checklist reports, parent daily reports, and reports by the child participants to assess outcomes. Because parents and children, and possibly the teachers (because they are contacted directly by therapists in PSST and PMT), know what treatments the children received, there is a chance that the measured outcomes are influenced somewhat by reporting artifacts. Ideally, one would like to see direct observations of child behavior at home and school, carried out by observers who do not know the children's treatment condition. When Guevremont and Foster (1993) used direct observations to assess outcomes of one problem-solving skills training program, they found considerably more modest gains than those found by Kazdin and colleagues; this suggests the potential importance of direct observational assessment by the Kazdin group or by others using their treatment approaches.

Problem-Solving Skills Training and Parent Management Training: Clinical Practice Issues

Finally, we consider issues of likely importance to practitioners who may want to consider incorporating PSST, or PSST plus PMT, into their clinical practice.

Clinical Representativeness of the Studies. Focusing first on the issue of external validity, we see a mixed picture in the studies by the Kazdin group. Participants in the early Kazdin studies were referred to an inpatient unit and treated there, and participants in the later studies were referred for outpatient care in the Yale Child Conduct Clinic. The clinic clearly has many strengths, and one of these is that the youngsters and parents treated there are community-referred and probably representative of many youths and families treated in everyday practice in service clinics. In other respects, the setting seems less representative of everyday practice. The therapists who provide PSST and PMT were selected and trained specifically for the treatment research program; they have been trained to a high standard of proficiency in these two treatments and in applied behavior analysis, and their case loads may not include the diversity that characterizes most everyday clinical practice. All this makes good sense, given the goals of the program, but it also means that we do not have sufficient experience yet to know what level of effort is required, and what level of treatment outcomes might be obtained, if the treatments were administered by representative staff in a conventional service clinic.

Implementability of the Treatment Programs. As for the PSST and PMT treatments, their use in service-oriented clinics, particularly in an era of managed care, might pose some significant challenges. Sheer duration of the treatments could be an issue. Kazdin (1996) notes that "Although treatment can be completed within a period of eight months, recruitment of cases and delays (e.g., not showing up for treatment, seasonal holidays, vacation breaks during the summer) conspire to extend the duration of the treatment to 10–12 months" (p. 392). Under managed care efficiency requirements, such lengthy treatment may be difficult to support. Therapist training requirements are also rather substantial for PSST and PMT. Therapists in the Child Conduct Clinic have master's degrees in one of the mental health professions, and then "They undergo an additional period of training of approximately 18 months. Repeated practice, viewing of sessions of others, and simulated treatment is completed before a therapist is assigned a patient. Supervision of the initial treatment case consists of viewing live sessions (through a video system) and discussing concretely all facets of the session" (Kazdin, 1996, p. 389). A more recent description (Kazdin, 2003) suggests that duration may have been reduced to about 6–12 months. Even this reduced investment in training, combined with the exclusive use of PSST and PMT, and the exclusive focus on conduct disorder, may not be feasible in some clinics. The staff-client ratio used in the Child Conduct Clinic – with one therapist for the child and one for parents – may also be hard to replicate in some productivity-conscious clinics.

On the other hand, as Kazdin (1996, pp. 402–3) has noted, the procedures his program uses to train therapists, assign them to cases, and monitor and supervise their performance could, in principle, be implemented in practice settings, and doing so might well enhance the effectiveness of the care in those settings. An important general point is that the procedures used in carefully executed treatment outcome research, although they may not be representative of usual clinical practice, may also help inform practice. That is, it may be that such procedures represent what is needed to produce very substantial benefit in many cases; the fact that procedures in conventional clinical care of children involve so much less time and expense than the research-based procedures may be one reason why the outcomes found for conventional care have not been very encouraging thus far (see Chapter 1; Bickman, 1997; Weisz et al., 1995a).

This reasoning aside, the person-power and expense associated with PSST and PMT are substantial and perhaps off-putting to clinic administrators with limited budgets and stringent productivity rules. Justifying the added expense would require strong evidence that the associated treatment gains are remarkable. As Kazdin and colleagues are careful to note in their studies, most of the children in even their best-outcome groups typically remained above the normal range in the severity of their antisocial behavior after treatment. A significant exception is found in the most recent study by Kazdin et al. (1992), in which a majority of children treated with a combination of PSST and PMT fell within the normal range by the end of treatment and at a one-year followup; it may be that such a double dose of treatment will be required to generate the striking improvements needed to persuade clinic decision makers.

Finally, an issue of practical importance to clinicians who would like to learn PSST and PMT is the availability of treatment materials and training opportunities. Although both PSST and PMT have a core set of treatment sessions (20 for PSST, 16 for PMT), and both are guided by manuals, the manuals describing the specific contents of the sessions are not readily obtainable, to date. And therapists seeking training materials and training programs may have difficulty finding either. Thus, dissemination of PSST and PMT remains a significant challenge for practitioners interested in pursuing these approaches.

How to Find Out More about PSST and PMT

Descriptions of PSST and PMT, and the rationale for each, can be found in a recent chapter by Kazdin (2003). To place the treatment programs in the context of the broader literature on conduct problems and conduct disorder, see the 1995 book by Alan E. Kazdin, *Conduct Disorder in Childhood and Adolescence* (2nd ed.; Sage), and his 1997 chapter entitled "Conduct disorder across the lifespan," appearing in the book, *Developmental Psychopathology: Perspectives on Adjustment, Risk, and Disorder* (New York: Cambridge University Press).

13

Multisystemic Therapy for Antisocial and Delinquent Youth

Like all of us, troubled children and teens are embedded within complex social systems. Each youngster's behavior reflects his or her own attributes interacting with characteristics of the family, peer group, neighborhood, school, and so forth. With antisocial and delinquent youths, there are often problems at (and between) multiple levels of the social system. Yet most of the tested treatments for conduct problems focus on only one or two of the layers. Anger management programs, for instance, focus treatment mainly on the individual youths who have problems in self-control (see Chapter 8). Other programs emphasize parent training and the parent-child relationship (see Chapters 9, 10, and 11). Still other programs focus on the family system (see Chapter 9) or pair youth training with parent training (see Chapter 12). In contrast to these approaches, multisystemic therapy (MST), to which we now turn, is an attempt to reach out and touch most of the major social systems that envelop antisocial and delinquent youth.

Included in the purview of MST are such social systems as the youth's family, family support network, school, neighborhood, peer group, and in many cases, probation officer and juvenile justice system. The MST therapist has a complex job, one that may not include much time in a clinic office and may not entail waiting for troubled clients to come in seeking help. Instead, much of the therapist's work day is spent in the settings where the young clients live their lives, and the people with whom the MST therapist talks include many of those who touch the young clients' lives. The particular intervention procedures used in any individual case are drawn from an array of empirically based techniques, most often those described in this book. As might be expected, this kind of multisetting, multimethod approach is complex; it requires considerable skill and ingenuity on the part of the therapist, and often a skilled supervisor. In this chapter, we examine the procedures used in MST, and the evidence on their effects.

Ecological Model

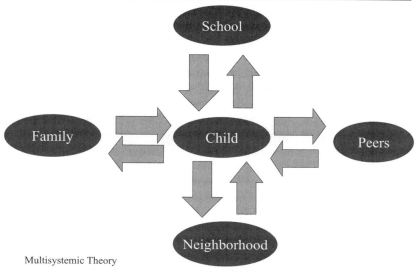

Multisystemic Theory

FIGURE 13.1. Part of the ecological model that guides multisystemic therapy. The individual youth is surrounded by elements of the social environment that influence the youth's behavior and are in turn influenced by the youth. [Reprinted with permission from Scott W. Henggeler.]

Multisystemic Therapy: Conceptual Basis and Procedural Overview

A core idea at the heart of MST is the notion that youth antisocial behavior is multidetermined – that is, shaped and maintained by multiple elements of the youth's social world – and that the impact is reciprocal, in that the youth both receives and exerts influence. This perspective is illustrated in Figure 13.1. The arrows in the figure reflect the reciprocity of influence between youth and parts of the social environment. Naturally, the situation is more complex than this figure can capture. There are many more environmental systems at play than those shown in the figure; for example, extended family members, religious leaders, various professional agencies, and even parole officers may play important roles. In addition, the various individuals and systems to which the youth and family are connected interact with one another. Antisocial behavior can result from this interplay of youth, key individuals, and social systems, but figuring out how is part of the detective work of MST. Once the MST therapist has an understanding of how the individuals and systems have converged to produce undesirable behavior, the task becomes one of reforming the environment, inducing change in individuals and systems at points where there is some give and where change can have a desirable impact on the youth.

The theoretical foundation underlying MST is a combination of general systems theory (von Bertalanffy, 1968) and Bronfenbrenner's (1979) theory of social ecology. A major intellectual contribution of systems theory has been its rich conceptualization of causality. In contrast to more binary, mechanistic, and linear causal notions, systems theory describes causality in terms of the reciprocal influence of multiple interacting forces. Thus, instead of arguing that A causes B, which in turn causes C, the systems theorist argues that A, B, and C all influence one another, and that any specific behavior is likely to have multiple causes, some arising from the interplay of A, B, and C. Such thinking has influenced multiple disciplines within the sciences, including schools of psychotherapy that emphasize causal interplay among members of the family system rather than focusing on "pathology" within an individual (see e.g., Bateson, 1972; Minuchin, 1974). Applying this interplay notion to the case of a delinquent youth, for example, a therapist might consider not only how parental disciplinary practices influence the youth, but also how the youth's behavior influences the parents, and what broader function the youth's behavior may serve in the family system, including siblings and extended family.

Bronfenbrenner's (1979) theory of social ecology also contributed importantly to the development of MST. In Bronfenbrenner's view, the individual's ecosystem is "a set of nested structures, each inside the next, like a set of Russian dolls" (p. 3). The innermost doll is the developing individual, who is both influenced by and continually influencing other elements or layers of the ecosystem. While this supposition is also an element of systems theory as applied to family therapy, the social ecological perspective is notable for the emphasis it places on not only family systems but also layers of the environment that are more distal from the child. For example, a youth's school achievement might depend as much on ties between the school and home as on what is directly taught to the child in class; and a youth's social behavior might be influenced by environmental forces that the child does not touch directly, such as the parents' place of employment, or the parents' experience as victims of racism. One other principle of Bronfenbrenner's (1979) social ecology that has special significance for MST is that an individual's development and behavior can only be fully understood when viewed within its naturally occurring context. Following this credo, the ideal MST therapist enters and works hard to understand the multiple settings in which troubled and troubling youths live their lives.

Multisystemic Therapy: In Brief

Designed for . . . . Seriously antisocial, delinquent youth, at high risk of out-of-home placement (e.g., in a corrections facility), often with prior arrests; ages 12–18

Number of sessions . . . . . Highly variable; sessions are combined with various brief contacts (some by phone) and diverse environmental interventions; typical treatment duration is about 60 hours (plus phone contact and collateral meetings) spanning 3–5 months

Session length . . . . Highly variable; range is about 10 minutes to several hours, with mean > one hour

Session participants . . . . Therapist with parents, with youth and parents, with youth and family, with family members and extra-family systems (e.g., teachers, neighbors)

Theoretical orientation . . . . . Emphasizes empirically tested procedures that are mainly behavioral (operant), cognitive-behavioral, and pragmatic family therapies

Treatment elements:

1. Therapist carries out assessment, to map (a) youth, family, and system strengths; and (b) the connection between the youth's identified problems and his or her social systems (family, school, neighborhood, peer group, etc.).
2. Therapist together with parents, youth, and others in the social systems, designs interventions to help the social systems support responsible youth behavior and discourage irresponsible behavior.
3. Therapist has sessions with family members, to coordinate implementation of the planned interventions, evaluate their progress, adjust them as needed.
4. Therapist has multiple weekly contacts with family, in person or by phone, and is available to family through cell phone/pager at all times, for consultation on problems, crises.
5. Weekly supervision with an MST expert, and on-call supervision available to therapist at all times, through cell phone/pager.
6. Establish family connections to community support systems, and introduce other changes to support staying power and generalization of treatment effects.

Treatment classified by Task Force as . . . . Probably Efficacious (Brestan & Eyberg, 1998)

Key resource for potential users . . . . . Henggeler, S. W., Schoenwald, S. K., Borduin, C. M., Rowland, M. D., & Cunningham, P. B. (1998). *Multisystemic Treatment of Antisocial Behavior in Children and Adolescents*. New York: Guilford. Henggeler, S. W. & Schoenwald, S. K. (1998). *Multisystemic Therapy Supervisory Manual: Promoting Quality Assurance at the Clinical Level*. Charleston, SC: Family Services Research Center, Medical University of South Carolina.

Multisystemic Therapy: Treatment Procedures

The specific procedures used by MST therapists vary widely from case to case, with the particulars depending on input from the therapist, supervisor, and key figures in the youth's social environment. Thus, in contrast to most of the evidence-based treatments, MST is not guided by a detailed manual that prescribes the contents of each treatment session and specifies the sequence of procedures to be followed (see Scientific Issues, later in this chapter). Indeed, there is much more to MST than formal sessions; a therapist's typical workday may consist of numerous contacts with a variety of key players in family, school, and other systems, developing, refining, assessing, tweaking, and reassessing various changes designed to redirect the young client. A central feature of MST is its emphasis on changing the social ecology of youngsters and their families, so as to discourage problem behavior and promote positive adjustment. Here we discuss how this emphasis shapes practice.

Techniques and Principles of the MST Program. The MST therapist works to create change in the environmental systems in which the youth is embedded. The specific techniques and procedures used to create these changes tend to be those supported in the scientific literature on treatment outcome. In most cases, the treated youth lives at home during treatment, though often there is an imminent risk of out-of-home placement (e.g., incarceration, group home, psychiatric hospital), and preventing such placement is frequently a goal of MST. Thus, an intensive family-based treatment delivery model is stressed. The model includes the following elements:

- Low case loads, typically no more than three to six families for a full-time therapist
- Placing interventions within the family's natural environment (e.g., home, school, neighborhood)
- Time-limited treatment, typically three to five months per family
- Support teams of therapists, with three to four practitioners per team
- Scheduling of meetings at the family's convenience, including evenings and weekends
- Multiple contacts each week (in person or by phone) between therapist and family
- Therapists available to the families 24 hours, 7 days per week

This level of intensity and therapist commitment may sound expensive, but Henggeler and colleagues (1998, see pp. 43–4 and Chapters 9–10) make the case that costs are actually much lower than the residential treatment alternatives often used with the severe cases they treat. Moreover, they argue, having therapists do their work in the youth's home enhances the relationship of therapist to family and generates particularly valid assessment of treatment progress (e.g., direct in-home observation of whether parental discipline and youth compliance have improved).

Given the flexibility and case-specific nature of the treatment procedures used in MST, perhaps the best way to describe the assessment and treatment approach is to discuss the nine general principles (from Henggeler et al., 1998) that define how MST is intended to be done.

1. *Use assessment to understand the fit between youth problems and social context.* In carrying out assessment, the MST therapist proceeds inductively, gathering information on the youth's situation, strengths, and needs, as seen by the youth, family members, peers, school personnel, and others in the neighborhood or community, and then integrating those inputs into a picture of how the youth's behaviors make sense within their context. Formal psychological testing is rarely a part of MST assessment; instead, discussion and direct observation in the natural settings of the youth's life are nearly always used. How might these approaches make serious conduct problems understandable? As an example, a teenage girl's violent behavior may begin to make sense as the therapist learns that her parents model physical violence when they argue, that both parents and school staff use ineffective disciplinary procedures, and that the girl's peer group admires her violence and rewards her with deference. The therapist integrates such information to form hypotheses about the youth's behavior, and to design (with the family's help) intervention procedures that will create a mismatch between undesirable behavior and the youth's social milieu. For this violent girl, such interventions might well include working with parents to establish ground rules for their own arguments (e.g., not in front of their daughter, and no physical aggression), to teach them effective behavior management methods (a la Patterson or Webster-Stratton – see Chapters 9 and 11), and to limit and closely monitor their daughter's peer contacts, ruling out association with peers who support her violence.

2. *Emphasize the positive and build on strengths.* Therapists who work with multiproblem youth and families can easily become preoccupied with the negative – for example, the parents' drug use, the youth's profanity and disrespect, the run-down and dangerous neighborhood – and this can create a negative perspective that spills over into interactions with the youth and family. To counter this tendency, and foster positive collaboration with families, MST therapists are taught to identify positives and strengths, to reframe negative information in realistically positive ways, to find things the youth or family is doing right and praise the success, and to generally present a "can do" attitude. Despite numerous negatives, strengths may be found in a family's cohesiveness, a youngster's athletic ability, or the

availability of a strong, stable, and loving grandparent. In addition, even parents who have poor child behavior management skills can be "caught" setting limits or rewarding appropriate behavior by their child, and praised for doing so. It is common for distressed multi-problem families to hear the problems reviewed, and to grow pessimistic; one job of the MST therapist is to provide hope by modeling an upbeat, optimistic attitude that can generate energy for change.

3. *Design interventions to promote responsible behavior and discourage irresponsible behavior by family members.* MST emphasizes encouraging responsible behavior much more than curing psychopathology. The therapist works on helping parents meet their responsibilities as role models and limit-setters in their children's lives. Discouraging parents' uncontrolled anger outbursts and teaching them solid principles of child behavior management fall into this category. In addition, the therapist works with adults in the young person's environment to structure contingencies that will foster responsible youth behavior. The guidelines for contingency setting are consistent with behavioral parent training principles covered in Chapter 9, but MST also stresses giving the youth input into rules and ensuring that the youth understands the rationale behind rules.

4. *Make interventions present-focused, action-oriented, and specific-goal-directed.* In contrast to treatments that unearth and focus on events in the past, sometimes the distant past, MST emphasizes the here and now. Although a previous experience of child abuse may be very significant for an aggressive teen client, the MST therapist would be less likely to focus on that experience than on current contingencies in the environment that appear to sustain the aggression. On the other hand, the previous abuse might well be a focus if its effects are central to understanding the youngster's current functioning or if they undermine current treatment. MST is also action-oriented. It involves repeated trials of this sequence: (1) hypothesize, (2) plan a change, (3) try the plan, (4) evaluate its outcome. Thus, passivity is discouraged, some problem-solving strategy is always being tried, and results are continually being assessed. This serves to keep the family engaged and reinforced by ongoing evidence that things are changing. The MST therapist also works with the family to target specific goals, goals of two types. *Overarching goals* are those the family aims to attain by the end of treatment (e.g., Julius will pass tenth grade). *Intermediate goals* reflect the nitty-gritty details needed if the overarching goal is to be attained (e.g., finish homework every night, study for tests, parents reward Julius for his academic efforts, parents talk with Julius's teacher at least once each month). How to tell if a goal is specific enough to meet MST criteria? Find out whether therapist, parents, and youth can all tell whether the goal has been met.

5. *Target sequences of behavior within and between parts of the ecosystem that maintain problem behavior.* Because serious problems in youth usually reflect the interplay of multiple layers in the ecosystem, the solution to those problems is apt to require intervention within and between layers. Accordingly, interpersonal transactions are seen within the MST model as the key mechanism by which treatment goals are achieved. For example, MST therapists often try to empower parents to separate their child from deviant peers while facilitating connections with prosocial peers, and building a good working relationship between their child and school personnel.

6. *Make interventions developmentally sensitive.* MST therapists aim for interventions that are sensitive to the developmental level and functional capacities of the key players – both the youth and others in the surround who are enlisted to play a role. Thus, while goals for a 13-year-old may appropriately focus on school achievements, school-related goals may seem unrealistic for a 17-year-old who needs job skills to enter an adult world. And a treatment that involves keeping a daily diary would be inappropriate for a youth who can barely read and write. Developmental considerations are important for the adults in the youth's treatment plan, as well. For example, a very young mother may be closer developmentally to her child than to most adults, and may tend to relate to her child like a competitive older sibling. Grandparents, even if they are good at grandparenting, may lack the energy needed to be primary caregivers to delinquent youth; so, if a youth's parents are incapable of providing appropriate guidance, a treatment plan might entail caregiving roles for an aunt or uncle, with grandparents in an ancillary helping role.

7. *Structure interventions so as to require daily or weekly effort by family members.* MST client families are not seen as passive recipients of the therapist's expertise. Rather, family members help design the change process, and make it happen, through regular effortful behavior, ideally every day. In one case, for example (see Henggeler et al., 1998), an adolescent girl was given daily household chores, and her grandmother monitored their completion daily, providing rewards as earned; on any day when chores were not done properly, the grandmother called the girl's custodial aunts to jointly select an appropriate consequence from a menu of options. In addition, the aunts monitored the girl's social behavior at school via daily contact with school personnel, and meted out appropriate consequences on a daily basis. The aunts also maintained daily contact with the girl's mother, to shore up her efforts to abstain from drug use. In addition, the therapist was in daily contact with either the grandmother or an aunt for regular updates and consultation on any problems.

Such daily monitoring and troubleshooting helps ensure that family members and the therapist stay on the same page, share common and timely information, and quickly detect any nonadherence to the treatment plan. The daily contact also provides ongoing outcome assessment, and frequent opportunities for positive feedback to family members. These daily encounters underscore an empowering message: family members are the primary agents of change.

8. *Assess intervention effects continuously and from multiple perspectives.* The frequent, often daily contact among participants in treatment helps to ensure continuous evaluation of how the treatment elements are working, and whether retooling is needed to prevent slippage. Validity of the evaluation is enhanced by drawing from multiple perspectives – the youth, family members, key figures in the school and neighborhood, and physical indicators as needed (e.g., random urine screens to check for drug use).

9. *Promote generalization and maintenance of gains by empowering caregivers to address family members' needs.* The Achilles' heel of many treatments is that their effects fade quickly after termination, once the therapist is no longer involved. The MST approach is designed to tackle this problem by shifting the power to fix problems from the therapist to the caregivers over the course of treatment. Therapists are taught to refrain from setting goals for a family and from riding in on a white horse and creating change through the force of their own skills and personality. Instead, the therapist's role is to collaborate with caregivers and nurture their ability to design solutions and see them through to success (e.g., teaching problem-solving skills that can be applied to a broad variety of problems – see Chapter 12). In areas where the family members cannot go it alone and clearly need help from others, the therapist works to ensure that those others are enlisted from the family's natural environment (e.g., extended family members, friends, neighbors, members of a local church), so the help can be sustained when the therapist is no longer there. Indeed, treatment should not end until those resources are in place and working well.

Supervision of MST therapists. Supervision plays a central role in MST. Indeed, one of the most important documents in the MST armamentarium is the manual describing the supervision process (Henggeler & Schoenwald, 1998). Typically, a team of three to four clinicians meets with an experienced MST supervisor weekly for 1.5–2 hours, to discuss 12–15 cases. For therapists working in remote sites, supervision is done by phone. Questions like these may be discussed in supervision:

• How does this youngster's behavior make sense in the context of his or her social ecosystem?

- What repeated patterns of family interaction have you seen that might explain the behavior?
- How do the caregivers and youth interact with community, school, and employers?
- What strengths do you see in the youth, family members, and others in the social system that could be used to support positive change?
- What are the family's goals for treatment?
- What is your treatment plan, and are family members invested in this plan? If not, what can be done to get you and the family in sync? (Alter the plan? Strengthen your alliance with family members?)
- What have the youth and family members done this week to achieve intermediate goals?
- What have you done this week to support the family in achieving these goals?
- If there are problems in implementing intervention plans, or the intervention is not producing change, what is the problem, and what must be done to address the problem?
- What is being done to build an alliance with social resources (e.g., school personnel, church members) the family will need for support when you (the therapist) are no longer involved?

The supervision process generates case-specific recommendations intended to maximize outcomes for each client family. It is also a venue for monitoring therapist adherence to core MST principles. More broadly, supervision is a therapist development tool, a way to help clinicians grow the conceptual and behavioral skills needed to implement MST effectively.

Individually tailored contents of MST interventions, rooted in the empirical literature. Thus far, we have emphasized primarily the principles and structure of MST. The content is more difficult to cover in any comprehensive way, because content is tailored to fit the people and circumstances of each case, and thus varies from case to case. As a general rule, the MST therapist works with the key players in a case to identify goals, and identifies treatment methods that the empirical literature suggests will be effective in reaching those goals. In principle, then, the therapist draws from a treatment method armamentarium that is as large as the empirical literature; in practice, over the course of its evolution, MST has come to emphasize a subset of the tested treatment methods – for example, operant, cognitive-behavioral, and certain systems-oriented approaches. Thus, when a youngster's delinquent behavior can be linked partly to poor parenting skills, as is often the case, the MST therapist may well structure interventions patterned after the kinds of parent training procedures discussed in Chapters 9 and 12 of this book. Those procedures, emphasizing operant principles and the judicious use of reinforcement contingencies, are apt to be combined with a cognitive and social emphasis. For example, the therapist may explore the youth's cognitions that lead to violent outbursts, and also parents' cognitions that may interfere with effective discipline (e.g., "The only way to get a child to behave is to beat him."). The social emphasis will likely include a search for others who can encourage and support a parent's effort to change disciplinary practices.

Often, a youth's problems will be connected, in part, to problems in the parents' relationship. When this is the case, the MST therapist draws techniques from the empirical literature on marital therapy (see Baucom et al., 1998), to improve communication and problem solving and thus enhance the relationship. Youngsters referred for MST may be bonded with delinquent peers who model and reinforce antisocial behavior, and they may have troubled, often volatile relationships with nondelinquent peers; so, the MST therapist may need intervention procedures derived from the literature on peer relations and social problem solving (e.g., Kazdin, 1996; see Chapter 12). Interventions to address academic deficiencies require a different base of literature (e.g., Lyon & Cutting, 1998). MST-referred youth or their parents can also manifest a variety of individual dysfunctions, even including depression and anxiety; for these dysfunctions, the MST therapist may embark on individual sessions patterned after such empirically tested procedures as cognitive behavioral therapy (see Chapters 3, 4, and 5) and using such familiar procedures as structured sequential problem solving (i.e., describe the problem, determine goals, generate alternative solutions, evaluate the solutions, choose one of them, design and practice a plan, implement the plan – see similar steps in Chapter 12).

An important point to emphasize is that, even when the MST therapist derives specific techniques from specific empirically supported therapies, the way the techniques are applied will be adjusted to fit the core MST principles outlined earlier. Thus, for example, even marital therapy or CBT for depression will be structured so that it targets clearly defined observable problems, is present-focused, addresses events within and between layers of the social system, requires daily or weekly effort (e.g., homework), and is monitored regularly though daily therapist contacts (for case illustrations, see Henggeler et al., 1998, Chapters 3–8).

Multisystemic Therapy: Outcome Studies Testing the Effects

Across a series of outcome studies, Henggeler and colleagues have shown beneficial effects of MST on several kinds of outcomes among youth and families confronting several different types of problems. The most substantial and well-replicated effects have involved families of seriously delinquent youth, with the typical participant being a youngster who has been arrested at least once. There are three core criteria for success with such youth: at home, in school, and out of trouble (Scott Henggeler, personal communication, 1997). Although delinquent youth are the primary focus of MST research, and of this chapter, we will note, in passing, a few of the additional applications of this treatment approach that have been put to empirical test.

Early Studies and the Evolution of MST: Delinquency, Child Maltreatment, and Sex Offenses. *Initial MST study: a quasi-experiment with inner-city delinquent youth.* The first study of MST (Henggeler et al., 1986) used a quasi-experimental design to test the treatment with inner-city delinquent youth averaging about 15 years of age (84% male; 65% African American, 35% Caucasian; 62% father-absent; mean family size 6.4 members). Referred from the Memphis (Tennessee) Metro Youth Diversion Project, the youths averaged about two arrests each, with a mean seriousness rating of 9.1 per arrest, on a scale in which assault/battery was 8 and murder was 17. In this initial study, MST (then called family-ecological treatment) was provided to all of a referred sample, whose outcomes were then compared to those of a nonrandom comparison group – that is, Memphis youths receiving usual treatment through the correctional program, with family demographics and arrest records resembling those of the MST sample. At the end of treatment, the MST group showed fewer behavior problems on all dimensional scales of a parent-report checklist, and more positive changes on multiple observational measures of youth-mother interaction, than the usual treatment group.

Although the nonrandom design of this study limits conclusions that can be drawn from the findings, the study contributed importantly to the evolution of MST, in at least two ways. Henggeler et al. (1986) originally conceived their treatment as office-based, but many families of the young offenders would not come to the therapists' offices; this dilemma prompted the home-based, community-based model of treatment delivery that has persisted to this day. In addition, the findings of this study, showing a decline in youth behavior problems coincident with observed improvements in mother-youth interaction patterns, supported the notion that intervention based in the family and addressing the family system might well be associated with positive changes in youth behavior.

First randomized trial, with maltreating parents. The first truly randomized trial of MST (Brunk et al., 1987) was focused not on youthful offenders but on abusive and neglectful parents of children in the elementary school age range (averaging about 8 years old). Some 76% of the identified parents were mothers, 55% of the identified maltreated children were boys, and the families were 57% Caucasian, 43% African American. The study pitted MST against an unusually strong comparison condition: behavioral parent training, based in part on Patterson's work (see Chapter 9). Parents in both treatment conditions reported decreased psychiatric symptomatology, reduced overall stress, and reduced severity of identified problems, and parent training proved superior on some measures. However, observational measures of parent-child interaction showed better outcomes for MST than for parent training, particularly on dimensions the literature links to risk of maltreatment. Specifically, the MST-treated families, compared to parent-training families, showed more effective parental management of child behavior, less passive noncompliance by children, and greater responsiveness of formerly neglectful parents toward their children.

Testing MST with juvenile sex offenders. In one other early study, Borduin et al. (1990) presented what may well be the only published randomized trial of treatment for juvenile sex offenders. The offenders were all boys, averaging 14 years of age (62% Caucasian, 38% African American); they had committed crimes ranging from exhibitionism to rape and molestation of young boys and girls. The youths and families were randomly assigned to home-based MST (37 hours on average) or to individual outpatient counseling provided by community-based mental health professionals (45 hours on average). Assessment of recidivism rates over the three years after treatment showed that fewer youths in the MST condition had been rearrested for sexual crimes and that the frequency of sexual crimes was lower in the MST condition (means: 0.12 vs. 1.62). Sex offending is widely regarded as highly treatment-resistant; this study represents a rare challenge to that pessimistic view.

First randomized trial of MST versus usual care in the juvenile justice system. Although MST has been tried with maltreating parents and youthful sex offenders, the most common application of the treatment is with delinquent youth who have committed primarily nonsexual offenses. In the first article reporting a randomized trial with delinquent youth of this type, Henggeler et al. (1992) compared MST to the usual care provided through the South Carolina Department of Youth Services (see next section). The treated youth averaged 15 years of age (77% were boys; 56% African American, 42% Caucasian, and 2% Hispanic American), and had more than three previous arrests (all including at least one felony) and more than nine weeks of prior incarceration. More than half had been arrested for violent crime, including manslaughter, assault and battery with intent to kill, and aggravated assault.

Families randomly assigned to MST had an average of 13 weeks of treatment, including 33 hours of direct contact with their therapist. Families randomly assigned to the Department of Youth Services (DYS) usual treatment condition all received court orders that included specific stipulations (e.g., curfew, school attendance) and were monitored by probation officers, who met with the youths at least once a month. Posttreatment and follow-up comparisons showed that MST was more effective than usual DYS services at reducing rates of criminal activity and institutionalization. At about 60 weeks after referral, group comparisons showed that MST families reported greater cohesion than the usual services group, who actually reported a decline in cohesion over time. Importantly, the MST group had about half as many arrests and far fewer weeks incarcerated (5.8 vs. 16.2) than the usual services group. At 60 weeks, 68% of the usual services group had been incarcerated, compared to only 20% of the MST group. There was also evidence of reduced drug use in the MST group, compared to the DYS services group (see Henggeler, Borduin et al., 1991). And findings of a 120-week followup (Henggeler, Melton et al., 1993) suggested that the MST intervention had genuine holding power. By the end of this follow-up period, the MST group had half the rearrest rate of the usual services group (39% of the MST group remained unarrested versus only 20% of the DYS group).

Second randomized trial with delinquent youth: the Missouri Delinquency Project. In a second randomized trial with seriously delinquent youth, Borduin et al. (1995) used a considerably stronger comparison condition and a longer follow-up period to assess effects with a young offender sample in Missouri. As in the Henggeler et al. (1992) study in South Carolina, the youths averaged 15 years of age (68% were boys; 70% were Caucasian, 30% African American). All had arrest records (minimum of two arrests, average of four); average severity of offenses was at the level of assault and battery, and all participants had been incarcerated for at least four weeks previously.

These severely delinquent youth were randomly assigned to either MST or an individual therapy intervention that "was selected to represent the usual community treatment for juvenile offenders" (Borduin et al., 1995, p. 571) in the judicial district of this study, and arguably in many other judicial districts as well (see Henggeler, 1989). The therapists for the individual therapy condition were from local mental health outpatient agencies and from the treatment services branch of the juvenile court; their theoretical orientations were an eclectic blend of psychodynamic, client-centered, and behavioral approaches. Focusing on personal, family, and academic issues, the individual therapists "offered support, feedback, and encouragement for behavior change" (p. 571). A core difference between the two treatment conditions was that individual therapy focused on the individual youth whereas MST focused on the systems in which the youth was embedded. Notably, individual therapy cases received more hours of treatment than did MST cases (29 vs. 24 hours for therapy completers).

Parent report measures and direct observations of parent-child interactions, shortly after treatment ended, showed much more favorable results for the MST youngsters and parents than for cases treated with individual therapy. MST cases showed declines in youth behavior problems and in parent psychopathology, and positive changes in observed parent-youth interaction – including increased supportiveness and decreased conflict and hostility. By contrast, the individual therapy group either showed no change or grew worse on these measures from pre- to posttherapy.

While these findings were valuable, the most important practical objective of the Borduin et al. (1995) study was to reduce criminal recidivism in youth who were clearly at high risk for reoffending and rearrest. To assess outcomes on this front, Borduin et al. compiled arrest records over an unusually long follow-up period of four years posttreatment; the evidence they collected provided strong support for MST. The overall comparison of all who had begun MST versus all who had begun individual therapy showed much lower rates of rearrest for the MST group (26% vs. 71%). In a particularly interesting breakdown of the arrest data, Borduin et al. presented "survival curves" showing the percent who remained unarrested at various intervals posttreatment, and with curves drawn separately for those who completed MST versus individual therapy, those who began but dropped out of MST versus individual therapy, and those who had been eligible for participation but refused treatment from the outset of the project. Comparison of these survival curves, presented here in Figure 13.2, showed that both MST completers, and MST dropouts, showed lower rates of rearrest than the remaining three groups. Interestingly, even those who had started MST but dropped out showed a marginally more favorable survival pattern ($p < .09$) than those who had started and completed individual therapy.

Additional analyses of the Borduin et al. (1995) data revealed a number of other encouraging patterns. First, even those MST youth who had been rearrested during the follow-up period were arrested less often, and for less serious and less violent offenses, than those youth in the individual therapy condition who had been rearrested. Second, the effects of the MST intervention were similar across different age levels (12–17 years at the beginning of the project), genders, racial groups (Caucasian vs. African American), and pretreatment arrest histories. Third, as reported by Henggeler et al. (1991), MST youth were less likely than individual therapy youth to be rearrested for substance-related offenses (4% vs. 16%).

MST as an alternative to psychiatric hospitalization. Since the publication of the important studies by Henggeler et al. (1992) and Borduin et al. (1995), the MST research group has continued to generate new evidence on the range and limits of treatment application. For example, recent studies have assessed the viability of home-based MST as an alternative to inpatient hospitalization for psychiatric emergencies (Henggeler et al., 1999b; Schoenwald, Ward et al., 2000). Youngsters ages 10–17 (mean 13.0 years; 65% male; 64% African American, 34% Caucasian, 1% Asian American) who had been approved for emergency hospitalization because of suicidal or homicidal ideation, psychosis, or threat of harm to self or others, were randomly assigned to be admitted to the hospital or to receive MST. At outcome assessment, about four months later, 57% of the MST group had avoided hospitalization altogether, and total days in the hospital had been reduced by 72% for the full MST group compared to the initial

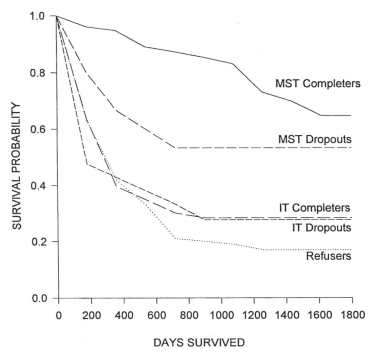

FIGURE 13.2. Rates of arrest survival (i.e., remaining unarrested) over a five-year period following treatment in the Missouri Delinquency Project. Youths who completed Multisystemic Therapy (MST) were least likely to be rearrested, followed by those who began but dropped out of MST. Higher rates of rearrest were found for youths who received individual therapy (IT), regardless of whether they completed or dropped out, and for youths whose parents refused treatment of any kind. From Borduin, C. M., Mann, B. J., Cone, L. T., Henggeler, S. W., Fucci, B. R., Blaske, D. M., & Williams, R. A. (1995). Multisystemic treatment of serious juvenile offenders: Long-term prevention of criminality and violence. *Journal of Consulting and Clinical Psychology, 63,* 569–578. Copyright © 1995 by the American Psychological Association. Reprinted with permission.

hospitalization condition; and MST costs were slightly lower than costs in the hospitalization condition ($5,954 vs. $6,174). MST proved superior in reducing youngsters' externalizing symptoms and improving family functioning and school attendance, and in generating consumer satisfaction; but hospitalization was linked to bigger gains in youths' self-esteem. Other research has focused on how outcomes are influenced by the degree of therapist adherence to MST principles, and on how transportable the treatment model is to therapists not directly supervised by the treatment developers. We will discuss the findings of this work under Scientific Issues later in this chapter.

Summary of the Clinical Trials Evidence. The base of evidence on MST and its effects is substantial, and notable for the diversity of problems with which the treatment program has shown beneficial effects. Best known for its power to reduce recidivism among juvenile offenders, MST has also been shown to reduce illicit substance use, to reduce sex offenses, to change patterns of interaction between maltreating parents and their children in ways likely to reduce the risk of maltreatment, and to produce better outcomes than hospitalization for youth experiencing psychiatric emergencies. A particular strength of the evidence on reduction in arrests is the long-term follow-up periods over which effects have been demonstrated, suggesting a holding power unmatched by other treatments in the field. Another significant strength of the work is that MST has been compared not to inert no-treatment or waitlist conditions, but rather to active alternatives, some of which – (individual therapy in Borduin et al. (1995), inpatient hospitalization in Henggeler et al. (1999b) and Schoenwald, Ward et al. (2000)) – represent strong doses of what youngsters would ordinarily receive in the absence of any research project.

What about Sal? Applying Multisystemic Therapy

Sal's situation illustrates the concept of multidetermination, discussed earlier, and fits well within the precepts of general systems theory (von Bertalanffy, 1968) and social ecology (Bronfenbrenner, 1979). Among the multiple elements of Sal's social system that may play causal or maintaining roles in his current behavior are an uninvolved father who presents a poor role model for an adolescent boy, a mother who lacks both parental authority and child management skills, a mother and father whose poor marital relationship undermines their capacity to collaborate as parents, school personnel who have dealt with Sal by punishment and suspension but not with a systematic plan, and inadequate collaboration between school and parents. In the center of this system is Sal, who has never developed study skills and thus does poorly in his schoolwork, and whose attitude and combative style have become entrenched. His cognitive set to interpret ambiguous social events in a negative or threatening way has helped fuel an explosive, aggressive style that has led to rejection by most of his prosocial peers. By default, he has connected to deviant peers, who provide both role modeling and reinforcement for his own deviant behavior. This kind of systemic dilemma is grist for an MST therapist's mill, as we can illustrate by imagining that Sal's behavior with his antisocial peers has led to an arrest for assault, and that the judge in the case gives Sal's family the option of home-based MST as an alternative to placing Sal in a juvenile facility. The choice was an easy one for Sal's mother.

Although she is relieved to have the MST option, Sal's mother doesn't know quite what to expect when the therapist visits the family for the first time. One of her first impressions is that the therapist seems to respect rather than blame the family, and to sympathize with their dilemma. In fact, the therapist seems to see Sal's behavior as the result of many different factors, some of which are not even in the family. As for the individual family members, the therapist asks them to say what their goals are for this process. Sal's mother can't remember being asked this question by any of the other specialists she has seen. She is stunned, and touched, to hear her husband say, "I wish I could be a better dad for Sal."

The therapist sets out to learn about the different systems that touch on Sal's life, by reviewing records at school and home, meeting with Sal and the key players in his social system (e.g., family members, school personnel, and even some of Sal's peers), directly observing social exchanges (e.g., Sal's interactions with his mother, peers, and staff at school), and developing a picture of how Sal's behavior makes sense within its social context. To the therapist, it makes sense that Sal would connect with deviant peers because they are the only ones who appear to accept him, and there are no negative consequences for associating with them. His aggressive behavior makes sense because it is rewarded by the compliance and deference of the youngsters he threatens, it is supported by his deviant peer group, it is one of the few kinds of behavior at which he currently excels and which thus give him a feeling of mastery, it leads to punishment by school staff in a form that Sal actually finds rewarding (i.e., suspension, so that he does not have to go to school), and it leads to no significant negative consequences at home. In these and other respects, Sal's behavior fits his social ecology well.

As part of the assessment process, the MST therapist prepares a summary of the initial goals of the treatment participants, and of strengths and weaknesses in each layer of the youth's social system. Here is a partial list of the goals:

Initial Goals/Desired Outcomes

Participant	*Goal*
1. Sal	Mother to "get off my case," quit nagging and complaining.
	Father and Uncle Al to do things with me.
	School staff to stop watching me all the time, and stop blaming me for stuff.
2. Mother	No more school suspensions for Sal.
	Sal to "listen to me, and do what I say."
	Husband to help control Sal.
3. Father	Wife and Sal to stop bickering, arguing.
	Be a better dad for Sal.
4. Uncle Al	Help Sal get on track so he doesn't "waste his life."
5. School staff	Stop Sal's extreme aggressive behavior; otherwise, remove him from the school permanently.

The summary of strengths and weaknesses focuses on features at each level of the youth's system that might support positive change, and those that might undermine efforts to change. A partial summary might look like this:

Individual (Sal). *Strengths.* History of above-average grades in elementary school (suggests capacity to pass academic work); physical strength and better-than-average athletic ability; loves to work on cars.

Weaknesses/Needs. Explosive temper, starts fights at school, history of suspensions. Does not comply with school rules, including homework. Disrespects and disobeys mother. Hangs out with risky peers.

Family. *Strengths.* Mother works, graduated from high school, provides for basic needs of family, loves Sal and wants to help him succeed in life. Father is a Vietnam veteran who has been drinking too much ever since returning from the war with an injury that provides disability payments. He wants to be a better father, and wants Sal to grow up to "make more of his life than I did." The fact that he is home much of the day could be an advantage if he gets engaged in helping with Sal. Uncle Al, who Sal likes and respects, is a self-employed auto mechanic who makes a reasonable living, cares about Sal, wants to help him, and has a house and repair shop near Sal's house.

Weaknesses/Needs. Mother lacks confidence and knowledge of child behavior management principles, and has lost control of Sal. Father is uninvolved, withdrawn into beer drinking, poor role model, and thus far has not devoted energy to making things better. The marital relationship between mother and father is unsatisfying to both and hampers parental teamwork in dealing with Sal. Uncle Al, though a potential resource, does not know how to help Sal.

School. *Strengths.* Deals decisively with aggressive behavior. One teacher and one coach have taken a special interest in Sal. School is near Sal's home.

Weaknesses/Needs. Principal has threatened permanent expulsion; deals with Sal through punishment only. History of negative interactions between school staff and Sal, and little history of working together with Sal's mother to solve problems.

Community. *Strengths.* Neighbors next door and across the street like Sal's mother, sympathize with her, and are willing to help. Nearby youth center has free sports and social activities closely supervised by adults. County mental health department is sponsoring a free program called the Community Reinforcement Approach (CRA) for substance abuse, at a nearby mental health center; evidence on this program suggests it might help Sal's father.

Weaknesses/Needs. Some of Sal's antisocial peers live nearby. A drug-dealing corner is three blocks from Sal's house, and there is gang graffiti on walls in the neighborhood.

Working from such information – on goals, strengths, and weaknesses – the MST therapist, Sal, Sal's mother and father, Uncle Al, and the supportive coach and teacher from Sal's school, develop a plan for how to proceed. Consistent with the second and third core principles of MST (discussed earlier in this chapter), the therapist's contacts with participants are designed to promote responsible behavior by building on systemic strengths like those noted here, and by fitting intervention objectives to identified goals and strengths of the participants. These ideas are put into action in several ways in Sal's case. Here are a few examples.

Intervention Elements. *Focus on the family, using behavioral and cognitive-behavioral principles.* The most important system in Sal's life is his immediate family. The therapist places special emphasis here. Sal's father contributes little at the outset, but he had stated in the initial family interview that one of his goals was to be a better father. So, the therapist asks him what would need to be changed for him to reach this goal. A surprisingly revealing conversation follows. Dad is ashamed of his drinking, which he knows is excessive, and he thinks the drinking would need to be under control if he is to be a good father. He also knows he should be more involved in his son's life, but he says he doesn't know how to deal with a disobedient son short of yelling, or simply avoiding contact.

Building on this outpouring, the therapist gets Dad to commit first to sharply limiting his beer intake. Together, they draw up a behavioral contract, saying what the limit is and noting consequences for Dad if he does and doesn't stick to the limit. He agrees that if he slips, he will enroll in the Community Reinforcement Program for substance abuse, which is offered at the local mental health center. The therapist also begins cognitive-behavioral work with Dad. One focus is Dad's idea that the only ways to survive contact with his son are to yell at him or ignore him. With the therapist's nudging, Dad makes a list of things he and Sal have done together in the past that seemed to go well – a fishing trip, building a model car together, and a surprisingly long list of other activities. By drawing up such a list, they begin challenging the validity of this core idea that yelling and ignoring are the only two ways to interact with Sal.

Sal's mother says that she needs more skills in managing Sal's behavior, and Dad agrees that he could use those skills, too. So, the therapist begins working with both of them on basic contingency management principles (see Chapter 9) and how they might be applied with Sal at home. In addition, both agree to enroll in a parenting effectiveness program offered at Sal's school. Even before initiating the behavioral skill building for Mom and Dad, though, the therapist sits in on enough family interactions to carry out a simple functional analysis of the pretreatment contingencies at home. One telling observation was that when Sal is behaving badly, he receives attention from one or both parents 98% of the time, albeit in the form of complaints, threats, and yelling, whereas when Sal behaves appropriately, he gets parental attention only 15% of the time. So, if Sal finds attention more rewarding than being ignored, as many youngsters do, a case could be made that behaving inappropriately is more rewarding than being well-behaved. The functional analysis also shows that serious conduct problems, such as fighting at school and being suspended, lead only to parental rebukes and some yelling, but not to the loss of any really valued privileges, such as television time or weekend movies. Moreover, good weeks at school, with no discipline problems, earn Sal nothing. The therapist uses information like this to plan changes in contingencies at home. The basic idea is to identify incentives Sal really values, and make these strictly contingent on Sal's behavior. Appropriate behavior needs to become more rewarding, and bad behavior less rewarding, than is currently the case for Sal. Making these changes fits perfectly into the parents' efforts to learn behavior management skills, and apply them to Sal.

The therapist sees this joint work by the parents on behavioral skills as one step toward building a more cooperative relationship. As another step in the same direction, at the therapist's suggestion, the contract for Dad's drinking includes "favorite meal" rewards for sticking to his limit, with Mom being the one who will prepare the meal. The therapist also works on the relationship more directly, using a behavioral marital therapy approach. This involves having the two identify some changes in the other that they believe would help the relationship, with each spouse committing to make some of the requested changes. The two had never even considered marital therapy previously, but it seems to make a positive difference even in the first month, and the gains continue to accumulate in later weeks. Even Sal notices the difference. One day he comments at dinner, "What happened? You guys aren't yelling at each other so much."

While there do seem to be genuine improvements in the marital relationship and in Mom and Dad's ability to work as a team vis-à-vis Sal, the therapist is aware that there is some risk of relapse on Dad's part. With this possibility in mind, the therapist has already begun thinking of another family resource that may be mobilized if needed: Uncle Al. Sal likes Uncle Al, wants to spend more time with him, and loves working on cars. Uncle Al is concerned about Sal, wants to help him, and has a small auto repair business. Strengthening the connection between Sal and Al could make for good role modeling of mature male behavior, foster development of a close confidant relationship with someone Sal respects, and provide opportunities for socially acceptable, constructive activity that can lead to skill building, increased self-esteem, income, and perhaps even future job prospects for Sal. An additional benefit is that more time spent working on cars with Al would mean less time spent with antisocial peers. However, all this must remain in the therapist's back pocket for the time being. To bring Al into the picture at this point might risk undermining Dad and resurrecting the self-doubts that immobilized him for so long.

Working on the intersystem connection between family and school. In addition to within-system (in this case, within-family) interventions, MST therapists place a premium on building and strengthening connections between systems. Much needed in Sal's case is a good working connection between family and school. With this aim in mind, the therapist and Sal's parents arrange a planning meeting with the coach and teacher who have shown an interest in Sal; included in the meeting is the assistant principal, who is the primary disciplinarian at school. In this meeting, the group agrees to a set of specific expectations for Sal's behavior at school (e.g., obeying staff, no verbal or physical aggression toward peers, no association with three specific antisocial peers), and they arrange for a daily report from school to home regarding whether Sal has met the expectations, and for specific consequences; for example, TV time and funds for weekend movies are made contingent on meeting school expectations. At the meeting, two additional directions are discussed: (1) having the coach who is interested in Sal try to draw him into a sport, such as football; and (2) arranging for tutoring, to help Sal get back on track academically (recall that he did make above-average grades in elementary school, suggesting potential).

Working on the family-neighborhood interface. One of the hardest parts of the treatment plan to implement and sustain will be keeping Sal away from his antisocial buddies. This may also be one of the most important parts of the plan because peers can have such a powerful impact in adolescence. To maximize the prospects, the therapist arranges for periodic meetings of Sal's parents with other parents they know in the neighborhood, including parents of Sal's current peer group. Carefully avoiding blame, the therapist helps guide the discussion to what he already knows the parents are concerned about: the fact that when certain combinations of kids are together (Sal included), inappropriate behavior often results, and things seem to be getting worse as these youngsters grow older and harder to handle. The parents identify specific combinations of youths who should not be together, and they design a system for monitoring where their youngsters are, and with whom. They also assemble a phone list, so each set of parents can call the others when trying to locate their teens. The system may not be perfect, but it feels good to Sal's mom and dad to have this shared understanding with other parents. At least they have allies in the struggle.

Turning parents into teachers. Finally, at the center of Sal's social system is Sal himself, a youngster whose problem behavior is connected in part to his thoughts and feelings. To address those inner processes, the therapist identifies two evidence-based treatment procedures that might be helpful: identifying and altering maladaptive cognitions and doing systematic problem-solving. Consistent with the MST aim of empowering parents, the therapist also teaches Sal's parents the relevant skills, so they can teach them to their son. One focus of this work is Sal's cognitions. He tends to see himself as persecuted (e.g., by nosy school personnel, by peers who disrespect him), and he interprets ambiguous social encounters in negative ways (e.g., interpreting an accidental collision with another boy as an intentional attack). Sal's parents learn to help their son examine and reshape such distorted cognitions (see procedures discussed in Chapter 8). Another focus is problem-solving skills training (see Chapter 12) – generating multiple possible solutions to problems, identifying the pros and cons of each, choosing one, and trying it out. This skill could help Sal resolve interpersonal encounters without resorting impulsively to aggression and violence. So, while environmental changes are set in motion, the parents are also trained to work with Sal on two specific skills related to how he thinks about things.

Overall, the intent of the MST therapist is to (1) put in motion a set of intervention processes that address, and link together, different layers of Sal's social system (e.g., Sal, his family, his school, his neighborhood); (2) carry out ongoing evaluations of the impact of these processes (e.g., regular reports from parents and school personnel) so as to establish which ones are working; (3) where interventions are not working, identify reasons and address them by altering the intervention; and (4) empower key players in the social system (e.g., mother, father, school teacher, and coach) to address family needs themselves, to enhance treatment generalization and maintenance when the therapist is no longer involved. Whether MST can turn Sal around is hard to say; but according to the MST model, the chances increase to the extent that the interventions deal not only with Sal but also with the social ecosystem in which his problems have been developed and sustained.

Troubleshooting: Common Treatment Problems and Recommended Solutions. MST therapists work with unusually difficult cases, most tougher than Sal's, so it is no surprise that they face a variety of obstacles and challenges. Here we note a few of the most common difficulties and some ways of coping recommended by the experts.

- *Parents who are ready to give up on their child.* Because families are typically referred to MST after their child has been in trouble multiple times for diverse reasons, the MST therapist may well find the parents demoralized, exhausted, even saying "I can't deal with this kid any longer." Expert MST supervisors counsel that the best initial response is one of empathy and validation. The message to parents needs to be, "It's appropriate for you to feel this way; any parent would." Beyond this, the therapist's goal needs to be restoring hope and renewing energy the parents will need to continue coping. One way to do this is through concrete help that quickly demonstrates the benefits of the therapeutic connection. As an example, the therapist may take the children (the MST case and siblings) on outings, so the parents can have time for themselves away from the stress. Moral support can also help, as when the therapist leaves a note telling the parents, *"I'm thinking about you today, and here is what I've been thinking: A lot of parents would have quit by now; what a blessing for Sal that he has you."* Moral support can also take the form of reframing, as when one MST therapist supported a father's firmness by saying, *"You are willing to risk losing your son's love to do what's best for him."* Note that such reframing cannot just be a technique; there must be a core of truth if the new way of thinking is to come across as authentic.

- *Parents who lack core behavior management skills.* Parents referred to MST sometimes have very low levels of behavior management skills. They may be too lax, too punitive, too erratic, or unsure how to set up contingencies. Some of the gap in skills can be addressed through traditional behavioral parent training (see Chapters 9, 13, and 15), but a specific task that can focus the process nicely is that of developing a behavior contract. In that process, specific management problems have to be addressed with specific solutions. How to identify positive behavior to reward when most of what the parents want is reduced negative behavior? The contract can specify rewards for such positives as keeping curfew, passing drug screens, and even reducing the level of marijuana found in successive drug screens. What if the youth won't say what rewards he wants? Then identify his highest-frequency behaviors (e.g., television, phone time with friends) and make those the rewards. What if "everything has already been taken away," so there are no costs to exact for contract violations? Then points can be offered toward something the youth wants and didn't dream he could have – new sports shoes, for example – with points earned or lost depending on behavior.

- *Parents who lack a support system.* MST often leans heavily on the family support system, but some families don't seem to have one. The MST therapist can do several things to address the gap. One is to look for informal resources the parents may not yet have called on – extended family members who are willing to help but haven't been asked, or a good friend at work. Another is to look for burned bridges – past events that have left parents estranged from neighbors or extended family members – and help parents find ways to make amends and repair ruptures. A third approach is to find more formal networks in which acceptance and help are highly likely. Examples include community-based parent support groups and church-related family programs.

- *Therapists who feel overwhelmed.* MST therapists have a tough job, and some can become overwhelmed and demoralized, just like parents can. Weeks of being paged in the middle of the night to deal with family emergencies can leave a therapist sleep-deprived and exhausted. Weeks of working with an unresponsive family can make a therapist feel inept. Learning that an MST client has just been charged with breaking and entering, or even murder, can leave a therapist feeling like a total failure. The MST supervision system (Henggeler & Schoenwald, 1998) is designed to address a variety of problems at the therapist level. Supervisors sometimes operate as "therapists' therapists," focusing on anxiety management skills (e.g., for worry over what the young client may do next), identifying and modifying maladaptive cognitions (e.g., self-attributions for youth behavior the therapist could not possibly have prevented), and even teaching systematic problem-solving skills. As an example, excessive therapist paging by the parents may prompt examination of the relationship the therapist has created with the parents. Perhaps parent work needs to focus more on increasing self-reliance and independent problem solving. Movement in that direction could be good for the parents, taking them where they ultimately need to be skillwise, and good for the therapist, reducing the onslaught of calls. To support effective problem solving with families, supervisors may well attend some of the parent or family sessions with the therapist, to observe the interactions firsthand and to model useful ways of coping.

Multisystemic Therapy: Scientific Issues

Multisystemic therapy is different enough from other interventions for conduct problems and antisocial behavior to pose some rather distinctive scientific issues. One of these issues is replicability of the treatment across settings and therapists. In the treatment research literature, a premium is placed on spelling out treatment procedures in therapist manuals, to support precise replication from one therapist and setting to the next. This is a reasonable expectation for treatments that involve preplanned procedures carried out in a more or less uniform way across different treated individuals. However, specifying procedures and their temporal order may be difficult in the case of MST, which (1) makes therapists and supervisors responsible for selecting from an array of evidence-based treatments, (2) expects therapists to tailor interventions to fit individual youngsters and their social ecology, (3) emphasizes ongoing assessment of outcome, and changes in the treatment plan when current procedures are not working. As an alternative to the kinds of manuals that are most common in our field, the MST group, following Piercy (1986), has "manualized" their treatment principles, as detailed near the beginning of this chapter.

Conceptually, this approach makes sense as a middle ground between a detailed manual of session-by-session treatment steps and a vague statement of treatment philosophy. However, because a primary purpose of manualization is to facilitate replication of treatment procedures across settings and therapists, the real test of the MST manual of principles will be whether it is sufficiently structured to generate faithful replication. Recent studies by Henggeler, Melton et al. (1997) and Henggeler, Pickrel, and Brondino (1999) indicate that when therapists do not have regular consultation with experts in MST, outcomes are disappointing, particularly on such important measures as criminal activity. This suggests the possibility that the individually tailored, highly flexible and fluid nature of MST may require more involvement of highly trained experts than may be necessary for simpler, more lock-step and readily manualizable intervention programs. This, in turn, suggests that, for MST, manualizing or otherwise describing what the expert supervisors do to guide therapists may be as important as manualizing therapist procedures. The treatment designers appear to agree. They have argued that treatment manuals are "necessary, but far from sufficient" (Henggeler & Schoenwald, 2002, p. 419). To complement their treatment manual, they have refined and documented their supervision procedures (see Henggeler & Schoenwald, 1998), and described how to implement them (see e.g., Henggeler & Schoenwald, 2000). Finding the combination of treatment manualization, therapist training, and supervision structure needed to make MST reliably transportable to new therapists in new settings will certainly be one of the most significant challenges facing this research group in the years ahead.

The subject of replication relates to another aspect of MST: the nature of the component interventions employed by MST therapists. The general orientation of the MST developers has been to build on the empirical literature where possible, selecting treatment procedures as needed from among the pool of empirically tested methods. This philosophy does appear to be applied rather consistently. For example, MST therapists are taught to work with youth who show cognitive distortion by using cognitive behavioral procedures to identify and address the distortions, and elsewhere to use modeling, role-play exercises, behavioral contingencies, self-monitoring and self-instruction, and problem-solving training (see Chapters 2, 3, 4, 5, 8, and 12). Some of the procedures (e.g., problem-solving training) come close to specific programs that have indeed been tested empirically; others appear to be developed on a somewhat ad hoc basis by therapist and supervisor, and in ways that may not correspond very closely to the specific tested interventions described in this book. As an example, helping youngsters control their anger is discussed in the MST literature and procedures are used in the treatment, but it appears that they are not the specific, manualized procedures for anger control that have been tested most systematically (i.e., those described in Chapter 8 of this book). Perhaps the use of general intervention principles to devise ad hoc procedures for each youth is precisely the right approach given the individualized treatment focus of MST. Or perhaps closer attention to specific manualized treatments that have been tested and reported in the literature would strengthen the impact of MST. This remains an empirical question worthy of study in the future.

Another useful direction for the future will be a continued and extended effort to identify treatment moderators. In the MST research to date, such potential predictors as youth age, gender, race, social class, and arrest history, have been assessed, but none of these variables has been found to predict outcomes (see Borduin et al., 1995; Henggeler et al., 1992). These findings are valuable in suggesting that MST can be beneficial across a rather broad range of youth characteristics. However, it seems likely that any intervention program will have certain boundary conditions, limits beyond which the program is not so beneficial. These boundary conditions may consist of not only client and family characteristics, but also therapist factors, setting conditions, and the interplay of factors across these and other dimensions (e.g., whether client and therapist are matched or mismatched for ethnicity). The information obtained in the extant MST database includes numerous potential moderators that have not yet been formally analyzed (e.g., parent educational attainment, number of children in the family, whether two parents are in the household), and future research might well expand this archive. As the popularity of MST grows, and corresponding requests for training and dissemination increase, it will be increasingly important to know the range of youth, family, therapist, and situation characteristics within which the treatment program has beneficial effects and outside of which the program may be less helpful.

One other important task on the scientific front will be the identification of mediators of change related to MST outcomes. Because MST is linked so directly to a specific systems-ecological causal model (see earlier discussion), and because relevant measures of functioning in youth, family, and other systems are collected at multiple time points, together with such outcome data as arrest records, the raw material needed for mediation analysis is present in the extant database of the MST research group. Appropriately, a research team from the MST group is one of the few in the youth treatment outcome field to have applied the most refined formal quantitative procedures for mediation assessment. Huey et al. (2000) used two samples of juvenile offenders to assess the mechanisms through which MST reduced delinquent behavior. One sample included 57 mostly rural, male, African American youths who had been arrested for criminal offenses and had been randomly assigned to MST; the other sample included 54 mostly urban, male, Caucasian youth offenders who met diagnostic criteria for substance use or dependence and had been randomly assigned to MST. In multiple tests, across the two samples separately, Huey et al. found that therapist adherence to the principles of MST was associated with improved family relations (i.e., measures of family cohesion, family functioning, and parental monitoring of youth behavior) and decreased youth contact with antisocial peers, which in turn were associated with decreased delinquent behavior at outcome assessment. Importantly, a formal test of mediation (Holmbeck, 1997) supported the idea that changes in family relations and delinquent peer affiliation mediated the relation between adherence and reductions in delinquent behavior. These findings represent a significant advance in our understanding of how MST actually works to reduce delinquent behavior. The Huey et al. (2000) study, together with a recent mediational analysis by Eddy and Chamberlain (2000; see Chapter 9), should help point the way to a new generation of research on mechanisms of change in child and adolescent treatment (see Weersing & Weisz, 2002, for a review).

Multisystemic Therapy: Clinical Practice Issues

From a practitioner's perspective, MST may be viewed with a combination of relief and worry. Many will certainly feel relief to discover a treatment program designed to grapple with some of the most difficult youth, and with the complexity of real life in clinical care and the juvenile justice system. Most practitioners recognize that each disturbed or disturbing youth is embedded within multiple layers of social context, and that each layer – family, school, peer group, juvenile justice system, etc. – is relevant to understanding and intervening with the youth. However, most evidence-based treatments have tended to simplify by emphasizing a single element of the system, most often the youth or the parent. Such simplification may serve important purposes (e.g., helping making treatments manualizable and replicable), but may also seem rather artificial to some practitioners.

MST cannot be faulted for oversimplification. It deals with the nitty-gritty of real life at multiple levels of the youth's social system, and it does not ignore factors that are relevant to the youth's problems because they cannot be dealt with in a clinic office. Instead, MST therapists try to identify all the elements of the system that may be important in understanding and treating the youth, fashion ad hoc treatment plans from a broad empirical base, and take their treatments into the home, school, and neighborhood. The evidence thus far is that these interventions produce very positive effects, at least when supervised by the treatment developers and their colleagues.

Practitioners discussing evidence-based treatments often express concern that the treatment procedures are so specific, and therapist flexibility so constrained, that treatment benefit may be confined to a narrow range of youngsters. For example, many treatments have been tested primarily with Caucasian youngsters, raising questions about whether benefits would be replicated with minority youth. And some of the literature on child psychotherapy links favorable treatment outcomes to high levels of family resources (e.g., middle and upper socioeconomic status) and low levels of child problem severity prior to treatment. MST is designed to permit considerable therapist flexibility, in part to serve the goal of adapting treatment to client and family characteristics as needed, to foster treatment benefit across a variety of youth and families. The evidence thus far points to success in attaining this goal, with tests generally showing similar outcomes for African American and Caucasian youth, for boys and girls, for youngsters of different ages within the adolescent range and different levels of pretreatment problem severity, and for families across a range of socioeconomic status levels. Moreover, the breadth of outcomes on which MST has shown positive effects is impressive, encompassing violent and assaultive behavior, sex offenses, substance use and abuse, and even parental maltreatment. From the evidence thus far, the effective range of treatment benefit from MST appears quite broad.

Of course, to obtain effects on these measures, MST requires that therapists have what may appear to be modest caseloads and heavy time commitments to each client family, with daily contact and 24-hour/day availability, and this raises the question of cost. Isn't MST inordinately expensive? Not if one compares it to the cost of the alternatives for many severely delinquent youth (see Schoenwald et al., 1996). A comparison offered by Henggeler et al. (1998, pp. 43–4) uses current costs to estimate that a team of three MST therapists can treat 50 families per year for $5,000 per family, for an annual total of $250,000. That cost would be more than offset by preventing even as few as seven youths from placement in a residential treatment center at $40,000 per placement, a total cost of $280,000. Moreover, these figures are dwarfed by the cost of incarceration (estimated at $100/day); in the Henggeler et al. (1992) clinical trial, MST was associated with a mean reduction in incarceration of 73 days per offender over the 59-week follow-up period. An additional point worth noting is that when MST reduces criminal behavior, it reduces such crime-linked costs as medical care for victims, property damage and loss, and lost work time and productivity among the victims of crime. Among the available treatments used to reduce serious criminal activity by adolescents, MST has been rated as the most cost-effective by the Washington State Institute for Public Policy (1998).

Another kind of cost that may concern practitioners is the human toll, for the therapists on the front lines. Research findings from the MST group have already shown that the successful therapist will need to be one who works hard to adhere closely to a demanding set of principles. Moreover, being an MST therapist can give new meaning to the terms "full-time" and "on call." One former MST therapist with whom I talked recently told me that after a year on duty she had to find another job, because she was "a nervous wreck." Being on call at all hours for most of the week meant that she could be paged in the middle of a deep sleep, or while eating out with friends. She often needed to cancel plans or drop what she was doing to go help a family deal with a crisis, or talk a youngster out of an angry rage. She all but stopped eating out, because worrying that a call would interrupt her meal made the experience unappealing. A number of these problems may reflect an idiosyncratic, poorly designed on-call schedule, or perhaps a way of working with the family that has inadvertently encouraged dependency (see Troubleshooting, earlier in this chapter). However, there may also be good and poor fits between MST and various personality types. It may be, for example, that people with a high worry threshold and an ability to focus exclusively on the activity at hand (seeing a case, or eating out with friends) are better suited to roles as MST therapist than are people who worry easily and have difficulty compartmentalizing. Even where the personality fit is ideal, therapist stints on the front line may need to alternate with other roles to avoid a high burnout rate.

Another practical concern is that therapists who want to learn the principles and procedures, but who do not have access to training and supervision from the treatment originators and developers, may have real difficulty. The MST research group has taken pains to study this issue, particularly in recent years, examining the impact of MST as delivered under varying levels of contact with the treatment developers and experts. Unfortunately, the evidence suggests that the benefits of MST may be rather sharply reduced if therapists do not have regular guidance from MST developers or experts (e.g., Henggeler et al., 1999a). Prompted in part by these findings, and in part by heavy demands for training from around the world, the MST research group has now made dissemination research a major focus of their agenda (see Schoenwald, Henggeler, & Brondino, 2000; Schoenwald & Hoagwood, 2001). The results of this ongoing work, in the years ahead, may enrich our understanding of the path from research to practice in youth mental health care.

How to Find Out More about Multisystemic Therapy

An excellent description of the principles and practices of MST, the evolution of the program, and its research support can be found in *Multisystemic Treatment of Antisocial Behavior in Children and Adolescents* (Henggeler, Schoenwald, Borduin, Rowland, & Cunningham, 1998). A key complement to this book is Henggeler and Schoenwald's (1998) *Multisystemic Therapy Supervisory Manual: Promoting Quality Assurance at the Clinical Level*, the document that guides the all-important therapist supervision process. A recent summary review of research on MST can be found in Henggeler and Lee (2003). Two web sites (www.msitinstute.org and www.mstservices.com) provide information on the program, materials, and training opportunities.

SECTION F

CONCLUSION

14

Evidence-Based Youth Psychotherapies

Strengths, Limitations, and Future Directions

In this book, we have examined a variety of evidence-based psychotherapies for children and adolescents. The therapies encompass the four broad clusters of problems and disorders that account for most referrals for outpatient child and adolescent mental health care: anxiety, depression, ADHD, and conduct problems and conduct disorder. The descriptions and critiques in each of the chapters have revealed several strengths and several limitations in each of the specific treatments and in the evidence base bearing on each of them. In this final chapter, I adopt a broader focus, describe some important strengths and gaps in the literature more generally, and highlight some issues that need special attention in future treatment development and in future treatment research. I also propose a specific model for treatment development and testing, one that I believe could contribute significantly toward bridging the gulf that still exists between clinical research and clinical practice.

Strengths of the Evidence on Youth Psychotherapy Effects

The broad evidence base on youth treatment, surveyed in Chapter 1, and the specific treatments and the research on them, discussed in subsequent chapters, shows substantial strengths – strengths that represent good news for all of us who care about youth mental health care.

Overall Magnitude and Durability of Treatment Effects. First, the meta-analytic findings we reviewed in Chapter 1 showed that the average effect of youth treatments tested in peer-reviewed studies is quite respectable, falling between commonly used benchmarks for medium and large effects (Cohen, 1988). Treatment effects have also proven to be durable, with little drop-off in benefit over the five to six months that is common in posttreatment follow-up assessments.

Specificity of Treatment Effects. The meta-analytic findings have also pointed to considerable specificity in treatment impact. In general, youngsters treated with tested interventions show more improvement in the problems that were targeted in treatment than in other problem areas. This supports the idea that improvements in those treated are not just broad, general changes associated with feeling better in a vague or diffuse way, but are instead focused changes reflecting the particular goals of the treatments used.

Coverage of Conditions and Age Groups. Beyond the meta-analyses of Chapter 1, the specific evidence-based treatments discussed in Chapter 2 and beyond show several encouraging characteristics. One of these is coverage. The evidence-based treatments include interventions for anxious youth, depressed youth, youngsters with significant conduct problems, and youngsters diagnosed as having ADHD. The treatments span the age range from preschool through late adolescence, and most have been tested with samples that include girls and boys and at least some ethnic variation. The breadth of age and problem focus almost certainly means that evidence-based treatments now exist, in principle, for a very substantial percentage of preschool through high school-age youth who are referred for treatment in service settings. There are significant gaps in coverage, of course, and we note some of these later in the chapter.

Varied Models of Treatment Delivery. Another strength of the treatments reviewed in this book is the creative array of treatment delivery models employed. The traditional weekly office visit model still predominates, but investigators have clearly begun to push the boundaries, with tests of more intensive approaches geared to school breaks and summer camp programs (Chapter 7), parent discussion group treatment in which core skills training is embedded in videotaped vignettes (Chapter 11), interventions providing behavioral training and support for biological parents (Chapters 6, 9, 10, and 12) and foster parents (Chapter 9), treatment supplements in the form of posttherapy booster sessions (Chapters 5 and 7) and parent sessions as complements to child sessions (Chapters 3 and 5), and a peripatetic therapist-in-the-youth's-environment model (Chapter 13). It is clear from this diversity of approaches that treatment developers are increasingly concerned not only about what the content of treatment should be, but also about how best to deliver that content. While the variations show intriguing diversity, it remains true that the most common model of treatment delivery is the once-weekly office visit, a fact that we consider later in the chapter.

Varied Approaches to Assessing Treatment Benefit. The investigators who study the evidence-based treatments have used an increasingly rich array of methods to assess treatment effects. More and more, over the years, we see outcome assessment that relies on multiple informants, some of whom do not know whether the youth they report on received treatment. Increasingly, we see outcome assessment that includes direct observation of child (and sometimes parent) behavior rather than relying on what children and parents report about their behavior. While research sophistication has improved over the years, refinements are needed, as we discuss later.

Increasing Efforts to Make Treatments Accessible to Practice. Another dimension along which treatment research has moved in recent years is that of clinical utility. As I have noted in the Clinical Practice Issues section of various treatment chapters, practitioners have to consider more than just the empirical evidence on outcome when they decide whether to adopt particular treatment approaches. Moreover, the extent to which treatments, once adopted, are carried out as their manuals specify, may depend on numerous factors other than the scientific support the treatment has generated. Adoption and successful implementation may often depend significantly on such practical matters as the availability of therapist manuals and youth materials, whether training is accessible and affordable, how long it takes to learn the program and to deliver it to the average child and family, and whether youngsters and their parents like it enough to show up and stay the course. In recent years, treatment developers have shown increased attention to such matters in designing their programs and in assessing outcomes. Treatment program web sites advertise available treatment materials and training programs, and treatment developers describe their treatments in a variety of professional meetings. These are important steps. Other measures may well be needed, as we discuss later in the chapter.

Issues That Need Attention in Future Research

As we have seen, there is some genuine good news to celebrate in regard to treatment development and research findings on child and adolescent psychotherapy. This is evident in the broad view taken in Chapter 1 and in the treatment-specific chapters that follow. However, as will always be true, the scientific evidence can be improved, and so can the treatments. To help stimulate such improvements, I have listed in Table 14.1 ten directions for the next generation of research on evidence-based youth treatment. In what follows, I will explain the basis for these ten points.

1. Building Evidence-Based Treatments for a Broadened Array of Problems and Disorders. First, although the problems and disorders addressed by current evidence-based treatments do appear to encompass concerns that bring a majority of clinically referred youth into treatment, significant gaps in coverage can be identified. As one example, eating disorders pose

TABLE 14.1. *Steps toward Strengthening Research on Child and Adolescent Psychotherapy*

1.	Building Evidence-Based Treatments for a Broadened Array of Problems and Disorders
2.	Learning about the Impact of Co-Occurring Problems and Disorders
3.	Expanding the Array of Treatment Models Tested
4.	Identifying Necessary and Sufficient Conditions for Treatment Benefit
5.	Enriching Our Understanding of the Effective Range of Specific Treatments
6.	Understanding Change Processes That Mediate Treatment Outcome
7.	Increased Attention to Therapeutic Relationship and Alliance Building
8.	Using Larger Samples and More Potent Comparisons
9.	Studying the Effects of Treatments in Real-World Practice Contexts
10.	Revisiting the Model That Guides Treatment Development and Testing

sinister risks; the annual mortality rate in 15–24-year-old females diagnosed with anorexia is more than 12 times the rate for this age/gender group from all other causes (Sullivan, 1995). Yet treatment testing has moved slowly, with only a few investigators focusing on anorexia (e.g., Robin, Bedway et al., 1996), and even less attention to bulimia in youth.

With few exceptions (see e.g., Azrin et al., 1994), potent treatments for substance-abusing youth are rare, particularly for users of harder drugs such as cocaine. Also with few exceptions (e.g., Borduin et al., 1990), the literature lacks successes in the treatment of youthful sex offenders. And despite attempts by several research teams, we still lack interventions for suicidal youth that clearly reduce the risk of further attempts (see Weisz & Hawley, 2002). Indeed, a recent review of youth suicide intervention research concluded that, "In general, control conditions are just as effective at reducing suicidal behavior as experimental conditions" (Miller & Glinsky, 2000, p. 1131).

Large numbers of boys and girls are referred for mental health care following maltreatment, but there is much work to be done before we understand how to identify the most beneficial treatments for these youngsters. The task is complicated by the heterogeneity of the forms maltreatment can take, and the heterogeneity of responses youngsters may show, ranging from anxiety and depressive disorders to conduct problems and overly sexualized behavior. One treatment development strategy recommended by experts (e.g., Saywitz et al., 2000) is to extend and modify treatment models from mainstream intervention research, as when abuse-specific CBT has been used to treat posttraumatic stress disorder in sexually abused children (e.g., Cohen & Mannarino, 1996). A broad range of maltreatment experiences and youth sequelae still await the application of this promising strategy.

Finally, most successful treatment of ADHD with behavioral methods has been confined to preadolescents; the behavioral treatments that work within that age range have not traveled well up the developmental path into adolescence (see Barkley, 1997, p. 5). Limited success of psychosocial treatments with ADHD in teens may make stimulant medication the evidence-based treatment of choice by default (Weisz & Jensen, 1999).

To put the coverage issue more broadly and more starkly, there are well over 100 disorders in the DSM-IV (American Psychiatric Association, 1994, 2000) that can be applied to children and adolescents, and our list of evidence-based youth treatments to date encompasses only a small percentage of these. The development of these treatments has begun, appropriately, with a focus on relatively high-prevalence conditions; in the future, that focus will need to broaden.

2. Learning about the Impact of Co-Occurring Problems and Disorders. Most of the treatments described in this book focus on a single problem (e.g., fear of dogs) or disorder (e.g., conduct disorder) or a homogeneous cluster (e.g., disobedient, disruptive, and aggressive behavior). Extensive evidence (e.g., Anderson et al., 1987; Angold et al., 1999; Jensen & Weisz, 2002) shows that most youngsters with problems do not come in neat, one-diagnosis packages, but in heterogeneous combinations. Youngsters diagnosed with ADHD often meet criteria for oppositional defiant disorder or conduct disorder as well; conduct disorder is often combined with depression; and so forth. Rates of such comorbidity are striking in community samples, and markedly higher in clinical samples (Angold et al., 1999; Jensen & Weisz, 2002; Weisz, 2000). Indeed, it is not unusual for youth in such clinical samples to meet criteria for three or more DSM diagnoses concurrently.

Will a treatment designed for youth depression work with depressed youngsters who also have severe conduct problems, combined with ADHD? Can a single treatment address all three problems concurrently? Questions like these are useful targets for the next generation of research. Such questions are difficult to answer now, because so many studies to date have (a) failed to carry out pretreatment assessments for problems or disorders other than the one targeted in treatment; (b) explicitly excluded youth with potentially interfering comorbid problems or disorders; (c) focused treatment on one problem or disorder without trying to address co-occurring problems or disorders; or (d) failed to assess, at posttreatment, problems or disorders other than the one targeted by the treatment. In the future, these design features will need to change if we are to understand how treatments work in the context of comorbid conditions.

3. Expanding the Array of Treatment Models Tested. The current array of evidence-based treatments, like research on youth treatment generally, is heavy on behavioral and cognitive-behavioral treatments, and light on nonbehavioral approaches. Psychodynamic, client-centered, existential-humanistic, and other nonbehavioral schools of psychotherapy are barely evident in the list of treatments covered in this book, and they are represented in fewer than a fourth of the studies reviewed in the primary meta-analyses (Casey & Berman, 1985; Kazdin et al., 1990a; Weisz et al., 1987, 1995). By contrast, the nonbehavioral approaches are more often favored and more often used than the behavioral in everyday clinical practice (Kazdin et al., 1990b; Weersing et al., 2002).

Thus, a useful direction for the future will be for researchers to broaden the range of models encompassed in their tests, including more of the approaches that service providers currently emphasize. Failure to expand our work in this way may help perpetuate a perception by some practitioners that research lacks relevance to their work (see e.g., Cohen et al., 1986; Garfield, 1996; Havik & VandenBos, 1996; Morrow-Bradley & Elliott, 1986). Finding questions of common interest to both researchers and practitioners seems a critical goal at this juncture, and broadening the array of treatment approaches tested is one eminently logical way to pursue that goal.

4. Identifying Necessary and Sufficient Conditions for Treatment Benefit. Most of the extant evidence-based youth treatments are rather omnibus, or even blunderbus in form, packing a variety of concepts and skills into one program, with termination considered appropriate only when all the components have been covered. For some of these treatments, all the elements may well be needed, but often the evidence base is too poorly developed to reveal just which elements are truly necessary or whether a subset of them might actually be sufficient to produce most of what can be gained from the treatment. Indeed, it is the absence of such a clear picture that often stimulates development of multicomponent interventions; new concepts and skills are added when in doubt, because it seems that they may help, and it probably can't hurt.

One result of this process may be treatments that have a good deal of adipose tissue, elements that do not actually contribute much to the outcomes achieved. As a matter of principle, given the time and expense associated with treatment, we need treatments that are as fat-free and efficient as possible. Indeed, treatments that fall short of this goal are apt to clash with the current emphasis, in clinical practice, on managing costs. Increasing treatment efficiency will likely enhance the attractiveness of the interventions to practitioners, improve the teachability of the procedures, and increase the likelihood that they will reach the children and families who need them. Of course, many of the elements of treatment may not enhance outcome directly but still be important to retain. For example, some elements of treatment may contribute to or enhance the acceptability of treatment, minimize dropout rates, or increase patient and therapist compliance with the regimen. Research will need to be designed so as to detect these important contributions as well.

In our field, a traditional pathway to understanding which treatment elements are actually contributing to outcomes is dismantling research, in which different treatment components are broken apart and tested separately. In principle, such research should provide the key to understanding necessity and sufficiency in treatment. However, the task is complex when many elements are involved in the same treatment, because the number of combinations multiplies quickly. Moreover, different subgroups of youths may differ from one another in their responsiveness to different subsets of treatment components. All of this means that the dismantling process may be particularly challenging for some of the more complex treatments. Nonetheless, the potential benefits make the job worth doing.

5. Enriching Our Understanding of the Effective Range of Specific Treatments. A fifth area needing increased attention is moderation of treatment effects. For each treatment, we need to know as much as possible about the range of youth clinical and demographic characteristics within which the treatments produce benefit and outside of which benefit diminishes. Even the best-supported treatments are helpful for some conditions but not others, and with benefit constrained by comorbid conditions: age, socioeconomic status, ethnicity, family configuration, or other clinical and demographic factors; but, with a relatively small number of exceptions noted in the previous chapters of this book, research to date has left us rather poorly informed about such constraints. Racial, ethnic and cultural factors, for example, are embedded but unexamined in most of our treatment outcome research, and this makes it difficult to know how robust most treatment effects are across various population groups (Weisz, Huey, & Weersing, 1998).

At this early stage in treatment development, most tested treatments have not been designed to take into account broad variations in language, values, customs, child-rearing traditions, beliefs and expectancies about child and parent behavior, and distinctive stressors and resources associated with different cultural traditions. The interplay between such factors and treatment characteristics may influence the relationship between child/family and therapist, the likelihood of treatment completion versus dropout, and the outcome of the treatment process. We need research assessing the extent to which treatment persistence, process, and outcome are associated with race, ethnicity, culture, and a variety of other child and family characteristics.

6. Understanding Change Processes That Mediate Treatment Outcome. We also need close and sustained attention to the change processes in treatment that actually account for observed outcomes. At present, we know much more about what outcomes are produced by our treatments than about what actually causes the outcomes (Kazdin, 2000; Shirk & Russell, 1996; Weersing & Weisz, 2002). If we fail to identify core causal processes, we risk a proliferation of treatments administered somewhat superstitiously because studies show they work, but without an understanding of the change processes therapists actually need to effect to produce results.

To understand how the treatments actually work, we need a generation of research testing hypothesized mediators of outcome. The procedures needed for carrying out such tests have been well described (Baron & Kenney, 1986; Holmbeck, 1997), and potentially useful evidence exists in greater volume than is generally recognized (Weersing & Weisz, 2001). At least two recent studies have adhered closely to the Baron and Kenney procedures. As we noted in Chapter 13, Huey et al. (2000) found that decreased affiliation with delinquent peers mediated reductions in delinquent behavior among youths treated with multisystemic therapy. As we noted in Chapter 9, Eddy and Chamberlain (2000) found that improved family management skills and reductions in deviant peer associations mediated the effects of their behaviorally oriented treatment foster care program on adolescent antisocial behavior. We need more such analyses focused on hypothesized mediators of change in other treatments (e.g., changed cognitions in cognitive-behavioral treatment for youth depression). Failure to test rigorously for mediation limits the field in a very significant way, creating a vacuum within which faulty assumptions about the nature and causes of change may sprout and thrive.

While mediation tests have real value, a case can be made that such tests alone cannot yield a complete understanding of causal mechanisms and change processes. Critical logical and design issues may well need to be addressed to fill out the picture, and this will likely require going beyond prevailing methods of mediator detection. For present purposes, let us note that with increased understanding of the mechanisms underlying therapeutic change, the prospects will increase for us to (a) understand and address impediments, stalls, and failures in treatment; (b) train therapists by teaching them what change processes they need to effect rather than simply what techniques to use; and (c) identify cross-cutting principles that can be used in designing, refining, and possibly combining interventions.

7. Increased Attention to Therapeutic Relationship and Alliance Building. The treatments described in this book are particularly strong at the level of procedural description – that is, what steps to take and techniques to use – but not so strong in helping therapists build a warm, empathic relationship and a strong working alliance with children and their families. This gap is striking in light of the widespread belief that the quality of the therapeutic relationship or alliance is important to success in most treatment encounters. Indeed, many child therapists rate the therapeutic relationship as more important than the specific techniques used in treatment (Kazdin et al., 1990; Motta & Lynch, 1990; Shirk & Saiz, 1992), and some treated children may agree, even those treated by the well-supported treatments described in this book. Kendall and Southam-Gerow (1996), for example, found that children treated for anxiety disorders using the Coping Cat program (see Chapter 3) rated their relationship with the therapist as the most important aspect of treatment.

What we lack thus far is a strong body of evidence (a) clearly defining what a positive therapeutic relationship consists of, (b) establishing how best to measure it, (c) identifying therapist characteristics and behaviors that foster it, and (d) testing the extent to which it actually predicts outcome when evidence-based treatments are used. All four issues warrant close attention in the next generation of research on evidence-based care.

8. More Potent Comparisons: Improved Power and Stronger Control Conditions. Improvements in basic sampling and study design could greatly strengthen the body of evidence on treatment impact. First, study samples need to be larger than has been the case in many trials to date. Naturally, relatively large samples are needed for the kinds of dismantling, moderator, mediator, and alliance tests just discussed; but a more general benefit of large samples is that they generate more reliable estimates of the true impact of treatment than do small samples. This fact is illustrated in Figure 14.1. The figure shows what is called a funnel graph, this one from McLeod and Weisz (in press), based on a collection of 118 published youth treatment outcome studies. As the figure illustrates, smaller samples (shown at the bottom of the graph) are associated with heterogeneous, unreliable estimates of effect size, and as sample size increases, effect size estimates stabilize. Our work (e.g., McLeod & Weisz, in press; Weisz et al., 1995b) suggests that about half the published studies in the field have employed samples small enough that their effect size estimates may not be very reliable.

A shift in the basic design of most treatment trials could also strengthen the database. The most common experimental design in the field pits an active treatment against a waitlist control condition. Waitlist comparisons are useful in controlling for spontaneous improvement over time, but they have little placebo value because participants know they are not receiving treatment; thus, treatment and waitlist participants cannot be naïve to their treatment condition. Designs that compare a target treatment to an active, credible placebo condition generate more interpretable findings than waitlist designs.

A case could be made that the most valuable design for the next generation of research is one in which youngsters needing treatment are randomized either to the target treatment or to the usual care provided in relevant treatment settings. There the question of interest would be a very practical one: Does this particular target treatment improve on the status quo – that is, does it produce better outcomes than the treatments already in use? Another way to frame the question: Can the target treatment produce

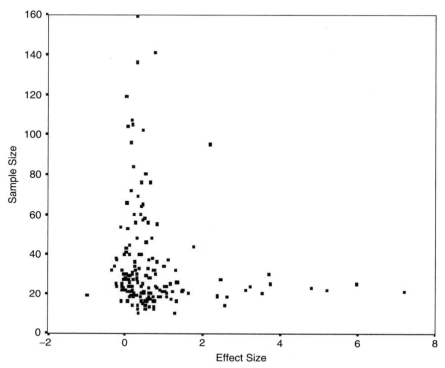

FIGURE 14.1. A funnel graph showing the relation between sample size and effect size within a sample of 118 published youth psychotherapy trials (from McLeod & Weisz, in press). Smaller sample sizes are associated with heterogeneous effect sizes; larger samples generate more stable effect size estimates.

better outcomes than the treatment-referred youngsters would be likely to receive in usual clinical practice? In cases where the answer is yes, the findings generate their own rationale for dissemination of the new treatment.

9. Studying the Effects of Treatments in Real-World Practice Contexts. Discussion of the treatment versus usual care design brings us to a broader theme. In the treatment literature, both psychotherapeutic and medical, a distinction is drawn between two very different forms of outcome research noted previously in this book. In *efficacy designs*, experimental control is used to test treatment impact under carefully arranged idealized conditions – for example, with just the right kind of clients selected, often with potentially troubling comorbidities excluded, with treatment done by particularly skilled therapists who are selected and paid by the researcher and trained to deliver the target treatment as faithfully as possible, and with arrangements designed to keep therapists functioning at their best and treated clients engaged. In *effectiveness designs*, intervention effects are assessed under ordinary clinical conditions, with treatment delivered to average or representative patients or clients, by average or representative practitioners, working under conditions that reflect typical practice realities (e.g., large caseloads, clinic productivity pressures). Given the nature of the research conducted to date, we know a good deal about the efficacy of our tested treatments; we know far less about their effectiveness. This is a problem in its own right, but I believe it also contributes to a number of other problems, including the fact that evidence-based treatments have enjoyed only limited dissemination to date. We will return to this issue later in the chapter.

One way to address this problem is to make treatment outcome research look more like clinical practice than it has in most instances to date. To the extent that we focus treatment trials on clinic-referred youngsters, treated by clinical practitioners, in the settings and under the conditions of real-world practice, we will be able to answer important questions about the impact of our treatments in the world of everyday clinical care. How effective are our tested treatments when they are taken out of efficacy designs and placed in real-world clinical practice? Inquiring minds want to know. Researchers can help.

10. Revisiting the Model That Guides Treatment Development and Testing. Focusing on the need for effectiveness testing brings us to a more fundamental question for the field: Is the scientific model that has guided the development and testing of most evidence-based psychotherapies the most appropriate and useful framework for our field? The prevailing model is one derived largely from research on biological interventions, such as medication. It may not be ideal for interventions that are primarily psychological, behavioral, and social in their focus. This may be a good time to take stock, to consider whether a different model of treatment development and testing could be helpful to the field. To understand why a different model may be needed, let us now consider the status of evidence-based treatments in the world of clinical practice.

Evidence-Based Youth Treatments and Clinical Practice Realities

Although research findings on the treatments surveyed in this book have been generally positive, practice patterns in general continue to emphasize clinically derived procedures pulled together in eclectic fashion by individual therapists. Child and adolescent clinicians, for the most part, have not incorporated most evidence-based procedures into their practice. Indeed, even clinical training programs seeking to emphasize such treatments have major difficulty identifying clinical supervisors from the community who have the expertise needed to supervise trainees in the treatments.

TABLE 14.2. *Evidence-Based Treatments: Why Not Widely Used in Practice?*

1.	Natural time course of the research-dissemination-practice sequence
2.	Evidence not required for practice – i.e., no FDA for psychotherapies
3.	Multiple guidelines and lists, no consensus
4.	Disciplinary boundaries – psychology and psychiatry versus others
5.	Limited practitioner and public awareness of evidence-based treatments
6.	Limited promotion, no "pharmaceutical industry for psychotherapies"
7.	Substantial training requirements (versus pills)
8.	Few incentives to change current practice, many disincentives
9.	Practitioner concerns about rigidity, relevance, appropriateness, of manualized treatments
10.	Medical-pharmaceutical model of treatment development and testing may not be ideal

As we have seen in the book, research has produced potentially bene-ficial treatments for the primary mental health problems that bring most young people into clinics – for example, conduct problems, oppositional behavior, ADHD, depression, fears, and anxiety – but when youngsters with such problems do go to clinics, even today, they are not likely to receive the treatments reviewed in this book. In fact, most of the evidence-based treatments continue to be used mainly in universities and research programs, not in everyday clinical practice. To be sure, the treatments are sometimes featured in lectures, in-service meetings, and continuing educa-tion programs, but widespread dissemination, training, and deployment to practice settings has not happened. To put it in terms my children might use, researchers gave a party, but most clinicians stayed home. Why?

Why Such Limited Dissemination and Deployment of Evidence-Based Treatments? Certainly there are many answers to this question, but I would like to highlight a few, listed in Table 14.2. First, and perhaps least trou-bling of all, is the fact that there is a natural time course for the movement of treatments from research to practice. It may take months to develop a good idea for a treatment program, a year or more to pilot the program and develop a manualized protocol, another year or two to write grant applica-tions and secure funding for a formal test, five or six years to complete the clinical trial, two years to complete analyses and go through the journal review process, and another year before the article appears in print. This is only for the first clinical trial. More years are required to build a body of evidence, and then for word on the treatment program to reach busy prac-titioners. Some of the gap between scientific findings and practice patterns can certainly be attributed to the time this sequence of events requires.

A second impediment to dissemination is that, unlike medications, which cannot be legally prescribed in the absence of FDA approval (see

Food and Drug Administration, 1997), psychosocial treatments are not required to be based on scientific evidence. Thus, there is no sanction against the use of untested treatments, and these now proliferate. Third, while the various mental health disciplines do have practice guidelines, practice parameters, and lists of empirically supported treatments, there is no interdisciplinary consensus as to the most appropriate standard; in the absence of consensus, practitioners who would like their work to reflect the scientific evidence, and parents who seek the best-supported treatment for their child, may find it difficult to be sure which treatments warrant emphasis.

Another crossdisciplinary issue is that most of the evidence-based treatments grow out of research done by psychologists and psychiatrists, whereas more than half the mental health visits in North America involve specialists outside these two professions, many of whom were trained in traditions that do not emphasize research as the principal path to effective treatment. Differences in disciplinary traditions can be difficult to reconcile. The fifth and sixth factors in Table 14.2 are closely related. Practitioners and parents have only limited awareness of evidence-based treatments, in part because large-scale dissemination efforts have not been central to the agenda of treatment developers. Those of us who do the research have little training, and sometimes (as in my case) little competence, in dissemination, promotion, or advertising. More importantly, because there are no large industry profits to be made from psychotherapy, we lack the potent dissemination engine (with drug representatives, television advertising, etc.) that the pharmaceutical industry uses to spread the word about new drugs to practitioners and the public.

A seventh factor is an important reality constraint: for those practitioners who want to adopt treatments that are supported in research tests, the training and supervision required to attain proficiency in those treatments are substantial. As a point of comparison, consider the physician's relatively simpler task of learning to prescribe a new medication appropriately. Even for that learning task, pharmaceutical companies provide abundant opportunities and incentives, including academic detailing, in which company representatives teach by shadowing physicians throughout parts of their workday. Nothing comparable exists for psychotherapies, and for some of the therapies no form of training is available. Eighth, there are few incentives, currently, for practitioners to change their practice patterns, and numerous disincentives – including the discomfort of giving up familiar and trusted procedures, the cost of training and supervision in new approaches, and the lost income from suspending or reducing current practice – to do new learning.

The last two reasons listed in the table are logically linked to one another: some practitioners have concerns about the clinical relevance and appropriateness of this new generation of treatments, and some of these concerns may reflect limitations in the model researchers have been using to develop and test the treatments. We turn now to a few illustrative clinician concerns about these treatments, some thoughts about their concerns in relation to current work by my own research team, and a discussion of models for treatment development and testing.

Practitioner concerns. Some practitioners are not attracted to this new generation of manualized treatments because of concern that the treatments may not be very relevant to the work they do or appropriate for the clients they treat. The specific concerns are diverse, but among those frequently mentioned are (1) that the use of manual-guided, empirically tested treatments may limit therapists' opportunities for creativity and innovation; (2) that manual adherence will constrain the therapist's ability to individualize treatment and thus interfere with development of a productive therapeutic relationship; (3) that most of the treatments have been tested with relatively simple cases at low levels of psychopathology and may not work with more severe cases; (4) that the treatments tend to focus on single problems or disorders and thus may not work with comorbid cases; and (5) that the complexity and volatility of clinically referred individuals and their families make each session unpredictable and a predetermined series of session plans unworkable (for details on some of these arguments, see Addis & Krasnow, 2000; Addis, Wade, & Hatgis, 1999; Garfield, 1996; Havik & VandenBos, 1996; Strupp & Anderson, 1997).

Some of these concerns may be not be realistic appraisals, and certainly not all of them fit all of the tested, manual-guided treatments equally well. However, I think it would be a mistake to simply dismiss the clinicians' points. If the evidence-based treatments are to make their way into practice settings, it will almost certainly be necessary to understand and address the concerns that make some practitioners reluctant to use the treatments. Indeed, some of the concerns may help inform significant improvements in treatment design. This is the impression my research colleagues and I are forming as we engage in research intended to take tested treatments into community clinics and assess their effectiveness there.

Our current research: putting science into practice, and learning from the process. In two current studies, my research team and I are taking empirically tested cognitive-behavioral treatments for youth anxiety (the Coping Cat program; Kendall, 1994; see Chapter 3) and for youth depression (Primary and Secondary Control Enhancement Training, or PASCET; Weisz, Thurber et al., 1997; see Chapter 4) into community clinics in Los Angeles, training and supervising clinic therapists in their use, and applying the treatments exclusively to children referred through normal community channels independent of our study (i.e., we do not advertise or recruit). Youths ages 8–15 who meet diagnostic criteria for the study are randomly assigned to receive either the manual-guided CBT or the usual clinical care already being provided in the clinic. Therapists who provide the treatment are the regular staff and trainees of the participating clinics, with each therapist having been randomly assigned to (1) be trained in the evidence-based CBT treatment, or (2) continue to treat children with their usual approach.

The study is teaching us a good deal about the challenges faced by therapists who try to fit the manualized treatments into their clinic routines, their demanding workloads, and the complex array of life circumstances their clients present. For example, the manuals require presession preparation and postsession recordkeeping that is often difficult for fully booked therapists to manage. And the referred youngsters the therapists treat in the clinics do seem rather different from those treated in many university trials. As an example, comorbidity is pronounced in the clinic cases; the anxiety and depressive disorders that are the focus of the study are typically mixed with oppositional defiant disorder, conduct disorder, or ADHD. More than 60% of our anxious youth and more than 80% of our depressed youth also meet criteria for at least one of those three DSM-IV disruptive behavior disorders. The parents, too, tend to differ from the often middle-class volunteers who answer ads for university clinical trials. Financial and social stresses and time pressures in the family members' lives can lead to missed appointments and premature termination and can undermine parents' ability to support the treatment process in ways such as helping the child with therapy homework.

What we are learning is that even treatment programs that are supported by evidence can face challenges when used in typical practice settings. I strongly believe that empirical testing is critical if we are to develop beneficial treatments. However, a critical question, in my view, is what approach to empirical testing will give us the best treatments? The challenge of fitting lab-tested treatments into real-world practice has led me to wonder whether the primary model that has guided the development and testing of psychotherapies for decades is well-suited to the task.

The medical-pharmaceutical model. Most of the treatments reviewed in this book have been developed and tested via more or less the same model that has guided medical and pharmaceutical research for years. That model – we will call it the *medical-pharmaceutical (MP) model* – may work reasonably well for biological interventions, but it may not be quite as well-suited to the production of clinic-worthy psychotherapies. The MP model involves a stepwise sequence in which experimental treatments and their protocols are first developed in the laboratory, and then tested via an extensive array of laboratory efficacy experiments (see Greenwald & Cullen, 1984; National Institutes of Health, 1994). In this MP model, it is only at the later stages of testing, after extensive efficacy research, that the intervention is brought into community settings "to measure the public health impact" (Greenwald & Cullen, 1984).

The MP model may work reasonably well for interventions that operate directly on the biological system – for example, psychoactive drugs and medical procedures for cancer treatment – or other targets of impact in which differences between lab and clinic conditions may not greatly alter the intervention effect. Under such conditions, relegating effectiveness tests to the very latest stages of treatment development and research may be reasonable, because the intervention may require relatively little modification to be brought to scale successfully in real-world clinical contexts. (Recent evidence on stimulant treatment of ADHD in community settings does suggest, though, that the "bringing to scale" process can be quite necessary, and challenging even if the treatment involved is a medication [MTA Cooperative Group, 1999].)

The gap between lab and clinic appears to be quite wide in the case of psychotherapies, much wider than with biologically focused treatments. For psychotherapies the gap includes (1) psychological and social characteristics of the treated individuals (e.g., with clinic-referred youth more severely disturbed, more likely to meet criteria for a diagnosis, more likely to have comorbidities, and more likely to drop out of treatment); (2) characteristics of their families (e.g., more parental psychopathology, family life event stressors, and perhaps even child maltreatment); (3) reasons for seeking treatment (e.g., not recruited from schools or through ads, but referred by caregivers because of unusually serious problems or family crisis, or even court-ordered); (4) the settings in which treatment is done (e.g., more financial forms to complete, more bureaucracy, and sometimes a less welcoming approach in the clinic); (5) the therapists who provide the treatment (e.g., not grad students or research assistants hired by and loyal to the advisor and committed to her or his treatment program, but rather staff therapists who barely know the treatment developer or the specific treatment, and who may well prefer different treatment methods anyway); (6) the incentive system (e.g., not paid by the treatment developer to deliver her or his treatment with close adherence to the manual, but paid by the clinic to see many cases and with no method prescribed or preferred); and (7) the conditions under which therapists deliver the treatment (not grad students' flexible time, but strict productivity requirements, paperwork to complete, and little time to learn a manual or adhere closely to it).

Perhaps these many differences between therapy in efficacy research and therapy in actual clinical practice are too pronounced to be bridged as simply the final step at the end of a long series of efficacy experiments. Perhaps the number of dimensions along which treatment would need to be changed to bridge the lab-to-clinic gap makes the task of moving from efficacy trials to clinic-based effectiveness tests so complex that the task needs to be made an integral part of the treatment development process. Indeed, the very real-world factors that experimentalists might view as a nuisance (e.g., child comorbidity, parent pathology, life stresses that produce no-shows and dropouts, therapists with heavy caseloads) and thus attempt to avoid (e.g., by recruiting and screening cases, applying exclusion criteria, hiring their own therapists), may in fact be precisely what we need to include, to understand, and to address, if we are to develop psychosocial treatment protocols that fit well into everyday practice. Treatments that cannot cope with these real-world factors may not fare so well in practice, no matter how beneficial they are in efficacy trials.

A Deployment-Focused Model of Treatment Development and Testing. Given the importance of developing treatments that are robust in clinical practice, there may be some value in considering a shift from the traditional MP model to a different perspective on treatment development research. The model I envision is one that brings treatments into the crucible of clinical practice early in their development and treats testing in the practice setting as a sequential process, not as a single final phase. I call this perspective the *deployment-focused model (DFM) of treatment development and testing.* A primary goal of the DFM is to outline a process by which treatments that show beneficial effects in efficacy trials can be adapted for testing and use in the practice contexts and conditions for which they are ultimately intended. A testable premise underlying the model is depicted in Figure 14.2. The figure reflects the idea that an evidence-based treatment (EBT in the diagram) that has fared quite well in efficacy trials may have potential to be beneficial in a practice context, but that the potential is most likely to be realized if the treatment has undergone subsequent adaptation to practice

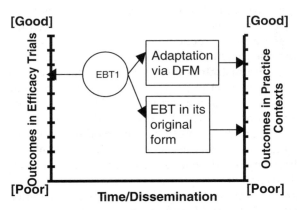

FIGURE 14.2. A testable proposition underlying the deployment-focused model of treatment development and testing. After successful efficacy testing, evidence-based treatments may need to undergo adaptation to the real-world clients and conditions for which they are intended. Treatments thus adapted may fare better in true effectiveness tests than evidence-based treatments that remain in their efficacy-tested form.

conditions. As the figure suggests, the effects of an evidence-based treatment that is moved into a practice context are expected to be more modest if the treatment is moved in its original efficacy-tested form than if it first undergoes the kinds of practice adaptations proposed in the DFM.

An alternative perspective. Of course, the DFM reflects only one view of how the transition from research to practice might operate. Some in the clinical research community believe that concerns about the gap between research and practice conditions are overblown, that efficacy-tested manuals can travel well from research to practice settings, and that once most treatments have been shown to be beneficial under controlled efficacy test conditions they can be taken into the field and applied effectively in clinical practice (see discussion in Addis et al., 1999; Chambless, 1996). In support of this view, one could argue that the best version of a treatment to bring to practice is precisely the version that has been tested and shown to work. This perspective might be called the *efficacy transfer model*. This is certainly a respectable perspective. Indeed, I do believe that clinical practice outcomes could be markedly improved for many boys and girls by a faithful application of such treatment procedures as those described in this book, many of which are supported by efficacy trials. My goal here is to offer a proposal for what I suspect may be a more optimal way to create effective treatments for use in clinical practice. At the very least, my hope is to offer heuristically useful ideas to stimulate further discussion.

Goals of the deployment-focused model. The proposed DFM is explicitly geared to ensuring that tests in practice settings do occur, and thus to the production of psychotherapies that work well in those settings. The model is guided by four primary aims: (1) producing treatments that can fit smoothly into everyday practice, working well with clinic-referred individuals treated in clinic settings by practicing clinicians; (2) generating evidence on treatment outcome in actual clinical practice, the kind of evidence clinicians and clinic administrators most need in order to assess the value of the treatments for their settings; (3) prompting direct tests of whether evidence-based treatments can outperform usual care in practice contexts; and (4) producing a body of evidence on the nature, necessary and sufficient components, boundary conditions (i.e., moderators), and change/causal processes (i.e., mediators) associated with treatment impact that will be especially strong in external validity, because it is derived from research in the practice context.

The fourth point warrants comment. As noted earlier, we need evidence from dismantling research to help us identify necessary and sufficient treatment components, from moderator tests to help us identify the effective range of benefit, and from mediator tests to help us identify change processes that account for treatment effects. However, within what kinds of designs will we generate the most useful answers to questions about necessary and sufficient components, moderators, and mediators? In my

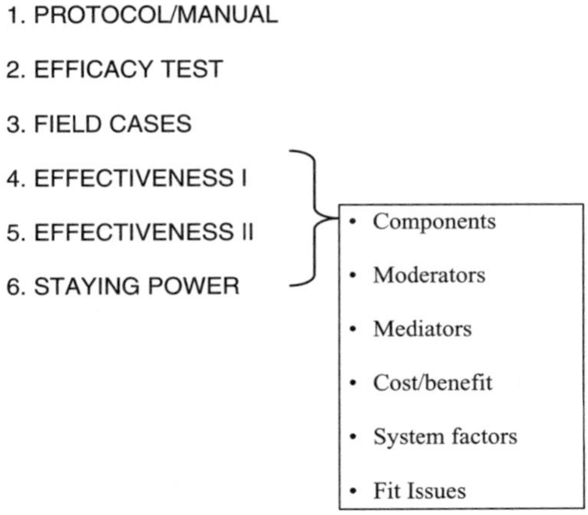

1. PROTOCOL/MANUAL

2. EFFICACY TEST

3. FIELD CASES

4. EFFECTIVENESS I

5. EFFECTIVENESS II

6. STAYING POWER

- Components
- Moderators
- Mediators
- Cost/benefit
- System factors
- Fit Issues

FIGURE 14.3. Steps and procedures in the deployment-focused model (DFM) of treatment development and testing.

view, the answers generated via efficacy designs may differ substantially from the answers one might generate through studies with referred youth treated by practitioners in genuine practice conditions, and the second set of answers will be more relevant than the first to our need to understand real-world treatment effects. Thus, even the kinds of research questions that have thus far been addressed primarily within efficacy designs (e.g., component effects, moderators, mediators) may actually be more profitably addressed in effectiveness studies designed to represent the clients, therapists, and contexts of clinical practice. The DFM is intended to generate precisely that kind of research, beginning rather early in the development and testing process. The model entails six steps of treatment development and testing, as shown in Figure 14.3.

Step 1: Theoretically and clinically guided construction, refinement, and manualizing of the treatment protocol. The initial step is the development, refinement, pilot testing, and manualizing of the treatment protocol. Theory and evidence on the nature and treatment of the target condition, the clinical literature (e.g., published case studies), and input from clinicians who have treated youngsters with that condition, are used to guide the design of treatment components and to plan clinically sensitive ways of presenting those components in sessions. Ideally, feedback from experienced clinicians who treat the target condition is used to refine the procedures, language, and supporting materials. The goal is production of (a) a treatment protocol that is well-grounded in the theoretical and empirical literature on the target condition (e.g., depression); (b) a manual that conveys the treatment components clearly to the therapist, and includes clinically appropriate means of presenting those components to the clients; and (c) engaging and clinically appropriate supporting materials (e.g., youth's practice book) that convey key ideas, and related exercises, directly to the participants. The treatment protocol should grow out of a clearly articulated model of the condition being treated, and of the mechanism(s) by which change in that condition is brought about through the treatment protocol.

Step 2: Initial efficacy trial under controlled conditions to establish evidence of benefit. Next, an initial group-design efficacy trial is used to assess whether the treatment (compared to a control group) can produce beneficial effects with recruited symptomatic youth who are treated under controlled laboratory conditions. The focus here is on symptomatic study volunteers, not clinically referred cases, because it is important in the initial test to avoid the risk of exposing severely disordered individuals who seek clinical care to a totally untested intervention. Step 2 research addresses this ethical issue, helping to determine whether the program is sufficiently promising when delivered under optimal experimental conditions to warrant further development and testing in clinical practice settings with referred youth.

Step 3: Single-case applications in practice settings, with progressive adaptations to the protocol. The third step is a series of single-case pilot tests with clinic-referred individuals, treated in clinical settings by research-affiliated therapists who know the protocol well. The setting(s) should be representative of those in which the treatment developer intends ultimately for the treatment to be used. Ideally, there is dual supervision – that is, one supervisor from the research team who is expert in the treatment protocol plus a second who is an experienced clinic staff member – to ensure (a) faithfulness to the core principles and the model of change that guides the treatment protocol, and (b) appropriateness of the treatment for, and goodness-of-fit with, the clinical setting and the community of the child and family. Throughout this process, successive modifications are made in the specifics of the treatment protocol and procedures, to satisfy (b), while adhering to (a). Changes are anticipated in the nature of the treatment elements, the ways the elements are presented to the clients and their family members, and the materials used to guide therapists and clients through the treatment. In this regard, the Stage 3 process can guide an important decision as to the type of manualizing best-suited to real-life practice, with choices ranging from highly structured, session-by-session instructions (Clarke et al., 1990) to broad treatment principles with illustrations of how to apply them (Henggeler, Schoenwald et al., 1998), and with various manual formats (Chorpita, 1998) as viable candidates for "best-fit" with the treatment setting. Stage 3 will be most informative to the extent that it encompasses a range of clients differing in such characteristics as age, gender, ethnicity, culture, and pattern of comorbidity.

Step 4: Partial effectiveness tests. The fourth step involves a series of group-design studies testing the newly adapted treatment protocol in ways that entail selected elements of representative clinical care. The idea is to explore, in stepwise fashion, the extent to which the protocol works (a) with referred youngsters, (b) when used in clinical care settings, (c) when used by representative practitioners, and (d) when compared to usual care in the practice settings of interest. Tests that encompass all these elements concurrently would risk a loss of inferential power because if such tests showed that the target treatment did not outperform usual care it would be difficult to discern the reason; such findings might reflect inappropriateness of the protocol for referred youths, a mismatch between protocol and constraints of the treatment setting, or clinician difficulties in using the procedures. To maximize learning in regard to prospects and problems of the protocol, tests in Step 4 will need to focus on the various elements of effectiveness testing, considered separately and eventually in strategically selected combinations. The specific structure of the tests in Step 4, and their sequential order, would depend, of course, on the nature of the protocol, the nature of the context for which it is ultimately intended, and the goals of the intervention developer. A common goal across these variations, however, would be sequential testing that examines the protocol in relation to key elements of representative clinical practice and eventually positions the protocol for a full test of effectiveness and disseminability in Step 5.

Step 5: Full tests of effectiveness and dissemination. Step 5 entails a series of group-comparison clinical trials, with the target treatment provided to clinic clients, in the clinic, by clinic staff therapists trained to proficiency in the protocol. As in Step 4, clients are randomly assigned to either the target treatment or usual care. A key goal is to assess the effectiveness and disseminability of the treatment program under the most representative clinic conditions possible. Success is assessed in two ways: (a) a test of whether trained staff practitioners actually adhere to the manual in their treatment sessions, and (b) a test of whether clients treated by the manual-trained staff practitioners show greater treatment gains than clients treated by staff practitioners employing their usual treatment approaches.

Step 6: Tests of goodness-of-fit and sustainability in practice contexts. The final step involves a genre of research focused on the relation between the treatment program and the practice contexts in which it is employed. One aim will be to identify factors that predict (a) the likelihood that practitioners will use the protocol, (b) the degree to which those who do use it will adhere to the manual, and (c) the extent to which use of the protocol improves youth outcomes. An overarching focus will be assessment of the protocol's staying power – that is, its continued use, with treatment integrity and youth outcomes maintained – over time in various settings. Certainly one ultimate test of the usefulness, useability, and likely long-term impact of the treatment protocol is the extent to which mental health service providers continue to use it with fidelity and to produce positive outcomes, after the researchers have left the scene. The likelihood of such long-term staying power is apt to increase to the extent that the treatment program has been designed to mesh well with the clients, families, therapists, settings, and conditions of real-world clinical practice.

Additional foci throughout Steps 4, 5, and 6: Components, moderators, mediators, cost-benefit, system factors, and fit issues. There is much additional learning that can be done within the studies conducted in Steps 4–6. As shown in Figure 14.3, an important goal is to use variations in the design and measures of these studies to (1) ascertain the necessary and sufficient components of our complex treatment packages, (2) identify moderators of outcome that set boundaries around treatment impact, (3) assess whether proposed mediators of treatment outcome do in fact mediate, (4) assess treatment costs in relation to benefits, (5) investigate which organizational factors in the systems and settings where the treatments are used (e.g., community mental health clinics, inpatient psychiatric units, primary care clinics, schools, social service agencies) relate to how effectively the treatments are used, and (6) test variations in treatment procedures, packaging, training, and delivery designed to improve fit to various settings in which the treatment is deployed. The aim is to generate a rich mosaic of information about the target treatment, its most essential ingredients, the factors that enhance or undermine its success, the boundary conditions therapists need to know when deciding whether to use it with children of particular demographic and clinical characteristics, the change processes that account for its effects, and procedural modifications that can magnify treatment effects or extend their duration.

Of course, current efficacy research already includes numerous dismantling studies and has begun to include tests for potential moderators and mediators. Indeed, some might argue that efficacy studies are the most appropriate context for such work. As noted previously, I am not so sure. In general, I think we need to ask ourselves whether the most valid answers to questions about treatment outcome, component contributions, moderators, and mediators are really more likely to come from research with recruited samples seen under controlled lab conditions or from referred samples seen under genuine clinical practice conditions.

Questions and Answers about the Deployment-Focused Model of Treatment Development and Testing. Three questions about the model and its application warrant attention here.

1. *How does the model relate to untested clinically derived treatments?* What implications does the model have for clinically derived treatments that are already being delivered in practice settings but that have not been previously tested? Certainly such treatments can be put on track for testing,

but perhaps with a somewhat different emphasis than for the kinds of treatments presented in this book. The fact that the clinically derived treatments are already in clinical use may mean that some of the work of fitting the treatment to the practice setting has already been done. For these treatments, Step 1 may be not so much a matter of creating a manual from scratch as describing in detail what is currently being done in the treatment. The newly minted manual would need to be field tested (Step 3), but the process may well lead to less modification than would be the case for treatments not derived from practice. Certainly the full range of empirical testing described in the model, from Steps 2–6, should apply to clinically derived treatments.

2. *How does the model relate to current treatments that already have an evidence base?* Most of the treatments described in this book already have a manualized protocol, and most have had the benefit of multiple efficacy trials – a kind of extended version of Step 2 in the model. In some cases, elements of clinical representativeness also have been a part of these trials; for example, some have involved clinically referred youths with severe problems. What may remain are opportunities to bring the treatments more fully into the effectiveness domain, perhaps beginning with field cases (Step 3), then proceeding to effectiveness tests (Steps 4 and 5) with referred youth, treated by average clinicians, in representative service settings, under practice conditions. In other words, the model is probably potentially relevant to most current treatments that have already been tested, at least to the extent that the treatment developers agree with the goals of the model.

3. *How does the model relate to tested treatments that are designed to use alternate sites and models of delivery?* An especially interesting question arises regarding treatments that are designed to use sites and models of delivery that bypass conventional service settings. As an example, consider the ADHD Summer Treatment Program developed by William Pelham and described in Chapter 7. In all the tests of this program, ADHD youngsters have been treated by supervised BA-level counselors in summer day camp settings. This is certainly not conventional clinical practice, but it may be the right context for this particular program. From the perspective of the DFM, the critical question is, "How does the treatment developer intend for the treatment to be used ultimately – that is, with which kinds of youth, treated in which settings, by what kinds of providers, and under what conditions?" To the extent that the context of the Pelham et al. (1998) treatment outcome research matches the context in which Pelham et al. intend for their program to be used outside of their research, an argument could be made that their work is already consistent with the core values of the DFM.

Another instructive example is the case of multisystemic therapy (MST; Henggeler et al., 1998; Chapter 13). Most tests of MST have involved therapists who are not a part of the conventional mental health or juvenile justice systems, but who are hired and trained by MST researchers. The training is extensive, and supervision can be as well. Moreover, the work of the therapist – visiting the youth's life settings, working with influential adults in multiple systems, being on call at all hours – goes well beyond what most therapists do in conventional clinical practice. To the extent that MST developers believe that the way they deliver treatment in their research resembles the way it should be delivered in everyday practice outside of research, their research may already be consistent with DFM goals. On the other hand, if MST were ultimately intended for delivery by community mental health center staff, then the DFM would suggest that such staff should be the ones delivering MST in the empirical tests of the treatment. The basic premise of the DFM is that whatever the treatment developer's goal is regarding ultimate deployment of his or her treatment program, that goal should be reflected in the way treatment development, refinement, and testing are conducted.

Summary

The evidence on treatments for children and adolescents includes more than 1,500 treatment outcome studies. Several hundred of these have qualified for inclusion in meta-analyses; these have generated medium-to-large effect sizes, and the effects have shown specificity to the treated problems and holding power over the five- to six-month follow-up periods that are characteristic in the field. In this book, we have described, illustrated, reviewed, and critiqued some of the strongest of the specific evidence-based treatments for youth. Taken together, these treatments have been designed to address the problems and disorders that appear to be the most common causes of referral for clinical care.

   While noting that the scientific literature and the treatments described here have numerous strengths, I have also tried to note gaps in the portfolio. For example, some particularly ominous conditions – such as, substance abuse, bulimia, suicidal behavior, and adolescent ADHD – need increased attention, and we need more treatments designed to cope with covariation among problems and comorbidity among disorders. The research focus also needs to encompass nonbehavioral treatment models that are widely used but untested. In addition, for treatments that are well-supported, we need a refined understanding of which components are actually necessary, what boundary conditions (e.g., age, ethnicity, culture, family configuration, therapist characteristics) limit the range of effects, and what change processes mediate treatment impact. We need research that can help us understand what a good therapeutic relationship is, how to produce it, and how it relates to treatment outcomes. We also need to complement our emphasis on treatment efficacy with evidence on effectiveness with referred youth, treated by practitioners, under typical practice conditions.

A significant concern is that most evidence-based treatments are not reaching most referred youngsters. Many of our best-tested treatments continue to be used almost exclusively in university research settings, and the great majority of referred youth continue to receive interventions that have never been tested in a clinical trial. There are certainly many reasons for this state of affairs, but one important cause may be that the medical-pharmaceutical model that has guided so much of psychosocial treatment, development, and research may not be well-suited to the task.

As an alternative, I have suggested a deployment-focused model of treatment development and testing. The model is put forth to encourage both the developmental steps and the kinds of research needed to create treatments that are well-suited to the real-world applications their developers intend for them. A basic premise of the model is that our research needs to engage the clients, providers, settings, and conditions toward which our treatments are ultimately aimed. When this happens, we are apt to discover multiple obstacles to clinical use, have multiple opportunities to address those obstacles, and thus find ways to shape the treatments to fit their intended use. The process is reminiscent of habit #2 in Stephen Covey's *The Seven Habits of Highly Effective People*: "Begin with the end in mind." This concept can be applied to the development of highly effective interventions. If we intend for our treatments to have impact on real-world clinical care, perhaps we should design our treatments and shape our research with that end in mind.

Concluding Comment: Supporting Not a List of Specific Treatments, But an Approach

One final point warrants emphasis here. The list of evidence-based treatments described and evaluated in this book is best viewed as a first-wave collection. These treatments are likely to be of real benefit to many youngsters and families facing a variety of problems and disorders. However, exact composition of the list will inevitably evolve over time as more studies are completed and the evidence base changes. This is in the nature of the scientific process. New treatments will be added in future iterations, and it is possible that one or more of the treatments that look strong today may drop off the list if adverse evidence accumulates. The point of this book, then, is certainly not to reify any particular treatment or any particular list of them. The book is devoted not to a list but to a process: identifying and selecting beneficial treatments by looking to the hard evidence on their effects, evidence derived from fair tests.

Like democratic elections and the jury system, treatment outcome research is not perfect, but it is probably a better approach than the alternatives. An important challenge for the future will be to make the findings of that research accessible to clinicians who want it to inform their practice. An equally important challenge will be to make the realities of practice evident to researchers who want their work to be clinically relevant; this seems essential if evidence-based treatments are to be built that fit smoothly into clinical settings and work well with the youngsters and parents who go to those settings seeking help. In short, if we want more evidence-based practice, we may need more practice-based evidence.

References

Abikoff, H., & Gittelman, R. (1984). Does behavior therapy normalize the classroom behavior of hyperactive children? *Archives of General Psychiatry, 41,* 449–454.

Abramowitz, A. J., & O'Leary, S. G. (1990). Effectiveness of delayed punishment in an applied setting. *Behavior Therapy, 21,* 231–239.

Abramowitz, A. J., O'Leary, S. G., & Futtersak, M. W. (1988). The relative impact of long and short reprimands on children's off-task behavior in the classroom. *Behavior Therapy, 19,* 243–247.

Abramowitz, A. J., O'Leary, S. G., & Rosen, L. A. (1987). Reducing off-task behavior in the classroom: A comparison of encouragement and reprimands. *Journal of Abnormal Child Psychology, 15,* 153–163.

Achenbach, T. M. (1991). *Manual for the Child Behavior Checklist/4–18 and 1991 profile.* Burlington: University of Vermont, Department of Psychiatry.

Achenbach, T. M., & Edelbrock, C. S. (1983). *Manual for the Child Behavior Checklist and Revised Child Behavior Profile.* Burlington, VT: University Associates in Psychiatry.

(1986). *Manual for the Teacher's Report Form and Teacher Version of the Child Behavior Profile.* Burlington: University of Vermont, Department of Psychiatry.

Achenbach, T. M., & Howell, C. T. (1993). Are American children's problems getting worse? A 13-year comparison. *Journal of the American Academy of Child and Adolescent Psychiatry, 32,* 1145–1154.

Achenbach, T. M., McConaughy, S. H., & Howell, C. T. (1987). Child/adolescent behavioral and emotional problems: Implications of cross-informant correlations for situational specificity. *Psychological Bulletin, 101,* 213–232.

Addis, M. E., & Krasnow, A. D. (2000). A national survey of practicing psychologists' attitudes toward psychotherapy treatment manuals. *Journal of Consulting and Clinical Psychology, 68,* 331–339.

Addis, M. E., Wade, W. A., & Hatgis, C. (1999). Barriers to dissemination of evidence-based practices: Addressing practitioners' concerns about manual-based psychotherapies. *Clinical Psychology: Science and Practice, 6,* 430–441.

Adesso, V. J., & Lipson, J. W. (1981). Group training of parents as therapists for their children. *Behavior Therapy, 12,* 625–633.

Albano, A. M., & Barlow, D. H. (1996). Breaking the vicious cycle: Cognitive-behavioral group treatment for socially anxious youth. In E. D. Hibbs & P. S. Jensen (Eds.), *Psychosocial treatments for child and adolescent disorders: Empirically based strategies for clinical practice* (pp. 43–62). Washington, DC: American Psychological Association.

Albano, A. M., Chorpita, B., & Barlow, D. H. (1996). Childhood anxiety disorders. In E. J. Mash & R. A. Barkley (Eds.), *Child psychopathology* (pp. 196–241). New York: Guilford.

Alexander, J. F., & Parsons, B. V. (1973). Short-term behavioral intervention with delinquent families: Impact on family process and recidivism. *Journal of Abnormal Psychology, 51*, 219–225.

(1982). *Functional family therapy: Principles and procedures*. Monterey, CA: Brooks/Cole.

Alexander, J. F., Barton, C., Schiavo, R. S., & Parsons, B. V. (1976). Systems behavioral intervention with families of delinquents. *Journal of Consulting and Clinical Psychology, 44*, 656–664.

Alexander, J., Waldron, H. B., Newberry, A. M., & Liddle, N. (1990). The functional family therapy model. In S. G. Alfred & S. Friedman (Eds.), *Family therapy for adolescent drug use* (pp. 183–199). Lexington, MA: Lexington Books/D.C. Heath and Company.

Allen, M. (1991). Crafting a federal legislative framework for child welfare reform. *American Journal of Orthopsychiatry, 61*, 610–623.

American Academy of Child and Adolescent Psychiatry. (1997). AACAP official action: Practice parameters for the assessment and treatment of children and adolescents with bipolar disorder. *Journal of the American Academy of Child and Adolescent Psychiatry, 36*, 138–157.

American Academy of Pediatrics. (2000). Clinical practice guideline: Diagnosis and evaluation of the child with attention deficit/hyperactivity disorder. *Pediatrics, 105*, 1158–1170.

American Psychiatric Association. (1987). *Diagnostic and statistical manual of mental disorders* (3rd ed., rev.). Washington, DC: Author.

(1994). *Diagnostic and statistical manual of mental disorders* (4th ed.). Washington, DC: Author.

(1995). Practice guidelines for the treatment of patients with substance use disorders: Alcohol, cocaine, opioids. *American Journal of Psychiatry, 152* (suppl. 11), 1–59.

(2000). *Diagnostic and statistical manual of mental disorders* (4th ed., rev.). Washington, DC: Author.

Anastopoulos, A. D., Barkley, R. A., & Shelton, T. L. (1996). Family-based treatment: Psychosocial intervention for children and adolescents with attention deficit hyperactivity disorder. In E. D. Hibbs & P. S. Jensen (Eds.), *Psychosocial treatments for child and adolescent disorders: Empirically based strategies for clinical practice* (pp. 267–284). Washington, DC: American Psychological Association.

Anastopoulos, A. D., Shelton, T. L., DuPaul, G. J., & Guevremont, D. C. (1993). Parent training for attention-deficit hyperactivity disorder: Its impact on parent functioning. *Journal of Abnormal Child Psychology, 21*, 581–596.

Anderson, J. C., Williams, S. M., McGee, R., & Silva, P. A. (1987). DSM-III disorders in preadolescent children: Prevalence in a large sample from the general population. *Archives of General Psychiatry, 44,* 69–76.

Angold, A., Costello, E. J., Burns, B. J., Erkanli, A., & Farmer, E. M. Z. (2000). Effectiveness of nonresidential specialty mental health services for children and adolescents in the "real world." *Journal of the American Academy of Child and Adolescent Psychiatry, 39,* 154–160.

Angold, A., Costello, E. J., & Erkanli, A. (1999). Comorbidity. *Journal of Child Psychology and Psychiatry, 40,* 57–87.

Ashcraft, C. W. (1971). The later school achievement of treated and untreated emotionally handicapped children. *Journal of School Psychology, 9,* 338–342.

Avenevoli, S., & Steinberg, L. (2001). The continuity of depression across the adolescent transition. In H. Reese & R. Kail (Eds.), *Advances in child development and behavior* (pp. 139–173). New York: Academic Press.

Axline, V. (1969). *Play therapy.* New York: Ballantine.

Ayllon, T., Layman, D., & Kandel, H. J. (1975). A behavioral-educational alternative to drug control of hyperactive children. *Journal of Applied Behavior Analysis, 8,* 137–146.

Azrin, N. H., Donohue, B., Besalel, V. A., Kogan, E. S., & Acierno, R. (1994). Youth drug abuse treatment: A controlled study. *Journal of Child and Adolescent Substance Abuse, 3,* 1–16.

Baer, R. A., & Nietzel, M. T. (1991). Cognitive and behavioral treatment of impulsivity in children: A meta-analytic review of the outcome literature. *Journal of Clinical Child Psychology, 2,* 400–412.

Bandura, A. (1971). *Psychological modeling: Conflicting theories.* Chicago: Aldine-Atherton.

(1973). *Aggression: A social learning analysis.* Englewood Cliffs, NJ: Prentice-Hall.

(1977). Self-efficacy: Toward a unifying theory of behavioral change. *Psychological Review, 84,* 191–215.

(1986). *Social foundations of thought and action.* Englewood Cliffs, NJ: Prentice-Hall.

Bandura, A., & Adams, N. E. (1977). Analysis of self-efficacy theory of behavioral change. *Cognitive Therapy and Research, 1,* 287–308.

Bandura, A., Grusec, J. E., & Menlove, F. L. (1967). Vicarious extinction of avoidance behavior. *Journal of Personality and Social Psychology, 5,* 16–23.

Bandura, A., & Menlove, F. L. (1968). Factors determining vicarious extinction of avoidance behavior through symbolic modeling. *Journal of Personality and Social Psychology, 8,* 99–108.

Bandura, A., & Walters, R. H. (1963). *Social learning and personality development.* New York: Holt, Rinehart, and Winston.

Bank, L., Marlowe, J. H., Reid, J. B., Patterson, G. R., & Weinrott, M. R. (1991). A comparative evaluation of parent-training interventions for families of chronic delinquents. *Journal of Abnormal Child Psychology, 19,* 15–33.

Barabasz, A. F. (1973). Group desensitization of test anxiety in elementary school. *The Journal of Psychology, 83,* 295–301.

Barkley, R. A. (1981). *Hyperactive children: A handbook for diagnosis and treatment.* New York: Guilford.

(1997). *Defiant children: A clinician's manual for assessment and parent training.* New York: Guilford.

(1997a). Behavioral inhibition, sustained attention, and executive functions: Constructing a unifying theory of ADHD. *Psychological Bulletin, 121,* 65–94.

(1997b). *Defiant children: A clinician's manual for assessment and parent training,* 2nd edition. New York: Guilford.

(1998). Attention-deficit/hyperactivity disorder. In E. J. Mash & R. A. Barkley (Eds.), *Treatment of childhood disorders,* 2nd ed. (pp. 55–110). New York: Guilford.

Barkley, R. A., Anastopoulos, A. D., Guevremont, D. C., & Fletcher, K. F. (1992). Adolescents with attention-deficit hyperactivity disorder: Mother-adolescent interactions, family beliefs and conflicts, and maternal psychopathology. *Journal of Abnormal Child Psychology, 20,* 263–288.

Barkley, R. A., Guevremont, D. C., Anastopoulos, A. D., & Fletcher, K. E. (1992). A comparison of three family therapy programs for treating family conflicts in adolescents with attention-deficit hyperactivity disorder. *Journal of Consulting and Clinical Psychology, 60,* 450–462.

Baron, R. M., & Kenny, D. A. (1986). The moderator-mediator variable distinction in social psychological research: Conceptual, strategic, and statistical considerations. *Journal of Personality and Social Psychology, 51,* 1173–1182.

Barrett, P. M. (1991). *Management of childhood anxiety: A family intervention programme.* Nathan, Australia: Griffith University.

Barrett, P. M., Dadds, M. R., & Rapee, R. M. (1991). *Coping koala workbook.* Nathan, Australia: Griffith University.

Barrett, P. M., Dadds, M. R., & Rapee, R. M. (1996). Family treatment of childhood anxiety: A controlled trial. *Journal of Consulting and Clinical Psychology, 64,* 333–342.

Barrett, P. M., Rapee, R. M., Dadds, M. M., & Ryan, S. M. (1996). Family enhancement of cognitive style in anxious and aggressive children. *Journal of Abnormal Child Psychology, 24,* 187–203.

Barton, C., & Alexander, J. F. (1980). Functional family therapy. In A. S. Gurman & D. P. Kniskern (Eds.), *Handbook of family therapy.* New York: Bruner/Mazel.

Barton, C., Alexander, J. F., Waldron, H., Turner, C. W., & Warburton, J. (1985). Generalizing treatment effects of functional family therapy: Three replications. *The American Journal of Family Therapy, 13,* 16–26.

Bateson, G. (1972). *Steps to an ecology of the mind.* New York: Ballantine.

Baucom, D. H., Shoham, V., Mueser, K. T., Daiuto, A. D., & Stickle, T. R. (1998). Empirically supported couple and family interventions for marital distress and adult mental health problems. *Journal of Consulting and Clinical Psychology, 66,* 53–88.

Baum, C. G., & Forehand, R. (1981). Long-term follow-up assessment of parent training by use of multiple outcome measures. *Behavior Therapy, 12,* 643–652.

Baumrind, D. (1967). Child care practices anteceding three patterns of preschool behavior. *Genetic Psychology Monographs, 75,* 43–88.

Beck, A. T. (1967). *Depression: Clinical, experimental, and theoretical aspects*. Philadelphia: University of Pennsylvania Press.

Beck, A. T., Rush, A. J., Shaw, B. F., & Emery, G. (1979). *Cognitive therapy of depression*. New York: Guilford.

Bernal, M. E., Klinnert, M. D., & Schultz, L. A. (1980). Outcome evaluation of behavioral parent training and client-centered parent counseling for children with conduct problems. *Journal of Applied Behavior Analysis, 13*, 677–691.

Bernstein, G. A., Borchardt, C. M., & Perwien, A. R. (1996). Anxiety disorders in children and adolescents: A review of the past 10 years. *Journal of the American Academy of Child and Adolescent Psychiatry, 35*, 1110–1119.

Bickman, L. (1996). A continuum of care: More is not always better. *American Psychologist, 51*, 689–701.

Bickman, L., Guthrie, P. R., Foster, E. M., Lambert, E. W., Summerfelt, W. T., Breda, C. S., & Heflinger, C. A. (1995). *Evaluating managed mental health services: The Fort Bragg experiment*. New York: Plenum Press.

Bickman, L., Noser, K., & Summerfelt, W. T. (1999). Long-term effects of a system of care on children and adolescents. *Journal of Behavioral Health Services Research, 26*, 185–202.

Bickman, L., Summerfelt, W. T., Firth, J. M., et al. (1997). The Stark County Evaluation Project: Baseline results of a randomized experiment. In C. T. Nixon & D. A. Northrup (Eds.), *Evaluating mental health services: How do programs work in the real world?* (pp. 231–258). Thousand Oaks, CA: Sage.

Birmaher, B., Brent, D. A., Kolko, D., Baugher, M., Bridge, J., Holder, D., Iyengar, S., & Ulloa, R. E. (2000). Clinical outcome after short-term psychotherapy for adolescents with major depressive disorder. *Archives of General Psychiatry, 37*, 29–36.

Birmaher, B., Ryan, N. D., Williamson, D. E., Brent, D. A., Kaufman, J., Dahl, R. E., Perel, J., & Nelson, B. (1996a). Childhood and adolescent depression: A review of the past 10 years, Part I. *Journal of the American Academy of Child & Adolescent Psychiatry, 35*, 1427–1439.

Birmaher, B., Ryan, N. D., Williamson, D. E., Brent, D. A., & Kaufman, J. (1996b). Childhood and adolescent depression: A review of the past 10 years, Part II. *Journal of the American Academy of Child & Adolescent Psychiatry, 35*, 1575–1583.

Bjorkqvist, K., Osterman, K., & Kaukiainen, A. (1992). The development of direct and indirect aggressive strategies in males and females. In K. Bjorkqvist & P. Niemala (Eds.), *Of mice and women: Aspects of female aggression* (pp. 51–64). New York: Academic Press.

Bloomquist, M. L., August, G. J., & Ostrander, R. (1991). Effects of a school-based cognitive-behavioral intervention for ADHD children. *Journal of Abnormal Child Psychology, 19*, 591–605.

Borduin, C. M., Henggeler, S. W., Blaske, D. M., & Stein, R. J. (1990). Multisystemic treatment of adolescent sexual offenders. *International Journal of Offender Therapy and Comparative Criminology, 35*, 569–578.

Borduin, C. M., Mann, B. J., Cone, L. T., Henggeler, S. W., Fucci, B. R., Blaske, D. M., & Williams, R. A. (1995). Multisystemic treatment of serious juvenile offenders: Long-term prevention of criminality and violence. *Journal of Consulting and Clinical Psychology, 63*, 569–578.

Bornstein, B. (1949). Analysis of a phobic child. *Psychoanalytic Study of the Child, 3–4*, 181–226.

Bowers, D. S., Clement, P. W., Fantuzzo, J. W., & Sorensen, D. A. (1985). Effects of teacher-administered and self-administered reinforcers on learning disabled children. *Behavior Therapy, 16*, 357–369.

Breiner, J., & Forehand, R. (1981). An assessment of the effects of parent training on clinic-referred children's school behavior. *Behavioral Assessment, 3*, 31–42.

Brent, D. A., Holder, D., Kolko, D., Birmaher, B., Baugher, M., Roth, C., Iyengar, S., & Johnson, B. A. (1997). A clinical psychotherapy trial for adolescent depression comparing cognitive, family, and supportive therapy. *Archives of General Psychiatry, 54*, 877–885.

Brent, D. A., Kolko, D. J., Birmaher, B., Baugher, M., Bridge, J., Roth, C., & Holder, D. (1998). Predictors of treatment efficacy in a clinical trial of three psychosocial treatments for adolescent depression. *Journal of the American Academy of Child & Adolescent Psychiatry, 37*, 906–914.

Brent, D. A., Roth, C. M., Holder, D. P., Kolko, D. J., Birmaher, B., Johnson, B. A., & Schweers, J. A. (1996). Psychosocial interventions for treating adolescent suicidal depression: A comparison of three psychosocial interventions. In E. D. Hibbs & P. S. Jensen (Eds.), *Psychosocial treatments for child and adolescent disorders: Empirically based strategies for clinical practice* (pp. 187–206). Washington, DC: American Psychological Association.

Brestan, E. V., & Eyberg, S. M. (1998). Effective psychosocial treatments of conduct-disordered children and adolescents: 29 years, 82 studies, and 5,272 kids. *Journal of Clinical Child Psychology, 27*, 180–189.

Brettschneider, C. L. (2001). *Punishment, property, and justice.* Burlington, VT: Ashgate Publishing, Ltd.

Brinkmeyer, M. Y., & Eyberg, S. M. (2003). Parent-child interaction therapy for oppositional children. In A. E. Kazdin & J. R. Weisz (Eds.), *Evidence-based psychotherapies for children and adolescents* (pp. 204–223). New York: Guilford.

Bromfield, R. (1992). *Playing for real: The world of a child therapist.* New York: Dutton.

Bronfenbrenner, U. (1979). *The ecology of human development.* Cambridge, MA: Harvard University Press.

Brunk, M., Henggeler, S. W., & Whelan, J. P. (1987). Comparison of multisystemic therapy and parent training in the brief treatment of child abuse and neglect. *Journal of Consulting and Clinical Psychology, 55*, 171–178.

Burns, B. J., Costello, E. J., Angold, A., Tweed, D., Stangl, D., Farmer, E. M. Z., & Erkanli, A. (1995). Children's mental health service use across service sectors. *Health Affairs, 14*, 147–159.

Bussing, R., Zima, B. T., Perwien, A. R., Belin, T. R., & Widawski, M. (1998). Children in special education programs: Attention deficit hyperactivity disorder, use of services, and unmet needs. *American Journal of Public Health, 88*, 880–886.

Butler, L., Miezitis, S., Friedman, R., & Cole, E. (1980). The effect of two school-based intervention programs on depressive symptoms in preadolescents. *American Educational Research Journal, 17*, 111–119.

Camp, B. (1977). Verbal mediation in young aggressive boys. *Journal of Abnormal Psychology, 86*, 145–153.

Camp, B., & Bash, M. A. (1981). *Think aloud: Increasing social and cognitive skills: A problem-solving program for children.* Champaign, IL: Research Press.

Campbell, S. B. (1990). *Behavior problems in preschool children: Clinical and developmental issues.* New York: Guilford.

Campbell, S. B., & Ewing, S. M. (1990). Follow-up of hard-to-manage preschoolers: Adjustment at age 9 and predictors of continuing symptoms. *Journal of Child Psychology and Psychiatry, 31,* 871–889.

Cantwell, D. P., & Baker, L. (1989). Stability and natural history of DSM-III childhood diagnoses. *Journal of the American Academy of Child and Adolescent Psychiatry, 29,* 691–700.

Carlson, C. L., Pelham, W. E., Milich, R., & Dixon, M. J. (1992). Single and combined effects of methylphenidate and behavior therapy on the classroom behavior, academic performance, and self-evaluations of children with attention deficit-hyperactivity disorder. *Journal of Abnormal Child Psychology, 20,* 213–232.

Carlson, C. L., & Tamm, L. (2000). Responsiveness of children with attention deficit-hyperactivity disorder to reward and response cost: Differential impact on performance and motivation. *Journal of Consulting and Clinical Psychology, 68,* 73–83.

Casey, R. J., & Berman, J. S. (1985). The outcome of psychotherapy with children. *Psychological Bulletin, 98,* 388–400.

Caspi, A., Elder, G. H., & Bem, D. J. (1987). Moving against the world: Life-course patterns of explosive children. *Developmental Psychology, 23,* 308–313.

Chamberlain, P. (1990). *Teaching and supporting families: A model for reunification of children with their families.* Grant No. 90CW0994, Administration for Children, Youth, and Families, Child Welfare Services, Human Development Services, Department of Health and Human Services.

(1994). *Family connections: A treatment foster care model for adolescents with delinquency.* Eugene, OR: Castalia Publishing Company.

(1996). Intensified foster care: Multilevel treatment for adolescents with conduct disorders in out-of-home care. In E. D. Hibbs & P. S. Jensen (Eds.), *Psychosocial treatments for child and adolescent disorders: Empirically based strategies for clinical practice* (pp. 475–495). Washington, DC: American Psychological Association.

Chamberlain, P., Moreland, S., & Reid, K. (1992). Enhanced services and stipends for foster parents: Effects on retention rates and outcomes for children. *Child Welfare, 71,* 387–401.

Chamberlain, P., & Reid, J. B. (1991). Using a specialized foster care treatment model for children and adolescents leaving the state mental hospital. *Journal of Community Psychology, 19,* 266–276.

(1998). Comparison of two community alternatives to incarceration for chronic juvenile offenders. *Journal of Consulting and Clinical Psychology, 66,* 624–633.

Chamberlain, P., & Smith, D. K. (2003). Antisocial behavior in children and adolescents: The Oregon multidimensional treatment foster care model. In A. E. Kazdin & J. R. Weisz (Eds.), *Evidence-based psychotherapies for children and adolescents* (pp. 282–300). New York: Guilford.

Chambless, D. L., Baker, M. J., Baucom, D. H., Beutler, L. E., Calhoun, K. S., Crits-Christoph, P., Daiuto, A., DeRubeis, R., Detweiler, J., Haaga, D. A. F., Bennett Johnson, S., McCurry, S., Meuser, K. T., Pope, K. S., Sanderson, W. C., Shoham, V., Stickle, T., Williams, D. A., & Woody, S. R. (1998). Update on empirically validated therapies II. *The Clinical Psychologist, 51,* 3–16.

Chorpita, B. F. (1998). *Modular cognitive behavior therapy for child and adolescent anxiety disorders.* Unpublished manuscript, University of Hawaii at Manoa.

Chorpita, B. F., Yim, L. M., Donkervoet, J. C., Arensdorf, A., Amundsen, M. J., McGee, C., Serrano, A., Yates, A., & Morelli, P. (2002). Toward large-scale implementation of empirically supported treatments for children: A review and observations by the Hawaii Empirical Basis to Services Task Force. *Clinical Psychology: Science and Practice, 9,* 165–190.

Christensen, A., Johnson, S. M., Phillips, S., & Glasgow, R. E. (1980). Cost effectiveness of behavioral family therapy. *Behavior Therapy, 11,* 208–226.

Clarke, G. (1991). *Adolescent depression health class curriculum.* Portland: Oregon Health Sciences University.

Clarke, G., Hawkins, W., Murphy, M., & Sheeber, L. B. (1993). School-based primary prevention of depressive symptomatology in adolescents: Findings from two studies. *Journal of Adolescent Research, 8,* 183–204.

Clarke, G., Hawkins, W., Murphy, M., Sheeber, L. B., Lewinsohn, P. M., & Seeley, J. R. (1995). Targeted prevention of unipolar depressive disorders in an at-risk sample of high school adolescents: A randomized trial of a group cognitive intervention. *Journal of the American Academy of Child and Adolescent Psychiatry, 34,* 312–321.

Clarke, G., Hops, H., Lewinsohn, P. M., Andrews, J., Seeley, J. R., & Williams, J. (1992). Cognitive-behavioral group treatment of adolescent depression: Prediction of outcome. *Behavior Therapy, 23,* 341–354.

Clarke, G., & Lewinsohn, P. M. (1991). *The adolescent coping with stress class: Leader manual.* Portland: Oregon Health Sciences University.

Clarke, G., Lewinsohn, P., & Hops, H. (1990a). *Leader's manual for adolescent groups: Adolescent coping with depression course.* Eugene, OR: Castalia Publishing Company.

(1990b). *Student workbook: Adolescent coping with depression course.* Eugene, OR: Castalia Publishing Company.

Clarke, G. N., DeBar, L. L., & Lewinsohn, P. M. (2003). Cognitive-behavioral group treatment for adolescent depression. In A. E. Kazdin & J. R. Weisz (Eds.), *Evidence-based psychotherapies for children and adolescents* (pp. 120–134). New York: Guilford.

Clarke, G. N., Rohde, P., Lewinsohn, P. M., Hops, H., & Seeley, J. R. (1999). Cognitive-behavioral group treatment of adolescent depression: Efficacy of acute treatment and booster sessions. *Journal of the American Academy of Child & Adolescent Psychiatry, 38,* 272–279.

Cobham, V. E., Dadds, M. R., & Spence, S. H. (1998). The role of parental anxiety in the treatment of childhood anxiety. *Journal of Consulting and Clinical Psychology, 66,* 893–905.

Cohen, J. (1988). *Statistical power analysis for the behavioral sciences* (2nd ed.). Hillsdale, NJ: Erlbaum.

Cohen, J. A., & Mannarino, A. P. (1996). A treatment outcome study for sexually abused preschool children: Initial findings. *Journal of the American Academy of Child and Adolescent Psychiatry, 35,* 42–50.

Cohen, L., Sargent, M., & Sechrest, L. (1986). Use of psychotherapy research by professional psychologists. *American Psychologist, 41,* 198–206.

Cunningham, C. E., Bremner, R., & Boyle, M. (1995). Large group community-based parenting programs for families of preschoolers at risk for disruptive behavior disorders: Utilization, cost-effectiveness, and outcome. *Journal of Child Psychology and Psychiatry, 36*, 1141–1159.

Dadds, M. R., Heard, P. M., & Rapee, R. M. (1992). *The role of family intervention in the treatment of child anxiety disorders: Some preliminary findings.* Unpublished manuscript, Albert Einstein College of Medicine.

Danforth, J. S., Barkley, R. A., & Stokes, T. F. (1991). Observations of parent-child interactions with hyperactive children: Research and clinical implications. *Clinical Psychology Review, 11*, 703–727.

DeFries, Z., Jenkins, S., & Williams, E. C. (1964). Treatment of disturbed children in foster care. *American Journal of Orthopsychiatry, 34*, 615–624.

Dodge, K. A., Bachorowski, J., & Newman, J. P. (1990). Hostile attributional biases in severely aggressive adolescents. *Journal of Abnormal Psychology, 99*, 385–392.

Dodge, K. A., Bates, J., & Pettit, G. S. (1990). Mechanisms in the cycle of violence. *Science, 250*, 1678–1683.

Dodge, K. A., & Coie, J. D. (1987). Social information-processing factors in reactive and proactive aggression in children's peer groups. *Journal of Personality and Social Psychology, 53*, 1146–1158.

Dodge, K. A., & Crick, N. R. (1990). Social information-processing bases of aggressive behavior in children. *Personality and Social Psychology Bulletin, 16*, 8–22.

Douglas, V. I. (1972). Stop, look, and listen: The problem of sustained attention and impulse control in hyperactive and normal children. *Canadian Journal of Behavioral Science, 4*, 259–282.

Drabman, R. S., Spitalnik, R., & O'Leary, D. (1973). Teaching self-control to disruptive children. *Journal of Abnormal Psychology, 82*, 10–16.

DuPaul, G. J., & Eckert, T. L. (1997). The effects of school-based interventions for attention deficit hyperactivity disorder: A meta-analysis. *School Psychology Review, 26*, 5–27.

DuPaul, G. J., Guevremont, D. C., & Barkley, R. A. (1992). Behavioral treatment of attention-deficit hyperactivity disorder in the classroom. *Behavior Modification, 16*, 204–225.

Durlak, J. A., Fuhrman, T., & Lampman, C. (1991). Effectiveness of cognitive-behavior therapy for maladapting children: A meta-analysis. *Psychological Bulletin, 110*, 204–214.

Durlak, J. A., Wells, A. M., Cotton, J. K., & Johnson, S. (1995). Analysis of selected methodological issues in child psychotherapy research. *Journal of Clinical Child Psychology, 24*, 141–148.

Dush, D. M., Hirt, M. L., & Schroeder, H. E. (1989). Self-statement modification in the treatment of child behavior disorders: A meta-analysis. *Psychological Bulletin, 106*, 97–106.

D'Zurilla, T. J., & Nezu, A. (1982). Social problem solving in adults. In P. C. Kendall (Ed.), *Advances in cognitive-behavioral research and therapy* (pp. 107–126). New York: Academic Press.

Ecton, R. B., & Feindler, E. L. (1990). Anger control training for temper control disorders. In E. L. Feindler & G. R. Kalfus (Eds.), *Adolescent behavior therapy handbook*. New York: Springer Publishing Company.

Eddy, J. M., & Chamberlain, P. (2000a). Family management and deviant peer association as mediators of the impact of treatment condition on youth antisocial behavior. *Journal of Consulting and Clinical Psychology, 68*, 857–863.

Egeland, B., Kalkoske, M., Gottesman, N., & Erickson, M. F. (1990). Preschool behavior problems: Stability and factors accounting for change. *Journal of Child Psychology and Psychiatry, 31*, 891–909.

Eisenstadt, T. H., Eyberg, S., McNeil, C. B., Newcomb, K., & Funderburk, B. (1993). Parent-child interaction therapy with behavior problem children: Relative effectiveness of two stages and overall treatment outcome. *Journal of Clinical Child Psychology, 22*, 42–51.

Ellis, A., & Harper, R. A. (1961). *A guide to rational living*. New York: Lyle Stuart.

Evans, M. E., Armstrong, M. I., Dollard, N., Kuppinger, A. D., & Wood, V. M. (1994). Development and evaluation of treatment foster care and family-centered intensive case management in New York. *Journal of Emotional and Behavioral Disorders, 2*, 228–239.

Eyberg, S. M. (1988). Parent-child interaction therapy: Integration of traditional and behavioral concerns. *Child and Family Behavior Therapy, 10*, 33–46.

Eyberg, S. M., Bessmer, J., Newcomb, K., Edwards, D., & Robinson, E. (1994). *Manual for the Dyadic Parent-Child Interaction Coding System-II*. Social and Behavioral Sciences Documents (Ms. No. 2897). Available from Sheila Eyberg, University of Florida, Gainesville.

Eyberg, S. M., Boggs, S. R., & Algina, J. (1995). New developments in psychosocial, pharmacological, and combined treatments of conduct disorders in aggressive children. *Psychopharmacology Bulletin, 31*, 83–91.

Eyberg, S. M., & Calzada, E. J. (1998). *Parent-child interaction therapy: Procedures manual*. Gainesville: University of Florida.

Eyberg, S. M., Edwards, D., Boggs, S. R., & Foote, R. (1998). Maintaining the treatment effects of parent training: The role of booster sessions and other maintenance strategies. *Clinical Psychology: Science and Practice, 5*, 544–554.

Eyberg, S. M., & Matarazzo, R. G. (1980). Training parents as therapists: A comparison between individual parent-child interaction training and parent group didactic training. *Journal of Clinical Psychology, 36*, 492–499.

Eyberg, S. M., & Robinson, E. A. (1982). Parent-child interaction training: Effects on family functioning. *Journal of Clinical Child Psychology, 11*, 130–137.

Eysenck, H. J. (1952). The effects of psychotherapy: An evaluation. *Journal of Consulting Psychology, 16*, 319–324.

(1960). The effects of psychotherapy. In H. J. Eysenck (Ed.), *Handbook of abnormal psychology: An experimental approach*. London: Pitman Medical Publishing.

(1966). *The effects of psychotherapy*. New York: International Science Press.

Feehan, C. J., & Vostanis, P. (1996). Cognitive-behavioural therapy for depressed children: Children's and therapists' impressions. *Behavioural and Cognitive Psychotherapy, 24*, 171–183.

Feindler, E. L. (1979). *Cognitive and behavioral approaches to anger control training in explosive adolescents*. Unpublished doctoral dissertation, West Virginia University, Morgantown.

(1995). An ideal treatment package for children and adolescents with anger disorders. In H. Kassinove (Ed.), *Anger disorders: Definition, diagnosis, and treatment*. Taylor & Francis.

Feindler, E. L., Ecton, R. B., Kingsley, D., & Dubey, D. R. (1986). Group anger-control training for institutionalized psychiatric male adolescents. *Behavior Therapy, 17,* 109–123.

Feindler, E. L., & Guttman, J. (1994). Cognitive-behavioral anger control training for groups of adolescents: A treatment manual. In C. W. LeCroy (Ed.), *Handbook of child and adolescent treatment manuals.* New York: Lexington Books.

Feindler, E. L., Marriott, S. A., & Iwata, M. (1984). Group anger control training for junior high school delinquents. *Cognitive Therapy and Research, 8,* 299–311.

Feindler, E. L., & Ovens, D. (1998). *Cognitive-behavioral group anger management for youth.* Unpublished treatment manual. Long Island University, New York.

Feshbach, S. (1970). Aggression. In P. H. Mussen (Ed.), *Carmichael's manual of child psychology* (pp. 159–259). New York: Wiley.

Firestone, P., Kelly, M. J., & Fike, S. (1980). Are fathers necessary in parent training groups? *Journal of Clinical Child Psychology, 9,* 44–47.

Fischer, J., Anderson, J. M., Arveson, E., & Brown, S. (1978). Adlerian family counseling: An evaluation. *International Journal of Family Counseling, 6,* 42–44.

Flannery-Schroeder, E. C., & Kendall, P. C. (2000). Group and individual cognitive-behavioral treatments for youth with anxiety disorders: A randomized clinical trial. *Cognitive Therapy and Research, 24,* 251–278.

Flavell, J. H., Miller, P. H., & Miller, S. A. (1993). *Cognitive development* (3rd ed.). Englewood Cliffs, NJ: Prentice-Hall.

Fleischman, M. J. (1979). Using parenting salaries to control attrition and cooperation in therapy. *Behavior Therapy, 10,* 111–116.

Fletcher, K., Fisher, M., Barkley, R. A., & Smallish, L. (1996). A sequential analysis of the mother-adolescent interactions of ADHD, ADHD/ODD, and normal teenagers: Neutral and conflict discussions. *Journal of Abnormal Child Psychology, 24,* 271–298.

Food and Drug Administration. (1997). Regulation requiring manufacturers to assess the safety and effectiveness of new drugs and biological products in pediatric patients. *Federal Register, 62,* 43900–43916.

Foote, R., Eyberg, S., & Schuhman, E. (1998). Parent-child interaction approaches to the treatment of child behavior problems. In T. H. Ollendick & R. J. Prinz (Eds.), *Advances in clinical child psychology* (Vol. 20, pp. 125–151). New York: Plenum.

Forehand, R., & King, H. E. (1974). Preschool children's noncompliance: Effects of short-term behavior therapy. *Journal of Community Psychology, 2,* 42–44.

(1977). Noncompliant children: Effects of parent training on behavior and attitude change. *Behavior Modification, 1,* 93–108.

Forehand, R., & Long, N. (1988). Outpatient treatment of the acting out child: Procedures, long-term follow-up data, and clinical problems. *Advances in Behaviour Research and Therapy, 10,* 129–177.

(1996). *Parenting the strong-willed child: The clinically proven five-week program for parents of two- to six-year-olds.* New York: Contemporary Books.

Forehand, R., & McMahon, R. J. (1981). *Helping the noncompliant child: A clinician's guide to parent training.* New York: Guilford.

Forehand, R., Sturgis, E., McMahon, R., Auguar, D., Green, K., Wells, K., & Breiner, J. (1979). Parent behavioral training to modify child noncompliance: Treatment generalization across time and from home to school. *Behavior Modification, 3,* 3–25.

Forgatch, M. S., & Martinez, C. R. (1999). Parent management training: A program linking basic research and practical application. *Tidsskrift for Norsk Psykologforesing, 36,* 923–937.

Forgatch, M. S., & Patterson, G. R. (1989). *Parents and adolescents living together, part 2: Family problem solving.* Eugene, OR: Castalia Publishing Company.

Frank, J. D. (1973). *Persuasion and healing: A comparative study of psychotherapy.* Baltimore: Johns Hopkins University Press.

Freedheim, D. K. (Ed.). (1992). *History of psychotherapy: A century of change.* Washington, DC: American Psychological Association.

Freud, S. (1909). Analysis of a phobia in a five-year-old boy. In *Standard Editions of the complete psychological works of Sigmund Freud* (Vol. 10). London: Hogarth Press, 1955.

Frick, P. J. (1998). Conduct disorders. In T. H. Ollendick & M. Hersen (Eds.), *Handbook of child psychopathology* (3rd ed., pp. 213–237). New York: Plenum Press.

Funderburk, B. W., Eyberg, S. M., Newcomb, K., McNeil, C. B., Hembree-Kigin, T., & Capage, L. (1998). Parent-child interaction therapy with behavior problem children: Maintenance of treatment effects in the school setting. *Child and Family Behavior Therapy, 20,* 17–38.

Furman, W., & Gavin, L. A. (1989). Peers' influence on adjustment and development: A view from the intervention literature. In T. J. Berndt & G. W. Ladd (Eds.), *Peer relationships in child development* (pp. 319–340). New York: Wiley.

Gadow, K. D. (1986). *Children on medication: Hyperactivity, learning disabilities, and mental retardation* (Vol. 1). San Diego: College Hill Press.

Garber, J., Keiley, M. K., & Martin, N. C. (2002). Developmental trajectories of depressive symptoms, attributions, and stress during adolescence. *Journal of Consulting and Clinical Psychology, 70,* 79–95.

Garfield, S. L. (1996). Some problems associated with "validated" forms of psychotherapy. *Clinical Psychology: Science and Practice, 3,* 218–229.

Garland, A. F., & Zigler, E. (1993). Adolescent suicide prevention: Current research and social policy implications. *American Psychologist, 48,* 169–182.

Gittelman, R., Abikoff, H., Pollack, E., Klein, D. F., Katz, S., & Mattes, J. (1980). A controlled trial of behavior modification and methylphenidate in hyperactive children. In Whalen, C. K. & Henker, B. (Eds.), *Hyperactive children: The social ecology of identification and treatment* (pp. 221–243). New York: Academic Press.

Gordon, D. A., Graves, K., & Arbuthnot, J. (1995). The effect of functional family therapy for delinquents on adult criminal behavior. *Criminal Justice and Behavior, 22,* 60–73.

Gottman, J., Notarius, C., Gonso, J., & Markman, M. (1976). *A couples' guide to communication.* Champaign, IL: Research Press.

Graziano, A. M., & Mooney, K. C. (1980). Family self-control instruction for children's nighttime fear reduction. *Journal of Consulting and Clinical Psychology, 48,* 206–213.

Greenwald, P., & Cullen, J. W. (1984). The scientific approach to cancer control. *CA- A Cancer Journal for Clinicians, 34,* 328–332.

Guevremont, D. C., & Foster, S. L. (1993). Impact of social problem-solving training on aggressive boys: Skill acquisition, behavior change, and generalization. *Journal of Abnormal Child Psychology, 27*, 13–27.

Haley, J. (1976). *Problem-solving therapy: New strategies for effective family therapy.* San Francisco: Jossey-Bass.

Hanf, C. (1969, April). *A two-stage program for modifying maternal controlling during the mother-child interaction.* Paper presented at the meeting of the Western Psychological Association, Vancouver, British Columbia, Canada.

(1970). *Shaping mothers to shape their children's behavior.* Unpublished manuscript, University of Oregon Medical School.

Hanf, C., & Kling, J. (1974). *Facilitating parent-child interaction: A two-stage training model.* Unpublished manuscript, University of Oregon Medical School.

Havik, O. E., & VandenBos, G. R. (1996). Limitations of manualized psychotherapy for everyday clinical practice. *Clinical Psychology: Science and Practice, 3*, 264–267.

Hazelrigg, M. D., Cooper, H. M., & Borduin, C. M. (1987). Evaluating the effectiveness of family therapies: An integrative review and analysis. *Psychological Bulletin, 101*, 428–442.

Henggeler, S. W. (1989). *Delinquency in adolescence.* Newbury Park, CA: Sage.

Henggeler, S. W., Borduin, C. M., Melton, G. B., Mann, B. J., Smith, L. A., Hall, J. A., Cone, L., & Fucci, B. R. (1991). Effects of multisystemic therapy on drug use and abuse in serious juvenile offenders: A progress report from two outcome studies. *Family Dynamics of Addiction Quarterly, 1*, 40–51.

Henggeler, S. W., & Lee, T. (2003). Multisystemic treatment of serious clinical problems. In A. E. Kazdin & J. R. Weisz (Eds.), *Evidence-based psychotherapies for children and adolescents* (pp. 301–322). New York: Guilford.

Henggeler, S. W., Melton, G. B., Brondino, M. J., Scherer, D. G., & Hanley, J. H. (1997). Multisystemic therapy with violent and chronic juvenile offenders and their families: The role of treatment fidelity in successful dissemination. *Journal of Consulting and Clinical Psychology, 65*, 821–833.

Henggeler, S. W., Melton, G. B., & Smith, L. A. (1992). Family preservation using multisystemic therapy: An effective alternative to incarcerating serious juvenile offenders. *Journal of Consulting and Clinical Psychology, 60*, 953–961.

Henggeler, S. W., Melton, G. B., Smith, L. A., Schoenwald, S. K., & Hanley, J. H. (1993). Family preservation using multisystemic treatment: Long-term follow-up to a clinical trial with serious juvenile offenders. *Journal of Child and Family Studies, 2*, 283–293.

Henggeler, S. W., Pickrel, S. G., & Brondino, M. J. (1999). Multisystemic treatment of substance abusing and dependent delinquents: Outcomes, treatment fidelity, and transportability. *Mental Health Services Research, 1*, 171–184.

Henggeler, S. W., Rodick, J. D., Borduin, C. M., Hanson, C. L., Watson, S. M., & Urey, J. R. (1986). Multisystemic treatment of juvenile offenders: Effects on adolescent behavior and family interaction. *Developmental Psychology, 22*, 132–141.

Henggeler, S. W., Rowland, M. D., Randall, J., Ward, D. M., Pickrel, S. G., Cunningham, P. B., Miller, S. L., Edwards, J., Zealberg, J. J., Hand, L. D., & Santos, A. B. (1999). Home-based multisystemic therapy as an alternative to the hospitalization of youths in psychiatric crisis: Clinical outcomes. *Journal of the American Academy of Child and Adolescent Psychiatry, 38*, 1331–1339.

Henggeler, S. W., & Schoenwald, S. K. (1998). *Multisystemic therapy supervisory manual: Promoting quality assurance at the clinical level.* Charleston: Family Services Research Center, Medical University of South Carolina.

(2002). Treatment manuals: Necessary, but far from sufficient. *Clinical Psychology: Science and Practice, 9,* 419–420.

Henggeler, S. W., Schoenwald, S. K., Borduin, C. M., Rowland, M. D., & Cunningham, P. B. (1998). *Multisystemic treatment of antisocial behavior in children and adolescents.* New York: Guilford.

Hibbs, E. D., & Jensen, P. S. (Eds.). (in press). *Psychosocial treatments for child and adolescent disorders: Empirically based approaches* (2nd ed.). Washington, DC: American Psychological Association.

Hinshaw, S. P. (1987). On the distinction between attentional deficits/hyperactivity and conduct problems/aggression in child psychopathology. *Psychological Bulletin, 101,* 443–463.

(1994). *Attention deficits and hyperactivity in children.* Thousand Oaks, CA: Sage.

Hinshaw, S. P., & Anderson, C. A. (1996). Conduct and oppositional defiant disorders. In E. J. Mash & R. A. Barkley (Eds.), *Child psychopathology.* New York: Guilford.

Hinshaw, S. P., Henker, B., & Whalen, C. K. (1984). Self-control in hyperactive boys in anger-inducing situations: Effects of cognitive-behavioral training and of methylphenidate. *Journal of Abnormal Child Psychology, 12,* 55–77.

Holmbeck, G. N. (1997). Toward terminological, conceptual, and statistical clarity in the study of mediators and moderators: Examples from the child-clinical and pediatric psychology literatures. *Journal of Consulting and Clinical Psychology, 65,* 599–610.

Holmbeck, G. N., & Updegrove, A. L. (1995). Clinical-developmental interface: Implications of developmental research for adolescent psychotherapy. *Psychotherapy, 32,* 16–33.

Horn, W. F., Ialongo, N., Greenberg, G., Packard, T., & Smith-Winberry, C. (1990). Additive effects of behavioral parent training and self-control therapy with attention deficit hyperactivity disordered children. *Journal of Clinical Child Psychology, 19,* 98–110.

Horn, W. F., Ialongo, N., Popovich, S., & Peradotto, D. (1987). Behavioral parent training and cognitive-behavioral self-control therapy with ADD-H children: Comparative and combined effects. *Journal of Clinical Child Psychology, 16,* 57–68.

Hoza, B., Pelham, W. E., Jr., Sams, S. E., & Carlson, C. (1992). An examination of the "dosage" effects of both behavior therapy and methylphenidate on the classroom performance of two ADHD children. *Behavior Modification, 16,* 164–192.

Hsu, L. M. (1989). Reliable changes in psychotherapy: Taking into account regression toward the mean. *Behavioral Assessment, 11,* 459–467.

Huey, S. J., Henggeler, S. W., Brondino, M. J., & Pickrel, S. G. (2000). Mechanisms of change in multisystemic therapy: Reducing delinquent behavior through therapist adherence and improved family and peer functioning. *Journal of Consulting and Clinical Psychology, 68,* 451–467.

Humphreys, L., Forehand, R., McMahon, R., & Roberts, M. (1978). Parent behavioral training to modify child noncompliance: Effects on untreated siblings. *Journal of Behavior Therapy and Experimental Psychiatry, 9,* 235–238.

Jacob, T., Magnussen, M. G., & Kemler, W. M. (1972). A followup of treatment terminators and remainers with long-term and short-term symptom duration. *Psychotherapy: Theory, Research, and Practice, 9,* 139–142.

Jensen, A. L., & Weisz, J. R. (2002). Assessing match and mismatch between practitioner-generated and standardized interview-generated diagnoses for clinic-referred children and adolescents. *Journal of Consulting and Clinical Psychology, 70,* 158–168.

Jones, M. C. (1924). A laboratory study of fear: The case of Peter. *Pedagogical Seminary, 31,* 308–315.

Kahn, J. S., Kehle, T. J., Jenson, W. R., & Clark, E. (1990). Comparison of cognitive-behavioral, relaxation, and self-modeling interventions for depression among middle-school students. *School Psychology Review, 19,* 196–211.

Kane, M. T., & Kendall, P. C. (1989). Anxiety disorders in children: A multiple-baseline evaluation of a cognitive-behavioral treatment. *Behavior Therapy, 20,* 499–508.

Kanfer, F. H., Karoly, P., & Newman, A. (1975). Reduction of children's fear of the dark by competence-related and situational threat-related verbal cues. *Journal of Consulting and Clinical Psychology, 43,* 251–258.

Kaslow, N. J., & Thompson, M. P. (1998). Applying the criteria for empirically supported treatments to studies of psychosocial interventions for child and adolescent depression. *Journal of Clinical Child Psychology, 27,* 146–155.

Kaufman, L., & Wagner, B. (1976). Barb: A systematic treatment technique for temper control disorders. *Behavior Therapy, 3,* 84–90.

Kazdin, A. E. (1993). Treatment of conduct disorder: Progress and directions in psychotherapy research. *Development and Psychopathology, 5,* 277–310.

(1995a). Child, parent, and family dysfunction as predictors of outcome in cognitive-behavioral treatment of antisocial children. *Behaviour Research and Therapy, 33,* 271–281.

(1995b). *Conduct disorders in childhood and adolescence* (2nd ed.). Newbury Park, CA: Sage.

(1996). Problem solving and parent management in treating aggressive and antisocial behavior. In E. D. Hibbs & P. S. Jensen (Eds.), *Psychosocial treatments for child and adolescent disorders: Empirically based strategies for clinical practice* (pp. 377–408). Washington, DC: American Psychological Association.

(1997a). Conduct disorder across the lifespan. In S. S. Luthar, J. A. Burack, D. Cicchetti, & J. R. Weisz (Eds.), *Developmental psychopathology: Perspectives on adjustment, risk, and disorder* (pp. 248–272). New York: Cambridge University Press.

(1997b). Parent management training: Evidence, outcomes, and issues. *Journal of the American Academy of Child and Adolescent Psychiatry, 36,* 1349–1356.

(1998). *Research design in clinical psychology* (3rd ed.). Needham Heights, MA: Allyn & Bacon.

(2000a). Developing a research agenda for child and adolescent psychotherapy. *Archives of General Psychiatry, 57,* 829–835.

(2000b). *Psychotherapy for children and adolescents: Directions for research and practice.* New York: Oxford University Press.

(2001). *Behavior modification in applied settings* (6th ed.). Pacific Grove, CA: Wadsworth.

(2003). Problem-solving skills training and parent management training for conduct disorder. In A. E. Kazdin & J. R. Weisz (Eds.), *Evidence-based psychotherapies for children and adolescents* (pp. 241–262). New York: Guilford.

Kazdin, A. E., Bass, D., Ayers, W. A., & Rodgers, A. (1990). Empirical and clinical focus of child and adolescent psychotherapy research. *Journal of Consulting & Clinical Psychology, 58,* 729–740.

Kazdin, A. E., Bass, D., Siegel, T., & Thomas, C. (1989). Cognitive-behavioral therapy and relationship therapy in the treatment of children referred for antisocial behavior. *Journal of Consulting and Clinical Psychology, 57,* 522–535.

Kazdin, A. E., & Bootzin, R. R. (1972). The token economy: An evaluative review. *Journal of Applied Behavior Analysis, 3,* 343–372.

Kazdin, A. E., & Crowley, M. J. (1997). Moderators of treatment outcome in cognitively based treatment of antisocial children. *Cognitive Therapy and Research, 21,* 185–207.

Kazdin, A. E., Esveldt-Dawson, K., French, N. H., & Unis, A. S. (1987a). Problem-solving skills training and relationship therapy in the treatment of antisocial child behavior. *Journal of Consulting and Clinical Psychology, 55,* 76–85.

(1987b). Effects of parent management training and problem-solving skills training combined in the treatment of antisocial child behavior. *Journal of the American Academy of Child and Adolescent Psychiatry, 26,* 416–424.

Kazdin, A. E., Siegel, T. C., & Bass, D. (1990). Drawing on clinical practice to inform research on child and adolescent psychotherapy: Survey of practitioners. *Professional Psychology: Research & Practice, 21,* 189–198.

(1992). Cognitive problem-solving skills training and parent management training in the treatment of antisocial behavior in children. *Journal of Consulting and Clinical Psychology, 60,* 733–747.

Kazdin, A. E., & Wassell, G. (2000). Therapeutic changes in children, parents, and families resulting from treatment of children with conduct problems. *Journal of the American Academy of Child and Adolescent Psychiatry, 39,* 414–420.

Kazdin, A. E., & Weisz, J. R. (1998). Identifying and developing empirically supported child and adolescent treatments. *Journal of Consulting and Clinical Psychology, 66,* 19–36.

Kazdin, A. E., & Weisz, J. R. (Eds.). (2003). *Evidence-based psychotherapies for children and adolescents.* New York: Guilford.

Kelleher, K. J. (1998, November). *Use of services and costs for youth with ADHD and related conditions.* Paper presented at the NIH Consensus Development Conference on Diagnosis and Treatment of Attention Deficit Hyperactivity Disorder, Bethesda, MD.

Kelley, M. L., & McCain, A. P. (1995). Promoting academic performance in inattentive children: The relative efficacy of school-home notes with and without response cost. *Behavior Modification, 19,* 357–375.

Kendall, P. C. (1981). Cognitive-behavioral interventions with children. In B. B. Lahey & A. E. Kazdin (Eds.), *Advances in clinical child psychology* (Vol. 4, pp. 53–90). New York: Plenum Press.

(1994). Treating anxiety disorders in children: Results of a randomized clinical trial. *Journal of Consulting and Clinical Psychology, 62,* 100–110.

Kendall, P. C., Brady, E. U., & Verduin, T. L. (2001). Comorbidity in childhood anxiety disorders and treatment outcome. *Journal of the American Academy of Child and Adolescent Psychiatry, 40,* 787–794.

Kendall, P. C., & Braswell, L. (1985). *Cognitive-behavioral therapy for impulsive children.* New York: Guilford.

Kendall, P. C., Chu, B., Hayes, C., & Nauta, M. (1998). Breathing life into a manual: Flexibility and creativity with manual-based treatments. *Cognitive and Behavioral Practice, 5,* 177–198.

Kendall, P. C., Flannery-Schroeder, E., Panichelli-Mindel, S. M., Southam-Gerow, M., Henin, A., & Warman, M. (1997). Therapy for youths with anxiety disorders: A second randomized clinical trial. *Journal of Consulting and Clinical Psychology, 65,* 366–380.

Kendall, P. C., Kane, M., Howard, B., & Siqueland, L. (1990). *Cognitive-behavioral treatment of anxious children: Therapist manual.* Ardmore, PA: Workbook Publishing.

Kendall, P. C., & Southam-Gerow, M. A. (1996). Long-term followup of a cognitive-behavioral therapy for anxiety disordered youth. *Journal of Consulting and Clinical Psychology, 64,* 724–730.

King, N. J., Meitz, A., Tinney, L., & Ollendick, T. H. (1995). Psychopathology and cognition in adolescents experiencing severe test anxiety. *Journal of Clinical Child Psychology, 24,* 49–54.

King, N. J., & Ollendick, T. H. (1997). Annotation: Treatment of childhood phobias. *Journal of Child Psychology and Psychiatry, 38,* 389–400.

Klein, N. C., Alexander, J. F., & Parsons, B. V. (1977). Impact of family systems intervention on recidivism and sibling delinquency: A model of primary prevention and program evaluation. *Journal of Consulting and Clinical Psychology, 45,* 469–474.

Kondas, O. (1967). Reduction of examination anxiety and 'stage fright' by group desensitization and relaxation. *Behaviour Research and Therapy, 5,* 275–281.

Kratochwill, T. R., & Levin, J. R. (1992). *Single-case research design and analysis: New directions for psychology and education.* Hillsdale, NJ: Erlbaum.

Lahey, B. B., & Loeber, R. (1994). Framework for a developmental model of oppositional defiant disorder and conduct disorder. In D. K. Routh (Ed.), *Disruptive behavior disorders in childhood* (pp. 139–180). New York: Plenum Press.

Larson, J., & Lochman, J. E. (2002). *Helping school children cope with anger: A cognitive-behavioral intervention.* New York: Guilford.

Last, C. G., Hersen, M., Kazdin, A. E., Francis, G., & Grubb, B. (1987). Psychiatric illness in the mothers of anxious children. *American Journal of Psychiatry, 144,* 1580–1583.

Leaf, P. J., Alegria, M., Cohen, P., Goodman, S. H., Horwitz, S. M., Hoven, C. W., Narrow, W. E., Vadem-Kierman, M., & Reiger, D. A. (1996). Mental health service use in the community and schools: Results from the four-community MECA Study. (Methods for the Epidemiology of Child and Adolescent Mental Disorders Study.) *Journal of the American Academy of Child and Adolescent Psychiatry, 35,* 889–897.

Lehman, A. E., Postrado, L. T., Roth, D., McNary, S. W., & Goldman, H. H. (1994). Continuity of care and client outcomes in the Robert Johnson Wood Foundation program on chronic mental illness. *Milbank Quarterly, 72*, 105–122.

Lehrman, L. J., Sirluck, H., Black, B. J., & Glick, S. J. (1949). *Success and failure of treatment of children in the child guidance clinics of the Jewish Board of Guardians: Analysis and followup of cases closed between April 1, 1941, and March 31, 1942.* Research Monograph No. 1, 1–87.

Leitenberg, H., & Callahan, E. J. (1973). Reinforced practice and reduction of different kinds of fears in adults and children. *Behaviour Research and Therapy, 11*, 19–30.

Levitt, E. E. (1957). The results of psychotherapy with children: An evaluation. *Journal of Consulting Psychology, 21*, 189–196.
(1963). Psychotherapy with children: A further evaluation. *Behaviour Research and Therapy, 60*, 326–329.

Levitt, E. E., Beiser, H. R., & Robertson, R. E. (1959). A follow-up evaluation of cases treated at a community child guidance clinic. *American Journal of Orthopsychiatry, 29*, 337–349.

Lewinsohn, P. M., Antonuccio, D. O., Steinmetz-Breckenridge, J. L., & Teri, L. (1984). *The coping with depression course: A psychoeducational intervention for unipolar depression.* Eugene, OR: Castalia Publishing Company.

Lewinsohn, P. M., Biglan, A., & Zeiss, A. (1976). Behavioral treatment of depression. In P. Davidson (Ed.), *Behavioral management of anxiety, depression, and pain* (pp. 91–146). New York: Bruner/Mazel.

Lewinsohn, P. M., Clarke, G. N., Hops, H. & Andrews, J. (1990). Cognitive-behavioral treatment for depressed adolescents. *Behavior Therapy, 21*, 385–401.

Lewinsohn, P. M., Clarke, G. N., & Rohde, P. (1994). Psychological approaches to the treatment of depression in adolescents. In W. M. Reynolds & H. F. Johnston (Eds.), *Handbook of depression in children and adolescents* (pp. 309–344). New York: Plenum Press.

Lewinsohn, P. M., Clarke, G. N., Rohde, P., Hops, H., & Seeley, J. R. (1996). A course in coping: A cognitive-behavioral approach to the treatment of adolescent depression. In E. D. Hibbs & P. S. Jensen (Eds.), *Psychosocial treatments for children and adolescent disorders: Empirically based strategies for clinical practice* (pp. 109–135). Washington, DC: American Psychological Association.

Lewinsohn, P. M., Rohde, P., Hops, H., & Clarke, G. (1991). *Leader's manual for parent groups: Adolescent coping with depression course.* Eugene, OR: Castalia Publishing Company.

Lewinsohn, P. M., Sullivan, J. M., & Grosscup, S. J. (1980). Changing reinforcing events: An approach to the treatment of depression. *Psychotherapy: Theory, Research, and Practice, 17*, 322–334.

Lewis, S. (1974). A comparison of behavior therapy techniques in the reduction of fearful avoidance behavior. *Behavior Therapy, 5*, 648–655.

Liddle, B. & Spence, S. H. (1990). Cognitive-behaviour therapy with depressed primary school children: A cautionary note. *Behavioural Psychotherapy, 18*, 85–102.

Linn, J. L., & Stark, K. D. (1990). *Childhood depression and social skills disturbances.* Unpublished manuscript, University of Texas at Austin.

Lochman, J. E. (1985). Effects of different treatment lengths in cognitive behavioral interventions with aggressive boys. *Child Psychiatry and Human Development*, 16, 45–56.

Lochman, J. E., Barry, T. D., & Pardini, D. A. (2003). Anger control training for aggressive youth. In A. E. Kazdin & J. R. Weisz (Eds.), *Evidence-based psychotherapies for children and adolescents* (pp. 263–281). New York: Guilford.

Lochman, J. E., & Breyer, N. L. (1977). Contingency contracting. In D. Upper (Ed.), *Perspectives in behavior therapy*. Champaign, IL: Research Press.

Lochman, J. E., Burch, P. R., Curry, J. F., & Lampron, L. B. (1984). Treatment and generalization effects of cognitive-behavioral and goal-setting interventions with aggressive boys. *Journal of Consulting and Clinical Psychology, 52*, 915–916.

Lochman, J. E., Fitzgerald, D. P., & Whidby, J. M. (1999). Anger management with aggressive children. In C. Schaefer (Ed.), *Short-term psychotherapy groups for children* (pp. 301–349). Northvale, NJ: Jason Aronson.

Lochman, J. E., Lampron, L. B., Burch, P. R., & Curry, J. F. (1985). Client characteristics associated with behavior change for treated and untreated aggressive boys. *Journal of Abnormal Child Psychology, 13*, 527–538.

Lochman, J. E., Lampron, L. B., Gemmer, T. C., & Harris, S. R. (1987). Anger coping intervention with aggressive children: A guide to implementation in school settings. In P. A. Keller & S. R. Heyman (Eds.), *Innovations in clinical practice: A source book* (Vol. 6). Sarasota, FL: Professional Resource Exchange.

Lochman, J. E., Lampron, L. B., Gemmer, T. C., Harris, S. R., & Wyckoff, G. M. (1989). Teacher consultation and cognitive-behavioral interventions with aggressive boys. *Psychology in the Schools, 26*, 179–188.

Lochman, J. E., Nelson, W. M., & Sims, J. P. (1981). A cognitive-behavioral program for use with aggressive children. *Journal of Clinical Child Psychology, 10*, 146–148.

Loeber, R. (1990). Development and risk factors of juvenile antisocial behavior and delinquency. *Clinical Psychology Review, 10*, 1–41.

———. (1991). Antisocial behavior: More enduring than changeable? *Journal of the American Academy of Child and Adolescent Psychiatry, 30*, 393–397.

Loeber, R., & Dishion, T. J. (1983). Early predictors of male delinquency: A review. *Psychological Bulletin, 94*, 68–99.

Long, P., Forehand, R., Wierson, M., & Morgan, A. (1994). Does parent training with young noncompliant children have long-term effects? *Behaviour Research and Therapy, 32*, 101–107.

Lonigan, C. J., Elbert, J. C., & Bennett-Johnson, S. (1998). Empirically supported psychosocial interventions for children: An overview. *Journal of Clinical Child Psychology, 27*, 138–145.

Lyon, G. R., & Cutting, L. (1998). Treatment of learning disabilities. In E. J. Mash & L. C. Terdal (Eds.), *Treatment of childhood disorders* (2nd ed.). New York: Guilford.

Mann, C. (1990). Meta-analysis in the breech. *Science, 249*, 476–480.

Mann, J., & Rosenthal, T. L. (1969). Vicarious and direct counterconditioning of test anxiety through individual and group desensitization. *Behaviour Research and Therapy, 7*, 359–367.

Marlatt, G. A., & Gordon, J. R. (1985). *Relapse prevention: Maintenance strategies in the treatment of addictive behaviors*. New York: Guilford.

Martin, B. (1977). Brief family intervention: Effectiveness and the importance of including father. *Journal of Consulting Psychology, 6*, 1002–1100.

McAllister, L. W., Stachowiak, J. G., Baer, D. M., & Conderman, L. (1969). The application of operant conditioning techniques in a secondary school classroom. *Journal of Applied Behavior Analysis, 2,* 277–285.

McCain, A. P., & Kelley, M. L. (1993). Managing the classroom behavior of an ADHD preschooler: The efficacy of a school-home note intervention. *Child and Family Behavior Therapy, 15,* 33–44.

McCullough, J., Huntsinger, G., & May, W. (1977). Self-control treatment of aggression in a 16-year-old male: Case study. *Journal of Consulting and Clinical Psychology, 45,* 322–331.

McLeod, B., & Weisz, J. R. (in press). Increasing the accuracy of treatment effect estimates in youth therapy trials: Using dissertations to assess and address publication and file drawer bias. *Journal of Consulting and Clinical Psychology.*

McMahon, R. J., & Davies, G. R. (1980). A behavioral parent training program and its side effects on classroom behavior. *B. C. Journal of Special Education, 4,* 165–174.

McMahon, R. J., & Forehand, R. (1984). Parent training for the noncompliant child: Treatment outcome, generalization, and adjunctive therapy procedures. In R. F. Dangel & R. A. Polster (Eds.), *Parent training foundations of research and practice* (pp. 298–328). New York: Guilford.

(2003). *Helping the noncompliant child: Family-based treatment for oppositional behavior* (2nd ed.). New York: Guilford Press.

McMahon, R. J., Forehand, R., & Tiedemann, G. L. (1985, November). *Relative effectiveness of a parent training program with children of different ages.* Presented at the annual meeting of the American Association for Behavior Therapy. Houston, TX.

McMahon, R. J., Tiedemann, G. L., Forehand, R., & Griest, D. C. (1984). Parental satisfaction with parent training to modify child noncompliance. *Behavior Therapy, 15,* 295–303.

McMahon, R. J., & Wells, K. C. (1998). Conduct problems. In E. J. Mash & R. A. Barkley (Eds.), *Treatment of childhood disorders* (2nd ed., pp. 111–207). New York: Guilford.

McNeil, C. B., Eyberg, S., Eisenstadt, T. H., Newcomb, K., & Funderburk, B. (1991). Parent-child interaction therapy with behavior problem children: Generalization of treatment effects to the school setting. *Journal of Clinical Child Psychology, 20,* 140–151.

McNeil, C. B., & Hembree-Kigin, T. (1995). *Parent-Child Interaction Therapy.* New York: Plenum Press.

Meichenbaum, D. (1977). *Cognitive behavior modification: An integrative approach.* New York: Plenum Press.

Menzies, R. G., & Clarke, J. C. (1993). A comparison of *in vivo* and vicarious exposure in the treatment of childhood water phobia. *Behaviour Research and Therapy, 31,* 9–15.

Milich, R., & Landau, S. (1982). Socialization and peer relations in hyperactive children. In K. D. Gadow & I. Bialer (Eds.), *Advances in learning and behavioral disabilities* (pp. 283–340). Greenwich, CT: JAI Press.

Miller, A. L., & Glinski, J. (2000). Youth suicidal behavior: Assessment and intervention. *Journal of Clinical Psychology, 56,* 1131–1152.

Miller, L. C., Barrett, C. L., Hampe, E., & Noble, H. (1972). Comparison of reciprocal inhibition, psychotherapy, and waiting list control for phobic children. *Journal of Abnormal Psychology, 79*, 269–279.

Minuchin, S. (1974). *Families and family therapy*. Cambridge, MA: Harvard University Press.

Morrow-Bradley, C., & Elliott, R. (1986). Utilization of psychotherapy research by practicing psychotherapists. *American Psychologist, 41*, 188–197.

Motta, R. W., & Lynch, C. (1990). Therapeutic techniques vs. therapeutic relationships in child behavior therapy. *Psychological Reports, 67*, 315–322.

MTA Cooperative Group. (1999). A 14-month randomized clinical trial of treatment strategies for attention-deficit/hyperactivity disorder. *Archives of General Psychiatry, 56*, 1073–1086.

Mufson, L., & Dorta, K. P. (2003). Interpersonal therapy for depressed adolescents. In A. E. Kazdin & J. R. Weisz (Eds.), *Evidence-based psychotherapies for children and adolescents* (pp. 148–164). New York: Guilford.

Mufson, L., Weissman, M. M., Moreau, D., & Garfinkel, R. (1999). Efficacy of interpersonal psychotherapy for depressed adolescents. *Archives of General Psychiatry, 56*, 573–579.

Murphy, C. M., & Bootzin, R. R. (1973). Active and passive participation in the contact desensitization of snake fear in children. *Behavior Therapy, 4*, 203–211.

National Institutes of Health. (1994). Behavioral therapies development program. *NIH Guide, 22*, No. 26.

Nelson, R. O., Lipinski, D. P., & Boykin, R. A. (1978). The effects of self-recording training and the obtrusiveness of the self-recording device on the accuracy and reactivity of self-monitoring. *Behavior Therapy, 9*, 220–228.

Novaco, R. (1975). *Anger control: The development and evaluation of an experimental treatment*. Lexington, MA: D. C. Heath.

Obler, M., & Terwilliger, R. F. (1970). Pilot study on the effectiveness of systematic desensitization with neurologically impaired children with phobic disorders. *Journal of Consulting and Clinical Psychology, 34*, 314–318.

Oden, S., & Asher, S. R. (1977). Coaching children in social skills for friendship making. *Child Development, 48*, 495–506.

O'Leary, K. D., Pelham, W. E., Rosenbaum, A., & Price, G. (1976). Behavioral treatment of hyperkinetic children: An experimental evaluation of its usefulness. *Clinical Pediatrics, 15*, 510–515.

Ollendick, T. H., & Cerny, J. A. (1981). *Clinical behavior therapy with children*. New York: Plenum.

Ollendick, T. H., & King, N. J. (1998). Empirically supported treatments for children with phobic and anxiety disorders. *Journal of Clinical Child Psychology, 27*, 156–167.

Patterson, C. (1979). Rogerian counseling. In S. H. Harrison (Ed.), *Basic handbook of child psychiatry: Therapeutic interventions* (Vol. 3, pp. 203–215). New York: Basic Books.

Patterson, G. R. (1976). *Living with children: New methods for parents and teachers*. Champaign, IL: Research Press.

(1982). *A social learning approach, Vol. 3. Coercive family process*. Eugene, OR: Castalia Publishing Company.

Patterson, G. R., & Chamberlain (1992). A functional analysis of resistance: A neo-behavioral perspective. In H. Arkowitz (Ed.), *Why don't people change? New perspectives on resistance and noncompliance.* New York: Guilford.

Patterson, G. R., Cobb, J. A., & Ray, R. S. (1973). A social engineering technology for retraining the families of aggressive boys. In H. Adams & L. Unikel (Eds.), *Issues and trends in behavior therapy* (pp. 139–224). Springfield, IL: Charles C. Thomas.

Patterson, G. R., DeBaryshe, B. D., & Ramsey, E. (1989). A developmental perspective on antisocial behavior. *American Psychologist, 44,* 329–335.

Patterson, G. R., & Forgatch, M. S. (1975). *Family learning series* (Five cassettes). Champaign, IL: Research Press.

(1987). *Parents and adolescents living together–Part 1: The basics.* Eugene, OR: Castalia Publishing Company.

(1985). Therapist behavior as a determinant for client noncompliance: A paradox for the behavior modifier. *Journal of Consulting and Clinical Psychology, 53,* 846–851.

Patterson, G. R., & Gullion, M. E. (1968). *Living with children: New methods for parents and teachers.* Champaign, IL: Research Press.

Patterson, G. R., Littman, R. A., & Bricker, W. (1967). Assertive behavior in children: A step toward a theory of aggression. *Monographs of the Society for Research in Child Development, 32* (No. 5, Serial No. 113).

Patterson, G. R., Ray, R. S., & Shaw, D. A. (1968). Direct intervention in families of deviant children. *Oregon Research Institute Research Bulletin, 8,* 1–11.

Patterson, G. R., Reid, J. B., & Dishion, T. J. (1992). *A social learning approach. 4. Antisocial boys.* Eugene, OR: Castalia Publishing Company.

Paul, G. L. (1967). Outcome research in psychotherapy. *Journal of Consulting Psychology, 31,* 109–118.

Peed, S., Roberts, M., & Forehand, R. (1977). Evaluation of the effectiveness of a standardized parent training program in altering the interaction of mothers and their noncompliant children. *Behavior Modification, 1,* 323–350.

Pelham, W. E. (1993). Pharmacotherapy for children with attention-deficit hyperactivity disorder. *School Psychology Review, 22,* 199–227.

(1999). A summer treatment program for children with behavior problems: Efficacy, effectiveness, costs, and managed care. In T. H. Ollendick (Chair), *Implementing empirically supported treatment for children in applied settings.* Symposium conducted at the meeting of the Association for the Advancement of Behavior Therapy, Toronto.

Pelham, W. E., & Bender, M. E. (1982). Peer relationships in hyperactive children: Description and treatment. In K. Gadow & I. Bialer (Eds.), *Advances in learning and behavioral disabilities* (Vol. 1, pp. 365–436). Greenwich, CT: JAI Press.

Pelham, W. E., Gnagy, E. M., Greiner, A. R., Hoza, B., Hinshaw, S. P., Swanson, J. M., Simpson, S., Shapiro, C., Bukstein, O., & Baron-Myak, C. (2000). Behavioral vs. behavioral and pharmacological treatment in ADHD children attending a summer treatment program. *Journal of Abnormal Child Psychology, 28,* 507–525.

Pelham, W. E., Greiner, A. R., & Gnagy, E. M. (1998). *Children's summer treatment program manual.* Buffalo: State University of New York at Buffalo.

Pelham, W. E., & Hoza, B. (1996). Intensive treatment: Summer treatment program for children with ADHD. In E. D. Hibbs & P. S. Jensen (Eds.), *Psychosocial treatments for child and adolescent disorders: Empirically based strategies for clinical practice* (pp. 311–340). Washington, DC: American Psychological Association.

Pelham, W. E., & Milich, R. (1984). Peer relationships in hyperactive children. *Journal of Learning Disabilities, 17,* 560–567.

Pelham, W. E., Schnedler, R. W., Bender, M. E., Nilsson, D. E., Miller, J., Budrow, M. S., Ronnei, M., Paluchowski, C., & Marks, D. A. (1988). The combination of behavior therapy and methylphenidate in the treatment of attention deficit disorders: A therapy outcome study. In L. Bloomingdale (Ed.), *Attention deficit disorder* (Vol. 3, pp. 29–48). London: Pergamon.

Pelham, W. E., Wheeler, T., & Chronis, A. (1998). Empirically supported psychosocial treatments for attention deficit hyperactivity disorder. *Journal of Clinical Child Psychology, 27,* 190–205.

Pennington, B. F., & Ozonoff, S. (1996). Executive functions and developmental psychopathology. *Journal of Child Psychology and Psychiatry, 37,* 51–87.

Pfiffner, L. J., & McBurnett, K. (1997). Social skills training with parent generalization: Treatment effects for children with attention deficit disorder. *Journal of Consulting and Clinical Psychology, 65,* 749–757.

Pfiffner, L. J., & O'Leary, S. G. (1993). Psychological treatments: School-based. In J. L. Matson (Ed.), *Hyperactivity in children: A handbook* (pp. 234–255). Boston: Allyn & Bacon.

Pfiffner, L. J., O'Leary, S. G., Rosen, L. A., & Sanderson, W. C. (1985). A comparison of the effects of continuous and intermittent response cost and reprimands in the classroom. *Journal of Clinical Child Psychology, 14,* 348–352.

Piercy, F. P. (1986). *Training manual: Purdue brief family therapy.* West Lafayette, IN: Center for Instructional Services.

Pisterman, S., McGrath, P., Firestone, P., Goodman, J. T., Webster, I., & Mallory, R. (1989). Outcome of parent-mediated treatment of preschoolers with attention deficit disorder with hyperactivity. *Journal of Consulting and Clinical Psychology, 57,* 628–635.

Pisterman, S., Firestone, P., McGrath, P., Goodman, J. T., Webster, I., Mallory, R., & Goffin, B. (1992a). The effects of parental training on parenting stress and sense of competence. *Canadian Journal of Behavioural Science, 24,* 41–58.

———. (1992b). The role of parent training in treatment of preschoolers with ADDH. *American Journal of Orthopsychiatry, 62,* 397–408.

Pollard, S., Ward, E. M., & Barkley, R. A. (1983). The effects of parent training and Ritalin on the parent-child interactions of hyperactive boys. *Child and Family Behavior Therapy, 5,* 51–69.

Prout, H. T., & DeMartino, R. A. (1986). A meta-analysis of school-based studies of psychotherapy. *Journal of School Psychology, 24,* 285–292.

Puig-Antich, J., & Chambers, W. (1978). *The schedule for affective disorders and schizophrenia for school-aged children.* Unpublished interview schedule, New York Psychiatric Institute, New York.

Quay, H. C. (1997). Inhibition and attention-deficit hyperactivity disorder. *Journal of Abnormal Child Psychology, 25,* 7–13.

Rapport, M. D., Murphy, H. A., & Bailey, J. S. (1980). The effects of a response cost treatment tactic on hyperactive children. *Journal of School Psychology, 18*, 98–111.

——— (1982). Ritalin vs. response cost in the control of hyperactive children: A within-subject comparison. *Journal of Applied Behavior Analysis, 15*, 205–216.

Rehm, L. P. (1977). A self-control model of depression. *Behavior Therapy, 8*, 787–804.

Rehm, L. P., Kaslow, N. J., & Rabin, A. S. (1987). Cognitive and behavioral targets in a self-control therapy program for depression. *Journal of Consulting and Clinical Psychology, 55*, 60–67.

Reid, M. J., & Webster-Stratton, C. (2001). The Incredible Years parent, teacher, and child intervention: Targeting multiple areas of risk for a young child with pervasive conduct problems using a flexible, manualized treatment program. *Cognitive and Behavioral Practice, 8*, 377–386.

Reinecke, M. A., Ryan, N. E., & DuBois, D. L. (1998a). Cognitive-behavioral therapy of depression and depressive symptoms during adolescence: A review and meta-analysis. *Journal of the American Academy of Child and Adolescent Psychiatry, 37*, 26–34.

——— (1998b). Meta-analysis of CBT for depression in adolescents: Dr. Reinecke et al. reply. *Journal of the American Academy of Child and Adolescent Psychiatry, 37*, 1006–1007.

Reisman, J. M. (1973). *Principles of psychotherapy with children*. New York: Wiley.

Renaud, J., Brent, D. A., Baugher, M., Birmaher, B., Kolko, D. J., & Bridge, J. (1998). Rapid response to psychosocial treatment for adolescent depression: A two-year followup. *Journal of the American Academy of Child and Adolescent Psychiatry, 37*, 1184–1190.

Reynolds, W. M., & Coats, K. I. (1986). A comparison of cognitive-behavioral therapy and relaxation training for the treatment of depression in adolescents. *Journal of Consulting and Clinical Psychology, 54*, 653–660.

Richters, J. E. (1993). Community violence and children's development: Toward a research agenda for the 1990s. *Psychiatry, 56*, 3–6.

Ritter, B. (1968). The group desensitization of children's snake phobias using vicarious and contact desensitization procedures. *Behaviour Research and Therapy, 6*, 1–6.

Roberts, M. C. (1994). Models for service delivery in children's mental health: Common characteristics. *Journal of Clinical Child Psychology, 23*, 212–219.

Robin, A. L. (1981). A controlled evaluation of problem-solving communication training with parent-adolescent conflict. *Behavior Therapy, 12*, 593–609.

Robin, A. L., Bedway, M., Siegel, P. T., & Gilroy, M. (1996). Therapy for adolescent anorexia nervosa: Addressing cognitions, feelings, and the family's role. In E. D. Hibbs & P. S. Jensen (Eds.), *Psychosocial treatments for child and adolescent disorders: Empirically based strategies for clinical practice* (pp. 239–262). Washington, DC: American Psychological Association.

Robin, A. L., Kent, R. N., O'Leary, K. D., Foster, S., & Prinz, R. J. (1977). An approach to teaching parents and adolescents problem-solving communication skills: A preliminary report. *Behavior Therapy, 8*, 639–643.

Robinson, E. A., & Eyberg, S. M. (1981). The dyadic parent-child interaction coding system: Standardization and validation. *Journal of Consulting and Clinical Psychology, 49*, 245–250.

Rogers, T. R., Forehand, R., Griest, D. L., Wells, K. C., & McMahon, R. J. (1981). Socioeconomic status: Effects on parent and child behaviors and treatment outcome of parent training. *Journal of Clinical Child Psychology, 10,* 98–101.

Rosen, L. A., O'Leary, S. G., Joyce, S. A., Conway, G., & Pfiffner, L. J. (1984). The importance of prudent negative consequences for maintaining the appropriate behavior of hyperactive students. *Journal of Abnormal Child Psychology, 12,* 581–604.

Rothbaum, F., Weisz, J. R., & Snyder, S. (1982). Changing the world and changing the self: A two-process model of perceived control. *Journal of Personality and Social Psychology, 42,* 5–37.

Rubin, K. H., Bream, L. A., & Rose-Krasnor, L. (1991). Social problem solving and aggression in childhood. In D. J. Pepler & K. H. Rubin (Eds.), *The development and treatment of childhood aggression* (pp. 219–248). Hillsdale, NJ: Erlbaum.

Rule, B. G., & Nesdale, A. R. (1976). Emotional arousal and aggressive behavior. *Psychological Bulletin, 83,* 851–863.

Russ, S. W. (1998). Psychodynamically based therapies. In T. H. Ollendick & M. Hersen (Eds.), *Handbook of child psychopathology* (3rd ed., pp. 537–556). New York: Plenum Press.

Russell, R. L., Greenwald, S., & Shirk, S. R. (1991). Language change in child psychotherapy: A meta-analytic review. *Journal of Consulting and Clinical Psychology, 59,* 916–919.

Saile, H., Burgmeier, R., & Schmidt, L. R. (1988). A meta-analysis of studies on psychological preparation of children facing medical procedures. *Psychology and Health, 2,* 107–132.

Sayger, T. V., & Horne, A. M. (1987, August). *The maintenance of treatment effects for families with aggressive boys participating in social learning family therapy.* Paper presented at the annual meeting of American Psychological Association, New York.

Saywitz, K. J., Mannarino, A. P., Berliner, L., & Cohen, J. A. (2000). Treatment of sexually abused children and adolescents. *American Psychologist, 55,* 1040–1049.

Schlichter, K. J., & Horan, J. J. (1981). Effects of stress inoculation on the anger and aggression management skills of institutionalized juvenile delinquents. *Cognitive Therapy and Research, 5,* 359–365.

Schoenwald, S. K., Henggeler, S. W., & Brondino, M. J. (2000). Multisystemic therapy: Monitoring treatment fidelity. *Family Process, 39,* 83–103.

Schoenwald, S. K., & Hoagwood, K. (2001). Effectiveness, transportability, and dissemination of interventions: What matters when? *Psychiatric Services, 52,* 1179–1189.

Schoenwald, S. K., Ward, D. M., Henggeler, S. W., Pickrel, S. G., & Patel, H. (1996). Multisystemic therapy treatment of substance abusing or dependent adolescent offenders: Costs of reducing incarceration, inpatient, and residential placement. *Journal of Child and Family Studies, 5,* 431–444.

Schoenwald, S. K., Ward, D. M., Henggeler, S. W., & Rowland, M. D. (2000). MST vs. hospitalization for crisis stabilization of youth: Placement outcomes 4 months postreferral. *Mental Health Services Research, 2,* 3–12.

Schuhmann, E. M., Foote, R. C., Eyberg, S. M., Boggs, S. R., & Algina, J. (1998). Efficacy of parent-child interaction therapy: Interim report of a randomized trial with short-term maintenance. *Journal of Clinical Child Psychology, 27,* 34–45.

Schwartz, A. J., Gladstone, T. R. G., & Kaslow, N. J. (1998). Depressive disorders. In T. H. Ollendick & M. Hersen (Eds.), *Handbook of child psychopathology* (3rd ed., pp. 269–290). New York: Plenum Press.

Scott, S., Spender, Q., Doolan, M., Jacobs, B., & Aspland, H. (2001). Multicentre controlled trial of parenting groups for childhood antisocial behaviour in clinical practice. *British Medical Journal, 28*, 1–6.

Shadish, W. R., Montgomery, L. M., Wilson, P., Wilson, M. R., Bright, I., & Okwumabua, T. (1993). Effects of family and marital psychotherapies: A meta-analysis. *Journal of Consulting and Clinical Psychology, 61*, 992–1002.

Shapiro, A. K., & Shapiro, E. (1998). *Powerful placebo: From ancient priest to modern physician.* Baltimore: John Hopkins University Press.

Shapiro, D. A., & Shapiro, D. (1982). Meta-analysis of comparative therapy outcome studies: A replication and refinement. *Psychological Bulletin, 92*, 581–604.

Shepherd, M., Oppenheim, A. N., & Mitchell, S. (1966). Childhood behavior disorders and the child-guidance clinic: An epidemiological study. *Journal of Child Psychology and Psychiatry, 7*, 39–52.

Sheslow, D. V., Bondy, A. S., & Nelson, R. O. (1983). A comparison of graduated exposure, verbal coping skills, and their combination in the treatment of children's fear of the dark. *Child and Family Behavior Therapy, 4*, 33–45.

Shirk, S. R. (Ed.). (1988). *Cognitive development and child psychotherapy.* New York: Plenum Press.

Shirk, S. R., & Russell, R. L. (1996). *Change processes in child psychotherapy: Revitalizing treatment and research.* New York: Guilford.

Shirk, S. R., & Saiz, C. C. (1992). Clinical, empirical, and developmental perspectives on the therapeutic relationship in child psychotherapy. Special issue: Developmental approaches to prevention and intervention. *Development & Psychopathology, 4*, 713–728.

Shure, M. B. (1996). *Raising a thinking child: Help your young child to resolve everyday conflicts and get along with others.* New York: Pocket Books.

(1999). Preventing violence the problem-solving way. *Juvenile Justice Bulletin,* April 1–11. Publication of the U.S. Department of Justice, Office of Juvenile Justice and Delinquency Prevention, Washington, DC.

Shure, M. B., & Spivack, G. (1972). Means-ends thinking, adjustment, and social class among elementary school-aged children. *Journal of Consulting and Clinical Psychology, 38*, 348–353.

Silverman, W. K., & Ginsburg, C. S. (1995). Specific phobias and generalized anxiety disorder. In J. S. March (Ed.), *Anxiety disorders in children and adolescents* (pp. 151–180). New York: Guilford.

Silverman, W. K., & Kurtines, W. M. (1996a). *Anxiety and phobic disorders: A pragmatic approach.* New York: Plenum Press.

(1996b). Transfer of control: A psychosocial intervention model for internalizing disorders in youth. In E. D. Hibbs & P. S. Jensen (Eds.), *Psychosocial treatments for child and adolescent disorders: Empirically based strategies for clinical practice* (pp. 63–81). Washington, DC: American Psychological Association.

Skinner, B. F. (1953). *Science and human behavior.* New York: Macmillan Co.

Sloan, M., Jensen, P., & Kettle, L. (1999). Assessing services for children with ADHD: Gaps and opportunities. *Journal of Attention Disorders, 3*, 13–29.

Smith, M. L., & Glass, G. V. (1977). Meta-analysis of psychotherapy outcome studies. *American Psychologist, 32*, 752–760.

Smith, M. L., Glass, G. V., & Miller, T. L. (1980). *Benefits of psychotherapy*. Baltimore: Johns Hopkins University Press.

Smoll, F. L., & Smith, R. E. (1987). *Sports psychology for youth coaches*. Washington, DC: National Federation for Catholic Ministry.

Smyrnios, K. X., & Kirkby, R. J. (1993). Long-term comparison of brief versus unlimited psychodynamic treatments with children and their parents. *Journal of Consulting and Clinical Psychology, 61*, 1020–1027.

Snyder, J. J., Edwards, P., McGraw, K., Kilgore, K., & Holton, A. (1994). Escalation and reinforcement in mother-child conflict: Social processes associated with the development of physical aggression. *Development and Psychopathology, 6*, 305–321.

Spirito, A. (1999). Introduction. *Journal of Pediatric Psychology, 24*, 87–90.

Spivack, G., Platt, J. J., & Shure, M. B. (1976). *The problem-solving approach to adjustment*. San Francisco: Jossey-Bass.

Spivack, G., & Shure, M. B. (1982). The cognition of social adjustment: Interpersonal cognitive problem-solving thinking. In B. B. Lahey & A. E. Kazdin (Eds.), *Advances in clinical child psychology* (Vol. 5, pp. 323–372). New York: Plenum Press.

Stark, K. D. (1990). *Childhood depression: School-based intervention*. New York: Guilford.

Stark, K. D., & Kendall, P. C. (1996). *Treating depressed children: Therapist manual for "ACTION."* Ardmore, PA: Workbook Publishing.

Stark, K. D., Kendall, P. C., McCarthy, M., Stafford, M., Barron, R., & Thomeer, M. (1996). *ACTION: A workbook for overcoming depression*. Ardmore, PA: Workbook Publishing.

Stark, K. D., Reynolds, W. M., & Kaslow, N. J. (1987). A comparison of the relative efficacy of self-control therapy and a behavioral problem-solving therapy for depression in children. *Journal of Abnormal Child Psychology, 15*, 91–113.

Stark, K. D., Rouse, L. W., & Livingston, R. (1991). Treatment of depression during childhood and adolescence: Cognitive-behavioral procedures for the individual and family. In P. C. Kendall (Ed.), *Child and adolescent therapy* (pp. 165–206). New York: Guilford.

Stark, K. D., Swearer, S., Kurowski, C., Sommer, D., & Bowen, B. (1996). Targeting the child and family: A holistic approach to treating child and adolescent depressive disorders. In E. D. Hibbs & P. S. Jensen (Eds.), *Psychosocial treatments for child and adolescent disorders: Empirically based strategies for clinical practice* (pp. 207–238). Washington, DC: American Psychological Association.

Strayhorn, J. M., & Weidman, C. S. (1989). Reduction of attention deficit and internalizing symptoms in preschoolers through parent-child interaction training. *Journal of the American Academy of Child and Adolescent Psychiatry, 28*, 888–896.

Stroul, B. A., & Friedman, R. (1986). *A system of care for children and youth with severe emotional disturbances* (rev. ed.). Washington, DC: Georgetown University Child Development Center, CASSP Technical Assistance Center.

Strupp, H. H., & Anderson, T. (1997). On the limitations of therapy manuals. *Clinical Psychology: Science and Practice, 4*, 76–82.

Sturm, R., Ringel, J., Bao, C., Stein, B., Kapur, K., Zhang, W., & Zeng, F. (2000). *National estimates of mental health utilization and expenditures for children in 1998.* Working paper No. 205. Research Center on Managed Care for Psychiatric Disorders. Los Angeles, CA: RAND.

Sullivan, P. F. (1995). Mortality in anorexia nervosa. *American Journal of Psychiatry, 152,* 1073–1074.

Swanson, J. M., McBurnett, K., Christian, D. L., & Wigal, T. (1995). Stimulant medication and treatment of children with ADHD. In T. H. Ollendick & R. J. Prinz (Eds.), *Advances in clinical child psychology* (Vol. 17, pp. 265–322). New York: Plenum.

Szatmari, P. (1992). The epidemiology of attention-deficit hyperactivity disorders. In G. Weiss (Ed.), *Child and adolescent psychiatric clinics of North America: Attention-deficit hyperactivity disorder* (pp. 361–372). Philadelphia: Saunders.

Task Force on Promotion and Dissemination of Psychological Procedures, Division of Clinical Psychology, American Psychological Association. (1995). Training in and dissemination of empirically validated psychological treatments: Report and recommendations. *The Clinical Psychologist, 48,* 3–23.

Taylor, T. K., Schmidt, F., Pepler, D., & Hodgins, H. (1998). A comparison of eclectic treatment with Webster-Stratton's Parents and Children Series in a Children's Mental Health Center: A randomized controlled trial. *Behavior Therapy, 29,* 221–240.

Treadwell, K. R. H., & Kendall, P. C. (1996). Self-talk in anxiety-disordered youth: States of mind, content specificity, and treatment outcome. *Journal of Consulting and Clinical Psychology, 64,* 941–950.

Tuma, J. M., & Sobotka, K. R. (1983). Traditional therapies with children. In T. H. Ollendick & M. Hersen (Eds.), *Handbook of child psychopathology* (pp. 391–426). New York: Plenum Press.

Turkewitz, H., O'Leary, K. D., & Ironsmith, M. (1975). Generalization and maintenance of appropriate behavior through self-control. *Journal of Consulting and Clinical Psychology, 43,* 577–583.

Van Houten, R. (1983). Are social reprimands effective? In S. Axelrod & J. Apsehe (Eds.), *The effects of punishment on human behavior.* New York: Academic Press.

Van Houten, R., Nau, P. A., MacKenzie-Keating, S., Sameoto, D., & Colavecchia, B. (1982). An analysis of some variable influencing the effectiveness of reprimands. *Journal of Applied Behavior Analysis, 15,* 65–83.

von Bertalanffy, L. (1968). *General systems theory.* New York: Braziller.

Vostanis, P., Feehan, C., Grattan, E., & Bickerton, W. (1996b). A randomised controlled outpatient trial of cognitive-behavioural treatment for children and adolescents with depression: 9-month followup. *Journal of Affective Disorders, 40,* 105–116.

(1996b). Treatment for children and adolescents with depression: Lessons from a controlled trial. *Clinical Child Psychology and Psychiatry, 1,* 199–212.

Walker, H., & Buckley, N. (1971). *Teacher attention to appropriate and inappropriate classroom behavior: An individual case study.* Unpublished manuscript, CORBEH, Department of Special Education, University of Oregon.

Washington State Institute for Public Policy. (1998). *Watching the bottom line:*

Cost-effective interventions for reducing crime in Washington. Olympia: Evergreen State College.

Watson, J. B., & Rayner, R. (1920). Conditioned emotional reactions. *Journal of Experimental Psychology, 3,* 1–14.

Webster-Stratton, C. (1981a). Modification of mothers' behaviors and attitudes through a videotape modeling group discussion program. *Behavior Therapy, 12,* 634–642.

(1981b). Videotape modeling: A method of parent education. *Journal of Clinical Child Psychology, 10,* 93–98.

(1982a). Teaching mothers through videotape modeling to change their children's behavior. *Journal of Pediatric Psychology, 7,* 279–294.

(1982b). The long-term effects of a videotape modeling parent-training program: Comparison of immediate and 1-year follow-up results. *Behavior Therapy, 13,* 702–714.

(1984). Randomized trial of two parent-training programs for families with conduct disorders children. *Journal of Consulting and Clinical Psychology, 52,* 666–678.

(1985). The effects of father involvement in parent training for conduct problem children. *Journal of Child Psychology and Psychiatry, 26,* 801–810.

(1990). Enhancing the effectiveness of self-administered videotape parent training for families with conduct-problem children. *Journal of Abnormal Child Psychology, 18,* 479–492.

(1992a). Individually administered videotape parent training: "Who benefits?" *Cognitive Therapy and Research, 16,* 31–35.

(1992b). *The incredible years: A troubleshooting guide for parents of children ages 3–8 years.* Toronto: Umbrella Press.

(1994). Advancing videotape parent training: A comparison study. *Journal of Consulting and Clinical Psychology, 62,* 583–593.

(1996). Early intervention with videotape modeling: Programs for families of children with oppositional defiant disorder or conduct disorder. In E. D. Hibbs & P. S. Jensen (Eds.), *Psychosocial treatments for child and adolescent disorders: Empirically based strategies for clinical practice* (pp. 435–474). Washington, DC: American Psychological Association.

(2001). *Leader's guide, the parents and children series: A comprehensive course divided into four programs.* Seattle: University of Washington.

Webster-Stratton, C., & Hammond, M. (1997). Treating children with early-onset conduct problems: A comparison of child and parent training interventions. *Journal of Consulting and Clinical Psychology, 65,* 93–109.

(2001). Preventing conduct problems, promoting social competence: A parent and teacher training partnership in Head Start. *Journal of Clinical Child Psychology, 30,* 283–302.

Webster-Stratton, C., Hollinsworth, T., & Kolpacoff, M. (1989). The long-term effectiveness and clinical significance of three cost-effective training programs for families with conduct-problem children. *Journal of Consulting and Clinical Psychology, 57,* 550–553.

Webster-Stratton, C., Kolpacoff, M., & Hollinsworth, T. (1985). Self-administered videotape therapy for families with conduct-problem children: Comparison with two cost-effective treatments and a control group. *Journal of Consulting and Clinical Psychology, 56*, 558–566.

Webster-Stratton, C., & Reid, M. J. (1999, November). *Treating children with early-onset conduct problems: The importance of teacher training.* Paper presented at the Association for the Advancement of Behavior Therapy, Toronto, Canada.

(2003). The Incredible Years parents, teachers, and children's training series: A multifaceted treatment approach for young children with conduct problems. In A. E. Kazdin & J. R. Weisz (Eds.), *Evidence-based psychotherapies for children and adolescents* (pp. 224–241). New York: Guilford.

Webster-Stratton, C., Reid, M. J., & Hammond, M. (2001a). Preventing conduct problems, promoting social competence: A parent and teacher training partnership in Head Start. *Journal of Clinical Child Psychology, 30*, 283–302.

(2001b). Social skills and problem-solving training for children with early-onset conduct problems: "Who benefits?" *Journal of Child Psychology and Psychiatry, 42*, 943–952.

Weersing, V. R., & Brent, D. A. (2003). Unpacking cognitive-behavioral therapy for adolescent depression: Comparative efficacy, mediation, moderation, and effectiveness. In A. E. Kazdin & J. R. Weisz (Eds.), *Evidence-based psychotherapies for children and adolescents* (pp. 135–147). New York: Guilford.

Weersing, V. R., & Weisz, J. R. (2002). Mechanisms of action in youth psychotherapy. *Journal of Child Psychology and Psychiatry, 43*, 3–29.

Weersing, V. R., Weisz, J. R., & Donenberg, G. R. (2002). Development of the Therapy Procedures Checklist: A therapist-report measure of technique use in child and adolescent treatment. *Journal of Clinical Child and Adolescent Psychology, 31*, 168–180.

Weiss, B., Catron, T., Harris, V., & Phung, T. M. (1999). The effectiveness of traditional child psychotherapy. *Journal of Consulting and Clinical Psychology, 67*, 82–94.

Weiss, B., & Weisz, J. R. (1990). The impact of methodological factors on child psychotherapy outcome research: A meta-analysis for researchers. *Journal of Abnormal Child Psychology, 18*, 639–670.

Weiss, G., & Hechtman, L. (1993). *Hyperactive children grown up* (2nd ed.). New York: Guilford.

Weisz, J. R. (1990). Development of control-related beliefs, goals, and styles in childhood and adolescence: A clinical perspective. In Schaie, K. W., Rodin, J., & Schooler, C. (Eds.), *Self-directedness and efficacy: Causes and effects throughout the life course* (pp. 103–145). New York: Erlbaum.

(2000). President's message: Lab-clinic differences and what we can do about them: I. The clinic-based treatment development model. *Clinical Child Psychology Newsletter, 15*, 1–10.

Weisz, J. R., Donenberg, G. R., Han, S. S., & Weiss, B. (1995a). Bridging the gap between laboratory and clinic in child and adolescent psychotherapy. *Journal of Consulting and Clinical Psychology, 63*, 688–701.

Weisz, J. R., Han, S. S., & Valeri, S. M. (1997). More of what? Issues raised by Fort Bragg. *American Psychologist, 52*, 541–545.

Weisz, J. R., & Hawley, K. M. (2002). Developmental factors in the treatment of adolescents. *Journal of Consulting and Clinical Psychology, 70*, 21–43.

Weisz, J. R., Huey, S. J., & Weersing, V. R. (1998). Psychotherapy outcome research with children and adolescents: The state of the art. In T. H. Ollendick & R. J. Prinz (Eds.), *Advances in Clinical Child Psychology, Volume 20* (pp. 49–91). New York: Plenum Press.

Weisz, J. R., Jensen, A. L., & McLeod, B. D. (in press). Milestones and methods in the development and dissemination of child and adolescent psychotherapies: Review, commentory, and a new deployment-focused model. In E. D. Hibbs & P. S. Jensen (Eds.), *Psychosocial treatments for child and adolescent disorders: Empirically based strategies for clinical practice* (2nd ed.). Washington, DC: American Psychological Association.

Weisz, J. R., & Jensen, P. S. (1999). Efficacy and effectiveness of child and adolescent psychotherapy and pharmacotherapy. *Mental Health Services Research, 1*, 125–157.

Weisz, J. R., McCarty, C. A., Eastman, K. L., Suwanlert, S., & Chaiyasit, W. (1997). Developmental psychopathology and culture: Ten lessons from Thailand. In Luthar, S. S., Burack, J., Cicchetti, D., & Weisz, J. R. (Eds.), *Developmental psychopathology: Perspectives on adjustment, risk, and disorder* (pp. 568–592). Cambridge, England: Cambridge University Press.

Weisz, J. R., Rothbaum, F. M., & Blackburn, T. F. (1984a). Standing out and standing in: The psychology of control in America and Japan. *American Psychologist, 39*, 955–969.

——— (1984b). Swapping recipes for control. *American Psychologist, 39*, 974–975.

Weisz, J. R., Southam-Gerow, M. A., & McCarty, C. A. (2001). Control-related beliefs and depressive symptoms in clinic-referred children and adolescents: Developmental differences and model specificity. *Journal of Abnormal Psychology, 110*, 97–109.

Weisz, J. R., Stevens, J. S., Curry, J. F., Cohen, R., Craighead, E., Burlingame, W. V., Smith, A., Weiss, B., & Parmelee, D. X. (1989). Control-related cognitions and depression among inpatient children and adolescents. *Journal of the American Academy of Child and Adolescent Psychiatry, 28*, 358–363.

Weisz, J. R., Suwanlert, S., Chaiyasit, W., & Walter, B. R. (1987). Over- and undercontrolled referral problems among children and adolescents from Thailand and the United States: The wat and wai of cultural differences. *Journal of Consulting and Clinical Psychology, 55*, 719–726.

Weisz, J. R., Sweeney, L., Proffitt, V., & Carr, T. (1993). Control-related beliefs and self-reported depressive symptoms in late childhood. *Journal of Abnormal Psychology, 102*, 411–418.

Weisz, J. R., Thurber, C. A., Sweeney, L., Proffitt, V. D., & LeGagnoux, G. L. (1997). Brief treatment of mild to moderate child depression using primary and secondary control enhancement training. *Journal of Consulting and Clinical Psychology, 65*, 703–707.

Weisz, J. R., Walter, B. R., Weiss, B., Fernandez, G. A., & Mikow, V. A. (1990). Arrests among emotionally disturbed violent and assaultive individuals following minimal versus lengthy intervention through North Carolina's Willie M. Program. *Journal of Consulting and Clinical Psychology, 58*, 720–728.

Weisz, J. R., & Weiss, B. (1989). Assessing the effects of clinic-based psychotherapy with children and adolescents. *Journal of Consulting and Clinical Psychology, 57*, 741–746.

——— (1991). Studying the "referability" of child clinical problems. *Journal of Consulting and Clinical Psychology, 59*, 266–273.

(1993). *Effects of psychotherapy with children and adolescents*. Newbury Park, CA: Sage.

Weisz, J. R., Weiss, B., Alicke, M. D., & Klotz, M. L. (1987). Effectiveness of psychotherapy with children and adolescents: A meta-analysis for clinicians. *Journal of Consulting and Clinical Psychology, 55*, 542–549.

Weisz, J. R., Weiss, B., & Donenberg, G. R. (1992). The lab versus the clinic: Effects of child and adolescent psychotherapy. *American Psychologist, 47*, 1578–1585.

Weisz, J. R., Weiss, B., Han, S. S., Granger, D. A., & Morton, T. (1995b). Effects of psychotherapy with children and adolescents revisited: A meta-analysis of treatment outcome studies. *Psychological Bulletin, 117*, 450–468.

Weisz, J. R., Weiss, B., Wasserman, A. A., & Rintoul, B. (1987). Control-related beliefs among clinic-referred children and adolescents. *Journal of Abnormal Psychology, 96*, 58–63.

Wells, K. C., & Egan, J. (1988). Social learning and systems family therapy for childhood oppositional disorder: Comparative treatment outcome. *Comprehensive Psychiatry, 29*, 138–146.

Wells, K. C., Forehand, R., & Griest, D. L. (1980). Generality of treatment effects from treated to untreated behaviors resulting from a parent training program. *Journal of Clinical Child Psychology, 9*, 217–219.

White, J. L., Moffitt, T. E., Earls, E., Robins, L., & Silva, P. A. (1990). How early can we tell? Predictors of childhood conduct disorder and adolescent delinquency. *Criminology, 28*, 507–533.

Wilson, G. T. (1985). Limitations of meta-analysis in the evaluation of the effects of psychological therapy. *Clinical Psychology Review, 5*, 35–47.

Wilson, P. H. (1992). *Principles and practice of relapse prevention*. New York: Guilford.

Wiltz, N. A., & Patterson, G. R. (1974). An evaluation of parent training procedures designed to alter inappropriate aggressive behavior of boys. *Behavior Therapy, 5*, 215–221.

Witmer, H. L., & Keller, J. (1942). Outgrowing childhood problems: A study of the value of child guidance treatment. *Smith College Studies in Social Work, 13*, 74–90.

Wolpe, J. (1958). *Psychotherapy by reciprocal inhibition*. Stanford, CA: Stanford University Press.

Wood, A. W., Harrington, R., & Moore, A. (1996). Controlled trial of a brief cognitive-behavioural intervention in adolescent patients with depressive disorders. *Journal of Child Psychology and Psychiatry, 37*, 737–746.

Yeh, M., & Weisz, J. R. (2001). Why are we here at the clinic? Parent-child (dis)agreement on referral problems at treatment entry. *Journal of Consulting and Clinical Psychology, 69*, 1018–1025.

Yu, P., Harris, G. E., Slovitz, B. L., & Franklin, L. (1986). A social problem-solving intervention for children at high risk for later psychopathology. *Journal of Clinical Child Psychology, 13*, 30–40.

Zangwill, W. M. (1984). An evaluation of a parent training program. *Child and Family Behavior Therapy, 5*, 1–16.

Zoccolillo, M. (1993). Gender and the development of conduct disorder. *Development and Psychopathology, 5*, 65–78.

Author Index

Subject Index

multiple treatments, 13
Multisystemic Therapy (MST), 415–6, 454
  antisocial behavior and, 414–28
  applying, 430–1
  assessment process, 431
  brief description, 416–7
  clinical practice issues, 441–3
  conceptual basis, 415–6
  costs of, 442
  delinquency and, 414–28
  ecological model, 415
  family, 435
  goals, 420–1
  information on, 428–43
  Missouri Delinquency Project, 427, 429
  moderators in, 440
  outcome studies, 424–30
  potential moderators, 440
  principles of, 418–24
  replication and, 439
  school and, 435
  scientific issues, 438–41
  supervision of, 422
  therapists and, 422, 437, 442, 469–70
  treatment manuals, 438–9
  treatment procedures, 418–24

nature, and psychotherapy, 5–6
negative reciprocity, 285
negative reinforcement, 284–5
negative spin, 105
negative thoughts, 106, 135, 153
negotiation, 136–7, 139, 154–7
neutral behaviors, 289
neutral condition, self-talk, 56
no contingency condition, 226
non-directive supportive condition, 147
non-focused intervention, 145–6
noncompliance, 216–7, 334
  antecedents of, 319
  commands and, 320
  conduct and. *See* conduct problems
  consequences and, 321
  defiance. *See* Defiant Children program
nondirective supportive therapy, 146, 148
nonspecific effects, 18
novelty game, 41

observational learning, 83. *See* modeling
Oedipal complex, 28
office visit, 448

one-on-one therapy, 365
one-way glass, 350
oppositional defiant disorder, 173–4, 252, 326, 336–7
out-of-home settings, 292
overanxious disorder, 75–6. *See* anxiety
overarousal, 277
overdetermined behavior, 178
overeating, 101

Parent-Child Interaction Therapy (PCIT), 313–4, 327–8, 331, 335–7, 339, 348–9, 352
  applying, 339–45
  brief description, 329
  clinical practice issues, 349–51
  conceptual basis, 327–8
  effects lasting, 346
  HNCP, 317, 328, 350
  information on, 351–2
  outcome studies, 335–9
  Patterson method, 348
  PDI and, 338
  procedural overview, 327–8
  scientific issues, 345–9
  statistical methods for testing, 347
  time-out procedure, 334
  treatment problems, 344–5
  treatment procedures, 329–35
parent-directed interaction (PDI), 328, 333–5, 339
parent management training (PMT)
  clinical practice issues, 411–3
  common treatment problems, 408–9
  conduct disorder, 387–401
  outcome studies, 396–405
  PSST and, 387–401, 405
  scientific issues, 409–11
parent training, 353–86
  ADHD and, 172–91
  behavioral. *See* Behavioral Parent Training
  conduct problems, 283–305, 387–401
  counteractions, 301
  family treatment and, 283–305
  Patterson group, 283
  sequential approach, 288
  STP and, 224, 239
  See also parents; *specific treatments*
parents, 57–8, 159, 290
  adolescents and, 139
  alpha commands, 333
  anxiety and, 79–80, 86